Kit Carson & the Indians

Kit Carson & the Indians

Tom Dunlay

University of Nebraska Press

Lincoln & London

Library of Congress

Cataloging-in-Publication Data

Dunlay, Thomas W., 1944–

Kit Carson and the Indians / Tom Dunlay.

p. cm.

Includes bibliographical references and index

ISBN 0-8032-1715-3 (cl.: alk. paper)

ISBN 978-0-8032-6642-1 (pa.: alk. paper)

ISBN 0-8032-6642-1 (pa.: alk. paper)

1. Carson, Kit, 1809–1868—Relations with Indians.

2. Pioneers—West (U.S.)—Biography. 3. Scouts

and scouting—West (U.S.)—Biography.

4. Navajo Indians—Wars. 5. Navajo

Indians—Relocation. I. Title.

F592.C33 D86   2000

978'.02'092—dc21

[B]   99-085995

FOR ED

CONTENTS

ILLUSTRATIONS

Following p. 254

The Dime Novel Carson, 1874

One of the earliest photographs of Carson, c. 1845

John C. Frémont, c. 1849

Carson and Alex Godey, 1844

Sagundai

Maria Josefa Jaramillo Carson, with child, c. 1850

Carson as an Indian agent, c. 1854

James Henry Carleton, 1866

Colonel Carson of the First New Mexico Volunteer Cavalry, c. 1865

Kit Carson at Adobe Walls, November 1864

Ouray, 1866–67

Carson as a brigadier general, 1866

Carson, c. 1867

One of the last photographs of Carson, 1868

PREFACE

The writing of this book might be attributed to an unidentified virus. I did not idolize Kit Carson as a child, though I must have read some biography or other of him. My interest in the Old West, however, developed very early, thanks to the ubiquitous cowboy heroes of the era, to the many Western movies in which the cavalry arrived at the last minute to save the beleaguered white folks, and to my father's reading of Mari Sandoz and Stanley Vestal, among others. The librarians at the Cordelia B. Preston Memorial Library in Orleans, Nebraska, directed me to good, serious books (I was that sort of kid), and I read David Lavender's *Bent's Fort*, Gene Caesar's *King of the Mountain Men* (about Jim Bridger), Bernard DeVoto's *Across the Wide Missouri*, and Jack Schaefer's *Company of Cowards*, all of which took a permanent grip on my imagination, for better or worse. By the time I was in college I had a strong interest in the era of the mountain men and in the Indian wars, especially those before 1865, in which, of course, Kit Carson figured prominently.

I can, however, date the beginning of my special interest in Kit Carson rather precisely. In May 1969 I drove my brother down to Lincoln, Nebraska, to attend a friend's air force commissioning ceremony at the University of Nebraska, and while there I purchased at the Nebraska Bookstore a copy of the first edition of Harvey Carter's *"Dear Old Kit"*. Carter's evaluation of Carson and his dismissal of some of the more absurd legends that had accumulated around the man both entertained me and gave me a new idea of what being a historian meant. Kit's varied and exciting career, including his transition from simple, buckskin-clad trapper to military commander and eventually brigadier general, was fascinating as a tale of adventure and for its seeming incongruity. At the same time, as I now realize, Carson seemed a hero who was not hopelessly larger than life, and his modesty and refusal to revel in his fame pleased me, as perhaps it was bound to please someone reared in rural Nebraska.

Over the years, as I very slowly developed into a historian, I collected references on Carson without any serious intention of writing a book about him, especially after the appearance of Thelma Guild and Harvey Carter's biography in 1984. I was aware, of course, of the increasing chorus of criticism directed at him for his role in the Indian wars of the 1860s, part of the wave of revisionism in Western history. I myself had written a book about the role of Indian scouts and auxiliaries in the Indian wars, which might or might not be considered revisionist, but I considered the more scathing attacks on Carson to be both misdirected and based upon a lack of understanding of the period as well as of the man.

In the winter of 1994 I contracted some mysterious bug and tried to wait it out instead of getting proper medical treatment. While I lay around home with a fever, I reread some of my Carson collection, and about the same time I read Philip Collins's *Dickens and Crime*. I suspect that it was the latter work, focusing on the great novelist's interest in, and ideas about, crime, criminals, and punishment, that led me to the idea of a work on Carson that, instead of being a full biography, would concentrate on his relations with, and his thinking about, Indians, the source of all the latter-day controversy, and the decline of his reputation. Of course, my approach to Carson and the Indians turned out to be very different from Collins's treatment of Dickens and crime; Carson's relations with Indians were a central feature—almost the main theme—of his life, and an examination of his character as well as his actions became necessary. As usual, my original idea could not be confined to the modest scope I intended. I decided early that a chronological, rather than a topical, organization would be necessary, to illustrate how Carson's involvement with Indians reflected the stages of his own life. If it was necessary for me to be in a feverish state to get inspiration, I hope this origin is not too evident in the book itself.

A major theme of this work was stated by Robert Utley, much better and more succinctly than I could, in his "plea that Kit Carson be allowed to live in his own world rather than in yours or mine."[1] Nineteenth-century America was not our America; if we must make an effort in writing Western history to understand the Indian cultures and viewpoints, so we must also make an effort to understand an Anglo-American culture deceptively similar in many ways to our own, yet often very different in its perceptions and priorities. Carson's contemporaries, as I point out, had no great trouble reconciling his frequent involvement in violence with their perception of him as kind, courteous, gentlemanly, and even tenderhearted. Today a great segment of our culture, intellectuals and academics especially, finds such a reconciliation virtually impossible. The belief that violence of any kind, no matter what the circumstances or the perceived justification, must be condemned unequivocally has much to recommend it. But historians cannot pretend that this proposition was as self-evident to nineteenth-century Americans as it is to some in the late twentieth.

As I point out, the spectrum of Anglo-American attitudes toward Indians in Carson's time also cannot easily be compared to our own. Most white people then had no doubt of their right and ability to judge Indians and other "non-whites" on a comparative basis by the standards of their own indubitably superior culture, just as they judged European immigrants. Attitudes toward Indians were profoundly ambivalent, more so than I could show in a book of any reasonable length, but in spite of expressions of unease, regret, and even shame at the treatment of the Native Americans, there was never any serious chance in the 1800s of acceptance of any outcome other than white domination and exploitation of the continent.

Writing this book has made me aware of the problem posed by Gale Christianson, biographer of Isaac Newton and Loren Eiseley:

> Weighing the thoughts and deeds of other human beings out of the context of their times is both dangerous and unfair. By the same token, when motives and actions are regarded primarily within their historical setting, critical evaluation is at a discount, rendering history useless as a moral as well as an intellectual pursuit.[2]

I can only hope I have charted a safe course between these two extremes. I would like to reiterate, however, what I state in the conclusion: that in evaluating Carson's life, even according to latter-day standards, one should consider not how he measures up against a standard few today can meet but where he started out—his upbringing, his backcountry culture, and the general consensus of his society regarding Indians—and where he arrived.

In writing my study of Indian scouts, I became aware of just how complex the attitudes of frontiersmen and Indian fighters were toward those varied groups and individual humans lumped together as "Indians": how frequently their relationships ranged from hostility to some to warm attachment toward others, and how surprisingly seldom the most experienced and knowledgeable of them were true, unqualified "Indian-haters," believing whole-heartedly that the only good Indian was a dead one. Studying Kit Carson, especially in the context of his experiences as a mountain man, only confirmed that observation. We should be wary of attributing to trappers, traders, and scouts our own ideas of multiculturalism and a strict, uncompromising attitude of racial egalitarianism and tolerance—of imposing on them an ideology formulated in another era. Yet we should also be wary of lumping people of another time with the doctrinaire racists and others we wish to condemn in our own time, of using them as substitutes for our own contemporary demons—as the gentleman I refer to in the first chapter did when he compared Kit Carson to Oliver North. The Kit Carson of legend, and to a great extent the Carson of fact, was an example of what Richard Slotkin calls "the man who knows Indians"—the character "whose experiences, sympathies, and even allegiances fall on both sides of the Frontier." This frontier hero, whose fictional model is James Fenimore Cooper's Hawkeye, "stands between the opposed worlds of savagery and civilization, acting sometimes as mediator or interpreter between races and cultures but more often as civilization's most effective instrument against savagery—a man who knows how to think and fight like an Indian, to turn their own methods against them."[3] Slotkin's primary interest lies in the Frontier Myth, and although he notes the frontier hero's possible role as mediator, his emphasis is on the violent role of the conqueror. In reality, many such characters found themselves playing both parts, according to the demands of the occasion and their own inclinations. We see Kit Carson negotiating with Indians on occasions even in his younger days, as when he avoided conflict with Apaches on his courier missions for Frémont and when he served as General Kearny's guide. In his later life, his service as Indian agent, treaty negotiator, and government adviser on Indians alternated with his services as scout and soldier. There was no question about his final allegiance because, as I point out, the "middle ground" became an increasingly hard place to inhabit, and the boy brought up at Boonslick could not be in doubt about his ultimate choice.

When Douglas Southall Freeman finished his massive biography of Robert E. Lee (published in 1934), he wrote that he had been "fully repaid" for his efforts "by being privileged to live, as it were, for more than a decade in the company of a great gentleman."[4] No biographer today would dare to write thus about his subject if he hoped to be taken seriously. Nonetheless, spending so much time with Kit has been an interesting experience, increasing my understanding of Western history and requiring me to examine some of my own attitudes and assumptions. In my first chapter I assert that Carson was a more complex person than allowed for by either hero-worshipers or critics; I have found that I was more right than I knew when I first wrote those words. Instead of the picturesque, quaint old scout, wholly predictable in his straightforward actions and uncomplicated ideas, I found a man trying to deal with complex moral issues and intractable real-life problems that would try anyone's conscience, judgment, and resolution.

This book was not meant to be the definitive biography of Kit Carson; at this writing Marc Simmons is at work on what may prove to be that volume. My intention from the first was to produce a study devoted to Carson's relations with Indians, but it proved impossible to deal with that subject satisfactorily without understanding something about his character and the environment that shaped him. From his childhood in a community "forted" against Indian attack to his last journey to Washington as a dying man with a Ute delegation, Carson was intimately involved with Indians in almost every imaginable way. Inevitably, the book became a study of his life, focused as much as possible on that one, central aspect.

I also do not claim to have written the definitive account of the Navajo campaign of 1863–64, which awaits a historian capable of integrating both the documentary record and Navajo tradition to produce a synthesis characterized by knowledge, judgment, balance, and compassion. I had anticipated having to confront, point by point, Clifford Trafzer's *The Kit Carson Campaign*. However, once I had read Lawrence Kelly's article "The Historiography of the Navajo Roundup" and articles by R. C. Gordon-McCutchan and Marc Simmons in the same collection, I concluded that the work of critiquing Trafzer's book step by step had been done and did not need repeating. I then felt free to tell the story my way, though my debt to Kelly, in particular, will be evident to anyone who knows the subject.[5]

I have been conscious throughout of having to argue against accepted myths, conventional wisdom, and popular misconceptions about Kit Carson. I fear that that consciousness has shaped the book more than might have been desirable. I have probably analyzed Kit's actions and attitudes far more than he ever found it necessary or even possible to do; I have had a lot more leisure for it than he generally had. I do not apologize for having devoted so much space to the deeds and motives of an illiterate frontiersman who accidentally became famous; that accident gives us a window through which to examine the world of a type of person common on the Indian-white frontier in America for well over two centuries. Most of these frontier people left us little or no record of their thoughts and activities. Only recently have historians begun to study them as other than romantic characters out of a colorful past.

My deepest interest lies in the people who lived in the past and the things they did, as opposed to contentious schools of thought among historians. Those contentions, however, have not been easy to avoid in writing about Kit Carson, and as I have said, the changing interpretations of his character and actions were what moved me to undertake this book.

There is a strong movement today, in historical writing in general and Western history in particular, toward the study of "ordinary" people instead of political, military, and social elites. Kit Carson was not ordinary in the sense of being obscure, but his story might be seen as that of an ordinary man—if there is such a thing—who lived an extraordinary life. Chance made him a celebrity and a symbolic hero, and so we have the chance to study the career of a man of modest origins, who had to meet extraordinary demands and of whom great things were expected. We can study his thinking on questions that were of great importance in his own time and that now are the subject of painful reevaluation by both scholars and the informed public. It is surely of some importance that an illiterate mountain man who spent much of his life in contact with Indians did not find either the pragmatic or the moral problems simple or easily solved and that he did not react entirely according to the simple, unexamined mindset often attributed to such people. There were, in fact, many people more or less like Carson in this, who lived on the frontier, or the "middle ground," and who did not find the situation as easy to deal with mentally as the dedicated reformers and assimilationists or as Senator Doolittle's Denver audience who, roused against the Indians, shouted, "Exterminate them! Exterminate them!" There are historians nowadays who contend that historical truth is really unattainable, that all we can study are the kinds of stories that people tell about the past, and their motives for telling the story in a particular way. However, most revision-ist Western historians still apparently believe that it is the historian's function to clear away myths, misconceptions, and falsehoods, popular and scholarly, to clarify at least some fragment or facet of the truth. I hope that this book can contribute something toward achieving that elusive goal.

ACKNOWLEDGMENTS

At the head of the list I must place Patricia and Scott Wendt of Bluestem Books in Lincoln, Nebraska. Both have probably heard more about Kit Carson than they ever wanted to know. Scott has proved his touch at locating Western materials and information that I despaired of finding. It was Pat who kept telling me that I should write more and keep on the job once started, and her reward was to find herself involved in the production of the "hard copy" of "Dunlay's Damned Book." I also owe them both, and William Wood, for helping pick things up after a minor disaster at my place.

Professor Fred Luebke of the University of Nebraska–Lincoln was no longer my official adviser when he put me on the trail of indispensable information regarding the Kit Carson controversy of recent years; he did it anyway. Following that trail brought me into contact with R. C. Gordon-McCutcheon and Skip Miller of the Kit Carson Historic Museums in Taos, New Mexico. I was able to use the museum archives and to read the articles for *Kit Carson: Indian Fighter or Indian Killer?* well before publication. Frank Torres at Fort Union National Monument helped me obtain a photograph of one of the paintings at the museum.

Marc Simmons, who is at work on a Kit Carson biography of his own, was very generous in providing information and exchanging ideas. I wish I could feel I had repaid him. Jennifer Bosley at the Colorado Historical Society located the microfilm of Carson's Fort Garland correspondence and ensured that I got copies.

Characteristically, I have either forgotten or failed to obtain the names of a number of people who helped me. These include the security chief at Fort Lyon Veterans Hospital (who knew more about Kit Carson than anyone else there), Maureen at Canyon de Chelly, and the New Mexico state archivist who pointed me toward other special material.

The staff of the interlibrary loan service at Love Library, University of Nebraska–Lincoln, deserve special thanks, particularly Lisa Parr.

The staff of the liver transplant unit at the University of Nebraska Medical Center at Omaha, including Doctor Byers Shaw, Doctor Tom Wood, Laurie Williams, Beth Hamm, and many others, should receive my thanks, since without them this book truly would not have been written. Doctors Joseph Stitcher, Robert Settles, and Stephen Youngberg in Lincoln have done their share in keeping me alive and functioning, not to mention providing medical advice about Kit Carson's last illness.

Regina Loffland, formerly of Taos and now of Sedona, Arizona, I would like to thank for encouragement, for advice, and for reminding me to follow my heart.

My brother, Edward Louis Dunlay, provided much assistance, financial and otherwise. Without him, too, this book would never have appeared. I have dedicated it to him.

Thomas William Dunlay
Lincoln, Nebraska
February 1999

Kit Carson & the Indians

Carson: I came to this country in 1826, and since that time have become pretty well acquainted with the Indian tribes, both in peace and at war.

> Testimony of Colonel Kit Carson,
> *Report on the Condition of the Indian Tribes*

George Bent: The Cheyennes call him Little Chief and the old men still talk about him today.

> George E. Hyde, *Life of George Bent*

We Navajos will never have the heart to forgive Kit Carson — he has done the damage already.

> Tiana Bighorse, *Bighorse the Warrior*

1. Will the Real Kit Carson Please Stand Up?

> *Carson*: Gentlemen, that thar may be true,
> but I hain't got no recollection of it.
> Henry Inman, *The Old Santa Fe Trail*

In the fall of 1851 a young American writer who had gained some fame for his books based on his experiences as a sailor and his travels in the South Seas published a novel about whales and whaling, among other things. The writer, of course, was Herman Melville and the novel was *Moby-Dick*. To prove that whaling was a sufficiently elevated subject for literature, he wrote a chapter called "The Honor and Glory of Whaling," in which he more than half humorously dragged in the name of every mythological figure who could conceivably have anything to do with his topic, including "Perseus, St. George, Hercules, Jonah, and Vishnoo!" Hercules he characterized as "that antique Crockett and Kit Carson." Melville clearly assumed that his American readers, at least, would recognize the names of the American heroes he ranked with Hercules and would consider the comparison, if fanciful, not wholly inappropriate.

But who were these Americans deemed worthy to stand with the Greek hero, "that brawny doer of rejoicing good deeds"? In 1851 Davy Crockett was fifteen years dead in the Alamo, the manner of his passing having turned a folksy, tall-tale-telling Indian fighter and congressman into one of the great dead. A series of Davy Crockett almanacs telling ever-taller tales of his imaginary exploits was keeping his memory green.[1]

But Christopher "Kit" Carson was very much alive in 1851 and living in Rayado, New Mexico. He was in his early forties, barely ten years older than Herman Melville, and some of his most notable exploits were still ahead of him. In fact, Melville had already mentioned Carson two years before, in a review of Francis Parkman's *The California and Oregon Trail*, where he said of Parkman's hunter and guide Henry Chatillon: "He belongs to a class of men, of whom Kit Carson is the model; a class, unique and not to be transcended in interest by any personages introduced to us by Scott."[2]

In the Kit Carson Home and Museum in Taos, New Mexico, one may see a bill of lading for the clipper ship *Kit Carson*, which sailed from Boston for San Francisco in 1855—a ship named for a man who made only one sea voyage in his life and who vowed never to take another. In 1849 two works of fiction were published in which Carson appeared as a character, Emerson Bennett's *The Prairie Flower* and Charles Averill's paperback *Kit Carson, The Prince of the Goldhunters*, made into a play the next year. This was the beginning of a series of what were later called dime novels featuring Carson, with titles like *Kiowa Charley, the White Mustanger; or, Rocky Mountain Kit's Last Scalp Hunt, Kit Carson's Bride; or, The Flower of the Apaches, Red Knife; or, Kit Carson's Last Trail*, and *The Fighting Trapper; or, Kit Carson to the Rescue*, plus works more specifically aimed at boys.[3]

The first full-length biography of Carson, which drew heavily on Kit's own dictated autobiography, was DeWitt Clinton Peters's *The Life and Adventures of Kit Carson, the Nestor of the Rocky Mountains, from Facts Narrated by Himself*, which appeared in 1858, before the subject was fifty. Three more books, by Charles Burdett, Edward S. Ellis, and John S. C. Abbott, had appeared by 1873, just five years after Carson's death.[4]

The first biography based on serious, broad research, Edwin L. Sabin's *Kit Carson Days*, was published in 1914. Carson's own autobiography appeared in versions edited by Blanche C. Grant (1928) and Milo M. Quaife (1935). Stanley Vestal (Walter Stanley Campbell), not a man to let the facts spoil a good story, produced *Kit Carson, The Happy Warrior of the Old West*, in 1928. Biographies varying in scholarship and literary value have continued to appear, their basically positive view of Carson indicated by the titles of the more significant: *Great Westerner: The Story of Kit Carson, Kit Carson: A Portrait in Courage, "Dear Old Kit": The Historical Christopher Carson*, and *Kit Carson: A Pattern for Heroes*.[5]

Besides all of the above, there was an enormous body of juvenile literature of mixed quality honoring Carson as a "pattern for heroes" for boys, and not only in his native land. At his home in Taos one may view works in French, German, Portuguese, Gujarati, Hindi, Singhalese, Arabic, and Japanese recounting Kit's exploits.

Obviously then, by the time he reached middle age, Kit Carson had become a true example of an old cliché: he was a legend in his own time, and he would remain a legend long after his death. Besides the biographies, he figured prominently in fur trade histories like Bernard De Voto's *Across the Wide Missouri* (1947) and David Lavender's *Bent's Fort* (1954), and in works of fiction like Jack Schaefer's *Company of Cowards* (1957).[6]

The adobe house in Taos where Carson lived much of his later life competes with Taos Pueblo and the homes of literary and artistic figures like D. H. Lawrence and Ernest Blumenschein as a tourist attraction, as does his grave in a park bearing his name near the center of the town. A river in Nevada and the capital of that state bear his name, as do the military base of Fort Carson and the town of Kit Carson in Colorado, Carson County in Texas, and the Carson National Forest in New Mexico. Kit Carson's place as a national hero was secure for at least a century after his death in 1868.

It would be misleading to imply that a change took place overnight, but one indicator of shifting attitudes that attracted great attention was the 1970 publication of Dee Brown's *Bury My Heart at Wounded Knee.* Presented as "An Indian History of the American West," the book narrates the western Indian wars from 1862 to the final tragedy at Wounded Knee in 1890. Relentlessly critical of whites and sympathetic to the Indians, it appeared at precisely the right moment of national self-doubt and "agonizing reappraisal" and permanently changed many people's view of the "Winning of the West." In Brown's chapter on the final Navajo war, Kit Carson played a prominent role as the field commander who finally defeated the Navajos. Brown saw the Navajos' fate as a terrible martyrdom, although he was less critical of Carson than of his military superior, General James Carleton. Brown characterized Carson as a man who liked Indians and had lived and married among them. Although he had become famous and respected, he had never, Brown wrote, overcome "his awe of the well-dressed, smooth-talking men at the top," and this awe made Carson act as Carleton's tool in inflicting much suffering on the Navajos. Brown also noted trader and Indian agent William Bent as a friend of the Cheyennes who "tried to do the best he could for them," without mentioning that Bent and Carson were old friends and in thorough agreement about the white men's treatment of Indians and about the policy the government should pursue to mend the situation.[7]

In 1972, at Colorado College in Colorado Springs, associate professor of anthropology Shirley Hill Witt persuaded the college ROTC to remove a display honoring Kit Carson, declaring that she found it offensive to have "a terrorist and a killer displayed with honor." This action prompted the leading authority on Carson's life to spring to his defense, but Professor Hill's description of Kit Carson as "a genocidal racist" perfectly encapsulated a common view of the man in the late twentieth century.[8]

On PBS recently, a folksinger introduced his song by explaining that he had always believed that Kit Carson was one of the good guys who wore a white hat. Then he had become acquainted with a Navajo Indian, who told him the truth about Kit and his treatment of the Navajos. Now, on the authority of this one source, he knew that Carson was a villain, rather like Colonel Oliver North! The song depicted Carson as having undertaken the campaign against the Navajos on his own initiative, apparently knowing that he had thereby damned himself at least historically. On a recent visit to Taos, I was told by a bookstore proprietor that he had decided to advertise on the local radio station the fact that his store was located across the street from Kit Carson Park; the radio people told him that they preferred to avoid mention of Kit Carson because he was so controversial.

In an introduction to *Piñon Country*, Haniel Long's 1941 depiction of the Upper Sonoran life zone of Arizona and New Mexico and its people, Tony Hillerman, the popular mystery writer whose stories are set on the Navajo Reservation, found Long's praise of Kit Carson "hard to swallow." "Navajos," Hillerman wrote, "remember Carson as a pretended friend who betrayed them, swept his troops through their territory, killing all who didn't escape, destroying their homes, cattle, and crops with a savage scorched-earth campaign worthy of Genghis Khan and then herding the survivors into captivity." Hillerman blamed Long's error on his writing "before our consciousness (and conscience) was raised on the subject of the white man's behavior and motivation in the frontier Indian wars."[9]

Scholarly works have demonstrated the same sort of shift in attitude. In a study of American Indian population history since 1492, Russell Thornton describes Kit Carson as "infamous among American Indians" (of all tribes, presumably) and says that besides having "pillaged the land and destroyed crops and livestock until the Navajo were brought to the brink of starvation . . . Carson killed a good many Navajos as well during this period of 'warfare.' " Thornton describes the suffering of the Navajos at Bosque Redondo without mentioning General James Carleton, implying that Carson was solely responsible for that episode.[10]

In *The Civil War in the American West*, Alvin Josephy surveys all the military campaigns of the period 1861–65 west of the Mississippi. In writing of the Navajo campaign, he acknowledges that in 1862 "the Rio Grande settlements were suffering intensely from resumed Navajo attacks," which he blames on the attacks of Hispanic New Mexicans on the Navajos. His description of the military operations details the "scorched earth" campaign, the suffering this entailed for the Navajos, and the "Long Walk" and confinement at Bosque Redondo. He is far less severe in his criticism of Carson than Hillerman or Thornton, observing that many knew him as "dear old Kit," but concludes that Carson's respect for military authority and his loyalty to General Carleton "made him an instrument of Carleton's inflexible will, and an enemy whom the Navajos and other Southwestern tribes would never forgive."[11]

The central work in the attack on Carson, however, is Clifford Trafzer's *The Kit Carson Campaign: The Last Great Navajo War*. Trafzer's first sentence acknowledges that "Kit Carson stands as one of the most famous figures in the history of the American West," and he ranks Kit's fame with that of Davy Crockett, Wyatt Earp, and Billy the Kid, all of whom, "like many of the 'infamous' people of the West had something in common—they were killers." The Navajo Indians, Trafzer asserts, have never shared the white people's view of Carson as a heroic figure. Trafzer's history of the Kit Carson campaign of 1863–64 places a major share of the blame for what happened to the Navajos on Carson.[12]

Trafzer also allots a large share of blame to General Carleton, whom he characterizes as "an unscrupulous, ambitious, selfish man, whose bearing radiated an abrasive, tyrannical personality"—an assessment that certainly reflects the opinion of many of the general's contemporaries, and he also describes Carleton as "savage-minded," a term he would undoubtedly not use to describe any Indian leader. Carson also receives his share: "Kit was a simple man of 'sound' character (except that he killed people from time to time, particularly Indians)." Carson was "easily impressed" by people like Carleton, who had formal education and social standing; he often yielded to "casual adulation" and was easily "persuaded and maneuvered through words of praise, flattery, and commendation. In short, Carson was Carleton's tool. . . . Because of his loyalty to his country and his friend, his thirst for adventure, and his innate sense of duty . . . Carson would carry out a brutal campaign against the Navajos." None of these conclusions about Carson's character and motivation, it should be noted, are really proven; they are only asserted.[13]

Trafzer's research and his conclusions have been severely criticized by scholars like Lawrence Kelly. Near the end of his book, Trafzer seems to have had some second thoughts, for he admits that "Carson was not a ruthless murderer, and he did not condone those who were," and he notes with approval Kit's condemnation of Colonel John Chivington, the perpetrator of the Sand Creek Massacre against the Cheyennes in 1864.[14]

Nonetheless, it appears that Carson is on the verge of taking over the place formerly held in Western historiography by Colonel Chivington as the designated villain of the Indian wars for his attack on Southern Cheyennes under a flag of truce. A recent defender of Chivington even dismisses the testimony against him by Carson, "who was personally responsible for the starvation and freezing deaths of thousands of Navajos."[15]

Considering all the above, it is perhaps not surprising that by 1986 a reviewer of Thelma Guild and Harvey Carter's biography of Carson could confidently write that Kit's campaigning against the Mescalero Apaches and Navajos "has proved detrimental to whatever remains of his popular reputation," and describe him as "a good company man, one who may doubt but who will in the end obey orders regardless of their rightness."[16]

An observer from another country and culture, reviewing the material presented here so far, might ask, "What's going on here?" Anyone who has lived in the United States for the last thirty years, however, will know perfectly well what is going on and why it has affected Kit Carson's reputation. The middle and late 1960s marked a major intellectual and popular shift in attitudes about our country and its history and a serious reevaluation of many cherished beliefs and values, including our views on the status and treatment of groups who had not shared all the benefits American society was believed to bestow. Blacks and American Indians were prominent among the groups whose standing and past experience came up for extensive review. The conquest of the continent, including the American West, commonly viewed as a triumph for American democracy, progress, and opportunity, looked rather different if one tried to imagine the viewpoint of the original inhabitants. Francis Jennings described the English settlement on the continent as "the invasion of America," and viewed the land not as "virgin" but as "widowed," deprived of its inhabitants, first by disease and then by war and dispossession.[17]

Inevitably, the entire history of Indian–white relations in the United States came under scrutiny. There had indeed been attacks on federal government policy toward Indians and on the attitudes and actions of the white population generally for many years, by historians whose work received little attention outside of specialized circles. By the early 1970s, however, the rise of a militant, articulate Indian movement added force to a shift in emphasis toward the suffering and dispossession of American Indians and the selfishness, violence, and racial prejudice of American whites.

The change was bound to affect the historical reputation of Kit Carson. In 1928 Stanley Vestal declared Carson to be "the symbol of the American frontier, as Odysseus was of the Greek seafarings," and asserted that "it is important that we understand and love the thing he represents." But if that frontier experience became, instead of something to love, something to be ashamed of, then what of Kit Carson?[18]

In a new preface to the 1991 edition of his "Dear Old Kit," originally published in 1968, Harvey Carter noted that the first edition had met criticism from those "who were not content with a hero as ordinary as the actual historical person but who wished to worship him as a superman who never failed and could do no wrong." The second edition, Carter feared, would face "the new mythmakers who regard Carson as an inhuman monster who starved, beat, and killed untold numbers of Navajo Indians and enslaved those who survived." In the original work Carter noted that Carson's early biographers had depicted him as "the greatest single factor in reducing the Indian population of Western America." This dime-novel image was all very well for much of the nineteenth-century audience, but in the late twentieth century such a reputation would not do.[19]

There were those within the historical profession who challenged the attack on Carson's good repute. Following the 1972 incident at Colorado College noted above, Harvey Carter, professor emeritus there, whose "Dear Old Kit" included the definitive version of Carson's autobiography, published an article defending the "Slandered Scout"; it appeared in the *Denver Westerners' Brand Book*, which assured that it would have a sympathetic audience but not the broad one that Carter might have hoped for. Carter made some good points within the limited space available, and also made plain the extent to which he identified himself with Carson and resented attacks on the man as attacks on his own scholarship and judgment. Born in the first decade of the twentieth century, Carter may not have fully perceived the radical—in the true sense of the word—nature of a later generation's developing criticism of Carson and of the western experience.[20]

Guild and Carter's 1984 biography, *Kit Carson: A Pattern for Heroes*, intended in part to answer such criticism and was factually the best and most authoritative to date, but it had to divide attention between a definitive factual account of Carson's life and a favorable presentation of his actions. Their assertion that Carson was not responsible for the Navajos' suffering at Bosque Redondo prompted the reviewer already quoted to charge them with "an extremely restricted sense of 'responsibility,'" and to wish for more speculation on Carson's motivations and for "intelligent insights on the sociocultural milieu which accorded this unlikely man fame."[21]

In 1992 R. C. Gordon-McCutchan, director of the Carson Historic Museums in Taos, reportedly heard a woman standing outside the Carson home declare, "I will not go into the home of that racist, genocidal killer." Hearing this prompted him to organize a conference held at Taos in July 1993, titled "Kit Carson: Indian Fighter or Indian Killer?" The avowed purpose of the conference was to reverse the current negative perception of Carson, and several respected Western history scholars, including Robert M. Utley, Marc Simmons, and Lawrence Kelly, presented papers directed to that end. Clifford Trafzer, whose work was sharply criticized by some of the speakers, was invited but did not attend. Other scholars asked to observe also were not present, among them Patricia Nelson Limerick, one of the most respected among the newer Western historians, and some Navajo scholars. One of the Navajos, anthropologist Harry Walters, remarked, "It's like trying to rehabilitate Adolf Hitler." Limerick saw no reason why "aging historical figures" like Carson had to be "gussied up," and said, "I think Kit Carson would be very angry that these wimpy intellectuals feel it necessary to be defending him." Limerick, who as a professor of history presumably qualifies as an intellectual herself, seems to have envisioned an unrepentant Carson indignant at having his bloody triumphs against the despised "redskins" misrepresented or even denied by misguided scholars. Another New Western historian, Ramón Gutierrez, opined: "It's the old white men angry that they're losing control over the world."[22]

There was obviously a more basic debate going on between schools of thought in Western history, and Carson, as so often in his lifetime, led the way because of his status as one of the greatest heroes of the older Western tradition. Apparently, for many of his critics, the question "Indian Fighter or Indian Killer?" was meaningless, proposing a distinction that embodied no real difference, since all violent actions against Indians by whites, under whatever circumstances, were equally reprehensible. Nonacademics, unacquainted with disagreements inside the ivory tower, were surprised that the discussion over the character and actions of an illiterate frontiersman dead for well over a century could provoke not "a productive, scholarly debate" but "an old-fashioned schoolyard brawl."[23]

But while disputes between so-called traditionalists and New Western historians, and debates over deconstructionism and presentism, may entertain those directly engaged, there are those who, perhaps naively, would simply like to know the truth about Kit Carson. Was he the simple, brave, noble hero admired by several generations of Americans; or was he a "genocidal racist," contemptuously slaughtering those unfortunate enough to have darker skins than his own; or was he the tool of ruthless agents of Manifest Destiny, carrying out unconscionable orders? Or is it possible that he has been both praised as a hero and damned as a villain for things he never did and attitudes he never held?

There are two stories about Carson that seem to bear on these questions. The first is told by Carson himself in his autobiography. In November 1849 he served as a scout for a force of U.S. dragoons that pursued a group of Jicarilla Apaches on the plains of northeast New Mexico; the Jicarillas had attacked a small wagon train on the Santa Fe Trail, killing a trader named James White and several others and carrying off Mrs. Ann White. It was the most difficult trail that he ever followed, Kit observed, but the hope of rescuing the woman spurred them on. When the column overtook the Indians, the commanding officer ignored Carson's desire to attack immediately and tried to parley. The Jicarillas instead prepared to flee, firing on the troops, who then charged. The Indians were scattered, but Ann White was found dead with an arrow in her heart, apparently killed while trying to escape. In the debris of the camp was the loot from the wagon train, including, Carson says, "a book, the first of its kind I had ever seen, in which I was made a great hero, slaying Indians by the hundred." The book may have been Charles Averill's *Kit Carson, Prince of the Gold Hunters*; its discovery prompted some uncomfortable thoughts in the real Kit: "I have often thought that as Mrs. White would read the same, and knowing that I lived near, she would pray for my appearance and that she would be saved."[24]

Patricia Limerick sees this episode as part of a pattern of betrayal — of the gap between the way printed words have described the West and the often disillusioning reality. On a more individual level, however, one may view it as Carson's first encounter with the uncomfortable aspect of his own fame — the raising of expectations that neither he nor any other man could possibly live up to.[25]

The second story appears in DeWitt Clinton Peters's biography of Carson, and since Peters relied heavily on Carson's recollections, this story may also have come from him. In 1850 Kit and a friend, Tim Goodale, took a herd of mules from New Mexico to Fort Laramie to sell to travelers on the California and Oregon Trails. People passing through the post were naturally excited to hear that the famous scout was there, and the mountain men present amused themselves by pointing out various buckskin-clad passersby as the great man. One traveler "fresh from the canebrakes of Arkansas" was, however, directed to the real Kit. He immediately went over and asked, "I say, stranger, are you Kit Carson?" Kit replied that he was, and the Arkansawyer looked over the man before him, about five-foot-five, stocky and bowlegged, and altogether unimpressive. "Look 'ere, stranger," he said, "you can't come that over me, any how. You ain't the kind of Kit Carson I am looking for." Kit then turned and pointed to a large, impressive trader in suitable prairie garb who was walking by, and the hero-worshiper went off to gaze upon his hero.[26]

The story is one of several that show Carson's mixture of embarrassment and amusement at his own fame, and the self-deprecating way he reacted to such displays of adulation. It also shows one of the reasons why so many people liked Kit. Here, it might be taken as an illustration of our central problem. In his own time and since, a great many people, like the man from Arkansas, have gone looking for a particular kind of Kit Carson and have refused to accept any substitute that does not fit their preconceptions.

For many Americans, of course, "Kit Carson" is simply a name vaguely associated with some sort of Western heroism. In the summer of 1994 I encountered a woman with some knowledge of Western history who asked why Carson had killed all those buffalo. Obviously she was thinking of William F. "Buffalo Bill" Cody. Others, with vague memories of a misbegotten 1950s television series, may associate him with law enforcement, like Wild Bill Hickock. It may be helpful, therefore, to survey, very briefly, Carson's career in chronological order.

Christopher Houston Carson was born in Kentucky on December 24, 1809; his family moved to the Missouri frontier in 1811, and there he grew up. His father died in 1818, and in 1824 Kit was apprenticed to a saddlemaker. He ran away from his apprenticeship in 1826 and went west on the Santa Fe Trail to New Mexico. After a few years of miscellaneous labor he became a Rocky Mountain fur trapper—a "mountain man"—pursuing the life of a trapper and hunter until 1842. He then became a guide and scout for the government explorer John Charles Frémont, whose published reports, including accounts of Carson's daring exploits, made him nationally known. With Frémont he was involved in the conquest of California during the Mexican War and performed more actions that enhanced his fame. For the next few years he resided in New Mexico with his wife, Maria Josefa Jaramillo, whom he had married in 1843, ranching and serving as a scout for the army. In 1854 he became government agent for several Indian tribes in northern New Mexico Territory, including Utes, Jicarilla Apaches, and the people of Taos Pueblo. With the coming of the Civil War in 1861 he became colonel of a regiment of New Mexico volunteers that participated in driving Confederate invaders out of the territory, and for the remainder of the war he was involved in campaigns against various southwestern tribes, including Navajos, Mescalero Apaches, Kiowas, and Comanches, as the principal field officer for General James Carleton, the commander in New Mexico Territory. At the close of the war he received the brevet rank of brigadier general. He continued in military service until 1867, commanding in southern Colorado, and also advised the government on Indian problems and participated in efforts to negotiate peace with different Indian tribes; then he left the service because of failing health. He soon accepted appointment as superintendent of Indian affairs for Colorado and accompanied a Ute delegation to Washington, but soon after his return to Colorado, and a month after the death of his wife, he died at Fort Lyon, Colorado, on May 23, 1868, from the rupture of an aortic aneurysm.[27]

It is not proposed to recite every detail of Carson's life but to examine his actions and his attitudes regarding the western American Indians he encountered at the various stages of his career. Carson's personality, as far as we can know it, is obviously relevant here; so is the historical context in which he acted and thought. If we cannot understand how the world may have looked to him and his contemporaries, then we will have trouble understanding why they did many of the things they did. Tired as the cliché is, the past is indeed another country.

Carson, it seems fairly certain, was at least a functional illiterate; reading was either very hard for him or impossible. The only specimens of handwriting certainly his are signatures, almost always written "C. Carson." His perception of the world was limited to what he could observe for himself and what he could learn directly from those around him. The intellectual and cultural movements of his time could affect him only indirectly. He spent most of his life in parts of North America remote from the centers of civilization and revolutions in industry and technology. He was born in the same year as Abraham Lincoln, Charles Darwin, Edgar Allan Poe, Alfred, Lord Tennyson, and William E. Gladstone, but the only one of these great contemporaries we can be sure he ever heard of was Lincoln.[28]

Yet Kit Carson did not live in a timeless, unchanging Never-Never Land "Wild West." The West he knew was very much subject to historical change, which profoundly affected his life. The ways in which he adapted to these changes were often representative of what was happening in the West, and make his life a paradigm of the whole process of American expansion in the early and middle nineteenth century.

Stephen Tatum describes the man who made these adaptations as an "unlikely man" to be a hero. The reaction of the skeptical Arkansawyer at Fort Laramie was shared, less vehemently, by many of Carson's contemporaries. There is a remarkable consistency to the reactions of people who met him after he achieved fame. William Tecumseh Sherman was a regular army lieutenant serving in California in 1848 when Carson rode into Monterey with mail from the East. "His fame was then at its height, from the publication of Frémont's books," Sherman recalled, "and I was very anxious to see a man who had achieved such feats of daring among the wild animals of the Rocky

Mountains, and the still wilder Indians of the Plains." Carson proved wholly different from Sherman's expectations: "I cannot express my surprise at beholding a small, stoop-shouldered man, with reddish hair, freckled face, soft blue eyes, and nothing to indicate extraordinary courage and daring. He spoke but little, and answered questions in monosyllables."[29]

Another lieutenant, with a somewhat less distinguished future, who met Carson in California in 1848 was George Douglas Brewerton, who also had certain definite expectations about the hero: "The Kit Carson of my imagination was over six feet high—a sort of modern Hercules in his build—with an enormous beard, and a voice like a roused lion. . . . The real Kit Carson I found to be a plain, simple unostentatious man; rather below the medium height, with soft, brown curling hair, little or no beard, and a voice as soft and gentle as a woman's."[30]

Clearly, Brewerton, Sherman, and the Arkansan at Fort Laramie expected someone like the "half-horse, half-alligator" frontiersman of popular myth, a compound of Davy Crockett, Mike Fink the Mississippi keelboater, and the "Big Bear of Arkansaw"—the loud, boastful, hard-living, casually violent westerner who could whip his weight in wildcats and who delighted in the slaughter of Indians. This uncouth stereotype was well established in popular culture by the mid–nineteenth century; it did owe something to the actual behavior of some assertive backcountry types, and some men on the frontier did their best to live up to it. It was the prototype for the dime-novel Kit Carson of a few years later who made his first appearance in Emerson Bennett's *The Prairie Flower* (1849), where he was an "incarnate devil in an Indian fight," who had "killed and scalped more savages in the same number of years than any two hunters west of the old Mississippi."[31]

Kent Steckmesser, Daryl Jones, Richard Slotkin, and Darlis Miller have all examined aspects of Carson's career as a dime-novel hero. Steckmesser and Slotkin both emphasize the blood-and-thunder aspect of the character, and Slotkin points out how "grossly racist" the dime-novel Carson is.[32]

But the real Kit Carson, seen in the flesh, could only disappoint such expectations; he was short, clean-shaven when possible, soft-spoken, modest, and rather uncommunicative. (At five-foot-five Carson was not remarkably short for his day; the majority of recruits for the Union and Confederate armies were between five-foot-five and five-foot-nine, so Kit hit the low end of the average.) But there was another literary model for the frontier hero available, one to which the modest, unaffected, and quietly courteous Carson could more easily be assimilated.[33]

The most famous American author of the nineteenth century, translated into any number of foreign languages, was James Fenimore Cooper, and he created perhaps the most famous American literary character of all time, a buckskin-clad frontiersman who embodied all the natural, untutored virtues. Natty Bumppo, variously called Deerslayer, Pathfinder, Hawkeye, Leatherstocking, and Long Rifle, owed something to Daniel Boone, but Cooper admitted that he was essentially a product of the imagination. Cooper himself explained that he was trying to create "a character that possessed little of civilization but its highest principles as they are exhibited in the uneducated, and all of savage life that is not incompatible with these great rules of conduct, . . . [one] removed from all the temptations of civilized life, placed in the best associations of that which is deemed savage."

Cooper's hero is modest, scrupulous, honorable, brave, and philosophical, very careful to point out that he is a white man, not a "half-breed," and that he has a different standard of conduct because of his white "gifts" from the Indians. This was important to readers in post-Revolutionary America, where the "white Indian," the "renegade" who fought as an Indian against the white frontier, like Simon Girty and Walter Butler, was a figure of unmitigated evil. But Natty Bumppo is a man who lives with Indians, who survives and makes his living by skills learned from Indians, and who can truthfully say that his best friends are Indians. He admires Delawares and Mohicans exceedingly, while despising Iroquois and Hurons, a fact that is not irrelevant to a study of Kit Carson.[34]

Cooper's Leatherstocking novels featuring Natty Bumppo, published between 1823 and 1841, were widely read, extravagantly admired as authentically American romances rivaling those of Scott, and condemned as offering a hopelessly idealized portrait of the American Indian. A literate young man like George Brewerton was surely thinking of them when he wrote that Carson, "the hero of a hundred desperate encounters, whose life had been spent amid wildernesses, where the white man is almost unknown, was one of Dame Nature's gentlemen — a sort of article which she gets up occasionally, but nowhere in better style than among the backwoods of America." Brewerton, it should be noted, grew up in an army family on the Atlantic coast, not "among the backwoods of America."[35] The same year Brewerton met Carson, the *Rough and Ready Annual* provided a sketch of the new hero and asserted, "In the school of men thus formed by hardship, exposure, peril, and temptation, our hero acquired all their virtues and escaped their vices."[36]

Another young man who met Carson in California during the Mexican War was Navy Lieutenant Edward Fitzgerald Beale, who shared some hard, dangerous traveling with Kit. Years later, defending his departed friend against slander by poet Joaquin Miller, Beale declared, "Carson was a man cleanly of mind, body, and speech, and by no means a Border ruffian. He had no gift of swearing." Beale further asserted that Carson had "a calm, dignified, sweet nature," and apostrophized him thus: "Dear old Kit! . . . Oh, wise of counsel, strong of arm, brave of heart and gentle of nature, how bitterly you have been maligned."[37]

In 1866 painter Worthington Whittredge went on a tour of the eastern Rockies and New Mexico. Whittredge says, "I had all my life wanted to meet a man who had been born with some gentle instincts and who had lived a solitary life, either in the woods or somewhere where society had not affected him and where primitive nature had had full swing of his sensibilities." The "wild characters" Whittredge met in the West were not what he was looking for: "I wanted to see a man of more modesty and more truthful turn of mind. The nearest approach to such a character I ever met with was Kit Carson, the famous scout."[38]

From Cooper's explanation of what he was trying to do, we can see the mold that Carson seemed to these observers to fit. If he was not a boastful, belligerent "border ruffian," there was another convenient category for him. Those who met Carson in the latter part of his life generally saw him in the Cooperian mode. The fact that none of them specifically compared him to Leatherstocking, while employing the language and images of his creator, suggests how well-established, and how taken for granted, the archetype was in American culture. It was in this genteel mode that his nineteenth-century biographers depicted him. Like the man from Arkansas, they knew what kind of Kit Carson they wanted to see, and Kit's outward personality allowed them to find the resemblance to Cooper's hero without too much strain.[39]

Still, we must remember that these contemporary witnesses, like many others, had one great advantage over us, over Carson's later critics and admirers alike: they actually knew the man. Some of them only met him briefly and were happy to have their preconceived ideas confirmed. Others, however, like Brewerton and Beale, or like John Frémont, knew him for extended periods of time, and traveled with him under trying conditions. Perhaps some of them were not overly sensitive to the wrongs done to Indians. Yet the cumulative testimony in Carson's favor is hard to ignore. After a difficult trip from California to New Mexico over the Old Spanish Trail, including tense encounters with Indians, Brewerton judged Carson well suited to the office of Indian agent, which required "great tact, much common sense, and a fair amount of judgement." In his account of the journey he had noted Kit's courage and boldness, and his caution, but he found him endowed with other qualities as well.[40]

Edward Beale, remembering his own trip through the southwestern desert with Carson, was even more fulsome. When he was sick, Kit had cared for him "as tenderly as a woman," giving Beale the last drop of water from his canteen. "Oh, Kit! I think again of afterwards on the bloody Gila, where we fought all night and travelled all day, with each man his bit of mule meat, and no other food, and when, I so worn from a hurt could go no further, begged you to leave me there and save yourself, I see you leaning on that old, long Hawkins gun of yours, (mine now) and looking out of those clear blue eyes at me with a surprised reproach, as one who takes an insult from a friend." In our day such prose as this arouses instant suspicion, but in the nineteenth century it was the appropriate way to express deep emotion.[41]

Jessie Benton Frémont, the explorer's wife, was another writer of purple prose, and she too was impressed with more than the obvious "manly" virtues in Carson. She credited him with a "merry heart" and "that most lovable combination of a happy and reasoning patience under trial, with quick resource and a courage equal to all proof." She also remembered the kindness he showed when her firstborn son — Kit's godson — died as an infant. "You were the first to warn me that my oldest boy could not live," she wrote to him years later. "I always think of you in connection with that poor suffering baby." Jessie and her husband were publicists and politicians, but there was no political advantage to be gained when she assured Kit that, if he died first, "There will be two friends here to feel that something has been taken from them not to be replaced."[42]

These admiring contemporaries and later biographers share one other characteristic with those who despise Carson as a racist and a practitioner of genocide, besides their tendency to see what they want and expect to see. They virtually all portray an uncomplicated Carson who is all of one piece and whose actions are wholly consistent with the character they assign to him. He is a man of simple nobility and courage who can be depended on to do the right thing under the most difficult circumstances, or he is a callous, brutal racist, or the easily manipulated agent of the genocidal policies of his superiors, representing the worst aspects of white Anglo-America. He is either/or. He is never seen as a man who had to make hard, complex, often ambiguous moral choices like the rest of us, who had to face the frustration of grappling with intractable circumstances, who was capable of growth, of learning and modifying his ideas.

Worthington Whittredge offers an unusual dimension of Carson's character. He reveals how Carson gave him a detailed description of a sunrise he had seen once in the Sangre de Cristo Mountains, "how the sun rose behind their dark tops and how it began little by little to gild the snow on their heads, and finally how the full blaze of light came upon them . . . and he wanted to know if I couldn't paint it for him." Granting that Whittredge may have gilded the account a little, this is the only source I have seen that gives any indication that Carson had any appreciation of the beauty of the landscapes among which he spent so much of his life. Except for that conversation, and the artist's recording of it, we would have no idea that Carson had any aesthetic sense. It was not what most people were interested in hearing about the great scout and Indian fighter.[43]

This study has two aspects, which are necessarily intertwined. One is to place Carson in his historical context, remembering that he lived in the early and middle nineteenth century, not in the late twentieth, and that this is more than a matter of dates. The other purpose is to study what Carson actually did and said, to see how far he conforms to the stereotype of the "genocidal racist." The intention is not to write a simple brief for the defense but to try to understand Carson in his human complexity.

The focus will be on Carson's relations with Indians, as far as can be judged from what he thought and did. Carson was first of all a man of action, and his actions, as recounted by himself and others, are the primary evidence. They ought to be seen, not only as the bare facts of what happened, but as they would have appeared to contemporaries, white and Indian, and to Indians of different tribes—for different tribes might have viewed the same act quite differently. The Navajo campaign was not unique or unprecedented, and it was not undertaken simply out of motiveless malice, or a generic, undifferentiated white "racism," however much ethnic or racial prejudice may have played its part. A verdict should not be pronounced on that campaign on the basis of secondhand accusations of "genocide" or invocations of the names of Genghis Khan or Adolf Hitler, without a detailed knowledge of the unique history of New Mexico, of the history, strategy, and tactics of Indian-white conflicts in the West, and of the actual events of the Navajo campaign.

Since World War II the word *genocide* has been used to raise the consciousness of members of the dominant culture to the very real historical injustices suffered by Native Americans in the centuries since Columbus. But the word originally had a very particular and restricted meaning, derived from what the Nazi regime in Germany tried to do to the Jews of Europe. A recent, scholarly definition is that genocide is "a form of one-sided mass killing in which a state or other authority intends to destroy a group, as that group or membership in it are defined by the perpetrator."[44]

James Axtell, one of the leading historians of Indian-white relations in colonial North America, points out that the definition "excludes from consideration the victims, civilian or military, of two-sided war, of any natural or unintended disaster, and of any individuals or 'loose cannons' acting outside the orders of the state or political authority." (Colonel John Chivington might be placed in the last category; he was certainly disavowed by the federal government.) Axtell, who can hardly be accused of lack of either sympathy or indignation in his writing on Indians, insists that "we must not apply [the term *genocide*] wholesale to every Indian death in the colonial period. To do so is to dilute our moral vocabulary to insipidity and to squander its intellectual and emotional force."[45]

Fritz Stern, historian of twentieth-century, Germany, has made the same point: "Out of respect for the dead, we should adopt a moratorium on facile analogies with unique suffering; the memory of that past should not be dissipated by mindless invectives."[46]

One of the commonest "facile analogies" is that between the Indian wars and the Vietnam War. For the generation to whom that war was an unforgettable trauma—the author's generation—the comparison seems irresistible. One historian who makes that association most explicitly, drawing a clear line of succession from colonial Indian-white conflicts to Vietnam, all part of an unbroken chain of white American racism and imperialism, is Richard Drinnon. Regarding Kit Carson, he writes, "Carson's Long Knives were forerunners of the Burning Fifth Marines," who, he informs us, had "the habit of burning at least half the [Vietnamese] villages they passed through."[47]

Obviously there are many acts deserving condemnation that do not fall under the classification of genocide, and many also that do not require comparison with Vietnam, except in the universal terms of human suffering. Some historical comparisons appear in this book, but I do not mean to suggest that exact analogies can be drawn between, say, Bosnia in the 1990s and New Mexico in the 1860s. Comparisons can be made between different Indian-white conflicts at different periods of history. Indian raids on frontier Missouri in Carson's childhood surely influenced his later actions; the relations between mountain men and Indians, hostile and friendly, which he participated in during his young manhood, I will argue, did influence him. The conduct of the Seminole War in Florida in 1835–42 is not irrelevant to the Navajo wars of the 1850s and '60s, and neither, certainly, is the conduct of Indian wars in the trans-Mississippi West from 1848 to 1890. The whole history of Indian-white interaction on the frontier is more complex than many writers are prepared to admit. In the Missouri of Kit's youth and the New Mexico of his maturity, and certainly in the Rocky Mountains during his first adult experiences, Indians were both enemies and allies, and those who knew most about the subject saw well beyond the broad classification *Indian* to distinctions that were more important and sometimes literally vital.

It is not always possible to reach definitive, infallible conclusions about the thoughts and actions of historical characters, even in the unlikely event that we could get past all our preconceived ideas about what they did, and should have done. Inevitably, the record is less than complete, especially in Carson's case. His illiteracy means that all that he said and thought comes down to us through interpreters, who may have altered the record, intentionally or otherwise. His official correspondence as an Indian agent and soldier was all taken down by clerks of varying ability. His spoken words, including official testimony, were taken down by others and reported according to the style of the various scribes. Even his autobiography, which stops short of the most controversial period of his life, was dictated to his Indian agency clerk.

His autobiography is one of the essential sources for any attempt to understand Carson. His amanuensis, John Mostin, apparently attempted to turn Carson's colloquial speech into more or less standard English, not always successfully. Carson clearly intended to provide a plain, factual narrative of his life to 1856, without literary flourishes or philosophical asides. Like many another autobiography, it is sometimes notable for what it does not say; yet Kit does often make his attitudes and reactions to specific situations clear.

Because of the way in which the document was produced, it is important not to read too much into matters of style and choice of words. Literary scholar Martin Green, in his study of American adventure literature, is perhaps the only one to evaluate Carson's autobiography as literature, in a volume that also covers selected works by such writers as Cooper, Irving, Richard Henry Dana, Melville, Parkman, Mark Twain, Theodore Roosevelt, Hemingway, Faulkner, and Norman Mailer. Certainly he does not consider Carson the peer of any of these in literary skill, but he points out that Kit was a more authentic adventurer than any of them. Therein lies the problem, for Green finds Carson to lack "moral delicacy, generosity, or passion," the reason being that "Carson was a real hero of adventure, and heroes are not notable for such qualities." Green seems unaware of the definitive version of the autobiography in Carter's *"Dear Old Kit"*, and his blanket judgment on heroes suggests that he too has found the Carson he was looking for. Aware of Carson's illiteracy, he cannot help holding the man responsible for matters of style and tone that Green views as proof that Carson was a callous, vindictive brute. He does not quote D. H. Lawrence, but he seems to have in mind the Englishman's famous definition, based on Cooper's hero, of "the essential American soul": "hard, isolate, stoic, and a killer." Carson, like the other authors, appears as an illustration of Western civilization as "a society obsessed by and addicted to the lust for power." Yet Green's comments are valuable as indications of a certain viewpoint, and will be alluded to on occasion.[48]

Carson seldom makes general observations about "Indians" as a group, and when he does it is usually in reference to a specific event or problem, as when he gives his opinions on Indian-white relations in New Mexico in the 1850s at the end of the autobiography—opinions at some variance with ideas he expressed later. He never says anything about Indians as harsh as Francis Parkman's remark that, after a few weeks or months on the prairie, one "begins to look upon them as a troublesome and dangerous species of wild beast." Nor does he utter any observation about any tribe, even the Blackfeet, like that of Mark Twain about the Gosiute Indians: "The bushmen and our Goshoots are manifestly descended from the self-same gorilla, or kangaroo, or Norway rat, whichever animal-Adam the Darwinians trace them to."[49]

Innumerable observers noted Carson's reticence. The account of James Meline, who met him in 1866, is typical: "He is one of the few men I ever met who can talk long hours to you of what he has seen, and yet say very little about himself. He has to be drawn out. I had many questions to ask, and his answers were all marked by great distinctness of memory, simplicity, candor, and a desire to make some one else, rather than himself, the hero of his story." Some people could draw Carson out, others could not, finding him, as William T. Sherman did, monosyllabic.[50]

One reason for this reticence will be apparent to those Americans who have grown up among country people (the real thing, not media caricatures). Such people, confronted by those who assume a superiority based on social standing or education, or urban sophistication, often prefer not to waste their time trying to communicate. With those who take them as they are and speak as one person to another, they can communicate quite well, but they show a deep reluctance to brag, to "blow their own horn." Those who too obviously patronized the quaint, unpolished scout, Carson probably did not consider worth his time. Hero-worshipers he could treat as he did the army officer who met him with the words, "So this is the great Kit Carson, who has made so many Indians run!" "Yes," replied Kit, "sometimes I run after them, but most times they war runnin' after me."[51]

Carson's fame depended less on what he said about himself than on what others, starting with John Frémont, said about him. Without the chance of his meeting and taking employment with the explorer, he might have ended up as just another old mountain man, sitting around the plaza in Taos, telling stories about his mountain days. Carson has often been compared to Daniel Boone, and certainly each became a representative figure, symbolizing a heroic era of westward expansion. Boone represented the trans-Appalachian frontier in its crucial first settlement in Kentucky, and the holding of that settlement in the face of Indian hostility; he symbolized the permanent frontiersman, whose restless search for freedom paradoxically opened new lands to civilization. Carson, representing the trans-Mississippi West, was one of the trappers who first ventured into the Rockies. As a guide and scout he "led the way" for Manifest Destiny; as an Indian fighter he consolidated the conquest. Before the era of the badmen and the gunfighters, he was the supreme western hero.

Boone owed his first fame to John Filson, whose sketch of his life in a promotional work on Kentucky caught the public imagination, leading to more imaginative biographies, and even a mention in Byron's *Don Juan*, besides helping to inspire Cooper in the creation of Natty Bumppo. Boone was neither the first to explore Kentucky, nor the first settler there, nor the supreme Indian fighter; indeed, he seems to have killed very few Indians, and enjoyed at least intermittently friendly relations with some throughout his life.[52]

Carson, his more recent biographers have agreed, was neither a leader nor an outstanding figure among the mountain men, simply a good trapper and a reliable man—a good man to have on your side in a fight, but not a superman. Like Daniel Boone, he was elevated by accident to preeminence as a symbolic hero. If the selection of a hero tells us something about the society that selects him, then so does the rejection of one. The dime-novel Carson represented endless adventure and the solution of problems by ready violence, applied chiefly to "lesser breeds." The more genteel Carson was "one of Dame Nature's gentlemen," with none of the vices and all of the virtues of the trapper and the scout, the fit champion of his people. The Carson now rejected is a brutal racist who carried out genocide against innocent people who had the misfortune to stand in the way of a self-appointed "superior race"; he thus becomes a scapegoat for the sins of our fathers, and the representative of much we wish to reject in our present society.

Like the traveler from Arkansas, many people have searched for the kind of Kit Carson they wanted, whether a dime-novel hero, Natty Bumppo in the flesh, or a Nazi in buckskins. Instead of these cardboard figures, let us take Carson seriously as a man, and try to find out what really was the relationship, or relationships, between him and the American Indians among whom he spent his life. It may not be possible to recover the full truth, and there may be times when the only possible conclusion is that of Saint Paul: "I do not know; God knows." But the attempt to discover the truth may be more interesting than the easy stereotype, for all that.

Carson's life can be divided fairly adequately into six periods. First comes his backcountry boyhood in Missouri, then his years as a mountain man, then his service as a guide and scout for Frémont and others, a period of some seven years as an Indian agent, his military service as an officer of New Mexico volunteers during the Civil War, and the last years when he was both soldier and peacemaker. The divisions are somewhat arbitrary, but they will be seen to correspond to real changes, not only in Carson's life but in the world he knew.

2. Backcountry

Carson: I was born on the 24 Decr. 1809 in Madison
County, Kentucky. My parents moved to Missouri when I
was one year old. They settled in what is now Howard County.
For two or three years after our arrival, we had to remain
forted and it was necessary to have men stationed
at the extremities of the fields for the protection
of those that were laboring.

Harvey L. Carter, *"Dear Old Kit"*

The words quoted above are all that Carson tells us about his family or his childhood—all that he either cared to talk about or thought people would be interested in. It is a classic American story as it stands, of course, with the hero's birth in the "dark and bloody ground" of Kentucky, the Anglo-Americans' first salient west of the Appalachians, and the move west to a new frontier, with the hardy pioneers "forted" in their little stockades against Indian attack, persevering in spite of the danger. Even allowing for Carson's usual reticence, it shows what impressed him most in those early years when he became aware of the world outside the family circle.

There was a great deal more behind that brief paragraph, naturally—things that Carson considered self-evident or commonplace, things that he assumed no one would want to hear, or were no one's business, things perhaps that he did not care to remember. He was not a self-conscious literary artist, trying to let people know how he came to be who he was, or inviting their sympathy. He does not tell us about the fear and insecurity a small boy might feel when he realized why his family and their neighbors were forted, and why men were stationed to protect the workers in the fields; obviously he never forgot the impression these things made on him, either.

The Carson family had settled in the Boonslick (or Boone's Lick) area in what is now central Missouri. Except for trading establishments on up the Missouri River, they were the farthest western white settlements in Missouri, and among the farthest in the United States. (They were, in fact, on land that the Sac and Fox Indians claimed and had not yet ceded to the United States.) Kit could have learned much of that anecdotally when he was a little older, along with something of family history and the general history of the Anglo-American frontier. There was a good deal he could not know, however, that is now available to us, that helps explain how the Carsons got to Boonslick, a long way from Kentucky, and a lot farther from Ulster and from Dumfriesshire in Scotland.[1]

The Carson family were what we have come to call "Scotch-Irish," lowland Scots who migrated to northern Ireland and then to the British colonies in America, chiefly settling in the frontier regions. David Hackett Fischer, however, in his study of British folkways in America, sees the Ulster Scots as only part of a great "North British" migration to America in the eighteenth century. The emigrants came from the Scottish lowlands and the adjacent Border counties of England, and also included inhabitants of northern Ireland who were chiefly natives or descendants of natives of those regions. These people shared much the same culture and outlook on life, a culture as distinctive and persistent, says Fischer, as those of the New England Puritans, Virginia Cavaliers, or Delaware Valley Quakers.[2]

Fischer and others see the people of the Anglo-Scottish border as possessing a common and distinctive culture, shaped by centuries of conflict between the two kingdoms and by persistent border raiding even in times of official peace. In war, they were a great military asset to their respective kingdoms; in peace, they were a perpetual nuisance to law and order. Religious conflict produced a region whose inhabitants, however bitterly opposed to each other, were also more like each other than any others in Britain. George MacDonald Fraser, who is one of them, says of their modern descendants, "They are not, to put it as tactfully as possible, the most immediately lovable folk in the United Kingdom."[3]

In the late seventeenth century Alexander Carson, Kit's great-grandfather, was a Presbyterian minister in Dumfriesshire, on the north side of Solway Firth in the West March of Scotland. Presbyterians suffered political and religious disabilities, and poverty was also common in the border regions. For whatever reason, Alexander Carson emigrated to Ulster by 1700, like many of his co-religionists. In Ireland, of course, they found more religious and political conflict, and they did not become more accommodating. (We can only imagine Alexander's reaction if he could have known that his great-grandson would not only be baptized by a popish priest but would marry a papist, and a Spanish-speaking one at that.) The Ulster Presbyterians held the north for Protestantism, of course, and went right on holding it when the rest of the world had ceased to care, but economic conditions there caused many to join the great North British migration to the New World.[4]

Alexander Carson took himself and his family to Lancaster County, Pennsylvania, perhaps between 1738 and 1748. Like so many North Britons, he settled in the "backcountry," the western frontier of the British colonies from Pennsylvania on south. His son William moved to North Carolina before 1761, and William's son Lindsey would eventually move to Kentucky. The Carsons were following exactly the path of so many of their people, as traced by Fischer: "They gradually became the dominant English-speaking culture in a broad belt of territory that extended from the highlands of Appalachia through much of the Old Southwest." Fischer notes that the backcountry was a "debateable land," like the British borderlands, where proud Indian nations with warrior traditions of their own disputed possession with the newcomers. It was in this "debateable land," Kentucky specifically, that Christopher Carson first saw the light of day on Christmas Eve, 1809.[5]

DeWitt Clinton Peters, seeking to flesh out Kit's meager account of his early years, made much of his birth state: "Indeed, in America, to be a native of the state of Kentucky, is to inherit all the attributes of a brave man, a safe counselor and a true friend." But the ways of the Kentuckian, the Carsons' kind of Kentuckian at any rate, were in fact the ways of the backcountry.[6]

Regarding the folkways of the backcountry, Fischer observes that a culture enduring generations of "chronic insecurity . . . develops an ethic that exalts war above work, force above reason, and men above women." The same insecurity prevailed on the Kentucky and Missouri frontiers, at least during the first part of Kit's boyhood.[7]

Lindsey Carson, Kit's father, was born in North Carolina in 1754. When he was a child of about six, there was war with the Cherokees on the North Carolina border; when he became a man the colonies revolted against Great Britain, which led to a bitter guerrilla war between Whig and Tory, in which Lindsey participated. He moved to Kentucky in 1792, when the Indian-white conflicts there were just beginning to wind down. In 1793 his first wife died, leaving him with five children, and in 1796 he married Rebecca Robinson, who bore him ten more, including Christopher, the sixth.[8]

Kit was only a year old when his family moved again in 1811, to the Boonslick country of Missouri. Anglo-Americans had begun moving to the region west of the Mississippi in the 1790s, when it was still part of Spanish Louisiana; Daniel Boone left Kentucky in 1799 and took up a Spanish land grant along the Missouri River. The Boonslick area took its name from salt licks, a resource that two of Boone's sons began to exploit in 1805. Permanent settlement in the area began just a year before the arrival of the Carsons in 1811, the year the traveler Henry Marie Brackenridge noted "a flourishing settlement" of seventy-five families living mostly on the banks of the Missouri in the space of four or five miles. They constituted the westernmost settlement in the territory of Missouri; many of them were from Kentucky, and like the Kentucky pioneers, they "forted up" in stations formed of groups of cabins arranged in an enclosure completed by a stockade. There were three significant ones in the immediate area—Cooper's Fort, Fort Kinkead, and Fort Hampstead. They would need those forts, for Boonslick was about to become part of a combat zone in a guerrilla war.[9]

Americans blamed this development on British influence over the Indians, but there was, of course, far more history behind it. Since the Revolution the Indians west of the Appalachians had steadily lost ground to the whites. Kentucky and Tennessee were gone, and so were large parts of the Old Northwest; portions of the tribes from those territories had moved west of the Mississippi to maintain their way of life. In 1804 the Sacs and Foxes had signed a treaty giving up much of their land east of the Mississippi and a portion of Missouri. The tribes were losing their economic self-sufficiency, becoming dependent on trade goods; in return for tribal annuities, the government induced leaders to sign away large tracts of land. The first decade of the nineteenth century witnessed the rise of Tecumseh, the Shawnee spokesman for Indian unity, and his brother, the "Prophet" Tenskwatawa, who preached spiritual renewal and a return to traditional values. They were not the first, but the most famous, Indian leaders to combine political and spiritual appeals in an attempt to turn the tide. Practical realities forced them to become allies of the British.[10]

Missouri had some twenty thousand white inhabitants when the War of 1812 began; the legislature estimated in 1814 that they were confronted with six thousand Indian fighting men. No major battles took place there, just intermittent raids and persisting insecurity. The Sacs and the Kickapoos were especially active, with Winnebagos, Potawatomis, Ioways, and others joining in. Louis Houck, the most thorough historian of early Missouri, has a chapter on the War of 1812 filled with accounts of Indian raids, many of them in the Boonslick area, not by armies of thousands of warriors, or even hundreds, but highly mobile, elusive parties of twenty or thirty.[11]

Paul Horgan writes of Cooper's Fort in 1812 as "a little United States community medieval in self-sufficiency and commonness of task." In fact, the fort was dependent on the larger society for many things, but the image of a medieval castle under siege might have seemed apt to the folk within. Other accounts confirm Kit's childhood memories of being "forted" and of men guarding the farmers in the fields.[12]

The year Kit was four, 1814, was especially bad in the Boonslick region; the settlers on the south side of the Missouri abandoned their homes and took refuge in the stockades on the north side. In April, Captain Sarshall Cooper was killed inside Cooper's Fort when an Indian under cover of night and storm reached the wall and fired through a chink between the logs, killing Cooper at his own fireside. A raid in early summer cost three whites their scalps, and a herd of horses and other plunder were carried off. In August the trader Manuel Lisa visited the area and found the settlers holed up in their forts, while the Indian raiders roamed about stealing horses, killing cattle, and also killing any settler caught outside a stockade. At Christmastime, when Kit turned five, they killed William Gregg and carried off his young daughter; she was recovered, but for a little boy there was one more thing to fear.[13]

In October, Lindsey Carson, who had been serving with the militia even though he was sixty that year, was with a small party looking over land when they were jumped by Indians. William McLane was killed, and the Indians, "so it is said," cut out his heart and ate it. Lindsey lost two fingers of his left hand to a bullet that cut away most of the stock of his rifle. One version of the story, perhaps an exaggerated version of another episode, has him killing two of the attackers, one with his rifle and the other in hand-to-hand combat with the Indian's own knife. Kit was surely old enough to remember his father coming home with a bloody, bandaged hand; certainly he saw that mutilated hand daily for the next few years, and heard often enough the tale of how it came to be so.[14]

Even after the United States and Great Britain made peace at the end of 1814, the Kickapoos, stubbornly hostile to those they called the "Big Knives," kept up raids in Missouri for another year before peace came to the western settlements. We read that Kit took a turn at guard duty. If there is any truth in this, we get a picture of a little boy "helping" his father, being allowed to sit up with him on guard until he fell asleep, and perhaps learning a lesson about a man's responsibilities. Lindsey Carson, certainly an old man for his time but a member of the militia, was active in defending the community. He set an example that Kit may have remembered when he himself was past fifty, and when he might have preferred staying at home to campaigning against Indians.[15]

The lesson that a boy might learn about Indian-white relations from these experiences was a hard one. The fears that frontier whites nourished about Indians were not simply racist fantasies, projections of their own unacknowledged, unacceptable impulses onto the Other— although such transference certainly nurtured and exacerbated those fears. The fear and the hatred were based on the harsh and terrible experience of decades of intermittent border warfare. Obviously, the Indians had their own experience, harsher and more terrible, of the other side of that frontier. William Foley, writing of precisely that period in Missouri history, says, "There were many atrocities and brutalities on both sides, but none of the participants seemed able to find a permanent solution that did not require the other's destruction. Despite a genuine desire to save the Indians, U.S. officials always eventually acquiesced to the demands of the more powerful white settlers. Their plans for persuading the Indians to abandon their traditional ways and to adopt those of the white world were unrealistic and doomed to fail."[16] As an adult, Kit Carson would confront every one of those harsh realities, and it would one day be his turn to search for that elusive solution.

Kit Carson's boyhood Missouri was far from Boone's Pennsylvania, in miles and in years of blood and anguish, but in Missouri, too, Indians and whites interacted in complex ways. The Shawnees who had removed to Missouri in the late 1700s sought to stay on good terms with their white neighbors, resisting the appeals of their fellow tribesman, Tecumseh, to unite against them. White and Shawnee children played together, and the two peoples intermarried on occasion, as they had for generations in the backcountry—and not invariably was the husband white and the wife Indian. There were Sacs and Foxes on the Missouri River who did not join their Illinois kinsmen in hostility toward the whites in 1812, and during the war the authorities carefully cultivated the friendship of the Osages living west of the settlements as a counter to the hostile tribes.

After Manuel Lisa reported the grim state of affairs at Boonslick in August 1814, the authorities dispatched Colonel Henry Dodge with 350 mounted rangers to their relief. With Dodge were some forty or fifty friendly Shawnees (perhaps including some Delawares), acting as guides and scouts. Working with local militia under Captain Benjamin Cooper, they overtook and captured some hostile Miamis. Dodge promised the Miamis safety, but after the rifle of a dead Boonslick man was found in the hostile camp, Cooper and his men wanted to kill them. Dodge pointed his sword at Cooper's chest and told him he would have to take the consequences if a shot was fired. Cooper's party backed off, and Dodge later considered saving the prisoners one of the things of which he was proudest.[17]

The vengeful reaction of Cooper's militia to learning that the prisoners had killed their neighbor was not remarkable, either on the frontier or in human history. Dodge's action was not really remarkable either, for he was a "border captain," with some knowledge of Indians, and he was working with the friendly Shawnees, who did not want the Miamis killed and would be outraged if the white chief did not keep his word. The presence of the Indian allies is the aspect of the affair that may surprise those who are not familiar with the history of Indian-white conflict in North America, but that was the most commonplace part of the whole business.

Some Indians were the allies of whites in virtually every Indian-white conflict in American history, and in virtually every conflict between whites in America through the Civil War. Cortés conquered the Aztec empire with thousands of Indian allies, and the Spanish empire was extended northward by a few Europeans and many Indian allies and workers. New Mexico, isolated at the far northern end of the empire, was held with the help of Pueblo auxiliaries. Most of the English colonies had some Indian allies to help defend their frontier, and sometimes depended more on them than on their militias. As the colonial powers fought to dominate the continent, they sought the aid of Indian allies, who sought their own advantage in the struggle. During the Revolutionary War, Britain incited Indians to attack the American frontiers, and continued to do so long after the two countries officially made peace. Indians, in fact, continued to be a significant factor in the power politics of North America until the final peace between Britain and the United States in 1815.[18]

Frontier rangers like Dodge's men were both the shield and the cutting edge of the white frontier for many years, and they were often more trusted by the frontier people than regular troops. Only well into the nineteenth century did the regulars largely take over their functions. One might expect them to be the most irreconcilable of Indian-haters, and certainly they could act with great brutality on occasion. All the same, cooperation between the races had been common since the seventeenth century, when Captain Benjamin Church, fighting in King Philip's War in New England, had organized a unit of rangers (not yet known by that name) that included whites and friendly Indians and gradually recruited prisoners from the enemy, who became his most effective men. Robert Rogers's famous corps of rangers in the French and Indian War included a company of Stockbridge (Mohican) Indians. In the Cherokee war on the Carolina border during Lindsey Carson's childhood, the regular British troops who burned the Cherokee towns were accompanied by rangers and friendly Indians, including Catawbas, Mohawks, Stockbridges, and Chickasaws. During the Revolutionary War, George Washington wanted to use his frontier riflemen and Indian allies to harass the British troops, who, he believed, were deathly afraid of them. Even the Texas Rangers, who ruthlessly prosecuted the Indian-white struggle from the 1830s on, frequently cooperated with Indian allies of various tribes.[19]

This seeming paradox becomes understandable if we remember two things, the first being that virtually no Indian war in any region ever ranged all the Indians of the region in unity against the whites; there were always those who, for reasons of their own, chose the white man's side. Second, among the frontier rangers and especially their leaders there were always a considerable number who had lived and worked with Indians, who had learned from them and counted themselves the friends of some Indians, and perhaps the enemies of their friends' enemies. James Fenimore Cooper was closer to the truth here than many of his critics. Benjamin Church is described by two present-day scholars as "a man not deterred by religious or racial antipathy from forming close ties with Indians," and as one who "approached them as one desiring to live on equal terms among them, neither as missionary nor, initially, as conqueror." James Smith led a group of frontier rangers called the "Black Boys" (because they painted their faces in Indian fashion) in western Pennsylvania in the 1760s; he had been a captive during the French and Indian War. Smith explained, "I taught them the Indian discipline, as I knew of no other at that time." Captain Jack Hays of the Texas Rangers, scourge of the Comanches in the 1840s, was on friendly terms with both the Lipans and those Delawares who had moved to Texas; he reportedly once accompanied some Delawares on a war party against Comanches, and Lipans operated with his Rangers.[20]

When Ethan Allen wanted to persuade the Caughnawaga Indians to join his Green Mountain Boys against the British, he wrote them, "I always love Indians and have hunted a great deal with them I know how to shute and ambush just like Indian . . . my men fight so as Indians do and I want your Warriors to join with me and my Warriors like brothers and ambush the regulars." James Smith concluded that "the Indian discipline" was much better suited to "the woods of America" than that of the British army. Many historians have noted how frontier Anglo-Americans adopted Indian ways of war; James Axtell has perhaps analyzed the phenomenon most thoughtfully. Frontier rangers, even more than most other backcountry folk, were often considered "white Indians" by easterners. They wore Indian moccasins, breechclouts, and hunting shirts (often in green or brown shades for camouflage), carried tomahawks, sometimes painted their faces, took scalps, and above all followed the Indian practices of stealth, concealment, mobility, ambush, and surprise attack on enemy villages. Axtell rightly emphasizes that much of this was purely pragmatic, the adoption of Indian means for white ends, and did not imply that the frontier whites had truly become Indians; as he points out, if the white man's foot was on the Indian's neck, it was little consolation to the Indian if the foot was wearing a moccasin.[21]

It is likely that young Kit Carson, growing up in the Boonslick country, heard about Henry Dodge's expedition, if he did not see the rangers and their Shawnee allies himself, and that he heard about Dodge's confrontation with Captain Cooper over the Miami captives, from the point of view of the Boonslick militia. We cannot know his reaction to such a tale, nor can we know how much of the frontier tradition of Indian warfare and Indian-white cooperation, given above, he consciously learned. These attitudes and practices, however, were pragmatic responses to recurring situations, and were also examples of how people in close and continuing contact, even when hostile, will tend to become more like each other, in ways both positive and negative. These same patterns would recur in Carson's adult life, often with a special intensity.

On a more personal level, Christopher Carson was a boy growing up in a backcountry community, shaped by the ways and values of that time and place and culture. The tale of his helping defend the fort by firing through a loophole sounds a bit dubious, considering his age at the time of the serious Indian raids around Boonslick. We are also told of his playing with Indian children (perhaps friendly Sacs and Foxes who lived on the Missouri, or visiting Osages); this would not have been an unusual experience for a frontier child, but we do not know how extensive it was; if true, it could have taught him that not every Indian was an enemy to be feared and fought.[22]

If the evidence about Kit's childhood is scanty, there is considerable information about the way backcountry people reared their children. David Hackett Fischer writes, "The rearing of male children in the back settlements was meant . . . to foster fierce pride, stubborn independence and a warrior's courage in the young." Self-control and restraint of anger were less emphasized. Male children were taught to defend their honor: "Honor in this society meant a pride of manhood in masculine courage, physical strength and warrior virtue." John Bowers, a twentieth-century child of the backcountry culture of eastern Tennessee, puts it this way: "Where I come from, males were taught from the cradle on to engage in roughhouse and blood-causing sports, never to back down from a fight, and to bond to the death with those who carried your blood and spoke with your accent. Loyalty and perseverance were two much-loved traits."[23]

One consequence of this emphasis on self-assertion and honor was a high level of individual violence. William Foley notes that in territorial Missouri, "fighting, brawling, and killing became more commonplace. . . . The semisavage lifestyles and erratic ways that made these rugged pioneers excellent woodsmen did not necessarily make them model citizens." While the lower orders brawled, the gentry settled "personal insults and affronts" by dueling. It was in the nineteenth century that American courts made a significant alteration in the English common law, which had held that a man in danger of his life from another's violence must make every possible effort to flee and escape his assailant, and was only entitled to use deadly force if he had his "back to the wall" and there was no other recourse. American courts increasingly ruled that a man going about his own lawful business had no absolute duty to flee someone who threatened his life, but could defend himself by killing his attacker, who was held responsible for his own death. Although the doctrine was eventually extended throughout the country, one senses the influence of the backcountry concept of a man's honor.[24]

Backcountry violence was often retaliatory, justified in the eyes of people who believed in enforcing their own ideas of justice; logically, the violence could also be anticipatory. Fischer refers pointedly to "the border variant of the golden rule—do unto others as they threatened to do unto you." "Lynch's law" originated in the backcountry, and justice was conceived of as, above all, retribution for wrongdoing—a kind of justice the individual was justified in taking into his own hands. Not surprisingly, that vigilante justice was applied even more freely to those who, like Indians, were outside the white community.[25]

Yet the violence had a pragmatic side, too. Andrew Jackson, the quintessential backcountry leader, knew how to use his temper to get what he wanted through intimidation. Backcountry wisdom held that, allowing for the demands of honor, one should consider the chances of winning before getting into a fight. Chivalry had little part in it all; one fought in order to win. The backcountry accepted the wisdom of the proverb, "He who fights and runs away / Will live to fight another day." Kit Carson in his maturity would come to exemplify that teaching; he may have remembered it on a windy Texas plain one day in 1864.[26]

There was more to backcountry teaching than violent assertiveness, of course. Honor was also a matter of keeping one's word and telling the truth. John Frémont would remark that "With me, Carson and Truth are one," and Kit would take pride in doing what he had promised. Honor was about loyalty to one's kin and one's chief, and Carson's loyalty to certain leaders, notably Frémont and James Carleton, would affect his historical reputation. Memory was important in an oral culture, and Carson's memory was often remarked upon.[27]

A man's character is not simply stamped out from the template of his culture. If one could create a model backcountry product, Carson would not fit the model in many respects, nor would any other man of the time and place. Abraham Lincoln, also born in backwoods Kentucky in 1809, and Nathan Bedford Forrest, born in Tennessee in 1821, grew up in a very similar environment, and each, like Kit, lost a parent at an early age; yet each turned out very differently. Josiah Gregg, born some three years before Carson, also grew up in the Boonslick region, and he too went west on the Santa Fe Trail, but Gregg became an intellectual and a scientist and wrote *Commerce of the Prairies*, the first comprehensive study of the Santa Fe trade and of New Mexico in English. The modest, quiet, reticent Carson described by so many was not the stereotypical assertive, touchy man of violence that one might expect from a superficial reading of Fischer (or some of Carson's latter-day critics). John Bowers's words, quoted above, on the fundamentals of backcountry rearing, appeared in an article about Sergeant Alvin York, the strikingly modest, unpretentious, and devoutly religious World War I hero from east Tennessee, whom Bowers considers a "prototypical" product of his culture. Carson was reared in a culture where violence was perfectly acceptable in defense of honor or to exact justice for serious wrongs. This "folkway" colored his view of the world and of his own experience. Carson would exhibit various backcountry traits in his life, and he was certainly capable of violence on occasion, but we must never forget the irreducible individuality of him or any other person.[28]

Lindsey Carson was fifty-five when his son Christopher was born. A man who sires a child at a relatively late age may be an especially stern father, being remote from his own childhood, or an especially indulgent, grandfatherly one; we do not really know which, if either, was true of Lindsey. What evidence we have about Kit himself as a father suggests that he was affectionate and permissive. Rafael Chacón describes him as lying on an Indian blanket in front of his army quarters with his pockets full of candy and lumps of sugar: "His children would then jump on top of him, and take the sugar and candy from his pockets and eat it. This made Colonel Carson very happy, and he derived great pleasure from these little episodes." General William T. Sherman visited Fort Garland, Colorado, while Carson commanded there in 1866, and later described Kit's children as "wild and untrained as a brood of Mexican mustangs. One day these children ran through the room in which we were seated, half clad and boisterous." Kit may have ruled with a freer hand than he ever knew as a child. The effect on him of being squeezed in by so many older siblings we also cannot fully assess.[29]

Lindsey Carson's death unquestionably influenced the life of Kit, who was eight years old at the time. Pioneer farms east of the Great Plains had to be cleared of timber, mainly by fire; in September 1818, a limb from a burning tree fell and killed Lindsey instantly.[30]

As a man, Carson would become attached, in some degree or other, to various authority figures: Ewing Young, Jim Bridger, Charles Bent, John Frémont, and James Carleton. The idea that he was searching for a father is hampered somewhat by the fact that Frémont and Carleton, though in positions of command, were younger than Carson, and Frémont may have tried to cast *Carson* in the role of the mentor, the wise old scout. As will be seen, Carson certainly did differ, sharply on occasion, with some authority figures.

Rebecca Robinson Carson was left with at least eight children, one born a week after her husband's death. She must have relied heavily on the older children for help, but after four years she remarried. This was another event that surely affected young Kit, now verging on adolescence. Tradition says that at about thirteen he became hard to handle—not exactly a startling development at that age—and lived with his brother William for a while. For a time he was a ward of a neighbor.[31]

One thing that seems fairly certain is that he did not learn to read or write, at least not to any very useful extent. We have only his signature in his own hand, and no reliable indication of any literacy. He had the retentive memory of a man who cannot rely on written records, he needed a clerk to help with his paperwork as an Indian agent, and he liked being read to, according to Jessie Frémont. Seeing a picture of Mazeppa bound to his horse in a volume of Byron's poems, he told her, "Read it out to me—you will read it quicker than I can!" Either he could not read at all and did not like to admit it, or reading was hard, slow work. It is possible that he was to some degree dyslexic, and that handicap could account for his humility and seeming deference to better-educated folk.[32]

Kit was probably smaller than the average male; "small of his age but thick-set" was the way David Workman, his master, described him when he ran off at sixteen. It cannot be said that he compensated for his size by being a bully or a clown. There is little information about him as a young man, except for what he provides himself, but he does describe instances of reckless behavior, and we will see one notable episode where he asserted himself very much in the fashion of the cocky short guy.[33]

Kit's family had something quite different in mind for him from what he became. Deciding that he should learn a useful trade, they apprenticed him at the age of fourteen to a saddler, David Workman, in nearby Franklin, Missouri. The location, if not the choice of occupation, was fateful, for Franklin was not only an important town in the Boonslick region; it was the head of the Santa Fe Trail.[34]

3. Mountain Man

Carson: Yes, sometimes I run after [Indians],
but most times they war runnin' after me.
Edwin L. Sabin, *Kit Carson Days*

There are two kinds of people:
those who divide people into two different kinds,
and those who don't.
Attributed to William James

While Kit Carson learned saddle-making in David Workman's shop, the country itself, like the young apprentice, was on the edge of great change. It was becoming more industrialized, politically democratic, and continental in reach. The debate over Missouri's admission to the Union as a slave state was a more ominous development. In the mid-1820s, white Anglo-America was still on the eastern edge of the trans-Mississippi West. Missouri and Louisiana were still the only states west of the great river. Large Indian nations remained east of the Mississippi, until Andrew Jackson implemented his removal policy in the 1830s. Two major Indian-white conflicts, the Black Hawk War and the Second Seminole War, were yet to be fought in the East. Illinois and Wisconsin, the theater of the first war, were still "the West," and would be until the Civil War.

Officially, the country's boundaries reached west to Mexican Texas and the Continental Divide. Practically, Missouri was a salient of white settlement on the far side of the river. The Louisiana Purchase was hardly a generation past. Lewis and Clark had gone to the Pacific in 1804–6, and on their heels American trappers and traders had moved up the Missouri all the way to the headwaters in present Montana, some of them crossing to the sea. The War of 1812 cut this development short. The U.S. Army established Fort Atkinson above the mouth of the Platte in 1819, and Major Stephen Long explored parts of the southern

Great Plains in 1820, concluding that they were useless for agricultural settlement.

In the early 1820s, however, a few Anglo-Americans moved not only onto the Great Plains but well beyond them, into the Rocky Mountains and what was then northern Mexico, and these movements largely determined where and how Kit Carson would spend his life. In 1821 a party of American traders from Missouri reached Santa Fe and found a market for American goods. A little later other Americans, also based in Missouri, reopened the fur trade on the upper Missouri River and in the Rocky Mountains. Out of these two commercial enterprises would come the vanguard of American continental expansion, much of the romance of the Old West, and what Herman Melville called that "class of men, of whom Kit Carson is the model"—the mountain men.

David Workman, Kit later acknowledged, was a good man, but saddle-making did not suit the youngster, and rather than "pass my life in labor that was distasteful to me," he ran away. Workman waited a while and then, apparently only to satisfy a legal obligation, he advertised and offered a one-cent reward for returning Kit—not much inducement even then. In August 1826, Kit went west on the Santa Fe Trail, headed for New Mexico[1]

The Santa Fe Trail opened a generation before the Oregon and California Trails. It was not a road for homeseekers, although many who traveled it did, like Carson, find a home in New Mexico; it was a road for traders, linking two widely separated and very different frontiers, eventually penetrating deep into northern Mexico. It made backcountry Missouri the gateway to an international market, and for many backcountry boys it was the pathway to adventure and a wider world. Franklin was its head in its first years, and it was a natural way out for a restless, discontented teenager.[2]

This is not the place to describe the life of the trail, or the "black-eyed señoritas" of Santa Fe that many authors have lingered over, but the trail did take the sixteen-year-old Kit Carson into a strange culture with a different language (which seems quickly to have become his second tongue). It also brought him to Taos, where he would eventually make his home, and where he joined the second Anglo-American thrust into the Far West, the fur trade.

The fur trade and the Santa Fe trade were linked from the first, many major and minor characters figuring in both. Goods hauled over the Santa Fe Trail were often exchanged for beaver pelts rather than Mexican silver. American trappers based in Taos exploited the beaver streams of Colorado and Utah before the more famous mountain men of the Rendezvous system got to them. As David Weber says, Taos "became the most important permanent market and supply depot for trappers between Fort Vancouver on the Pacific and St. Louis on the Mississippi." At the extremity of Spanish-American settlement, Taos was as much a frontier settlement as Boonslick, though much older. The Indian Pueblo had been there since perhaps the fourteenth century. Ranchos de Taos dated from about 1776, and Don Fernando de Taos, the community now known simply as Taos, from the 1790s.[3]

Kit Carson spent the winter of 1826–27 at Taos, at the home of an old Boonslick neighbor, Matthew Kinkead, one of the Americans already resident in the town. He did not become a trapper immediately, being, as Guild and Carter note, "too small, too young, too green"; he spent the next few years in one sort of labor or another on the Santa Fe Trail and its southern extension. In 1829 he got the opportunity for which he had probably been waiting, and joined Ewing Young's trapping party headed for the Gila River. He would come to exemplify, in the eyes of many people, the mountain man.[4]

This class of men became the objects of romanticizing at an early date. Fictional or semifictional works about mountain men, by authors like Timothy Flint, Albert Pike, George Frederick Ruxton, and Sir William Drummond Stewart, began appearing in the early 1830s. Pike, Ruxton, and Stewart had the advantage of personal acquaintance with them. But the principal early source of the romanticized mountain man, before Kit Carson's sudden rise to fame, was one of America's most distinguished authors, Washington Irving. His two fur trade histories, *Astoria* (1836) and *The Adventures of Captain Bonneville* (1837), gave Americans a glimpse of a world far beyond what they were accustomed to think of as the western frontier, and of men living a strange and (from a safe distance) romantic life. His view of the trapper as an adventurous free spirit, untrammeled by the bonds of conventional eastern society, reveling in adventure, whiskey, and Indian and Hispanic women, has persisted to the present day.[5]

Some scholars have discerned no less than three stereotypes of the mountain man. The first, according to William Goetzmann, is the romantic, indeed epic, hero depicted by Irving as leading a "wild, Robin Hood kind of life." The second is the man who is outside the bounds of decent society, daring but degraded, both a Caliban and "one of the saddest heroes in all history," the destroyer of the environment that gives him his freedom, exemplified in fiction by Boone Caudill, the hero of A. B. Guthrie's *The Big Sky*. Goetzmann proposes a third stereotype, the "Mountain Man as Jacksonian Man," an "expectant capitalist" who went to the Rockies seeking opportunity.[6]

Harvey Carter and Marcia Spencer have argued that the "expectant capitalist" image applies better to some fur trade leaders than to the rank and file. They agree with Goetzmann in attributing the heroic stereotype in the first instance to Washington Irving, finding the origin of the second, degraded image in certain writers who visited the West in the 1840s, after the decline of the fur trade, and encountered the last diehards still clinging to the old way of life. Their mountain man is indeed a man with a wanderlust, valuing his freedom, who did engage in perilous encounters with men and animals and romantic ones with Indian and Mexican women, who did drink when he had the chance, but whose delinquencies were no worse than those of men in the settled areas.[7]

Our concern is the mountain men's relations with the Indians among whom they lived and worked, and thus certain observations on these stereotypes seem relevant. Goetzmann presents a statistical analysis of the lives of 446 mountain men, showing how many moved on to other occupations and how few stayed on as lifelong trappers. Under the category of "persons killed in the fur trade" he gives the figure of 182—a mortality rate of roughly 41 percent. Not all of these were killed by Indians; accidents, disease, grizzly bears, and other wild animals must account for many of these deaths. James Ohio Pattie, possibly not the most reliable of witnesses, looked back in 1830 at the men who had come to the mountains with him and lamented, "Some had died by lingering diseases, and others by the fatal ball or arrow, so that out of 116 men, who had come from the United States in 1824, there were not more than sixteen alive." Artist Alfred Jacob Miller, who attended the 1837 Rendezvous and talked with the trappers as well as painting them, believed that forty or fifty mountain men a year were killed by the Blackfeet. Being a mountain man was obviously a little different from keeping a store in Cincinnati, and the "expectant capitalist" who sought his opportunity in the mountains was the product of a slightly more rigorous process of self-selection than usually applied. Lewis Garrard, one of the authors credited with contributing to the "daring but degenerate" image, declared that a mountain man could "tear off a bloody scalp with even a grim smile of satisfaction." George Frederick Ruxton, also viewing the remnant mountain men of the 1840s, judged that "Constantly exposed to perils of all kinds, they become callous to any feeling of danger, and destroy human as well as animal life with as little feeling as they expose their own." The callousness that Garrard and Ruxton noted may have been similar to that of the combat veteran who tries to build a wall between his emotions and the events outside, particularly the loss of comrades and the need to kill.[8]

The mountain man was heroic, Harvey Carter and Marcia Spencer argue, because he was a distant wayfarer, like Odysseus, but also because he engaged in personal combat, like the heroes of the *Iliad*. He was a degenerate brute, for some contemporaries and later critics, because he callously took human life, and casual about killing because his victims were only Indians.[9]

There is some question about how many trappers actually engaged in combat; of some three thousand men estimated to have been Rocky Mountain trappers in the period, Carter and Spencer believe only about 40 percent actually fought, with a somewhat higher percentage for elite leaders. Still, trapper memoirs like Kit Carson's indicate that the memoirists were engaged in mortal combat on a number of occasions. Those who ventured into areas like the Blackfoot country, as Carson did, were probably more sure of violent encounters. Here, as in other respects, mountain men were probably more diverse than the hero-brute stereotypes allow for.[10]

Certainly mountain men did fight Indians. They took scalps, and they admittedly sought violent retribution for acts of violence or theft by Indians. However, to imagine the mountain men as buckskin-clad death squads roaming the West slaughtering the inhabitants in accordance with an "only good Indian is a dead Indian" philosophy is seriously mistaken. The relationship between the mountain men and the Indians was far more complex than that, and their interactions were of every kind imaginable.

Winfred Blevins writes, "The mountain-man era was not just another phase of domination and exploitation of the Indians by whites. It was an exception to that overwhelming pattern." Although this is a sweeping statement, the relationship of the trappers and the Indians, if not entirely unique, was governed by factors different from those prevailing on most Indian-white frontiers in Anglo-American history, producing, by necessity, different ways of seeing and treating each other.[11]

The two groups were not meeting on the frontier as commonly defined by white historians of the nineteenth and much of the twentieth centuries: the clearly defined line between "civilization" and "savagery," between "white" and "red." Only in a limited sense were they even meeting on the frontier as more recently defined: the zone where widely differing cultures meet and interact. The mountain men were hundreds of miles beyond the Anglo-American settlement frontier at its farthest extension in Missouri. The three thousand mountain men who roamed the Rockies and other trapping grounds from the 1820s to around 1840 were tied to the world economy by their need for supplies, but in other respects they were quite isolated from their parent society. During the entire period, only one United States military force was launched in support of fur traders—Colonel Henry Leavenworth's 1823 expedition against the Arikaras in South Dakota—and it was not a great success, nor did it come near the Rockies. A few military escorts for Santa Fe trains and a few marches of dragoons to "show the flag" barely came in sight of the mountains before 1840. The mountain men were on their own.[12]

As Blevins says, "So few men could not possibly force their way through the mountains. . . . So they were compelled, from the beginning, to try to get what they wanted by friendship, persuasion, and trade." On occasion, they did force their way through the mountains, obtained what they wanted through violence, but they could not do so consistently. Quite simply, they were in the Indians' world. To survive for any length of time there they must live by the Indians' rules and not forget they were there for the business of trapping beaver. Jim Bridger's fur brigades trapped in the face of Blackfoot hostility in the 1830s, but only as a desperate measure prompted by the decline of beaver and intense competition between fur companies, and he knew that he could fall back on the Crow country or other areas where he and his men would be more welcome. If the trappers had been on terms of mortal hostility with every tribe in the mountains, their whole enterprise would have been hopeless.[13]

Howard Lamar sees the period of the mountain men and Indian traders up to the mid-1800s as "an era when whites [and Indians] could mingle, trade, and live—however uneasily—in some sort of frontier modus vivendi," which was most true in the days of the mountain men.

William Swagerty argues that the fur trade had to be "bicultural and symbiotic" in order to succeed in the West, and he finds the mountain men to be "more open-minded and sensitive to other cultural viewpoints than any other social group entering the West during the nineteenth century," a characteristic he sees as partly the result of the small numbers of trappers in the mountains. Circumstances forced the trappers, in that brief period, to live in something like what Richard White calls the "Middle Ground," his definition of the reciprocal relationship worked out by the natives and the French and then British traders and officials in the Great Lakes region from the seventeenth to the early nineteenth century, when both Indians and Europeans had to modify their view of each other "as alien, as other, as virtually nonhuman," and seek "accommodation and common meanings." A major difference is that the Great Lakes Middle Ground, in spite of major changes, endured well over a century; that of the Rocky Mountain trappers and traders was encompassed by the lifetimes of Kit Carson's generation.[14]

In the 1860s Frances Fuller Victor took down the reminiscences of the old mountain man Joe Meek, then a solid citizen of Oregon. In describing the Rendezvous of 1833 on the Green River in southwest Wyoming, she names the different companies present, and then notes casually "the usual camp of Indian allies." The Indians may have included Shoshones, Crows, Bannocks, Nez Perces, and Flatheads; they were there first of all to trade, but to call them allies of the whites at the Rendezvous is not inaccurate, even though some of them—such as Crows and Shoshones—were not friendly to each other. Many of them had fought as allies of the whites before and would again, for they had enemies in common.[15]

The first true mountain man was John Colter, a member of the Lewis and Clark Expedition. When the explorers were returning from the Pacific in 1806, they met two white trappers going up the Missouri into previously unknown country to try their hand at beaver trapping. Colter, having already spent over two years away from white civilization, asked the two captains for permission to take his discharge and join them. He spent another four years in the mountains and had several near-fatal encounters with the Blackfeet, including his famous naked "race with death" from Blackfoot pursuers. These incidents pointed the way to the future of the mountain fur trade, and one was especially portentous. In 1808 Colter was traveling with a party of Flatheads and Crows on the Gallatin River in Montana when they were attacked by Blackfeet. Colter found it necessary to fight alongside his companions and was wounded in the leg. The episode antagonized the Blackfeet, but it was a symbol of the relationship that would develop between the mountain men and various tribes.[16]

The friendly relations between the mountain men and certain tribes were based on pragmatic considerations. The mountain men were few in number and worked in small, dispersed groups. It was not only desirable but an absolute necessity that they have friends with whom they could take refuge, with whom they could travel in dangerous country, and who would fight beside them when the necessity arose. For the Indians, too, there were good reasons for making such alliances.

In reality, the Indians dominated the region and were the determining factor in much that happened. Blevins says that the Indians viewed the mountain man with both awe and contempt: awe because he possessed technological marvels that they could only regard as evidence of great supernatural power—"medicine"; contempt because he would give away these marvels for something as mundane as sexual intercourse. Anthropologist John Ewers writes that the Indians first viewed white men as semidivine, possessed of great power for good or ill; closer acquaintance showed them that whites were human, all too human, and they began to judge them by their own ethnocentric criteria, and inevitably found them wanting.[17]

Granted that white men were less than ideal human beings from the Indian point of view, there were still at least two excellent reasons for some tribes to be on good terms with them. First, white traders and trappers had a great variety of goods that the Indians could not possibly produce themselves: cloth, beads, mirrors, metal pots, tools of many kinds, knives, tomahawks—all items that could enhance the quality of life. They also had alcohol, which traders saw as an indispensable article of traffic, but which some tribes nonetheless refused for years. Above all, the white men had guns and ammunition, a special consideration for the tribes of the northern Rockies, because for many years the Blackfeet had blocked their access to direct trade with the Hudson's Bay and North West companies in Canada, while themselves enjoying the advantages of such trade, including the possession of firearms to use against the mountain peoples. The Flatheads, Nez Perces, Shoshones, Kutenais, and others all suffered from the power of the Blackfeet, whom John Ewers describes as "the dominant military power on the northwestern plains." It was no accident that these mountain tribes became the friends and allies of the mountain men, and also no accident that the Blackfeet became their bitter enemies.[18]

This implies other reasons for friendship and alliance with the whites. The mountain men were not intruders in a peaceable kingdom; in most of the places they went, war was a well-established state of affairs. "Indeed," wrote Colonel Henry Atkinson in 1820, "there is scarcely a tribe but what is at war with some one or more tribes." Tribes fought for possession of horses, for control of hunting grounds, and for revenge. This state of affairs had existed for centuries, long before the appearance of the whites, though their presence and their trade may have, as Anthony McGinnis says, "complicated, changed, and intensified intertribal warfare."[19]

For western Indians of the 1800s the concept of "Indian" or "Indianness" had little meaning. Unlike the native peoples east of the Mississippi, who had had centuries of conflict and dispossession to awaken ideas of racial solidarity, the western tribes still identified themselves exclusively by their tribal affiliation. They were proud of being Crow, Blackfoot, Shoshone, Sioux, or Comanche; being "Indian" was meaningless. As late as the 1880s, W. P. Clark, in his study (based on years of firsthand research) of the Indian sign language, the principal means of intertribal communication on the Great Plains and adjacent mountain regions, could find no sign for the concept "Indian"; the people so called "always specify the tribe." John Ewers has coined the term *tribocentric* to describe their attitude.[20]

If the different tribes regarded each other thus, then it was not hard to regard the white men as just another tribe, their language and ways only a little stranger than those of other tribes in the mountains. Different tribes made alliances based on convenience and common interest, just as nations have done throughout history. Crees and Assiniboines were allied against the Blackfeet, the Blackfeet were allied with the Atsinas (Gros Ventres to the mountain men), and the Shoshones (Snakes) were for a time allied with the Flatheads, Nez Perces, and Kutenais. The Crows and Flatheads were united against the Blackfeet in the 1808 battle that enlisted John Colter. Similar alliances prevailed in other parts of the West, like the Kiowa-Comanche alliance on the southern plains. These partnerships did not compel action on all members of a tribe; there would be no Indian equivalent of the Normandy landing against an enemy tribe, but there were many common defensive and some offensive actions.[21]

Although we must avoid any notion that the mountain men were supermen, each capable of slaying his dozens and hundreds of "redskins," as the dime novels would picture Kit Carson doing, they were nonetheless potentially valuable allies. Warren Ferris of the American Fur Company believed that an experienced mountain man could learn to follow a trail and detect the presence of danger as well as any Indian. The trapper generally carried a muzzle-loading "plains" rifle, the legendary Hawken or some other make, usually over .50 caliber, and with it he must have had some skill, since he lived by hunting. If not the superweapon of some tall tales, it was more accurate and longer-ranged than the trade muskets most commonly carried by Indians, though slower-firing than bows and arrows.[22]

Lewis Saum sees the mountain men as "the lowest echelon of the English-speaking fur trade," and their memoirs have a "deplorably sanguinary character." Their atypical role, as trappers not traders, "colored their thinking, and not to the red man's advantage." Although the mountain men's memoirs are certainly filled with bloody encounters, they are also filled with instances where Indians and white trappers cooperated in these same battles, and where they lived and worked together on more peaceful occasions.[23]

The most prominent example is the Rendezvous, the distinguishing feature of the fur trade in the central and northern Rockies in the 1820s and '30s. William Ashley and his associates, unable to establish themselves on the upper Missouri because of the hostility of the Arikaras, introduced two innovations in the fur trade in the mid-1820s. They decided to rely on white trappers instead of Indians as the primary suppliers of beaver pelts, and they dispensed with permanent forts as trading centers. The Rendezvous was an annual summer meeting of the trappers with supply trains brought west along the Platte River road by the fur companies. The first was held in 1825 and it was an annual event until 1840. The exact meeting place shifted from year to year, but the usual location was somewhere in southwestern Wyoming, along the Green River or a tributary, or in nearby areas in southeastern Idaho or northern Utah. This was the approximate location, as it happened, of a trading rendezvous where the Shoshones met with the Crows, Flatheads, and Nez Perces in the days before these tribes made direct contact with the whites. Perhaps Ashley was inspired by this Indian practice; if so, it was simply another example of whites benefiting from Indian example. Indians were always present in considerable numbers at the

Rendezvous, the Shoshones in particular, and commonly members of other tribes that traded in the area. Some of them traveled hundreds of miles at considerable risk. Tipis and Indians are prominent in Alfred Jacob Miller's paintings of the 1837 Rendezvous. Of the journey there he notes, "Indians encamped en route for the rendezvous were all about us, for this gathering at a fixed time brings them far and near." He estimated that some three thousand were present.[24]

Predictably, the traders judged Indians on the basis of their relations, friendly and cooperative or hostile and dangerous, with the whites, human and understandable considerations that took precedence over preconceived ideas based on literature or popular prejudice. Ethnocentrism and the strains of culture shock remained, but the hard facts of survival and business ruled day-to-day behavior and influenced emotion and judgment. An early casualty was the notion that Indians were simply "Indians." Fur traders and mountain men came to consider tribal distinctions as not only significant but literally vital. One survival skill a trapper had to learn was how to tell one tribe from another, preferably at a safe distance, knowing which tribes were likely to be friendly and hospitable, which definitely hostile, and which uncertain or dangerous to a lone man. The mountain man's emotional reactions to different tribes varied accordingly; even the most biased responded differently to a Flathead than to a Blackfoot.[25]

Certain tribes earned lasting enmity. The Arikaras, who attacked William Ashley's men on the Missouri in 1823 and were bitter enemies of traders for years thereafter, were regarded with both hatred and contempt, stigmatized as "the Horrid Tribe," a title also bestowed on the Blackfeet. Paiutes, the so-called Diggers of the Great Basin, with a very simple material culture and frequent clashes with whites, received sometimes brutal and disdainful treatment. But it was the Blackfeet who held pride of place as the bitter and persistent enemies of the "Big Knives"—the American trappers.[26]

Some historians trace this hostility to the penetration of the Blackfoot country by the Lewis and Clark Expedition in 1806, when Meriwether Lewis and three of his men killed one or perhaps two Piegan Blackfeet on the Marias River in Montana. In 1808 John Colter joined with Crows and Flatheads in a battle with Blackfeet. In 1810 the Missouri Fur Company established a post at the Three Forks of the Missouri to trap and trade with the mountain tribes—Shoshones, Flatheads, and Nez Perces—whom the Blackfeet had long raided, enjoying the advantage of numbers and firearms obtained from the British traders in Canada. Fearing the loss of their edge in weaponry, the Blackfeet harassed the post and forced its abandonment after a few months. When the Americans returned to the mountains in the 1820s, the hostilities resumed. The Americans believed the British encouraged this animosity, but in any case the Blackfeet saw American trade and friendship with their enemies as threatening, and the trappers' exploitation of beaver and game animals on their own hunting grounds made things worse. Later, they accepted an American Fur Company post in their country, but not the presence of the mountain men. "If you will send Traders into our Country we will protect them & treat them well; but for Trappers—Never," Blackfoot chiefs told a government agent in 1834. Alfred Jacob Miller, after conversations with mountain men in 1837, wrote of the Blackfeet: "They are the sworn enemies of all—Indians and white men alike. Their principal charge against the latter is that they trespass on their beaver streams, and that they have time and again warned them off,—threatening them with the consequences. To all this the beaver hunters pay no heed, and are knocked on the head at the handsome average of 40 or 50 per season." Miller clearly refers to Jim Bridger's trapping expeditions in Blackfoot country in the 1830s when, as Kit Carson says, "A trapper could hardly go a mile without being fired upon." The mountain men called the Blackfeet "Bug's Boys," which supposedly meant "the Devil's Own."[27]

With an enemy so detested, friends rated very highly. Even some very seasoned and cynical fur traders could not altogether resist the myth of the Noble Savage, at least where their favorite tribes were concerned. The Flatheads were depicted in glowing colors by almost every fur trade memoirist. Warren Ferris credited them with "humanity, courage, prudence, candour, forbearance, integrity, trustfulness, piety, and honesty," and added that they had never killed or robbed a white man or stolen a horse from one. The Nez Perces, also consistent friends of the whites, rated high, as did the Shoshones. Daniel Potts declared the Utes "an exception to all human kind, for their honesty." The Crows, who traded with the whites and were not actively hostile, but who would rob traders when the opportunity arose, were regarded more ambivalently. To Captain Benjamin Bonneville they were "fine martial-looking fellows," but "one of the most roving, warlike, crafty, and predatory tribes of the mountains."[28]

It was commonplace for white men with extensive experience among Indians to have favorite tribes, even to identify themselves with some tribe, and to despise others. James Fenimore Cooper, who could have known authentic frontiersmen while growing up in western New York around 1800, emphasized Hawkeye's warm friendship and admiration for Delawares and Mohicans and his distrust and disdain for Iroquois and Hurons. Certainly, some whites believed that "the only good Indian was a dead Indian." Their actions in accord with that philosophy, as at Sand Creek in 1864, are an undeniable part of American history. Yet the men who had the closest acquaintance with Indians tended to be more discriminating. We will see how Kit Carson came to regard the Utes.

Indians and mountain men not only traded and fought together but interacted in virtually every other way. Trapper memoirs are full of accounts of parties traveling together, for mutual security but also for social reasons, and trappers often wintered with Indians, again for security, sociability, female companionship, and simple comfort. Warren Ferris was sent by his employers to buy some articles from the Rocky Mountain Fur Company in early 1832 and found its brigade, probably including Kit Carson, camped on the Lemhi River in eastern Idaho with forty or fifty lodges of Flatheads and Nez Perces, passing the time "gambling and regaling each other with adventure stories." On Bear River in Utah in the spring of 1834, Osborne Russell found Andrew Drips of the American Fur Company with a party "consisting of about 60 whites and nearly as many half breeds who were encamped with 400 lodges of Snakes [Shoshones] and Bonnaks [Bannocks] and 100 lodges of Nez Perces and Flatheads." Joe Meek gives a lively account of trappers joining in a large Flathead and Nez Perce buffalo hunt in the fall of 1838, following the chief's directions as the Indian hunters were required to do, to insure the maximum kill of winter meat. "That war a sight to make a man's blood warm! A thousand men, all trained hunters, on horseback, carrying their guns, and with their horses painted in the height of Indians' fashion."[29]

These relationships depended upon the unwritten code of conduct. In 1839, certain trappers hanging out at Fort Davy Crockett, a ramshackle trading post on the Green River in northwest Colorado, lost some horses to Sioux raiders; they prudently left the Sioux alone and made up their loss by stealing from friendly Shoshones whose hospitality they had enjoyed. According to the traveler E. Willard Smith, "the trappers remaining at the fort expressed their displeasure so strongly at this act of unparalleled meanness that they [the offenders] were obliged to leave the party." Robert Newell expressed the mountain men's shock: "Shuch thing never has been Known until late." Joseph Walker, a prominent and respected leader, realized the Shoshones, by their own code, might take vengeance on any whites. Walker and a party of trappers including Joe Meek, Newell, and Kit Carson, pursued the miscreants, who holed up in an abandoned trading post. After some maneuvering, involving an attempt by the thieves to enlist some Utes on their side, Walker's party marched off with the horses and restored them to the Shoshones. Meek acknowledged that he and his comrades were "not anxious to spill" white men's blood, and the first consideration involved the security of nearby whites. All the same, bloodshed might have been necessary to redress the wrongs to friendly Indians. Walker was a man of unusually strong character, but it is worth noting that Kit Carson was among his supporters—a fact Kit does not mention in his autobiography.[30]

Obviously the standards applying to friendly Indians were different from those for enemies. Ornithologist John Kirk Townsend, at the Rendezvous of 1834, "listened to the recital of bloody and ferocious scenes, in which the narrators were the actors, and the poor Indians the victims, and I have felt my blood tingle with shame, and boil with indignation, to hear the diabolical acts applauded by those for whose amusement they were related." Quite possibly, the boys were pulling the greenhorn's leg a bit, but from the context it is clear that these stories were of encounters with Blackfeet, and Townsend acknowledged that "The Blackfoot is a sworn and determined foe to all white men."[31]

Fur trade literature clearly reveals that mountain men were capable of brutality toward Indians, and not only Blackfeet. Washington Irving relates an incident in which two Arikaras entered the camp of Captain Bonneville's trappers led by Daniel Adams. They were apparently creating a diversion while other Arikaras swept off the party's horses. Adams's men seized the two and said that they would kill them unless the other Arikaras returned the horses. During negotiations the Arikara leaders offered progressively larger numbers of horses in exchange, but the trappers insisted on the return of all. Refusing that demand, the raiding party departed with the animals, and the prisoners were killed. Irving had the story at second hand, and one may wonder if the Arikaras would really have sacrificed the lives of two of their tribesmen. In any case, the Arikaras were another tribe with whom the trappers had a special, mutual animosity, dating back to the attack on William Ashley's men in 1823.[32]

The commonest stereotype of Indians in nineteenth-century literature arose from the belief that they were uniquely vengeful, that they never forgot an injury or let pass an opportunity for revenge. Noah Webster, in his dictionary definition of *savage*, noted that the Indians of America were "implacably cruel and revengeful toward their enemies." Writing of "the Indian," Francis Parkman said, "With him revenge is an overpowering instinct; nay, more, it is a point of honor and a duty."[33] Anyone reading much of American frontier history is likely to conclude that the whites were equally obsessed with revenge; indeed, the "overpowering instinct" is fairly universal.

Many Anglo-American mountain men were from the backcountry of Missouri, Kentucky, and Virginia. Backcountry people were much inclined to redress wrongs by taking the law into their own hands. David Hackett Fischer sees this not as a "frontier" trait, since other frontiers saw relatively little of it, but a "tradition of retributive folk justice" brought to the southern backcountry from the Anglo-Scottish border. To men reared in this tradition, it seemed natural to act when "wronged." They argued that hostile Indians must be taught not to attack whites or no white man would be safe where he was so badly outnumbered. The Rocky Mountain trappers were far beyond any support from their own government, and there was no law-enforcement authority outside the tribe to provide justice. The Indian tribes operated on a retributive principle; one of the primary reasons for warlike expeditions by Indians was to seek revenge for previous losses. There were few large-scale battles or massacres, but those that did occur "kept the revenge cycle spinning endlessly," as Anthony McGinnis puts it.[34]

What Josiah Gregg said of the Santa Fe trader applied also to the mountain men with whom he was so closely associated: "He is in daily, nay, hourly exposure of his life and property, and in the habit of relying on his own arm and his own gun both for protection and support. Is he wronged? No court or jury is called to adjudicate upon his disputes or his abuses, save his own conscience; and no powers are invoked to redress them, save those with which the God of Nature has endowed him." All of this is perfectly understandable, but the possibilities of abuse are obvious. What is done to oneself or one's friends is intolerable; what one does to one's enemies is "justice." If all parties operate on the same principle, and no outside authority steps in, there is no logical end, unless one party overwhelms the other. Besides, the temptation in such a system is to apply what Fischer calls "the border variant of the golden rule—do unto others as they threatened to do unto you."[35]

Kit Carson was instructed in this doctrine on his first expedition as a trapper, with Ewing Young in 1829. Young (himself from the backcountry in eastern Tennessee) had sent a trapping party out from Taos toward the Colorado River. On Salt River in Arizona they were attacked by Apaches and forced to return to Taos. Young then set out with forty Anglo-Americans and French Canadians on the same route. They encountered what were assumed to be the same Indians on Salt River (supposedly, some of the same men were with the second party and could identify them), and Young ordered the majority of his men to conceal themselves so that the Apaches would think them weak. Carson says that Young "allowed them to enter the camp," which might imply either that they were attacking or that they came to parley. Then Young "directed the party to fire on them"; Carson says fifteen or twenty were killed. Carson, our main source for this affair, clearly had no doubt that these were the same Apaches who had made the previous attack, and that they intended to attack again. Certainly no one alive today is in a position to assert otherwise. Whether the example did any good might be questioned, since Carson says the party continued to be harassed by Indians as it moved toward the Colorado.[36]

Obviously, mountain men were capable both of violence and friendship toward Indians. But when all allowance is made for individual diversity, and for the force of circumstance, momentary rage and fear, and stubborn pride, what did mountain men really think about Indians? Bil Gilbert asserts that the Indians left their mark on the frontiersmen by turning some of the most noted of them into "pseudo-Indians," not renegades but "Indian lovers in many senses of the word." He declares that the mountain men "provided nearly all the visceral Indian lovers in the American westering movement." Joseph Walker, married to a Shoshone, would seem to fit this description, for on a trip back to Missouri to visit relatives he was asked when he was coming back to civilization to settle down; he replied that he was going back to live with the Indians because "white people are too damned mean."[37]

The assertion that some white men became "white Indians" is nothing new. John Faragher points out how the frontier hunters of Daniel Boone's generation learned from Indians and assimilated many of their ways. It was a concern of easterners, from colonial times on, that the frontier population, especially hunters and others on the very fringes, was becoming uncivilized and even a danger to settled society. In 1836 Washington Irving expressed the apprehension that "this immense wilderness of the far West," not being susceptible to cultivation and civilization, might become the abode of "new and mongrel races . . . the remains of broken and almost extinguished tribes; the descendents of wandering hunters and trappers; of fugitives from the Spanish and American frontiers; of adventurers and desperadoes of every class and country, yearly ejected from the bosom of society into the wilderness." Certainly all the elements Irving listed were present in the Rockies and on the Great Plains at the time he wrote.[38]

It may be wise here to recall James Axtell's caution that whites often adopted Indian means to serve white men's ends. However much the mountain men might adopt Indian ways, it could still be argued that their essential attitude remained racist. This study has tried to discern mountain men's attitudes from their actions, since they were, first of all, men of action. But what prejudices and preconceptions may have underlain these actions, beyond their obvious pragmatism? Were they, to use the latter-day word and concept, racists?[39]

Richard Drinnon, in his study of "the metaphysics of Indian-hating and empire-building," distinguishes sharply between racism and ethnocentrism. Ethnocentrism is the "inner-centeredness of a group united by social and cultural ties," the belief of virtually all ethnic groups that their people and their ways are good and right, and that others who deviate from them are not only different but somehow not quite right. Racism, Drinnon suggests, is the "habitual practice by a people of treating, feeling, and viewing physically dissimilar peoples—identified as such by skin color and other shared hereditary characteristics—as less than persons." One reason Drinnon makes this distinction is that he is aware that Indians were as ethnocentric as anyone else, and he wishes to present racism as a phenomenon unique to Western European civilization—the result of sexual and other repressions—and all other peoples as the victims of European, and especially white American, villainy. Nonetheless, the distinction seems intellectually valid. Racism implies a more formal, all-encompassing set of attitudes, not susceptible to contrary evidence, though evidence can always be produced to support it. Ethnocentrism, however—the assumption that there is something wrong with Those People because they are different and do things differently—is the essential prerequisite of racism. The question is, were Kit Carson and his fellow mountain men racists, or did they simply have ethnocentric prejudices like the rest of the human race?[40]

The very years that Carson spent in the mountains saw the rise of an "American school" of ethnology that supplied scientific support for the idea that "races" were separate species, some distinctly and unalterably inferior to others, with "whites" superior to all others. This notion challenged the Biblical teaching of common descent from Adam and Eve but was still attractive for many reasons. Supposedly, this doctrine arose from the need to justify the existence of slavery, but Reginald Horsman argues that it developed in part as a justification of Manifest Destiny. The period saw the removal of thousands of Indians from east of the Mississippi and American expansion at the expense of Mexico, and it was more comfortable to believe that those who lost out in this process were doomed by their own inherent inferiority. While Kit Carson trapped in the Rockies in the 1830s, a distinguished anatomist and ethnologist, Dr. Samuel Morton of Philadelphia, was measuring the skulls of American Indians and writing his book *Crania Americana*, published in 1838. Morton concluded that the intellectual faculties of Indians were "of a decidedly inferior cast when compared with those of the Caucasian and Mongolian races." The "inaptitude of the Indian for civilization" seemed to Morton undeniable; they had learned nothing from two centuries of contact with whites.[41]

Such doctrines, however welcome among the East's intellectual and political elite, had little circulation in the Rocky Mountains. There were educated men among the trappers; Osborne Russell writes of the "Rocky Mountain College" and of debates in winter quarters in which "some of my comrades who considered themselves classical Scholars have had some little added to their wisdom." Russell himself spent one winter reading Byron, Shakespeare, Scott, the Bible and commentaries, "and other small works on Geology Chemistry and Philosophy." One trapper working out of Fort Davy Crockett in 1839 had been a student at the University of Jena in Prussia. There is no evidence, however, that Dr. Morton's work or others of that ilk found their way so far west. If they had, Kit Carson could not have read them.[42]

Richard Drinnon would argue, however, that racist attitudes and practices were well established in America before the rise of "scientific" racism, which indeed only built on and confirmed popular beliefs. Deep-seated and sometimes virulent prejudices were common among white Americans well before the second quarter of the nineteenth century, prejudices little subject to examination and reinforced by such psychological mechanisms as projection. The question is how much these prejudices were subject to alteration, or at least modification and moderation, by experiences that would put them to the test, or at least make their translation into action undesirable.[43]

In a famous study of the psychology of colonization, Octave Mannoni argues that Europeans who went out to established colonies sought to compensate for an inferiority complex by living among people whom they could treat as unquestionably inferior, while they assumed a superiority just as unquestionable. But whites who went west in the days of the expanding frontier were generally looking not for an opportunity to lord it over "inferiors," but for economic opportunity or personal freedom. Certainly, frontier settlers most often desired the absence, not the presence, of Indians, no doubt a racist attitude. To Mannoni, however, it is the dependence of the "natives" that is gratifying to the European, assuaging his feelings of inferiority. As John Ewers notes above, the Indians came to judge whites by their own ethnocentric criteria and found whites wanting. The mountain men, instead of dominating the land with their power, were a small minority in a region controlled by Indians. The Indians had no conception of the larger society from which the mountain men came, or of the sheer numbers of white Americans in the East. It may be that some violent acts by mountain men were prompted in part by frustration at the Indians' failure to recognize the white man as superior and to treat him as such. But the situation did not offer the trapper much easy balm for feelings of inferiority.[44]

Winfred Blevins acknowledges that the mountain men had their full share of prejudices: "The talk of the trappers was full of references to everyone who was not like them; John Bull got it as fully as the 'niggur' who got it as fully as the red man who got it as fully as the 'greaser' who got it as fully as the 'Frenchy.'" In 1846 Francis Parkman stopped off at the multiethnic trading community that became Pueblo, Colorado. There he concluded, "The human race in this part of the world is separated into three divisions, arranged in the order of their merits: white men, Indians, and Mexicans, to the latter of whom the honorable title of 'whites' is by no means conceded." Parkman had his own heavy load of prejudices, but there is ample confirmation that Anglo-Americans of the time often rated Indians—friendly Indians at least—higher than Hispanics, especially Hispanic men.[45]

The Rocky Mountain fur trade was anything but a haven of ethnic purity. Circumstances required the mountain men to associate with friendly Indians in business, social life, and war. Perhaps no group of whites had such close association with Indians in so many different ways. As noted above, the mountain men themselves were a highly diverse group. The majority of them were either Anglo-Americans (many from Virginia, Kentucky, and Missouri), French Canadians, or French speakers from the Mississippi valley (often Missourians). About 15 percent may have been Europeans, like the Irish-born Tom Fitzpatrick. Jim Beckwourth and Edward Rose were noted mountain men with African ancestry, and some others appear briefly, at times anonymously, in the records, often referred to as "mulattoes," which means that today they would be classed as African-Americans. Hispanics were often associated with mountain men, although David Weber, the authority in this area, believes they were generally servants rather than trappers. At least one New Mexican, Mariano Medina, was definitely a trapper. The Hudson's Bay Company employed Polynesians from Hawaii as boatmen in the Pacific Northwest. A mountain man determined to be a racist would have plenty of opportunity for practice.[46]

More important here is the fact that a number of mountain men were, in fact, Indians. Some of those designated as "Frenchmen" were of mixed ancestry, "half-breeds" in the parlance of the times, reflecting the long interaction of French speakers and Indians in the fur trade of the Mississippi and Missouri Valleys and Canada. Whether they were classed as "white" or "Indian" depended to a great extent on their cultural affiliation. A few Indians from western tribes became closely associated with white trappers. Warren Ferris tells of a Shoshone named Cut Nose who joined the whites and dressed like them: "He is an excellent hunter and has often rendered them important services." Osborne Russell says that the Nez Perces whom Bridger's men protected from the Bannocks were "numbered among our trappers." Russell also records a Nez Perce as being on "our side," that is, with Bridger's brigade, and being killed in a fight with Blackfeet in 1836. The whites called one Nez Perce "Kentuck" because he kept trying to sing the song "The Hunters of Kentucky"; whether or not he actually worked as a trapper, he was in Tom Fitzpatrick's camp at the 1834 Rendezvous.[47]

More important numerically as trappers were members of eastern tribes, often partially assimilated to white men's ways, who functioned as white mountain men did and were closely associated with them. The

North West and Hudson's Bay companies brought numbers of Iroquois trappers from Catholic settlements on the St. Lawrence to the Pacific Northwest early in the 1800s; they were trapping the western slope of the Rockies years before the Americans. Pierre's Hole in Idaho, the site of two rendezvous, was named for "Old Pierre" Tevanitagon, an Iroquois trapper killed by the Blackfeet. Some, including Old Pierre, deserted the Hudson's Bay Company to work with the Americans and live as free trappers. Antoine Godin, an Iroquois trapper, started the Battle of Pierre's Hole in 1832 by killing an Atsina chief in revenge for the earlier death of his father. Kit Carson later described the Iroquois he knew as "good hunters, good shots, and brave warriors."[48]

Members of other eastern tribes, like Potawatomis and Ioways, appeared in the mountains, but the most prominent were Shawnees and Delawares, especially the latter. The Delawares are almost ubiquitous in the fur trade literature, either in separate parties or in association with white trappers. Western tribes commonly regarded them as white men, as in their dress and equipment—including the rifles they knew well how to use—they appeared to be. (They themselves took pride in being Indians and thus, they said, being less vulnerable to Indian tactics than white men.) Migrating west from the Delaware River Valley in front of the white advance, they were by the early 1800s largely west of the Mississippi. Some had been with Henry Dodge's rangers sent to relieve the Boonslick settlers in 1814, and their role as scouts for the whites would continue. They were found on frontiers from Kansas to Texas, often acting as intermediaries between whites and local tribes, and their hunting parties ranged into the Rockies and on to the Pacific. Their prowess as warriors was respected and feared by western tribes.[49]

Among Delawares with whom Kit Carson apparently associated in his trapping years were Manhead and Tom Hill. Hill later settled for a while among the Nez Perces, where he opposed the presence of missionaries, then participated with whites in the conquest of California. Joe Meek was distressed by the death of Manhead at the hands of Blackfeet, for he and the Delaware had been through some rough experiences together, and he did not think the killers had suffered sufficiently in the engagement. He and another mountain man went back, therefore, and stole a number of horses from the Blackfoot camp, a form of revenge Manhead might have considered appropriate.[50]

About 1837 a party of seventeen white trappers joined six Delawares led by Jim Swanock on an expedition into Blackfoot country. The whole party recognized Swanock as their leader, and he saved them from a trap set by the Blackfeet. It is difficult to see how much further acceptance could go than for white men of that era to accept the leadership of an Indian. Osborne Russell tells of an occasion when an old Iroquois trapper he calls "our leader" led white trappers in a fight with Blackfeet on the Madison River.[51]

Roger Barker, in a study of the effect of frontier environments on behavior, notes that in these areas there are fewer people to do what needs to be done. Therefore, each person becomes more valuable, and there is a greater need to tolerate personality differences. In Barker's words, "On the frontier the balance of questioning is less toward What kind of person is he? and more toward What has to be done? and Can he do this job?" The mountain man's bid for survival enforced tolerance, if not democracy.[52]

Warren Ferris was asked to take a small party through a hundred miles of potentially hostile Arapaho country to recover a cache of American Fur Company pelts. The men he picked were two Delawares, a Shawnee, and two French Canadians, "all men who had seen death in all its forms and could look it steadily in the face if necessary, yet men of great caution and vigilance who had all shown great presence of mind on trying occasions." It was not an occasion for indulging ethnic or racial prejudices, even if Ferris had been so inclined. The episode would seem to illustrate Barker's thesis very neatly.[53]

A major form of interaction between Indians and mountain men remains to be dealt with: the relations between mountain men and Indian women. A significant feature setting the Rocky Mountain fur trade frontier apart from many others in American history was the almost complete lack of Anglo-American women, a point ignored by studies that deny the uniqueness or the isolation of the mountain men by emphasizing their economic aspirations or their integration into the world economy. This lack was a major factor in pushing Indians and whites into a closer relationship. It is no secret that trappers and fur traders had sexual relations with Indian women; part of the reason that more literary authors referred to the Rendezvous as "saturnalia" was because of the casual indulgence of white men in sexual relations for which they exchanged trade goods. Reverend Samuel Parker, after attending the 1835 Rendezvous, charged them with "unrestrained dissoluteness," and added that "their demoralizing influence with the Indians has been lamentable." He acknowledged that they lived hard, dangerous lives; indeed, their conduct was probably much like that of soldiers or sailors and other men far from home and the company of women for long periods. Kit Carson admitted, "Trappers and sailors are similar in regard to the money that they earn so dearly, daily being in danger of losing their lives . . . they think not of the hardships and danger through which they have passed, spend all they have and are ready for another trip." It was commonly acknowledged that they spent a good deal of that money on those they generally called "squaws."[54]

Not all these connections were casual, however. It was not just brief sexual encounters with Indian women that scandalized easterners; it was the frequency with which mountain men married Indians and had children with them. William Swagerty found that nearly 40 percent of their first marriages were to Indians, 19 percent to New Mexicans, and only 16 percent to Anglo-Americans. Shoshones ranked first among marriage partners, followed by Sioux, Flatheads, Arapahos, Nez Perces, and, interestingly, Blackfeet. Even more trappers married women of mixed ancestry. Clearly, mountain men were not following a rigid color line in their domestic lives. Considering the distance they lived and worked from the Anglo-American settlements, it is not likely that they would have, although Swagerty finds that Anglo-American mountain men were somewhat more reluctant to marry Indians than were French speakers or Europeans. About one-third of the Anglos made first marriages to Indians, as compared to roughly half of his sample of all ethnic groups.[55]

This may mean a bit less than it might seem to; men have very commonly shown a willingness to establish relations with women of groups they otherwise deemed inferior. Trappers' marriages with Indians were rarely solemnized in churches, at least not until some time later; in the eyes of white, Christian society, they were not marriages at all. The test would be in their long-term treatment of both the women and their children. Swagerty finds that the average marriage lasted fifteen years and produced three children. Only about 10 percent separated from the first wife, but Swagerty, admitting his information may be unreliable, says as many as one in five mountain men may have left their first wives, or vice versa. The whole subject of fur trade marriages and family relations has received more attention from Canadian scholars than from Americans, which in itself may be significant. The "squaw man" and the "half-breed" generally have not been admired figures in American literature or society. Kit Carson's nineteenth-century biographers would ignore his Indian marriages, though dime novelists apparently had fewer difficulties with such matters.[56]

Carson twice married Indian women, first Waanibe (Singing Grass), an Arapaho, then Making-Out-Road, a Cheyenne. Isaac Rose, a fellow mountain man but not the most reliable of witnesses, says that there was a temporary relationship with a Shoshone woman, whom Kit left when he decided to make a trip to Taos because he was "not willing to take an Indian wife among the Mexican Senoras." Rose's amanuensis definitely plagiarized from Frances Fuller Victor and may have done so from Peters or other Carson biographers; he may have lifted this tale from a cheap biography. Carson seems to have married Waanibe in 1835 or not long thereafter; she died between 1839 and 1841. The only picture we have of their life together comes from a story John Frémont heard from Edward Beale. In 1847 Carson was staying at Senator Thomas Hart Benton's house in Washington, and seemed to be troubled about something; Beale asked him about it, and Carson explained that the ladies of the house might not like to associate with him if they knew that he had had an Indian wife. He added, "She was a good wife to me. I never came in from hunting that she did not have the warm water ready for my feet." When it is remembered that a trapper spent hours wading in cold mountain streams setting traps, besides hunting in all kinds of weather to provide food for his family, we can see that this was no small matter.[57]

Carson says nothing of Waanibe, or of his second Indian wife, in his autobiography. The sense that these relationships would not be acceptable to respectable folk, such as the readers of the biography that DeWitt Peters expected to write from Carson's recollections, may account for this reticence. The second marriage, to Making-Out-Road, was not a success; apparently she divorced him after the fashion of her people, by putting his belongings outside their tipi near Bent's Fort. He seems to have concealed this second match from female relatives in later life, during his marriage to Josefa Jaramillo. Carson and Waanibe had two daughters, only one of whom, Adaline, survived early childhood. The marriage to Making-Out-Road may have been intended to provide them with a mother. Carson accepted his responsibility to them. The younger child apparently was looked after by his New Mexican family until she was scalded to death in an accident. Adaline he took to Missouri to be cared for by his sisters. Later she was enrolled at a Catholic "female seminary," and after Carson had married and settled down permanently in New Mexico, he brought her there to live with him. On the face of it, he did all that he could, as a single father and later one often gone on long journeys. What growing up without parents as a "half-breed" in Missouri may have cost Adaline we cannot know. She was characterized later as "a wild girl"; her first marriage broke up and she died in her early twenties in California. There seems no reason, however, to doubt Kit's good intentions within the limits of nineteenth-century ideas about child-rearing. He had every reason to think that the wandering lifestyle that he necessarily pursued through the 1840s precluded his caring for her himself, and he probably doubted his ability, as a male, to raise her properly. She received a much better formal education than he ever had.[58]

As the Rocky Mountain fur trade waned in the 1840s, many mountain men settled down in multiethnic trading communities like Pueblo, Hardscrabble, and Greenhorn in Colorado, or Robertson, near Fort Bridger in Wyoming. Taos and other northern New Mexico communities served a somewhat similar purpose for some mountain men, especially those who, like Kit Carson, had married Hispanic women. These communities were near the mountains, allowing hunting trips and perhaps some trapping, and they were places where Indian or Hispanic spouses and children of mixed heritage were less subject to the discrimination of latecoming Anglo-Americans, who were sometimes leery of old "mountaineers," with their strange ways and stranger families.[59]

It seems safest to conceive of mountain men's attitudes toward Indians as a spectrum that ranges from the near-complete assimilation of a few to the contempt and casual brutality of others. But that view must be modified by the fact that "Indian" is too broad a category to be meaningful in many of the situations that the mountain men found themselves in. Behavior that was appropriate with one group of Indians was wholly inappropriate with another. People with whom one had socialized, traveled, shared winter quarters, hunted and eaten buffalo, fought alongside, and who were perhaps relatives by marriage, were to be regarded and treated very differently from those who, if met, would probably try to steal one's horses and take one's scalp. William Swagerty, who has already noted the social adaptability of the mountain men, adds that their sexual habits "clearly reveal a compromise between Euroamerican Christian norms and mores and those of the various Indian cultures of the American West and Mid-west." That last generalization might be extended to their behavior in general.[60]

This was the social environment is which Kit Carson spent the years of his young manhood, from the age of nineteen until he was past thirty. Whatever notions about "Indians" he may have had, shaped by backcountry tradition and a frontier Missouri boyhood, would have been tested and modified, if not necessarily completely altered, by the years that brought him to maturity, the exact result depending on his individual personality. As noted, Carson's first lesson as a mountain man was that of retaliation against the Apaches, carried out by Ewing Young in 1829. He then accompanied Young's party to California, where a less typical experience awaited. Some Indians attached to one of the Catholic missions, Mission San José, ran away and took refuge in a village of Miwok Indians, who were not friendly to the mission or the Hispanic Californios. Some Californios and some mission Indians went after them, and these in turn got help from a friendly village. After being beaten off by the village of refuge, the pursuers applied for help to Young's party, and Young sent Carson and eleven others to assist. After a daylong fight, in which the Miwoks "lost a great number of men," according to Kit, the attackers burned the village. The next day, after a threat that "we would not leave one of them alive," they secured the return of the runaways.[61]

It is hard to see the point of mixing in this quarrel. Guild and Carter attribute it to Young's (and Carson's) slave-state origins; returning a runaway might have seemed a social duty. Perhaps, on the other hand, it was just a means of gaining the goodwill of the local Hispanic population. By this period, many non-mission Indians and runaways were in fact engaged in raiding the Californios. The expedition was against one group of Indians in company with men of another; once again, the lines of "racial" division were blurred.[62]

Soon after, another group of Indians (Carson does not name any of these California tribes) ran off most of the Young party's horses. Carson was one of the twelve riders who pursued them one hundred miles into the Sierra Nevada. They caught the thieves feasting on some of the horses, killed eight, and took three children prisoners, who presumably found their way into servitude among the Californios, very likely at a mission. The trappers had applied the rule of not allowing Indians to get away with an offense; the loss of most of the party's horses would have been similarly punished by most of the Indian tribes that the mountain men were acquainted with.[63]

Returning from California, the Young party crossed the Mojave Desert to the Colorado River, where it camped and trapped. One day while most of the group were checking their traps, young Kit was apparently left in charge of the camp and the few men remaining. A large number of Indians (again of an unnamed tribe), whom Carson estimates at five hundred or more, visited the camp. The trappers kept a watchful eye on them, and detected concealed weapons. Carson "considered the safest way to act was not to let the Indians know of our mistrust and to act in a fearless manner." Through a Spanish-speaking Indian, he told them they must leave inside ten minutes: "If one should be found after the expiration of that time, he would be shot." One would imagine that the Indians gathered from this that the white men were a bit mistrustful. They left and there was no bloodshed. The twenty-year-old Kit had shown that he could keep his head and act decisively; he had also displayed the caution which would be so prominent a characteristic in later years. As to whether the danger really existed, he was in a better position to judge than anyone living well over a century later. The Indians might have carried concealed weapons because they distrusted the white men, but the latter were entitled to their doubt. Carson had managed to avoid a violent encounter that could have ended very badly for him and his outnumbered comrades, but the full implications of that lesson would not become apparent in his life until years later. There is reason to believe, however, that Young was already coming to regard him as one of his most reliable men.[64]

Young's men returned to New Mexico in the spring of 1831, sold their furs, and had a high time until the money ran out. Kit soon joined a party of Rocky Mountain Fur Company trappers in Santa Fe and journeyed north into the heart of the Rockies, the "Rendezvous Country" where the most famous mountain men (at least in the eyes of latter-day historians) had been pursuing their trade since the mid-1820s. Trappers shifted about from Taos and the southwestern trapping grounds to the Rendezvous and the northern Rockies with complete freedom, especially if they were free trappers like Carson, bound to no company. Taos and the Rendezvous were the two poles of the mountain fur trade for a decade and a half. It would be a few years before Kit attended a Rendezvous, but his career as a mountain man was well launched.[65]

This journey took Carson as far north as Jackson Hole, Wyoming, and the Salmon River in Idaho. He records no personal conflict with Indians, but four or five of his party were killed by Blackfeet while hunting. This was apparently the same Rocky Mountain Fur Company party that Warren Ferris found encamped with the Flatheads and Nez Perces that winter, "gambling and regaling each other with adventure stories," so Kit was learning another side of life in the Rocky Mountains, an aspect he does not mention, undoubtedly because it was so utterly ordinary.[66]

In 1832 he left the Rocky Mountain Fur Company and joined the party of John Gantt, which took him into Colorado. The party spent the winter of 1832–33 on the upper Arkansas River, near present Pueblo, and while there lost some of its horses to a Crow raiding party. Inevitably, there was a pursuit by twelve men, including Carson, also accompanied by two Cheyennes—Black White Man and Little Turtle—although the Cheyenne account differs from Carson's in various details. They followed the Crows through the snow and were able to sneak up on their camp and secure the horses. According to Carson, the men who had lost their horses and recovered them were willing to leave it at that, but those who had not personally lost any animals, including Kit himself, wanted something more: "We were determined to have satisfaction, let the consequence be ever so fatal." The trappers marched on the Crow "fort," a log enclosure, and a dog gave the Crows warning. Carson says that the whites opened fire as the Crows were getting up, killing most of those in that camp—the surprise attack at dawn traditional in guerrilla warfare. The survivors fled to a second Crow fort nearby. As it was now daybreak, the Crows could see how few trappers were actually present and decided to attack; they lost several more men. The whites were finally forced to retire but had suffered no losses. Carson's autobiography notes, "In the success of having recovered our horses and sending many a redskin to his long home, our sufferings were soon forgotten." George Bent, the half-Cheyenne son of William Bent, gives a slightly different version, which he says Carson told him; Bent recorded the tale some forty years after Carson told it to him. He says that the two Cheyennes ran the horses off while the Crows and Carson's party were actually engaged, and that only two Crows were actually killed. Carson would seem to be more worthy of trust on the details, but the casualty toll may not have been as large as his account makes it sound. As Bent says, everyone on both sides kept jumping about to disturb the enemy's aim.[67]

Martin Green takes this episode as a prime example of Carson's brutal amorality. He takes *satisfaction* as the key word, "with its debased-chivalric connotation of a code of honor." But chivalry, as understood by the readers of Sir Walter Scott, had nothing to do with it, although the actual medieval knights, or Anglo-Scottish "border reivers," might have understood it very well. It was the backcountry code of retributive justice, the refusal to let somebody get away with something at your expense. The affair was a bloody exercise in retribution, and Carson must bear his share of the responsibility, which as far as his dictated account goes, caused him no qualms. One must remember, however, the presence of the two Cheyennes; Carson's, or his scribe's, use of the word *redskins* gives a misleading impression of a specifically racial animus. The animus was against those (expletive) Crows who stole our horses, and the Cheyennes saw no reason not to participate on the side of their friends the trappers. By their code, which the mountain men had largely adopted, horse thieves who got caught paid the penalty the pursuers were able to inflict, the same penalty the Crows would have inflicted on anyone they caught stealing their horses. All the plains tribes engaged in these horse raids, and all of them punished raiders who did not get away in the same fashion. Even if white Christians were brought up in a different tradition—which is doubtful in the case of backcountry men like Carson—the mountain men were far from an environment where such standards seemed to apply and where wrongs could be righted by sheriffs and courts.[68]

Carson devoted considerable space in a relatively brief memoir to this episode, indicating that, though it was not his first fight, it was important to him. George Bent's version of the affair makes Carson the leader of the mountain men, something not apparent from Kit's own account. Although the Bent version is clearly inaccurate in some respects—he has the year wrong and believes Carson was working for the Bent brothers at the time—it would explain why this fight received so much space if it was the first time Kit was in charge in an engagement with Indians, and why he felt so much satisfaction with the result. Beyond that, one should perhaps be wary of reading too much into an account dictated by an illiterate man to a clerk, and both perhaps bored at times with the task. It would certainly be unwise to assume, as Martin Green does, that a lack of expression of feelings (like horror or remorse, for instance) means that Carson was incapable of such feelings. His satisfaction, and relief, may be that of a young man who has been in combat with an enemy superior in numbers and has come off victorious and without losses. If he was actually in charge of the party, he may have been unwilling to shrink from combat in his first "command." As Harvey Carter points out, the mature Carson might well have been willing to take the horses and leave well enough alone. Moreover, if the trappers had simply taken the horses and fled, the Crows would likely have pursued them, and then they would have had to fight a larger party capable of surrounding them, without the advantage of surprise. Carson makes no mention of such a pragmatic consideration, though it is hard to believe that it did not occur to someone in the white party. In spite of his habitual modesty, here Kit may have preferred to remember their motives as more purely "heroic." This winter began a long association between Carson and the Southern Cheyennes, which deepened when he later worked for the Bents at their fort on the Arkansas and married Making-Out-Road. In George Bent's words, written early in the twentieth century, "The Cheyennes call him Little Chief and the old men still talk about him today."[69]

Joe Meek recalled another violent encounter with Indians later that year (1833), which Carson did not mention. According to Meek, he, Carson, Levin Mitchell, and three Delawares named Manhead, Jonas, and Tom Hill all made an excursion into Comanche country, somewhere south of the Arkansas River. South of the Arkansas a large number of Comanches attacked—Meek says two hundred—and since the mules they were riding could not possibly outrun the Comanche horses, the mountain men cut the animals' throats and used them as a breastwork to fight behind. Each time the Comanches charged, only three men would fire their rifles, taking out the leaders each time. The Comanches' horses were spooked by the smell of the mules' blood and would not close with the enemy. Although the trappers suffered from the sun and thirst, the Comanches finally gave up and rode off. The little party then had a thirsty hike back to water and the mountains. There are some doubtful aspects to this story; Meek gives the year as 1834, which is impossible since neither he nor Carson could have been in the area that year. Harvey Carter believes it could have taken place in the spring of 1833, because Meek often gets dates wrong, and other events he relates shortly after occurred in that year. Meek also says they killed forty-two Comanches, a dubious figure. Mitchell, Manhead, and Tom Hill are otherwise documented, although no other source ties them to such an episode. Carson's failure to mention it does not absolutely disprove its occurrence—he fails to mention at least one other Indian battle he probably fought in 1839. To the Comanches, the trappers would have been intruders on their hunting grounds, although they did not need such a motive for attacking a small party from which they could seize some loot and win some glory. It could be, of course, that Meek made the whole thing up, or more likely that something similar occurred but he added Carson to the company after the fact because of his fame.[70]

While Kit and his companions continued trapping in the Colorado mountains, there were two incidents in which unnamed Indians attempted to steal their horses, and in each case one thief was killed. Shortly thereafter Carson and three companions spotted four mounted Indians, and he proposed that they charge them, assuming that these Indians were the group that had made the attempts on their horses; the assumption was correct, but the decision was a near-fatal mistake. In Carson's words:

> [W]hen near we found we had caught a tartar. There were upwards of sixty Indians. They had surrounded us and our only chance to save our lives was a good run. We done so, the Indians firing on us from all directions. We run the gauntlet for about two hundred yards, the Indians were often as near as twenty yards of us. We durst not fire, not knowing what moment our horses might be shot from under us and the idea of being left afoot, your gun unloaded, was enough to make any man retain the shot which his gun contained. We finally made our escape and joined the party at the camp. One of the men was severely wounded, it being the only damage we received.

Carson surely realized later that the incident was a classic example of the use of a decoy to lure an enemy into an ambush, a tactic commonly employed by the plains tribes and many other horse-warrior peoples throughout history. (It may even have been the origin of the old expression he used about catching a Tartar, since the Mongols often practiced it on a far larger scale.) These Indians had just made another unsuccessful attempt at capturing the main party's horses and were seeking compensation: "They made a very good attempt, but thank God, failed." The whole affair shows that the young Kit—now twenty-three—was still impetuous and combative, and that his later caution was well learned.[71]

After trapping in Colorado for a while longer, Carson and some of his friends headed to Taos to sell their pelts and enjoy themselves. Kit then joined a company of trappers under Richard Lee and journeyed north through Colorado to northeastern Utah, wintering near a trading post belonging to Antoine Robidoux. During the winter a California Indian working for Robidoux made off with six horses belonging to the trader, who then asked Kit to pursue the thief and recover them—an indication that Carson was considered a particularly reliable man, one who could follow a trail and take care of himself. He set out, accompanied by a Ute Indian, whose horse gave out after a hundred miles. "But I was determined not to give up the chase." He overtook the thief: "Seeing me by myself [he] showed fight. I was under the necessity of killing him."[72]

We need not doubt the necessity, and few of his contemporaries would have doubted the justice of dealing with a horse thief in this manner, but anyone considering Carson's relations with Indians would note that to this point, so far as his account goes, they chiefly involved violence. Carson does seem to have gotten into more than his share of deadly encounters, and his autobiography might justify Lewis Saum's complaint about the "deplorably sanguinary character" of mountain men's writings. Carson, however, gives this impression in part because he does not bother to mention ordinary, friendly encounters with Indians. He says nothing about spending his first winter in the northern Rockies among the Flatheads and Nez Perces, and he mentions the fact that his camp of the winter of 1833–34 was near a Ute village only because his companion in the pursuit of the horse thief was from that village. Nor does he mention other friendly dealings with the Utes during this period, nor their guiding him through the mountains, although the Utes apparently had pleasant recollections of trading with him, finding that the little white man with the easily remembered name of Kit Carson was honest. It was the exciting, violent episodes, when his life was at stake and luck or skill brought him through, that were memorable; these were the tales that trappers told around campfires. The everyday business of trading and living with Indians would surely not interest anyone reading his account, and the tales men told of their encounters with Indian women were not suitable for a respectable nineteenth-century audience. Carson did not keep a journal like Osborne Russell, nor did he have the literary sense of Warren Ferris, or Joe Meek's amanuensis, Mrs. Victor, that prompted them to include enlivening detail about a mountain man's life. Carson does note how Jim Bridger's men wintered on the Powder River in, apparently, 1837–38; he says, "Near our encampment was the Crow Indian village. They were friendly and [we] remained together during the winter." That the two camps, mountain men and

Crows, would cooperate in case of a Blackfoot attack did not need to be mentioned any more than the daily socializing that undoubtedly took place.[73]

"Old Gabe" Bridger was one of the great names among the mountain men, more famous in written history than any of them except Carson, and much more prominent than Kit at the time. Signing up with him meant going in harm's way, and Carson would add quite a few more violent encounters to his autobiography in the next few years. Bridger's specialty was trapping in the Blackfoot country around the headwaters of the Missouri in western Montana, a guarantee of danger and insecurity. Bernard DeVoto says that Bridger liked to kill Blackfeet, but there were more compelling reasons for entering the hunting grounds of the trappers' most inveterate enemies. In the early and mid-1830s the region was still well stocked with beaver, unlike areas such as the Snake River country, which had been badly depleted by the competing companies.[74]

This was the period of which Carson said, "A trapper could hardly go a mile without being fired upon." He was with a party of fifty men, but to trap profitably they had to go out in vulnerable groups of two or three. The hunt was so dangerous and unprofitable that they finally broke off and went into winter quarters on the Snake River. In February 1835 Blackfoot raiders stole eighteen of their horses. After a difficult pursuit through the snow, the two sides held a parley, the mountain men demanding their stolen horses. The Blackfeet were unwilling to return all the animals, and negotiations broke down: "We broke for our arms, they for theirs." Carson had just fired his rifle to protect a friend, Mark Head, when he saw a Blackfoot aiming at him. He tried to dodge, but "the ball grazed my neck and passed through my shoulder." The trappers drew off and spent a very cold night without fires, for fear of offering a target to the enemy. Carson "passed a miserable night from the pain of the wound, it having bled freely, which was frozen." The ball probably came from a trade musket of aproximately .60 caliber, capable of inflicting a terrible wound at close range. This was by far the most serious injury Kit ever suffered in all his battles.[75]

At the Green River Rendezvous of 1835 occurred one of the most famous incidents of Carson's life, one not directly relevant to the study of his relations with Indians but certainly relevant to any assessment of his character. One of the trappers present was an American Fur Company man whose name is usually spelled Shunar (probably Chouinard). Carson describes him as "a large Frenchman one of those overbearing kind and very strong. He made a practice of whipping every man that he was displeased with, and that was nearly all." After having beaten two or three men one day, and probably having had a few drinks, Shunar announced that he could beat any Frenchman and could handle Americans with a switch—a general challenge to any man on the scene, "making his brag" as it was called. Carson says, "I did not like such talk from any man, so I told him that I was the worst American in camp. Many could t[h]rash him, only [they did not] on account of being afraid, and that if he made use of any more such expressions, I would rip his guts." This sounds like a variation on Carson's usual modesty; he was physically the least impressive American present, but he was still able to take care of any loud-mouthed Frenchman. The threat to "rip his guts" was the standard sort of remark on such occasions.[76]

Shunar immediately got his horse and rifle and rode out to fight. Carson also mounted and took the first weapon handy, a pistol (better suited to mounted combat in any case). Carson

> demanded if I was the one which he intended to shoot. Our horses were touching. He said no, but at the same time drawing his gun so he could have a fair shot. I was prepared and allowed him to draw his gun. We both fired at the same time; all present said but one report was heard. I shot him through the arm and his ball passed my head, cutting my hair and the powder burning my eye, the muzzle of his gun being near my head when he fired. During our stay in camp we had no more bother with this bully Frenchman.

Carson's account, elaborated in Peters's biography, was the standard one until 1914, when Edwin Sabin published his biography *Kit Carson Days*.[77]

Sabin's version claims that Carson had not just wounded his opponent but killed him. Sabin relied on the recollections of Smith H. Simpson, who had known Carson in Taos in the 1850s and '60s, and who gave what he said was the story Kit told him. Simpson understood that the two men were at odds over an Indian woman whom he believed to be Waanibe, the "Arapaho belle" Carson later married. In his 1928 Carson biography, Stanley Vestal elaborated on this story, based on what he said was the version told him by an Arapaho he knew early in the twentieth century, and by George Bent. According to this account, Shunar had tried to rape Waanibe, and the Frenchman's challenge only offered Kit a convenient occasion for revenge. In the actual duel, says Vestal,

Carson first wounded his opponent, then went back to his lodge to get another pistol, which he used to finish the job. Vestal then has his hero say, apologetically, "Shucks, boys, I ought to ha' throwed him the fust shot!"[78]

No one has yet demonstrated that Arapahos were present at the 1835 Rendezvous (some of the tribes present there were on hostile terms with them), but it is always possible that the difficulty had something to do with a woman. Carson is reported as saying that this was his only "serious personal quarrel," meaning the only fight in which he was motivated by a purely personal dispute with his opponent. Moreover, he is said to have expressed his animosity toward Shunar whenever he told the story. The only reason he gives for the fight is that "I did not like such talk from any man," and it is entirely possible that the spectacle of a big man bullying others and bragging about it—besides the sneer at Anglo-Americans—touched a raw nerve. Or the retrospective animosity could have sprung from the fact that Shunar, as Kit saw it, tried to sneak his shot while pretending to back down; that could also explain why he might be angry enough to kill the man after wounding him. Carson would often express his scorn at what he deemed cowardly conduct, and perhaps it was this biting outrage that struck his listeners. Harvey Carter argues that this lasting animosity is psychologically more consistent with Carson's having let his opponent live, since there was no point in being angry with the man once he had killed him, although Shunar's wound would seem to even the score for most offenses. Carson's statement that "During our stay in camp we had no more bother with this bully Frenchman" makes more sense if Shunar was alive but chastened than if he was dead.[79]

There are two other apparently firsthand eyewitness accounts of the fight. Isaac Rose has Shunar mounted on his horse when issuing his challenge and says that the Frenchman was acting out of chagrin that he, Rose, had beaten him at trapping beaver. As indicated earlier, Rose cannot be taken as a wholly independent witness, since his amanuensis James Marsh clearly drew on Frances Victor's book about Joe Meek and probably on Peters's biography of Carson. Rose, or Marsh, adds details not found elsewhere, such as Carson's wearing "a peculiar smile, as though he was about to perpetrate some excellent joke," when going into a fight, and Carson's asking, while the Frenchman was being carried away by his friends, if Shunar was satisfied, or wanted another shot. Shunar, he says, begged his companions not to let Carson near him. Marsh spells the name "Shonare," suggesting that Rose did say something about the duel, and that Marsh spelled the name phonetically.[80]

A more reliable account, at least one much closer to the event, is that of the Reverend Samuel Parker, a missionary stopping over at the Rendezvous on the way to Oregon. Parker, the original source for Shunar's name, offers his story as "a specimen of mountain life"; he has Shunar, "the great bully of the mountains," offering his challenge on horseback, Carson telling him "if he wished to die he would accept the challenge," and the two mounted men, as in Carson's story, close together and firing at the same instant. Shunar was wounded; his bullet missed Carson. While Carson went for another pistol, "Shunar begged that his life might be spared." With those words Parker ends his account of the fight, and goes on to a lengthy disquisition on the wild and dissolute ways of the mountain men. At the end of a long paragraph, he writes, "They would see 'fair play,' and would 'spare the last eye'; and would not tolerate murder, unless drunkeness or great provocation could be pleaded in extenuation of guilt." This ending may seem ambiguous, the question of Shunar's survival depending on whether Carson was drunk or could be considered as suffering great provocation. But when Parker's book was published in 1838, Kit Carson was still an obscure trapper whose name, as far as Parker could know, was unlikely ever to appear again in print. Parker was not protecting the reputation of a national hero, and since he clearly regarded the mountain men as a dissolute, lawless lot who corrupted the Indians, a murder would prove his case even better than a brawl. Granted, he tried to be fair and point out their better side, as in the remarks quoted above, but if he did not want to tarnish Carson's good name, why mention his name at all?[81]

Stanley Vestal scorns Parker's version, considering his own Indian informants more reliable; he believes Parker was not an actual eyewitness, and that the mountain men concealed the truth from him: "Rough men do not tell all they know to a parson." This does not explain how these rough men (unanimously considerate of the parson's sensibilities), in a gathering the equivalent of a very small town, could give Parker a fairly circumstantial account of the fight and yet keep him from learning the most significant fact about it, namely the death of one of the principals. It is noteworthy that Parker gives a more detailed description of Shunar's wound than does Carson. Parker says, "C.'s ball entered S.'s hand, came out at the wrist, and passed through the arm above the elbow." Carson's biographers have not considered how the preacher came by this knowledge, but there is an obvious explanation. Parker's companion on his journey was Dr. Marcus Whitman, who was a physician as well as a missionary. While at the Rendezvous, Whitman earned considerable goodwill for the missionaries by operating on Jim Bridger, removing a Blackfoot arrowhead that "Old Gabe" had carried in his back for three years. Thereafter, Parker says, "calls for surgical and medical aid were constant every hour of the day." Surely Whitman was called upon to tend to the wounded Shunar, if the Frenchman was alive to be treated, and this would be the source of Parker's detailed knowledge of the wound. Those who prefer Shunar dead to Shunar living can still say that this was a postmortem examination, perhaps conducted to see if there were signs of life, but then why describe the arm wound in detail and not mention the mortal one?[82]

The fact remains that there are only three accounts of the duel that can possibly be considered firsthand—Carson's, Parker's, and Rose's—with the reservations indicated about the last. They all indicate, if not as explicitly as one might wish, that Carson did not kill Shunar after wounding him. The explanation of the story that Shunar was killed may be that his wound became infected or gangrenous and that he died some time later, which would be entirely possible, even with medical treatment, given the state of knowledge about infection at the time. A large-caliber, soft-lead bullet, mushrooming as it hit bone, could inflict terrible damage on a limb. It might also be pointed out that, in such circles, an injury could be considered part of the fair risks of a brawl, but a killing, especially of a defenseless man, would call for revenge by the dead man's friends.[83]

In Carson's autobiography, the chronology of the four years after the Rendezvous of 1835 becomes a bit confused. Perhaps in 1836, he married Waanibe. He spent two seasons trapping for the Hudson's Bay Company out of Fort Hall in Idaho, and a good part of the rest of the time as a free trapper with the brigades of Jim Bridger and his associates, first working for their own company and then for the American Fur Company. Trapping with Bridger meant, again, trapping in Blackfoot country, on the upper Yellowstone and around the Three Forks of the Missouri, wintering on the Yellowstone or with the Crows on the Bighorn or Powder Rivers.[84]

David Wishart observes, "There was an air of desperation surrounding this final stage of the Rocky Mountain Trapping System." The trappers were pursuing an ever-dwindling supply of beaver. There were still some rich streams in the Blackfoot lands, but the price was high, as the Blackfeet still objected bitterly to the invasion of their hunting grounds and depletion of their game by people they already detested as the friends and suppliers of their enemies. Of one of these trips, with a brigade one hundred strong, Carson says, "We had met with so much difficulty from the Blackfeet that this time, as we were in force, we determined to trap wherever we pleased." This was the mountain men's attitude: they had the right to trap where they pleased, if they were strong enough to assert it. They had always believed this, and in the case of the Blackfeet they had nothing to lose, since the tribe had been hostile to trappers for the last thirty years. Whatever consideration they might have shown to a friendly tribe—and friendliness was defined in part by willingness to let them trap and winter on tribal territory—did not apply to Blackfeet. They were not troubled by violating the territory of the "horrid tribe."[85]

Flatheads, Nez Perces, and other mountain tribes had for years hunted buffalo on the plains, in country claimed by the Blackfeet, often in allied groups conducting their hunts like military operations, sometimes joining with the Crows. Once again, the mountain men followed Indian practice, although the Indians were seeking food and other necessities of life, while the trappers sought a commercial resource. But the beaver, of course, was vital to the mountain men's way of life, and perhaps their attachment to that life might be measured by the risks they took. It may be that the trappers conducted their operations with greater persistence and aggressiveness than the Indians.[86]

A brief encounter with Blackfeet on the Yellowstone in 1837 moved Robert Newell to comment, "Thare is no more dangerous a Country than this at present in these parts or even in North America," a remark that makes clear the trappers' sense of insecurity in or near Blackfoot country. Mountain men seem to have regarded these areas, on the Missouri headwaters and the upper Yellowstone, as a combat zone, where battle was the rule and it was wisest to get in the first shot. Frances Victor, citing Joe Meek, typifies their attitude thus:

They knew that among these unfriendly Indians, not to attack was to be attacked, and consequently little time was ever given for an Indian to discover his vicinity to a trapper. The trapper's shot informed him of that, and afterwards the race was to the swift, and the battle to the strong. Besides this acknowledged necessity for fighting whenever Indians were met with in the Blackfeet and Crow countries, almost every trapper had some private injury to avenge.

Therefore, Victor writes, the mountain men were quite ready to shoot into an Indian camp, if their own position was advantageous. Besides, she admits, Meek and some others were ready to fight "for the fun of it." This is a description of a war, Us against Them. Here in Blackfoot country, at least, the mountain men did "force their way through."[87]

Bridger's men were the usual mixed lot, the majority undoubtedly French-language speakers and Anglo-Americans. There may also have been some mountain Indians, Nez Perces or others, and at least one black man. There was evidently a considerable contingent of Delawares—one source says as many as forty—and Joe Meek mentions some Shawnees. Meek tells of some Delawares using horses to decoy Blackfeet into an ambush, with the result that "there was one less Blackfoot thief on the scent after trappers." This too suggests a wartime mentality.[88]

Both Kit Carson and Osborne Russell tell of a fight on the Madison River in which the trappers attacked a large Blackfoot village. Russell says that Bridger wanted to avoid an encounter, but his men protested "against trying to avoid a village of Blackfeet which did not contain more than 3 times our numbers." The result was a pitched battle among rocks where the Blackfeet took a position and the trappers charged, one charge being led by an old Iroquois trapper. In this fight Kit rescued Cotton Mansfield, then had to be rescued himself by David White. As Mansfield's horse went down and the Blackfeet came for his scalp, he called out, "Tell Old Gabe [Bridger] that Old Cotton is gone," but Carson spoiled his exit line. Carson called it "the prettiest fight I ever saw." The wars of the twentieth century have made such language suspect, but in the 1800s men were more frank about such emotions. The trappers were the aggressors, but they assumed that the same Blackfeet would attack their small trapping parties if left alone. Carson says, "This ended our difficulties with the Blackfeet for the present hunt," and that was what they had in mind.[89]

In another battle the trappers, having detected a Blackfoot camp, attacked them on an island in the Yellowstone. This was the fight in which Manhead, the Delaware leader, whom Carson called "a brave man," was mortally wounded by a poisoned musket ball. Meek says they gained no great advantage, but "the camp of Bridger fought its way past the village, which was what they must do, in order to proceed." A few days later, a large force of Blackfeet appeared. Bridger's men threw up log fortifications, but the Blackfeet interpreted a grand display of the aurora borealis as a bad omen and withdrew.[90]

The late 1830s witnessed the decline of what David Wishart calls the Rocky Mountain Trapping System, the combination of white trappers who remained in the mountains for long periods with the annual Rendezvous, which supplied them and provided a market for their furs. A change in fashion to silk hats caused a decline in demand for beaver pelts at the same time that the supply had greatly diminished from overtrapping. The mountain men had destroyed the foundation of their way of life. If they were "expectant capitalists," there was no longer a fortune to be made in the mountains. Some tried to diversify, in ways desirable or undesirable. A few became "scalp hunters" in northern Mexico. Others turned to stealing horses in California, in alliance with Utes. During this period Carson traveled with a party to the Southwest to trade with the Navajos, his first known contact with them. For a time he hunted and trapped out of Fort Davy Crockett in Brown's Hole on the Green River in northwest Colorado. Apparently, he attended the last Rendezvous in 1840, on Green River. It was a sad, subdued affair; "times was certainly hard no beaver and every thing dull," in Robert Newell's words. It was the last time any company would find it worthwhile to send supplies to the mountain men.[91]

At the Rendezvous of 1838, Captain John Sutter, later of Sutter's Fort in California, bought an Indian boy from Carson, either directly or through another mountain man. Guild and Carter argue that mountain men frequently bought children who were captives among various tribes to save them from mistreatment or death. There was an extensive trade in captives among plains, southwestern, and mountain tribes, in which Hispanic New Mexicans also participated. There is no indication that Carson had gone in for slave-trading as a business; a servant, as opposed to a wife, was not a very practical indulgence for a trapper. We do not know whether this was a compassionate or a commercial venture for Carson, but it is hard to see how he could be certain of making a profit when he acquired the boy.[92]

While Carson was operating out of Fort Davy Crockett in 1839, he was involved in two incidents he does not mention in his autobiography. One was an encounter on the Little Snake River in northwest Colorado with Sioux raiders, who fired into the camp of seven trappers and two women (perhaps including Waanibe) and killed one man. He did tell E. Willard Smith about it at the time, and he apparently gave an account of the same incident to James Meline much later, in 1866, though details differ between the two writers. Meline's version gives a rare, convincing example of Carson's speech.

"Why yes," he said, "I am up to a good many of their tricks, but they fooled me once—they fooled me pretty bad that time. I'll tell you about it. . . . As I lay by the fire, I saw one or two big wolves sneaking about camp—one of them quite in it. Gordon wanted to fire, but I would not let him, for fear of hitting some of the dogs. I had just a little suspicion, that the wolves might be Indians, but when I saw them turn short round, and heard the snap of their teeth, as the dogs came too close to one of 'em, I felt easy then, and made sure it was a wolf. The Indian fooled me that time. Confound the rascal,"—becoming animated—"confound the rascal, do you think he had n't two old buffalo bones in his hand that he cracked together every time he turned to snap at the dogs? Well, by and by we dozed off asleep, and it was n't long before I was awoke by a crash and a blaze. I jumped straight for the mules, and held 'em. If the Indians had been smart, they'd a had us all, but they run as soon as we fired. They killed but one of us—poor Davis. He had five bullets in his body, and eight in his buffalo robe. . . . They tried to waylay us next morning, but we killed three of 'em, including their chief."

Kit was clearly exasperated by the ruse that fooled him, but could not withhold his admiration.[93]

The other episode was the one in which he participated under Joseph Walker in recovering the horses stolen by trappers from friendly Shoshones. Carson may simply have considered the affair unimportant, since no casualties resulted, or he may have forgotten. However, one of the party of horse thieves was an old friend, Dick Owens, or Owings, later Kit's comrade on Frémont's expeditions. He may have preferred not to remember an occasion when they were on opposite sides and might have shot each other, and which did not reflect well on Owens. If shame at opposing fellow white men caused him to conceal the incident, he was rather late in showing it.[94]

According to Robert Newell, some of these same horse thieves went off to California "for the purpose of robbing and Steeling." Such actions were a symptom of the decline of beaver trapping, but Carson did not take up this new occupation. After hunting for some time around Fort Davy Crockett and Robidoux's fort in Utah, he headed for Bent's Fort in Colorado. It was probably about this time that Waanibe died, leaving Carson with two small children.[95]

Bent's Fort, or Fort William, a virtual adobe castle on the Arkansas River, had been founded by Bent, St. Vrain and Company in 1833, and was now both a major trading post for the southern plains tribes and the principal stopping point on the Mountain Branch of the Santa Fe Trail. Lying on what was then the U.S.–Mexican border, it was the only real rest and resupply point between the Missouri frontier and Santa Fe. The company was an important participant in both the Indian and Santa Fe trades. It had an especially close relationship with the Southern Cheyennes, and William Bent, who managed the post, had married into the tribe. He and Kit Carson, who were virtually the same age and both rather short, would become lifelong friends. In later years, when he had become an acknowledged public authority on Indians, Kit would insist that Bent's expertise and influence were superior to his. In a few years Carson would marry the sister-in-law of William's older brother and partner, Charles Bent. Of the brothers and their partner, Ceran St. Vrain, he would say, "Their equals were never in the mountains."[96]

Carson would work as a hunter for the fort, providing meat for its staff, for just eight months in 1841 and 1842. It was during this period that he married the Cheyenne woman Making-Out-Road, a brief and unsuccessful venture. Apparently, there was also a brief relationship with a Hispanic woman named Antonia Luna at about this time. In the spring of 1842 he journeyed to Missouri, visited relatives, and left his older daughter, Adaline, with them. His relationship with the Bents would continue, and they would play an important part in his life.[97]

The first period of Carson's adult life—his years as a mountain man—was coming to an end. Looking back on it in his autobiography, he would say, "It has now been 16 years I have been in the mountains. The greatest part of that time passed far from the habitations of civilized man, and receiving no other food than that which I could procure with my rifle."

He was now thirty-two, at a time when many of a man's attitudes and standards are fairly well set. The half of his life he had passed as a mountain man was a formative period, teaching him lessons he never forgot, even if he later modified his ideas, as some men do and some never manage. He is reported as saying, "The happiest days of my life were spent in trapping." This was the nostalgia of an aging, indeed dying, man for his youth, but apparently he remembered those days of danger and hardship, days of close, day-to-day intimacy with Indians, positively. So what was the legacy of those years in the mountains, and how did they shape him?[98]

Howard Lamar says that it is useless to argue about whether mountain men were noble or degraded because we have little or no record about most of them. Leroy Hafen's great biographical compendium is disproportionately devoted to the better-known, better-documented figures. There were many, especially among the French speakers and those who were not "white," who left little or no record, like the handful of African descent who appear occasionally in the records. We know little or nothing about most of the Indian mountain men—Delawares, Shawnees, or indigenous mountain tribesmen—for the same reason.[99]

The mountain men lived in an environment that severely tested the American cultural-historical tendency to place people in distinct ethnic and racial categories. The famous dictum that "the only good Indian is a dead Indian" was put into that form, or nearly so, after the Civil War by General Philip Sheridan, but the basic idea had a long history on the frontier. Whether or not Sheridan meant it, there were undoubtedly many white people who did, people who wanted the Indians entirely gone from any area where white people might possibly want to settle, and who believed that their disappearance from the earth would be a positive good. Mark Twain found them all "treacherous, filthy, and repulsive." But the mountain men could not really afford this kind of thinking, comfortingly simple though it might be. To work and survive in the Rocky Mountains in the 1820s and '30s required a greater degree of discernment, even from men not naturally inclined to be so discerning.[100]

They had to adopt many Indian ways of dressing, eating, even of relating to the natural world. The Indian skills of trailing, scouting, observing, must become second nature. Washington Irving insisted, based on the evidence of Benjamin Bonneville and others, that "it is a matter of vanity and ambition with them to discard everything that may bear the stamp of civilized life, and to adopt the manners, dress, gesture, and even walk of the Indian. You cannot pay a free trapper a greater compliment, than to persuade him you have mistaken him for an Indian brave." Biculturalism, in the sense of living on the borderline between cultures, had been common in the fur trade, especially among French traders, since the days of the *coureurs de bois*. A substantial proportion of the mountain men were French speakers, and the others fell, in their individually varying degrees, into the same pattern. For outside observers, then and later, as Howard Lamar says, "The very biculturalism that the French traders practiced became in the mountain men either repulsive depravity or extreme romance." He adds, "Indeed, the taboo against the Indian life style was remarkably similar to the taboos against the way mountain men lived."[101]

Western Indian cultures varied widely in their attitude toward war, from the essentially defensive posture of most Pueblo communities to the martial spirit and glorification of the individual warrior seen among many Great Plains peoples, but nearly all the tribes the mountain man was likely to come in contact with practiced some form of warlike activity. In practicing violence against some Indians, therefore, the trappers were not introducing some new aberration into the plains or mountain environment.

There was little that Carson had experienced in the mountains, any more than in his backcountry boyhood, that would have led him to forswear violence. He would continue to see it as sometimes necessary for self-preservation, as justified retaliation, and as a means for solving problems not susceptible to other solutions. Mountain men agreed that the western Indians held an entire tribe responsible for the deeds of particular members. This was the reason Joseph Walker, Carson, and others were ready to confront other white men to restore horses stolen from friendly Shoshones, who otherwise would hold all white men responsible. Mountain men, as Marc Simmons points out, often acted on the same principle, especially with the Blackfeet. They saw no alternative, given their own small numbers and the lack of any higher authority to enforce justice, than to make their own justice, as Indian tribes did with each other. As Anthony McGinnis points out, the revenge cycle kept spinning. Eventually, Carson would come to understand the defects in the system, but there is little evidence of this as he entered his thirties.[102]

Carson certainly had a number of violent encounters with Indians during his years in the mountains. Some were clearly instances of self-defense, as in the "mule fort" episode with the Comanches. Others, like the fight with the Apaches led by Ewing Young, were perceived as self-defense, and it is difficult now to say whether the trappers were right or wrong. Pursuits of horse thieves, and retaliation against them, were considered justifiable by both Indians and whites at the time. The attack on the Crow horse thieves in Colorado is harder to justify, if the horses could have been recovered without bloodshed; the trappers may simply have wanted to fight an inevitable battle under the most favorable circumstances, but Carson gives no reason for fighting except the desire for "satisfaction." The Cheyennes who accompanied the trappers would have treated the Crows the same way. In the Blackfoot country the mountain men assumed they were in a war zone, where it was wisest to get in the first shot against an unconditional enemy, though a special animosity toward Blackfeet was clearly involved.

Although the nineteenth-century notion of Indians as uniquely war-like is wrong, the fact of widespread intertribal warfare is undeniable. Mountain men adapted themselves, perhaps all too readily, to this as-pect of the environment. They constantly moved across Indian hunting grounds, for there was little country that could not be considered the territory of some tribe. They aggressively entered the country of the Blackfeet, as other Indians also did. As noted earlier, mountain men often fought as allies of Indians, and often fought for the reasons Indians did. Retribution for attacks on themselves followed the practice both of the Indians and of the culture from which many of them came. They had their full share of prejudices, but they were not practicing genocide, nor did they seek to conquer the Indians, to dispossess them, or to change their culture; the supposed "inaptitude of the Indian for civilization," in Dr. Morton's phrase, was not their concern. At the end of the fur trade era, the Indians were still independent and in control of their territories. Undeniably, some of the mountain men showed a casualness about taking human life that betrayed their backcountry origins.

One effect the violence of the mountain years would have on Carson (and many other old trappers) was to make him habitually cautious, vigilant, and mistrustful, especially where Indians were concerned. He could not forget the price to be paid, which he had seen paid by friends, for carelessness. George Nidever summed it up: "In an Indian country one cannot take too many precautions, and I owe my life many times over to my habitual vigilance and caution in all my movements while in the mountains. Of the many trappers that I have known that were killed in the mountains by Indians, a very large proportion of them were careless and imprudent in their habits." Thomas Jefferson

Farnham's observation of mountain men led him to this conclusion: "Habitual watchfulness destroys every frivolity of mind and action. They seldom smile: the expression of their countenance is watchful, solemn, and determined. They ride and walk like men whose breasts have so long been exposed to the bullet and the arrow, that fear finds in them no resting place." "Watchful, solemn, and determined" might describe the countenance that Kit Carson shows in many of his photographs.[103]

Those who knew Kit Carson in his maturity frequently mention his caution and watchfulness. George Brewerton remembered Kit sleeping with his saddle-pillow placed "to form a barricade for his head," with his pistols half-cocked above it and his rifle under his blanket at his side, and how he would not expose himself in the full glare of the campfire. "I doubt if he ever knew what fear was, but with all this he exercised great caution." Worthington Whittredge, staying with him in Santa Fe in 1866, noted, "He never turned in without examining his revolver and placing it under his pillow, and he awakened at the slightest noise."[104]

For a twentieth-century American to sleep in secure surroundings with a revolver under his pillow would be taken as an indication of paranoia or an obsession with firearms—probably both. For Carson it was a survival habit picked up by sheer necessity, a ritual without which he would have felt uncomfortable, though he knew perfectly well that there was little danger of Indian attack in Santa Fe. Many western Indian tribes lived in a state of insecurity similar to that of the mountain men. Meriwether Lewis almost failed in making initial contact with the Shoshones because of their dread of the Blackfeet and other enemy tribes. Benjamin Bonneville found the Nez Perces, while he spent the winter with them, under continual harassment by the Blackfeet. Carson had adapted to that environment, and he never ceased to be cautious in dealing with Indians, never forgot the hard lesson that contact with people of a very different culture could be dangerous. Nearing fifty, he admitted to Albert Richardson "that when a boy he was daring and reckless; but now when traveling he exercised great vigilance, having seen many of his comrades killed by Indians through their own carelessness."[105]

As noted, Carson's own autobiography, concentrating on exciting and often bloody episodes, gives an unbalanced impression of a mountain man's life. He chose not to mention his Indian wives, nor the fact—so commonplace to him—that the trappers routinely engaged in intercourse, of various kinds and in various senses of the word, with Indians in their daily lives. He mentions Bridger's men traveling with a village of Flatheads and Pend d'Oreilles, and wintering with Crows, but this sort of thing was too ordinary for frequent notice.[106]

Martin Green, in an interesting insight, sees the mountain men as the counterparts of the Russian Cossacks. The Cossacks were Russians and other Slavs who, for various reasons including the oppression of serfdom, fled their society to live among the nomads of the steppe, adopting many of the customs, the dress and fighting methods, even the words of the nomads, and intermarrying with them to produce a new and distinct people. We have noted Washington Irving's concern that "this immense wilderness of the far west" might become the home of "new and mongrel races," descended from trappers, fugitives, and Indians. Nothing of the sort happened, of course. The Cossacks originated in the fifteenth and sixteenth centuries and retained a distinctive identity until the twentieth. The mountain men, even if we include the trappers who followed in the footsteps of Lewis and Clark before the War of 1812, flourished for little over thirty years. People of mixed ancestry did not play the prominent role in American history that the métis did in the Canadian West, not because there were no such people but because cultural and social pressures forced them to become "Indian" or "white" (or "Mexican"), to identify themselves with one or the other distinct and separate group, as defined by Anglo-American society. Had the expansion of the Anglo-American settlement frontier been delayed for a much longer period, it might have been different. As Howard Lamar suggests, "possibly a line of métis or halfbreeds would have existed from Oklahoma to Saskatchewan."[107]

Would Kit Carson have been part of that mixed, multicultural society, or would he have moved on to the settled, respectable life, like a good Jacksonian man? All he really says about the change in his life in the early 1840s is that "Beaver was getting scarce," and that it was "necessary to try our hand at something else." Mountain men were not fleeing anything like serfdom, though a few no doubt sought escape from outstanding warrants or other social or domestic difficulties or, like young Kit, apprenticeship or an onerous occupation. How many more attractive options were there for an illiterate man whose chief occupational skills fitted him for a life no longer economically feasible? His job as a hunter put those skills to use, and, like many other old mountain men, he soon found further employment for his hard-won knowledge as a guide and scout.[108]

Carson's years as a mountain man were a mind-expanding experience. He was exposed to different cultures in a way that would not have been possible in frontier Missouri (although his home state, with its French-speaking population and contact with Hispanic New Mexico and neighboring Indians, was a more cosmopolitan place than one might imagine). As William Swagerty points out, the mountain men were not conquerors trying to impose their values or their political and social dominion. Carson and his fellows lived for a time on a "middle ground," as Richard White would have it, of cultural accommodation, where whites and Indians had to give a degree of recognition to each other's humanity. Howard Lamar says, "Trade was the one successful means of communication between the world of the Indian and the world of the white." The trader and the mountain man "had to know and tolerate two worlds, whereas the farmer did not, for he had no need for the Indian." Carson would live to see the relatively tolerant, sometimes violent, but often accommodating world of the trader and the mountain man replaced by one in which the attitudes of those who had "no need for the Indian" were dominant. He would be an instrument of that change, one of the men who had to deal with its consequences, and one of those trying to moderate between the two worlds. His life would become a microcosm of the historic changes sweeping over the West, although he would never have imagined such a grand outcome when he took his daughter Adaline back to his family in Missouri in the spring of 1842.[109]

4. Guide and Scout

Carson: He was a brave Indian, deserved a better
fate, but he had placed himself on the wrong path.
Harvey L. Carter, *"Dear Old Kit"*

. . . the fulfillment of our manifest destiny to overspread
the continent allotted by Providence for the free
development of our yearly multiplying millions.
John L. O'Sullivan, *Democratic Review*, 1845

KIT AND THE PATHFINDER

Carson's trip back to Missouri in the spring of 1842 was fateful. At that point in his life he was thoroughly obscure, an illiterate trapper who had spent his entire life in the backcountry settlements of Missouri or their New Mexican counterparts, or in Indian country far beyond the Anglo-American settlement frontier. He had been mentioned briefly in one published book, as a leading figure in a brawl. His principal employment through his adult life was becoming economically obsolete. He had two children to support and a limited number of possibilities for doing so. There were hundreds of men very much like him in the West, scattered from Missouri to California, either looking for new opportunities or trying to cling to the old way of life. There was no particular reason to assume that Kit Carson would not end up like many of them, eking out some kind of living in northern New Mexico, remembered by his neighbors and descendants and receiving perhaps the briefest mention in some fur trade histories, completely overshadowed by such figures as Jedediah Smith, Tom Fitzpatrick, Joseph Walker, and Jim Bridger.

What happened instead was that Carson became the most famous of the mountain men, the one whose name was instantly recognizable, so that Herman Melville, just seven years after that return to Missouri, could describe him as the model of that whole "class of men." He would become famous, not just for the statutory fifteen minutes, but for the rest of his life and beyond. That fame would give him the respect not just of the general public but of political and military leaders, so that he became a man from whom heroism was routinely expected. More than a warrior hero, he would be regarded as an expert, the Old Scout who could be called upon not only for heroic achievement but for wise counsel, whose opinion on Indians, in peace or in war, was of special and unquestioned value. For many people he would be Cooper's brave, wise, and noble frontier hero in the flesh. His first biographer summed it up by calling him "the Nestor of the Rockies." He would often deprecate his fame, but it would help ensure employment for most of his later life; it would also place on him a burden of expectations that he would try conscientiously to fulfill. It would sometimes force him to be absent from his growing second family when he would have preferred to be at home. Ultimately, it would give him a leading role in a tragedy.

There was nothing remarkable in Carson's becoming a guide and scout; the same course was followed by a number of his fellow mountain men, including Jim Bridger and Tom Fitzpatrick. The unpredictable development of his fame resulted directly from Kit's meeting on a Missouri River steamboat with Lieutenant John Charles Frémont of the U.S. Army. Behind that meeting and its consequences, however, was the whole process of American expansion, which had already shaped Carson's life and would continue to do so. A few years before his birth, the United States had gained formal title to the Louisiana Purchase, a vast tract of land consisting essentially of the western drainage of the Mississippi; that development had brought Lindsey and Rebecca Carson and their family to the Boonslick country. In 1842 there were only three states in that tract—Louisiana, Arkansas, and Missouri—and the enormous expanse of the Great Plains beyond was still the exclusive homeland of many thousands of Indians. Yet in just a few more years the United States would expand explosively, extending its sovereignty to the Pacific. Afterward, the whole process would seem inevitable, but it resulted from the conscious desires of many people, ordinary citizens and frontier settlers but also leading men in politics and government. Texas, formerly a province of Mexico, had been an independent republic dominated by Anglo-Americans for six years in 1842, its annexation to the United States delayed only by opposition to the expansion of slavery. The Oregon country—later Oregon, Washington, and Idaho—was officially under the joint sovereignty of Britain and the United States, but actually the only non-Indian authority in the region was the Hudson's

Bay Company. The huge expanse of country west from Texas to the Pacific was officially part of Mexico, but only in coastal California and the Rio Grande valley in New Mexico did Mexico exercise any sort of authority. The coastal areas in California and Oregon appeared much more attractive to Anglo-Americans than the "Great American Desert" that supposedly encompassed the Great Plains and the mountain regions beyond.

Many Americans, then, were eyeing those territories. By 1842 the government's interest in the country west of the frontier settlements was sufficiently great, and sufficiently open, that Lieutenant Frémont was on his way to the mouth of the Kansas River on the Missouri to organize and lead a government-sponsored expedition west to South Pass and the Continental Divide. He was an officer in the Corps of Topographical Engineers, an elite body of men charged with mapmaking, who would dominate official exploration of the West in the mid-1800s.[1]

Of their meeting Carson says simply that he had spent a few days in Saint Louis "and was tired of remaining in settlements." He took passage on a steamboat, presumably to reach Independence, Missouri, from which he would return to New Mexico, "and—as luck would have it—Colonel Frémont, then a Lieutenant, was aboard of the same boat." At some point Carson learned that Frémont would be leading an expedition and would need a guide. "I spoke to Colonel Fremont, informed him that I had been some time in the mountains and thought I could guide him to any point he would wish to go. He replied that he would make inquiries regarding my capabilities of performing that which I promised. He done so. I presume he received reports favorable of me, for he told me I would be employed." Frémont promised Kit one hundred dollars per month, an impressive salary for the time.[2]

Frémont's characteristically more expansive account says that Carson was returning from putting his daughter in a convent school in St. Louis. "I was pleased with him and his manner of address at this first meeting. He was a man of medium height, broad-shouldered and deep-chested, with a clear steady blue eye and frank speech and address; quiet and unassuming." He goes on to speak of Carson's "modesty and gentleness" and his "straightforward nature." The meeting, says Frémont, was the beginning of "our enduring friendship."[3]

Possibly, the meeting was not quite as casual as Carson makes it sound; perhaps he was on that steamboat for the purpose of meeting the leader of the proposed expedition, and even asked the unnamed persons of whom Frémont made "inquiries" to give "reports favorable of me." His well-attested modesty and distaste for bragging do not mean that he had no eye at all for his own advancement.

Both men, in fact, were headed for fame, in part because of this meeting. Frémont, and his wife and father-in-law, would make the name Kit Carson so instantly recognizable that he could be mentioned in the same sentence with Davy Crockett and even Hercules. Frémont would become not only "the Pathfinder"—another echo of Cooper—but a presidential candidate, a general, a millionaire, a center of political controversy, and the defendant in a sensational trial involving other national figures—all in all, a nearly perfect American celebrity.

Carson certainly returned Frémont's regard; in 1856 he would say of his old commander:

> All that he has or ever may receive, he deserves. I can never forget his treatment of me while in his employ and how cheerfully he suffered with his men while undergoing the severest of hardships. His perseverance and willingness to participate in all that was undertaken, no matter whether the duty was rough or easy, is the main cause of his success. And I say, without the fear of contradiction, that none but him could have surmounted and succeeded through as many difficult services, as his was.

Carson's praise gives important clues to Frémont's success as an explorer and as the leader of a small group of men.[4]

It is not necessary here to analyze Frémont's character in depth, although his complex personality, and the remarkable ups and downs of his life, have made him a natural target for biographers. What is important here is the interaction of Frémont and Carson as it affected the Indians they encountered, and the effect of their association on Carson's later career. No one seems to doubt that Frémont was responsible for Carson's rise to fame, and many historians have agreed with Allan Nevins that it was "a rare stroke of luck" for Frémont that brought the two together. Nevins sees their friendship as the result of "the magnetism of opposites." Carson, he says, was "cool, quiet, observant, and determined, while Frémont was quick, sensitive, passionate, and impetuous." Nevins sees Carson as notable for "stability and balance," the qualities in which he finds Frémont most deficient, and praises Kit's "rugged honesty, his transparent sincerity, his gentleness and kindliness (save to Indians and Mexicans, whom he regarded as most frontiersmen did), his loyalty and reliability." Nevins's qualification regarding Carson's "gentleness and kindliness" is, of course, precisely where the present work comes in, and it will be necessary to test that qualification regarding the period of Carson's service with Frémont and his other stints as a guide and scout in the 1840s and '50s.[5]

Frémont's most recent biographer, Andrew Rolle, finds him "a bird of rare plumage," whose "bland and gentlemanly" exterior concealed "destructive forces" raging within. Like Nevins, Rolle sees him as unstable, and also as childish, rebellious, and narcissistic, qualities Rolle traces to his subject's loss of his father at the age of five and to his illegitimate birth. That he had real gifts as an explorer and scientist Rolle acknowledges. Before meeting Carson, Frémont had already attracted favorable attention for his exploration and mapmaking on the northeastern Great Plains, and had demonstrated the other side of his character by being expelled from college and by eloping with Jessie Benton, the teenage daughter of Senator Thomas Hart Benton of Missouri, a man who possessed the power to ruin him, but who instead became the promoter of his career after a reconciliation. If it is not necessary to probe Frémont's character so deeply as Nevins and Rolle try to do, it seems fair to say that his sense of the possible was often flawed, and that he not infrequently acted like a "loose cannon."[6]

In regard to how the association of the two men affected the Indians they encountered, Rolle makes his opinion plain. Carson, he says, was Frémont's "hit man," killing Indians with his leader's instigation. Carson "did not hestitate to chastise natives who took vengeance on white parties." Rolle seems to assume that Indians only attacked whites as retaliation for white men's wrongdoing, which seems as unwise as the contrary assumption so often made by nineteenth-century whites. Ironically, however, Kit would assert something similar regarding certain Indian tribes. Rolle refers to Carson's involvement in burning a California Indian village while he was with Ewing Young in 1830, in such a way as to suggest that Carson was solely responsible, and without noting that the burning followed a battle in which there were Indians on both sides.[7]

Carson, while with Frémont, was indeed involved in several incidents of violence with Indians, but the impression given by Rolle that Frémont rode about the West pointing out Indians for Carson to shoot, or nodding approvingly while Kit shot them on his own initiative, is badly misleading. Most of these incidents occurred in California and

Oregon during Frémont's third expedition, and they will be dealt with in due course. There were no such episodes during the first expedition, although the possibility existed and was successfully avoided. All of the violence cannot be excused, but none of it was purely gratuitous, and the circumstances and how they appeared at the time are highly relevant to any evaluation of Carson's character and his relations with Indians.

Frémont's "First Expedition" set out from Chouteau's Landing on the Missouri on June 6, 1842. With the party, besides Carson, were a number of Anglo-American and French-speaking frontiersmen, including Kit's friend Lucien Maxwell and Basil Lajeunesse, whom Frémont considered one of his best men and whose death Carson would one day bloodily avenge.[8]

Frémont's official second in command was the Prussian cartographer Charles Preuss, who would keep a valuable diary of this and Frémont's next expedition. Preuss was one of the few people who associated with Kit Carson for an extended period who seems to have had an unfavorable opinion of him, and that opinion was related in part to Kit's attitudes toward Indians. But Preuss had a poor opinion about much linked with the expedition, including its leader, whom he refers to in some of his earliest entries as "that childish Frémont," and "a foolish lieutenant." Preuss had a melancholy temperament and his discontent, as he recognized, was related to his being the odd man out in the party, an educated European ill-adapted to wilderness life among rough American backwoodsmen: "The dreariest and most miserable aspect of this journey," he wrote, "is that there is no human being with whom I can converse in some way. I should be satisfied if I had only a single German comrade." He judged Carson the only good buffalo hunter in the group, but saw him as biased and unduly apprehensive regarding Indians. Neither Carson nor Frémont seems to have been aware of Preuss's jaundiced view of them. Frémont praised him for his "faithful and valuable service" and the "cheerful philosophy of his own which often brightened dark situations," and saw him as one "of those who were comrades, and part with me." Carson, telling of an occasion when Preuss was lost for four days and found his way back, says, "We were all rejoiced at his return, for the old man was much respected by the party." (The "old man" was six years Kit's senior.)[9]

The expedition followed the route of the fur company caravans, the future Oregon Trail, up the Platte and the North Platte toward South Pass. Carson disposes of the whole affair in two and a half paragraphs;

Frémont is considerably more verbose and dramatic. He recalls one occasion when a member of the party rode in shouting that he had seen a war party of twenty-seven Indians. Carson mounted the nearest horse and rode off to scout the situation. The twenty-seven Indians proved to be six elk, but the event provided Frémont with the occasion for some fine writing: "Mounted on a fine horse, without a saddle, and scouring bareheaded over the prairies, Kit was one of the finest pictures of a horseman I have ever seen." These lines, in Frémont's official report, mark the real beginning of Carson's apotheosis as a frontier hero. They might have described a figure in one of the livelier paintings by Charles Deas, William Ranney, or Arthur Tait, who in this and the next decade gave Americans an image of the West featuring mounted, buckskin-clad frontiersmen scouring over the prairies.[10]

Barring such momentary excitements, the trip was routine until a few days before they reached Fort Laramie. Then, near Chimney Rock in western Nebraska they met Jim Bridger, who informed them that the Oglala Sioux and the Cheyennes in the area were in a hostile mood. Some of their warriors had been on an expedition beyond the Divide and on Little Snake River had attacked a party led by Henry Fraeb, for whom Carson had worked several years earlier. Fraeb's party was in company with a band of Shoshones, and in true fur trade fashion the combined forces drove off the attackers, causing them some casualties. (Fraeb was also killed.) Now a large number of Sioux and Cheyennes were gathered to seek satisfaction from both whites and Shoshones.[11]

Frémont was absent from the main party on a side trip when the meeting with Bridger took place. When he rejoined at Fort Laramie he found his command agitated, some of them insisting on returning to Missouri. Frémont consulted with Bridger, Carson, and other experienced men at the fort. Bridger did not think such a small party as Frémont's could safely venture farther west. Tom Fitzpatrick had taken a group of emigrants on past Laramie to Oregon, the Sioux letting him pass because of their regard for him, but they had sworn no other whites would go through. In Frémont's words: "Carson, one of the best and most experienced mountaineers, fully supported the opinions given by Bridger, of the dangerous state of the country, and openly expressed his conviction that we could not escape without some sharp encounters with the Indians. In addition to this, he made his will." Making a will was perhaps prudent for a man with two small children, but it did nothing for the party's morale. There is no indication that Carson considered quitting. He had signed on with Frémont, and his word and his pride were both at stake; that was enough for a backcountry man. Carson himself says nothing about the will; he may have found it embarrassing to recall, in the light of later events, or it may simply have been one of those personal matters that was nobody else's business.[12]

Several Sioux chiefs at the fort also warned Frémont that he should not try to pass westward. The explorer, by his own account, gave them an eloquent oration, rebuking them and telling them that he was bound to continue: "Whatever a chief among us tells his soldiers to do, is done. We are the soldiers of the great chief, your father." Carson summarized Frémont's words: "Frémont informed them that he was directed by his government to perform a certain duty, that it mattered not what obstacles were in his advance, . . . that he would accomplish that for which he [was] sent or die in the attempt; and if he failed, by losing his party, his government would eventually punish those that caused the failure." Apparently Frémont made an impression; at any rate, the Sioux attack failed to materialize.[13]

That Frémont pressed forward, despite the advice of men as experienced and knowledgeable as Bridger and Carson, was characteristic. That he got away with it confirmed his propensity for pushing ahead regardless of the odds. Carson was sufficiently impressed that he gave as much space to Frémont's speech as to the rest of the first expedition, which he summarized thus: "We continued our march [and] arrived at the South Pass. Frémont accomplished all that was desired of him and then we returned. Arrived at [Fort] Laramie sometime in September. During the expedition I performed the duties of guide and hunter. I, at Laramie, quit the employ of Frémont, he continuing his march for the States taking nearly the same route as that by which he had come." There was, however, a bit more to it than that, though none of it involved any trouble with Indians.[14]

They marched west through South Pass to the Wind River Mountains, where Frémont took a group, including Carson and Preuss, to climb to the heights. During the climb, Preuss records, Frémont thought Carson was going too fast and the two had an argument, with Frémont putting another man in Carson's place in the lead. The quarrel was quickly made up: "One claimed he had not meant it as the other assumed, and [Frémont's] headache was relieved," in Preuss's words. Probably the altitude made both men irritable, but the episode shows that Carson was not always meekly subservient to those in authority. Neither makes any mention of what they no doubt regarded as a minor difference. Preuss says that Frémont became angry with Carson again when Kit moved the main camp while the leader was still climbing mountains, but that Frémont cooled down and treated Carson amiably. The reason, Preuss implies, was that Carson was indispensable: "To be sure, what could we have done without him in the prairie? How could we get back if we lost our only good buffalo hunter?"[15]

Shortly after these episodes, when they pitched camp, they found the remains of an Indian camp. Preuss relates, "Kit, who otherwise makes a great to-do about such things in order to make himself important, said that the lodges were those of a weak, miserable tribe of Snake Indians." Here Preuss shows his reaction to Carson's habitual caution where Indians were concerned. The guide's concern about the Sioux danger, manifested at Fort Laramie, and no doubt other unrecorded admonitions and precautions, seemed to Preuss to be overblown, especially after the Sioux attack did not happen. Preuss would eventually conclude that this attitude was simply a prejudice, that Kit saw "a murderer in every miserable human being." The Prussian had no way of knowing how much harsh experience lay behind Carson's apprehensions, and it would be late in Frémont's next expedition before he began to understand.[16]

Carson left Frémont's party at Fort Laramie in September 1842, and may have spent the next few months hunting and trapping. He reappears in Taos in February 1843 on the occasion of his next and final marriage. On the sixth of February he was married in the parish church to Maria Josefa Jaramillo. Cristobal Carson was described in the parish register as "a native of Missouri in North America and a resident of this town of Our Lady of Guadelupe." The bride had not reached her fifteenth birthday; Kit was thirty-three. Josefa, as she was usually called, was by all reports a beautiful young woman—taller, by some accounts, than her husband. Lewis Garrard, seeing her some four years later, wrote, "Her style of beauty was of the haughty, heart-breaking kind—such as would lead a man with a glance of the eye, to risk his life for one smile." Some early photographs, believed to be of her, certainly show a very attractive woman.[17]

Josefa's father, Francisco Jaramillo, was apparently a respectable but not wealthy man; her mother, Maria Apolonia Vigil, belonged to a family of large landowners in the Rio Arriba, the Rio Grande valley north of Santa Fe. Her older sister, Maria Ignacia, had for some years been the common-law wife of Kit's friend and sometime employer, Charles Bent, which presumably explains how they met. The match may indicate the regard that Bent had for Carson; whether Kit thought of marrying the boss's sister-in-law as a means of advancement seems impossible to know. Marriages between Anglo-American and French-speaking trappers and traders and New Mexican women had become common in northern New Mexico since the opening of the Santa Fe Trail. Some of these unions, like Kit's, were consecrated by the church, and some, like Bent's, were not.[18]

We know virtually nothing of the details of the courtship. Carson mentions the marriage once in his autobiography and says nothing more; it was private business, and the usual literary sentiments about "my beloved wife" were beyond him. That there was a church wedding, the only kind available in New Mexico at the time, suggests that Kit insisted on doing the right thing, since there was no such formality in the union of Charles Bent and Josefa's sister. On the other hand, Ignacia was a widow in her twenties when she took up with Bent, while Josefa was a young girl presumably still under her parents' care. Cohabitation without marriage was common in nineteenth-century New Mexico, one reason being the fees necessary for a religious ceremony. Kit had smoothed the way by being baptized into the Catholic faith. According to the parish record, the baptism was performed conditionally, since he had been baptized "according to the rite of the Anabaptists," on January 28, 1842, over a year before the marriage. This may be evidence that the marriage had been planned for some time, and that there had been a delay to allow the bride to mature a bit, or perhaps an unplanned delay for Frémont's first expedition. However, the other records near the baptismal entry are dated 1843, so the pastor may have made the error, common early in a new year, of writing down the old year. On the other hand, Carson's age is given as thirty-two, which would fit the 1842 date.[19]

What Josefa thought about marrying a short, bowlegged Anglo eighteen years her senior is also unknown. Career opportunities for women in New Mexico, or Missouri for that matter, in the nineteenth century were limited, and a good steady husband was likely the best option available, or even imaginable. Neither in New Mexico nor in backcountry Missouri at that time was marriage for a woman so young altogether remarkable. In 1828 another Anglo-Hispanic marriage took place in which the bride was twelve. In any case, Kit and Josefa's union lasted twenty-five years, until they both died within a month of each other, and it produced seven children.[20]

Carson's last marriage, like his Indian marriages, does not in itself prove lack of prejudice; as noted, men have often been willing to consort with or marry the women of peoples they considered inferior. Anglo-American men of this period often took the somewhat illogical position of regarding Hispanic women much more highly than Hispanic men, praising the beauty, charm, and tenderheartedness of the former while condemning the latter as treacherous, cowardly, and possessed of almost every other contemptible quality. Many Americans of the period, as Francis Parkman noted, ranked Indians higher than New Mexicans. But Carson lived much of his life in regions where Spanish-speaking people were a decided majority. Spanish was his second tongue, and some judged that he spoke it better than he did English. Indeed, his last words were in Spanish. There are recorded instances where he expressed the common Anglo contempt for Mexican courage, and other times when he said just the opposite. Records do not indicate that he treated Hispanics in the harsh and brutal fashion attributed to his friend Lucien Maxwell—except in one notable incident, under unique circumstances. We will see at least one occasion on which he risked his life to right a wrong done to New Mexicans, and on others he took the same risk to protect them from Indians and from Anglo-Americans. He was a man of action, and his actions must speak for him.[21]

One of those occasions took place just a few months after his marriage. In April 1843 he left for the United States with Charles Bent and Ceran St. Vrain and one of their caravans. At the Arkansas River in southwest Kansas they met a force of U.S. dragoons commanded by Captain Philip St. George Cooke, who informed them that a group of Texans, led by one Jacob Snively and operating under the authority of the president of the Republic of Texas, was lurking in the area. They intended to seize a westbound wagon train led by the brother of Governor Manuel Armijo of New Mexico; the governor was held responsible for the brutal mistreatment of a party of Texans who had unsuccessfully invaded New Mexico in 1841, and Cooke believed that the Texans would either kill the New Mexicans with the Armijo train or take them hostage. Cooke could not offer protection beyond the Arkansas, the international boundary, and the people of the caravan wanted Kit to ride to Santa Fe with a message asking the governor to send a military escort. They offered him $300, and "I agreed to carry it."

He set out with his friend Dick Owens by way of Bent's Fort. There he was informed that there was danger from Utes along the route. Owens stayed at the fort, but Kit continued, William Bent having given him a fast horse: "I started, discovered the Indian village without them seeing me, passed them during the night, arrived safely at Taos." This would have offered a novelist like Cooper material for several paragraphs at least; Kit treats it as routine.[22]

Armijo had in fact already set out with a few hundred men to meet the train, but his advance guard was defeated by Texans and he lost heart and turned back. Kit's message was supposed to induce him to try again. The governor sent Carson a message to carry to the caravan and he set out again with a New Mexican companion. On the way they encountered a large group of Utes.

> The Mexican advised me to mount my horse and make my escape, that the Indians had no horse that could catch him and, as for him, he thought the Indians would not injure him and they, in all probability, would kill me. I considered the advice very good and was about to mount my horse. I changed my mind and thought how cowardly it would be in me to desert this man that so willingly offered to sacrifice his life to save mine. I told him no, that I would die with him.

The Utes pretended friendship, and the leader, "the old rascal," offered his hand and then seized Kit's rifle. "We tussled for a short time and I made him let go his hold." The Indians circled about waving their guns, trying to get in a position where they could fire without losing any of their men. "They remained around us about a half hour and seeing but little hopes of their being able to kill us without losing two of themselves, they left." Carson devotes enough space to this incident to suggest that it made a special impression on him; it must have been a long half hour. He is honest enough to admit that his first impulse was to take the Mexican's advice and run for it, perhaps thinking of his young bride back in Taos, but this was not acceptable. Frustratingly, Carson does not even record the name of the man who was ready to sacrifice his life for him, and for whom he was ready to return the favor. On reaching Bent's Fort, he learned that Captain Cooke had encountered and disarmed the Texans, sending them home. Twice in a few days Carson had risked his life to protect New Mexicans, and twice experience, skill, and judgment—and some luck—had brought him through. The first time he had had monetary inducement, but the second time only his sense of honor impelled him.[23]

That not every American would have acted as Carson did is shown by the fact that the Texans who defeated Armijo's advance were, in fact, stray mountain men, "Texans" for the nonce, recruited for Snively at various trading posts in Colorado; Charles Bent had had to persuade some of his own employees not to join them. Moreover, when Kit arrived in Taos carrying his message, he found that the attack had provoked an anti-American riot in the town, causing some resident Anglos to flee. Carson does not even mention these matters; he evidently had no particular sympathy for the raiders, nor did the riot offer any excuse not to aid his Mexican companion. The episode with the Utes, which would permanently have prejudiced many men, did not prevent him from later holding that tribe in higher regard than perhaps any other he had met.[24]

When Kit arrived at Bent's Fort, he learned that John Frémont had passed through on another expedition. He rode on up to Pueblo to see the explorer: "My object was not to seek employment. I only thought that I would ride to his camp, have a talk, and then return. But when Frémont saw me again and requested me to join him, I could not refuse, and again entered his employ as guide and hunter." Undoubtedly the pay was good, but when a man who has just married a beautiful young woman eighteen years his junior suddenly takes a job that will keep him away for at least several months, there must be something about the job that is powerfully attractive—and the man must have a fair amount of confidence in both himself and his wife. In fact, he would be gone a year.[25]

Frémont's "Second Expedition" was a considerably more ambitious undertaking than the first. He had some forty men with him, including the old mountain man Tom Fitzpatrick, and the melancholy Prussian, Charles Preuss. Equipment included an instrument cart and a small mountain howitzer to impress the Indians. Shortly after Carson joined, Frémont hired another hunter, a young Missouri Frenchman named Alexis Godey, who was apparently known to Carson. Frémont's instructions were to connect the territory he had surveyed in 1842 with the surveys of Commander Wilkes of the U.S. Navy on the Pacific coast, "so as to give a connected survey of the interior of our continent." The orders came from the chief of the Corps of Topographical Engineers, but the idea was that of Senator Thomas Hart Benton, Frémont's father-in-law and a fervent expansionist.[26]

They traveled north to the Oregon Trail in Wyoming, already being traveled by emigrants to the Pacific Northwest, inspected the Great Salt Lake, then followed the trail more or less to Fort Vancouver on the Columbia River, the Hudson's Bay Company's headquarters in the Northwest. Then they dropped southward through central Oregon to explore the Great Basin east of the Sierra Nevada. They crossed the Sierra in winter, another instance of Frémont's determination and recklessness. After an arduous passage over the mountains, they reached California and Sutter's Fort, and traveled south along the San Joaquin Valley. In Southern California they traversed the Mojave Desert and followed the Old Spanish Trail into southern Nevada and on into Utah, where they left the Spanish Trail and traveled through the parks of the Colorado Rockies. The party celebrated Independence Day, 1844, at Bent's Fort, after which Carson left for Taos while Frémont continued on to the United States. Kit had been gone from home for almost exactly a year.[27]

In his official report Frémont presented the expedition as a grand romantic adventure, but he also recorded scientific and geographical data that were only vaguely known before, or not known at all. Among other things, he was the first to inform the outside world of the existence of the Great Basin, a vast area east of the Sierra Nevada that had no outlet to the sea. Most of what he saw and reported was already known to the mountain men, but he gave it a scientific precision and helped draw the public's attention westward.[28]

The expedition generally managed to avoid conflict with Indians, with some conspicuous exceptions, one of which would have a great influence on Kit Carson's future fame. Before that, they would meet many Indians without bloodshed. A meeting with some Cheyennes and Arapahos who were returning in a bad mood from an unsuccessful raid on the Shoshones ended peacefully because, Frémont believed, they were intimidated by the howitzer. Some Shoshones, in their turn, thought the expeditionary party might be hostile Indians because it carried an American flag, apparently a custom with the Sioux and some others. This, too, turned into a friendly encounter. In the Blue Mountains of Oregon they camped where the only water was far below in a ravine. Carson and Preuss, among others, volunteered to go down with buckets and get water.[29]

At Klamath Lake in southern Oregon they met the Klamath Indians. This was another friendly encounter, with no hint of the later events that would lead Frémont to declare these people "noted for treachery," and that would stir both him and Carson to bloody retribution, and Carson to describe them with perhaps the harshest words he used for any Indians. They then moved down the eastern side of the Sierra Nevada, looking for the mythical Buenaventura River. Satisfied that it did not exist, Frémont turned west, determined to cross the Sierra, even though winter was at hand. He was really going far beyond his original orders, for he could have returned to the States at this point, but he was determined to go on to California, whatever the risk. The crossing was an arduous passage of a month and a half through the snow, during which they were reduced to eating mule and dog meat.[30]

During the mountain passage Frémont fell into an icy stream and Carson plunged in after; the explorer does not actually admit that Carson saved his life, but the gesture was no doubt much appreciated. A few days later, when they feared that they would lose all their remaining animals to starvation, Frémont heard a shout from Carson: "Life yet, life yet; I have found a hill-side sprinkled with grass enough for the night." They had already caught a view of the valley below, with the coast range beyond, which Carson recognized from his trip to California with Ewing Young: "There," he said, "is the little mountain—it is fifteen years ago since I saw it; but I am just as sure as if I had seen it yesterday." In his autobiography Carson says simply, "Our feelings can be imagined when we saw such beautiful country." Some of the men became "insane," and it was at this time that Preuss was lost for four days. They reached Sutter's establishment on the Sacramento River with less than half of the horses and mules with which they had started across the mountains. The whole trip showed the negative as well as the positive side of Frémont's leadership—the refusal to accept limitations as well as the ability to triumph over difficulty.[31]

Their journey up the San Joaquin Valley was an easy jaunt by comparison, though they had to go far south to find a way east not blocked by snow. Eventually they took the Old Spanish Trail, which went from Santa Fe to southern California, describing a great curve through Colorado, Utah, and southern Nevada. In spite of the name, suggestive of conquistadores and missionary friars, it had really been in regular use only since the previous decade, when it was opened by American trappers. Now pack trains from New Mexico, laden with woolen goods, traveled to California to purchase horses and mules to drive back. It was on this trail that the party's first violent encounter with Indians occurred, one that would move Frémont to some of his purplest prose, and do much to insure Kit Carson his place as a popular hero.[32]

On April 24, 1844, on the Mojave River, the party encountered two New Mexicans, Andres Fuentes and an eleven-year-old boy named Pablo Hernandez, the survivors of a party of six that had included Fuentes's wife, Pablo's parents, and Santiago Giacome. They had been part of a larger caravan bound eastward for New Mexico and had gone on ahead to find better grass. At a place called the Archilette, or Resting Springs, they were attacked by a band of Indians. Fuentes and the boy escaped, but the others were killed, and the attackers carried off their horses and mules. The next day the party picked up the trail of the stolen animals, and Carson and Godey, with Frémont's agreement, volunteered to accompany Fuentes to recover them. In Carson's words, "Godey and myself volunteered with the expectation that some men of our party would join us. They did not."[33]

Carson and Godey were not going to back out, however, so the three set off; Fuentes's horse soon gave out and so the other two continued. After a cold night without making a fire, for fear of being seen, they went on and found the Indians feasting on the meat of some of the stolen animals. Godey and Carson crawled up on the horse herd in the dark, like any plains horse-stealing party, but the animals spooked and the Indians were aroused. Carson's account is almost clinical:

> We now considered it time to charge on the Indians. They were about thirty in number. We charged. I fired, killed one. Godey fired, missed, but reloaded and fired, killing another. The remainder ran. I took the two rifles and ascended a hill to guard while Godey scalped the dead Indians. He scalped the one he had shot and was proceeding towards the one I had shot. He was not yet dead [and] was behind some rocks. As Godey approached he raised [and] let fly an arrow. It passed through Godey's shirt collar. He again fell and Godey finished him.

They then gathered up the animals and returned to the main party, taking with them a young boy abandoned by the fleeing Indians.[34]

Frémont's version of the story is predictably more colorful, but substantially the same, except that he says that the second man Godey scalped was still alive, although hit twice, and he "sprang to his feet, the blood running from his skinned head, uttering a hideous howl." An old woman shrieked at them from the mountainside where she had fled. "The frightful spectacle appalled the stout hearts of our men; but they did what humanity required, and quickly terminated the agonies of the gory savage." On the return to camp, says Frémont, "Two bloody scalps, dangling from the end of Godey's gun, announced that they had overtaken the Indians as well as the horses." Over forty years later Frémont's memoirs included an illustration depicting that return, showing both men mounted, Godey smiling with the two scalps blowing in the wind, Carson with his arms raised and hat waving in triumph. However accurate the picture, it shows the importance of the event for Frémont.[35]

Carson and Godey, Frémont says, had ridden about a hundred miles in thirty hours on their mission. Unlike Carson, he was not content with a factual description, and his reflections on the affair point up a contrast in attitudes between his time and ours:

> The time, place, object, and numbers considered, this expedition of Carson and Godey may be considered among the boldest and most disinterested which the annals of western adventure, so full of daring deeds, can present. Two men, in a savage desert, pursue day and night an unknown body of Indians into the defiles of an unknown mountain—attack them on sight without counting numbers—and defeat them in an instant,—and for what? To punish the robbers of the desert, and to avenge the wrongs of Mexicans whom they did not know. I repeat: it was Carson and Godey who did this—the former an American, born in the Boonslick country of Missouri; the latter a Frenchman, born in St. Louis—and both trained to western enterprise from early life.

Frémont would copy the same words from his report into his memoirs some forty years later. Barring certain gory details, his whole account might have come from one of Cooper's novels, and his reflections on it leave no doubt that he saw the whole episode in that heroic light.[36]

Charles Preuss, however, saw the matter in a very different light, and his reflections might have been designed for one of Carson's twentieth-century critics. Earlier he had written that, "Unlike Kit, I don't see a murderer in every miserable human being," clearly a reflection on Carson's habitual caution and his admonishments to his comrades. His version of the fight is contemptuous:

> Two scalps from the hands of Alex Godey. Are these whites not much worse than the Indians? The more noble Indian takes from the killed

enemy only a piece of the scalp as large as a dollar, somewhat like the tonsure of a priest. These two heroes, who shot the Indians creeping up on them from behind, brought along the entire scalp. The Indians are braver in a similar situation. Before they shoot, they raise a yelling war whoop. Kit and Alex sneaked, like cats, as close as possible. Kit shot an Indian in the back; the bullet went through under the chest, and the Indian was able to run two hundred feet and get behind a rock. In the meantime, Godey had missed the other Indian, but loaded again and ran after him. Without knowing it, he passed within a few paces of the rock, from which the wounded Indian shot an arrow close past Godey's ears. Turning, he first dispatched this one, and then he shot the running Indian. Thus he was entitled to both scalps, for according to Indian custom the scalp belongs to the one who makes the kill. Godey rode into camp with a yelling war cry, both scalps on a rod before him. Kit was somewhat disgruntled because of his bad luck.

There may be some personal animosity in Preuss's denunciation of the two, but he raises issues that are clearly relevant to our subject.[37]

It is hardly surprising that Preuss, a genteel European unused to violence, should be disgusted when he saw two men with whom he had associated for months ride into camp shouting triumphantly, with two bloody human scalps dangling before them. Scalping was a product of a milieu with which he had no experience and was as repugnant to him as to any twentieth-century American. Whatever its origins, it was practiced in this period by both frontier whites and many of the Indians with whom they came in contact, and it would have seemed unremarkable to Carson and Godey. For the whites it lacked any religious connotation it may have had for Indians and perhaps expressed contempt for the victim; it was considered appropriate in Indian warfare, not elsewhere. Preuss's notion that the Indians would have proceeded in a "more noble" manner, taking a smaller scalp and giving fair warning with a "war whoop," shows his ignorance of the realities of frontier warfare. How else were two men to take on thirty—if we accept Carson's figure—except by "creeping up on them from behind?" Carson's account indicates that they intended to make off with the horses without seeking "satisfaction." Only when the Indians were alerted did they think it necessary to fight, relying on surprise and a bold front to prevail. Carson gives no indication that he was actually disgruntled that Godey got both scalps;

he admits quite frankly that he had not finished the man he shot, which some of his old associates would have found embarrassing. There is no clear evidence that Carson ever personally took a scalp; there is also no compelling reason to suppose that he did not, though his leaving Godey to perform the operation in this case might indicate that he had no particular relish for the practice.

The difference in perceptions between Carson, Frémont, and Preuss is still present today. Frémont saw the action of Carson and Godey as chivalrous and disinterested, a righting of wrong and restoration of property to Fuentes and the orphaned Pablo Hernandez—property that may have represented the whole of their worldly goods. Preuss was disgusted by what he saw as a barbarous act, though perhaps more repelled by the manner than the substance of it. For Kit it was yet another pursuit of horse thieves, like so many he had taken part in, the principal difference being that here he had no personal interest in the matter but acted, as Frémont says, to avenge the wrongs done to Mexicans he did not know. There was no authority to whom the injured could apply for justice on the Old Spanish Trail; victims and their defenders must make their own rough justice.

When members of the expeditionary party reached the site of the attack on the New Mexicans, they found the bodies of the two men, "naked, mutilated, and pierced with arrows." The two women were not found, but Frémont's imagination painted a lurid picture of their fate. Young Pablo Hernandez wept, crying out, "*Mi padre! Mi madre!*" Frémont declares, "When we beheld this pitiable sight, and pictured to ourselves the fate of the two women, carried off by savages so brutal and so loathsome, all compunction for the scalped-alive Indian ceased; and we rejoiced that Carson and Godey had been able to give so useful a lesson to these American Arabs, who lie in wait to murder and plunder the innocent traveler." These reflections were understandable on such an occasion, but similar rationalizations appear rather frequently in Frémont's writings. This sort of condemnation is notably lacking in Carson's autobiography, or in most of his other recorded statements, for all his wariness where Indians were concerned. Perhaps it was simply that he lacked Frémont's rhetorical gifts, but the contrast is striking.[38]

Carson, in fact, reports that another party following them found the two women dead, "their bodies very much mutilated and staked to the ground," perhaps as vengeance for the deaths of the two men killed by Godey and Carson. Kit simply records the fact, without any general reflections, but Frémont in his later memoirs writes of what seems to be the same atrocity as if he had seen the bodies himself, which he apparently had not, and gives it as a motive for a later attack on Indians having no connection with the affair.[39]

A few days later, Frémont's explorers encountered a group of Paiute Indians they believed to be the same people who had killed the New Mexicans. Frémont says, "Towards us their disposition was evidently hostile, nor were we well disposed toward them." Each man was carrying arrows in his hand ready for instant use; in all fairness, the wariness was probably mutual. Frémont says, "I was forcibly struck by an expression of countenance resembling that in a beast of prey; and all their actions are those of wild animals. Joined to the restless motion of the eye, there is a want of mind—an absence of thought—and an action wholly by impulse, strongly expressed, and which constantly recalls the similarity." (One wonders what the Paiute chief saw in Frémont's face.)

In spite of Frémont's warnings, the chief, with a few others, pushed into the party's camp, contemptuous of the white men's weapons, indicating that he had many more men, and that they had their own weapons. Frémont says that he had difficulty restraining his own men, especially Carson, "who felt an insult of this kind as much as if it had been given by a more responsible being." "Don't say that, old man," said Carson, "don't you say that—your life's in danger"; he spoke in English, but his meaning must have been clear. Frémont gave a worn-out horse to the Indians for food, and the encounter passed off without violence. Both Frémont's and Carson's reactions were obviously caused by a combination of apprehension, wounded pride at the chief's arrogance, and the conviction that these were the people who had killed the New Mexicans a few days before. Carson, an old poker player, may have decided that a good bluff was in order. If he did feel the insult, then one could say that he had recognized the chief's humanity, in a way that Frémont did not, and reacted like a true backcountry man. One is not insulted by an animal. Nonetheless, they sensibly avoided a fight. Kit does not even mention the episode.[40]

Just a few days after this, on the Virgin River in northwest Arizona, their luck ran out. Baptiste Tabeau, one of the party, went back a short distance to a former camp to look for a strayed mule without telling anyone and did not return. Carson took a few men to search for him, but all they could find were signs of his body falling from his horse and a great deal of blood, enough to make it certain he was dead. Carson says, "I was grieved on account of the death of the Canadian. He was a brave, noble-souled fellow. I had been in many an Indian fight with him and I am confident, if he was not taken unawares, that he surely killed one or two before he fell." Apparently Kit had known Tabeau in his trapping days, and now he was seeking what consolation he could find. Nothing could be done, since their horses were too worn out to mount a pursuit.[41]

Frémont's words are probably accurate in gauging the party's feeling: "Men, who have gone through such dangers and sufferings as we had seen, become like brothers, and feel each other's loss. To defend and avenge each other, is the deep feeling of all." Preuss was shocked out of his humanitarianism: "May God have mercy on the Paiutes who fall into our hands now. They lurk like wolves among the rocks along the road. . . . When I think of what happened to Tabeau, I must say that I was lucky that I did not fare worse during the four days in the mountains. Suppose those Indians had been like the Paiutes?" Preuss still did not consider all Indians to be alike, but he was perhaps beginning to understand Carson's ingrained caution. Again, these Paiutes may have been antagonized by earlier travelers on the Old Spanish Trail. Utes often raided the Great Basin peoples for captives to sell to New Mexicans, and the New Mexicans sometimes carried out their own raids; the Paiutes could not have regarded strangers in their territory with equanimity. None of that would have made Tabeau's comrades feel any better, but there were no immediate consequences—those would come when Carson was in the area a few years later.[42]

Frémont's men left the Old Spanish Trail near its turn southeast toward New Mexico and moved on to Sevier River and Utah Lake. On the way they encountered the famous Ute chief Wakara, noted for his slave raids on the Paiutes and his horse-stealing expeditions to California, sometimes in company with former trappers; Frémont found him "quite civil." While they were still among the Utes of the region, Preuss records, "Kit received as a gift from an old acquaintance a piece of venison, which was excellent."[43]

Within a few days more, Preuss recorded another incident involving Carson and the Utes:

Kit bought an Indian boy of about twelve to fourteen years for forty dollars. He is to eat only raw meat, in order to get courage, says Kit, and in a few years he hopes to have trained him, with the Lord's help, so that he will at least be capable of stealing horses. He actually eats the raw marrow, with which Kit supplies him plentifully. He belongs to the Paiute Nation, which subsists only on mice, locusts, and roots, and such a life as the present must please him very much.

Apparently, the boy was one of the numerous Paiute captives whom the Utes took for sale, part of the extensive network of such trading in the West at the time, a practice established before Europeans came to the country. Preuss was willing to believe that the boy was better off than he would have been if Kit had refused to buy him. In fact, an instance is recorded of a Ute killing a child in rage because some Mormons refused to buy it, although this occurred some years later under changed conditions. Reportedly, Paiutes sometimes sold their children when conditions were especially difficult in their harsh environment. As with the Indian boy sold to John Sutter, we do not know to what extent the transaction represented compassion or commerce on Kit's part. The remark about training the boy to steal horses may be taken as Kit's way of kidding the solemn German; it could indicate that the future he had in mind for the youngster was not one of simple servitude. Marrow was often eaten raw, and considered a delicacy.[44]

The expedition moved on into the Colorado Rockies. The scouts saw signs of an Arapaho village, which they were anxious to avoid because they were coming from the country of the Utes, the Arapahos' enemies, and might be accused of giving them arms. When they did meet the Arapahos, they took up a defensible position and negotiated safe passage, giving presents to seal the bargain. Then they met some trappers who said that two of their friends had been killed by these same Arapahos. Shortly thereafter, separate parties of Arapahos and Utes appeared, each wanting Frémont to join in attacking the other. The explorer avoided making a choice, and the party continued to Bent's Fort. Kit did not consider any of these later encounters with Indians worth mentioning; they were perfectly routine to him.[45]

From Bent's Fort, Carson returned to Taos, having been gone a year. At his rate of pay with Frémont, he should have earned at least $1,200, an impressive sum at the time. Perhaps this helped him justify to Josefa why he had been absent for most of their marriage to date. He stayed at home in Taos from July 1844 until the next March, or at least most of the time; that fall the Santa Fe trader James Josiah Webb met Kit traveling with friends from Pueblo to Taos and received from him this characteristic advice: "Look out for your har, boys! The Utes are plenty about here." In March 1845, Carson says, "Dick Owens and I concluded that, as we had rambled enough, that it would be advisable for us to go and settle on some good stream and make us a farm."[46]

The site they chose was across the Sangre de Cristo Mountains from Taos: "We went to Little Cimarron, about 45 miles east of Taos, built ourselves little huts, put in considerable grain, and commenced getting out timber to begin our improvements. Remained till August of the same year." In classic pioneer fashion Kit was recapitulating the family experience on a new frontier; like Lindsey Carson at Boonslick, he was putting in a crop and clearing land. But settling down was not in the cards for him yet. Events were occurring far to the east, south, and west that would prevent that and change his whole life.[47]

In Washington, the government ordered the publication of *Report of the Exploring Expedition to the Rocky Mountains in the Year 1842, and to Oregon and North California in the Years 1843–'44*, by Brevet Captain J. C. Frémont. Except for the brief mention in Samuel Parker's book in 1838, this was the first time that the name Kit Carson appeared in print, unless one counts the notice in a Missouri newspaper of his running away in 1826. Ten thousand copies of Frémont's report were printed in 1845, and other editions followed. Two years later David Coyner, introducing another book of western adventure, would write, "Any publication, throwing any light upon that vast wilderness between the States and the Pacific, and calculated to open its secrets, will be read with interest." This certainly proved true with Frémont's publication, a combination of scientific and geographical information with hardship and adventure, told in a most readable fashion. Scholars have speculated on whether John Frémont or Jessie Benton Frémont had more to do with the actual authorship, but here it is important that the work made Kit Carson a public figure, the first stage in his becoming the symbolic frontiersman, the model mountain man, guide, and scout of the trans-Mississippi West.[48]

Thanks to Frémont's work, people like William T. Sherman and George Brewerton within a few years would be eager to meet the great scout, and they would be astonished that the hero of such adventures would turn out to be, in Sherman's words, "a small, stoop-shouldered man, with reddish hair, freckled face, soft blue eyes, and nothing to indicate extraordinary courage and daring." Brewerton would expect, on the basis of the same document, a man "over six feet high—a sort of Hercules in his build—with an enormous beard, and a voice like a roused lion." Obviously, Frémont's brief physical description of the man had not made the same impression as his account of Carson's deeds.[49]

Writing on the frontier myth in *The Fatal Environment*, Richard Slotkin titles a section "Frémont and Carson: Heyward and Hawkeye in California." Slotkin explicitly compares Cooper's hero and the young officer who plays the conventional romantic role in *The Last of the Mohicans* on the one hand, and Kit Carson and John Frémont on the other. The analogy calls for Carson, the old, experienced westerner, to educate Frémont, the young eastern gentleman, in the ways of the wilderness; the young hero then gets the girl and makes his fortune while the old scout remains a marginal character, heroic but not suitable for romance. The comparison between the two books may be just a bit overdrawn, for the central character of Frémont's report is John Charles Frémont, who is already possessed of courage, strength of will, and wilderness skill. All the same, Kit is depicted as "one of the finest pictures of a horseman I have ever seen." He jumps into an icy steam to save Frémont (who never quite admits that he needed saving), he helps inspire the party in crossing the Sierra and finds grass to keep the animals alive, and above all, he and Godey take on many times their number of Indians to avenge the deaths of the New Mexicans and recover their horses. Within two years of the Pathfinder's report, Carson would be recognized by sailors on the Pacific coast as "memorable for his adventures in the mountains with Col. Frémont." In less than a decade and a half, he would be the subject of a biography of over five hundred pages.[50]

By an irony Frémont certainly never intended, Carson's fame would eventually outshine his own. The explorer's future ventures—politics, the military, finance, and even in exploration—would prove less successful and would provoke controversy that would leave him with an equivocal, though still glamorous, reputation. Carson, as Slotkin points out, "had the wisdom or the good fortune to remain in the West, among the scenes that had been part of his legend from the start."[51]

CALIFORNIA CONQUERED

Frémont's next venture, which would develop both the glamor and the controversy to their full extent, began as his first report was reaching the public. James K. Polk, who became president in 1845, was dedicated to an avowedly expansionist program, including the annexation of Texas, Oregon, and California. Texas joined the Union almost immediately by treaty. Negotiations were opened with Great Britain over Oregon. Mexico refused even to negotiate over California or the Texas boundary, and war began to seem likely. In the midst of these events, Frémont started west on his third expedition, with sixty-two white men and twelve Delaware Indians.[52]

Carson says simply, "The year previous, I had given my word to Frémont that, in case he should return for the purpose of making any more explorations, that I would willingly join him." Frémont sent word from Bent's Fort about the beginning of August 1845 that he was indeed headed west again. "Then Owens and I sold out, for about half it was worth, and we started to join Frémont and we both received employment." Also with the party were Kit's old friend Lucien Maxwell and a tough young man from Tennessee named Thomas Salathiel Martin, who would leave an interesting account of the expedition. Charles Preuss had chosen to remain in the East.[53]

Kit had given his word, and we can only guess what part adventure, good wages, and attachment to Frémont each played in his keeping it. Frémont says only, "This was like Carson, prompt, self-sacrificing, and true."[54]

Alex Godey was also with the expedition, and Frémont devotes some space to comparing him, Carson, and Owens. All three, he thought, might have become marshals under Napoleon. "Carson, of great courage; quick and complete perception, taking in at a glance the advantages as well as the chances for defeat; Godey, sensible to danger, of perfect coolness and stubborn resolution; Owens, equal in courage to the others, and in coolness to Godey, had the *coup-d'oeil* of a chess-player, covering the whole field with a glance that sees the best move." Allowing for the romanticism of this undoubtedly sincere tribute (and the likelihood that its author saw himself in the Napoleonic role), it is interesting that, in Frémont's view, Carson was not distinguished, like the other two, for coolness. It would seem that the Carson Frémont knew, for all his caution in Indian country, was still combative and even impetuous, as in the confrontation with the Paiute chief. The ability to size up "the advantages as well as the chances for defeat," however, would become apparent to others in time.[55]

Frémont's first expedition had been confined to territory officially recognized as part of the United States. The second had entered both the "jointly occupied" Oregon country and Mexican territory, compiling geographical information but also exploring travel routes that could be used by American settlers and acquiring useful military intelligence. The third expedition would go much further, not so much in geographical as in political and military terms. Frémont, and Carson, would be involved in acts that were highly controversial as they became part of America's westward expansion in the age of Manifest Destiny. They would also become involved in far more conflict with Indians than on the previous two expeditions, and some of their acts would be more questionable, at least by later standards.

Although the ostensible purpose of the third expedition, like the previous ones, was exploration, there is reason to believe that Frémont had other instructions from persons in high places, from Senator Benton and perhaps from President Polk himself. He certainly seems to have believed that he was expected to act on his own initiative in case of war with Mexico, which seemed increasingly likely. Being Frémont, he would push whatever understanding or instructions he did have to the limit. His written orders, however, did not direct him anywhere near California, where his most spectacular and controversial acts would occur.[56]

The expedition's first act was to cross the Great Basin. Its encounters with Indians there were not violent. Frémont made his Delawares give back the bow and arrows that they had taken from a lone Indian, and the men fed an aged woman who came upon their camp, catching Carson and all the other alert frontiersmen by surprise. When they reached the Sierra Nevada, Frémont told them that they were going to cross into California.[57]

The crossing of the mountains was remarkably easy, compared to the previous expedition. Frémont took fifteen men, including Carson, Maxwell, Owens, and Godey, for the crossing, sending the remainder of the party, with Joseph Walker as a guide, around the southern end of the mountain range. On the west side of the Sierra, however, occurred the first incidents that would set the tone for the third expedition's relations with Indians. Owens, Maxwell, and two Delawares, while scouting ahead, were attacked by perhaps a hundred Indians, and had to be relieved by Frémont and the rest of the party. Frémont calls them "Horse-Thief" Indians, former mission dwellers who had taken to the mountains and were now engaged in raiding the Hispanic settlements for horses, which served as food as well as transportation. Many groups in the interior engaged in these raids, greatly increasing the insecurity of the Hispanic population, to whom the distant Mexican government, only tenuously in control of California, offered little protection.[58]

Maxwell's biographer says that Frémont had apparently taken it upon himself to punish the Indians for stealing horses from American settlers in the vicinity, acting as if the country was already under the control of the United States and he had authority to protect settlers. Even so, his behavior was not so very different from that of Ewing Young a decade and a half earlier. Shortly after, Maxwell, who was ahead of the party, had an encounter with a lone Indian; they shot it out on foot and Maxwell won.[59]

Frémont's party now journeyed south to rejoin the main group. While searching for the others, the explorers had an encounter that Carson describes very briefly: "[W]e came on a party of Indians, killed five, and returned to the fort." Frémont does not even mention this incident in a fairly detailed account of the trip, but he does note that they had been harassed by Indians who killed or tried to steal their animals. He probably reacted to this harassment in what they all considered self-defense.[60]

Frémont's actions in the next weeks—early 1846—are not directly relevant to our theme. The Mexican governor had first allowed the expedition to remain in California and purchase supplies but then, becoming aware of the increasing chance of war between the two countries, ordered him out. Frémont took a defiant stand on a mountaintop, then was forced to back down in the face of superior force and march off to the north, up the Sacramento River. His expedition spent much of April 1846 near the ranch of Peter Lassen, and there occurred one of the more dubious episodes in Frémont's relations with Indians.[61]

Carson's account is brief, but not wholly dispassionate:

During our stay at Lawson's [Lassen's], some Americans that were settled in the neighborhood came in stating that there were about 1000 Indians in the vicinity making preparations to attack the settlements; requested assistance of Frémont to drive them back. He and party and some few Americans that lived near started for the Indian encampment. Found them to be in great force, as was stated. They were attacked. The number killed I cannot say. It was a perfect butchery. Those not killed fled in all directions, and we returned to Lawson's. Had accomplished what we went for and given the Indians such a chastisement that [it] would be long before they ever again would feel like attacking the settlements

Harvey Carter and Thelma Guild, always favorably disposed toward Carson, find this "preventive expedition" hard to justify. Other writers have been scathing regarding the affair and Carson's part in it.[62]

Frémont misplaces this episode in his memoirs, indicating that it occurred after his return from Oregon a few months later. This was when open hostilities between the Americans and Mexicans in California had commenced, and he suggests that the Mexican commander intended to incite the Indians to attack the American settlers. Whether a failure of memory or a deliberate distortion is responsible, Frémont's chronology is almost certainly wrong. He says that, according to the settlers, "the Indians of the valley were leaving their rancherias and taking to the mountains; a movement which indicated preparations for active hostility." According to these reports, they had killed an Indian boy employed at one of the ranches who had refused to accompany them, an ominous development if true. Frémont goes on to expound on "the barbarities of Indians, some of which I had seen, and towards women so cruel that I could not put them upon paper. An Indian let loose is of all animals the most savage. He has an imagination for devilment that seems peculiar to him, and a singular delight in inflicting suffering." He goes on to a description of the scene of the attack on the New Mexican party on the Old Spanish Trail, avenged by Carson and Godey on the second expedition, including the women staked to the ground, whom he probably had not seen. This sort of denunciation of "Indians" in general, without differentiation, as peculiarly cruel and capable of inflicting unmentionable horrors on women is commonplace in nineteenth-century American writing. The assumptions it reflects are grossly indiscriminate and designed to incite hatred; they fed the fears of frontier whites and were used to justify violent acts against Indians. In spite of his apparent misrepresentations, Frémont may still have believed he was justified in this attack.[63]

Thomas Martin's version adds information not given by Carson or Frémont. He apparently had no more doubts than they that the attack was justified by the Indians' intention of attacking the settlers. He says that Frémont denied the settlers' request officially, "as he had no right to fight the inds."—that is, he was a U.S. Army officer in Mexican territory. Therefore, Frémont "told us that those who wished [to] take part in an expedition against these indians he would discharge, and take us again afterwards." All but four of the men in the party took up the offer. According to Martin, "We found the indians to the number of 4000 to 5000 on a tongue of land between the bends of the river, having a war-dance preparatory to attacking the settlers." The advance-guard of thirty-six men charged on sighting the Indians, firing a volley and killing twenty-four, then charging with sabers (the only indication that the party possessed such weapons). After three hours' fighting, "We had killed over 175 of them." Martin's statistics are highly questionable. Even Carson's figure of one thousand Indians present seems too high, especially if he was referring to fighting men. Very few Indian-white engagements in the West would have yielded an Indian casualty toll anywhere near 175; the Indians would not remain on the scene to suffer such losses. Martin's figure for the total number of Indians is so unlikely as to make his "body count" highly suspect. Frémont gives no figures, but emphasizes the dispersion of the Indians, minimizing the casualties by implication.[64]

The men with Frémont believed that they were making a justified preventive strike to discourage the Indians from any idea of attacking the settlers in the area. Neither Martin nor anyone else addresses the question of whether women and children were killed along with men of fighting age. These would certainly have fled first, with the men covering their retreat as best they could. Carson's description, "It was a perfect butchery," does not prove anything one way or another. Martin Green sees in Carson's phrase an expression of satisfaction at the completeness of the slaughter. The words could be those of John Mostin, Carson's scribe, but they are sufficiently forceful and striking to justify taking them as Carson's own. That does not mean that Carson was gloating over the "butchery." Ordinary Americans even today use the word *perfect* to mean "complete" and "unmitigated," without expressing any approval, as in "a perfect mess." Carson does not enter here into the explicit detail he devotes to other Indian fights, including the battle with the Klamaths he describes a little later, perhaps because he did not care to recall exactly what had happened. One possible explanation of his reticence, and Frémont's elaborate justifications, may be that, although they considered the attack justifiable in itself, things got out of hand and the settlers (and perhaps some expedition members) engaged in "a perfect butchery," far beyond what Kit thought necessary.[65]

As we do not know enough to say whether or not women or children were killed in the attack, we cannot say positively whether the Indians actually intended to attack the white settlers. Thomas Martin says they were holding a war dance, but it is highly unlikely that he or anyone else with the party knew what a war dance of these Indians looked like. Frémont says they had feathers on their heads and their faces were painted black, "their war color," which would have signified the intent of some plains and mountain tribes, but not necessarily these Indians. They may have gathered for some ceremonial or social purpose having nothing to do with hostile intentions. (These people have been identified as either Maidu or Wintu by different authors.) As noted, a number of interior California tribes in this period were engaged in attacking Hispanic settlements near the coast, so hostile intent is by no means out of the question. Sutter's settlement had also been raided by horse thieves on occasion. It is entirely possible, of course, that some white settlers had been guilty of acts that infuriated the Indians to the point of retaliation; this would be a recurring pattern in California, as elsewhere in the West in coming years. If the Indians had stolen or killed stock belonging to white Americans, the whites would have been likely to react in a way that could in turn arouse the Indians—another all-too-common frontier scenario.[66]

It may be wise, then, to refrain from dogmatism about the absolute right or wrong of this incident. Carson's motives for participating, however, are not hard to imagine. It was probably the first time since his boyhood that he had seen Anglo-American settlers, people not very different from his old Boonslick neighbors, in apparent danger of Indian attack. The boy who remembered being forted for two or three years was bound to spring to the defense of people with whom he could so readily identify. In later years Kit would become more skeptical about the fears of frontier whites, more ready to see their part in provoking Indians, but he would never be able to regard these dangers with the objectivity possible to a historian more than a century removed from such events.

After this battle Frémont's party moved on north, leaving California for Oregon in reluctant compliance with the orders of the Mexican authorities. The men had reached Klamath Lake when the course of larger events overtook them. The "messenger of destiny" was Lieutenant Archibald Gillespie, United States Marine Corps, sent to California with some sort of special instructions for Frémont from the government in Washington, the exact nature of which has remained mysterious. Arriving in California, he set out with a few men to overtake Frémont. Finding that he was being followed by hostile Indians, he sent two of his men ahead to catch Frémont and request a meeting. The explorer took

GUIDE AND SCOUT

ten men, including Carson, and hastened to find the marine, "having but poor faith in the Klamath Indians," in Carson's words.[67]

Frémont would take the instructions he received as his warrant to seize California. First, however, would come another bloody encounter with Indians. The night of the meeting with Gillespie, as Frémont admits, he failed to set a guard, probably preoccupied with the thought of great events unfolding. The cautious Carson probably went to bed thinking that the commander would take this obvious precaution, especially in the known presence of Indians who were not trusted. Instead, he was awakened by "a noise as of an axe striking, jumped up, saw there were Indians in camp, gave the alarm." The Klamaths had attacked, and the noise was the tomahawking of Basil Lajeunesse and Denny, one of the Delawares. Crane, another Delaware, jumped up and took five arrows in his body, as the Klamath chief was shot down. Carson's rifle had been damaged, and he had only a pistol, with which he fired at the chief, only cutting loose his tomahawk. Maxwell and Joseph Stepperfeldt shot the chief, of whom Carson says, "He was the bravest Indian I ever saw. If his men had been as brave as himself, we surely would all have been killed." Godey, finding something wrong with his gun, stepped into the firelight to examine it, exposing himself to enemy fire; the exasperated Carson cried out, "Look at that fool. Look at him, will you?"[68]

The attackers were beaten off. The next morning the party found that they had three men dead—Lajeunesse, Denny, and Crane—and one Delaware wounded. Although Carson later spoke with respect of the bravery of the dead Klamath chief, at the time he relieved his feelings by knocking the dead man's skull to pieces with his own tomahawk; Sagundai, one of the Delawares, scalped him. (Martin Green notes this action as an instance of Carson's brutality, without making it clear that the man was already dead or that Carson had just seen three comrades killed.) Some ten years later Kit would describe the meeting with the Klamaths during Frémont's second expedition in these words: "We pronounced them a mean, low-lived, treacherous race, which we found to be a fact after we were in their country in 1846." These are the harshest words to be found in his autobiography about any group of Indians. Even so, unlike some of Frémont's gratuitous generalizations, it is directed at one particular group of Indians, not at all. It was probably prompted by their betrayal after showing hospitality toward Gillespie shortly before the attack, and after Frémont's having given them some meat, tobacco, and knives.[69]

We do not have any account giving the Klamaths' reasons for the attack. Guild and Carter suggest that the news of Frémont's attack on the Indians in California had "spread like wildfire" and prompted the Klamaths to make a preemptive strike on a party they regarded as hostile and dangerous. Lawrence Keeley lists the Klamaths among the numerous notably aggressive peoples around the world who frequently engaged in offensive raiding, and who were centers of areas of especially intense warfare. Hudson's Bay Company men and a few American travelers had clashed with the Indians in southern Oregon a number of times since the 1820s. Carson and his comrades, of course, could not see things dispassionately. After the Klamath assault, Frémont says, "For the moment I threw all other considerations aside and determined to square accounts with these people before I left them." He would apply the old rule of the mountain men, the frontier, and the backcountry—the rule so frequently followed by the Indians themselves—the law of retribution.[70]

Frémont talked with Swanock, the Delaware leader, and with Sagundai. They expressed a desire for revenge on the Klamaths. Frémont allowed them to remain behind to set an ambush for any Klamaths who appeared at the abandoned camp. Soon after the whites marched off, a volley was heard, and the Delawares returned with two scalps. "Better now," Swanock said, "very sick before, better now." Thomas Martin, however, says that some whites, apparently including himself, remained with the Delawares, and that nine Klamaths died. In spite of Frémont's frequent praise for "his" Delawares, he shows a tendency to attribute to them the more questionable or "barbaric" acts of his party.[71]

This was not to be the extent of the party's revenge, however. They were headed around the lake, toward the Klamath village on an inlet. Frémont says that he sent Carson and Owens ahead with ten men, including Thomas Martin, to reconnoiter but to avoid combat until the main party could come up; Carson remembers being told to "act as I thought best" if seen by the Indians. On coming on a village of about fifty lodges: "By the commotion in their camp I knew that they had seen us and, considering it useless to send for reinforcements, I determined to attack them, charged on them, fought for some time, killed a number, and the balance fled." Thomas Martin says, "Kit Carson proposed that we should charge down on them without waiting for the arrival of the rest of the company." According to Martin, they rode their horses into a stream that was much deeper than expected and got their powder wet, "and we would have been in a fine fix, if the rest of our party had not arrived at this moment." That agrees with Frémont, who says the main body came up in time to join the fight, but disagrees with Carson, who says that Frémont arrived "too late for the sport." Frémont, as he rode up, saw a dead Indian in a canoe: "On his feet were shoes which I thought Basil [Lajeunesse] wore when he was killed."[72]

Whether or not Frémont was on time for the "sport," Carson takes responsibility for what ensued. There was a great deal of camp equipage and fishing gear at the site, large stores of fish, and the houses of the village itself, woven of flags (cattails). Carson says, "I wished to do them as much damage as I could, so I directed their houses to be set on fire. The flag being dry it was a beautiful sight. The Indians had commenced the war on us without cause, and I thought they should be chastized in a summary manner. And they were severely punished." Thomas Martin says that most of the Klamaths escaped to the mountains, but a few hid in clumps of cedar and were killed by the Delawares. He mentions an old Indian woman found dead in one of the canoes but otherwise says nothing about casualties among women and children, seeming to imply that this one woman was exceptional. Frémont says in his memoirs that fourteen Indians were killed. When Jessie Frémont came to write an account based on her husband's recollections and on what she heard from Carson, she reported twenty-one Indians dead. She quotes Carson as telling her, "We gave them something to remember . . . the women and children we did not interfere with." She adds, " 'Interfere' had a narrower meaning to Carson than to us." The clear implication is that there was no deliberate attempt to harm the women and children, beyond destroying their homes and goods. If Jessie Frémont invented Carson's statement to protect his reputation and that of her husband, she was clever enough to include Carson's particular meaning of the verb *to interfere*. The circumstances, with Carson's detachment in "a fine fix" facing superior numbers of warriors until help arrived, would argue in favor of the noncombatants having time to get away.[73]

The whole affair was another example of the revenge cycle, no more edifying than it would have been on the Anglo-Scottish border or in the Blackfoot country. Carson's words, if his, about the "sport" of fighting the Klamaths and the "beautiful sight" of their burning houses, dictated a decade after the events, cannot be anything but repugnant; they referred to a particular group whom Carson and the others blamed for the deaths of their comrades. Of them, Carson says, "Of the three men killed, Lajeunesse was particularly regretted. He had been with us in every trip that had been made. All of them were brave, good men." In describing the burial of the three, Carson betrays his emotion, and that of the rest of the party, in an interesting way. The detachment that fought off the initial Klamath attack "would have taken the bodies to our camp, but on account of the timber being so thick, the bodies knocked against the trees and, becoming much bruised, we concluded to bury them when we did."

Kit had seen a good many dead bodies in his career up to 1846, but he was still not callous about those of dead friends (two of them Indians, be it noted), and he still found it necessary to explain, in a memoir that generally ignores such routine matters as burials, why they were interred in a hasty fashion. These feelings help us to understand, if not to excuse, the retaliatory attack on the Klamaths. If Jessie Frémont is to be trusted—and certainly she was not there—it was not an indiscriminate attack on all, regardless of age or sex, it was not "genocidal," and it was not carried out simply because the Klamaths were Indians. As usual, if there was to be any redress, it was in the hands of those who believed themselves wronged.[74]

After the fight they moved a mile or two from the village and camped. Frémont sent Owens back with about twenty men to watch for pursuers. When Owens sent word that some fifty Klamaths had returned to the village, Frémont hurried back to reinforce him with five or six men, including Carson and the Delawares Swanock and Sagundai. They encountered one Indian on the way whom they charged, Carson in the lead. Kit's gun misfired and he had to throw himself on one side of his horse in an attempt to avoid the Indian's arrow. Frémont fired, missed, and rode his horse over the warrior; Sagundai jumped from his horse and killed the man with a blow from his war club. Frémont says, "It was a narrow chance for Carson. The poisoned arrow would have gone through his body." Carson agreed, saying, "I considered that Frémont saved my life for, in all probability, if he had not run over the Indian as he did, I would have been shot." One reason for Carson's lasting loyalty to Frémont is probably to be found in this incident.[75]

The next day, as they headed south for California, Maxwell and Auguste Archambeau, in advance, encountered a lone Indian who fired arrows at them. They killed him—although, Carson insists, they had not intended him any harm—because he persisted in shooting at them, an understandable action considering recent events in the neighborhood.

The consequences of the battles already fought would continue to dog them. Passing down the Sacramento, they had to avoid an ambush by local Indians in a canyon. They went around and Carson, Godey, and another man pursued the would-be attackers. Carson relates, "One man, brave[r] than the rest, hid himself behind a large rock, and awaited our approach." The man fired arrows so rapidly that the whites had to retreat back out of his range. Then Carson fired his rifle: "My shot had the desired effect. He was scalped. . . . He was a brave Indian, deserved a better fate, but he had placed himself on the wrong path." Again, it may be unwise to read any strong regret into Carson's words, but it seems clear that he regarded this death as unfortunate necessity. The act itself, however, was performed with the efficiency of a veteran warrior. Carson could respect the courage of an enemy, but it would have been, for him, sheer foolishness to hesitate in the face of an armed and dangerous fighting man.[76]

The next day Stepperfeldt and another man killed an Indian they believed was attempting to steal a mule. This was the last such incident on Frémont's third expedition. The explorer's generally good record for avoiding trouble on his first two ventures had been drastically reversed during the third, and Frémont must bear some, if not all, of the responsibility. He and his men certainly did not create the hostility between the interior tribes of California and the Hispanic and Anglo-American settlers, and the party's response to attempts to steal its animals was the same as that of both Indians and whites of the time. Frémont's decision to launch an attack on the Indians near Lassen's ranch, to prevent an anticipated attack on white settlers, may have precipitated his later troubles.

On the return to California, Frémont plunged into the larger political and military arena. It is not necessary to describe in detail the involved story of the American conquest of California. To simplify greatly, Frémont, though unaware that war had, in fact, broken out on the Rio Grande between the United States and Mexico, chose to interpret his instructions from Washington as authorization to seize the province. He joined a group of American settlers who had already launched the "Bear Flag" revolt and declared California independent. At first, the American naval commander on the coast hesitated to support Frémont because he had no written orders, but eventually the navy joined in the act of conquest. Frémont believed he had forestalled British ambitions in the area by his prompt action.[77]

Only miniscule forces were involved in the military operations of the conquest and casualties were small. One incident that did occur, however, involved Carson in one of the darker episodes of his career. Two Americans were captured and murdered by Californios, and this led to an action that stained the repute of Frémont and his men more, for contemporaries, than all their Indian fighting. Three Californios—Francisco and Ramón de Haro and their uncle, Juan de los Reyes Berreyesa—were killed by a party of Frémont's men that included Carson. Although the essential fact is not in doubt, there is considerable difference regarding the details, which concern Carson's degree of responsibility. Frémont, noting the outrage his men felt over the deaths of the two Americans, says, "My scouts, mainly Delawares, influenced by these feelings, made sharp retaliation and killed Bereyasa and de Haro." Once again he attributes the most dubious acts of his party to the "savage" Delawares.[78]

Hubert Howe Bancroft has it that the three Californios landed from a boat and Carson asked Frémont if they should be taken prisoner; Frémont said, "I have no room for prisoners," so Carson and some others of the party shot them down as they approached. Told of the deed, Frémont nodded and said, "It is well." Bancroft's principal source, Jasper O'Farrell, said that Carson stated he had killed the three unwillingly at Frémont's order. Archibald Gillespie, some ten years after the event, gave an account in which Carson and his companions shot the men and then reported to Frémont, who asked, "Where are your prisoners?" Carson replied, "Oh, we don't want any prisoners; they lie out yonder." Frémont then gave approval, saying, "It is well!" Gillespie wrote his story during Frémont's presidential campaign of 1856 and was influenced by political and perhaps personal animosity, but his version actually reflects less discredit on Frémont, and more on Carson, than Bancroft's later version. Alex Godey, during the same campaign, defended Frémont by claiming the three resisted being taken prisoner.[79]

Carson, not surprisingly, does not mention this incident in his autobiography, although he refers to the killing of the two Americans that preceded it. He did, however, tell his version of the affair to W. M. Boggs, an old acquaintance and a relative of Charles and William Bent, in 1853. Unfortunately, Boggs did not record the extant version of the story until some fifty years after Carson told it to him, although he may have made notes at the time. According to Boggs, Carson and two comrades, Granville Swift and Jack Neil (apparently Samuel Neal), took the three Californios prisoner and Carson then asked Frémont what to do with them. Frémont replied, "Mr. Carson, I have no use for prisoners—do your duty." Kit returned to his companions, and they had "a short consultation" and shot the prisoners. Boggs, who says he had the story from both Carson and Swift, blamed Carson for "a cold hearted crime," and questioned Kit about it when he was in California in 1853, asking, "What did you kill them for when you had them in your power?" Carson then gave his version of the story, explaining that he and the others had been enraged by the murder of the two Americans, who had reportedly been killed in an especially atrocious fashion, being tied to trees and literally pulled apart by the lariats of the Californios. Carson said specifically that the three Californios were killed in retaliation for the manner in which the Americans had died. According to Boggs, it was Kit's older brother, Moses Carson, a California settler, who discovered the bodies of the two Americans and buried them, although it is not clear whether Kit had the story of their deaths directly from Moses at the time he took retribution. Boggs remained unhappy about the killing of the prisoners, but believed that Carson had done "many brave and generous deeds" in the rest of his life, and described him as having "a noble soul—none of your Buffalo Bill Show acting kind, but plain, little, brave Kit Carson, unassuming in manners."[80]

Boggs's account, as close as we are likely to get to Carson's version of the story, puts responsibility for giving the orders on Frémont—another reason for Kit to have kept silent about the matter—but does not completely absolve Carson, unless one accepts the notion that following orders relieves one of moral responsibility. Whatever the exact course of events, it seems plain that the act was the kind of battlefield retaliation so often carried out in war, by men enraged at the real or supposed acts of the enemy—retaliation that seems most often to fall on those innocent of the original atrocity.

Frémont rode into Monterey with a combined force including his explorers and some "Bear Flag" settlers, to the great interest of the townspeople and American and British sailors. The commander of the Royal Navy's Pacific squadron had arrived on a battleship shortly after the Americans seized the town, giving color to Frémont's claim to have saved California from the clutches of John Bull. A British naval officer was much impressed with the "true trappers, the class that produced the heroes of Fenimore Cooper's best works," with the Delawares, and with Kit Carson, who, he wrote, was as well known on the prairies "as the Duke [Wellington] is in Europe."[81]

Commodore John Sloat, the U.S. Navy commander who had been shocked to find that Frémont had no written authority for his acts, was shortly after succeeded by Commodore Robert "Fighting Bob" Stockton, an active, aggressive, and rather high-handed commander who found Frémont a man after his own heart and who somewhat irregularly organized the explorer's forces into the "Navy Battalion of Mounted Riflemen," with Frémont as major commanding, Archibald Gillespie and Richard Owens as captains, and Godey and Carson as lieutenants. The battalion, consisting of Frémont's original explorers and "Bear Flaggers"—old mountain men and other adventurous spirits among the American settlers, good men in a fight if not too amenable to discipline—was then transported by sea to San Diego to seize control of Southern California. This was Carson's only sea voyage, during which he was so seasick that he avoided ever making another. San Diego and Los Angeles fell quickly and bloodlessly under American control; the conquest appeared complete.[82]

Officer status, even in a rather ersatz organization, was not something that Carson could normally have expected, but he soon received an even higher compliment, and greater responsibility. Both Stockton, now the self-appointed governor of California, and Frémont decided that Washington must be informed as quickly as possible of events in remote California. They also decided that Carson should be sent overland with dispatches, accompanied by fifteen men, among them Lucien Maxwell and six Delawares. Frémont says that the assignment was both "to insure the safety and speedy delivery of these important papers," and "a reward for brave and valuable service on many occasions." Kit would be able to see his wife in New Mexico on the way. In Washington he would report directly, first to Senator Benton, and then to the president and the secretary of the navy. As Frémont says, "It was a service of high trust and honor, but of great danger also." Kit was expected to cross the entire continent and arrive quicker than a message could be sent by sea around Cape Horn; he believed that he could have done it in sixty days, except for an unexpected meeting.[83]

Carson and his men set out from Los Angeles on September 5, 1846, traveling across the desert to the Colorado River, then up the Gila River. Because their forced pace did not allow much time for hunting, they lived on dried meat and cornmeal; many of their riding mules wore out or were killed for food. Near the Santa Rita del Cobre copper mines in southwest New Mexico, they sighted an Apache village. According to Carson, they were at war. He knew that, if he either attempted to pass or remained where he was, they would spot him. "So I had a consultation with Maxwell and we came to the conclusion to take for the timber and approach them cautiously and, if we were seen, to be as close as possible to them at the time of discovery. We kept on, had arrived about 100 yards of the village when they saw us. They were somewhat frightened to see us. We said we were friends, were enroute to New Mexico, wished to trade animals. They appeared friendly." Carson's party carried out its trade amicably and proceeded on. The habitually wary Apaches might well have been frightened, or at least startled, to see strangers who had managed to approach within a hundred yards of their village. Trappers and traders like Carson and Maxwell did not automatically attack any Indians they saw. The Apaches might be at war with Mexicans, but that did not mean that an old mountain man could not work something out.[84]

Carson proceeded on to a meeting that would be fateful, for others even more than for himself. When war had broken out the previous May between Mexico and the United States, the government in Washington quickly ordered Brigadier General Stephen Watts Kearny, one of the army's most experienced frontier commanders, to take command of the Army of the West, consisting of half of the First Dragoon regiment and a body of Missouri volunteers, and proceed west on the Santa Fe Trail. He was to march to Santa Fe, occupy New Mexico, detach a force to take Chihuahua, and move on to California. While larger forces engaged the main Mexican armies, Kearny was to seize the fruits of Manifest Destiny. The conquest of New Mexico proved easy enough because Governor Armijo's will to resist collapsed and so did that of his forces as a consequence. Leaving his Missourians to deal with hostile Indians and to occupy Chihuahua, Kearny then set out with five companies of dragoons to take possession of California. On October 6, 1846, near Socorro, New Mexico, on the Rio Grande, he met with "Carson, the celebrated mountain man and his party," as one of the command recorded in his diary.[85]

The seizure of California by the U.S. Navy was something that Kearny might have anticipated but could not have counted on until he was informed of the fact by Carson. He now made two significant decisions: one was to send back all his force but two companies of dragoons, who would escort him to California to establish American rule there according to his orders; the other was to take Carson back with him as guide over the desert route Kit had just traversed, giving the dispatches to his own guide, Tom Fitzpatrick, to take to Washington. The first decision proved unfortunate for reasons neither Kearny nor Carson could have known at the time. The second was an obvious and sensible one, given Carson's knowledge of the route, but caused Kit considerable unhappiness. In his autobiography he says only, "He ordered me to join him as his guide. I done so, and Fitzpatrick continued on with the despatches." However, in a statement given to assist Frémont at his court-martial, Carson declared that he was very unwilling to obey Kearny's orders because they would require him to violate his pledge to Stockton and Frémont to deliver the dispatches in person: "I was pledged to them, and could not disappoint them; and, besides that, I was under more obligations to Colonel Frémont than to any other man alive." In fact, Carson considered disobeying Kearny's order, slipping away from the general's camp, and continuing on to Washington. Maxwell talked him out of it, and he returned west with Kearny. Since he was officially an officer, this decision probably saved him some trouble in the end, though it delayed his reunion with Josefa for some months. The authenticity of his statement, at least regarding his difference with Kearny, has been questioned because of the statement's use in Frémont's defense, but it seems consistent with Carson's frequently expressed loyalty to his leader and with his backcountry sense of honor. Carson was certainly useful to Kearny's force beyond his services as a guide. When some Apaches appeared along the Gila, he went to meet them and persuaded one to come into the dragoon camp in spite of the Indians' obvious unease. Peaceful passage was assured and the troops were able to trade for a few badly needed mules. This is yet another episode that Kit does not bother to mention.[86]

When Kearny's command reached California, it found the situation greatly changed from when Carson had left. Many Californios in the south had risen against the American occupation and the area had to be reconquered by the combined efforts of the navy, commanded by Stockton, and Kearny's little force of dragoons. Most of this campaign is not directly relevant to our subject, although Carson was in the thick of it, starting with the Battle of San Pasqual (December 6, 1846) in which the dragoons were very roughly handled by Californio lancers. Some historians have held Carson partially responsible for Kearny's decision to engage in this battle, in spite of the poor condition of his little force after their desert journey, because Kit supposedly told Kearny that the Californios would not put up much of a fight. This may be true but Kearny was, of course, responsible as commander for his own decision. After the battle, when the dragoon force was in desperate condition and surrounded by the enemy, Carson, Navy Midshipman Edward Fitzgerald Beale, and an Indian were sent out to carry an appeal for help to Commodore Stockton in San Diego. They slipped through the Californios, in spite of the reported warning to his men by Andrés Pico, the enemy commander, that Carson was with the Americans and they must watch out or "*Se escapará el lobo* (The wolf will escape)." Beale at one point believed that they were trapped and wanted to fight it out, but Carson declared, "No; I have been in worse places before, and Providence has always saved me." The Indian, whose name (recorded neither by Carson nor Beale, but by a sailor with the fleet) was Che-muc-tah, got through before either of the white men.[87]

Once the forces of Kearny and Stockton were united, they set about reconquering Southern California. In their march on Los Angeles, Carson acted as a scout and participated in the two small battles at San Gabriel and La Mesa. George Downey, one of the sailors fighting on land, saw Carson as "the coolest of all the cool ones that ever was in a fight." According to Downey: "Whenever the Mexicans were nearest there was Kit, with his eternal pipe stuck in his mouth, never removing it, but to fire his rifle, and every time he brought his man. He would then resume his pipe and go on loading as coolly as if he were shooting ducks for amusement." Los Angeles fell on January 10, 1847. Thereafter, the commanders fell to fighting among themselves full time, with unfortunate results for all, particularly Frémont.[88]

In the meantime, Carson was otherwise occupied. In February 1847 he was ordered east with dispatches for the War Department, and set out accompanied by Navy Lieutenant Beale, his companion on the courier mission after San Pasqual. Carson's account of the journey is characteristically brief and factual, Beale's just as characteristically highly colored. Beale was still in bad physical shape from their earlier ordeal, so bad that Carson says, "I did not think that he could live." At first he had to lift the younger man on and off his horse. They followed roughly the same route as Kit's first, abortive trip east, up the Gila through Arizona. Carson says he took care of Beale "and paid to him as much attention as could [be] given to anyone in the same circumstances and, before our arrival [he had] got so far recovered that he could assist himself." As Beale remembered it:

> Oh, Kit, my heart beats quicker, even now old fellow, when I think of the time twenty-five years ago, when I lay on the burning sands of the great desert, under a mesquite bush, where you had tenderly as a woman would have laid her first born, laid me sore from wounds and fever on your only blanket . . . and then under that sun of flame and on those burning sands, without a thought of ever seeing water again, you poured upon my fevered lips, the last drop of water from your canteen.

Possibly Beale exaggerated what to Kit was a fairly routine situation. On the Gila they were attacked by Indians, presumably Apaches, who shot arrows into their camp. Carson ordered his men to take cover behind their packsaddles and keep quiet so as not to draw fire, and not to return fire but to wait until the enemy approached and use their rifles as clubs. The Indians, seeing they were accomplishing nothing, withdrew. Beale is brief about the fight, but this is the occasion of his reference to the time "on the bloody Gila, where we fought all night and travelled all day, with each man his bit of mule meat, and no other food." In the same article, Beale also tells us how Carson "mourned like a woman, and would not be comforted" on the battlefield at San Pasqual, "not for those who had fallen, but for the sad hearts of women at home." Allowing for Beale's flourishes, we still get a picture of a Carson rather different from the callous killer, lacking in "moral delicacy, generosity, and passion," depicted by writers like Martin Green. Beale tells another story of how Carson caught an army sergeant apparently threatening a sick man with a knife and whipped out his pistol, declaring, "Sergeant, drop that knife, or 'by the Splendor of God,' I'll blow your heart out." The oath, the only one Beale ever heard Kit use, was "that of William the Conqueror," which the naval officer had read to him out of *Tristram Shandy*. Carson clearly believed in putting his "generosity and passion" into forceful use, and his words undoubtedly had the desired effect.[89]

Carson also gave the Beale family an account of the fight on the Gila that was preserved, giving a rare sample of his speech:

> Things whirring like birds on the flight wuz flying over us as I wuz trying to sleep by the campfire and Ned [Beale] was sleepin or

leastwise he wuz snorin. Then suddenly he sits up and says, "What's that Don Kit?" and I says, "Them's arrers" and they wuz and could you believe it before I could hold him down Ned was wrapping his buffalo robe around him and standing in the fire kicking out the embers. "Now," sez he, as them arrers came whizzin along like a raft of geese going south before er North wind. "Now," sez he, "Don Kit, they won't be able to get our directions any more and you know they don't dare rush us"; then he tumbled down on the ground and went on with his sleepin.

As many noted, Carson in telling a story was likely to make someone else the hero. This sample suggests that he, the product of an oral culture, had his gifts as a storyteller, and also had an eye for the ludicrous side of things.[90]

When Carson reached Taos in early April 1847, he learned of the revolt that had taken place there in February against American rule, carried out by some local New Mexicans and Indians of Taos Pueblo, in which Charles Bent, appointed governor of New Mexico by Kearny, and several other Americans and New Mexicans friendly to them had perished. Josefa Carson, staying at her brother-in-law's house, had been a witness and testified against the killers at their trial.[91]

During his visit to Washington, Carson stayed at Senator Benton's home, where he became friends with Jessie Benton Frémont. She was already disposed by her husband's stories to view Kit as a hero, and that impression remained. Like so many others, he was exasperated by the delays and evasions of politicians and bureaucrats, and she recorded his opinion of such people: "With their big houses and easy living they think they are princes, but on the plains we are the princes—they could not live there without us." It is not surprising that she found him to appreciate Robert Burns's verses declaring, "A man's a man for a' that." She also says that he enjoyed hearing her read Byron's "Mazeppa." The illustration of Mazeppa tied naked to the back of a horse prompted his exclamation, "It looks like Indian-work—they're devils enough for just such work as that." He understood Mazeppa's desire, as described by the poet, for revenge on the enemies who had treated him so: "That's so, that's so! He knows how a man feels. That's the way I felt. Until I paid them back, after the Blackfeet destroyed my caches and carried off my furs and skins. But I came back. I thanked them for their conduct. I had to wait. I had to wait for the right men to help punish the thieves.

Then my time came, and we left mourning in their tribe." The story accords with the mountain men's doctrine of retaliation, but it should be noted that Carson records no such incident in his autobiography, and that Jessie Frémont commits a number of errors in her reminiscent chapter on Kit.[92]

Kit had two interviews with President Polk, giving him Frémont's side of the dispute with Kearny over who was in fact governor of California, the explorer or the general. The president gave him a lieutenant's commission, dated June 9, 1847, in the Regiment of Mounted Riflemen, a regular army unit formed the previous year for frontier service, in which Frémont had already been commissioned lieutenant colonel; neither would ever actually serve with the regiment. Eventually, after much delay, Carson was ordered to return to California, again carrying dispatches. Edward Beale went with him as far as St. Louis, then had to turn back because of illness. From Fort Leavenworth Carson had an escort of fifty men from a Missouri volunteer regiment. With them he had a short engagement near Pawnee Rock on the Arkansas in Kansas when some Comanches tried to run off the stock of a nearby government wagon train. He managed to recover the stock but lost two of his horses because their riders, fighting dismounted, dropped their reins to fire; his mentioning the matter shows his disgust at their amateurishness.[93]

From Santa Fe he continued west with a group of hired civilians on the Old Spanish Trail. Near the Virgin River he met some three hundred Indians who wanted to enter his camp. He refused permission, telling them that they had recently killed seven Americans, and that he knew their plan was to enter his camp pretending friendship and then kill his whole party: "I told them to retire, if not, I would fire on them. I was compelled to fire. One Indian was killed and the balance went off." Carson once again had no doubt that the Indians—presumably Paiutes—had hostile intentions and had understood him perfectly. Once again, he was in a better position, on the basis of experience, to make that judgment than anyone a century and a half removed from the scene. He arrived in California in October 1847, at which time he met Lieutenant William T. Sherman. The winter he spent in charge of a detachment of dragoons at Tejon Pass, watching for Indian raiders, and in the spring he again started east on another dispatch-bearing mission, this time accompanied by Lieutenant George Brewerton, who left a detailed account of the trip and of Carson.[94]

Like Edward Beale, Brewerton clearly saw Carson as a hero, and their journey together did nothing to alter that notion. Though astonished at first meeting to find the heralded Kit so unprepossessing, he nonetheless found him fully up to expectation in action. They set out along the Old Spanish Trail, accompanied by a mixed party including some of Frémont's men. It was on this trip that Brewerton noted Kit's great caution: his sleeping with his saddle-pillow placed as a barricade, his keeping his guns ready to his hand, his refusing to expose himself in the light of the campfire any longer than it took to light his pipe. He knew they were traveling through the country of the Paiutes, with whom he had experienced so much trouble. Their first meeting with Paiutes, however, passed off peacefully, with pipe-smoking and talk, although Kit charged them to their faces with attacks on travelers. One young Indian, however, tried to steal a cup by flinging it into some bushes across a stream. One of the party, "an old mountaineer," forced him to recover it under threat of death, apparently with no interference from Carson.[95]

Smoke signals informed other Paiutes along the trail of the party's presence. On their next meeting with Paiutes, Carson found their conduct so suspicious that he kept one of them, a young man, as "a sort of hostage for their good behavior during the night." The Indian himself maintained his calm, although he had to reassure his people once that he was still alive. The next morning he was allowed to go, with an old pair of trousers as a gift. On the Virgin River, where Baptiste Tabeau had been killed in 1844, they found that their camp was being watched by a lone Indian, "who had reconnoitred our position with the view of stealing the animals." Carson, Brewerton, Auguste Archambeau, and a man named Lewis followed his tracks and when they saw him, "evidently badly frightened, and running for his life," they opened fire. Lewis shot him in the shoulder, but he nonetheless made his escape. There is nothing very attractive in the picture of four men with rifles, all presumably good shots, firing on one fleeing man armed only with a bow and arrows. It is entirely possible that they were right, and that he was a horse thief, or a scout for others with hostile intent. The fact that he had evidently spied on their camp without showing himself made them suspicious, especially after previous incidents in this vicinity. Possibly, he was simply a hunter anxious to find out who these strangers in his country were and unwilling to show himself until he could be sure of their intentions. Tabeau's death in the same area four years earlier was important to their reaction, for several of the party had been with Frémont and had known Tabeau. They were disposed to believe, because of the location, that this man was one of the band that had killed their friend. There is no way of knowing. Under the circumstances, they had no inclination to give him the benefit of a doubt.[96]

They pushed on, had a friendly meeting with Wakara's Utes, and from other Utes in the Wasatch Mountains were able to obtain meat and fish when in need. Crossing the Grand River on rafts, they lost one with rifles and saddles, and Brewerton nearly lost his life; another party of Utes rendered assistance. In the San Luis Valley in southern Colorado they found Indian sign. "Look here," said Kit, "the Indians have passed across our road since sun-up, and they are a war-party, too; no sign of lodge poles, and no colt tracks; they are no friends, neither: here's a feather that some of them has dropped. We'll have trouble yet, if we don't keep a bright look-out." A party of New Mexican traders warned them that trappers had been attacked in the vicinity recently. When about fifty miles from Taos, they encountered a body of Indians; Carson says there were "several hundred, Utes and Apaches" (the latter presumably Jicarillas). Carson talked to the chief in the Ute tongue, and on finding the man did not understand (meaning that he was an Apache), said, "We are in for it at last." Carson describes his course of action: "We retired into the bush, would only allow a few of them to approach us, informed them that if they were friends they would leave, that we were naked and in a destitute condition, and could give them nothing. They evidently left us, when they saw we had nothing." Shortly after, they met a party of volunteer soldiers in pursuit of the Apaches, an indication that Carson's apprehensions were well-founded.[97]

Brewerton's version of the encounter is considerably more dramatic. He describes the Indians surrounding the party's position, yelling and brandishing their weapons, while Carson stood facing them:

> His whole demeanor was now so entirely changed that he looked like a different man; his eye fairly flashed, and his rifle was grasped with all the energy of an iron will. "There," cried he, addressing the savages, "is our line, cross it if you dare, and we begin to shoot. You ask us to let you in, but you won't come in unless you ride over us. You say you are friends, but you don't act like it. No, you don't deceive us so, we know you too well; so stand back, for your lives are in danger."

Brewerton says their ammunition was limited to three rounds apiece, but that would have cost the Indians more than they were willing to pay. As Carson said, the Indians could see they had nothing. He had made the best of an uncomfortable situation by good tactics and a bold front.[98]

When they arrived in Taos, Brewerton noted that "Kit was disposed to linger by his own fireside to the last moment which duty would permit," which was hardly remarkable considering that he and Josefa had been married five years and that he had been gone most of that time. After visiting Santa Fe, Carson pushed on, without Brewerton. The military commander at Santa Fe told him that his regular army commission had not been confirmed by the Senate, apparently part of the political fallout attending Frémont's court-martial. Friends advised Kit to give the dispatches to someone else to carry, under the circumstances. He says proudly that he decided to carry out his mission anyway.

> As I had been entrusted with the despatches, chosen as the most competent person to carry them through safely, I determined to fulfill the duty. . . . Having gained much honor and credit in the performance of all duties entrusted to my charge, I would on no account wish to forfeit the good opinion of the majority of my countrymen because the Senate of the United States did not deem it proper to confirm on me the appointment of an office that I never sought, and one which, if confirmed, I would have resigned at the termination of the war.

Carson was aware of the "honor and credit" he had gained through his service with Frémont. He took pride in carrying out his duty in spite of senatorial pettiness, in living up to the good opinion others had formed of him. It was a pride that led him to leave his young wife one more time, in spite of the reluctance that Brewerton noted. As for his commission, his experience in military service, especially his encounter with Kearny and the downfall of Frémont, not to mention the problems associated with his illiteracy, had probably convinced him that he was not cut out for a regular army career. Although Frémont later wrote that Carson, like Owens and Godey, could have earned a marshal's baton in the army of Napoleon, probably neither of them could have imagined at the time that Kit would one day be able to wear a brigadier general's stars on his shoulders.[99]

Having learned that there was trouble with the Comanches on the Santa Fe Trail, he avoided their country by going north along the South

Platte, the Platte, and the Republican Rivers through Nebraska and Kansas to Fort Leavenworth, then on to Washington. One item of news he carried was of the discovery of gold in California, though it is not clear that he was the first to bear that information to the East. He probably saw his daughter Adaline in Missouri going or coming back, but he makes no mention of her in his autobiography. In Washington he was reunited with John and Jessie Frémont, under unhappy circumstances. A court-martial had convicted the explorer of disobedience and, rather than accept the official reprimand, he had resigned from the army. The couple asked Kit to be godfather to their firstborn son, who would die in infancy.[100]

Ending his account of this last courier mission, Carson summed up his first period of government service: "I was with Frémont from 1842 to 1847. The hardships through which we passed I find it impossible to describe, and the credit which he deserves I am incapable to do him justice in writing. But his services to his country have been left to the judgement of impartial freemen, and all agree in saying that his services were great and have redounded to his honor and that of his country."

During that period much had changed, both for Carson and for the United States. A country that had been bounded by Texas and the Continental Divide now reached to the Pacific. Vast areas and great numbers of people—Indian, Hispanic, and mixed—had been brought under at least nominal U.S. sovereignty. The Great Plains, once officially regarded as a gigantic Indian reserve, would become a bridge to the West for Anglo-American settlers. The question of slavery or freedom in those territories would lead to civil war. Carson had willingly played his part in the process of Manifest Destiny. For the rest of his life he, like the rest of the country, would live with the consequences. On a personal level, Kit had gone from an obscure mountain man not much different, with his New Mexican wife and his part-Indian daughter, from many others, to a national figure, known to army officers, sailors, and the general public as "the celebrated mountain man." When he said that he was "under more obligations to Colonel Frémont than to any other man alive" he was probably thinking of how the Pathfinder saved his life, contributed to his financial security, made him an officer, as well as bestowing "much honor and credit." It was this fame that would transform his life, making him the representative frontiersman of the trans-Mississippi West and the living avatar of Fenimore Cooper's fictional hero.[101]

From now on, people in authority would repeatedly offer employment, ask advice, or assign missions to Kit Carson the Great Scout, missions usually involving Indians in one way or another. Carson's reaction to his fame, and the consequent demands and opportunities, would be a complex mixture. He would show an apparently consistent courtesy and friendliness toward his admirers coupled with a refusal to play the hero for them, a sometimes embarrassed and sometimes wryly humorous tendency to downplay his fame, and a conscientious desire to perform the duties people placed upon him.

Carson was very much what we have come to call "country," in an age when the attitudes and behavior that designated it were far more common. More than one witness described him as looking, in his later years, like an old farmer. The backcountry traits—the insistence on honor and manliness, the readiness to use violence in both self-defense and retaliation, and the modesty and self-deprecating humor—were all learned at an early age and integrated into his personality. The quiet, courteous Carson was the same man as the one who, backed only by a few half-armed men with three rounds apiece, could warn off 150 unfriendly warriors, or who could take satisfaction in wreaking retribution on Indians he believed had attacked his party and killed his friends without provocation.

RAYADO: THE OLD SCOUT SETTLES DOWN

The effects of Carson's new fame and status became apparent very shortly, as he sought to settle down. A story not confirmed by Kit has it that during the fall of 1848 he and some others, including Lucien Maxwell, were employed by William Bent to reopen a trading post that Bent, St. Vrain and Company had previously established and then abandoned in the Texas Panhandle on the Canadian River. After their arrival at the site, goes the tale, Jicarilla Apaches ran off all their animals except for two mules, forcing them to make a long hike back to Bent's Fort. On the way back they had to beat off an attack by Kiowas, killing three. The same post, Fort Adobe or Adobe Walls, would be very important to Kit on a later occasion, and then he would apparently have some knowledge of the area.[102]

During the winter of 1848–49, Carson notes, "I made two trips with Colonel Beall, 1st Drag[oon]s in command of troops in pursuit of Indians." Major Benjamin Beall commanded the detachment of dragoons then stationed at Taos. The Indians were apparently Jicarilla Apaches and perhaps Muache Utes, who had engaged in hostile acts against New Mexicans. Carson was employed as guide. Of the first expedition he says only, "After surmounting many difficulties and passing through severe hardships, we finally accomplished the object of the expedition and returned to Taos." On their return they came across a Jicarilla camp and captured two men, allegedly chiefs. Beall talked with them; they promised better behavior and were released. Some sources say this action was on Carson's advice; his apparent satisfaction with the results of the expedition would suggest that he at least approved of the release.[103]

In February 1849, Carson was again Beall's guide when the officer took two companies of dragoons to the Arkansas to require the tribes on the river to give up Mexican captives. They found there, Carson says, "four nations of Indians, some two thousand souls," presumably Cheyennes, Arapahos, Kiowas, and Comanches. Tom Fitzpatrick, now Indian agent in this area, strongly opposed any attempt by Beall to carry out his mission, for the Indians would not comply and the military force was not strong enough to fight them. Kit says that "the Agent, traders, and officers of his command" were all opposed to the attempt, but he does not say whether he agreed with them. Fitzpatrick and the traders were men of his own sort, and he generally indicated in his memoirs when he strongly disagreed with the action of an officer concerning Indians. In any case, Beall took their advice.[104]

The U.S. Army, having assumed responsibility for the security of the New Mexico frontier, would more and more be drawn into hostilities with Indians as the interests of Hispanic and Anglo settlers and those of the native tribes increasingly clashed, and Carson also would be drawn into these conflicts. He does not indicate whether Beall asked him to take service as a guide and scout (presumably with pay) or whether he offered his services. In the next few years, however, he would frequently be called on because of his reputation and proven performance.

In 1845 Carson had made a start at settling down, then had abandoned it to join Frémont's third expedition. Now, in the spring of 1849, he and Lucien Maxwell set out again to establish themselves permanently. As Kit explains, "We had been leading a roving life long enough and now was the time, if ever, to make a home for ourselves and children. We were getting old and could not expect to remain any length of time able to gain a livelihood as we had been [for] such a number of years." Maxwell's father-in-law, Charles Beaubien, had gained a large land grant in northeastern New Mexico from the Mexican governor, Manuel Armijo. A son having been killed in the 1847 Taos revolt, Beaubien now turned to his son-in-law to develop the land and earn a profit. Carson loaned some of the money he had earned with Frémont to Maxwell and moved across the mountains to join him.[105]

To do so, he had to turn down a request from his old friend and commander, John Frémont. In January 1849 the Pathfinder had stumbled into Taos in the wake of his disastrous Fourth Expedition, having failed in an attempt to cross the Rockies in southern Colorado in winter, losing many men to hunger and cold. Now he wanted Carson to accompany him and help complete the task, then move with his family to California. This time, however, Kit declined. He and Josefa cared for the haggard explorer at their house in Taos, but he was unable to "decide to break off from Maxwell and family connections," in Frémont's words. One wonders if Josefa, pregnant with their first child after nearly six years of marriage, put her foot down this time.[106]

Carson moved across the Sangre de Cristo range to the eastern foothills, where the mountains meet the plains, and settled with Maxwell on Rayado Creek, not far from the Santa Fe Trail. The location, amid mesas and grasslands, with the mountains to the west and a view of the Great Plains to the east, is as attractive as any to be found, even in New Mexico. Carson says only: "Arrived at Rayado, commenced building and making improvements, and were in a way of becoming prosperous." Once again he was following his father and making a home in a new land.[107]

But as at Boonslick forty years earlier, or as in Kentucky or Carolina or Pennsylvania before that, it was not a new land for a number of people already living there. For generations it had been the homeland of the Jicarilla Apaches. These people, speaking an Athapaskan language and thereby related to other groups called "Apaches" and to the Navajos, lived and hunted over a substantial part of northern New Mexico and southern Colorado. The center of the world, as they saw it, was near Taos. The band called the Llaneros, as their Spanish name suggested, hunted east of the mountains on to the Great Plains as far as the Texas and Oklahoma panhandles. Their villages lay along many of the streams flowing out of the mountains into the prairies. In the first years of American control of New Mexico, their way of life was still that of part-time farmers and hunters, but that way of life was under increasing threat from other peoples. Their only real allies were the Muache Utes, with whom they intermarried. The hostility of the Great Plains peoples—Comanches, Kiowas, Cheyennes, and Arapahos—made buffalo hunting a perilous enterprise. Raids by these tribes in the Jicarilla homeland made their traditional farming along the streams an increasingly insecure and uncertain source of food. Thus they were thrown back on the relatively scarce supply of game in the mountains, at a time when expanding Hispanic and Anglo-American activity in the region put pressure on that resource. It is not surprising that they came into conflict with newcomers who, after the American occupation of New Mexico, began settling in their territory, disrupting the supply of game and bringing herds of livestock (a tempting alternative food source) with them. Of course, any threat to livestock touches a raw nerve with herdsmen. The stage was set for another replay of the traditional frontier conflict, as hungry Indians—increasingly desperate as their options dwindled and the search for food became a constant struggle—confronted settlers both Anglo and Hispanic with their own frontier traditions of fighting back against attackers, and also faced the military defenders of those settlers.[108]

During his brief tenure as governor of New Mexico in 1846–47, Charles Bent described the Jicarillas as "an indolent and cowardly people, living principally by thefts committed on the Mexicans, there being but little game in the country through which they range, and their fear of other Indians not permitting them to venture on the plains for buffalo. . . . The predatory habits of these Indians render them a great annoyance to the New Mexicans." Bent recognized some of the sources of the problem, while he had also obviously adopted the prejudices of his Taos neighbors. Colonel George McCall, who inspected military posts in New Mexico in 1850, was even harsher in his view of the Jicarillas, "one of the most troublesome" divisions of the Apaches. They were "considered as incorrigible," and would "continue to rob and murder our citizens until they are exterminated." He could think of no means to save them. Kit Carson would become much more intimately involved with the Jicarillas than either Bent or McCall, and he would be nearly as critical of them, though he never favored their extermination.[109]

An early visitor to Rayado was the California-bound Charles Pancoast, whose party passed through in July 1849; he described the ranch and, impressed with "the famous Mountaineer," recorded Carson's view of the local Indian situation. The ranch house at the time was a two-story log cabin, surrounded by an adobe wall for protection, with several other adobe buildings about, plus corrals, stables, and a slaughterhouse—a blend of frontier Missouri and New Mexico. Carson, observed Pancoast, "had about him a dozen or more Americans and Mexicans and about twenty Indians, besides a number of Squaws, all to be fed at his table." Kit himself was "a superior representative of the genuine Rocky Mountain Hunter," clad in a buckskin coat and pants, with moccasins on his feet and a Mexican sombrero on his head, his hair down over his shoulders. At first, though he was hospitable and provided beef for his guests, he had little to say, but, sitting around the travelers' campfire, he opened up.

He spoke of the difficulties he had experienced in maintaining the lonely position he occupied and in protecting his Stock from the Raids of the Utes and other Indians. He had called in the aid of the U. S. Soldiers, and being thoroughly acquainted with the haunts of the Indians, he had punished them so severely that they had found it their best policy to make their peace with him. He now enjoyed their Friendship, and often gave them meat; and they no longer molested his stock, although they continued to steal that of others. However, he still kept a Guard on his Cattle by day and a Sentinel at night.

This sounds as much like a forecast of the next few years at Rayado as a description of the state of affairs in the summer of 1849; it would seem that the essential pattern was established early. Carson may have been speaking as much of his intentions and hopes as of what he had already accomplished.[110]

Biographer Lawrence Murphy notes that Maxwell's approach to Indian relations was essentially pragmatic. Indians would often drop by Rayado and would expect to be fed and provided with clothing and other goods, as they would have offered hospitality to visitors to their own camps. If refused, they might satisfy their needs by theft. At the same time, if stock was stolen or even given voluntarily, Maxwell could claim compensation from the government and demand that the military chastise any offenders. Many Plains Indians enjoyed Maxwell's hospitality at Rayado and at nearby Cimarron when he moved there. Some officials found his attitude contradictory, but an old mountain man would have seen it as good sense. How much this policy was determined by Maxwell, the major partner in the enterprise, and how much by Carson, is not evident, but there is no reason to suppose that the two friends differed on the essentials. Maxwell is characterized by his biographer as a strong-willed, even bullheaded man, sometimes violent and not easily swayed by the advice of others. But Carson was one man whom he respected and to whom he would listen. Kit's experience, writes Murphy, "proved valuable in warding off Indian attack and negotiating with the tribes that frequented the front range of the Rockies."[111]

The first serious interruption to the task of developing Rayado, as recorded by Carson, came in October 1849. The Santa Fe trader James White and his wife, Ann, their daughter, and a black woman servant, had traveled west with a caravan on the southern branch of the trail, then left the slow train and pushed ahead. Near Point of Rocks in northeast New Mexico, a band of Jicarillas attacked and killed White and the other men in the group, carrying off the women. The nearest troops were at Taos, and from there Captain William Grier led his company of the First Dragoons, with Antoine Leroux and Robert Fisher as guides, across the mountains to pursue the raiders and rescue the captives. When they passed through Rayado, Carson joined them. Kit found the camp where, in his words, "the murder had been committed." From there the column followed the trail for ten or twelve days. "It was the most difficult trail that I ever followed. As they would leave the camps, they, in numbers from one to two, went in different directions, to meet at some appointed place. In nearly every camp we would find some of Mrs. White's clothing, which was the cause of renewed energy on our part to continue the chase." Whether or not Kit remembered the kidnapping of Patsy Gregg from Cooper's Fort in December 1814, when he turned five, and the pursuit and rescue by Boonslick men, the situation was a classic frontier scenario. The abduction of white women and children by Indians stirred some of the deepest emotions of white men, and spurred them, as Carson notes, to supreme efforts.[112]

They came in sight of the Indian camp on the Canadian River near Tucumcari Butte, apparently achieving surprise. Kit says, "I was in advance, started for their camp, calling for the men to follow. The comdg. officer called a halt, none of them would follow me. I was informed that Leroux, the principal guide, told the officer in command to halt, that the Indians wished to have a parley."

The Jicarillas started packing their goods for flight, and a shot was fired that struck Captain Grier, causing no serious injury. The captain ordered a charge, but the delay allowed all but one of the Indians to escape. Kit continues: "In about 200 yards, pursuing the Indians, the body of Mrs. White was found, perfectly warm, had not been killed more than five minutes—shot through the heart with an arrow. . . . I am certain that if the Indians had been charged immediately on our arrival she would have been saved." Carson says he was sure that Grier and Leroux acted as they thought best, but he remained convinced that he had been right in his wish to attack immediately, and certainly the result could have been no worse than what actually happened—except, of course, from the viewpoint of the Jicarillas. The young girl and the servant were never found.[113]

Afterward, Carson chose to believe that Ann White was better off; she could not have lived long, he declared, because she had been treated so badly. "Her life, I think, should never be regretted by her friends. She is surely far more happy in heaven, with her God, than among friends of this earth." This is the only such religious sentiment in Carson's autobiography, although others would quote him as expressing religious ideas. A decade later he discussed the matter with James Meline, who stated, as on Carson's authority, "The poor lady was wasted, emaciated, the victim of a foul disease, and bore the sorrows of a life-long agony on her face, for when a woman captive has not the signal good fortune to be made the mistress of one savage, she becomes the prostitute of the tribe." Meline was stating bluntly what Carson avoided. It was the conventional wisdom that white women captives of Indians suffered "a fate worse than death," which was one reason why such strenuous efforts were made immediately to rescue them. Conceivably, Meline read more into Carson's resigned words than he explicitly said. Kit was trying to console himself, after all, for a failure, even though he held others responsible.[114]

There was a particular reason for Carson to seek consolation in this instance:

In camp was found a book, the first of its kind I had ever seen, in which I was made a great hero, slaying Indians by the hundred, and I have often thought that as Mrs. White would read the same, and knowing that I lived near, she would pray for my appearance and that she would be saved. I did come, but had not the power to convince those that were in command over me to pursue my plan for her rescue. . . . I presume the consciences of those that were the cause of the failure have severely punished them ere this.

The book was very likely Charles Averill's paperback *Kit Carson, Prince of the Gold Hunters*, published that year, one of the first works of fiction to exploit Carson's name.

In the early years of his fame Kit was confronted with one of its great drawbacks: the unrealistic expectations of people who knew him only through his legend. If Kit was ever tempted to believe the hype about himself, here was a sharp reminder of his human limitations. There was no proof that Ann White had read the book, but it obviously troubled him to think that he could have been the object of a desperate woman's hopes that he could not fulfill. He later declared that everything Averill wrote about him was false, and after being handed a copy, he reportedly threatened to "burn the damn thing." The rescue of white women taken by Indians was a major feature of the careers of the real-life Daniel Boone and the fictional Natty Bumppo, but Carson, putting forth his best effort, had not been able to emulate them.[115]

The Jicarillas related a different version of the affair a few years afterward. They claimed they had approached the White party peacefully and had been driven off, which provoked a fight in which the white men were killed. The Jicarillas had cared for Mrs. White and, said Chief Chacon, would have turned her over to the soldiers gladly if they had not been attacked. This was not what Carson, who had seen her dead body, believed. In later years, as we will see, he might have found the Jicarilla explanation of the original attack credible. Whether Leroux's desire for negotiations or Carson's more aggressive approach would have been better is hard to resolve. The shot that struck Captain Grier could have been fired by one excited warrior with an itchy trigger finger, but it was inevitably taken by the soldiers as a sign of hostile intent. In later years Carson would often manifest a less indulgent attitude toward the Jicarillas than toward the Utes; the fate of Ann White may have had something to do with this.[116]

If the dragoons had been stationed nearer than Taos, they could have responded more quickly to the White attack. The military authorities soon stationed troops at Rayado, perhaps at the urging of Carson, Maxwell, and Charles Beaubien. During the winter of 1849–50 a detachment of ten dragoons under Sergeant William Holbrook was present at Rayado. In the spring when some Jicarillas attacked, wounding two New Mexican herders and running off most of the ranch's stock, Carson and an old trapper named Bill New joined Holbrook's troopers in pursuit, overtaking the raiders after some twenty-five miles. Carson relates, "We approached the Indians cautiously and, when close, charged them; killed five, the other four made their escape." They returned with all but four of the horses, and also with the scalps of the five dead Indians. Sergeant Holbrook reported cheerfully that the scalps were taken as "a voucher"—proof of the kill—but Captain Grier, forwarding the sergeant's report, was careful to state that the trophies were taken by Mexican herders who came up after the fight ended. Since colonial times, whites on the frontier had considered scalping dead Indians as appropriate treatment for an enemy who also mutilated the dead (both sides thus perpetuating and exacerbating such practices), but a regular army officer knew his superiors might consider it unsuitable. There is no indication that Carson had anything to do with the scalping (he simply does not mention it), nor that he was particularly shocked by it, though he could have found such activity on the part of regular soldiers, mostly immigrants and eastern city boys—greenhorns to him—grimly amusing if not pretentious.[117]

In the summer of 1850, Kit and Tim Goodale took a herd of mules north to Fort Laramie to sell; this was the occasion on which he met the hero-worshiper from Arkansas who was unwilling to believe that the unimposing person before him was the great Kit Carson (see chapter 1). During the return trip he had to evade a group of hostile Indians, which necessitated spending an entire day up a cottonwood tree, keeping watch. "Sometimes I would fall asleep, and nearly fall," says Kit, "but would recover in time and continue my watch." During that same summer the army decided to station Captain Grier and two companies of the First Dragoons, with artillery, at Rayado. The move provided some protection for settlers in the area and for travelers on the Santa Fe Trail. The price of their supplies and housing was a source of income for Carson and Maxwell. Western settlers often tried to have soldiers stationed near them for just such pecuniary reasons, but there was soon proof that their presence was needed at Rayado. A raid by Jicarillas or Utes, perhaps both, carried off many of Maxwell's animals and killed Bill New, "a brave and experienced trapper" in Carson's words, and an army bugler. Carson, Maxwell, Beaubien, and other citizens petitioned the governor of the territory for help.[118]

The petition asked the governor to authorize a campaign by civilian volunteers. Frontier citizens often believed that they could do a better job of Indian fighting than regular troops, if the government would just turn them loose and give them rations, pay, and compensation for loss of horses or equipment. Calls for the raising of volunteer groups would recur during Indian-white conflicts, especially if the regulars did not immediately end the trouble. Such calls rose because of frustration, and the hope of making a few dollars, but also because citizens often believed the army was incompetent and too restrained in Indian-fighting. Volunteers would not be ready to make peace as soon as the Indians offered but would thoroughly chastise them. Carson, from his recorded words, seems to have had more confidence in and respect for regular officers than many frontier civilians did, although there were some he criticized scathingly, but he would in his autobiography express his belief in the efficacy of civilian volunteers like the Missouri frontier militia and rangers of forty years before, and in the need to chastise Indians thoroughly before accepting any peace overtures. Later on, he would modify these views in the light of experience. Citizen volunteers would be an important feature of campaigns in New Mexico into the next decade, campaigns in which Carson would play a prominent part.[119]

In the spring of 1851, Carson set off for Missouri to purchase supplies for Maxwell. He had finally decided to bring his daughter Adaline to New Mexico to live with him. As usual, in his autobiography he says nothing about the girl, who was probably about twelve at the time. His family, both in New Mexico and in Missouri, obviously knew about his Indian marriage and his part-Arapaho daughter, but it was a private matter. In fact, he mentions Josefa Jaramillo only once, and his other children not at all, in his autobiography. Also with the party returning to New Mexico was Kit's niece, Susan Carson, who had just met and married Jesse Nelson, a young friend of Carson's who had accompanied him on the trip. Susan also goes unmentioned in Kit's account of the journey, which leads one to wonder if he had somehow picked up the genteel convention of the time that a lady's name did not appear in print except when she married or died.[120]

The return trip was an eventful one. Carson decided to return by the Bent's Fort, or Mountain, Branch of the Santa Fe Trail, up the Arkansas into Colorado, then south through Raton Pass into New Mexico. In western Kansas his party met a village of Cheyennes. Carson had been acquainted with the tribe for twenty years, and his relations with them had always been friendly; two Cheyennes had fought beside him and other trappers against Crow horse thieves. What he did not know was that a military column, also headed for New Mexico under command of Lieutenant Colonel Edwin "Bull" Sumner, had antagonized these

Indians. One of the officers with the column, while intoxicated, had flogged a Cheyenne. This was a deadly insult; one Cheyenne did not strike another except under very special circumstances. As the first American to happen along, Kit was the scapegoat. This was the same law of retribution under which the mountain men, Kit included, had operated for years. As Marc Simmons observes, now that Kit was to be the object he found the situation not to his liking.[121]

Thinking the Cheyennes friendly, he asked some twenty who had followed him some distance from their village to come into camp and smoke. They began to talk among themselves in their own tongue, not realizing he understood Cheyenne.

> I understood them to say that while I would be smoking and not on my guard they could easily kill me with a knife, and as for the Mexicans with me, they could kill them as easily as buffalo. . . . I informed the Indians that [I knew not] the cause of their wishing my scalp, that I had done them no injury and wanted to treat them kindly, that they had come to me as friends and I now discovered that they wished to do me injury, and that they must leave. Any refusing would be shot, and, if they attempted to return, that I would fire on them.

Jesse Nelson gives a much more exciting account, with one Cheyenne brandishing a tomahawk around Carson's head and guns and arrows pointed. Ah-mah-nah-ko, one of the Cheyennes, now recognized Kit and calmed the situation for the moment, but he warned that the Indians would probably try an ambush later.[122]

Carson started on his way, and after dark he sent a rider to hurry to Rayado for assistance. The next morning he told some Cheyennes that his messenger had gone to Rayado for the troops, "and that among them I had many friends, that they would surely come to my relief, and if I were killed they would know by whom, and that my death would be avenged." The Cheyennes realized that it was too late to overtake the messenger, so they departed. Carson was quite certain that he and his party would have been killed but for the Indians' fear of the promised retaliation.[123]

Carson's rider caught up with Sumner's column on the third day, but the colonel would not send help, so the man rode on to Rayado, where Captain Grier sent a detachment of dragoons to Kit's assistance. When this force met with Sumner, the colonel decided to send a party from his own force along with them. Carson was sarcastic about this change of mind, saying, "The conscience of the gallant old Colonel then, I presume, troubled him." He concluded that Sumner thought that the officer in command of the detachment would receive credit for any fight with the Indians that occurred, and the colonel wanted to share that credit. "But to the Colonel I do not consider myself under any obligations; for by his conduct two days previously he showed plainly that by rendering aid to a few American citizens in the power of Indians, [who were] enraged by the conduct of some of his command, was not his wish."

Martin Green sees Carson's expression of anger here as a sign of "something boiling beneath," presumably some sort of suppressed, generalized hostility or rage. Considering the circumstances, especially since Carson's daughter and niece, in addition to himself, a friend, and some fifteen other people, were all endangered, Kit's anger seems entirely understandable. About the officer who flogged the Cheyenne in the first place he was even more scathing: "The cause to me [was] unknown, but I presume courage was oozing from the finger ends of the officer and, as the Indians were in his power, he wished to be relieved of such [a] commodity." Fighting Indians who were clearly threatening was one thing, but the officer's conduct was both bullying and cowardly, and therefore contemptible. It was an attitude that he would express even more memorably, regarding the conduct of Colonel John Chivington, some years later.[124]

One result of the Cheyenne incident was Carson's first encounter with the officer commanding the detachment that Sumner belatedly sent to his assistance, Captain and Brevet Major James Henry Carleton. He expressed warm gratitude toward Carleton and Lieutenant Robert Johnson, commanding the detachment from Rayado, and especially toward Captain Grier, who "showed his noble heart and that reliance can be placed on him in the hour of danger." Carson clearly approved highly of some army officers but was prepared to criticize others whose conduct he did not approve, even when they were in positions of authority.[125]

The next couple of years were active but devoid of Indian conflict. Kit and Maxwell organized one last trapping expedition into the Colorado mountains; he calls it a good hunt, but perhaps it was also a sentimental journey, the last visit to the days of youth. In 1853 he and Maxwell again pointed to the future by driving a herd of sheep to California by the standard route through South Pass and across the Sierra Nevada; a stronger sense of history and legend would have led him to drive cattle, of course. He found California changed beyond recognition by the gold rush: "When I first went over into California in 1829 the valleys were full of Indian tribes. Indians were thick everywhere, and I saw a great deal of some large and flourishing tribes. When I went there again in 1853, they had all disappeared, and when I inquired about certain tribes I had seen on the very spot where I then stood, was told by the people living there that they had never heard of them."

Of course, Carson had been in California much more recently than his 1829 trip with Ewing Young, and his sojourn with Frémont would have given him a hint as to what had happened to the Indians; even in five years the change had been drastic. The gold rush brought in huge numbers of Anglo-Americans, primarily young males without frontier experience, and the kind of conflict he had seen and participated in near Lassen's ranch had been repeated many times over. Combined with the effects of imported diseases, which caused the greater proportion of the casualties, the result was a disaster for California Indians. The miners generally saw the Indians as a dangerous nuisance (though some settlers viewed them as a labor force), to be eradicated if they objected in any way to their presence or conduct. What happened cannot be called true genocide, since it was not officially sponsored, but it was devastating all the same. Not all of the vanished Indians were necessarily dead; many had probably moved off into the mountains.[126]

A meeting he may have had in California could also have given him food for thought. His old comrade Edward Beale had been appointed federal superintendent of Indian Affairs for California and had arrived back in the state about the same time as Kit and his herd of sheep. Beale immediately set to work on a new government policy designed to prevent the complete destruction of California's Indians. In early September 1853 he began setting up, near Tejon Pass north of Los Angeles, an Indian reservation set aside for the Indians to settle and farm, in order to prevent the destructive conflicts between whites and Indians and protect the Indians from the devastating effects of contact with whites, such as alcoholism. Beale believed that the history of the California missions showed that these Indians could be induced to work hard and support themselves in a "civilized" fashion. The idea of "civilizing" the Indians had long been a major part of federal Indian policy, but the specific concept of the reservation was more recent, and Beale's Tejon project was one of the first attempts to put it into practice. Beale's reservation ran into many of the problems that dogged the system throughout its history: corruption and inefficiency on the part of many federal employees and hostility and land hunger on the part of many other whites.[127]

Kit Carson does not mention Beale on this trip, but he also fails to mention meetings that apparently took place with old friends and relatives settled in California (including his daughter Adaline). Beale was in San Francisco at about the time Kit visited the city, and they surely would have met if possible. Beale's experiment would inevitably have been a major topic of conversation, and Ned surely would have asked for his old friend's advice on any matter involving Indians. Tejon Pass would have been on Carson's likely route south to Los Angeles after he had visited his relatives, and he could have seen the reservation in its early stages. Here, Beale and others hoped, was the alternative to the fate that seemed to be overtaking the California Indians. Perhaps it also seemed to Carson to offer an alternative to the destructive conflicts and insecurity in New Mexico. At any rate, he would soon become a steadfast and persistent advocate of the reservation system.[128]

For the moment, he simply wanted to get back home. Maxwell took a ship from San Francisco to Southern California, but Kit made the trip on a mule, remembering the discomfort of his sea voyage in 1846, when "I swore it would be the last time I would leave sight of land." Then the two returned to New Mexico by way of the Gila River route through Arizona. In Santa Fe, Carson learned he had received an appointment as a federal Indian agent for the Muache Utes.[129]

Such appointments were a significant form of patronage for politicians, and it is a little hard to imagine that even someone with Kit Carson's credentials received one entirely unsolicited, though he gives no indication that he had sought the appointment. Assuming that he did, it suggests that he felt the need of a more secure source of income than offered by his investment in the Rayado operation. He had two children living at this time: Adaline, who was already married and living in California, and William, born in 1852. (Waanibe's second child died in Taos in 1843; Josefa's first child, named Charles after Charles Bent, had died before he was two.) The post offered a regular salary and work where his accumulated experience and expertise would be of first importance. The exact source of his appointment may be obscure. Thomas Hart Benton had lost his Senate seat and most of his political influence by opposing the expansion of slavery; John Frémont had served briefly as senator from California but had failed at reelection in

1852. Perhaps Edward Beale brought up Kit's name in the right places. Carson moved back to Taos from Rayado, putting him nearer the homes of most of his charges; whether or not he found this return attractive, it meant that Josefa would be closer to her family. He continued to be concerned with Maxwell's operations, and would assist his friend when he could, sometimes through the use of his office. Taos, however, would be his home base for much of the rest of his life. His wandering days were largely over.[130]

The appointment marked a departure in Carson's life in another sense. Since 1842 he had been periodically in the service of the federal government, with Frémont's expeditions and as a soldier in the Mexican War, then during the years at Taos and Rayado when on occasion his services were sought out by military commanders. Kit had so far followed a pattern of government employment when needed, like many old mountain men. An Indian agent, however, served for an extended period at a yearly salary, not as an intermittently hired expert. In fact, he would spend most of the rest of his life serving the United States government in some capacity, civil or military, and would die holding a government office. Howard Lamar describes him as "the perennial public servant."[131]

As a public servant, Carson would be concerned primarily with Indians and their relations with the government and the growing non-Indian population of the West. In the previous course of his life he had, so to speak, handled his relations with Indians on a case-by-case basis. If Indians were friendly, he responded in a friendly manner. If they were hostile, or he had reason to believe they intended to be, he would respond with the amount of threat or violence he and his associates considered necessary.

As an Indian agent, however, Kit would not only have to deal with particular cases but to consider long-range policy, not only responding to particular problems as they arose, but also considering how to solve or prevent those problems, and therefore what caused them in the first place. If he had not thought deeply or systematically about the larger implications of frontier expansion and Indian-white conflict before, now he would be driven to think about these matters. He would no longer be dealing simply with Indians, but with what would come to be known as "the Indian Problem."

5. Indian Agent

I do not know whether I done rite or wrong,
but I done what I thought was best.
Carson to James L. Collins, September 20, 1859

To establish order in this territory, you must either submit to these
heavy expenditures, or exterminate the mass of these Indians.
James S. Calhoun to Commissioner of Indian Affairs, March 30,
1850, Annie H. Abel, ed., *Official Correspondence of James S. Calhoun*

AN ALTERNATIVE TO EXTINCTION

Kit returned to his family in Taos on Christmas Day, 1853. He soon posted the required bond and took up his duties as Indian agent. His appointment had been dated March 1, 1853, but he had been gone on his California trip for months before he heard of it. That the job was kept open for him suggests the lack of any sense of urgency in Washington regarding Indian affairs in New Mexico—or perhaps any affairs whatever in that remote part of the national domain. With a largely Hispanic and Indian population and separated from the East by hundreds of miles of Great Plains traversed only by horse or wagon, New Mexico Territory (including present Arizona and southern Colorado) stood low on the list of the nation's priorities, except as a possible route to the Pacific Coast. The gold rush made California a state in 1850; New Mexico would wait for statehood until 1912, sixty-six years after Kearny's army entered Santa Fe.[1]

The low priority given New Mexico affected Carson's work as Indian agent in a number of ways. During his entire tenure he would operate out of his adobe house near the plaza in Taos. This was convenient for him, but it was also unavoidable since the government provided no quarters. For the Indians, as Carson would point out, it was considerably less convenient because they had to journey into Taos, which was not only time-consuming but exposed them to various risks and bad influences. The lack of an official headquarters was only one aspect of what Kit came to recognize as a thoroughly unsatisfactory situation for the agent, the Indians, and the government.[2]

Our image of an Indian agent in the West springs from the late nineteenth and early twentieth centuries. In that period, during the last Indian wars and afterward, Indians were confined to reservations within certain well-defined boundaries and as far as possible were expected to remain there, even forced to do so. Agents, backed either by the military or a police force made up of selected Indians, enforced or tried to enforce increasingly stringent control over people's daily lives. Rations of food and other goods, more or less adequate and frequently less, were doled out at regular intervals. Conditions varied greatly, but an agent held great power over the lives of the people committed to his care, acting as chief administrator, chief law enforcement officer, and judge. Eventually his powers extended to seizing children to be sent to school and prohibiting traditional religious ceremonies. Carson's position and his duties as Indian agent from 1854 to 1861 included almost none of these powers or duties. He had no reservation; no "agency" in the sense of a building or group of buildings housing himself, his office, and his staff; no staff except for one clerk; and little power to enforce his will. There was no school to send Indian children to, and probably the last thing on his mind was restricting the religious freedom of the people he dealt with.

Carson's job was in transition from the colonial and early republican position of an Indian agent as a diplomat representing his government among more or less sovereign tribes to the developing one of an agent as an administrator who actually exercised control over "his" Indians and directed them on the road to "civilization." Kit's powers and budget were limited, but he was nonetheless expected to prevent conflict as far as possible, to persuade the Indians to submit to the government's will, and to solve any problems arising from contact between Indians and whites.

As the duties of an Indian agent were in transition, so was United States Indian policy. Up to the mid-1840s, the government had operated on the assumption that there was a vast area west of the Mississippi that could be set aside indefinitely for the Indians, both those native to the region and tribes removed there from the eastern states. For decades, particularly during Andrew Jackson's administration, the "Great Father" sought to persuade or force eastern tribes to emigrate to the Great

Plains. Beyond the "Permanent Indian Frontier" they would be free from molestation and corruption by whites and could adopt white, Christian civilization at their own pace. The arrival of the United States in California and Oregon, and the establishment of the Mormons in Utah, changed the picture radically. The new settlements had to be connected to the East, and the government began considering possible routes for a Pacific railroad. As increasing thousands traveled west on the Oregon, California, and Santa Fe trails, possibilities for friction with Indians multiplied. White settlement on the Great Plains, which had seemed so far in the future, now became imminent; in fact, Kansas and Nebraska territories were organized the year Carson took up his duties as agent. In New Mexico there were long-established and complex patterns of contact and conflict involving Hispanic New Mexicans, Pueblos, Navajos, Apaches, and other plains and mountain peoples, conflicts that would intensify as Hispanic and Anglo-American settlement expanded, as at Rayado.

It became obvious that the old assumptions about removal to the permanent Indian territory beyond Missouri were useless; a new policy was necessary. All the problems the removal policy had been intended to solve remained. The resources of the government, civil and military, had not expanded in proportion to the expansion of territory and the number of Indians within that territory; in remote New Mexico neither the military nor the civil agents dealing with Indian affairs would have the resources they considered necessary.

Though the government Indian policy that developed from the mid-1840s on appears bewilderingly inconsistent in detail, there were certain persistent themes, based on widely shared assumptions about Indians and their relations with whites, which dominated Indian policy to near the end of the century. James Calhoun, who was superintendent of Indian Affairs in New Mexico in the early 1850s, and for a time territorial governor, stated many of these themes in recommendations to the commissioner of Indian Affairs in Washington in 1849 and 1850. Calhoun praised the Pueblos as relatively "civilized" folk who should be encouraged and protected by the government. In regard to the "wild" Indians—the plains tribes, Utes, Apaches, and Navajos—he declared that they "must be located and confined within certain fixed limits and there compelled to remain, and to build up Pueblos and cultivate the soil." Military force would be an essential component of this policy because the nomadic tribes would not cease raiding until convinced that the government could punish them for any aggressive act: "I could make treaties with all these tribes; and they would comply with every stipulation just so long as you have an arm raised to strike them; and no longer."

After they were confined within certain limits, their intercourse with whites restricted, and instructed and compelled to cultivate the soil, then they could be offered presents, but only food and "instruments of husbandry" because "they should be taught at once to rely upon their own industry." Indians thus confined and compelled to farm would require government support and assistance: "You would have to send men among them to teach them the use of agricultural implements, which should be furnished to them, and also, to direct their labor in the building of Pueblos." He thought it all might be accomplished for $100,000, and support for the Indians might be required for twelve months—estimates that proved hopelessly optimistic. But he insisted that far greater expenditure would result from the persistence of Indian-white conflict: "Expend your million now, if necessary, that you may avoid the expenditure of millions hereafter." There would be another consequence, Calhoun warned, if the government failed to make the effort: "To establish order in this territory, you must either submit to these heavy expenditures, or exterminate the mass of these Indians."[3]

Calhoun's proposals, in both their specifics and their underlying assumptions, reflect the essence of the Indian policy that grew up during the period in which he wrote, the period that witnessed the beginnings of the "fixed limits" reservation system. Because the Indians, not knowing what was good for them, were likely to object to this program, military force, or at least the threat of force, would probably be necessary to confine them on these reservations and make them stay there. They would have to be provided with food and tools to start with, until they learned how to support themselves, but they ought not to expect to be supported by the government without labor. Instructors would be necessary to show them how to farm and build permanent dwellings. Education in English, in the ways of American society, and in the Christian religion would ultimately transform them from "prim-itive" hunting folk and predatory raiders into "civilized" people. In the meantime, however, it would be necessary to separate them from white people in order to prevent the violent clashes that menaced, and infuriated, the frontier citizenry and ultimately proved so destructive to the Indians, and to preserve them from the corruption that such contact inevitably brought. Almost invariably, the common wisdom ran, the Indian learned the white man's vices and not his virtues, and became drunken, demoralized, dishonest, depressed, and infected with venereal disease.

Cultural relativism, now considered an indispensable part of the mindset of a Western intellectual, was rare in nineteenth-century America, when cultural and religious confidence were so much stronger. Some Romantics idealized the Noble Savage's freedom from civilized corruption, but the underlying Anglo-American values remained persistent and pervasive. Certainly the latter-day idealization of Indian culture as a desirable alternative to that of Anglo-America was seldom to be met with. No one, perhaps, cherished the ideal of the Noble Savage more than George Catlin, who devoted his life to preserving the images of the Indians for posterity, yet Catlin could write that "the Indian's mind is a beautiful blank, on which anything might be written, if the right mode were taken to do it." In any case, Catlin thought the "decent and modest, unassuming and inoffensive" Indians probably would remain "unconverted and uncivilized" by whites so full of "vices and iniquities."[4]

The debate over Indian policy in the nineteenth century was not over the value and integrity of the Indian cultures, or the morality of their conversion into Christian citizens. The debate was between those who believed that every effort should be made to save the Indians by transforming them, and those who declared such an effort to be quixotic and futile. The latter group could be divided, roughly, into those who thought that the Indians' disappearance was regrettable but inevitable, because of the "inaptitude for civilization" noted by Doctor Samuel Morton, and those who saw that disappearance as quite desirable and something to be facilitated, because "the only good Indian is a dead Indian."

In *Alternative to Extinction*, Robert Trennert argues that the reservation system as it developed in the later nineteenth century was essentially formulated in the years 1846 to 1851. His title underscores another controlling assumption of the men who developed the system and worked to make it a reality. As they saw it, the reservation was indeed the only feasible, realistic alternative to the extinction in store for the Indians. Certainly the Indian population was declining. Henry Dobyns declares flatly, "From the beginning of European colonization on the continent until the twentieth century, more Indians had died every year than were born." The steady curve of decline reached its nadir late in the nineteenth century. Causes included disease, warfare, the stress and disruption of removal, and change and degradation in traditional ways of life; disease was undoubtedly the greatest destroyer. By the mid-1800s, as Brian Dippie has shown, the theme of the "Vanishing American" was well established in American literature and thought. The major causes that whites assigned for the phenomenon were disease, alcohol, and warfare, both intertribal and interracial. Indians seemed, in words frequently used, to "melt away" before the "progress of civilization."[5]

Segregation on reservations was an idea whose time had come. The removal of eastern Indians to west of the Mississippi, certainly intended to open their lands to white settlement, was considered justified as a means of saving the Indians from decline. Some tribes had, in fact, removed themselves west to avoid white contact; others, like the Cherokees, who had adapted to white contact relatively well, were removed very much against their will. The example of California, where a sudden influx of large numbers of whites into areas with substantial Indian populations proved disastrous, showed all too well the dangers of large-scale, unregulated contact. In Florida, the growth of white population and the removal policy had led to the most expensive Indian war in American history, which ended just twelve years before Carson took up the duties of Indian agent. In New Mexico the United States had stepped into a series of conflicts of long standing which created a persisting insecurity. James Calhoun informed the government in 1850: "In travelling through this territory, you can not safely travel alone, and when in Indian country, an escort is absolutely necessary." That conditions for Indians were equally insecure was not stated. There were concrete examples in plenty, then, to lead thinking men to conclude that government action was necessary to protect both Indians and whites from the consequences of increasing, unregulated contact. The questions were: how to do it, and how much was it going to cost?[6]

Calhoun warned the commissioner that "you must either submit to these heavy expenditures, or exterminate the mass of these Indians." The word *genocide* had not been invented in the mid-1800s, but *extermination* was a word frequently heard in debates on the "Indian question," and it expressed the opinion of a vocal faction on the frontier, much more vividly than the later neologism. In July 1865 Senator James Doolittle addressed an audience of Denver citizens, declaring that "extermination for deeds into which Indians are driven by starvation is not only unjust, but criminally wrong." The audience's response was a shout of "Exterminate them! Exterminate them!" For many frontier whites, the idea of protecting Indians and fostering their transformation into productive, law-abiding citizens was not only chimerical but "criminally wrong." Indians were not only hopelessly degenerate and irredeemable, but an immediate, intolerable menace to decent white citizens. Colonel Chivington's reputed remark at Sand Creek, "Nits make lice," was already in use before that occasion, and it typified the attitude of this school of thought toward Indian women and children. Easterners who were shocked by such ideas were dismissed as ignorant sentimentalists whose ideas about Indians were derived from the novels of Cooper.[7]

Many whites who did not share such ideas were nonetheless fearful about the direction of Indian-white relations. Whatever the motives of the Indians, white citizens could not be expected to submit quietly to theft, destruction of property, or the killing and kidnapping of innocent people. An incident like the attack on the White caravan, and the captivity, abuse, and murder of Ann White, her child, and her servant, summed up for many all that they needed to know about Indians. Before 1846, the U.S. Army had policed the Permanent Indian Frontier, trying to keep a balance between whites and Indians. On occasion, as in California, they sometimes found themselves in the thankless position of trying to protect Indians from settlers. But there was no question that, in the end, their loyalty would be to white American society, that they must protect American citizens. In New Mexico that meant the Hispanic population and the Pueblos, who, being settled, agricultural folk, were "civilized" by comparison with the "wild" tribes. Had Indian "depredations" been simply racist fantasies based on projection, things would have been much simpler, but they were real enough, and people in fear for their lives, families, and property were not inclined to be objective. John Bourke, the soldier-chronicler of the Indian wars, pointed out that the courage and resourcefulness displayed by an Apache on a raid "would have been extolled in a historical novel" about Scottish Highlanders, "but when it was your stock, or your friend's stock, it became quite a different matter." Military men who were painfully aware of the reasons Indians had for many of their violent acts were nonetheless bound to act in defense of the frontier population that formed part of their own society. For Kit Carson, intimately acquainted with the reasons for violence on both sides, the response would be complex and, from the perspective of a much later, uninvolved historian, sometimes inconsistent.[8]

The possible use of force was an essential component of the developing Indian policy. Military force would be necessary to protect white citizens from Indian attack and to ensure that Indians remained confined on the reservations selected for them. Kit Carson pointed out what might not have occurred to many officials, that reservation Indians might also need protection from other Indians hostile to them. In the post–Civil War period, in the aftermath of the Sand Creek massacre and other battles, Indian rights advocates would become increasingly critical of the army, and the contest would intensify over whether the military or civilians should control Indian affairs. Before 1860 the question was slightly less intense, perhaps because the policymakers in Washington had not thought out all the implications of their theories. In 1849 the Office of Indian Affairs had been transferred from the War Department to the new Department of the Interior because of "war being the exception, peace the ordinary condition," as Senator Jefferson Davis argued. Senator Davis and his colleagues had perhaps not consulted the authorities in New Mexico. A few months after the passage of the bill authorizing the transfer, James Calhoun informed the commissioner of Indian Affairs: "The wild Indians of this country have been so much more successful in their robberies since Genl Kearny took possession of the country, they do not believe we have the power to chastise them." Robert Trennert points out that the warrior tribes "were undefeated and no peaceful persuasion . . . could convince these tribes to give up their heritage and traditional style of life and begin assimilation." The government had decided on policy but could only put it into effect when the tribes were forced to submit, "something that was not seriously contemplated at that time, but proved a bloody corollary of the program once inaugurated." That corollary would be very much a concern of Kit Carson's for the rest of his life.[9]

As the military arm of such a policy, the U.S. Army was not especially well prepared. At the close of 1853, just as Carson prepared to take up his duties as agent, the army had a total strength of about 10,500 soldiers, of whom 1,678 officers and men were stationed in New Mexico. Considering that this army was responsible for maintaining peace or "chastising" the Indians over the entire area from the Mississippi to the Pacific, it is possible to see why the reservation system was slow to go into effect, in New Mexico and elsewhere.[10]

Historians today treat the reservation system as a tragedy for the Indians, one in which they were brutalized by war, dispossessed of their land, subjected to great privation on the reservations, and then demoralized when their culture, the source of their sense of value, came under attack. It would be hard to deny any part of that indictment. A deep, largely unquestioned ethnocentrism lay at the very root of the policy. The people most passionately committed to saving the Indians were the most determined to change them, for they saw the transformation as the only hope of their salvation. Without discounting the tragedy, one must remember that the policy was indeed adopted, in Trennert's phrase, as an "alternative to extinction." What many critics of the reservation seem to have in mind as an implicit alternative is a cultural pluralism that would have been quite foreign to the thinking of the overwhelming majority of Americans in the nineteenth century. Moreover, and this is the crucial point, the changes that were taking place in the West as an inevitable concomitant of white expansion were already, even as Carson became an agent of the policy, making the traditional life of the Indians impossible. Carson would become increasingly aware of that underlying condition as he tried to carry out his duties in the next few years.

Self-serving motives played a major part in the formulation of Indian policy. Confining Indians on reservations, putting an end to the roving, hunting way of life many practiced (and all were thought to practice), freed the land for white occupation. That the white occupants would vote in states-to-be was not lost on the members of Congress who passed the bills necessary to implement the policy. They proved, overall, to be not so enthusiastic about the "heavy expenditures" that James Calhoun had advocated in 1850, and their readiness to economize on the support and assistance that were part of the program—and on the military forces necessary to carry it out—would be another reason why things did not go as smoothly as originally hoped.

Many see Kit Carson and other Indian agents as simply instruments of the dispossession of the Indians, cynically serving their masters at the expense of the people placed in their care and making a living while doing it. Many men sought the position of agent for just such a purpose, and made much more than their honest salaries in the process, thanks to corrupt arrangements with contractors and other profiteers. There is no evidence that Carson profited in this way, but as an agent he had a steady job, paying about $1,200 a year, a respectable salary at the time (substantially more than an army colonel earned). James Calhoun thought the pay and allowances of an agent would be insufficient in New Mexico, but it is doubtful if Kit had luxurious tastes. Carson was, after all, the descendent of generations of backcountry pioneers who had dispossessed Indians in Pennsylvania, Carolina, Kentucky, and Missouri. His parents had settled on unceded Indian land in Missouri; he himself had started a settlement at Rayado. Was he simply the servant of white expansion, using whatever influence he had with the Indians to facilitate their downfall? Since he never explicitly addressed the question, we must search for the answer in his actions and in what we can gather from his words about the problems he confronted, bearing in mind that the answer may not be as clear-cut as we might wish.

Carson was agent for the Muache Utes, the Jicarilla Apaches, and for Taos Pueblo; his geographical jurisdiction was simply the areas inhabited by these groups of Indians in northern New Mexico and in present southern Colorado, then part of New Mexico Territory. The Jicarillas and Utes were basically hunting peoples, although the former practiced some agriculture. Both moved about from place to place seeking game. They hunted buffalo on the plains when the hostility of the plains peoples allowed; otherwise they sought game in the mountains. As Carson several times pointed out, they had to disperse into small groups in order to hunt effectively in the mountains; in large groups they could not sustain themselves but would have to be fed by the government. The people of Taos Pueblo were sedentary farmers, although they hunted to provide meat. They supported themselves and lived on peaceful terms with their Hispanic neighbors, although like other Pueblo communities they had to worry about encroachments on their land holdings. They caused far less concern to the authorities than the Utes and Jicarillas during Carson's tenure as agent, and this is reflected in the modest part they play in his official correspondence.

The Utes and Jicarillas required more attention. In 1854 Governor and Superintendent of Indian Affairs David Meriwether informed the commissioner of Indian Affairs that "the Utahs are probably the most difficult Indians to manage within the Territory." As for the Jicarillas, "no other single band of Indians has committed an equal amount of depredations upon, and caused so much trouble and annoyance to the people of this Territory as the Jicarillas. . . . whenever there is any mischief brewing, invariably [the Jicarillas] have a hand in it." When Meriwether wrote, a war involving the Jicarillas and some Utes had been going on for several months.[11]

Kit's long residence in New Mexico, though highly intermittent before 1849, would have given him insight into the relations between the different peoples and the changes that were taking place. As Indian agent he would be even more intimately involved in the situation. Fortunately, his job required him to make regular reports and engage in considerable correspondence. Undoubtedly, a modern bureaucrat could generate more paperwork in a week than Carson did in seven years, but the documentation is still far beyond what he produced before 1854. This is the more fortunate because his autobiography takes us only to 1856. For the first time, we have some insight into his daily thoughts and actions, not as they were selectively recalled years later. The records show the thoughts and actions of a man responding to problems as they came up, thoughts and actions not always consistent for that very reason, but fairly consistent when seen as a whole. These reports were written for him by various scribes. The illiterate Carson had no choice but to employ someone to take down his thoughts, and one is left wondering at times how precisely the written words reflect his thinking. Overall the pattern of his thought seems consistent enough that we can assume that Carson had the various clerks read the letters back to him before he affixed his signature (consistently "C. Carson"), although vocabulary, grammar, and fluency varied considerably with the different amanuenses.[12]

The documents reveal Carson's basic acceptance of the main points of the government policy as developed from the mid-1840s on: removal of Indians to special areas—reservations—set aside at some distance from white settlement, the use of military force when necessary to confine Indians on these reservations, the need to convince Indians that the government had the power to punish them if they attacked whites, and the need and desirability of teaching them to support themselves by agriculture and to become "civilized." He would support this program for the rest of his life, by his actions and his words, and this fact raises some interesting questions, not only about Carson but about the policy itself and the conditions under which it was formulated.

Does Carson's adoption of the government program mean that he was "a good company man," carrying out policy regardless of his own doubts and parroting what his superiors wanted to hear, or does it simply indicate how pervasive and unquestioned was the ideology on which the policy was based? Or does it indicate that the policy, with all its gross faults (so obvious with hindsight) seemed to an experienced man to be the only feasible "alternative to extinction"?

Carson was not an exceptionally original thinker, capable of devising a brilliantly innovative solution to the problem, or of articulating it if he had. He had to work within what seemed to him to be the limits of the possible, based on his knowledge of all the peoples involved—a knowledge of Anglos, Hispanics, and disparate groups of Indians that was exceptional for whites in general and the agents of the Indian Bureau in particular. With or without profound empathy and insight, he surely appreciated the difficulties Indians would experience in shedding their own culture better than policymakers in Washington and Indian agents—often political appointees—just arrived from the East. As a mountain man and a guide for Frémont, he moved far beyond the settlement frontier, living and interacting with Indians in ways that were sometimes violent but often cooperative. After he settled down in New Mexico, the settlement frontier in a sense caught up with him. At Rayado he became a settler, trying to establish a claim to the land and at the same time, apparently, trying to live with the Indians on the basis of the fur trade modus vivendi: accommodation if possible and retaliation as deemed necessary. But he was now a part of the settlement frontier, and he saw at first hand the effects of contact between disparate groups of peoples who had conflicting needs and claims to the land, and no agreed-upon authority or mechanism for settling their conflicts—peoples whose traditions, established over generations, often led to violent redress of grievances.

Carson had been in the northern Rockies when the great smallpox epidemic of 1837 hit the peoples of the upper Missouri, decimating tribes like the Blackfeet. He had seen how the gold rush had virtually expunged the Indian populations from some parts of California. He himself had participated in an attack on California Indians who were perceived as a threat to white settlers, and apparently considered it justified. He had participated in Indian-white conflict in northeastern New Mexico. As an Indian agent he would see and take part in other conflicts between the expanding Anglo and Hispanic settlements and the increasingly hard-pressed but still unsubdued Indians. He would have frequent opportunity to hear the Indian side of the question.

There is no evidence that Carson ever explicitly questioned the legitimacy of white American expansion—which would have made him a rare bird indeed in his time—or felt that he questioned the right of white settlers to seek protection from Indians, or the right of the government and its military arm to provide protection. He would be an instrument of that military arm on many occasions. But he saw increasingly how hard-pressed the Indians were, and how, as he would later put it, the whites were "not willing to do them justice." He did not change sides and probably could not have imagined doing so. However, the idea that he fought Indians because of a generic frontiersman's belief that the only good one was a dead one, and because he liked having "an Indian for breakfast now and then," is hard to sustain if one examines the record.

Carson would become an earnest advocate of separating the Indians from the whites and establishing them on reservations, yet the Indians he looked after from 1854 to 1861 never had a reservation in that period. They continued roving freely over present southern Colorado and northern New Mexico, or as freely as advancing settlement, increasing scarcity of game, and the raids of Indian enemies from east and west allowed. They were to receive certain annuities from the government, chiefly in the form of food and clothing, and issuing these items was one of Kit's chief responsibilities, but the lack of areas especially set aside for them would be one of the persistent problems of his tenure as agent. Large portions of their homeland were part of grants that the Spanish and Mexican governments had given to prominent citizens over the years, and now, in the 1850s, settlers were actually moving into these areas, notably in the San Luis Valley, on the upper Rio Grande and its tributaries in southern Colorado.[13]

When William Carr Lane was governor of New Mexico in 1852–53, he negotiated a treaty with the Jicarilla Apaches that provided for them to be supplied with food for some five years, along with some breeding stock, while they settled down and started to farm. Without waiting for approval from Washington, Lane carried the agreement into effect, settling the Apaches on a farm near Abiquiu, New Mexico, employing farmers and laborers to teach them and construct buildings, and supplying provisions. As often happened, Congress failed to ratify the agreement. As Lane's successor, David Meriwether, noted, this "caused much embarrassment and difficulty"; the Indians (including others besides the Jicarillas) had received supplies for some four months, at a cost of $15–20,000. When Meriwether took office in 1853 as governor and ex officio superintendent of Indian Affairs for the territory, he had no Indian funds on hand and had to tell the Indians he had nothing for them. The farms were not producing enough for their support, and they had food for only a few weeks. They "began to complain of bad faith on the part of the United States, and to insist on a compliance with the stipulations of the compact." When Meriwether tried to explain why this was impossible, they wanted to know "how did their former Father [Lane] get money for this purpose." The result, as Meriwether noted, went beyond "embarrassment and difficulty," for the Jicarillas resorted "to theft and robbery upon the citizens of this Territory for a subsistence, which has continued up to this time [September 1854]."[14]

This particular debacle was not untypical of the course of U.S. Indian policy in the Southwest and elsewhere, where the combination of inattention and parsimony in Washington left local officials to struggle along the best they could. The Ute bands of Colorado and New Mexico would not be granted a reservation until 1868, when Kit Carson in his last days, and as his last government service, would play a part in establishing it. The Jicarillas would wait a good deal longer. Kit would first have to deal with the conflict partly caused by the failure of Lane's policy, and then try to maintain the uneasy peace that followed, acting not as the administrator of the "civilizing" process but as a negotiator, a distributor of the government's scant bounty, and sometimes as part of the "strong arm" that was the final arbiter between Indians and whites.[15]

The failure of the Lane treaties illustrated another essential flaw in the conduct of U.S. Indian policy. Government negotiators made treaties with Indian leaders as if the tribes were sovereign nations, yet the relationship between the government and the Indians was basically different. In earlier times Indian "nations" possessed a degree of independence and power that made it necessary to treat them as sovereign; by the mid-1800s this was no longer the case. Chief Justice John Marshall had defined them in 1831 as "domestic dependent nations"; as the century wore on, the emphasis would increasingly be on the adjective *dependent.* The treaty system, however, legitimized the white appropriation of Indian lands, since the Indians in theory signed over possession in return for payment of annuities, assignment of a reservation, and other considerations. In practice, each side expected the other to adhere rigidly to agreements based on deep lack of understanding. The Indians believed the "Great Father" could decide on a course of action and carry it out, having no understanding of the separation of executive and legislative powers or of the workings of a bureaucratic state. The Jicarillas' failure to understand why Meriwether could not supply their needs in accordance with Lane's promises demonstrated the problem beautifully. The whites in turn failed to understand that the "tribes" or "nations" they negotiated with were not the cohesive entities they imagined, and that the chiefs could neither speak for all their peoples nor compel their obedience to compacts they did not approve. Because each side believed that violations of the treaty by the other side abrogated the agreement, treaty-making tended to be a futile exercise, except insofar as it furthered the ultimate white goal of taking control of the land.[16]

The immediate consequences of these persistent misunderstandings fell on ordinary people, Indian and white, at the point of contact. In New Mexico in 1854 this meant war. Jicarillas were involved in raids on livestock and clashes with troops, culminating in a confrontation, on March 5, 1854, between U.S. dragoons under Lieutenant David Bell and Apaches led by Lobo Blanco. Five Apaches were killed, including Lobo Blanco. Some also believed that Chico Velasquez, a Muache Ute leader, had been involved in the various raids and had abandoned the Jicarillas just in time to avoid the consequences.[17]

Carson's first reports as Indian agent show him confronting these conflicts. Reporting Ute thefts of cattle to Governor Meriwether on January 20, 1854, he said he believed they were the work of a few, the majority being "as well disposed as ever," but also that "most of the depredations were committed from absolute necessity when in a starving condition." The latter point would become a constantly recurring refrain in his reports for the next seven years. A little later he reported the Muaches in "a very deplorable state," noted that he had fed them corn and wheat, and asked "to what extent I may go in supplying their wants, for if the Government will not do something for them to save them from starving, they will be obliged to Steal." This point too he would be constantly restating over the next several years.[18]

Just over two weeks after Bell's encounter with Lobo Blanco, Carson reported that he had just traveled two hundred miles through snow looking for Ute cattle thieves, and spoken with Jicarillas who admitted stealing cattle because "they were in a starving condition." The government should take some action to protect citizens and their property: "Humanity as well as the plighted faith of our government demands it." The basic reason was quite plain: "The game in the Utah country is becoming scarce, and they are unable to support themselves by the chase and the hunt." The choice for the government was also quite plain: "The government has but one alternative, either to subsist and clothe them or exterminate them."[19]

Kit had seemingly changed his mind about the good faith of the majority of the Utes in two months: "But it is my opinion after years of experience with the Indian character that before the Utahs can be made to respect treaties, citizens and their property, they should be severely chastised and punished, and be made to know and feel the power of the government; then, the policy of endeavoring to induce them to settle in Pueblos or villages might be attended with success." The apparent inconsistency over a few weeks' time may mean that he had come to believe that Chico Velasquez and his band were involved in the recent hostilities, and that some Utes were egging on the Jicarillas. He would continue to believe, in principle, that it was necessary at times to "chastise" some groups of Indians to convince them of the need to refrain from attacking whites.[20]

Just a few days later, however, he was writing of his council with some Jicarillas at Cantonment Burgwin, the military post near Taos. Their band was camped near Picuris Pueblo, trading with the local New Mexicans for food, "as they are in a starving condition." They denied any part in recent hostilities. Carson recommended the appointment of a special agent to stay with the Jicarillas and furnish them with food and give them good advice: "I believe if such a course were pursued the Apaches would soon become quiet and contented." Because of the lack of game in the region, "the government must either subsist them for the present or allow them to steal."[21]

Since Governor Meriwether had recently gone on leave, William Messervy was acting governor and superintendent. The lack of funds hamstrung the operations of the territorial government. The military commander at Cantonment Burgwin tried to bring the Jicarillas into the post for safekeeping, and they took alarm and fled. A force of sixty dragoons under Lieutenant Henry Davidson went in pursuit and overtook them at Cienguilla, in the mountains southwest of Taos, on March 30. The dragoons were soon outflanked and surrounded, suffering heavy casualties. Carson and Davidson had both participated in Kearny's march to California and the fight at San Pasqual, and Kit testified in his old comrade's favor at a court of inquiry into the affair. As Carson said later, "I know Davidson, having been in engagements when he done a prominent part, and I know him to be as brave as an officer can be." He even praised the lieutenant for refusing to take cover, something for which he had called Alex Godey a fool on an earlier occasion. Carson always admired a brave man, and he was loyal to his friends.[22]

One historian claims that Carson's remarks about chastising the Utes (addressed to his civilian superior just nine days before the battle) caused the military to launch the 1854 campaign against the Jicarillas, a different tribe. This would have required an unusual degree of speed and coordination between civil and military branches. Since Kit was writing to Messervy, trying to preserve peace with the Jicarillas, just three days before Davidson's engagement, the connection seems tenuous. Just the day before the fight, Messervy had ordered Carson, who was in Santa Fe consulting with him and who probably persuaded him to act, to return to Picuris and promise the Jicarillas a supply of food if they would remain peaceful; now it was too late. From Fort Union, Lieutenant Colonel Philip St. George Cooke set out with some two hundred dragoons and foot soldiers for Taos. There he picked up additional dragoons from Cantonment Burgwin, and a company of "spies and guides" consisting of thirty to forty New Mexicans and men of Taos Pueblo—a local version of the commands of rangers and Indians seen on so many frontiers. The captain of the "spy company" was James Quinn, a local lawyer and businessman, and the lieutenant was John Mostin, Carson's interpreter and clerk. Another recruit was Kit Carson, who reported, "I shall accompany the command as requested by Col. Cook u. s. a." Altogether, the force numbered about two hundred men.[23]

There is no evidence that Carson had any doubts about the propriety of his taking on this assignment. The two branches of government, civil and military, that dealt with Indian affairs were often in conflict, as he was well aware, but the formal questions of separation of powers and proper channels probably meant little to him, especially under the circumstances. He was basically the U.S. government's agent for controlling the Indians. The expedition, he was to say just two years later, was for the purpose of "giving them such chastisement as they deserved." In any case, once fighting had started, Anglos and Hispanics over a large part of northern New Mexico would be in danger—not just anonymous "settlers" but neighbors, friends, and relatives by marriage in the Taos area, the Rio Arriba, and the San Luis Valley. Lindsey Carson's son would find it hard to sit by in an office when his skills would be needed.[24]

The troops crossed the Rio Grande through high water, then entered the mountains on the west side of the river, struggling through rugged terrain covered with snow, all on short rations. Carson was impressed

with the soldiers' endurance and determination. Apparently the Jicarillas were surprised also, or perhaps they failed to realize how Carson
and the spy company aided the soldiers in tracking them down, though
Cooke says the snow made their trail easy to follow. The expedition,
the spy company in the lead, overtook the Indians on April 8 on the
Rio Ojo Caliente. Although Carson does not describe his part in the
fight, Captain Quinn says, "Carson had always been ahead with the Spy
Company and it being no time to swap knives we [he?] charged hard
on the leaft with the Mexicans and myself with my Pueblos." The Indian
women and children had fled and the men were covering their retreat.
They had good cover in the rocks; as Quinn remarks, "Carson thinking
the Spy Company needed support or that the horses and families would
escape us rode back to hurry up the troops." The Jicarillas lost only
a few men, but virtually all their camp equipment and provisions and
some horses. They were pursued, in Cooke's words, through country
where "a world of bleak snow spread unlimited to the West. . . . such
was the scene of the enemy's flight by moonlight; the tracks that bore
diminutive feet left a feeble memorial of its sufferings."

Some seventeen women and children were thought to have died of
cold and hunger in the mountains; they had dispersed in their usual
fashion. Carson says, "The Jicarilla Apache Indians are the worst that
are to be pursued. They always, after having been attacked, retreat in
small parties and have no baggage, and are capable of traveling several
days without food [so] that it is impossible for any com[man]d of regular
troops to overtake them, if they are aware of their being pursued." Kit
did not want the women and children to get away because if they were
captured the men would be more likely to come in and surrender. If
they were killed, on the other hand, as he would later point out, the
men would have nothing left to live for but revenge.[25]

Although Carson says nothing of his own role, Cooke wrote that
"Mr. Carson showed his well known activity and boldness." He ranked
Kit, along with the spy company and Captain Quinn, among those "on
whom I depended for showing me the way to the enemy." His part was
prominent enough that some Jicarillas apparently remembered the man
they called "Gidi" as the leader of the force sent against them.[26]

Yet, perhaps as a result of conversations with the officers of the
column, Kit was having some second thoughts within a few days of the
fight. Just four days later, he wrote Messervy from "Camp on Puerco"
saying,

Having become acquainted with the Commencement of the war on the Apaches about Taos, & accompanied Col Cooke in his present expedition, I have to report to you, just, that in my opinion, they were driven into the war, by the action of the officers & troops in that quarter;—that since they have been attacked, with loss of lives, property, & provisions;—vigorously pursued through the worst mountains I ever traveled through, Covered with Snow;—that their Sufferings & privations are now very great;—but that thinking there will be no quarter or mercy shown them, they will resort to all desperate expedient, to escape any sort of pursuit.

He had decided to leave the column and wait at Abiquiu for Messervy's instructions: "My opinion is that it would be best for them to be sent for, and a fair & just treaty made with them." On April 19, Carson reported that some of the troops had encountered a lone Ute and had taken his horse and weapons, after which he escaped. Kit immediately sent a runner to the Ute village to tell the Indian to come to the agency where he could get his horse back. Cooke, fearing the incident might lead the Utes to commence hostilities, asked Carson to go back to his agency and settle the "difficulty." The agent explained to the Utes that the soldiers had thought the lone Ute to be an Apache, and that the Americans did not mean them any harm. There was apparently little Ute participation in this stage of the war. Governor Meriwether credited this abstention to prompt action by the regular troops and militia, "together with the judicious management of agent Carson." Meriwether would seldom praise Carson again.[27]

There is an apparent inconsistency between Carson's opinion at the time that the Jicarillas had been driven into war and his later declaration in his autobiography that Cooke's column gave them "such chastisement as they deserved." Kit's rhetoric was sometimes tougher than his actions, and his opinions, like other people's, varied with immediate circumstances. It is possible that the Apaches who fought Davidson were not the same group that were pursued by Cooke; Carson himself questioned whether the former were involved in the raids that led to Lieutenant Bell's fight. Perhaps he thought the group Cooke attacked were the ones who started the trouble. Things were more complicated than simple tribal designations made them appear.[28]

Though Carson criticized the actions of some officers, he had high praise for those who came up to his standards, like Captain George

Sykes, who commanded the infantry with Cooke. As for Cooke himself, "He is as efficient an officer to make campaigns against Indians as I ever accompanied—that he is brave and gallant all know." This was especially high praise from Carson because Cooke had been one of General Kearny's chief backers in the controversy with Frémont. In the next campaign Carson would form a high opinion of another regular officer, and the relationship established between them would be fateful in several ways.[29]

Cooke had attempted to pursue the fleeing Jicarillas after the fight on the Rio Ojo Caliente, but was foiled by the terrain, the weather, and the scattering of the Indians—the common experience after an Indian fight. If the Apaches had not retained some good horses, Carson thought, "they would have been chastised in such a manner that war with that tribe would never again occur." Instead, there seemed to be a general war with the Jicarillas, and some feared a grand alliance of plains and mountain tribes, with Comanches, Kiowas, Arapahos, and Mescalero Apaches joining with Utes and Jicarillas. Reports of Jicarillas in the San Luis Valley prompted Cooke to order Captain James Carleton of the First Dragoons to take two and a half companies of his regiment and Captain Quinn's Spy Company north from Taos to intercept them. Once again Kit Carson was along as "principal guide."[30]

The march took Carleton's force north to the Sierra Blanca in Colorado, then east across the Sangre de Cristo range to the edge of the plains. Carson discovered the trail of three Indians; although it was old and "cold," he declared them to be Jicarillas, that being confirmed by discarded loot from the Cienguilla fight. Quinn's trailers led the column south to the Raton Mountains on the present Colorado–New Mexico border. Now occurred one of the legendary events of Carson's career. He saw the trail was fresh and told Carleton that they would overtake the Indians at about two o'clock in the afternoon. The officer, skeptical of such precision, "told me that if such would be the case that he would present to me one of the finest hats that could be procured in New York." The Jicarillas were found, at two o'clock, camped on a mesa at the northern end of Raton Pass. Considerable care was necessary to achieve surprise; Carson and Quinn's scouts took the lead. The dragoons made enough noise to warn the wary Apaches, but too late for them to avoid attack. Several Jicarillas were killed and a number of horses and much camp equipment captured. Some of the Pueblos set up an ambush and killed another Jicarilla who returned to camp after the troops left.[31]

According to Captain Carleton,

Kit Carson . . . who is justly celebrated as being the best tracker among white men in the world, says that in all his experience he never saw such wonderful trailing in his life as that accomplished by Captain Quinn and his Mexican Spy company. Carson willingly admitted that these men had kept on the track when he would have given up. Therefore, to Carson and Quinn is due all the credit for whatever successes the column may have had in finding the Jicarilla Apaches.

It was characteristic of Kit to give others as much credit as possible. He later declared, "It was entirely owing to the good management of Major Carleton that the Indians were discovered." Some time later he received the hat Carleton had promised, specially made in New York, and on the inside band was stamped,

At 2 o'clock
KIT CARSON
from
MAJOR CARLETON

The mutual esteem established between the two men would affect not just their lives but those of thousands of Indians in the next decade.[32]

Shortly after returning from this latest expedition, Carson wrote to Acting Governor Messervy about the danger to his friends at Rayado, requesting the governor to provide protection. A cynic might note that Lucien Maxwell would be able to sell food and forage to any troops stationed there, but Carson's real concern was for the residents there, including "an American Lady a niece of mine," and they could not leave "without sacrificing their all." The Boonslick boy could never forget the effect of Indian hostility on ordinary people like Susan Carson Nelson. It was the Comanches he was concerned about; regarding the Utes, he had already declared, "I have confidence in the good faith of the Utah Indians at present."[33]

THE AGENT AND THE GOVERNOR

The peaceful relations with the Utes were not destined to endure, however, and Carson would soon find himself involved in difficulties he was less well equipped to handle than Indian fighting or Indian diplomacy. In July of 1854, Governor David Meriwether returned from his leave in the East. Meriwether was a Kentuckian in his mid-fifties, and like most appointees to territorial office he was a politician, a good Democrat appointed by President Franklin Pierce. In his younger days, however, he had been an Indian trader on the Missouri, and had had dealings with the Otoes, Omahas, Pawnees, and Osages. In 1820 he was imprisoned by the Spanish authorities in New Mexico, having gone there before newly independent Mexico allowed trade with the United States. He would be governor of New Mexico from 1853 to 1857 and would be embroiled in various controversies, to be expected for any governor of that turbulent territory who took a stand on anything. One of the main sources of difficulty would be Indian affairs.[34]

The immediate problem arose from Governor Lane's unratified treaties and the resulting shortage of funds. The more basic problem with the Utes and Jicarillas was that, in Meriwether's words, "they depend on the chase and robbery for their subsistence." The Utes were at war with the Cheyennes and Arapahos, who had guns supplied by traders and government agents. "Consequently the Utahs dare not visit the buffalo country in search of food."[35]

Meriwether entered into negotiations with Chacon, a chief of the Jicarillas, who wanted to end hostilities but lacked the authority to compel obedience from all his people's warriors. Carson reported to Meriwether on September 30, 1854, that a party of Utes had visited him and expressed the desire to remain at peace: "They complain that they are very poor and the game is very scarce. . . . I would respectfully suggest that as the inclement season is now very near, that you, at as an early day as possible, call them together and make them presents of blankets, Shirts &c. I deem this to be a matter of great importance." Meriwether followed this advice, but the results were not what either of them anticipated.[36]

In early October, Carson set out to gather Utes for the council. The Utes were agitated, but Kit calmed them with "talk of the friendly feeling and good intentions of the government." They had stolen some property because one of their people had been killed by Mexicans. The Jicarillas, he reported, were still committing depredations "from necessity—as they are in a bad condition," and unless prompt measures were taken, "they will clean out this part of the country of its stock."[37]

The council was a lesson in unintended consequences. Meriwether distributed presents, including blanket coats for the head men. Unfortunately, smallpox soon broke out, and every chief who had received a coat died, leading the Utes to conclude that the coats were the source of the disease. To make things worse, one of the men who had killed the Ute whom Carson had mentioned made his escape and, as Kit said, "nothing more was attempted to be done to render justice to the Indians." It was next to impossible to convict or punish a white man for killing an Indian on the frontier. Kit's disgust is evident, even in the restrained words of his scribe. It was an especially bad time for such a failure of justice.[38]

In the meantime Carson had to report some misfortunes of the people of Taos Pueblo. Cheyennes and Arapahos killed twelve Taos men hunting in the Raton Mountains. "It is much to be regretted that among the Pueblo indians slain were a number who distinguished themselves in the late campaigns, under Col. Cooke and others, and rendered efficient service to the government in the Spy Company." He asked Meriwether to take steps so that "those northern tribes may not interfere with those of my agency." These men had been Kit's comrades in battle, besides being his responsibility as agent; a man looked out for his friends.[39]

Governor Meriwether blamed the Jicarillas, rather than Cheyennes or Arapahos, for the attack on the Taos hunters; one would suppose that the Taos men knew who their attackers were. The disagreement was prophetic of future discord between Carson and the governor. On Christmas Day, 1854, Jicarillas and Utes led by Blanco attacked the trading community at Pueblo on the upper Arkansas, killing all but four of the inhabitants. Carson, however, did not think many Utes of the Rio Grande, his immediate charges, were involved: "Blanco . . . I have never seen, nor does he often come about our settlements unless when he intends mischief."[40]

Meriwether responded by calling up a force of six companies of volunteers to serve six months, giving command to Charles Bent's old partner, Ceran St. Vrain. Carson fully approved, saying in his 1856 autobiography, "It was the only appointment of the Governor that met the approbation of the people. Many were surprised at his sound judgement in making such a noble choice." Kit also approved, at the time, of the enlistment of local volunteers to fight Indians; if the chastisement of the hostiles were left to the citizens, he declared, the latter would soon "bring them to subjection." Although Carson had a degree of respect for the regular army not common on the frontier, it would be some years before events caused him to modify his enthusiasm for volunteers.[41]

The volunteers, mostly Hispanic New Mexicans, together with another spy company, marched north to Fort Massachusetts and joined regular troops commanded by Colonel Thomas Fauntleroy. With the troops as surgeon was Carson's future biographer, Doctor DeWitt Clinton Peters. Carson accompanied the troops as they marched west across the San Luis Valley on March 14, 1855. He devotes some space to this campaign in his autobiography, mainly to praising officers, but says nothing of his own part. Apparently, it was he who found a large trail of Indians on the west side of the valley. They slept without fires that night to increase the chance of surprise.[42]

On March 19, with Carson in the lead, they pushed on to Saguache Pass, where they encountered a mixed band of Utes and Jicarillas led by Blanco coming down the pass toward them. The Indians drew up in line and taunted the troops in Spanish until the dragoons charged and scattered them. Two chiefs and six warriors were killed, and the rest scattered into the mountains, leaving their horses. The troops caught them again near Poncha Pass. Supposedly, some of the women killed their children to prevent their being taken prisoner.[43]

After the weary troops returned to Fort Massachusetts to refit, Fauntleroy and St. Vrain carried on separate operations, the former against the Utes and the latter against the Jicarillas east of the mountains. One of St. Vrain's men, Rafael Chacon, later recalled that Carson was with this force, leading some Pueblo scouts, but Kit himself says, "I did not accompany this expedition." They once again attacked an Indian camp, killed a few men, and captured horses and camp equipment.[44]

After these operations the Muache Utes sought peace and so did some Jicarillas. Carson later thought they had gotten off too easily; if the volunteers had been in service another three months, "there would never again have [been] need [of] any troops in this country. The Indians would have been entirely subjected and, in all probability, but few of them would be left to be of any trouble." This is the most "hard-line" statement in Carson's autobiography, and if it were the only one on the subject we had from him, it would justify the view of him as an Indian-hater and an advocate of genocide. Carson was referring to those Indians who had been actively engaged in hostilities, and who had not only massacred the people at Pueblo but attacked many others in northern New Mexico. As he saw it, there was a recurring cycle of such events:

As it is at present [1856], the Indians are masters of the country. They commit depredations as they please. Perhaps a command of troops will be sent after them. They will be overtaken, some of the property they stole recovered, and they make their escape unpunished. The superintendent will then call them in to have a grand talk. Presents are given, promises are made, but only to be broken when convenient. I can say that this country will always remain in its impoverished state as long as the mountain Indians are permitted to run at large, and the only remedy is [to] compel them to live in settlements, cultivate the soil, and learn to gain their maintenance independent of the general government.

This was a statement for his prospective biographer, not an official report, but it expressed ideas he also advocated in his official reports. Unless the government provided a reservation for the Indians, and a dependable means of subsistence, peace treaties were an exercise in futility. He was perfectly aware that the Utes and Jicarillas did not escape "unpunished" in the recent campaigns. In his annual report for 1855, written a few months after the military operations just described, and immediately after the making of the treaties he complained of, he declared that the Utes and Jicarillas were "Serious in that which they said," and "in all probability will remain friendly for a long period." He observed that the Indians now committing depredations "are those who have lost their families during the war. They consider that they have nothing to live for than revenge for the death of those of their families that were killed by the whites; . . . when they will ask for peace I cannot say." Carson knew quite well what the Indians had suffered in the war, and he understood why some of them kept on fighting. Many years later, Casa Maria, a Jicarilla, remembered that at the peace negotiations near Abiquiu one American asked, "Are these all there are left of you?" An Apache replied, "Yes, only so many." The American said, "You were nearly exterminated. Do not become enemies again. Many old men, children, and women, have died." Although it is not entirely clear from the context, Casa Maria may have been attributing these words to "Gidi," who was apparently Kit Carson. It was not a failure of empathy or even of imagination that prompted the diatribe in Kit's autobiography, but rather his frustration at the continued insecurity of life and property in New Mexico, the failures of the government's policies, and most particularly his deep differences with one man—David Meriwether.[45]

In his annual report for 1855, written in September, Carson noted that depredations continued. In forwarding the report to Washington, the governor appended a note: "Mr. Carson does not inform me which Indians committed these depredations, though the last part of his report would leave the impression they were committed by Jicarilla Apaches." Meriwether thought it more likely that Comanches were guilty, for it was "scarcely probable that the Apaches would be guilty of such acts after they had sued for peace . . . and then meet me in council but a few days thereafter . . . It is to be regretted that Agent Carson did not ascertain from the prisoners what Indians they were." Of course Carson could tell what tribe any prisoners belonged to. This message shows how matters stood between the governor and the Indian agent, and some of the reasons why. The Indians whom Carson refers to as desperately seeking revenge for the loss of their families were obviously those involved in the recent hostilities, that is, Jicarillas or Utes.

In his autobiography the following year, Kit writes, "The [Jicarilla] Apaches are now daily committing depredations." As Meriwether had just concluded a peace treaty with Ute and Jicarilla leaders, he found it hard to believe that they would be guilty of such acts and so placed the blame on the Comanches. In his report on the September treaty council, Carson said he believed the Muache Utes and Jicarillas "that were present were serious" and probably would "remain friendly for a long period." Those still raiding were not present, had nothing to live for but revenge, and "when they will make peace I cannot say." Meriwether perhaps committed the common error of assuming that the chiefs of a tribe could speak for, and dictate the actions of, their whole tribes, an odd error for an old Indian trader. Such differences of opinion were a major, but not the only, cause of the quarrel between Meriwether and Carson.[46]

At about the same time as this difference of opinion, Meriwether returned Carson's report of official expenditures to him, citing errors. He would do so on other occasions, complaining once to the commissioner of Indian Affairs that the expenditures for different periods were so mixed together "that it is impossible for me to understand them." In his own autobiography Meriwether comments that Carson's accounts "were always wrong." Corruption among Indian agents was a persistent scandal, some agents making their fortunes during their government "service" by creative bookkeeping and conniving with contractors—one reason why the Indian service was such an important field for political patronage. Meriwether, as critical of Carson in his memoirs as the latter was of the governor in his, never hints that Kit was guilty of anything worse than incompetence in this regard. Considering his obvious personal animosity, he would surely not have failed to mention any malfeasance. Meriwether had painful recollections of the deficit in Indian funds incurred by his predecessor, Governor Lane, and he was determined to keep his own books straight.[47]

The crisis in the relationship came, appropriately enough, at an Indian council. We have only Meriwether's account, for Carson says nothing of it. There is even doubt as to the year it occurred, whether at the 1855 treaty council with the Utes and Jicarillas or the next year. Meriwether says he set out for a council on the Chama River, taking an escort of dragoons and a herd of sheep to feed the Indians. Carson was not present the day the governor arrived, but many Indians were, and he gave them sheep to eat. The next day Carson arrived with Chief Tierra Blanca (Blanco), a forbidding figure scarred by smallpox and with only one eye. Meriwether turned the herd of sheep over to Carson, with instructions to give the Indians only ten or fifteen each morning. The next morning he found that Carson had given all the sheep to the Indians, "for which I lectured him in a mild manner for this disobedience of orders, whereupon he mounted a 'highhorse' and said he was the agent for these Indians and intended to dispose of them and the sheep as he thought proper." Meriwether says he let the matter go, telling the Indians the next morning that he had no more sheep. He and Carson then had a discussion about whose responsibility it was to provide food for the Indians, setting the tone for the rest of the council.[48]

The council commenced with a mutual exchange of prisoners. Shortly thereafter, there was an alarm—some young men riding in with the false report that Navajos were attacking. Then, says Meriwether, began "such a scene of confusion as I never witnessed in my life. Each Indian mounted his horse with his lance or other weapon, and hallooing as loud as he could yell, rode in different directions." The governor took his interpreter and went among the Indians, telling them that he had invited them to the conference and they would not be molested.

Seeing this, Carson came to me saying, "If you don't get under the bank of the river, these Indians will kill you." When I told him that I was not afraid of their hurting me, and directed him, as he spoke their language some, to go among them and try to quiet them. Instead of doing this, he lay under the bank of the river.

A detachment of dragoons investigated the reported attack and found nothing. After things quieted down, Tierra Blanca asked for more sheep, and when Meriwether said he had no more, "then Carson said that if he had been superintendent of Indian Affairs, as I was, these Indians should not go off hungry." The level of discourse declined from there on. Meriwether replied, "It is possible that if you had been superintendent of affairs, you might not have hidden under the bank of the river as you did."

> At this he became very abusive and said that he was not a damn fool like I was, to risk his life in the manner I did. I then informed him that he might consider himself suspended from his agency, and that he was no longer an Indian agent under me. To this he replied, "I'll let you see that you have no power to suspend me."

Then, says Meriwether, Carson "became so boisterous" that the governor had the officer commanding the dragoons put him under guard.[49]

After the council the governor's party returned to Santa Fe, and Meriwether preferred charges against Carson, "the first specification of which was disobedience of orders; the second, insubordination; the third, disrespectful conduct towards a superior officer; and the last was cowardice, in the presence of the Indians." The dragoon commander and others present, he says, supported his charges, saying that they only wondered at the governor's forbearance. Carson then had a friend write out a letter of apology which he signed, Meriwether noting scornfully that "Carson could not write a letter himself, but could only write his name at the bottom." In the letter he admitted he was in the wrong and begged to be reinstated in his post. The governor accepted the apology, and "I had no further difficulty with him during the remainder of my stay in New Mexico, except as to his accounts, which were always wrong."[50]

Meriwether dismisses Carson from his autobiography with these words: "Poor Kit was a good trapper, hunter, and guide, and in the latter capacity, while employed by Colonel Frémont had acquired a reputation which spoiled him, and which in after life and in a higher position he failed to sustain." The charge of being spoiled would have startled the many people who knew Carson as down-to-earth, modest, and self-deprecating. The charge of cowardice most would also have found astonishing, though many noted his caution and watchfulness. His defiance of the governor would not be so remarkable in the man who challenged Shunar and who warned an obstreperous Indian chief that his life was in danger. There are some problems with this account, however, starting with the fact that we have only Meriwether's version. As noted, it is not clear just when the incident happened, if it happened at all, in September 1855 or a year later.[51]

Neither Carson nor Meriwether has anything to say of such an incident at the Indian council of 1855, which they both mention attending, in their annual reports. Regarding the council of 1856, Kit mentions having been there at the start, but in a letter to the governor he indicates that he was not present when a Ute reportedly tried to kill Meriwether, having left before the meeting ended. His failure to mention such a confrontation as Meriwether describes would not be surprising, for being arrested and then forced to apologize in order to retain his post would have been humiliating in the extreme.[52]

Meriwether dictated his account some thirty years later, when he was in his eighties. Guild and Carter suggest that the story became greatly inflated, if not badly distorted, in his memory. Assuming that something happened between the two men at an Indian council, there are still problems with the details. How Meriwether could assure the Utes that they would not be harmed if they were under attack by Indians over whom he had no control is not clear, though probably he expected his dragoon escort to provide protection. In such a chaotic situation as Meriwether describes, with a battle apparently about to break out, it is not surprising that Carson would take cover. The danger would not have been from Utes intentionally trying to harm the governor (unless they thought he was trying to betray them because of their recent hostility), but from stray bullets and arrows, a danger more obvious to Kit than to his superior, whose Indian experience had not included battles. Carson had called his comrade Alex Godey a fool for standing exposed to enemy fire in firelight, so he might well have said the same to Meriwether when the other man remarked on his hiding behind a river bank. To impugn a backcountry man's courage was a mortal insult, as Meriwether, a Kentuckian, must have known. The man who challenged Shunar would have been more than "boisterous" in the face of such a charge, so it is not hard to believe that Kit said things that his superior found insubordinate and abusive.

It is not clear on what legal grounds a federal civil official might order the arrest of another civilian, his subordinate, by a regular army officer on charges of insubordination. The officer commanding the dragoon escort was Captain Richard Ewell, a future Confederate general and a veteran frontier officer. He and Meriwether, according to the latter, became good friends during the Kentuckian's governorship. Ewell and Carson were also acquainted, for the captain had assisted Kit in apprehending the men who plotted the robbery and murder of Santa Fe traders in 1850, and he had commanded the army detachment at Rayado in 1851. Ewell had a reputation for eccentricity and irreverence toward his own superiors, but it could be that his sense of hierarchy was offended by Carson's conduct toward the governor, especially if violence seemed possible. It could well be that the dragoon officer simply thought that it would be best to separate the two men until they had cooled down.[53]

The essential difference between Carson and Meriwether went deeper than angry words over courage and authority. They differed over the management of Indian affairs, a subject on which each considered his own judgment superior to the other's. If we accept Meriwether's version, he had trusted his own judgment in a dangerous situation involving Indians and, what would have been most galling to Carson, he was proved right. As Carson probably saw it, Meriwether took a foolish chance, striding about in the middle of an impending fight over which he had no control and, because the reported attack was a false alarm, he got away with it. His subsequent self-satisfaction and his insult to Carson's courage would have been intolerable, causing Kit to revert to behavior more characteristic of his younger days. Since Carson says nothing of the incident, we have no check on Meriwether's thirty-year-old memory of events, but we know that Kit had no good opinion of David Meriwether.

Carson was not the only Indian agent with whom Meriwether differed; the governor also found Abraham Mayers, agent for several of the pueblos, unsatisfactory. Meriwether found some of Mayers's statistical reports unintelligible, and when he asked the agent to procure documents relating to the Indian communities' land titles, Carson was drawn into the dispute. Kit declined to make a trip to Picuris Pueblo, not far from Taos, to obtain the relevant documents for Mayers, as he wrote to his fellow agent, because earlier expenses of his had been disallowed. His letter went on to Meriwether, who wrote Carson saying, "Letters of such character as yours to Agent Mayers will not deter me from a proper discharge of my duties." That shows well enough how matters stood between the two in the summer of 1856.[54]

One central problem between Carson and Meriwether related to Kit's need for assistance with his official paperwork. He had different assistants over his tenure as agent; John Mostin, who took down his autobiography, seems to have worked for him much of the time from 1855 until Mostin's death in 1859. In August 1855 Mostin is noted as the agency interpreter. Since Carson himself had some knowledge of the Ute language, spoke Spanish as many of the Indians did, and was well acquainted with the sign language that was the common mode of communication between different tribes, his need for an interpreter was certainly not as great as that of many agents who came west after receiving their appointments. Everyone who has studied Carson's career has concluded that the "interpreters" in fact took care of Kit's clerical work and made out his reports, to which he affixed his signature.[55]

Mostin or Carson apparently let the cat out of the bag in submitting accounts. Meriwether returned the accounts for correction, as on other occasions, complaining of "Charges for expenses of self and clerk at Santa Fe $13 when I am ignorant of any regulations which authorize an Agent to have a clerk." This reprimand came very shortly after the likely date of the alleged confrontation of Carson and the governor at the Indian council. Meriwether himself states flatly that "Carson could not write a letter himself, but could only write his name at the bottom." This is not to say that Mostin was totally unequipped to serve as an interpreter. Meriwether told the commissioner of Indian Affairs that Mostin "can neither speak the Indian or Spanish language as well as Mr. Carson, himself, but that he is a discharged soldier who is employed for his clerical service." As a discharged soldier he had probably spent some time in New Mexico, where the overwhelming majority spoke Spanish; he had also acted as a lieutenant in Quinn's spy company, in which the men were either Hispanic New Mexicans or Taos Pueblo men. In August 1855, Carson explained to Meriwether at some length why "I deem the services of an Interpreter indispensable even if he should not be acquainted with the languages of all the various tribes," because there was no one who understood all the required languages, and even a moderate knowledge of Spanish would be useful. The Indians were accustomed to being addressed through an interpreter on formal occasions, which would "add to the effect of the communications," and it was useful to have an assistant who could communicate with them if they came calling in his absence. But he was not telling the whole story. The regulations did not allow a clerk, which he needed, but did allow an interpreter.[56]

In any case, Meriwether did not buy it. In returning Carson's accounts on the occasion noted, he wrote that he had approved expenses for paying Mostin, "but I deem it my duty to inform you that I cannot do so again." Evidently, Mostin's performance was not up to Meriwether's standards, for the governor returned various reports to Carson for revision in 1855, saying of one, "I apprehend it will not prove to be such a document as is desired by the Department in Washington."[57]

One can imagine Carson's frustration. He undoubtedly believed that he understood the essential business of his job, dealing with Indians on a day-to-day basis, as well as anyone. His illiteracy, absolute or not, handicapped him in performing what he must have regarded as a secondary task and exposed him to the criticism of a superior who, he believed, knew far less about the Indians than he did. It was after four years as Indian agent that he wrote to the commissioner asking for "a copy of the Regulations of the Indian Department . . . for the use of this office," suggesting how much he knew about those regulations. Even the commissioner wrote to the acting governor on one occasion in 1856, noting that Carson had not "rendered any account or voucher" for the payment of his salary as required. Kit was clearly not a natural-born bureaucrat.[58]

Early in 1856, when Meriwether was again absent on leave, Carson wrote to the acting governor, W. W. H. Davis, about the point of contention. He noted that Meriwether, on departing for the States, had directed that Mostin be discharged, "To which Order I had no objections, & discharged him." Now large numbers of Indians were visiting the agency asking assistance, and Carson, needing help, requested permission to employ an interpreter. The next month, he hired C. Williams as "Assistant at this Agency."[59]

Meriwether probably did not take kindly to this attempt to circumvent him. A few months later, when the governor had returned to New Mexico, Carson wrote that he was leaving to distribute presents to the Indians on the Conejos River in the San Luis Valley. He pointedly remarked, "Not being allowed to employ any person I shall have to make the journey alone, but as I know the country over which I may have to travel I fear but little difficulty." Someone obviously wrote the letter for him, as Meriwether would have known.[60]

The final outcome of the Mostin affair appears in the record nearly three years later, in 1859, nearly two years after David Meriwether had left New Mexico for the last time. Carson wrote to the then superintendent, James Collins, transmitting "an unpaid account of John Mostin for services rendered in this Agency as Interpreter—":

Your predecessor ordered his discharge, on what grounds at the time I was at a loss to know—the benefit to the Ind. service, I have been since informed, was not taken into consideration by the Honrble, the late Supt. Ind. Affs. Meriwether, in ordering Mostin's discharge. He done it, having the power, to satisfy the ill feeling he bore towards Mostin and myself— If you read his communications to Ind. Dept. in regard to myself I have no doubt but you will be satisfied that such was the cause of his action towards Mostin—

Since it was impossible for one man to perform the duties of agent, "I kept Mostin in employ disregarding the order of the Supt. sooner than neglect the duties which I have sworn to truly perform." He now hoped that Mostin could be paid "for rendering govt. faithful service."[61]

Carson was accusing his former superior of trying to get him. Since Meriwether clearly knew that Carson could not do the indispensable paperwork without a clerk, depriving him of one would indeed make his job impossible. As in so many fields, the ability to do the work counted for less than the ability to do the paperwork. The governor must have known that someone was writing Carson's reports after Mostin's supposed discharge; so long as no charges were submitted to him, he could do little but criticize the reports. Was Mostin simply helping Kit out and supporting himself in some other way, or was the agent paying him out of his own pocket? Perhaps it was a little of both. Certainly Mostin took down Carson's autobiography in 1856. The account submitted in 1859 covered services for October through December 1855, and from August 1856 through May 1857, declared to be "actually necessary for the public service." It was in May of 1857 that Meriwether left New Mexico for the last time, and Carson was able to rehire his "interpreter" openly. If the account was paid, it did Mostin little good, since he died a few months later, on October 29, 1859, and Carson promptly hired J. F. Esmay in his place.[62]

Carson makes no mention of these personal differences, or even Meriwether's name, in his autobiography, but he makes his opinion of "the Superintendent" plain. Regarding an unnamed person who had injured him earlier, he said, according to Jessie Frémont, "If I ever have a chance, I will do him an honest injury"—an open, straightforward act of retribution. This he did in his autobiography, meant to provide information to his prospective biographer, Dr. Peters, where he openly criticized Captain Grier and Antoine Leroux for their part in the pursuit of the captors of Ann White, Colonel Sumner for his failure to send help when he was menaced by the Cheyennes, the unnamed officer whose mistreatment of a Cheyenne put him in danger in the first place, and most prominently Governor Meriwether. Peters muted his criticism, however, though he referred to Meriwether's "weak diplomacy" without mentioning him directly; this criticism was no doubt known to Meriwether, and is probably reflected in his verdict that Carson "failed to sustain" the reputation he had won with Frémont.[63]

Beyond their personal differences, however, was their substantial disagreement regarding the conduct of Indian affairs. Meriwether never mentions such differences in his criticism of Carson, attributing their difficulties to Kit's inefficiency and insubordination. Carson, on the contrary, says nothing of their personal difficulties in his autobiography, but devotes several paragraphs near the end of that document to criticizing his superior's official acts. No doubt Meriwether resented Carson's substantive criticism as well as his "insubordination" and "disrespectful conduct." Carson likewise took offense at Meriwether's harassment of him over red-tape issues, at the arrest and suspension at the Ute council (if this took place as the governor described it), and at the pursuit of an official policy that ran counter to his own judgment and advice. But the policy difference went to the heart of the problems of Indian-white relations in New Mexico and in the West generally.

As noted, Carson complained in his autobiography that, as of 1856, "the Indians are the masters of the country." They committed depredations, troops pursued them, some stock was recovered but the Indians escaped into the mountains. Then the superintendent—Meriwether—called them together "to have a grand talk. Presents are given, promises are made, but only to be broken when convenient." In his annual report of 1855, Carson had expressed faith in the sincerity of the Utes and Jicarillas at the council, but in 1856 he seemingly contradicted himself, in part: "The Apaches did not all come in at the time of the treaty. They were committing depredations. The fact was reported to the Superintendent but would [not] be believed. Treaty should not have been made with the Apaches. No faith can be placed in their promises." Here he seems to be speaking of the Jicarillas in general, not just a few desperate, vengeful holdouts.

The reason for the apparent change is plain: "The Apaches are now daily committing depredations. They go unp[un]ished and, in my opinion ere long they may again commence hostilities. The other tribes with whom the treaties were made I think will comply with their demands and will not again be hostile if the Government does not stop their supplies of provisions during such times as they cannot hunt." The last sentence was an important qualification, distinguishing sharply between the Jicarillas and the Utes, absolving the latter from any serious hostile acts since the treaty council and placing the blame on the Jicarillas. Carson would always maintain a special affection and a special concern for the Utes; like any old mountain man, he made clear distinctions between different groups of Indians, even those closely allied. In warning of the need to supply provisions, he put his finger on a major problem of Indian-white relations at the time and for many years to come.[64]

Carson accused Meriwether of buying off the Indians as a temporary expedient: "Those in power considered the Indians sufficiently punished; the Indians asked for peace, it was granted them." Carson believed, as did many whites of the time, that a military defeat severe enough to convince Indians of the futility of resistance was a necessary precondition of lasting peace, at least in some cases. People with warrior traditions might not give up their way of life unless they were genuinely convinced of the necessity. Carson understood from long experience that the warrior virtues were deeply embedded in the cultures of many tribes; these virtues were part of his own backcountry culture. At least some proponents of the reservation system realized that force would be necessary in some cases to insure the Indians' compliance. The Jicarilla war of 1854–55 was one of a series of conflicts in that decade, the first in the long list of Indian campaigns extending into the 1880s. General George Crook, one of the most effective commanders in the later Indian wars, who was also notably and outspokenly sympathetic to the Indians and critical of government policy, summed the situation up succinctly: "Of course, you have got to use a little force." In 1871 the Board of Indian Commissioners, a body of reformers and Indian rights advocates acting as semiofficial overseers of the Bureau of Indian Affairs, declared a "legitimate and proper" use of military force to be "compelling in the Indians an earnest desire for peace." But Kit Carson's actual application of force, based on his own judgment, would seem inconsistent from a later perspective.[65]

Carson also stated his opinion on the subject in his annual report for 1859. In reference to hostilities committed by Tabeguache Utes against miners in Colorado, he wrote:

Nothing has been done to make them cease from the commission of hostilities, or to teach them that when they rob and plunder our citizens they should expect prompt and severe punishment. . . . The consequences of letting these Indians go unpunished will be injurious. Other bands of Indians, seeing that depredations are committed by these with impunity, will soon follow an example so much in accordance with their habits and inclinations, and will only remain quiet so long as it suits their convenience.

Carson spoke in one report of 1857 of the Indians knowing "no law but that of retribution." He believed that they would understand the whites' retaliating for hostile acts, but if food and other goods were given to them without such retaliation, they would assume the whites were afraid of them. Yet Carson's actions in the case just cited, of the Tabeguaches, would not be perfectly consistent with his stated beliefs.[66]

The treaties that Meriwether negotiated in 1855 might seem fully in accord with the government's evolving reservation policy, with which Carson was in basic agreement. The Indians were to cease hostilities, give up their land claims, and agree to settle on a designated reserve, where they would begin farming and herding. The government would provide annuities, either given in the form of goods, or "expended for moral improvement and civilization." Spiritous liquors would be barred from the reservations and their intercourse and trade with whites would be regulated by the government. All of this was a rubber stamp of government policy, and echoes what Carson himself repeatedly recommended. Yet in this instance he objected strongly. Noting that the treaties were still unconfirmed by the Senate in 1856 (in fact, they never were confirmed), he declared, "They should not be. Such treaties were not of a character to suit the people."[67]

The Senate's failure, once again, to ratify the arrangements, which the government's representative on the spot had made with the Indians, points out one serious flaw in the execution of national policy. But Carson's objections were probably not on the same basis as those of the senators. He distrusted the Jicarillas: "No faith can be placed in their promises." One reason, as Carson was certainly aware, was that they had no united leadership that could enforce observance of peace terms on all their people. Beyond that was the Jicarilla belief that they had a right to whatever grew on their land, granted to them by the supernatural powers, including the livestock and crops that Anglo and

Hispanic ranchers thought belonged to *them*—a difference in viewpoint not easily reconciled. As long as their other food sources continued to dwindle, the problem would not go away. This was one of the difficulties that the reservation system was supposed to solve, but there was another difficulty with the Meriwether treaties. The Muache Utes were granted a reservation that included parts of the San Luis Valley already settled by whites. The Jicarilla reservation would be in the mountains west of the Rio Grande and northeast of the New Mexican town of Abiquiu, where some of the Apaches indeed settled in to await their rations, a few farming land loaned by friendly citizens. Others squatted near Taos and sold earthenware and the small baskets—*jicarillas*—that gave them their Spanish name. But, as Carson said, the treaties were "not of a character to suit the people." As noted, the Muache Utes were given land already settled by whites, a policy with little record of success in the history of the United States. New Mexicans in the Rio Arriba were loath to have the recently hostile Jicarillas settled near them, and Charles Beaubien, Lucien Maxwell's father-in-law, got up a petition with more than a hundred signatures to send to the president asking that the Jicarilla treaty not be ratified. Regardless of the justice of the matter, such sentiments did not bode well for the success of the arrangement.[68]

The close proximity of Indians and whites was one of the problems the reservation system was expected to solve. Such proximity increased the chances of friction, episodes of theft and violence on both sides, and the incidence of alcoholism and other white men's vices. The result was a pessimism about the adaptability of the Indians. Such pessimism also reflected the deep-seated Anglo-American uneasiness about interracial contact, and perhaps a broader tendency to solve social problems by segregating the people seen as deviant. The same America that produced the reservation system also developed the modern penitentiary and the insane asylum. Carson had a good deal to say on the subject, and his thoughts, although not remarkably original in the context of the time, were based on a degree of experience available to few government policymakers.

In 1857 he produced some of his most detailed statements on the subject. In June he wrote to the new superintendent of Indian Affairs for New Mexico, James Collins, "in regard to a system that should be adopted by the general government for the civilization of the Indians of this agency": "I should recommend in the first place they be removed as far as possible from the Settlements, let them be established in Pueblos, say the Muache band of Utahs in one, and the Jicarilla Apache band in another, and not less than a distance of five miles apart." There should be a military post nearby with farmers and "mechanics" to teach them to farm and to make necessary tools, and cattle and sheep to feed them and serve as a start for their herds. Then missionaries could "instruct them in the laws and rules of christianity." This was all virtually dogma among whites whose ideas of Indian policy went much beyond "extermination." Carson reiterated:

> Have no Mexicans to live near the Pueblos, for most of our difficulties is caused by them. They steal from the Indians, and the Indians know no law but that of retaliation, and from such acts commence hostilities with the Indian tribes and the United States, and as long as they remain near the Mexican settlements they will be furnished liquor, and the Jicarilla Apaches being notorios for drinking, will be always in difficulty with the citizens of the Territory.

This is one of the first times that Kit so emphatically blamed the New Mexicans, rather than the Indians, for causing hostilities, a theme that would recur in his reports and other official statements, and would be extended in time to Anglo-American settlers. In his autobiography he had recently said, "Every visit an Indian makes to a town, it is of more or less injury to him." Holding such ideas, it is hardly surprising that he regarded the reserves set up by Meriwether, so close to New Mexican settlements, with such disfavor.[69]

There was an inescapable corollary to this warning, of course. When Sam Houston was president of the Texas Republic, he reportedly observed, "If I could build a wall from the Red River to the Rio Grande, so high that no Indian could scale it, the white people would go crazy trying to devise means to get beyond it." From Kit's remarks about the Mexicans, one might not guess that among them he had friends and in-laws, as did that prominent citizen Charles (Carlos) Beaubien, who devised the petition against the Jicarilla reservation near Abiquiu. The boy from Boonslick (whose own parents had illustrated Houston's observation by settling on the unceded lands of the Sacs and Foxes) could surely sympathize with both the settlers' desire for land and their need for security from Indian hostility. Removing Indians as far as possible from contact with whites was the dearest desire of white farmers, ranchers, and miners, and so it is possible to be cynical about Carson's motives. But that land-hunger, it was becoming obvious, was another reason for separating Indians and whites. In the 1850s the Texans fulfilled Houston's prediction by forcing the federal government to cancel all reservations granted in the state, removing the inhabitants to Indian Territory, including some who had been allies of the Texans against the Comanches and Kiowas. Kit would never lose sight of the frontier settlers' need for safety, nor would he cease to discriminate among tribes on the basis of their degree of hostility to whites, but he would increasingly lay a large share of blame on the settlers.[70]

Carson ended that June 1857 report by reiterating, "In my opinion, I would respectfully suggest to your honor, the removal of all Indians of the Territory as far as can be practicably done from the settlements." Just two months later he repeated the same advice, in more detail, in his annual report for 1857. He believed that the Utes were more contented with the "presents" (annuity goods) they received in August than in previous years, and that the "citizens have no cause of complaint." He noted,

> Mohuache Utahs are not Indians that are addicted to the use of ardent spirits. But I fear, if they are permitted to visit the settlements as they desire, that in a few years they will become accustomed to the use of ardent spirits, and as Indians generally learn the vices and not the virtues of civilized men, they will become a degraded tribe, instead of being, as they are now, the most noble and virtuous tribe within our Territory.

Kit's language—or Mostin's—is the sort of thing Cooper might have had Hawkeye say in praise of his beloved Mohicans or Delawares. Other people, however, would record him as saying essentially the same thing about the Utes, if in more down-to-earth language. Here he asserts, "Prostitution, drunkenness, and the vices generally, are unknown among them." Thus many a trader and mountain man wrote of his favorite tribe. But action would be necessary to preserve this state of primitive virtue: isolation from white settlements, instruction in farming "to gain their subsistence" and reduce their dependence on the government. Not too much could be expected of the present generation, who were accustomed to living "by the chase and robberies committed on the neighboring tribes and the whites." But the "rising generation," having learned to support themselves by "honest labor," would "not depart therefrom" but would be proud to instruct their children in honest labor. Troops would have to be stationed among them for a time, to protect them from hostile tribes and to "show them that the government has the power to cause them to remain on the lands given them, and not to overreach on that of their neighbors."[71]

Carson's ideas, expounded twice within two months in 1857, suggest that he had been giving the matter considerable thought. He had been an Indian agent for over three years; he had spent over thirty years, off and on, in New Mexico; and he had had ample opportunity to observe the changes taking place on the frontier. His 1853 trip to California showed the devastation resulting from a sudden, massive, and unregulated influx of whites. The continuing insecurity in New Mexico showed the results of contact between Indians and a less explosive but persistently expanding white population. The problem existed in all the frontier zones of the West, and the United States government would have to deal with it.

Kit's solutions were certainly conventional, as were the words chosen by Mostin, or whoever wrote those documents. But the fact that he took the trouble to reiterate them suggests that he took them seriously, and that he wanted to convince the men who actually made policy of the importance of what he was saying. They may have been received ideas, based on ethnocentric assumptions and so pervasive that even an illiterate frontiersman in remote Taos could pick them up, but he seems to have adopted them as the best feasible solution to problems that he confronted daily. He was thoroughly familiar with the worst effects of those problems on all parties—bloodshed, robbery, captivity of women and children, perpetual fear and insecurity, impoverishment, and the degradation of dependency and drunkenness. The necessity of remote, self-sustaining reservations seemed to him obvious and inescapable. The consequences of failing to establish them—the destruction and even disappearance of the Indians through violence, disease, starvation, and alcohol—seemed equally obvious.

Carson specifically proposed his ideas for "the civilization of the Indians of this agency"—the Muache Utes and the Jicarilla Apaches being his official, immediate concern. Kit's reference to the Utes as "the most noble and virtuous tribe within our Territory," however uncharacteristic the language, indicates his special, Cooperish concern for them. They were "his" Indians, in a paternalistic sense; agents, like other government representatives, were addressed as "Father," and he was "Father Kit." Some of it was his conscientious need, as discerned by his biographers, to do his duty the best he could. Perhaps he was consciously telling his superiors what they wanted to hear, but if so he went to impressive length for a reticent man for whom the written word was not a natural means of communication. It is unlikely that the commissioner of Indian Affairs needed convincing, but perhaps the comfortable gentlemen in Congress, who made appropriations and approved treaties, and who had not yet approved a reservation or even built an agency for his Indians, did need it.

Carson, at any rate, had some basis for his difference with Governor Meriwether other than personal animosity. That personal feelings colored his attitude is evident, both in his official correspondence and in his casual references to the man. The state of feeling between the two was public knowledge, for it gave rise to rumors. In September 1856, Meriwether held a council with some Utes at Abiquiu at which he distributed annuity goods. Carson was present on the first day and then left. The next day a Ute, disgusted with the blanket he had received, which Carson says was old and worn, tore it up and made threats against Meriwether; some of his tribesmen restrained him. On September 17, Kit wrote to the governor: "I have received information from a friend in Santa Fe, that there is in circulation a report that I was instrumental of the disturbances among the Indians at the time they were receiving presents at Abiquiu. I was not present at the time of the disturbance and all that I know regarding them I have learned by enquiry this day." Carson said that after leaving the council he had heard that there was some disturbance, but he thought there was no use returning because it would be settled quickly. Inquiring into the matter, he had heard the story of the angry Ute getting his gun to kill Meriwether; the Indians concealed the true cause of the hubbub. Now Kit wanted to know if Meriwether had heard the story and if he believed it. "I feel deeply grieved to think that any one could be base enough to spread such a report and hope that credence would be given it. . . . I wish to defend myself of Such malicious injury that some bare faced Scoundrel has endeavored to do me."

He might well be concerned, but Meriwether wrote back that he had heard nothing of the report. If the governor had heard such a story and believed it, it is hard to see why, considering the general tone of his references to Carson in his own memoirs, he would have omitted it.[72]

As Meriwether dismissed Kit from his autobiography with a remark about how he had "failed to sustain" the reputation he had gained, so Carson discounted the governor soon after his departure in an official report about the continuing problems of contact between disparate peoples. He was forwarding to the new superintendent of Indian Affairs in New Mexico, James Collins, correspondence "in regard to a murder committed by one Benito Martinez of two Utah Indians." He wanted the correspondence sent to the commissioner in Washington, "as I wish his Honr. to know the course I pursued in regard to the apprehension of the murderer." With this in mind he added, "By this time I have no doubt, but his Honr. has come to a conclusion how to receive and place faith in the statements of his late Excellency Governor Meriwether." Kit was no doubt feeling particularly confident because he had recently received news of his reappointment as agent for another four years. Either Meriwether's adverse opinions had not been credited in Washington, or they had not been quite so negative as he had thought. After March 3, 1857, the offices of governor and Indian superintendent in New Mexico were separated, with James Collins taking the latter job. Whether this was a verdict on Meriwether's tenure or not, the previous arrangement obviously was not deemed satisfactory.[73]

In his autobiography, completed in 1856, Carson also had some last thoughts about Meriwether's stewardship. Regarding the distribution of annuity goods at Abiquiu, he complained,

> I cannot see how the Superintendent can expect the Indians to depart satisfied that he has called [them] to see him from a distance of two or three hundred miles, compelled [them] to go several days without anything to eat, unless they have carried it with them. . . . They could more than earn the quantity they receive in one day's hunt. . . . If presents are given them it should be taken to their country. They should not be allowed to come into the settlements, for every visit an Indian makes to a town, it is of more or less injury to him.

The poor quality and scant quantity of goods for the Indians was not wholly under Meriwether's control, since the congressional appropriation determined what could be spent, but the procedure was. Perhaps Carson voiced his opinion and had it rejected by his superior. He was not about to give Meriwether the benefit of a doubt.[74]

When Carson (with Mostin) finished his autobiography, the penulti-
mate paragraph was devoted to present personal circumstances, but it
included some further thoughts on Indian policy.

> I am now living in Taos, N. M., in the discharge of my official duties as
> Indian Agent. Am daily visited by the Indians, give to them presents,
> as directed by the Superintendent. I am opposed to the policy of
> having Indians come to the settlements, but as there are no agency
> buildings allowed to be built in the country of the Indians, necessity
> compels them to come to the towns.

There would be no agency buildings and no reservation for the Muache
Utes or the Jicarilla Apaches during Kit's tenure as agent. The Indians
must come to Taos, in spite of the disadvantages he pointed out.[75]

The early conclusion of Carson's autobiography is a major loss to
any student of his life, since he had another twelve years ahead of him,
and some of his most dramatic and controversial exploits lay ahead. We
do have official correspondence, of the sort lacking for his years as a
mountain man and guide, covering the years of service as an Indian
agent and later as a soldier. The completed autobiography was given
to Doctor DeWitt Clinton Peters, the admiring army surgeon, who in
1858 would publish the first full-length biography of Kit Carson, a work
of over five hundred pages titled *The Life and Adventures of Kit Carson,
the Nestor of the Rocky Mountains, from Facts Narrated by Himself.* Kit does
not seem to have received much financial benefit from it, but the scale
of the work suggests the fame he had already achieved, and the book
undoubtedly helped build his reputation, along with the more widely
available dime novels. Peters's likening of Carson to Nestor, the valiant
and wise old king of the *Iliad,* shows him already established in the
role of the old scout, shrewd, wary, and thoroughly versed in the ways
of the Indians as well as mighty in battle. In his first paragraph Peters
declared that a born Kentuckian, like Kit, possessed "all the attributes
of a brave man, a safe counselor and a true friend." For the rest of his
life people would expect Kit Carson to display these qualities as a matter
of course, and his role as a "safe counselor" on the subject of Indians, in
peace and in war, would be as important as his service as a warrior. Kit's
reported opinion of the biography was that "Peters laid it on a leetle
too thick."[76]

A photograph of Carson taken during his service as Indian agent shows him dressed up in his Sunday best, coat, tie, and hat—perhaps the New York hat from Major Carleton—and looking very much the solid, bourgeois citizen; he also had apparently been getting quite a bit of good New Mexican home cooking. Albert Richardson, who met him in 1859, described him as "a stout middle-aged man with straight brown hair, mild eye and kindly face. He wore a suit of gray, and looked like an Illinois farmer; but when he took off his hat his face and head indicated character." On foot he looked "stout and ungraceful," bowlegged, as he himself said, from years of riding with short stirrups like an Indian, but he was a skillful and reckless rider. Richardson, like so many others, noted that "Carson never spoke of his own exploits except in reply to my questions." Richardson continued: "He said that as a boy he was daring and reckless; but now when traveling he exercised great vigilance, having seen many of his comrades killed by Indians through their own carelessness. . . . Reading with difficulty, and writing little beyond his own name, he speaks fluently English, French, Spanish, and several Indian tongues, all acquired orally."

Marian Sloan, a little Anglo girl living in Santa Fe at this time, remembered him as "awkward and uncouth. Often he was coatless and perhaps did not own a tie. He spoke the Western vernacular." She thought him "a lonely man": "His was a great heart and very kind, yet he wore shyness before his face like a veil. Only with children and the child-like Mexicans was he able to lay that shyness aside."

The Carson of the later 1850s was obviously not cast, outwardly, in the mold of the great scout and Indian-fighter. He described his life as an Indian agent thus: "I frequently visit the Indians, speak to them about the advantages of peace, and use my influence with them to keep them satisfied with the proceedings of those placed in power over them." He was "daily visited by the Indians, give to them presents," words summing up much of his official activity in those years. Much of his correspondence is concerned with the visits of Indians to Taos, or his visits to them, and with the need to give them "presents," or simply to ensure that they were fed and clothed. Much of the rest of his paperwork concerned his efforts to prevent the frictions between Indians, Hispanics, and Anglos from generating serious hostilities. Keeping the Indians "satisfied with the proceedings of those placed in power over them," when he himself was not altogether satisfied with those proceedings, may have been a tedious task.[77]

Some of his work continued to concern the people of Taos Pueblo, although they were self-supporting and not involved in any overt conflicts with the citizenry. In July 1856 he wrote to the commissioner of Indian Affairs, sending him the names of fifteen Taos Indians who had served in José Maria Valdez's company in St. Vrain's battalion in the campaign of 1855, presumably so they could receive compensation. Later in the month he transmitted the claim of Juan Domingo Martín, "an Indian of the Pueblo of Geronimo de Taos": "I know the applicant and was on the campaign against the Indians with him. He is now perfectly blind from the effect of a wound received on Said campaign. I was present when he was injured— If he should be entitled to a pension please inform me of the course to be pursued. He is a very good Indian and I hope he may receive something from government in payment for the many services rendered before he lost his sight." (Here again is the word *perfectly*, in this case obviously not used to express approval or satisfaction.) Kit's description of him as a "good Indian" may smack of paternalism to a later generation, but he probably meant that he was like other comrades, white and Indian, casualties of battle who were "brave, good men." The two had fought together, and the agent was Martín's sole, and legitimate, means by which he could appeal for the compensation due him for his disabling injury received in federal military service. In May 1857 Carson sent to Superintendent Collins the applications for bounty land of fourteen Indians "that served during Ind. disturbances in N. Mexico during the years of 54 and 55 —"; bounty lands were a standard means of compensation for voluntary military service. On June 6, 1859, Carson wrote to Collins, noting that two and a half years after first raising the matter in January 1857, and six months after writing about it to the commissioner, he had "received no reply thereto. . . . The Indians are daily asking me if They are to receive Bounty— I would like to be able to give them correct information about this claim I forwarded." The slowness of the federal bureaucracy is obviously no new phenomenon.[78]

In September 1856 Carson wrote to his old friend William Bent, still trading on the Arkansas, asking him to speak to "the Indians in his neighborhood" about making peace with Taos Pueblo. Bent replied that the Cheyennes and Arapahos were willing to meet Taos representatives at his fort, adding that he would like Carson "to keep the Mexicans from coming down here and stealing horses from these Indians." Carson wrote to Governor Meriwether that the Pueblos wanted to send representatives, "but desire that I accompany them." Wary of the governor's close attention to his expense account, he said he would go "if you deemed it advisable for me to go," and would gladly "do all in my power to aid them in making a permanent treaty of peace and friendship with their ancient enemies, the tribes of the plains." Carson's old acquaintance with the Cheyennes and Arapahos probably moved the Taos leaders to ask for his assistance, trusting him to look out for their interests. Probably he was emphasizing through this means his value in Indian relations to a superior who had shown a serious lack of confidence. We will see other evidence that Indians trusted him in a similar situation. In 1858 Carson was able to bring about a successful peace conference between representatives of Taos and the two plains tribes.[79]

It was not the Taos Pueblo people, however, who were the source of Kit's major problems as agent. To judge from the paperwork generated from 1854 to 1861, it was the Utes and the Jicarillas, and their Hispanic and Anglo neighbors, who kept him busy. From his correspondence one becomes aware of how the world was changing in remote northern New Mexico. The hostility of the plains tribes, the expansion of the settlements, and the scarcity of game in the mountains (partly a consequence of that expansion), pushed the Utes and Jicarillas into increasing dependence on the bounty of the federal government, even while they ostensibly continued the traditional lifeway of nomadic hunters. The basis of that life was eroding; either they tried to supplement the diminishing supply of game with the white man's stock, leading to armed conflict, or they turned to the Great Father, and therefore to his representative, Father Kit.

Carson's descriptions of the problem become repetitious, but the repetition is itself eloquent. One of his first communications as agent, in January 1854, deals with the killing of four or five head of cattle and the theft of two horses by some Utes near Culebra. He believed that the thieves were "outcasts and vagabonds" who lived with the Jicarillas, the bulk of the Utes being "as well disposed as ever," but he added, "I have no doubt that the most of the depredations are committed from absolute necessity when in a starving condition." Soon after, he wrote that "the Muhuache Utah Indians are daily coming in here and state that they are in a very deplorable state." He was furnishing them with corn and wheat and wanted to know how far he could go in supplying them, "for if the Government will not do something for them to save them from starving, they will be obliged to steal." In March 1854 he reported the complaint of Juan Benito Valdez and Jesus Maria Sanches about the theft of thirty head of their cattle near Conejos in the San Luis Valley. Accompanied by a dragoon escort, he had searched unsuccessfully for the Indians to demand restitution, and turned back because of cold and snow, traveling two hundred ninety miles on horseback. The experience moved him to his first dissertation on what would become a familiar theme: something had to be done to protect the citizens and their property. Game was becoming scarce in the Ute country, and since the Indians could not support themselves by hunting, the government must "either . . . subsist and clothe them or exterminate them." Shortly after this communication, hostilities with the Jicarillas erupted, Carson having noted that they were "in a starving condition," and having tried to avert trouble by furnishing provisions. Much of his correspondence for the next seven years would be variations of the same theme.[80]

In October 1855, for instance, Kit noted that within five days he had been visited by three different parties of Utes and Jicarillas. He gave them food and clothing, "considering it beneficial for the public service." He assured the acting superintendent, W. W. H. Davis, that he would not give them anything else without instructions, but "I respectfully Suggest that those Indians be furnished with such articles as they actually need, until such time the treaty which they made be approved and they be settled in the Country allotted them." The treaty was Governor Meriwether's agreement, which was never ratified. Carson does not hint here at the disapproval of the treaty that he later expressed. Once again he pointed out the need to supply the Indians, the winter making it impossible for them to hunt successfully. If something was not done, "I am of the opinion that they will have recourse to appropriating the property of citizens of United States, and by their doing that may cause them to murder citizens." He noted "the damages which have been done by those Indians during the last war." Carson may well have grown weary of reiterating these points, for he would still be making them years later, even after his service as agent ended.[81]

Carson was writing about the interlocking effects of Indian-white contact on the frontier following the expansion of settlement. Most of his white contemporaries were most likely to become aroused over the effect of Indian depredations on innocent white people like Ann White, with whom they could easily identify and whose sufferings offended strongly held beliefs and values. Latter-day historians are more likely to concentrate on the injustices and sufferings inflicted on the Indians, far surpassing the troubles of the ultimately victorious whites. For Kit

Carson they were all inseparable facets of the same problem. He had both the advantage and the disadvantage of intimate acquaintance and involvement with each of the different peoples. He could not shed his personal identification with the settlers, Hispanic and Anglo, but neither could he ignore the grim circumstances that increasingly bore on the Indians. Neither the nature of his job nor the knowledge acquired by years of close interaction with the Indians, knowledge equaled by only a handful of white men, would permit the sort of distance from the Indians possible to most settlers, to say nothing of the distance from the problem enjoyed by twentieth-century historians.

In November 1855 he noted the theft of eight animals from the Utes and Jicarillas. Although the act had not occurred within the jurisdiction of his agency, he recommended action to apprehend the thieves:

You are aware that the late war with the Utah Indians was commenced by Mexicans living in the same vicinity—they killing a Utah for the purpose of getting his blankets. If Mexicans continue stealing from the Indians there is no telling to what it may lead—perhaps to war and bloodshed. An Indian cannot do without his horse, especially the Utahs who have always been accustomed to have them, if he loses his horse he loses the means by which he is to gain his subsistence and when lost necessity will compel him to steal.

Carson's disgust over the foolish or wanton acts of individual whites, acts that could mean "war and bloodshed" for many, would manifest itself increasingly. In the same letter he asked that he and another agent, Lorenzo Labadie, be furnished with copies of the main points of Meriwether's treaty, because many people were unaware of what he called "the main point . . . that is, the Indians [ought] to retain the property stolen by them during the war and the government pay the value of the property to their respective owners." If citizens relied on direct action to recoup their losses, serious trouble was likely.[82]

A few days later he asked authorization to employ a lawyer to recover from Antonio José Valdez a mule taken from the Ute chief Blanco, which Valdez claimed had been stolen from him. Blanco, the same man who led the attack on Pueblo just a year before, was now asking the agent for redress, "and I think with good reason." Carson believed that the Utes had observed the treaty faithfully, "and it will have a bad effect if they are allowed to think that the government is not prompt also to observe it." Carson did not doubt that Blanco had taken the mule from

Valdez in the first instance, but there were more important issues at stake, including the good faith of the government he represented.[83]

Carson was not unconcerned about the losses citizens suffered at the hands of Indians. A few days later he forwarded Vicente Martínez's claim for compensation for property taken by Utes and Jicarillas. After the end of the war of 1854–55, these reciprocal thefts of livestock, and occasional individual acts of violence rather than spectacular raids, would be the staple of his communications to higher authority, along with the constant visits of Indians in need of food and clothing. In March 1856 he again noted the "daily begging for food" of Utes and Jicarillas who were "in a deplorable condition," and had lost nearly all their horses during the winter. It would require five or six hundred dollars in the next two months "to Enable them to get allong." It was "very evident that they must be assisted or they will commence their depredations upon the inhabitants." He was unable to look for a site for an agency because of the snow. It would have been a waste of time in any case, since Meriwether's treaty would not be ratified, there would be no reservation, and the agency would still be at his home in Taos when he gave up the post of agent in 1861.[84]

What changed over those years was his emphasis regarding the troubles between whites and Indians. It was only a relative shift in emphasis, because Kit never forgot that white people suffered in Indian wars, and he could never simply say that they deserved what they got. It was obvious to him that the expansion of white settlement meant the displacement of the Indians, with pain and suffering on all sides. It would have been hard for him to assign collective guilt to all settlers. Eventually, however, he would impress listeners with his condemnation of what one witness called "the brutalities and barbarities of the border."

Carson continued to distinguish between groups of Indians on the basis of their actions and of his own prejudices. In August 1856 he wrote Meriwether of depredations by Jicarilla and Mescalero Apaches near Mora: "No murders were committed, but women were ravished, men flogged, and animals driven off— The people finding it useless to report the damage done them, there being but little hope of redress, is the reason of the particulars of the depredations Committed not being transmitted to me." Some visiting Jicarillas had made promises of good behavior, "but little faith Can be placed in the word of a Jicarilla." The Utes, he was convinced, would remain friendly. They complained, however, that their enemies on the plains received arms

INDIAN AGENT

and ammunition and they did not, and Kit thought their complaint justified. He feared that their not receiving "the same fostering care of the government as their enemies" would cause an outbreak. He hoped something might be done, "and I have not the least doubt, as your honor will shortly meet them in council, but that the cause of Arms &c. being retained from them and furnished others will be satisfactorily explained." The last sentence was a dig at Meriwether, but it also shows that he wanted the Utes, his friends and his responsibility, to have a chance to defend themselves.[85]

Carson's willingness to give the Utes the benefit of the doubt is evident. On Christmas Day 1856 he wrote that they promised "future friendship," and he had no doubt they would comply with their promises "if furnished food in Such quantities as they may actually require during the winter months." In the same letter he described a conversation with the head chief of the Muache Utes about the limits of the country claimed by the tribe. The chief, although not named, was probably Kaniache, with whom Kit became well acquainted during this period, and who would serve with him in the wars of the 1860s. The chief was not invariably friendly to whites and had indeed been wounded in a skirmish with some traders and their Arapaho friends a few months earlier. It seems, however, that he frequently visited Kit's house in Taos, and the two became friendly, which proved very much to Carson's benefit on one occasion. Chief Blanco, leader of the attack on Pueblo in 1854, came to Kit's house one day when Kaniache was also visiting, and without dismounting called the agent to the door. Blanco remained on his horse when the rest of his party dismounted, arousing the suspicions of both Carson and Kaniache. Blanco drew his gun, apparently to shoot Carson, and Kaniache quickly grabbed the weapon and pulled it from his grasp. Carson seems to have taken no action against Blanco, which could have sparked wider hostilities; indeed he does not mention the matter in his correspondence. It is unlikely that he forgot Kaniache's saving his life.[86]

One Ute leader was unhappy enough with Carson to try to kill him, and another saw him quite differently. There is only a little contemporary evidence of the tribe's view of him. In his annual report for 1858 as superintendent of Indian affairs for New Mexico, James Collins noted how he had met with the Capote Utes and Jicarillas at Abiquiu, urging them to make peace with the "Upper Arkansas Indians" (the Cheyennes and Arapahos). He found them "not only willing but anxious" to do so, and they agreed to meet their longtime enemies in council "provided

Agent Carson would accompany them and be present in the council." The hopes for peace were dashed by an inopportune Cheyenne incursion, but the condition on which the Ute and Jicarilla leaders were willing to meet the Cheyennes and Arapahos is testimony to their trust in "Father Kit." They were presumably aware of his old acquaintance with the two plains tribes, from each of which he had married wives, and of his knowledge of the Cheyenne tongue. They believed he would look out for their interests, and that his judgment was equal to his knowledge and trustworthiness.[87]

The Capote Utes, included in Collins's council, were not assigned to Carson's agency. However, they came to Taos on occasion for food, as in January 1857, "not being able to move to their proper agency on account of the weakness of their animals and the impassibility of the roads." Carson told them to come in and he would feed them until they could travel, "hoping that it may meet your approbation," as he wrote Governor Meriwether. His action suggests one reason why the Capotes would trust Kit's counsel in negotiations with their enemies. In the summer of 1858, when travel conditions were presumably not a problem, he reported that "Indians not thereto belonging frequent my Agency," specifically Capote Utes, causing him to fear a shortage of rations for issue. Perhaps they knew they would meet with a more sympathetic reception there than from their own agent or, to put it another way, perhaps they found Father Kit a soft touch.[88]

Of concern to Carson, because of the effect on the Utes, was the outbreak of renewed hostilities between the Navajos and the New Mexicans, and hence the involvement of the U.S. Army. This long-standing war had slacked off in the mid-1850s, thanks in part to the efforts of Navajo agent Henry Dodge, but matters deteriorated after Dodge's death in 1856, and with the mishandling of relations by the commander of Fort Defiance, Navajo and New Mexican raids on each other were soon in full swing. At the same time, the Navajos and Utes were also raiding each other. Early in 1858 Carson, in accord with the government policy at the time, had discussed with Ute leaders the possibility of their making peace with the Navajos; their reply was not enthusiastic: "They say that they have no particular desire to make peace, but as it is the wish of the government they will do so. I think that even if peace is made it will not be of long duration." In fact, the Utes walked out on the council when it was held in March, having no confidence in the Navajos. Kit did not think this an altogether bad thing:

The Utahs have no desire to make peace. They say the Navajoes, asking for peace, were at the same time committing depredations, such as stealing stock, murdering citizens of the U. S. & committing depredations in their (Utah) country— I am of opinion, for the benefit of the Utahs, that no treaty was concluded for it will prove more beneficial to them, and the same time be the cause (by the tribes being at war) of the Utahs not joining the Mormons.

White governments since colonial times had promoted conflicts between Indian tribes for their own ends—quite simply, to divide and rule. Carson was not wholly cynical in the matter, since he apparently shared the Utes' distrust of the Navajos; the former were his official concern and he was biased in their favor. The government apparently took the danger of Mormon subversion quite seriously; Kit noted that he had been "ordered to use all means in my power to prevent" the Utes from joining them. In February 1858, setting out for a visit to the Muaches, he asked for a cavalry escort, not for fear of immediate danger but because, "the Department being of opinion that the Utahs are being tampered with by Mormons," he wanted troops with him "so that they may know that troops are in readiness, at my disposal, and if they are guilty of any act against the United States, that it is in my power to punish them." Above all, Carson did not want to see another Indian war in northern New Mexico.[89]

In October 1858, Carson went to Abiquiu "for the purpose of procuring twenty Utahs to accompany the troops operating against the Navajo Indians, as guides and trailers." Neither the Utes nor the Navajos had any sense of solidarity against the whites, and the Utes found the chance of gaining glory and taking stock and captives from their enemies attractive. Kit had already noted at the end of September that "the Utahs are now in the Navajo country," implying that they were operating on their own, with or without official encouragement. In this instance he recruited two chiefs and eighteen warriors, whom he conducted personally to the department commander in Santa Fe. One of them was Kaniache, who returned in late November after serving with a "company of Spies" who scouted for the troops and killed three Navajos. Kaniache and his men, Carson reported, became "dissatisfied with the manner in which the campaign was conducted, not, I presume, being capable of appreciating the mode of operations of a regular army against a savage foe." They set off on their own and surprised five lodges of Navajos, capturing one woman and forty horses.[90]

They brought the woman to Taos to sell to a New Mexican purchaser, in accord with long-standing custom. As Carson reported to Collins, "I thought it better for the squaw to be with me than with Mexicans or Utahs. I therefore purchased her of the Utahs, gave them three horses and other articles, the sum of $300 in all. The squaw shall remain in my possession subject to your orders. I am ready to deliver her to the Navajos by their paying me the sum I gave for her or they may have her without paying the sum as you may direct." As noted, this was not the first time Carson had purchased a captive from Indians. We will see that the woman probably stayed with him for some years. This was not an isolated, individual act on Carson's part, but a reflection of the society in which he lived.[91]

There was a trade in captives among many Indian tribes of the West before the Spanish and other Europeans ever appeared there, and the New Mexican colonists readily adopted it. Spanish government policy declared it a Christian duty to ransom captives, who then were obligated to work off their ransom for their benefactors. Because it was officially prohibited to enslave Indians, this was one answer to the need for labor. Many were purchased from captors among the plains tribes, and the Utes captured people in the Great Basin for sale in New Mexico. As hostilities with the Navajos increased, it was natural to take or purchase captives from among the enemy. By the time Carson arrived in New Mexico, the custom was something practiced from time immemorial. The assumption, under the Spanish regime at any rate, was that when the ransomed captive had worked off his or her price, he or she was free. This commonly meant becoming part of the lower stratum of Hispanic society, or sometimes joining an Indian pueblo. Former captives were called *genízaros*, after the Turkish Janissaries, and some settlements were established especially for them, often as frontier outposts. These captives were clearly in servitude, and were not free to leave until they worked off their ransom. Many lost their tribal affiliation, especially if captured young. Yet the institution was substantially different from plantation slavery in the Old South. Freed *genízaros* were often employed as scouts and military auxiliaries, not a role the southern slaveholder was likely to consider for his human property. An Indian was in servitude not simply because of his race, but because of the circumstance of his captivity, often because a state of war existed with his people. Poor Hispanic folk could also be held in servitude for debt as peons, sometimes for life. It was the custom to baptize these captives, with their masters as godparents, incorporating them as part of the patriarchal family.[92]

Anglo-Americans who settled in New Mexico under Mexican rule or later seem to have had few qualms about adopting this practice. Of course many of them, like Carson, came from slaveholding states and would not have seen the servitude of non-whites as remarkable. Kit's friend, Lucien Maxwell, had Navajo children as servants in his homes at Rayado and Cimarron. It was reported that in the 1860s the governor of New Mexico and other territorial officials had them in their homes. The status of Navajos, direct enemies of New Mexico and often taken captive by New Mexicans and not by Indian intermediaries, may have been different from that of other ransomed captives, and they may have been, in Lawrence Murphy's words, "forced to carry out the most burdensome and disagreeable tasks with little hope of freedom." In a few instances they were set free by U.S. courts, but few of them would have been aware of this recourse.[93]

The parish records of Our Lady of Guadalupe Church in Taos show the baptism of three Navajos "in the charge of Cristoval Carson." Two were christened on December 23, 1860, by Father Gabriel Ussel, with Kit and Josefa's children William (Julian) and Teresina, both young children themselves, as godparents. The two young Navajos were Juan, age thirteen or fourteen, and Juan Bautista, age five. Father Ussel noted that the Carsons had adopted these children "according to the custom of the country." Ussel was not a native New Mexican but a Frenchman, part of Bishop John Lamy's program to reform the New Mexican church. If he found anything about the situation or the status of the youngsters improper, his disapproval was not strong enough to induce him to refuse baptism. On September 9, 1864, a twenty-year-old Navajo woman named Maria Dolores was baptized by Father José Maria Coudert, who noted simply that she had been "held for the last six years in the house of Kitt Carson and Josefa Jaramillo." From the dates, it seems likely that she was the woman Carson ransomed from the Utes in 1858. Concerning one of the two boys, probably little Juan Bautista, Kit's son Christopher Junior—also known as Kit—had a story he told many years later:

A party of Utes came along from a fight with Navajos. A three-year-old boy of that tribe had been captured. The Ute chief told mother that the boy was a bother to them and they intended to kill him. She knew an appeal for his life would be useless so she asked what they would sell him for. A horse was named as the price, which mother immediately gave them and took the boy into our home. Later father adopted him and gave him the name of Juan Carson. He lived to young manhood, married a Mexican girl, but not long afterward died. I have his picture.

The younger Kit would have been only two at the time of the boy's baptism, so his account of how the youngster came to the family was obviously based on what he remembered being told by his parents and siblings. That Kit Jr. still had Juan's picture in 1924, and that a photograph was made at all, shows that the boy meant something to him and to the rest of the family. Juan's marriage shows that, like so many other captives, he became a part of New Mexican society in a way not conceivable for a southern slave. Kit Jr. also tells how, during the Confederate invasion of 1862, his family fled from Taos, and his mother, for fear of meeting rebel stragglers, "concealed her valuables in the garments of a faithful Navajo girl servant [possibly Maria Dolores] she had raised from babyhood."94

The documentary evidence does not really reveal the attitude of Kit and Josefa Carson toward these Navajos in their home, whether they were first of all bond servants, captives ransomed out of compassion, or adopted family members. Their baptism was important, but it was not unusual—"the custom of the country," as Father Ussel noted. Kit claimed that it was better for Maria Dolores "to be with me than with Mexicans or Utahs," and he was probably right. By 1864, however, she had been with him for six years. During most of that time the Navajos and New Mexicans had been engaged in some degree of hostility, which would have made it difficult to return her to her people. There were a few months of relative peace in 1861, just at the time when the beginning of the Civil War was seriously disrupting conditions in New Mexico and Carson was becoming involved in military activities. Whatever the custom, it seems doubtful that a priest would have baptized someone her age if she had been obviously unwilling, however optimistic he may have been about her conversion. Female captives in such a situation are obviously vulnerable to sexual exploitation, and undoubtedly they often were in New Mexico. There is no evidence that this was the case with Maria Dolores. Those who wish to believe the worst about Carson are free to do so, but his known tender heart offers as good an explanation as any for the acquisition of the two boys, and of the young woman as well. It probably never occurred to him that anyone would find anything wrong with his solution to the problem of how they should be provided for. That there was anything wrong with cutting them off from their cultural heritage also probably never entered his mind.

It requires a real effort to recapture the world view of nineteenth-century New Mexicans, for whom the Navajos were not the victims of others' rapacity and racism but the scourges of New Mexico, perpetrators of innumerable raids in which thousands of head of horses, cattle, and sheep were carried off and hundreds of ordinary, unoffending people, herders, and inhabitants of small villages and ranchos were killed or made captive. To them it seemed reasonable and justifiable, a custom sanctioned by long practice, to exact some degree of retribution by taking Navajos captive in turn. That the Navajos would see the matter quite differently is obvious. That the practice was pernicious in the extreme, not least in the exacerbation of existing hatreds, is also obvious. It was a miserable situation, and Kit Carson would be deeply and crucially involved in its eventual resolution.

Carson certainly knew that the practice of captive servitude was often far from benign. In January 1859 he wrote to Superintendent Collins about "an Apache girl aged 11 or 12 years," who had been captured by U.S. troops ten years before and given to a New Mexican lady. She had come to Carson for protection: "The girl was nearly naked. Had on her person sign of maltreatment." He took her into his house and gave her clothing, intending, if Collins approved, "to give her to some respectable person that can give me good security of treating her properly." He noted that she "prefers returning to her people," but he apparently did not favor that step. Why the abused girl concluded that Kit was the person to appeal to is not known. He does not say why he did not favor returning her to the Apaches, or whether she was a Jicarilla (as seems likely) or of some other Apache group. Carson also says nothing about any living relatives. There were exchanges of captives after the end of hostilities in 1855. She was still a child and few nineteenth-century adults would have considered her wishes binding in such circumstances, not even the former runaway apprentice Kit Carson. The following April, Kit wrote Collins that he was sending the "Indian girl" to him with an escort, "for fear the Apaches, not knowing where she was going, might take her." Perhaps it was because she had been at least partially assimilated and baptized a Christian that neither man was willing to adopt what now seems the easy and obvious solution. The history of the Indian wars offers many instances, on both sides, of unwillingness to return assimilated child captives.[95]

Utes who were supposed to be assigned to the agency at Abiquiu continued to appear on Kit's doorstep asking for food, prompting him to complain in July 1858 about Diego Archuleta, the agent at the other post. Apparently, Collins raised some question about Kit's feeding these Indians, informing him that Archuleta had already provisioned them, for he wrote, "if the amount you state was judiciously given to the Indians of the Abiquiu Agency there would have been no necessity of Indians of said Agency coming to me for food, and I gave unto them as they appeared on the point of starvation. Whether Agent Archuleta acted discreetly or no in the issue of provisions I cannot say." He noted that he had three times the number of people to be fed at his agency, "not including those that frequent it," as at Abiquiu. While Kit did not have much to say about other officials of the Bureau of Indian Affairs in his correspondence as agent, he would eventually have a good deal to say about the shortcomings of those charged with executing government policy, another aspect of the "Indian problem" with which he was becoming well-acquainted.[96]

Shortly after, he expressed his opinion of a proposal for moving the Jicarillas to the agency at Abiquiu. They might go if the government promised to feed them, for there was not enough game in the vicinity of the town. They were willing to work; those around Taos were assisted by New Mexicans who bought their pots and baskets and hired them to work. They did not trouble him much for food but hunted around the Spanish Peaks and on the plains. It would not be practical to move them from the settlements "unless forming them in a settlement to be fed and guarded by govt. until able to feed and protect themselves." With the Utes it was different; in spite of his fondness for them, he noted, "They are in no way industrious. Provisions they expect of government, in fact they think presents are given them, through fear, to keep them at peace." Industriousness was defined in the white man's terms; the Utes were not interested in agriculture, however hard they might work at hunting, and getting them to change would be difficult. Once again he noted the scarcity of game in their country, compelling them to come to the settlements for food. "Such will be the case until colonized, and in colonies they will not remain unless troops are placed . . . to protect them from their enemies and then they will not remain if not compelled to do so. I am of opinion that for the benefit of the Indian, he should be made [to] do as government directs and not as he wishes himself." Carson here stated the essence of government policy for many years to come. The reservation system was designed to save the Indians in a particular fashion, whether the Indians liked the method or not. Kit believed in the inescapable necessity for such a policy as much as its formulators in Washington.[97]

In his annual report for 1858, Superintendent Collins wrote of the Muache Utes that, in the opinion of Agent Carson, "there is a growing spirit of insubordination strangely manifested among them, which he fears will have to be subdued by the military arm . . . before they can be induced to settle and become cultivators of the soil." Collins noted the ill effects of the Utes' contact with the settlements, especially drinking, as the reason they needed to be settled somewhere, also noting that they were becoming "less submissive" by such interaction. The communication from Carson cited just above may have been Collins's source, although Carson did not explicitly mention any "spirit of insubordination."[98]

In his own annual report for 1858, Carson asserted that the Indians had committed few depredations: "They stole some animals from the Mexicans, and the Mexicans also stole some from them. The Indians gave me the animals stolen by them, and I made the Mexicans return the animals they had stolen, thus satisfying both parties."

His principal concern in this report was the need for a permanent reserve.

It would promote the advance of civilization among the Indians of this agency if it were practicable that I could live with them. They have no particular place to reside, are of a roving nature, and an agent could not be with them at all times, so I have selected this place as the most proper for them to receive such presents of food as they need; and such will necessarily be the case until agency buildings are built. The Indians should be settled on reserves, guarded by troops, and made to cultivate the soil, because the required amount of provisions to be given them cannot be procured at any of the frontier settlements.

He returned yet again to his old refrain: "To keep the Indians from committing depredations on citizens, food by the government must be provided them, and liberally, there being no game of any consequence in the country through which they roam." He realized that the Utes and Jicarillas, especially the former, had no desire to settle down as farmers and would have to be compelled. He also knew that the current situation, besides being unsatisfactory for all concerned, could not endure indefinitely.[99]

Since Carson maintained that the Utes were committing few "depredations," the "growing spirit of insubordination" noted by Superintendent Collins presumably referred to dissatisfaction with the overall situation. Carson thought the Utes regarded government annuities as a form of "protection money," given out of fear to keep them peaceful, an attitude he probably found irritating, although he constantly repeated that it was, in fact, necessary to feed the Indians to keep them from making off with other people's livestock. His references to "punishing" or "chastising" the Indians, to show that the government had the power to enforce its wishes, came usually at periods when the Indians had committed violence or seemed likely to; to that he could never be indifferent. There is little evidence, however, that he habitually adopted the brusque, dictatorial style of some agents of the later reservation era. There are, instead, accounts of his spending hours in traditional council negotiations, smoking the pipe and conversing verbally or in sign language.[100]

The mutual "depredations" between the Indians and their white neighbors became an increasing concern for Carson. In August 1858 he noted seven head of animals stolen by Indians: "They have given them to me and I will deliver them to the owners." Citizens had stolen three animals from the Indians, "which I will endeavor to recover and return to them so that they may have no cause of dissatisfaction." At the end of the same year he noted that "the Indians under my charge have conducted themselves in a creditable manner," committing no depredations, and reporting no animals stolen from *them*. "If citizens do not steal from, or molest the Indians of this agency I would never have the duty to perform of reporting Indian depredations." He had "checked the desire of stealing from Indians" by recovering their lost property and returning it. He acknowledged that it was more difficult to recover animals stolen by Indians than by citizens. "So long as both citizens and Indians are honest their [*sic*] will not be much difficulty of keeping the Indians in their present friendly state." He did not want to be understood as accusing citizens in general of dishonesty:

"I only allude to a class of person, that unfortunately reside among us, who are, in the estimation of all intelligent persons, inferior to the Indian." Carson apparently had not come to the point of condemning the whole society to which he belonged for the state of the Indians or of Indian-white relations. There would have been little satisfaction and less hope in that, since he was engaged not in an intellectual exercise but in a search for practical solutions to immediate, pressing problems. In the same report, he recommended increasing the allowance of food for the next two months (January and February 1859) because of the poor condition of the Indians' horses: "If an Indian's horse is not fit for service he can aid but little toward his maintainance." These continual reflections on the theft of small numbers of animals, and on the well-being of horses, are far from the drama and heartrending tragedy of so many accounts of Indian-white relations on the frontier, but they represented a common reality, denoting the importance of these animals to stockraising communities, which only a few can appreciate today. To the Utes and Jicarillas, dependent on game and hence on mobility, their mounts were of vital importance. Carson's efforts to recover stolen animals were far from trivial in the eyes of the Indians and white people living in northern New Mexico.[101]

In 1886 General George Crook said that it was his policy not to give the Indians grievances to brood over. Seemingly small troubles could accumulate until one more proved too much and violence followed, "and the people at large, who never see anything but the last straw, exclaim, 'Why, what fiends to break out for such a trifle!' " Kit's frequent references to the satisfaction or dissatisfaction of the Indians regarding their annuities and the treatment they received, and his concern that the Indians not see the government as breaking faith with them, show how well he understood Crook's principle of settling grievances as soon as possible. He would also have understood another of the general's pronouncements: "No one else in the world is so quick to see and to resent any treachery as is the Indian. You can do nothing toward his management unless you have his confidence." Circumstances, however, would force Carson to agree with yet another of Crook's observations: "It is a poor sort of honor, though a popular one, which holds that decency is to be used only toward white folks, and that when you lie to an Indian or swindle him, it doesn't count."[102]

The underlying cause of dissatisfaction, of course, was that the Indians were being displaced in their own country by newcomers, were being circumscribed both physically and emotionally, deprived of their land and way of life and reduced to dependency. Carson was, of necessity, dealing with the resulting problems piecemeal, but he knew that some broader solution was necessary, and the need was becoming ever more acute. In November 1858 he had to write to Collins asking to draw on official funds to operate the agency: "I have nearly expended my available private funds and as I do not wish to incur any debts is my reason for addressing you." It is doubtful if he had anticipated having to spend his own money to keep the operation going when he took the job. Unwillingness to turn Indians away completely empty-handed seems a likely explanation. Through the winter of 1858–59 he continued to report "no depredations" by the Utes or Jicarillas. Again the following April he had to ask Collins for money, having spent "every dollar of my private money," because he always paid on the spot for purchases, "whether govt. money is in my hands or no." The Indians having departed, saying they would not return until July, he wrote, "God grant it— They have nearly worried me to death."[103]

In February Kit hurried to Rayado with twelve cavalrymen because of a report that Comanches were there, but the plains warriors had already departed, having been received hospitably and having caused no trouble. They said they had been told by "Mexican traders" that "in the spring U. S. troops would enter their country and there remain for the purpose of fighting them." Rayado residents had told them "that the talk of Mexican traders was not always to be relied on." These traders were the comancheros, New Mexicans who had traded with the Comanches since the two peoples had made peace in the 1780s. As hostilities between Anglo-Americans and Comanches intensified, the former, including Carson, would increasingly cast a jaundiced eye on the traders, who were suspected of trafficking in goods and stock stolen in Texas, besides providing the Indians with arms and information about military movements. U.S. troops were operating in Comanche country in 1858–59, striking their camps in Kansas and Indian Territory, though they were not based in New Mexico. In 1860, however, troops would march from New Mexico to attack the "Lords of the South Plains" on their home ground, and a few years later Kit would be bound east on a similar mission. The Comanches were starting to show

INDIAN AGENT

hostility toward New Mexico, but on this occasion the only Indians seeking trouble were fifteen Utes who arrived at Rayado at the same time as Carson, looking for the Comanches; Kit "told them that they ought not to be at war with other Indians unless the government wished it."[104]

About this same time, Kit traveled to Hatch's Ranch on the edge of the plains to meet some Comanche chiefs, who did not appear. Since the Comanches were not in any way part of his official responsibility, he may have been acting on a special request from either his superiors or the Utes. On the way back he passed through Mora, where the citizens were "in a great state of excitement" over the presence of Indians nearby and had called for troops. Mora was where "women were ravished, men flogged, and animals driven off" by Apaches in 1856, so the people's fear was understandable. The military commander, having just arrived from Fort Union, "offered me any military aid I should require," but Kit declined, "fearing that a display of troops would intimidate the Indians and cause them to flee to unprotected parts of the country where they would undoubtedly commit depredations." He proceeded to the Indians' camp, consisting primarily of Jicarillas and perhaps some Utes, who said they would go wherever Carson directed. He sent most of them west of the Rio Grande, some of the Jicarillas camping near Cienguilla, where he was sure "there will be no danger of any difficulty occurring caused by them" because they were used to living near New Mexicans in that area. Between the lines one can read the satisfaction of the old mountain man at having settled without trouble a situation that in the hands of someone less experienced might have led to bloodshed and destruction.[105]

The actions of traders were of concern closer to home. In 1856 a local justice of the peace, Jésus Maria Velasques, had informed Carson that two residents of Abiquiu, Pedro Leon Luhan and Tomás Chacon, were transporting lead, bullets, and powder into the Ute country, in such quantities that it was obvious they intended trading. Kit, however, knew that the Indians needed ammunition for hunting and self-defense against other Indians. But Velasques's concern shows how many settlers felt about armed Utes on the frontier, and neither Carson nor his neighbors could forget that some Utes had been using their guns for another purpose only recently. The free and easy frontier trade was also taking on another aspect as the settlement frontier pressed harder on the Indians.[106]

That pressure would soon increase dramatically, and it would be very much Carson's concern. In 1858 gold was discovered in the mountains of what was then the western part of Kansas Territory, soon to become Colorado. The Utes, already pressed by New Mexican settlement from the south, were now to be confronted with the sort of influx of whites that had swamped California, predominantly young males with little knowledge of Indians and inclined to think that there were no rules in the Wild West. Parties of hopeful prospectors would be swarming through the Utes' hunting grounds, some of them meaning no harm, but others all too ready to disregard the humanity, to say nothing of the sensitivities, of the inhabitants. In April 1859 Carson wrote that he was going on a trip "to recover Indian horses" and then would proceed to the mines: "My object is to prevent any difficulty arising between the miners and Utahs—." He had been informed that the miners intended to enter the Valle Salado, which he noted was "the only hunting ground the Muahuaches have. . . . should they on their arrival, find parties of whites thereon I fear difficulties would arise." The "difficulties" could be avoided, he thought, if both parties were informed first and did not meet unexpectedly. He also requested a leave of thirty or forty days, which does not suggest great apprehension.[107]

As Kit journeyed north, he met a traveler from the newly founded town of Denver who told him that miners had killed a Ute, and that the Utes were suspected of committing "many thefts." Carson obtained a small escort of soldiers from Fort Garland. When they discovered a large Indian trail, including the tracks of shod horses, he concluded that the Indians had been stealing from whites, but "not knowing whether blood had been shed on either side," he "thought it prudent to retreat." He explained that when a Ute died it was customary to kill one or more persons from another nation: "I have Known as many as four Mexicans to have been Killed as payment for loss of one Utah who died of disease." Since he did not know the attitude of the Utes at the moment and had only a small escort, he had made a "retrograde movement." This caution reflected the hard lessons of a lifetime. Kit was no longer a reckless, combative young mountain man, but a middle-aged family man who did not have to prove anything to himself or to others. If violence had already broken out, his value as a mediator, with little force behind him, would be limited.[108]

Just to illustrate his usual remarks about the difficulty the Utes had in subsisting themselves, he added that in a journey of 250 miles, "I did not see game enough to subsist two lodges one day." He also noted that he had sent word to the miners that they should treat the Indians "humanely." "If they endeavor to drive [out] the Indian he will object and do all in his power to retard their progress which can be easily done by him, being in his own country, & the miners necessarily divided in small parties and unacquainted with the country."[109]

A little later he learned that Arapahos, not Utes, had stolen horses from the miners, and the Utes had then stolen from the Arapahos. Some travelers who had just passed through the Valle Salado had spoken highly of the behavior of the Utes, being "more friendly and hospitable than the prairie Indians." Said Kit: "I think the Utahs will remain friendly so long as treated in proper manner by emigrants."[110]

Carson continued to express hope through June that all would be well, declaring that the Utes were "conducting themselves very well." Though granted leave at the end of June, he did not take it, having learned first that some Utes had stolen horses from miners, and then that two whites had been killed. Some two hundred miners were out seeking retribution. "Since the discovery of those mines," he wrote, "I feared such an outbreak. It has come sooner than I expected." Perhaps his earlier optimism had been whistling in the dark. His first reaction was to hope that the perpetrators, whom he believed to be Tabeguache Utes, would be "summarily punished." A brother of the deceased Muache chief Blanco accused the Tabeguaches and offered the services of Muaches against them: "He speaks sensibly saying that the whites not knowing the guilty from the innocent one is as likely to be punished as the other and as the Muahuaches are innocent it would be safer for them to accompany any expedition that may go against the Tabawaches than to remain in the country the expedition would pass through." Carson said he would ask the Muaches to come to the Conejos River, where he would speak with them.[111]

A week later, however, he had received information that "the Muaches were as much interested in the killing as the Tabawaches," and were trying to conceal the fact. He sent word to them that he would give them no food "till the matter was duly investigated, and that if guilty they would be punished." The murderers should be delivered up for punishment. Carson was probably angry at being lied to, but he insisted that "if the Utahs are allowed to go unpunished for such deeds there is no telling what next they may do." He wanted them to "feel the consequence of acting in bad faith." Breaking faith, to a backcountry man or an Indian, was a very serious matter indeed; the mountain men had depended on the observance of such rules, and reacted to their violation by seeking retribution. Carson asked Collins for instructions but said he had already informed the Muaches that the inescapable condition was that the murderers be given up.[112]

Carson believed, on the basis of information he had received, some of it from a Muache living at Taos Pueblo, that the killings were committed in the course of horse stealing, and that the Utes were the ones at fault. He touched on one of the hardest questions of Indian-white relations of the period: the administering of justice for individual acts. Carson knew well how hard it was to punish a white man for killing an Indian; he complained several times about the lack of justice in such cases. White perpetrators, if arrested, were likely to escape or to be acquitted by white juries. Indians, in turn, were deeply reluctant to give up members of their own tribe to white justice. There was no reciprocity, since white murderers were never turned over to Indian justice and seldom punished by whites. Moreover, just like the whites, Indians were reluctant to punish one of their own for killing an outsider. At the same time, the Indians were sometimes willing to accept the payment of blood money, which to the whites was wholly inadequate when one of their own was killed by an Indian.[113]

By mid-August, however, Kit had cooled down, as far as the Muaches were concerned, and was issuing their annuity goods as usual; the goods for the Tabeguaches he wanted kept at Taos "till such time as the band are properly disposed towards the U. S." He had heard that the Tabeguaches intended to fight, and that it would do no good for him to go and talk with them. The leader in the killing was the brother of the band chief and was unlikely to be given up. If he had to go see them, he would need "an escort sufficiently strong to intimidate them"; otherwise, he and the escort would likely be attacked, "and you can easily imagine the result." One can imagine David Meriwether's knowing smile if he had read those words, but Kit was not going to be a "damn fool" to no purpose. He urged that mounted troops be stationed on the Conejos to protect the frontier settlements.[114]

Both Carson and Collins took note of the troubles in Colorado in their annual reports for 1859. Collins declared his belief that Indians should always be "taught to respect an American wherever they meet one," and added, "My policy would be never to allow a murder or robbery to go unpunished." Having made it clear that he was not soft on Indians, Collins pointed out "that our countrymen often act with great imprudence in reference to the Indians," going into Indian country in small parties, "entirely beyond the reach of protection," with good horses, rifles, and other equipment offering temptation. "Men who are strangers to Indians, entirely unaccustomed to their habits and characters, are very apt, when they see one, in place of showing him some act of kindness, to insult him by driving or, perhaps, kicking him out of camp." The ideas Collins expressed are very similar to ones Carson had set out before and would again.[115]

Carson devoted most of his annual report for that year to the troubles in Colorado. He was now convinced that the Muache Utes had had no part in the troubles, except for one outcast from the band. The Muaches had come in and reported the circumstances to him, and he believed them. The principal men wanted peace and had decided to remain near the agency to prove their good faith, "and that I may be satisfied that they take no part with the perpetrators of these outrages." However, he reported, "the proceedings of the Tobawatches have been different." They had retreated to their country on the Grand River, and had sent word that if the authorities wanted them, they could send troops after them. All available troops, however, were campaigning against the Navajos. Kit believed that "the consequences of letting these Indians go unpunished will be injurious. . . . I have every reason to fear that in the spring they will visit us, and do much damage to the unprotected northern settlements of this Territory, in which marauding expedition they will be joined by the Muahuaches, if the latter band is not well treated during the winter."

In the last few years, however, few thefts had been committed by the Muaches, and Kit had been able to recover the animals taken. Contrary to an earlier observation, he reported, "In making these exchanges of property between the Mexicans and Indians, I meet with much more difficulty in tracing and recovering stock stolen from the Indians by Mexicans than from the Indians: the Mexicans seem mostly to have the advantage in these thefts." Carson knew all too well the obstacles the frontier settlers put in the way of keeping peace. The condition of the Indians themselves he saw as grim; the numbers of the Muaches and Tabeguaches, he believed, were in decline, from diseases and conflict with hostile tribes. The solution he proposed, as always, was that "they shall be settled on reserves, and compelled to cultivate the soil for their maintenance." They had no interest in "self-support," at least not of the sort whites recognized as such, and "they will continue to sink deeper into degredation, so long as a generous government, or their habits of begging and stealing, afford them a means of subsistence." Carson's mode of expression was ethnocentric, but the situation was surely as grim as his description.[116]

Carson, it should be remembered, was not describing a proudly independent people living and supporting themselves purely by hunting in the traditional way of their ancestors, but a people becoming increasingly dependent for subsistence on the government, which provided neither lavishly nor dependably. The expansion of white settlement into the mountains, which could only be expected to continue, would increasingly deprive them of their hunting grounds and freedom of movement. Their decline in numbers, to whatever cause it was attributed, could also be expected to continue until some change took place. Their continuing contact with whites promoted the spread of alcoholism. And as both New Mexican settlers and Colorado miners generated friction by impinging on their lands, renewed conflict was an ever-present possibility. Carson might be bound to the work ethic, but there were immediate, pragmatic reasons to want to see the Utes and Jicarillas settled at a distance from whites, where they could support themselves by farming.[117]

In late August 1859, Carson reported the killing of five white miners and two Indians in an attack by the Tabeguaches. He recommended no one be allowed to trade with these Utes, since they would only supply themselves with ammunition. He believed that if no action were taken the Tabeguaches would think the government timorous and attack the settlements. The Muaches he believed were acting in good faith, refusing to deal with the hostiles: "I will do all in my power to retain their friendship and keep them from joining the hostile band." Collins should take a strong escort when going to give presents to the Utes. To add a little more to Kit's difficulties, John Mostin was suffering from the ailment that would kill him in October, just when Carson planned to travel to Conejos to meet with the Muaches and warn them to have nothing to do with the Tabeguaches[118]

Superintendent Collins wanted Carson to join him in distributing goods to Utes at Abiquiu, presumably because of his knowledge and influence, but Kit had to give out goods to the Indians of his own agency at the Conejos River and did not think he could make both meetings. At the Conejos he found himself in the middle of another of those incidents that confirmed his belief that the different peoples should be separated.[119]

On September 14 near the village of San Antonio, in present southern Colorado near the Conejos, an Indian picked a roasting ear in a cornfield. A New Mexican followed him and, Carson reported:

> They had a few words & clinched, the Mexican was stabbed pretty severely in the back by an arrow, the Mexican then got a club and beat the Indian, from the effects of which he will in all probability die— The Indians immediately commenced surrounding fully armed, an express was sent for me I immediately proceeded to the place of difficulty and found them much enraged and I do believe if I had not gone the Indians would have massacred all in the town.

He was able to pacify them, and on the twentieth secured a promise that they would remain quiet. Many Muaches were on the Conejos awaiting the distribution of goods, and the situation remained tense. Apparently the Utes were supposed to wait for the distribution until Collins's arrival. Carson decided instead to issue the goods immediately so that the Indians would not have to remain in the area, "for if put off they would think I had some object in view such as calling troops &c." In words that might sum up his whole tenure as Indian agent, as well as the immediate situation, Kit said, "I do not know whether I done rite or wrong, but I done what I thought was best. It was impossible to keep the Indians there any longer therefore I made the issue." The rest of the report showed his concern that his initiative in this matter should not cause any financial problems or confuse the paperwork.[120]

In October came a break in the difficulties with the Tabeguache Utes. Carson left Taos on the twenty-fourth to travel to Abiquiu, where he stayed at the house of Albert Pfeiffer, then subagent for the Utes at that agency and later Kit's comrade in the Indian campaigns of the 1860s. From Abiquiu Carson wrote Collins that he intended to meet with the Tabeguache Utes and that it would be good if Collins could be there, but if he could not, "give to me & Pfeiffer authority to give them their gratification." He wanted "to start them up now that they are good & peaceably disposed." In his next monthly report he described having "a long talk" with the Tabeguaches: "They say they were not engaged in the massacre, and promising to act in good faith in the future. I accompanied them to the Conejos, and there delivered them their presents, I believing this to be the best course to be pursued with them —.... they promise to use their influence with all other bands, and make peace with the whites."

Kit says nothing about the chastisement he had earlier believed necessary for the Tabeguaches. Here he had seized an opportunity to pacify a group of Indians by hearing them out and, very likely, letting them know that they still had a chance to make peace and they had better take it. His initial reaction to the attacks on miners had been to take a hard line, but when he had to act, "the best course to be pursued" was that of negotiation. (In the same letter he reported the death of John Mostin on October 29, 1859.)[121]

At the end of November he was complaining of "much difficulty and trouble" caused by the almost daily visits of the Muaches. Conflicts with the plains tribes kept them from hunting and "they must be fed by Government." The activities of Indians farther away also caused problems; on a visit to Mora he took from a New Mexican, probably a comanchero trader, a white boy who, it later proved, had been captured by Kiowas at Fredericksburg, Texas. From the description Carson sent out, the boy's father, H. Hoerster, recognized him and wrote to Kit. Ransoming Texas captives had become frequent and fairly profitable in both New Mexico and Indian Territory as the unnamed comanchero would have known, although he may also have felt compassion for the boy. There is no sign that Kit saw any inconsistency in the retaining of Indian captives in the society in which he lived and the effort he made to return the Hoerster boy. In the same period he was inquiring, at the request of the government, into "the abduction of an American Lady from Texas," promising to do everything in his power.[122]

The usual problems continued as 1860 opened. Collins returned an account to him because of errors. Salvador Lucero complained that the Utes had stolen four head of his cattle, and Kit wrote, "He appears to be a very Candid Man, and his affidavit may be true." The theft of Lucero's animals he thought likely to be retaliation for the stealing of thirty Ute horses by Mexicans. The Indians continued to visit the Taos agency:

Scarcely a day passes but I have from five to twenty five to feed and take care of, their only resource is upon Government and as they come in I must provide for them and send them away, only to be visited again when their supplies are exhausted, and in this way some

INDIAN AGENT

band of them are my daily visitors. I have made the expenses as small as possible, but notwithstanding, they have been very heavy for the month.

Kit knew very well the Indian belief that those who were comfortable must assist those who were in need, but he had also been made aware that accounts must be kept in order and that the government's bounty was finite.[123]

In February 1860, Carson acknowledged receiving two land warrants for Indians, probably warrants for some of the Taos Pueblo men who had served in the campaigns of 1854–55 — nearly six years delayed. He wrote that he would "dispose of them to the best possible advantage and see that the Indians receive the full advantage of them." Probably the Indians did not intend to settle outside the pueblo but wanted the money from the sale of the warrants. Situations like this offered white men opportunities to cheat Indians, but nothing in Kit's record indicates that he would do this. Apparently Albert Pfeiffer had complained of having too many Tabeguache Utes descending on his agency for food, for Carson told Collins, "I do not know what more I can do than I am doing every day, it is very certain Mr. Pfeiffer cannot have them all, as there has not been a day for the last month but there has been a band of them at this agency." Wheat and corn were scarce and the price was going up, "but it Must be had at some price, and these Indians fed or they will steal." At the end of the month he noted that "no complaints of theft or other depredations have come to me." However, he had "a constant delegation calling for food," and since game was very scarce, he had to issue food daily "to keep them from starving or stealing." The Utes were "very anxious to go on the campaign against Navajos Inds." that was being planned. Later in the year, in fact, Kaniache and Carson's subagent, Albert Pfeiffer, would lead an officially sanctioned raid against the Navajos that would kill six and net nineteen captives, five hundred horses, and five thousand sheep. The connection between the raid and the scarcity of game was not stated, but the authorities no doubt preferred that the Utes satisfy their needs at the expense of a common enemy rather than from United States citizens.[124]

In April Carson again went to the Conejos River to meet Muache and Tabeguache Utes, whom he described as "in a poor condition." He did not have enough food for them all: "some twenty-five or thirty squaws went away without anything." All he could tell them was to hunt and supply their own needs. They were conducting themselves well, and he believed would continue friendly. "I have cautioned them against troubling or having anything to do with the Miners and they have promised me to do so." Any complaint he had about the shortage of supplies was implied rather than explicit, whatever he may have said to Collins in conversation. The superintendent was no more responsible for the congressional appropriation than he was.[125]

In June Kit made a trip to Pike's Peak and Denver to evaluate the situation there, finding "a very friendly feeling existing between the Utahs and Miners," a feeling he thought would continue "so long as the Miners are judicious in their intercourse with them." He wrote, "I have Cautioned them to be very discreet with the Utahs, and they have promised to treat them fairly and friendly so long as the Indians commit no depredations on them." It is not clear whether Carson was really as optimistic as he appears in this report. He certainly knew that it took only the irresponsible actions of a few on one side or the other to precipitate conflict. Relative peace with the Utes had been preserved since 1855 in spite of the strains his reports chronicled.[126]

These strains figured in his annual report for 1860. Once again he reported the Utes to be on friendly terms with the whites, but conditions for the Indians were getting worse:

The hunting grounds of the Tabahuaches being in the section of country where the whites are in search of gold, their game is becoming scarce; much of it having been killed by the settlers, and a great deal of it driven from the country. Hence it will be absolutely necessary to feed them during the approaching winter months. . . . They . . . do not appear to be entirely satisfied with the encroachments upon what they are accustomed to consider their rights; but as long as the whites do not interfere with them or sell them intoxicating beverages, I think they will continue friendly with the people.

The Muaches, whom earlier he had reported to be unaffected by alcohol, were now "constantly becoming more and more addicted to the use of ardent spirits." He had done everything he could to find out who was selling them the liquor, without success. Once again Kit proposed the only solution he could think of: "to have them settled on reserves, and furnished with a few good farmers and mechanics." Kit continued: "It is true that the older members of the tribes, who are confirmed in their present habits of life, might be obstinate in their resistance to the change; but they, in the course of nature, must pass away in a few years, and the young generation . . . can be educated in such a manner as to make them submit to the habits and customs of civilized life. To effect this reformation will be required the labor of years."

Carson was realistic regarding the conservatism of the older generation of Indians. Where the children were concerned, he sounds as optimistic as any well-meaning reformer in Boston or Washington. It is doubtful that he envisioned forcible carting off of Indian children to schools where they would be physically punished (a rarity among most Indians) for any failure to observe alien customs, or even for speaking their own language, and where many would die of tuberculosis and other diseases. The man who had not even managed to learn to read in his own language probably did not give the details of such education much thought. Perhaps he simply nourished the faith that many unlearned people have in the transforming power of education. Obviously, he did not subscribe to the idea, becoming more widespread just at this time, that Indians were incapable, because of inherent inferiority, of mastering the complexities of "civilized life."[127]

Carson really had little choice but to be optimistic, for the alternative he saw was grim. If the Indians were not fed, the Utes would "be reduced to the necessity of thieving and robbing," he said, and in a few years, they would "become victims of intemperance and its concomitant vices, which [would] reduce them to a condition of great depravity." Disaster could be staved off by "setting them apart to themselves," with farm tools and proper instruction. As for the Jicarilla Apaches, their condition was worse, if anything:

They are rapidly degenerating, their associations with the citizens of this territory proving to be a great bane to their naturally not very correct morals. We daily witness them in a state of intoxication in our plaza. No sacrifice is considered by them too great to be made in order to procure whiskey. . . . They are truly the most degraded and troublesome Indians we have in our department. A few days since one them was killed in a drunken spree by being stabbed by one of his own tribe with a large butcher-knife.

Pushing past the conventional, moralistic rhetoric, perhaps imposed on Carson by his amanuensis, we can easily see some of the reasons for his concern. After some six years as agent, during which conditions had deteriorated but little had been done toward a practical solution, he sounded a note of urgency: "Something must be done soon to remove them from contact with the settlements if we would avoid their utter ruin. If permitted to remain as they are, before many years the [Jicarilla] tribe will be utterly extinct."[128]

Carson's thoughts were those of a firsthand observer with unusually extensive experience and knowledge. The imminent extinction of Indian tribes, however, had been exercising a number of minds in the United States in the 1850s. The period witnessed the rise of a school of scientific racist thought, the "American school," which saw the different "races" of humanity as distinct species, separately created and endowed by their Creator with quite different intelligence and capabilities. The "school" in effect codified and validated popular prejudices, finding, to white men's gratification, that whites—Caucasians—had inherently greater mental capacities—literally, larger brains—and had developed a vastly superior civilization. Blacks were suited only to serve whites, and generally accepted their subordinate role with docility. Indians, more proud and stubborn, had repeatedly shown their inability to learn and adapt to civilization and were the same as they had always been, apparent exceptions being always the result of intermarriage. By the 1850s these ideas were not only widely accepted in intellectual and literary circles, but, some argue, significantly influenced U.S. Indian policy. Others claim that the people who made government Indian policy in that decade were largely unaffected by these ideas; their thinking was shaped by the optimism of the eighteenth-century philosophers about the perfectability of humanity, and by evangelical Christianity's emphasis on human brotherhood.[129]

The question was far from academic at the time, of course, for the scientific racists generally declared that the reformers' hopes of civilizing the Indians were chimerical, that concern for the Indians' well-being was mere "sentimentalism." The Indians' fate was "irrevocably sealed," in the words of one journal: "He must wane away and be extinguished at last." The belief that Indians could, and should, be "civilized" according to the white Anglo-American model—which now seems the height of racism, ethnocentrism, and cultural imperialism—was in fact the philosophy of those who opposed the predominant school of racism, the "American school," which enjoyed great scientific respectability. In practical terms, therefore, the assimilationist reformers opposed the notion that it was a waste of time and effort to try to save the Indians, and instead proposed government action, in the form of the reservation system, training in agriculture for self-support, and education.[130]

Kit Carson, the illiterate frontiersman living in remote Taos and dealing day by day with real Indians, would seemingly have had little to do with this sort of elevated scientific and philosophical debate. He obviously had read none of the books, journals, and official documents in which these differing ideas were presented. Many of the popular prejudices that scientific racism ratified were accepted without question in the society he grew up in and were probably questioned explicitly by few of those among whom he spent his life. Carson was directly engaged, however, in the human situations that made these questions more than academic. As so often in his life he was involved in the changes that were reshaping America and the questions that were part of the process. On one question he made his thinking plain: fearing the extinction of the Indians in his charge, he preferred action, trying to help them adapt to the drastic changes taking place in their world as a result of white expansion, as opposed to accepting the Indians' extinction and either sighing with regret or calling it good.

Carson's annual report for 1860 would be his last as agent for the Utes and Jicarillas. Before the next report, events would shift him into a very different field of public service, one that dime-novel readers might think more appropriate. But he served some seven years as an Indian agent, and those years were more than a humdrum interlude in a life of adventure, as most biographers have regarded them. If one is considering Carson's career from the standpoint of his relations with Indians, these years are of great significance. Up to 1854 he had been concerned with Indians as people living in areas where he himself traveled, worked, and lived. His relations with them ranged from battle to marriage, but the primary consideration was how they affected himself and his companions. With one group he might trade peacefully or spend the winter; another might steal his mount or menace his life. Distinguishing such groups was vital; he learned both the penalty for carelessness and the folly of easy generalization about "Indians."

When he became an Indian agent, his concern expanded to larger questions of Indian-white relations, of how Indians and whites on a changing frontier affected each other. He had to reconcile the goals of keeping the peace, protecting the Indians, and yet ultimately serving the interests of the white community. From the evidence, he found the task complex and frustrating. In some respects he was almost uniquely qualified for the job, by knowledge and long experience. Most Indian agents were easterners appointed for political reasons. John Greiner, Carson's predecessor as agent for the Utes and Jicarillas, said that he received his appointment "because I could sing a good political song," and that those appointed at the same time owed their jobs to knowing some politician. Carson, by contrast, could communicate with the tribes under his charge, was acquainted with them and with western Indians in general, and understood the intricacies of diplomacy between tribes. He also had a long acquaintance with the Hispanic folk who formed the great majority of the non-Indian people of New Mexico. Because of his reputation and his long association with the army, his ideas and advice were likely to be respected by civil and military officials—with the notable exception of Governor David Meriwether.[131]

Federal Indian policy seemed to consist of inconsistent half-measures, but there was, in fact, a "concrete policy" adopted by Washington. The problem was in the implementation, given the actual conditions and the less-than-malleable human material, Indian and white, found in New Mexico and elsewhere in the West. The Jacksonian policy of Indian removal was ostensibly intended to provide room enough and time for the Indians to adapt to white civilization, but national expansion in the 1840s created a whole new situation in which the West was to be settled, not in the remote future but in the next few decades. A situation arose in which the project of "civilizing" the Indians lost priority to the defense of the new frontiers. Yet the accomplishment of that project seemed even more needful, if the Indians were to be saved.[132]

The government had a duty to protect its citizens, and if they came into conflict with Indians, civil and military officials knew what their choice must be. In many cases they sought, as Carson did, to mediate and prevent conflict if possible. Military officers in some cases protected Indians from violent whites, and were bitterly criticized for doing so. Army officers and some civil officials were themselves bitterly critical of frontier whites, but ultimately the soldiers and officials represented white society against the "savage."

Carson did not make government policy, but he several times explained, through a scribe, what he thought that policy should be, apparently hoping to exert some influence. His ideas largely agreed with the broad outline of policy set out in Washington, a policy based on two basic goals that, if not absolutely incompatible, were hard to reconcile. They were, first, to ensure that the Indians gave up their claims to lands that the whites wanted with a minimum of danger and expense to settlers, and second, to prevent the extinction of the Indians.

For the policymakers, the solution was the reservation system, which would isolate the Indians and imbue them with Anglo-Saxon values. Many whites viewed that optimistic solution with contempt. Many, not all, white frontiersmen saw the extinction of the Indians as a most desirable end, and the sooner the better. Learned and articulate men in the East demonstrated the scientific fact of the Indian's inferiority. To assume otherwise was sentimentalism. Historians differ on how much the ideas of the scientific racists influenced government Indian policy. Interpretation may depend on how cynical one assumes officials were in their assertions of concern for the Indians.

Present-day criticism of nineteenth-century Indian policy rests on certain assumptions that, however valid they may be, would have seemed strange to Kit Carson's contemporaries. They include an ideal of multiculturalism, joined with an admiration for Indian culture for its presumed environmental wisdom, lack of materialism, and communitarianism. At the time, this vision was shared by a few Romantics like George Catlin, but did not much influence "practical" men and policies. Another assumption is that goodwill toward Indians necessarily encompassed all Indians under all circumstances, and entailed total pacifism and unwillingness to do violence to any Indians at any time. To the mountain men, who had the most notable record for sustained, intimate, and often friendly contact with Indians and for adopting at least some Indian values, this would have been a startling idea. How could one live in peace and harmony with Flatheads and Blackfeet at the same time?

Present-day critics have in mind, as an alternative to the reservation system, either that whites should have stayed out of the Indian country altogether, which they had no intention of doing, or that they should have exercised a strict respect and tolerance for Indian cultures and values, which was highly unlikely given their belief in the superiority of their own ways. White expansion altered the environment, destroying the game and grazing on which the Indians depended and limiting their movements. Some frontiersmen, like the mountain men, could adapt to living in harmony with some Indians, as Kit Carson and Lucien Maxwell tried to do at Rayado, with some limited success. In most cases friction developed and violence was likely to follow. The aggressors were often white men, but Indians had their own warrior values that allowed them to tolerate only so much at the hands of settlers. The hasty or irresponsible acts of a few could have heavy consequences for many, as in the case of the Ute beaten to death by the Mexican on the Conejos.

Carson, from the evidence of his reports and recommendations, accepted the general principles of the reservation system, realizing that the Indians would have difficulty accepting drastic changes in their way of life. That did not prevent him from advocating the system, for he believed that the alternative was worse: the progressive degradation and dwindling away of the Indians, accompanied by repeated outbreaks of conflict. The decimation of California's Indians and the slower erosion and guerrilla warfare of the New Mexico frontier were examples he could cite with some authority.

That Carson, with all his firsthand experience with Indians, accepted the essentials of the reservation system as fully as the frock-coated policy-makers in Washington is sobering. It suggests that certain assumptions about Indians and their contact with white civilization were so pervasive as to be almost inescapable. It also suggests that, given the conditions actually existing and the attitudes of the different parties, the reservation system, with all the harm that hindsight shows it did, may have been at the time the most realistic alternative to the extinction its proponents feared. Historians are rightly leery of the concept of inevitability, for it can be used to deny individual moral responsibility. But if anything seems inevitable it was white American expansion in the West. That was the "given" with which Indian agents like Carson worked.

Carson reiterated these ideas about reservations in reports to men who presumably already accepted them, probably because he was urging action. The government devoted the greatest immediate attention to tribes who seemed to be most directly in the path of the white advance, as on the eastern Great Plains or in California, but Carson saw that the situation in faraway, half-forgotten New Mexico was becoming urgent. During the seven years of his service, his agency remained at Taos, and no reserve was set aside for the Utes or the Jicarilla Apaches. Although Kit repeatedly pointed out the harm done to the Indians by their coming in to the settlements to receive their food and other goods, the government showed no haste to implement its declared policy. Governor Meriwether's treaties were never ratified by Congress, and Carson opposed these agreements because the designated reserves were too close to the settlements and included land already occupied by New Mexicans. Some of the people opposing the treaties were neighbors of his, like Charles Beaubien, and he was hardly ignorant of their self-interest. But his own opposition was consistent with his belief that the Indians could not "remain peaceable with these people." If the Indians occupied land New Mexicans had taken for their own, even for a few years, the ill-will generated would hardly make for peace. The Indians naturally harbored the same resentment, but it would do them little good to act on it. The friction and mutual thievery he witnessed constantly did not encourage optimism about the chance for peaceful coexistence. Even the Jicarillas, who had intermittently enjoyed a sort of symbiosis with New Mexicans in the Rio Arriba, had gone to war, or been pushed into it, in 1854.

Carson's tenure as an Indian agent taught him a great deal about the "Indian problem," but his course was essentially a holding action, an extended period of keeping the peace and providing for the most immediate needs of the Utes and Jicarillas. He also tried to arrange peace between the Indians of his agency and the plains tribes. After the conflicts of 1854–55 a tenuous peace did continue, at least in part due to Kit's efforts, and in part because of the impression made on the Indians by the military operations of those years. There are indications that some of the Utes, Jicarillas, and Pueblos respected and trusted him, even seeking his mediation with the plains tribes.

Because Kit's reports were written for him by more literate scribes, one must be cautious in ascribing meaning to subtleties of language. His attitude could probably be described as paternalistic, in the sense that he concerned himself with the well-being of the Indians and often thought he knew better than they what was good for them. He constantly insisted on the need to feed the Indians, almost invariably coupling this with the warning that, if not fed, they would steal to feed themselves, with potentially disastrous consequences. As another old mountain man, Paulino Weaver, said of the Yavapais and Walapais in Arizona in 1864, "It is hard to ceep a hunkry Indian from stealing and almost as hard to keep the whites from making an indiscriminade Sloughter of them for stealing." In his reports Carson had to justify, to superiors far from the scene, the filling of the Indians' constant requests for food, and to justify expenditures sometimes exceeding previous estimates. He had to emphasize that present expenditure could perhaps prevent much greater expense, and bloodshed, in the future. On occasion he spent his own funds, with no certainty that the government would reimburse him. He also had to justify, to the Indians, the actions of the Great

Father, however inconsistent and unfortunate they might appear, to keep them "satisfied," as he put it. Some years later Governor A. C. Hunt of Colorado had to explain to the Utes why the government did not fulfill the conditions of its treaties. He observed, "It is impossible to answer these complaints, for I know too well their justness; but as a true agent of the government I cannot admit the wrong, and I fear my attempted explanations but disgust the Indians instead of appeasing them." Kit never expressed his feelings so explicitly, but at times he surely found himself in the same equivocal position, trying to persuade the Indians to accept what he himself found unsatisfactory.[133]

Much of Carson's correspondence as agent had to do with the theft of livestock by both New Mexicans and Indians, no small matter to people so dependent on these animals. He spent considerable time tracking down stolen animals, checking brands and descriptions, and persuading those in possession of the creatures to give them up. He complained that it was harder to recover stock stolen by New Mexicans than that taken by Indians, and he declared once that if citizens would neither steal from nor otherwise molest Indians, he would never have to report Indian depredations.

One of Carson's biographers, Edwin Sabin, wrote that, as an Indian agent, "Kit Carson presented no startling theories, and none that was not tried out by Government." As noted, Kit's ideas agreed with the essentials of government policy set in Washington, and he only wished that the government would attend to carrying them out. Sabin, writing early in the early 1900s when the "Vanishing American" was still widely deemed headed for extinction, declared that Carson's efforts had been frustrated by bad white men and by the Indians' stereotypical penchant for the white man's vices, not his virtues. "He had been successful in killing the Indian," Sabin wrote, "he had not been successful in preserving the Indian." "Hopeless compassion" was Sabin's assessment of Kit's attitude. Carson most certainly experienced the frustration of a man dealing with a complex and often intractable situation, one often beyond his control and offering no perfect choices. We have seen what he thought needed to be done. Some respected scientific minds were insisting that there was no solution to "the Indian problem." Carson rejected that belief, whether because of human concern, because his job was to do something for them, or perhaps simply because, as with so many Americans, his reaction to a problem was to try to solve it.

It is hard to say whether he regarded his years as an agent as being as much of a failure as Sabin did. He would continue to be "the perennial public servant," and he would continue to be deeply concerned with Indians, but the relative peace of the Taos years was coming to an end. In a letter dated January 2, 1860, but more likely written in 1861, Kit told Superintendent Collins that he had no money; the Indians must wait until Collins let him know how much he could spend. "Owing to the present state of affairs in the East I do not think myself safe in advancing any money to the government purposes." If the revised dating is correct, then it is easy to identify the situation in the East that caused him to question if the government would be sending any money for the Indians. South Carolina had seceded from the Union on December 20, 1860, and word of the national turmoil in the wake of Lincoln's election would have reached New Mexico. The future of many things besides the government's Indian policy was in doubt. Kit, like so many other Americans, would find his whole future changed by the results of choices made in the coming months and years.[134]

6. Soldier

Carson: I don't like a hostile Red Skin any more
than you do. And when they are hostile, I've fit 'em—
fout 'em—as hard as any man. That's my business.
James F. Rusling in Edward S. Ellis, *The Life of Kit Carson*

. . . he could scarcely read or write but had wonderful influence
over the men. He was a genuine frontiersman and a splendid Indian
commander. The troops sometimes accused him of cowardice because
he was so cautious . . . on the march he would never build fires if
he wanted to surprise the enemy; he would creep up cautiously;
he whipped the Navajoes; he was a long time in New Mexico.
John Ayers, "A Soldier's Experience in New Mexico"

KIT GOES TO WAR

In the center of the main plaza in Santa Fe stands a monument commemorating those New Mexicans who fought and died for the Union during the conflicts of the 1860s. On two faces are inscriptions honoring the federal troops who fell fighting the "Rebels" at the battles of Valverde, Apache Canyon, and Glorieta in 1862; this is said to be the only Civil War monument in the country to bear the word *Rebels*. Another face bears the inscription:

TO THE HEROES

WHO HAVE FALLEN IN THE

VARIOUS BATTLES WITH [*excised*]

INDIANS IN THE TERRITORY OF NEW MEXICO

The missing word, chiseled out in the twentieth century, was SAVAGE. This monument, erected a few years after the end of the Civil War, reminds us just how terribly serious a business those battles were for the generation that fought them. Years before the reconciliation of North and South, Rebels were Rebels and hostile Indians were savages. This was their reality, and we cannot understand the actions of the people of those times if we forget that.

Indian-white conflict in the West intensified during the Civil War years, and although most regular army troops departed for the East, even larger numbers of wartime volunteer soldiers soon took their place. Whites continued to move west, and new gold discoveries from Montana to Arizona increased travel and settlement in areas where Indians lived. Six new territories and one new state were organized during the war. At the same time, the defects of the government's Indian policy—some the result of inefficiency, corruption, and lack of funds; some inherent in its basic conception—caused further deterioration in Indian-white relations. In the midst of all this, the Confederacy launched an invasion of New Mexico, with other western regions as further objectives. It was this last event that drew Kit Carson out of Taos, put him in uniform, and engaged him in the campaigns that would put the final crown on his fame—and would cloud his reputation a century later.

One episode symbolizing the choices the national crisis forced on people, even in faraway New Mexico, occurred in Taos sometime in 1861. Some Confederate sympathizers hoisted a Southern banner in the plaza, which prompted local Unionists to set up a cottonwood pole in a corner of the plaza flying the Stars and Stripes, which they guarded night and day. To this day the flag flies over Taos plaza twenty-four hours a day in commemoration of the event. Most versions of the story insist that Kit Carson was in the group of Union men, on the basis of a statement made fifty years later by Smith Simpson, one of the group. Simpson also prepared a list of the members, on which Carson's name does not appear.[1]

One characteristic story illustrates his Unionism, told by Luther Perry Wilmot, who as a young man spent some time during the winter of 1860–61 at a ranch near Greenhorn in the Colorado mountains on the upper Arkansas. Secession and civil war were in the air, and Wilmot was the only Northern man on the place, so he thought it best not to discuss the situation. Kit Carson dropped by and stayed for a while, playing poker for beans with the hands; he and the foreman "won all the beans." Wilmot found that he and Carson had something in common, besides an interest in shooting: "Kit was Loyal, but he was like me and would not argue the point."[2]

Kit had grown up in a slave state, and no state would be as bitterly divided by the war as Missouri, which endured years of guerrilla warfare.

Even families were divided—one of Kit's brothers fought for the Confederacy. Kit had been in the service of the federal government for years, but the same could be said of many men in the army and the Indian service who "went South." His contemporaries seem to have taken his loyalty to the "Old Flag" for granted; those who wrote anything about him were largely Union men and would have been surprised if Kit was not on their side.[3]

As the country headed inexorably into war, New Mexico began to feel the effects. A number of regular army officers serving in the territory resigned, including two department commanders in succession, and troops began to be withdrawn from the frontier outposts to concentrate for the march eastward. The Navajos and Apaches, concluding that the soldiers had given up, took heart; raids on settlers and their herds increased. However, the departure of the regulars for the East halted in the summer when a force of Texas cavalry under Lieutenant Colonel John Baylor entered the southern part of the territory by way of Franklin, Texas (El Paso), and seized the region around Mesilla, proclaiming it Confederate territory and capturing several companies of regular troops. Colonel Edward Canby, the departmental commander, not only retained the remaining regulars in New Mexico but ordered the organization of a force of volunteers and militia to meet the emergency.[4]

One of those who responded to the call was Kit Carson. In fact, he offered not only his own services but those of the Utes at the very beginning of the year, as the effects of the crisis on the army first became apparent. At this point he may have had in mind using the Utes against hostile Indians, but in August he would urge utilizing their services against the Confederates, under his leadership. Eventually, however, he would sign up for more conventional military duty.[5]

Colonel Canby feared, rightly, that the Confederates would send a much larger force than Baylor's few companies to invade the rest of the territory, and his regular force would be entirely inadequate to deal with them, so he started organizing volunteers and militia. As in the rest of the nation, these units were hastily raised and sketchily organized, armed, and trained, their officers being chiefly leading citizens or simply men who could recruit some followers. The majority of the New Mexico volunteers, numbering some 2,800 by February 1862, were Hispanic; the officers were a mixture of Hispanics and Anglos. Canby, like most regulars at the beginning of the war, had a poor opinion of volunteers in general, and a poorer one of native New Mexicans, whom he thought unlikely to be very useful against the Confederates, but perhaps serviceable against Indians or as auxiliaries.[6]

The First New Mexico Volunteer Infantry Regiment was organized in July and August of 1861 at Fort Union and Santa Fe. Its first commander was Charles Bent's old partner Ceran St. Vrain, who resigned at the end of September. One theory is that his name was used to draw in recruits but that it was intended from the first that the man who would take the regiment into action would be the original lieutenant colonel, Christopher Carson, who had resigned his position as Indian agent on May 24. If so, then it would seem that, in spite of Kit's national fame, his name was considered less of a draw in New Mexico than that of the prominent and wealthy St. Vrain, who was nearly sixty at the time. When he resigned, Carson was promoted to full colonel. Like most Civil War volunteer officers, Kit had no formal military training whatsoever.[7]

While the regiment was preparing for service, a rumor reached Fort Union that a force of Texans was marching up the Pecos or the Canadian River to attack the post. Kit offered to gather a force of Mexicans and Utes to run off the horses of the enemy, and Colonel Canby authorized him to send out spies and harass the Confederates; the rumor proved premature. In the past, white Americans had considered it unforgivable when other white men had led Indians against them (witness Jefferson's denunciation of George III in the Declaration of Independence for bringing in "the merciless Indian savages"), though they always recruited Indians themselves when possible and would do so in this war. Kit obviously had no qualms about leading the Utes against the Texans in the type of guerrilla operation for which they were well suited, and he evidently believed they would follow him.[8]

As a regimental commander, Carson was not likely to fit the regular army's prescription. His illiteracy handicapped him as an administrator. He knew nothing of close-order drill, in that day the basis of battlefield tactics in conventional warfare. His ideas on discipline, the regulars' highest value, were those of the backcountry individualist and the mountain man. Most of the formalities dear to the West Pointer's sense of order and propriety probably seemed silly to him. A few years later, when someone apologized for addressing him as "Colonel" instead of "General," as he had then become, he said, "Oh, call me Kit at once, and be done with it."[9]

Perhaps the most detailed description of Carson as a regimental commander comes from Edward Wynkoop, a Colorado volunteer officer who knew him in 1862 or shortly after, and who claims to have been "among his most intimate friends." He provides the usual description of a man whose appearance was "as unlike what the general idea would most naturally be of him [as] possible." His uniform "did not set well on him at all." He was "below the medium height, squarely built, slightly bowlegged and those members apparently too short for his body." His head and face, however, "made up for all the imperfections of the balance of his person." He was a moderate drinker but smoked "to a considerable extent," and Wynkoop never heard him swear. Wynkoop gives Kit the conventional attributes: he had "a heart as tender as the most sensative [sic] woman," "the courage of a Coeur de Leon," "the utmost firmness," and "the best of common sense."[10]

Having given these fairly standard tributes to "dear old Kit"—the term he considered "the most natural expression in referring to him"—Wynkoop then details some of the more amusing difficulties caused by Carson's lack of education and military training. He had a lieutenant whom Wynkoop calls "Mac" who was supposedly knowledgeable in military affairs, and whom Carson made drillmaster and "Fac-totum" in such matters. On one occasion the colonel decided that a deserter should be drummed out of the service without bothering with a court-martial (which might have imposed the death penalty), so Mac conducted the full ceremony for such occasions, with a band and guard detail. Unfortunately, Carson, observing the ritual, stepped up to the central figure, examined him, and exclaimed, "Why Mac, that ain't the man." The victim had been incarcerated only for drunkenness. Mac also marched his company to church for mass, and then had them present arms to the priest. Carson's comment on a complaint about this was, "Mac is a Military man and if he did present arms to the Priest it must be according to Army Regulations."[11]

Other sources confirm Wynkoop's portrait. A Confederate soldier wrote, following a comrade's description, "Kit Carson is a low, square-set old plain farmer-looking man with a slow, quiet speech and a good deal of accommodation." A California volunteer tells of an occasion when a number of Carson's men asked him to sign orders for them to be issued molasses by the commissary; he signed each order in good faith, then learned that they actually authorized the men to purchase whiskey. Thereafter Kit would not sign an order until his adjutant had read it.[12]

It would seem that discipline in the First New Mexico was not up to regular army standards, but the same could be said of many volunteer regiments of the Civil War. John Ayers, an officer with the New Mexico troops, insists that Carson "had wonderful influence over the men." Wynkoop notes that he had "a beautiful mild blue eye; but which would become terrible under some circumstances and like the warning of the rattlesnake always sounded the alarm before the spring," and that "he could punish with the utmost vigor a culprit who was deserving of the same."[13]

One of Edward Wynkoop's stories, though not directly related to military discipline, illustrates Kit's firmness. Carson and Wynkoop traveled to Albuquerque on an occasion when the Rio Grande was swollen by melting snow. As they prepared to swim their horses across, two boats were about to cross, carrying "gaily dressed Senoritas" who were going to mass in the town. As one boat pushed off, heavily loaded, "a rough looking Mexican Ranchero" jumped aboard. The boatman asked him to get out because he was endangering the women, but he refused.

> Kit Carson then approached and in a mild manner pointed out to him his wrong doings, but without avail,—he then spoke to him in a peremtory manner; the man was still obstinate, when like a flash of lightning Carson raised his sheathed sabre which he carried in his hand; struck him a tremendous blow along side of the head, knocking him headlong into the turbid waters of the Rio Grande; the fellow sunk like lead, when quicker than thought, Kit plunged headforemost after and dragged him out on the bank.

Obviously, the man who had challenged Shunar was still very much a part of the mild and easygoing Colonel Carson. Faced with a pigheaded, unreasonable, and perhaps drunken man who was endangering women by his actions, Kit reacted in backcountry fashion. If one ascribes his action to ethnic prejudice, then one must recall that the women he was protecting were also Hispanic. Kit took responsibility for his actions by rescuing the man. He was still the man who threatened to blow the heart out of a sergeant who was mistreating a sick soldier. It would have been a mistake for any of his men to presume too far on his easygoing demeanor.[14]

Armies always have the dilemma of balancing the roles of the "warriors" and the "managers," both of whom are indispensable. Without the managers an army cannot be organized, trained, or disciplined, nor can it be fed, clothed, armed, or moved about efficiently. But armies are intended to fight, and so they must also have leaders with the warrior spirit, who have the will and ability to fight and to get others to fight, too. It seems clear which type Carson belonged to, although his combativeness at this stage of his life was tempered by ingrained caution, to the extent that some would doubt his courage.[15]

Carson would have his chance to demonstrate battlefield leadership, for the Confederate government in the fall of 1861 organized an expeditionary force of three regiments of Texas cavalry under General Henry Sibley, a former U.S. dragoon officer, to march west and exploit Baylor's victory in southern New Mexico, intending to take possession of the entire territory. By January 1862 they were assembling near Mesilla, ninety miles south of the Union post of Fort Craig, where Colonel Canby concentrated his own forces. Canby had more troops than Sibley, but the majority were New Mexican militia and volunteers, in whom he had little confidence.[16]

The two forces maneuvered and skirmished for a few days in the vicinity of Fort Craig, then on February 21 met in full-scale battle at Valverde, on the east side of the Rio Grande a few miles above the fort. At first the battle was fought for the Union principally by the regular infantry, cavalry, and artillery, who pushed the Texans back away from the river. However, it soon became necessary to bring in the volunteers, and Canby ordered Carson to bring his regiment across the river and join the Union right.[17]

Carson and his men joined a force of regulars in forcing back the Confederate left, endangering the enemy's entire line. They beat off a Southern cavalry charge and were ready to push on when the Texans launched an all-or-nothing charge on the Union left and captured Canby's principal battery of artillery. The Federal battle line came apart and Canby had to order a retreat to Fort Craig.[18]

From most accounts, Carson and his regiment performed their duty admirably. Some sources report him shooting soldiers who wanted to flee from the battle, but these stories may grow out of the post-defeat denigration of the courage of the New Mexicans. One witness who was there reports him walking up and down the line, quietly encouraging the men, saying, "*Firme, muchachos, firme* [Steady, boys, steady]." Canby blamed the New Mexican volunteers for his defeat, but not Carson or his regiment.[19]

Valverde would be Carson's only engagement with the Rebels. After the battle Sibley's army marched north, bypassing Fort Craig. The Texans entered Santa Fe, but shortly afterward part of their force, heading east on the Santa Fe Trail, met a Union force of regulars and Colorado volunteers and fought two battles; they pushed the Federals back, but a detachment of Coloradans destroyed the Confederate supply train. The loss of their supplies reduced the Southerners to living off the country. Canby had supplies removed or destroyed as much as possible, and Sibley had to order a retreat. Canby then took his regulars from Fort Craig to operate against the enemy, leaving Colonel Carson in charge of the post and the bulk of the remaining volunteers. The Confederates retreated out of New Mexico, bypassing Fort Craig. With another column of Union troops advancing from California, Sibley's men had evacuated New Mexico and the El Paso area by June 1862.[20]

It was not the end of strife in New Mexico, however, nor of Kit Carson's military service. With the Texans gone (although the Union military would continue to fear their possible return for many months to come), New Mexicans and their Indian neighbors returned to more familiar modes of conflict, and Kit's services would be very much in demand. In truth, the older conflicts had never really ceased, and with the withdrawal of regular forces from many of the outlying posts in New Mexico and Arizona, the hostile bands of Navajos and Apaches intensified attacks on travelers, herds, and ranches. While Baylor's Texans occupied southern New Mexico, they had to fight Apaches there and in western Texas. Kit's brother, Moses Carson, was with a group of settlers who fled southern Arizona because of Apache hostility, suffering a number of casualties as they fought their way to Mesilla. The Southwest was as far from tranquility as ever. The New Mexico and California troops who had enlisted to fight the Confederates would spend the rest of their enlistments trying to subdue the Indians. As elsewhere in the West, Indian-white conflict intensified, with as many or more troops present as before the war, and a more energetic and single-minded white leadership directing operations. The level of violence increased as the Indians, at first encouraged by the retreat of the regulars, had to face more determined bluecoats, westerners with a less ambivalent attitude toward Indian-white conflict than the officers of the prewar regulars.[21]

New Mexico might be one of the remotest corners of the national domain, but it would have a military garrison larger than that of prewar days. In August 1862 the "California Column," a brigade of California volunteer troops sent east across the desert to help drive the Rebels from New Mexico, arrived on the Rio Grande. Their commander was an old acquaintance of Kit Carson's, James Carleton, with whom he had campaigned against the Jicarilla Apaches in 1854. Carleton was now a brigadier general of volunteers, and in September he would succeed Edward Canby in command of the Department of New Mexico.[22]

In the meantime, Canby had reorganized the New Mexico volunteers, culling out those officers and men deemed less effective from four regiments of infantry and consolidating what was left into a single mounted regiment, the First New Mexico Volunteer Cavalry, hoping to secure the services of one effective unit for Indian campaigns. The regimental commander was, one must assume, the senior New Mexico volunteer officer in whom Canby had the most confidence—Colonel Christopher Carson. Besides the First New Mexico, General Carleton would at one time or another have the services of a California cavalry regiment, and all or portions of one New Mexico, two California, and three regular infantry regiments. In the next few years they would conduct campaigns of unprecedented scope and intensity under Carleton's forceful, and many would say ruthless, leadership.

James Carleton would command in New Mexico for over four years. Though he never fought the Confederates, he became a dominating figure in the history of the Indian wars and of the Southwest. John Cremony, a California officer who was himself criticized by Carleton, credited the general with "acknowledged ability and apparent zeal," but accused him of "unscrupulous ambition and exclusive selfishness." Robert Utley, the foremost authority on the Indian wars of the period, says, "If the Army contained a career officer high or low who added to ability and zeal a deeper insight into the essential nature of Indian warfare, he left no evidence of the attainment." On the other hand, C. L. Sonnichsen, historian of the Mescalero Apaches, has written, "If [Carleton] had never come to New Mexico—if he had never had to function as God in a war-torn and distracted country—his determination and organizing ability might have been put to better use. He had intelligence and foresight, driving energy, and a consuming ambition to do well. . . . His trouble was that he could not admit an error, change his mind, or take a backward step." Arrell Gibson sees him as "a complex person, sensitive, creative, and highly intelligent yet devoid of compassion. He was vain, and his imperious manner . . . antagonized many people."

Kit Carson would be the principal field commander and most trusted subordinate of this man for over four years, and they would constitute a somewhat unlikely yet formidable team, in spite of great differences in personality, background, and training. Carson's obedient and loyal service under Carleton would make him, as a historical figure, something more than the Leatherstocking-cum-dime novel legend he might otherwise have remained, but many years later it would cast a shadow over his reputation, as a result of what contemporaries would regard as his crowning achievements.[23]

James Henry Carleton was born in Maine in 1814. As a young man he had literary aspirations, later fulfilled to some extent by magazine articles, professional and scientific papers, and one book on the battle of Buena Vista. After service in the Maine militia he obtained a regular army commission in 1839, in the First Dragoons, and served until his death thirty-four years later. Although he never attended West Point, he was in many ways the epitome of the frontier regular. His collaboration with Carson was a partnership of representatives of two sharply contrasting American folkways, the New England Puritan and the backcountry man. He was a man of broad interests within and without the bounds of his profession, and he had a good command of English prose. As Utley points out, he had acquired a clear understanding of the basic principles of Indian warfare. In a frequently quoted passage of instructions to a subordinate, he wrote:

The troops must be kept after the Indians, not in big bodies, with military noises and smokes, and the gleam of arms by day, and fires, and talks, and comfortable sleeps by night; but in small parties moving stealthily to their haunts and lying patiently in wait for them; or in following up their tracks day after day with a fixedness of purpose that never gives up. . . . Some flour, bacon, a little coffee, and sugar, thrown on a pack-mule, with the men carrying, say, two or three days' rations in their haversacks, and it will surprise the country what a few resolute men can do. . . . An Indian is a more watchful and wary animal than a deer. He must be hunted with skill; he cannot be blundered upon; nor will he allow his pursuers to come upon him when he knows it, unless he is the stronger. . . . I once, in this country, with some good trackers under Kit Carson, followed a trail of Apaches for over a fortnight. I caught them. Others can do as well.

However repugnant the comparison of Indians to wild game may be (and he had caught the close kinship of the skills of the hunter and the guerrilla warrior), Carleton had laid out the essential military requirements for success in such warfare: high mobility, preferably through use of pack animals; persistence; stealth and concealment, aiming at surprise; the necessity for good scouts and trackers; and the difficulty of forcing Indians to fight unless they were surprised or held the advantage. Carleton's mention of Kit Carson in these instructions shows clearly the impression their 1854 collaboration had made upon him, and suggests that Kit may have furthered the dragoon officer's education.[24]

Carson makes it plain that Carleton's "good management" in the 1854 operation impressed him, as did the officer's paying off his wager of a hat. The two were members of the same Masonic lodge in Santa Fe. Carson would be Carleton's loyal lieutenant for over four years, to the extent of remaining in the service when he would have preferred being at home with Josefa and the children. That loyalty, whether arising from personal regard, a sense of duty, the backcountry man's natural attitude toward the chief, or from agreement on certain essentials, would long after lead to charges that he was a compliant tool of Carleton's "genocidal" policies. It is the more surprising in that Carleton had a reputation as a disciplinarian, demanding and even harsh toward subordinates; the abrasiveness of his personality is evident in his correspondence, as are a broad authoritarian streak and a tendency toward what is now called micromangement. In his most familiar photographs he poses as the fierce warrior, looking as if he could glare through an adobe wall. He maintained a virtual military dictatorship over New Mexico during his years in command, keeping martial law in force and restricting travel, on the ground that the Confederates might once again invade (a concern that seems to have been genuine). His regime would arouse widespread and bitter opposition, partly based on his supposed Democratic partisanship, virtually defining territorial politics in those years. At first glance it might seem that Carson, with his informality and lack of concern for military forms and discipline, would not be happy working with such a man.[25]

If Carson seems to have been liked by most people who met him, Carleton more often aroused either respect or intense dislike. He seems, however, to have been a bit more complicated than his image allows. One subordinate during the war wrote to him for advice on a personal problem, "as I would have gone to an older brother." If one dismisses this man as a sycophant, there is also the case of William McCleave, one of the cavalry officers in the California Column. McCleave, an Irish immigrant, served as an enlisted man in Carleton's company in the First Dragoons before the war. In 1853 he and another dragoon got seriously drunk at Las Vegas, New Mexico, and the Irishman defied the captain's orders, saber in hand. Subdued, he was forced to walk to Fort Union tied behind a wagon. If Carleton were simply the unimaginative martinet of stereotype, one would expect McCleave to have been in his bad books for good. Regular officers sometimes showed surprising tolerance with men considered basically sound, however, and McCleave ended ten years of service in 1860 as first sergeant of Carleton's company, which is surely a tribute to both men. In 1861 he was appointed captain in the First California Cavalry, probably through Carleton's influence, was promoted later to major, and was one of Carleton's most trusted officers, eventually retiring from the regular army in 1879. It would seem that Carleton had a bit more imagination and flexibility than he might at first glance be credited with, and that he could recognize the abilities of subordinates who did not quite fit his own mold, fostering their careers and getting the most out of their strengths. (His enemies would of course have seen this as favoritism.) In Carson's case, this meant that the understanding of Indians and Indian warfare promised by his reputation, and confirmed for Carleton from personal observation, would be directed to the purpose for which he was suited, even if Kit himself lacked enthusiasm for the task.[26]

Carson would become the only former mountain man to play a prominent role as a military commander in the Indian wars. Other old trappers, notably Jim Bridger, would serve as scouts, but of all the men who had gained such knowledge of Indians, in peace and in war, in the mountain fur trade during the 1820s and '30s, only Carson would make the transition to military commander in the new era of intensified, polarized Indian-white conflict in the West. One reason was probably the dubious social standing of many old mountain men, limited by lack of education and their status as "squaw men." Age was another factor, for by the time these conflicts reached their height in the 1860s, most old mountain men were in fact old, or at least past the optimum age for military command under frontier conditions. Kit Carson, one of the younger generation of mountain men, was past fifty when the Civil War began. At the end of the war the average age of Union or Confederate major generals was forty-two and a half years, and the average for regimental commanders must have been considerably younger; Carson by that time had passed his fifty-fifth birthday and his health was beginning to break. By the mid-nineteenth century, moreover, Indian fighting was increasingly being taken over by the regular army, and frontier rangers and "border captains" were becoming relatively less important. It was the Civil War that temporarily reversed this trend and gave volunteers—citizen soldiers—the primary task of Indian fighting during the war years, making Kit Carson a military commander.[27]

Otherwise, the leading reasons for Carson's prominence in the Indian wars were his adaptability and, of course, his reputation. The fact that he was Kit Carson, the great scout and Indian fighter, unquestionably propelled him into a position he would not otherwise have held; once again, he was deemed indispensable and expected to perform great deeds. How else would an illiterate former trapper become a colonel and, eventually, a brevet brigadier general? This is not to say that Carson gained his position only because of the inflated notion that the public and influential persons had of him, as with certain other military commanders of the period. Both Canby and Carleton in succession chose him to command operations against hostile Indians, and they were both experienced military professionals with records of success in Indian campaigning. They were not impressionable hero-worshipers and both knew how to sideline an officer in whom they lacked confidence to an unimportant desk job, whatever his reputation. Instead, they gave Carson responsible leadership of the most important operations under their command.

Carson's standing became evident even before Carleton took command in New Mexico in September 1862. As soon as the Texans were expelled from the territory, Canby determined to conduct military operations against the Indians who were making the most serious raids on the settlements, the Navajos and the Mescalero Apaches, first concentrating on the Navajos. Carson would lead this campaign, while Lieutenant Colonel J. Francisco Chavez conducted a smaller operation against the Mescaleros. This fact should dispose of the notion of some writers that Carleton initiated these Indian campaigns primarily to occupy his restless troops. Canby issued the orders on September 9, 1862, shortly before relinquishing command to Carleton. Carleton would carry out the plan, with significant modifications, but Canby originated the strategy, intended to confine the Navajos to a reservation, which he had in fact formed at least a year before.[28]

Carleton made a significant change almost as soon as he took command on September 14; he decided to make the campaign against the Mescaleros his first priority, to settle matters with them decisively before undertaking the more demanding campaign against the Navajos. Therefore he ordered Carson, with five companies of his regiment, to reoccupy Fort Stanton, in the heart of Mescalero country in southeastern New Mexico. While Carson was on his way to Fort Stanton, Carleton prepared specific orders, labeled "extermination orders" by historians, for the conduct of the campaign.[29]

Carleton ordered some California troops to operate independently to the south of Carson's command, noting that they should hire good Pueblo or Mexican scouts. On October 12, Carson was ordered to make war upon the Mescaleros until further orders: "All Indian men of that tribe are to be killed wherever you find them. The women and children will not be harmed, but you will take them prisoners, and feed them at Fort Stanton until you receive other instructions about them." If the Indians sued for peace, Carson was to tell them that they had attacked the people of New Mexico at the time of the Texan invasion, in spite of a previous peace treaty, and were now to be punished. Carson was also to say that he himself had no power to make peace, and that the Apache chiefs must come to Santa Fe to discuss peace, but that

> you will keep after their people and slay them until you receive orders to desist from these headquarters; that this making of treaties for them to break whenever they have an interest in breaking them will not be done any more; that that time has passed by; that we have no faith in their promises; that we believe if we kill some of their men in fair, open war, they will be apt to remember that it will be better for them to remain at peace than to be at war. I trust that this severity, in the long run, will be the most humane course that could be pursued toward these Indians.

Carleton also ordered Carson, in the event of another Texan invasion, to harass the enemy's camps and run off their stock by night, and set the prairie on fire.[30]

These orders are harsh enough, although they do not quite merit the description of "extermination orders." The general made a point of saying that the women and children would not be harmed, but would be taken prisoners. His purpose was to force the Mescaleros to make a lasting peace by giving them no other way to escape the relentless destruction of their men. He believed, as he said in his orders, that if the army killed some of the men, the people as a whole would realize the necessity of keeping the peace. He also clearly believed that these Indians had previously made peace at their convenience, with no serious intention of keeping it when military operations against them ceased. His assertion that his "severity" would be "the most humane course" in the end may be hard to stomach, but he clearly meant that ending the conflict once and for all was better than allowing intermittent hostilities to continue indefinitely. A subordinate so inclined might have interpreted these orders as license to kill all or as many as possible of the men of the tribe; Carson did not so interpret them.

From the Mescalero viewpoint, naturally, recent history appeared somewhat differently than it did to Carleton. The Mescalero Apaches lived in the mountain ranges of southeastern New Mexico and western Texas, especially the Sierra Blanca, Guadalupe, and Davis ranges. They lived primarily by hunting and gathering the mescal plant, which gave them their Spanish name. They also had a well-developed tradition of raiding their neighbors, including the people of Mexico and New Mexico. The New Mexicans attacked the Mescaleros in turn, each group believing itself justified by the law of retaliation. In the mid-1800s the Mescaleros were caught in the same vise as the Jicarillas and other southwestern tribes, as expanding white settlement and travel reduced the supply of game, increased the contacts between whites and Apaches and hence the chances of conflict, and brought within their reach herds of livestock from which to make up the shortage of game. In 1854–55 they became involved in warfare with the U.S. Army, and a number of their chiefs made a treaty with Governor Meriwether by which they accepted a reservation in the area of the Sierra Blanca, where Fort Stanton was established to guard them. Although the treaty was never ratified, many of them lived for the next few years in an uneasy condition of peace, farming a little and subsisting otherwise on government rations; troops on occasion had to protect them from attack by citizens from Mesilla. At the same time, unsubdued bands from the Guadalupe and Davis Mountains continued raiding, and the reservation Indians were blamed. With the Confederate invasion, many assumed that the soldiers were gone and the whites in retreat, and the younger and more aggressive elements resumed raiding. They attacked Federals and Confederates impartially, wiping out one detachment of Texans who were not afraid of Indians, and drove recent settlers away from the Rio Bonito area.[31]

That the Mescaleros, or a considerable portion of the tribe, had resumed hostilities after making a peace treaty particularly irked New Mexicans, and General Carleton, although the bands from the southern mountains may have been responsible for a considerable portion of the raiding, and the chiefs who made the agreement had little control over the actions of other warriors in any case. But this last factor made any peace that did not give the government control over all the Mescaleros tenuous. To the New Mexicans, it seemed that the Apaches had taken advantage of their weakness at the time of the invasion. Superintendent James Collins, in his report for 1861, thought the present trouble had started with a fight between Apaches and Texans, but "since then they have inaugurated a series of depredations upon the Mexican settlements, having killed one man and stolen a considerable amount of property." All the crops and property of the settlers on the Rio Bonito had been "deserted and lost by the settlers in consequence of the hostility of the Indians." A year later Lorenzo Labadie, agent for the Mescaleros, found things no better. Labadie, a native New Mexican, would later become a defender of the Indians, but in his report for 1862 he noted that in August they killed some forty men and six children, and carried other children into captivity, besides stealing horses, mules, donkeys, cattle, and sheep. The Indians had given indications of a desire for peace, but Labadie thought, "It will hardly be safe to trust them until they have been punished for past offences." General Carleton agreed, believing that permanent peace would come from a thorough military defeat, bringing the Mescaleros under the power of the government. No peace overtures that did not involve such a surrender would be accepted, and military operations would continue until it was made.[32]

Some writers have it that Kit Carson was reluctant to fight the Mescaleros, believing that "the Indians could be brought to terms without a war," and that he was "shocked and embarrassed" at the "complete savagery" of Carleton's orders. They cite no evidence, however, to prove that this was Kit's attitude. He had said many times that he believed some tribes would accept reservation life only when they were decisively and unmistakably defeated. There is no good reason to think that he doubted the need for some sort of military operation against them. The dead men and captive children Labadie had referred to would have been a present reality to him. His actions during the campaign, however, would be substantially different from the program laid out by Carleton.[33]

Before Carson reached Fort Stanton, a force from his regiment clashed with some Apaches and claimed a victory; their leader was Captain James "Paddy" Graydon, who had distinguished himself in command of a scout company during the Confederate invasion. Two Apache chiefs, Manuelito and José Largo, and several other men were killed and others wounded. Graydon claimed he had been holding a parley and the Indians started the fight; another report had it that Graydon had treacherously attacked the Apaches under cover of a talk. Soon after, Captain William McCleave, leading some California troops, showed why Carleton trusted him by surprising a party of Mescaleros in the Sacramento Mountains and defeating them, killing a few and freeing some captives. The Indians fled over the mountains to Fort Stanton and promptly surrendered to Kit Carson.[34]

The situation was not quite what Carleton had envisaged. Instead of a protracted campaign, the Mescaleros, or a substantial portion of them, were already in Carson's hands. Kit sent three chiefs—Cadete, Chato, and Estrella—to Santa Fe to talk with the general. Taking Carleton's orders literally, he might have continued hostilities against the rest until peace was final, trying to kill as many of the men as possible. In fact, he did nothing of the sort, and it would have been foolish as well as inhumane to do so, when he already had them in hand. Either he simply chose to ignore his superior's orders or, more likely, he decided that those orders did not cover the present situation. Carleton must have imagined a situation where the Indians were still loose in the mountains while a few chiefs were trying to gain a cessation of military operations by making meaningless promises and hoping to be bought off, which is the way he depicted the previous history of Mescalero-white conflict in his orders. Instead, most of them were already in Carson's custody, and Kit had once again seized an opportunity to end the fighting, whatever he or anyone else had said before.[35]

Carleton never indicated that he was displeased with Carson's action. He told the chiefs that they and their people could surrender, but that they must go to a safe location where the troops would not confuse them with those still hostile. McCleave's Californians were ordered back to their base. The general told Carson, "If you are satisfied that Graydon's attack on Manuelita and his people was not fair and open, see that all the horses and mules . . . are returned to the survivors of Manuelita's band." Carleton proved curiously scrupulous for a man supposedly determined to exterminate the Mescaleros. Carson had been suspicious about the circumstances of Graydon's fight with Manuelito, and the general evidently did not think that Graydon had acted in the spirit and intent of his orders, whatever the captain may have thought. Graydon did not account for his actions, at least not in this world, for he became involved in a gunfight with a regimental surgeon, J. W. Whitlock, resulting from an argument over the Manuelito affair. Graydon took a wound that proved mortal, and Whitlock was shot a number of times by the men of Graydon's company. Carson called out other troops to disarm Graydon's men, denounced them, and reportedly threatened to shoot every fourth man; of course he let himself be talked out of it. The defects of discipline in the First New Mexico were painfully on display. Carleton wanted Graydon tried, but it was too late for that.[36]

Perhaps Carleton was kidding himself, and trying to evade responsibility, by taking this attitude toward Graydon's actions, but it seems that killing as many Indians as possible, by any means available, was not his plan after all. He was shocked by killing under a flag of truce, as opposed to a "fair and open" fight, and so was Carson. Aside from anything else, such acts would only arouse further hostility and make it harder to secure the surrender of the Indians. Carleton gave orders regarding a supply train sent to Fort Stanton at the end of November: "When the train starts to return, have all the Mescalero men, women, and children, of the peace party, with all their effects, come with this train. The women and children and baggage will be hauled in the wagons, and you will see that they have provisions enough to last them all to the Bosque Redondo." Carson was to continue operations against the unsurrendered Mescaleros, and any band that surrendered would also be sent to Bosque Redondo. "The result of this will be that, eventually, we shall have the whole tribe at the Bosque Redondo, and then we can conclude a definite treaty, and let them all return again to inhabit their proper country." In November 1862 he intended to return the Mescaleros to their homeland in the mountains when he believed peace was secure. That plan would soon change.

"Bosque Redondo" would shortly become the most notorious place name in New Mexico, but Carleton did not at first intend it as a permanent home for the Mescaleros. The Bosque Redondo, or Round Grove, on the Pecos River in the grasslands of eastern New Mexico, had long been a favorite camping place of the Mescaleros when they ventured onto the plains, and a meeting place of comancheros with their trading partners. Carleton first saw the site while making a survey of the Pecos in 1852, and he concluded it would be a good site for a cavalry post, strategically located with wood, grazing, and water available. Higher authority ignored his recommendation, but when Carleton returned to New Mexico as commanding general, he ordered the establishment of a post in October 1862, naming it Fort Sumner after Colonel Edwin Sumner. Before long he began to see other possibilities for the site, as a permanent, not temporary, home for the Mescaleros. Believing the place to have potential for agriculture, he apparently asked why the Apaches could not be settled right there, under the guardianship of the fort, and taught farming. There the experiment of civilizing the Indians could be carried out under controlled conditions, well removed from white settlements and under military supervision and protection. He would "have them, in short, become what is called in this country—a pueblo."[37]

The idea would be fateful, not only for the Mescaleros, but for the Navajos and, it may be, for western Indians in general. There was a notion among some Anglos in New Mexico at this time, apparently including Kit Carson, that the New Mexican Indian pueblos had been created by the Spanish, who were thought to have settled previously nomadic Indian hunters in these communities after their conquest in the early 1600s, converting them to Christianity and making the hunters into farmers. Because all Indians were assumed to be "uncivilized" hunters, there had to be some way to account for Indians who had permanent towns and relied primarily on agriculture. This belief ignored the immense variety of Indian cultures, and particularly the fact that the Pueblo peoples had practiced agriculture and built substantial towns centuries before any Spaniard ever saw the region. Carleton was well aware of this fact, although he still credited Catholic missionaries with making the Pueblos "christianized and partially civilized" and "very much above the nomadic Indians in point of intelligence and gentleness." It may be, however, that Carleton and others had heard, perhaps in a garbled version, of the genízaro communities the Spanish government founded in the 1700s, made up of former captives from plains and other tribes, now detribalized and to some extent assimilated into Hispanic culture. Carleton was ignoring great and ancient cultural differences between Apaches and Pueblos, believing that if some Indians could be civilized farmers, so could others. Soon he would try out his idea on a much larger scale.[38]

By March 1863 the majority of the Mescaleros were at Bosque Redondo; less than a hundred had taken themselves into the mountains of the New Mexico–Texas border and west of the Rio Grande, where they kept up raiding and kept the troops in those areas busy. While other soldiers of Carleton's command occupied themselves in operations against Apaches in southwest New Mexico and in Arizona (which became a separate territory in 1863, though still part of Carleton's jurisdiction), the general prepared for the campaign against the tribe he and many others saw as New Mexico's greatest enemy—the Navajos. As he explained to the adjutant general of the army at the beginning of February: "It may be set down as a rule that these Navajo Indians have long since passed that point when talking would be of any avail. They must be whipped and fear us before they will cease killing and robbing the people." He had no doubt who should command in this campaign. Kit Carson was still the indispensable man.[39]

Carson, however, did not see himself as indispensable and had other plans. It must have been an unpleasant surprise to the commanding general to receive Carson's letter of February 3, 1863, submitting his resignation, explaining that he had only delayed it because of the possibility of another Confederate invasion and the opportunity of "proving my devotion to that Government which was established by our Ancestors." In the event of another invasion, it would be his "pride and pleasure" to serve under the general's command, but "at present I feel that my duty as well as happiness, directs me to my home & family and trust that the General will accept my resignation." He expected to see Carleton shortly and discuss promotion in the First New Mexico with him. It was probably at this conference that the general persuaded Carson not to resign.[40]

Carson had joined the army to defend New Mexico from the Rebels and now that that danger had passed, he preferred life at home with his family to military glory. Strictly speaking, the army was not obliged to accept his resignation, but in that era such resignations by citizen soldiers were common enough and routinely accepted. Somehow Carleton got Kit to change his mind, probably by insisting that Colonel Carson's services were indispensable, that no one could equal his accumulated knowledge and experience, his "peculiar skill and high courage." Even a man who consistently deprecated his own reputation might be flattered by such talk, and of course Carleton would have made it a matter of duty. Navajo raids were a principal source of the persistent insecurity of life in New Mexico, and the general believed that only a decisive military campaign could end them.

Whatever Carleton's shortcomings, he was a professional soldier, conscious of serving a country torn by civil war and in danger of dissolution. Far from the great battlefields, he had charge of one corner of the national domain which it was his duty to protect and preserve, a point he surely made to Carson. Kit's letter of resignation had referred to "my devotion to that Government which was established by our Ancestors." He may have been thinking of Lindsey Carson, who had fought in the Revolutionary War.

Something besides Carleton's persuasiveness had caused Kit to reconsider resignation. When Kit was a small boy, Lindsey Carson, though nearly sixty, was a member of the Boonslick militia, helping defend the community from Indians, and had lost two fingers engaging the enemy. Now his son was past fifty and yearning for a quiet life at home, but his frontier community was under threat of Indian raids.

His contemporaries thought it natural that Kit Carson should be campaigning against Indians, but later generations, increasingly uneasy about the "Winning of the West" and still wishing to regard Kit as a hero, sometimes chose to believe that Carson, in William Keleher's words, "was not particularly enthusiastic" and doubted the need for military measures. Novelist Jack Schaefer depicts him as "reluctant to take the assignment," believing that "more understanding and some honest treaty-making would do the job without the use of gunpowder"; having accepted the assignment "under pressure," says Schaefer, Carson, "handicapped by Carleton's policies, bound by Carleton's orders," was "forced to make efficient use of considerable gunpowder."[41]

Recent writers and historians have simply denounced Carson as a brutal racist willing to carry out genocidal policies. Raymond Friday Locke, a historian of the Navajos, believes that Carson's reason for wanting to resign was "nothing so noble" as reluctance "to wage the savage war planned against the Navajos." Locke, who clearly does not want to give Carson credit for any admirable motives, argues that Kit was embarrassed by having been made to look foolish when his men took advantage of his illiteracy to get him to sign orders allowing them to purchase whiskey. If any episode during his service was embarrassing enough to make him want to resign, one would imagine it to be the gunfight between Captain Graydon and Surgeon Whitlock, ending with Graydon's company shooting Whitlock to pieces. Carson had quickly restored order, but he might well have become disgusted with the uncongenial task of maintaining discipline over an unruly, ethnically mixed body of men.[42] His proffered resignation alone should dispose of the notion that Carson, the "racist" and "Indian hater," could hardly wait for a chance to clean out the "redskins."

Carson made his views most explicit regarding the Navajo war in testifying before a congressional committee investigating Indian affairs in 1865. He gave a capsule summary of the situation and the reasons for the campaign as he saw them:

I know that even before the acquisition of New Mexico there had about always existed an hereditary warfare between the Navajoes and Mexicans; forays were made into each others's country, and stock, women, and children stolen. Since the acquisition, the same state had existed; we would hardly get back from fighting and making peace with them before they would be at war again . . . there is a part of the Navajoes, the wealthy, who wish to live in peace; the poorer classes are in the majority, and they have no chiefs who can control them.

In the same statement, Carson said he believed that most of the southern plains tribes were "compelled" to be hostile by the actions of whites, with the exception of the Kiowas, and that "justice demands that every effort should be made to secure peace with the Cheyennes and Arapahos before any war was prosecuted against them, in view of the treatment they have received." He thought that most difficulties with Indians at the time arose "from aggressions on the part of whites." It hardly seems that Carson believed that the only good Indian was a dead Indian, or that the sole cause of Indian-white conflict was the perversity of the Indians. He distinguished between groups of Indians, and for some reason he saw war with the Navajos, or with the Kiowas, in a different light from other such conflicts. (The Navajos and the Kiowas, it should be noted, were the Indians he had recently been fighting.)[43]

Just as government officials in the 1800s tried to devise a policy that could be applied uniformly to all tribes, so Americans in the twentieth century, as in the nineteenth, assume that all Indians faced exactly the same problems in confronting whites. Thus all Indian-white conflicts are viewed as exactly the same in origin and outcome, equally tragic and motivated, on the part of the whites, by the same discreditable motives. It is assumed, therefore, that anyone who took a sympathetic, or an unsympathetic, view of Indians would apply it equally to all, since they were all members of the same "minority." Whatever the merits of this concept for the early twenty-first century, it does not reflect nineteenth-century reality. There were many people who really did think that the only good Indian was a dead one, and there were advocates of Indian rights who saw all Indians as the victims of evil frontiersmen. As noted above, Kit Carson had moved some distance in the latter direction himself by 1865. But many frontiersmen learned, like him, to make distinctions between tribes and understood the complexity of relations between peoples. Kit was a longtime resident of New Mexico, and he was a friend and even admirer of the Utes, enemies of the Navajos, factors that could have prejudiced him. But clearly he saw the Navajo conflict as the product of a particular set of circumstances, not as just another instance of the general perfidy of Indians, or another opportunity to harry and destroy them. He seems to have viewed the Navajo campaign he waged in 1863–64 as a necessity.

The Navajos are today the most numerous Indian tribe in the United States. If not quite as universally identifiable as the war-bonneted plains warrior, the Navajo with his or her colorful blanket and turquoise jewelry has become a symbol of "Indianness." The beauty of the Navajos' art, the grandeur of their land, and the integrity of their culture and religion have inspired admiration among intellectuals and the general public. They are conflated in some minds with the Pueblos, in spite of great differences in language and culture, with the result that many are surprised to learn that the Navajos were a warrior people who raided their neighbors. Thus, when many learn that the people who "walk in beauty" were once harried by U.S. troops, that their crops and herds were taken or destroyed, that they were driven from their homes and forced on a "Long Walk" to a "concentration camp," where many died of disease and malnutrition, the reaction is likely to be horror and indignation. Learning that Kit Carson was the leader of the soldiers who made war on the Navajos causes many who previously believed that he was a hero to see him as either a genocidal racist or a precursor of those twentieth-century soldiers who claimed that they only carried out orders.

Since World War II obedience to orders has not been considered a defense against charges of atrocity. Professional soldiers of the 1800s, not imagining the full possibilities of ideologies of hatred stripped of the last rags of honor or Christian scruple, still held to an ideal of obedience and discipline as good in themselves. They considered a soldier absolved of responsibility if he carried out the orders of a lawful superior in wartime. U. S. Grant, criticized early in the Civil War for returning runaway slaves to their masters in accord with what was then official policy, wrote, "So long as I hold a commission in the Army I have no views of my own to carry out. Whatever may be the orders of my superiors, and law, I will execute." General George Crook, one of the frontier soldiers most outspokenly sympathetic toward Indians, is reported as saying, "The hardest thing is to go and fight those whom you know are in the right." Other American soldiers said something similar regarding the Indian wars. Kit Carson was certainly not a professional soldier, but he served within this climate of opinion.[44]

The Navajo campaign of 1863–64, the "Kit Carson Campaign," must be understood as part of a long and involved history of conflict in the Southwest. Reasonable men, not without prejudice but perhaps motivated by something more than blind racial hatred, could believe that a military operation against the Navajos was an unavoidable necessity, whether they were right or wrong in the light of later standards. The sort of war James Carleton and Kit Carson conducted in the Navajo country was in no way unique in the history of Indian-white conflict or of "irregular" warfare, nor was it genocidal in any meaningful sense of the word. It was the culmination of over a decade and a half of intermittent warfare between the U.S. Army and the Navajos, and of decades of conflict between those people and the New Mexicans. The pattern of conflict had been set, as Carson said, before the United States had acquired New Mexico, and the essential features of the campaign had been worked out well before General Carleton took command there.

AN HEREDITARY WARFARE

By 1863 the two peoples had over generations become locked into the kind of hostile relationship all too familiar in history. As Carson put it, "There had about always existed an hereditary warfare between the Navajoes and Mexicans." The origins of the conflict are subject to some scholarly debate. The Navajos, who call themselves the *Diné*,

are one branch of the Athapaskan language family, which also includes the Apaches. Their ancestors, most scholars agree, were relative
latecomers to the Southwest, arriving there from somewhere to the
north long after the Pueblo peoples had become sedentary farmers,
perhaps in the fifteenth century. There is some disagreement about
the early relationship between the two groups. It has been commonly
assumed, on the basis of later history, that the Athapaskans were always enemies of the Pueblos, raiding them as they did in historic
times. Jack D. Forbes contends that they coexisted in the region for
an extended period, their relationship being one of "peace and commerce," with occasional warfare. This changed, he believes, with the
arrival of the Spanish, whose slave raiding and "divide and conquer"
strategy turned the Apaches and Navajos into raiders and enemies of
the Pueblos.[45]

The Navajos had proved remarkably adaptable, taking in substantial
numbers of Pueblo people and elements of Pueblo culture, and also
adopting the animals the Spanish brought to the region—horses, sheep,
and cattle. They became, uniquely among North American Indians, a
pastoral people, with large herds and also fields of corn and wheat,
and even orchards. By 1800 they were well established in the area of the
present Four Corners, the meeting place of Arizona, New Mexico, Utah,
and Colorado. The history of their relationship with their Hispanic and
Pueblo neighbors, from the early 1700s on, consisted, in the words of
Raymond Friday Locke, "of little more than a long list of raids and
counter-raids, of expeditions and punitive expeditions." As Kit Carson
put it, "forays were made into each other's country, and stock, women,
and children stolen." Basically, the Pueblos and Hispanic people were
allies against the Navajos.[46]

The conflict might be seen as the traditional animosity between
sedentary farmers and pastoral nomads, which some scholars see as the
origin of true warfare in the Old World, now being replayed in the New,
although the New Mexicans had large herds, and the Navajos had their
own fields and were not truly nomadic. The pastoral folk often regard
the farmers with contempt; the Navajos and the Apaches reportedly
said that they allowed the Mexicans to live in order to raise stock for
them—a boast that Anglos were pleased to take literally. Even allowing
for particular, local circumstances, one can say the horse peoples of
both Old and New Worlds have very often been warriors and raiders of
their neighbors.[47]

There is really no doubt about the persistent hostility between the two peoples, but even at the time, and certainly since, there has been a question about which should bear the chief moral responsibility. In the twentieth century especially, the gnawing doubt about white America's treatment of the Indians has led many historians to shift that responsibility from the Navajos to the Hispanic New Mexicans and the military and civil officials of the U.S. government. Edward B. Spicer notes that Anglo interference was "questioned and resisted from the first."[48] Increasingly, profound doubt has been cast on the justification for the military campaigns against the Navajos by Carleton and others, and incidentally on the good repute of Kit Carson.

In New Mexico, as in so many such cases, there was no law or authority that all sides recognized as legitimate, impartial, and effective. Therefore, as Kit Carson observed, each side made forays into the other's country, stealing stock and captives. Kirby Benedict, chief justice of the territory, explained in 1865, "The Navajos were in the habit of making forays upon the ranches and settlements, stealing, robbing, and carrying away captives; the finding of herds and driving off sheep and other animals was carried on to a very ruinous extent; the killing of persons did not seem so much the object of their warfare as an incidental means of succeeding in other depredations."

Governor Henry Connelly agreed but pointed out the other side of the equation: "The Mexicans generally have been on the defensive. But sometimes they go after them to make reprisals, to get back their own, and to get what more they could. They mutually also captured and held as slaves the women and children of each other." The governor evidently knew whereof he spoke; according to Chief Justice Benedict, he had Navajo captives in his own household. As we have seen, Kit Carson also had in his charge three young Navajos. Both men would undoubtedly have said that they had taken these captives in because there was no other practicable way to care for them.[49]

When Navajo chief Zarcillos Largos said that his people had "just cause" for raiding the New Mexicans, he undoubtedly was referring to the raids of New Mexicans seeking livestock and captives. Governor Connelly, who thought the Navajos more successful in taking stock and the New Mexicans in taking captives, estimated there were from fifteen hundred to two thousand of the latter in New Mexico in 1865; Louis Kennon, testifying before the same committee, put the figure at five to six thousand. According to historian Marc Simmons, in many New

Mexico towns slaves were sold in the plaza after mass on Sundays; a rich man might place a special order for a Navajo woman to present to his daughter as a wedding gift. The men of the town of Cebolleta specialized in the taking and selling of such human merchandise. As noted, the Utes also took captives from the Navajos and sold them to New Mexicans, who considered themselves entitled to their services for having ransomed them. Louis Kennon declared, "I know of no family which can raise one hundred and fifty dollars but what purchases a Navajo slave, and many families own four or five—the trade in them being as regular as the trade in pigs or sheep." These practices obviously were not a secret, nor were they simply a fringe activity.[50]

Raids on the Navajos were part of the ongoing warfare between the two peoples. Albert Pfeiffer, as an agent for the Utes working under Carson, had participated with Kaniache in a raid on the Navajos in 1860, taking nineteen women and children captive, along with many horses and sheep. This was part of an army campaign against the Navajos in which the Utes served as auxiliaries. Military and government officials of Spain, Mexico, and the United States authorized raids by militia, citizen volunteers, Utes, and Pueblos as a means of augmenting the scanty forces of regular troops. Colonel Edwin Sumner, the military commander in New Mexico in 1851, was opposed to such irregular enterprises unless under strict army control, but later commanding officers accepted the need for combined operations by regulars, volunteers, and Indian allies. Both sides took captives, and both sides were reluctant to give them up as part of attempted peace settlements. The Navajo captives among the New Mexicans, as noted, were likely to be baptized and absorbed into the lower classes of Hispanic society. In the words of James Collins: "They are held and treated as slaves, but become amalgamated with the Mexicans and lose their identity." Much the same thing happened to most of the New Mexican captives among the Navajos. By the mid-1800s there was among the Navajos a whole clan called the "Mexican" clan, descendants of captive Hispanic girls and women, descent being reckoned through the mother. The fact that so many of the prisoners on both sides were young facilitated assimilation. The surviving families of the captives on both sides must have grieved in much the same way. No doubt the captors in both cases believed they had "just cause" since they were striking at the enemies of their people, and both sides were pleased at enriching themselves.[51]

The Dime Novel Carson. *The Fighting Trapper, or Kit Carson to the Rescue,* 1874.
Photograph from Albert Johannsen, *The House of Beadle and Adams and Their
Nickel and Dime Novels: The Story of a Vanished Literature*
(Norman: University of Oklahoma Press, 1950).

One of the earliest photographs of Carson, c. 1845,
in his mid-thirties. From the collection of the
Kit Carson Historic Museums, Taos NM.

John C. Frémont, c. 1849. Carson served as Frémont's guide
and scout on three exploring expeditions, and Frémont made Carson
the representative frontiersman. This item is reproduced by permission of
the Huntington Library, San Marino CA. 188 (1150A).

Carson and Alex Godey returning from their expedition against the
Indian raiders on the Old Spanish Trail, 1844, driving the recovered horses.
Godey has two scalps dangling from his rifle barrel. An artist's conception.
From John C. Frémont, *Memoirs of My Life* (Chicago: Belford, Clarke and Co.,
1887). Christlieb Collection, Center for Great Plains Studies,
University of Nebraska–Lincoln.

Sagundai, one of the Delawares who accompanied Frémont's Third
Expedition. From John C. Frémont, *Memoirs of My Life* (Chicago: Belford,
Clarke and Co., 1887). Christlieb Collection, Center for Great Plains Studies,
University of Nebraska–Lincoln.

(*opposite*) Believed to be a photograph of Maria Josefa Jaramillo Carson,
with child, c. 1850. From the collection of the Kit Carson Historic Museums,
Taos NM.

James Henry Carleton, commander of the Department of New Mexico
from 1862 to 1867; Carson's commanding officer in the Mescalero, Navajo,
and Kiowa-Comanche campaigns.
Courtesy Museum of New
Mexico, Neg. No. 22938.

(*opposite*) Carson as an Indian
agent, c. 1854, in his mid-forties.
From the collection of the Kit Carson Historic Museums, Taos NM.

Colonel Carson of the First New Mexico Volunteer Cavalry, c. 1865, in his mid-fifties. The effects of age and hard campaigning are evident. Courtesy Museum of New Mexico, Neg. No. 7151.

Kit Carson at Adobe Walls, November 1864. A twentieth-century painting by Nick Eggenhoffer. The artist has included the Indian scouts, at right; the ruined trading post; the mountain howitzers; the troopers fighting dismounted; and Carson on horseback giving orders.
Fort Union National Monument.

Ouray, Tabeguache Ute chief and ally of Kit Carson in keeping peace during Carson's command at Fort Garland co, 1866–67. Courtesy Colorado Historical Society, Neg. No. wpa1075 ibf Ouray.

Carson as a brigadier general, 1866, at fifty-six.
From the collection of the Kit Carson Historic Museums, Taos NM.

Carson c. 1867, at about fifty-seven.
The effects of his illness are beginning to show.
Courtesy Museum of New Mexico, Neg. No. 7152.

One of the last photographs of Carson, made during his trip to the East in 1868, at fifty-eight. It is also one of the best known images, and has shaped public perception of his appearance. In fact, he had clearly lost a great deal of weight and was a few months from death. Photo by James W. Black, Courtesy Museum of New Mexico, Neg. No. 13307.

The Americans—first the traders and trappers of the 1820s and '30s, then the soldiers and civil officials after 1846—brought their own baggage of historical experience and preconceptions about Indians. Their received view of history told them that Indians were savage folk, the enemies of settled, civilized people. Although most of them viewed "Mexicans" with an automatic contempt, they also saw them as people who lived in permanent houses and towns; who went to church, even if they were Catholic; who, alien as some of their ways were, were recognizably an offshoot of Western civilization. If they were under attack by Indians, then it was another chapter of a story familiar to Americans, who knew which side they were on. The Pueblos were a complication, but Anglos generally placed them in a special category, sometimes higher than the Hispanics, while viewing the "wild" tribes in the more familiar image. That the Pueblos frequently served as auxiliaries to American military expeditions also raised their standing.[52]

Anglos who had long resided in New Mexico, like Kit Carson, James Collins, and Governor Henry Connelly, were aware of the complexity and ambiguity of the relationships between the peoples. They had, however, become identified by marriage and other interests with the Hispanic people and to some extent shared their prejudices, though they could also criticize New Mexicans sharply. Recent arrivals, like the already-quoted Louis Kennon and Kirby Benedict, and soldiers like Edward Canby, often saw a lack of clear-cut moral differentiation between the two sides. What they could not see was an easy way to resolve these conflicts that would be truly even-handed and satisfactory to both sides.

It is a necessary simplification to speak of two sides in order to discuss the question at all. Designating two sides, Navajos and New Mexicans, implies two monolithic groups, all the members of each acting and thinking just the same. This was true neither of the Navajos nor of the New Mexicans. The Navajos were classed, in Spanish terminology, as *ricos*, the rich, and *ladrones*, literally "robbers." The former had great herds of horses, sheep, and cattle. The latter did not, and wished to acquire them; therefore they conducted raids on the herds of the New Mexicans, in the time-honored fashion of mounted pastoral folk. The ricos, already having wealth and status, found peace better than war; the retaliatory raids of New Mexicans fell most heavily on them, since they had the most to lose. But once the ricos had been despoiled, they could only recoup their losses by becoming ladrones. Thus the cycle became self-perpetuating.[53]

Captain John Pope, an army engineer, had spent two years in New Mexico when he submitted his ideas on the defense of the territory to his superiors in Washington in 1853. He was impressed by the Navajos' knowledge of agriculture and herding, and thought them more intelligent and "much farther advanced in civilization" than other New Mexico tribes. He believed they could easily be induced to settle in pueblos and so "be brought wholly under control." Pope considered the raiders to be a minority of the tribe, he guessed one-tenth, and he thought it "unreasonable and unjust to punish a whole tribe for the depredations of a few." "A few restless persons," he observed, might be found in any community, "and unless controlled by stringent laws . . . they are likely at any time to jeopardize the peace of their neighbors." This was a shrewd observation, one Pope could have applied as fairly to the New Mexican community. Those who actually raided the Navajos could not have been more than a minority of the male citizens; those who suffered by Navajo raids represented a much wider cross-section, for those raids extended over much of New Mexico, well east of the Rio Grande, and fell on the Pueblos as well as the Hispanic people.[54]

Pope also hit on one of the principal reasons for the recurring cycle of raiding and peacemaking:

> The great obstacle to any successful negotiation with them results from the peculiar form or rather want of form of their government. They are eminently democratic in their notions and recognize no control whatever. They are divided into numerous families and cliques and are only amenable to control through their personal interests. . . . In such a state of things it is impossible to make a treaty with them which is not likely to be violated.

Virtually all informed sources agree with Pope here. The Navajos were one people in language and culture, but they had no political unity. A Navajo chief might have influence because of his wealth and social standing, and of course his war record, but he was not in a position to give orders like an army officer, nor to enforce laws and allot punishments like a governor or a judge. Only the force of community opinion had the power to do that, and even the community could do little without a recognized enforcement mechanism. Whites who dealt regularly with Indians, like Captain Pope, came to recognize this fact, but they continued to make peace agreements with the Navajos, since they could see no other hope of breaking the cycle of hostilities with the military resources available. Thus they kept asking Navajo society to do things it was ill-equipped to do.[55]

There was a period in the mid-1850s when it seemed as if the cycle might slow down or even stop. Colonel Sumner established a military post, Fort Defiance, in the Navajo country in present northeast Arizona in 1851. In a few years the government agent, Henry Dodge, and the post commander, Captain Henry Kendrick, had established a modus vivendi with the Navajos that greatly reduced the hostilities. Incidents continued to occur, and New Mexican stockmen grazed their herds on Navajo lands, but there was a cessation of large-scale, persistent raiding. In 1855 Governor Meriwether made a treaty, setting aside a reservation for the Navajos and promising them annuities. Like his other agreements, it was criticized for giving the Indians too much land, and like the others, it was never ratified by Congress.[56]

Late in 1856 Henry Dodge disappeared on a hunting trip, apparently killed by Apaches. The next year, Captain Kendrick was transferred from Fort Defiance. For the Indians, personal relationships and trust were of primary importance, and in this instance they were right. Kendrick's successor, Captain William Brooks, managed to alienate the Navajos near the fort by killing Indian horses grazing on land used by the post. A Navajo then killed a black slave belonging to Brooks, and the captain demanded the surrender of the guilty man, though the Navajos offered blood money. The likelihood of a white man being punished for killing a black slave, it should be remembered, was at that time very slight. Brooks refused to accept an attempt to pass off a dead Mexican captive as the killer. The Navajos were simply unwilling to surrender one of their own for killing an alien. It was about this time that the Utes refused to make peace with the Navajos, and Kit Carson thought this might be just as well, both for the Utes and for the whites. These incidents and other clashes led to resumption of full-scale hostilities, in which forces of regular troops, New Mexicans, and Indian allies invaded the Navajo country and tried again to enforce peace on the white man's terms by force of arms. Once again the Navajos raided far and wide in New Mexico. Once again efforts to make peace were not successful for long.[57]

The last major campaign against the Navajos before Kit Carson's was that of Major Edward Canby in 1860–61. In form, if not in final result, it was very similar to Carson's three years later. Columns of regular troops, infantry and cavalry, New Mexican volunteers, Pueblos, and Utes acting on their own and as scouts for the troops scoured the country from September into the new year. Canby's instructions from the department commander were "to seize and destroy the crops of the Navajos." In the winter campaign three columns of regulars tried to squeeze the Navajos between them, while the Utes swept the country between the columns, taking horses, sheep, and captives. The Navajos avoided pitched combat, while harassing the columns when they could. The campaign became a matter of keeping the Navajos on the run, depriving them of as much of their crops and livestock as possible, driving them into the most desolate desert and mountain areas, where they suffered greatly as winter came on. Patrols kept in the field, moving as secretly as possible to achieve surprise. Units of citizen volunteers, with Pueblo allies joining them, were also in the field, in a fashion traditional since Spanish times, in spite of official doubts about their motives and susceptibility to control. This was the beginning of the period the Navajos called the *Nahondzod*, the "Fearing Time," extending to 1868 and the end of their captivity at Bosque Redondo.[58]

Canby's purpose was to force the entire Navajo people to surrender, which meant that they would have to agree to control the actions of the ladrones, even using force against them if necessary. By March 1861 he had secured the agreement of over thirty chiefs and was hopeful that peace might be maintained if the Navajos "can be secured from outside aggressions." Unfortunately, the army lacked the authority to control the attacks of New Mexican irregulars, and other matters soon distracted the regulars' attention.[59]

As Canby's campaign ended, the secession crisis was splitting the nation and the army officer corps. The peace arrangement quickly fell apart, due to actions by both sides, and Navajo raiding again scourged New Mexico. A crucial event was the outbreak of violence at Fort Fauntleroy in September 1861, when a dispute over a horse race led to fighting between New Mexico volunteers and Navajos. In October 1861, Superintendent James Collins reported on the new wave of raids: "The record of murders committed by them is truly frightful . . . this death list is not made up of a few lives lost. . . . Its number will extend to nearly three hundred for the past eighteen months. . . . One of two things will have to be done with them—a total breaking up of the nation, verging upon extermination, or placing them upon a reserve." Collins saw things no more cheerfully a year later: "Indeed, their hostilities are present to us in a more aggravated form that at the time of my report last year." The only thing to be done was "to let them be well punished by the military arm."

A year later a new superintendent of Indian Affairs, Michael Steck, had taken office and was making his annual report in September 1863. Steck had been a sympathetic agent for the Mescalero Apaches, and he was to become a bitter antagonist of General Carleton, so it is noteworthy that he saw the Navajo tribe as "the most formidable of all with which we have to deal." He thought, "The Indians, by their acts of wholesale destruction of life and property, and the general disregard they have exhibited of all former promises, have rendered themselves liable to severe punishment." Between 1860 and 1863 raids by different tribes had cost the lives of over two hundred "citizens, soldiers, and shepherds," and had taken at least five hundred thousand sheep and five thosuand horses, mules, and cattle. Most whites in New Mexico agreed with Steck, but there were a few exceptions.[60]

John Greiner, Carson's predecessor as agent for the Utes and Jicarillas, thought that peace might have been preserved in the 1850s if the successors of Agent Henry Dodge and Captain Henry Kendrick had been "persons of equal prudence"; he also saw "the capture of [the Navajos'] flocks and herds, and their women and children for servants" by New Mexicans as a principal cause of trouble. Another New Mexico resident, Louis Kennon, saw the Navajos as "the most abused people on the continent," and judged "that in all hostilities the Mexicans have always taken the initiative with but one exception that I know of." He believed that the New Mexicans had pressured the army into war in 1858, simply because "the Navajoes had a great many sheep and horses and a great many children," and that the troubles of that year at Fort Defiance were only a pretext covering this underlying motive for war.[61]

Navajo raiding caused serious loss of life and property in New Mexico, and had for many years, but Frank McNitt, an expert on the Navajo wars up to 1861, argues that "a state of constant warfare was contrary to Navajo nature and totally disruptive of normal Navajo life. Stock raisers and farmers could not live as raiding nomads or fugitives." The same, of course, applied to the stock raisers and farmers of New Mexico. The view that the interminable cycle of wars was primarily the fault of New Mexicans is one that appeals to many recent writers, who find the invariable cause of Indian-white conflict in the conduct of whites. This thesis is the basis for such highly critical histories of the Kit Carson campaign, the "Long Walk," and the Bosque Redondo exile as those by Lynn Bailey and Clifford Trafzer, and the hostile comments of many other writers already quoted. Most Anglo and Hispanic New Mexicans of the 1860s would have disputed such an interpretation vehemently.[62]

One contemporary observer who had enough experience to understand the problem and was at least not biased by personal ties to New Mexico was Colonel Edward Canby, who conducted the campaign of 1860–61. He would be killed in 1873 while attempting to negotiate a peace with the Modoc Indians of northern California, becoming the only serving U.S. general to be killed by Indians. He had been warned of possible treachery, but took the risk in the hope of ending the conflict. It would seem that he was not inflexibly committed to a military solution to Indian troubles. In the fall of 1861, while in command in New Mexico and preparing to resist the Confederates, he wrote to superior headquarters about the state of Indian-white relations in the territory:

The depredations of the Navajoes are constant. . . . Between the Navajoes and people of New Mexico a state of hostilities, with occasional intervals of peace, has existed almost since the first settlement of the country. Each party claims that the treaty of peace has been broken by the other, and it is impossible now, even if it were profitable, to inquire which is in the right. Each successive war has reduced the Navajoes in strength and wealth, and has, by reducing them to poverty, added to the strength of the ladrones, or war party. There is no doubt that many of these difficulties, if not caused, have at least been greatly aggravated, by the illegal acts of the Mexican people, and in some cases have been the direct cause of the difficulties that immediately followed them. The consequences of these acts have almost invariably fallen upon the portion of the Navajoes known as the peace party and upon those of the inhabitants who have property to lose, while the aggressors profit by the sale of their booty and captives. These acts are not restrained by the moral sense of the community, and so long as these marauders find a ready sale for their plunder and for their captives, it will be impossible to prevent these depredations and the consequent retaliation by the Indians.

Unless this system, "encouraged by the sympathies of the people and fostered to some extent by the Territorial laws," could be broken up, said Canby, "the country will be involved in interminable evils." He added, "Recent occurrences in the Navajo country . . . have so demoralized and broken up that nation, that there is now no choice between their absolute extermination or their removal and colonization at points so remote from the settlements as to isolate them entirely from the inhabitants of the Territory." Canby thought that the extermination of the Navajos, "aside from all considerations of humanity," would be a difficult task, for the country was "impracticable and destitute of resources for military operations," and the enemy would not stand and fight in any numbers, so any operations would become "a chase of individual thieves." Such Navajos as desired peace should be protected by the army until they could be placed on reserves at a distance from the New Mexicans "until they are able to sustain themselves as heretofore." This had been "repeatedly recommended by the superintendent of Indian affairs and the commanders of this department." It was the only policy that had any chance of success, and was recommended by "considerations of humanity, economy, and experience."[63]

A little earlier Canby had also written to Governor Connelly, explaining his project for separating the Navajo "peace party" from the ladrones, and for protecting the inhabitants of New Mexico from Indian raids. Canby lectured Connelly on the need for all citizens to support the law and the policy of the government: "Unless the illegal acts of a few vicious individuals are denounced by the moral sense of the community and enforcement of the laws aided by all, the best efforts that can be made to control the Indians and protect the inhabitants will be utterly fruitless." Canby was well aware of the moral complexities and ambiguities of the situation in New Mexico; he did not see a simple "savage"-versus-"civilized" picture. The next year, however, after the expulsion of the Texans and before being succeeded by General Carleton, Canby was, as noted, planning a renewed military campaign against the Navajos, with Kit Carson in field command. He apparently saw no other way to carry out his proposal to place the Navajos on reserves isolated from the New Mexicans, in order to insure lasting peace.[64]

Because Canby, not Carleton, made the original decision for a new Navajo campaign, the notion that the latter devised the campaign because of his unique and inflexible animosity toward Indians can be discarded—as can the theory that Carleton hatched a war simply to keep his troops from dangerous idleness. If Canby, with his clear and relatively unbiased appreciation of the situation in New Mexico, saw a military operation as necessary, then it may be that he simply could find no other solution, given the intractable conditions that existed. Carleton must have conferred with his predecessor before the change of command, and in any case he had also served for several years in New Mexico. Even if he was, as many historians would argue, more rigid and relentless and less understanding than Canby, it is hard to see how ensuing events could have been radically different, without a radical change in some of the major social, political, and military factors. No military commander in New Mexico would have sat by and let things go on as they were. A negotiated peace had been tried repeatedly, and no agreement had lasted.

That two department commanders in succession believed in the necessity for the campaign will not impress those who believe that all army officers operated on the principle that "the only good Indian is a dead Indian." Those who have made any detailed study of the Indian wars and of the frontier military know that this was far from true. Certainly army officers were as ethnocentric as their fellow Americans, but their opinions nonetheless ranged over a broad spectrum, encompassing every possible attitude except, it would seem, the dogged cultural relativism demanded of the modern intellectual. Both Canby and Carleton—and Kit Carson, though he was not making the ultimate decisions—had to operate within a narrow range of imaginable options, based on their understanding of a situation with deep historical roots.[65]

Another reason given for the Navajo campaign, and Carleton's other Indian campaigns, is that he wished to clear the way for the exploitation of mineral resources in western New Mexico and Arizona. A Navajo school textbook declares flatly, "Kit Carson's commanding officer, Gen. James Carleton, attacked the Navajos because he hoped to find gold and saw nothing wrong with killing people who got in his way." Like the idea that Carleton wanted to keep his troops busy, this theory ignores ample evidence of the damage caused in New Mexico by Indian raids, and it assumes that these campaigns were solely Carleton's idea, when we have seen that Edward Canby had similar plans. However, Carleton was very much interested in developing the mineral resources of the Southwest and did what he could to encourage and protect prospectors and miners. He offered help to a gold-seeking party in Arizona headed by the old mountain man Joseph Walker, and he ordered some of his California troops to prospect for gold in conjunction with escort duties. He wrote more than once to General Henry Halleck, general-in-chief of the army, about the discovery of "one of the richest gold countries in the world" on the Gila River, asking for more California troops who were "practical miners" to be stationed there. These troops could "exterminate" the Apaches there—almost his only use of the word *exterminate*—and colonize the area when discharged. "Do not despise New Mexico, as a drain upon the government," he told Halleck. "The money will all come back." He also wrote Secretary of the Treasury Salmon Chase about the region from the headwaters of the Gila to the Colorado, which was "uncommonly rich" in gold and other minerals. He sent Chase samples of gold and copper and suggested that the largest nugget go to Mr. Lincoln, to gratify him with the knowledge "that Providence is blessing our country, even though it chasteneth." Aside from drawing the attention of powerful people in Washington to himself and the importance of his remote bailiwick, these letters reflect Carleton's awareness that the Union, with its credit strained by the war, would greatly benefit from the discovery of new sources of wealth, which he could easily consider it his duty to facilitate. Some stories that he had his own investments in mining claims apparently arise from the claims of Henry Carleton, an entirely different person, but that he was interested in such investments and had made some by 1867 also seems clear.[66]

The viewpoint remaining to be considered regarding the origins and the justification for the Navajo campaign is, of course, the viewpoint of the Navajos—not the twentieth-century Navajos who, like the rest of us, look back on it through the haze of tradition and historical interpretations, but those who actually experienced the *Nahondzod.* Their opinions are scantily recorded; a few statements by chiefs and recollections of old people given long after are about all we have directly from that generation. Most Navajo evidence on the period has been filtered through one or more generations of storytelling before being recorded. In the 1940s Clyde Kluckholm wrote of the Navajo memory of the captivity at Fort Sumner (Bosque Redondo): "Even today it seems impossible for any Navajo of the older generation to talk for more than a few minutes on any subject without speaking of Fort Sumner. . . . One can no more understand Navajo attitudes—particularly toward white people—without knowing of Fort Sumner than he can comprehend Southern attitudes without knowing of the Civil War." Kluckholm wrote when the Long Walk and Fort Sumner were already eighty years in the past, and part of the living memory of only a very few Navajos, which surely testifies to the traumatic nature of the experience for them. At the same time, beliefs and traditions of southern white people of the late 1900s about the Civil War, while undoubtedly meaningful for them, and explaining much about their attitudes and politics, would not be accepted by historians as valid evidence about the details of Civil War history. The same caution must apply to Navajo traditions about the same time period.[67]

Navajo stories and traditions of the period have been collected in the twentieth century, and they undoubtedly give valuable insight into the experience of the *Diné*. They leave no doubt whatsoever that the *Nahondzod*, from about 1860 to 1868, the period of Canby's and Carleton's campaigns, the Long Walk to Fort Sumner, and the years at Bosque Redondo, was a terrible time for the Navajos, a time of fear, suffering, and loss. Kit Carson, however, can only be held responsible, at the most, for the first phase, the military campaign, since he was not in charge of the Long Walk and only briefly directed the Bosque Redondo reserve in its early phases. Late twentieth-century Navajos, nonetheless, have chosen to make him the villain of the piece. Once again his fame has made him the symbolic figure representing far more than himself. The same Navajo school textbook already cited quotes Tłááschchí'í Sáni on the cause of the Navajo war:

> There was a time when our ancestors hid like the deer in rocks and canyons because they were afraid of being captured, but it was their own fault. There were Navajos then who had nothing. No livestock of any kind. Building a hogan, planting a crop, hoeing—they never thought of it. Like coyotes or wolves that steal in the night, they were raiding the Utes. . . . Then there were Mexicans who lived along rivers east of Huerfano Mountain. They had stock in their corrals too. From as far as Black Mesa Navajos traveled over there like mice in the night and took it. So also with the whites. . . . It was robbery! They told fine stories about "going to war," but they were just saying that. They were stealing. Soon everyone turned against the Navajos, and the word got back to Washington. "If the Navajos stay out there, things will only get worse," they said. "Let's just round them up and get them off their land." That's when the army came looking for us.

Tłááschchí'í Sáni was eighty years old when he made his statement in 1980, which places his birth over thirty years after the return from Bosque Redondo. He was certainly much closer to the event than later generations, but he was still telling, after many years, the stories he had heard from people who experienced those times. It is noteworthy that he attributes the war to the attacks of Navajo raiders on Utes,

New Mexicans, and Anglos. He was not the only Navajo, relying on traditional accounts, to do so. Were he and others simply relaying what they were told, or were they making their own critical evaluation of received tradition?[68]

Navajo traditions of the *Nahondzod* have been collected at random by various persons, but the largest collection is in a volume titled *Navajo Stories of the Long Walk Period*, which was published by the Navajo Community College Press in 1973. That material, the editor notes, was "collected by Navajos from Navajos and translated by Navajos." More than forty Navajos, most of them elderly, recorded their versions of events over a century in the past, stories that had come down to them by word of mouth. It is a great pity that so little effort was made to collect such material earlier in the twentieth century—from those with personal memory of the events—as was done with Indian veterans of the plains wars. Interpretation of such stories is not easy. As Ruth Roessel notes in her introduction to *Navajo Stories*, they are not very specific as to time, and events of earlier wars, perhaps dating back to Mexican or even Spanish times, may be combined with those of Carson's campaign. Moreover, the Navajos probably did not distinguish, understandably enough, between the actions of Kit Carson's uniformed and relatively disciplined New Mexico volunteer regiment and those of irregular bodies of self-constituted "militia" raiders who acted on their own account.[69]

If nothing else, the diversity of these accounts proves once again that all members of an Indian tribe do not think in stereotyped fashion. That diversity is notable in the storytellers' views of the causes of the war. In Roessel's words, some narrators "place all blame squarely on the shoulders of the U.S. government, the white people, Mexicans and hostile Indian tribes." Others, however, place the blame on part or all of their own people, who raided other peoples without regard to the possible consequences for all Navajos. Howard Gorman, a member of the Navajo Tribal Council, explained:

> It began because of the behavior of a few *Diné*. A handful, here and there, riding horseback, killed white people and others that were traveling overland, and took their belongings. So the soldiers, commanded by Kit Carson, were ordered out.

Gorman particularly blamed a man named Double Face, "a very stubborn man, known as a thief and killer," and the group he led, for causing trouble: "Today, they would be referred to as gangsters." Rita Wheeler, relating the experiences of her ancestors, placed great emphasis on the attacks on the Navajos by Utes, Hopis, and other Indians:

> The reason why they came to raid was because of a few Navajo men who had gone out to raid other tribes. Some even went into the territory of the Mexicans and brought back horses. This created tension and soon brought these people into the Navajo areas, raiding and waging war upon families. That's when they really became our enemies.

Eli Gorman remembered what his father and others had told him:

> As time went on the *Diné* continued to raid, and the U.S. government was getting tired of the situation and looked at the Navajos as real potential troublemakers. A white leader probably said, "There is nothing but trouble ahead for them. We will have to round them up because, as time goes on, they will decrease in number. Many of them will be killed, especially the belligerent ones. If we round them up peaceful ones will not be killed; children will not be killed; only the warlike *Diné*. . . . ["] At least, that is what the old people used to tell me.

Hascon Benally, who would have been born around 1880, gave this version:

> Our late forefathers, those that were wise, begged their fellow *Diné* to stop going around stealing horses, sheep and cattle from the Mexicans; but the stealing went on. One of the men who was begging the *Diné* to quit stealing said, "Don't be sorry when we get enemies like a road covered with ice — starvation, poverty and cold. You will suffer; then you will understand."

Henry Zah had heard a similar explanation:

> More than a hundred years ago, we, the *Diné*, didn't have single strong leaders, and we lived like being on two paths or two separate ways, fighting and having wars with other tribes that lived in neighboring territories. For that reason, *Wááshindoon* (the United States government) took us to Fort Sumner a little over a hundred years ago. It was because of our own angriness. Old men and women folks told it that way — the ones who took the journey.

These and other Navajo storytellers differed as to the details of the origin of the wars, and on the proportion of raiders and troublemakers among the people as a whole. But they believed that the responsibility did not all lie on one side.[70]

It should certainly not be implied that the Navajos of an earlier generation uniformly accepted blame for their own troubles. As noted, their opinions were much more diverse than that. Others concentrated on the sufferings inflicted on their ancestors by their enemies. Some nursed a deep and persistent sense of wrong, voiced with particular force by Curly Tso:

> The government's reason seemed to be that the white people, coming this way, needed more land, and the Navajos were scattered out too far and lived on some of the best lands; so, in order to give the white people the land, plans were made by the government to kill most of the Navajos and send the rest to *Halgai Hatéél* (Wide Plains or Oklahoma), or perhaps, to round them up and force them to live close together like the Hopis. Personally, I often wondered, after I became aware of white men's laws, why our people were treated so unjustly. White Men make and preach about all kinds of laws, laws that protect individual rights; and where were these laws then? . . . the laws do not say to place blame and have innocent people suffer the consequences; and such was the case that the Navajo people went through.[71]

The belief that many innocent people suffered because of the acts of a few comes through clearly in a number of these accounts.

In late 1861 Colonel Edward Canby had declared, "There is now no choice between [the Navajos'] absolute extermination or their removal and colonization at points so remote from the settlements as to isolate them entirely from the inhabitants of the Territory." The suggestion that the forcible roundup and confinement of the Navajos was a humanitarian measure to avert their extermination must strike modern readers as either obtuse or cynically self-serving on the part of whites. Yet some Navajos in the twentieth century echoed it. Hascon Benally imagined the thinking of the U.S. government:

> It probably said, "What if the *Diné* vanish? It would be bad; so there must continue to be some *Diné*." . . . The government, thinking of assisting the Navajo people, said, "Some *Diné* probably are still alive; so scout them out and bring them in."

Dugal Tsosie Begay believed the same:

As the wars went on between us and the others, the number of our people decreased and the government noticed it. They talked about us and they said, "What if all Navajos starve to death, or what if they all are wiped out by other Indian tribes and the Mexicans? What's next?"

As the talk went on, it was decided from Fort Sumner that we be rounded up and taken to that place for security.

According to Frank Goldtooth:

When these tribes became extreme in fighting the Navajos, something called the government stepped into help us, to take us away from the enemies, to take us to a place called *Hwééldi* [Bosque Redondo]. We were in the hands of the government, and our order was to march to *Hwééldi* where we would be safe from our enemies.

Conceivably the speakers learned this interpretation in white-run reservation schools, but since they were speaking to fellow Navajos, it is hard to see why they would repeat it if they did not believe it, especially if family traditions were contrary. Apparently some Navajos in the decades after the Long Walk and Bosque Redondo believed that their condition at the time was desperate, and that the experience, bad as it was, perhaps saved them from something worse.[72]

Zonnie Ahtay (Pretty Girl) was born about 1845. When she was around seventy she told her experiences to a white friend:

Zonnie Ahtay was too young to remember the years when sheep and goats and cattle were plentiful and when they lived openly and without fear. . . . Many of her childhood memories are of hasty messengers arriving with messages of raiding parties of soldiers, Mexicans, or Apaches. Then would come the hurried bundling of blankets, pots, and food supplies . . . as they fled back into the mountains to a hidden cave, where they could find shelter until the raiders were gone.

Zonnie Ahtay's memories would have gone back well before the Carson or the Canby campaigns, covering the 1850s; she describes a condition of persistent fear and insecurity. Her father died when she was twelve or thirteen, around 1858, and her mother "became afraid that her two girls might be captured and taken away by the Mexicans or soldiers as many others had been." They moved west to the Hopi country, and Pretty Girl, now called Slim Woman, was adopted by relatives who had been impoverished by "soldier raids." They raised corn and beans, which they carefully concealed in pots underground: "They dared not stay close to their food supply, as this was near the Ute country where Ute and Apache raids were frequent." The Navajos were not passive victims: "They were tough and desperate and fought back as fiercely as they could, raiding and stealing whenever the opportunity presented itself." That they did so effectively, measured by the complaints of New Mexicans, we have already seen. We may understand why Canby would say that "it is impossible now, even if it were profitable, to inquire which is in the right," and why he believed that separating Navajos and New Mexicans and placing the former on a reserve where they could be guarded, and also protected, would be the only effective solution.[73]

The Navajos and New Mexicans were engaged in a war of attrition. The attrition was slow, but the Navajos, with perhaps twelve thousand people to some eighty thousand New Mexicans, were likely to lose in the long run, especially since the U.S. Army had become a factor. In the meantime, their progressive impoverishment inevitably turned more and more of them into raiders, causing much grief to New Mexicans. To reiterate, the lack of any central authority among Navajos made a binding, comprehensive peace extremely difficult to achieve. And New Mexicans, with their own wrongs to avenge, did nothing to discourage those among them who conducted their own raids. In the light of the facts, it might seem that Edward Canby was not simply abdicating moral responsibility by declining "to inquire which is in the right," but was recognizing the inability of such an inquiry to provide a solution.

The New Mexicans were not the only dedicated enemies of the Navajos. Their own accounts dwell as much on the attacks of their Indian enemies as on those of Mexicans and soldiers. The Utes were especially assiduous, both as allies of the army and on their own initiative, and of course they also saw themselves as avenging past wrongs. They had told Kit Carson that they could not make peace with the Navajos because they could not trust them; in other words, they recognized the same problem of lack of authority that the whites complained of. They would play their part in Carson's campaign, as in previous ones.

The Utes were not the only Indians at odds with the Navajos. The Pueblo villages had long suffered from Navajo raids, and they had often sent men to assist Spanish, Mexican, and U.S. expeditions against them. Erna Fergusson, writing about 1930, tells of how various Pueblo communities in their dances staged "most realistic sham battles between wild Indians and blue-coated Americans": "The Pueblos still remember that it was the United States troops who first gave them protection from the marauding Navajos and Apaches, and in these dramas their sympathy is with the soldiers." The historians of Santa Ana Pueblo, on the Jemez River near the Rio Grande, write that by the early nineteenth century, the Navajos "posed a major threat to the pueblo." Summer was the time "when Navajo and Apache raiders were most likely to attack Tamayame [Santa Ana] herds and herdsmen . . . Tamayame patrols on the trails, Tamayame farmers . . . and even, as the raiders grew more daring, the women and children at Tamaya [Santa Ana] itself." In turn, men of Santa Ana and other pueblos joined American military expeditions against the Navajos after New Mexico changed hands.[74]

The Pueblos closest to the Navajo country were Zuni, in western New Mexico, and the Hopi towns in northern Arizona, isolated on their mesas to the west of the main Navajo lands. Their nineteenth-century histories likewise present a long record of Navajo raids and Pueblo reprisals. In 1850 Navajos besieged Zunis for sixteen days, and the army sent ammunition to the Zunis to help out. In 1858, Zunis rescued some U.S. troops from Navajos. Although the Hopis had little official relation with the government or the army in those years, a delegation visited Governor Calhoun in August 1851. As he wrote, "They complained that the Navajos had left them exceedingly poor, and wretched, indeed, they did look." They too had suffered under Navajo attacks, and would until Kit Carson's campaign, in which both Zunis and Hopis would be active. Navajo Charlie Mitchell, who remembered those times, recalled in 1929, "all of the different peoples—the Utes and the Pueblo Indians, the White House people and the Isletas and those on the Rio Grande, the Jemez, the Santo Domingo . . . and the Zuñi and the Hopi and the Oraibi—all of those who live around us were put down toward us. And so this Navaho tribe, of which we are, thus was entirely alone." To all of them it probably seemed, as in the words of Ruth Underhill, that "the Navajos were reaping the harvest of the years they had been Lords of the Soil."[75]

There was nothing new in the use of Indian allies by white armies. Nor was there anything radically different about the kind of campaign ordered by Carleton and conducted by Kit Carson in the Navajo country in 1863–64. In tactics and strategy, it was very much like Canby's campaign of 1860–61, owing much to earlier experience of Indian warfare, and pointing the way toward future campaigns. Like those later wars, it has been labeled "genocidal" by historians. The conduct of this military operation has led to comparisons between Kit and such figures as Genghis Khan and Adolf Hitler. Such comparisons are usually made without detailed knowledge of what Carson actually did during the Navajo war, and without historical understanding of Indian-white warfare in general. Fortunately, scholars such as Robert Utley, Lawrence Kelly, Marc Simmons, and R. C. Gordon-McCutchan have studied Carson's conduct in some detail, and their work is utilized here.

In 1860, during Canby's campaign, Secretary of War John Floyd, a Virginia gentleman, sent orders to the commanders in New Mexico about the conduct of the war against the Navajos. The troops "should have as their object to inspire them with fear, by a few decisive blows for the destruction of life; and not impoverish them, by wantonly destroying their flocks and herds." As Utley remarks, "The Secretary thus exposed his ignorance of the realities of Indian fighting." Floyd imagined a series of "honorable" stand-up fights between the troops and Navajo warriors, in which the latter would be decisively defeated, with a loss of life that would induce them to give up the fight. But the Navajos, like most western Indians, would not fight pitched battles except where they had an overwhelming advantage or were trapped and had to defend their families. Canby found that they would not stay and fight because the extent and nature of their broad and rugged land, "impracticable and destitute of resources for military operations to a degree that can only be realized from personal observation," nearly always allowed them to escape. Canby's ethnocentric verdict was: "The Navajoes are too cowardly to fight in number . . . and any operations that may be carried on against them will ultimately resolve itself into a chase of individual thieves." The Navajos would not fight the white soldiers on the soldiers' terms, as long as they had superior mobility, knowledge of the country, and refuges in the mountains and canyons. It was the classic dilemma of a regular army confronting guerrillas in their own country, country ill-suited to conventional military operations.[76]

The solution adopted by Canby, and in turn by Carleton and Carson, was the classic one. The soldiers would destroy their herds and flocks and crops, the basis of their economy, and harass them in the summer and especially in the winter. The point was to deny them three vital things: subsistence, security, and sanctuary. Battle casualties might be few, but the toll of suffering on the whole population would ultimately force surrender. The same strategy, with local variations, would reappear in Indian campaigns for the next two decades. It was not new when Canby used it, however. In the Second Seminole War, in which Edward Canby served as a junior officer, Seminole raiders operating out of the swamps were a maddeningly elusive enemy; the army finally opted for small parties of soldiers and sailors to penetrate their sanctuaries, destroying their small cornfields, showing them they had no sanctuary.[77]

As Lawrence Keeley has pointed out, such a strategy results from civilized soldiers adopting the methods of their "primitive" enemies, increasing their mobility and concentrating their efforts on the enemy's manpower and economic resources: "By attrition, they gradually erode the primitives' small and inelastic manpower pool; by destruction of food and materiel, they exhaust the slim economic surpluses of the warriors, often inducing them to surrender to avoid starvation." These are, Keeley argues, the basic methods of primitive warfare.[78]

As the living conditions and subsistence of Indian tribes varied, so did the emphasis of army strategy. The Navajos were particularly vulnerable because of their large herds and flocks and their fields, which were obvious targets; the fields were immobile, and the cattle and sheep limited mobility and could be driven off by an enemy. The Apaches, relying largely on hunting and raiding, had to be pursued actively and constantly by army columns with inferior mobility; they would maintain their resistance long after the Navajos were subdued, and the army had to make extensive use of Apache scouts against them. The Great Plains tribes were also highly mobile and elusive, but their dependence on the buffalo proved an Achilles' heel.

Such a strategy was not consonant with conventional standards of warfare in the mid-nineteenth century, as Secretary Floyd's orders of 1860 suggest. Warfare was supposed to be carried on by bodies of armed men fighting pitched battles, each side trying to destroy enough of the enemy to force him to accept defeat, the way Union and Confederate commanders tried to win at Shiloh, Gettysburg, and Chickamauga, at a great cost in soldiers' lives. Such destruction of fighting men was honorable. The Indians' culture and small numbers, not to mention their lack of a government with coercive powers and lack of elaborate logistical support, all inclined them to the philosophy of living to fight another day. In the Civil War, to be sure, the Union increasingly directed its efforts toward destruction of the Southern resource base and the people's will to resist. This has been described as "total war," resembling World War II in erasing the distinction between soldiers and civilians, an interpretation that has in turn been questioned on the grounds that the destruction was much more selective and restricted than commonly portrayed. Historians have gone on from the idea of the Civil War as a total war to describe the Indian wars after 1865 as total wars, assuming that the example of war against civilians in 1861–65 taught the army the lesson they then applied to the Indian wars.[79]

This theory assumes that the "Indian Wars" designates a period after 1865, rather than a series of conflicts fought before, during, and after the civil conflict. William Skelton argues that army officers had concluded long before 1861, at least as early as the Seminole War of 1835–42, that conventional rules of war—"humane treatment of prisoners of war, protection of noncombatants and their property and food supplies, a general respect for one's opponents"—did not apply in Indian warfare. Both a low opinion of Indian character and the difficulty of getting Indians to fight on the white man's terms shaped this conclusion, though Skelton does not believe that army officers in general subscribed to the scientific racism that developed during the period. Army officers believed it necessary, if hostilities occurred, to apply overwhelming force, to convince the Indians that resistance was hopeless. Otherwise, the "hostiles" would make a temporary peace agreement they never intended to keep. The inability of tribal leaders to enforce peace agreements on all members of their tribes fostered this belief. If whites accepted a peace agreement prematurely, hostilities would only resume. It was in this belief that James Carleton was so determined to make peace with the Mescaleros only when they had all surrendered themselves into his power, and he would pursue the same policy with the Navajos.[80]

The Navajos became aware of Carleton's military preparations, made plain by the building of Fort Wingate in northwest New Mexico, and a delegation of eighteen chiefs came to Santa Fe in December 1862. Carleton reported: "I told them that they could have no peace until they would give other guarantees than their word that the peace would be kept . . . that we had no faith in their promises; that if they did not return we should know that they had chosen the alternative of war; that in this event the consequences rested on them." The "other guarantees" the general wanted consisted of the Navajos' agreement to move to

Bosque Redondo. A group of Navajos who had separated from the others and encamped near Cubero, according to their 1861 agreement with Canby, had already been ordered to move to the Pecos. Perhaps their example encouraged Carleton to expect the rest of the nation to submit, but if so, he was mistaken. The prospect of leaving their own country to live in a confined area, contrary to their customary way of life, was repugnant, indeed frightening. Further, it violated their profound religious attachment to their land, to them a sacred land between four sacred mountains, given to them by the supernatural powers. But this agreement to move was the only indication of peaceful intent that the commanding general would accept.[81]

One of the most difficult tasks of the army in Indian warfare was to separate the "hostiles" from the "friendlies" within a particular tribe. Since most army officers lacked the detailed knowledge necessary to make such a determination, and since most believed Indians to be "treacherous" and unreliable anyway, friendly actions and not just words were required. The problem of distinguishing actively hostile elements from the rest of the population has proved the stumbling block for innumerable antiguerrilla operations, and the tendency of soldiers to treat everyone in an alien population as hostile in such situations has commonly generated further hostility. Carleton had to distinguish the two or treat all Navajos as hostile; he also had to be able to protect those who did surrender from their enemies, or there would be no lasting peace, as Canby had pointed out. He apparently could think of only one way to do all this. In June 1863 he sent word to Delgadito and Barboncito, two prominent chiefs he had talked to in December,

> that all those Navajoes who claimed not to have murdered and robbed the inhabitants must come in and go to the Bosque Redondo, where they would be fed and protected until the war was over; that unless they were willing to do this, they would be considered hostile and would be proceeded against accordingly . . . that we have no desire to make war upon them and other good Navajoes; but that the troops cannot tell the good from the bad, and we neither can nor will tolerate their staying as a peace party among those against whom we intend to make war. Tell them they can have until the twentieth day of July of this year to come in . . . that after that day every Navajo that is seen will be considered as hostile and treated accordingly; that after that day the door now open will be closed.

Carleton had placed the Navajos between a rock and a hard place. His arbitrary deadline may not have meant much, unless it was explained carefully what day was meant, even assuming that the word could be disseminated throughout the Navajo country in a month's time. He was probably right in saying that his soldiers could not, and might not try to, distinguish between Navajos when the campaign began. Having decided that fighting was necessary, he could only make the distinction by separating the two groups and keeping the "friendlies" under surveillance. Otherwise, attacks on groups claiming to be at peace were sure to occur, the attackers claiming justification because of the supposed presence of a few men guilty of hostile acts; Sand Creek is only one of many such episodes during the Indian wars. Moving them as far as the Pecos was, of course, an indication of his eventual plan for them, and he probably could not understand just how reluctant they would be to make that move, or why.

Carleton had met Delgadito and Barboncito again in April 1863 near Cubero, and once again told them that the removal to Bosque Redondo was the condition of peace. They tried to find a compromise, but he would accept none. Barboncito declared that he would remain peaceably near Fort Wingate, even if he were killed, but that he would not move to the Pecos. In the same month the general ordered Carson to secure "ten of the best Ute warriors" and "four of the best Mexican guides": "We will have none but the best. Our work is to be thorough, and we must have men to do it."[82]

Carleton reiterated his July 20 deadline in his General Orders No. 15, dated June 15, 1863. In the very first sentence he declared, "For a long time past the Navajoe Indians have murdered and robbed the people of New Mexico." The order explained how he had told them that "binding guarantees" must be given for the future, and how instead "additional murders, and additional robberies have been perpetrated." Then he gave detailed instructions to Carson and the nine companies of his regiment, six mounted and three on foot, that were to join him for the campaign. (Four more companies were to operate from Fort Wingate.) Carson was to take his command, some 736 men, into northeastern Arizona and establish a military post at a site called Pueblo Colorado (at or near present Ganado, Arizona), which would be called Fort Canby.[83]

Carson, not just complying passively with orders, made his own contribution to the preparations for the campaign. He asked for authority to employ one hundred Utes as auxiliaries. To obtain the necessary funds Carleton forwarded the request to Washington, calling Carson "the distinguished commander of the expedition," and repeating the reasons Kit had probably given him: "The Utes are very brave, and fine shots, fine trailers, and uncommonly energetic in the field. The Navajoes have entertained a very great dread of them for many years. I believe one hundred Ute Indians would render more service in this way than double their number of troops. They could be mustered as a company or, preferably, could be employed as spies and guides." This would not be the only time that Carson would modify, or seek to modify, his superior's ideas when he thought necessary. One can only speculate on how much influence his advice had on the planning of the campaign, but this instance may indicate that he was more than just the faithful executor of ideas formulated solely by Carleton.[84]

THE FEARING TIME

Carson set off from Los Lunas, on the Rio Grande, on July 7, 1863, with part of his command. He marched by way of Fort Wingate to the site of Fort Defiance, Colonel Sumner's old post in Arizona near the present New Mexico boundary (at the present community of that name), where he arrived on July 20, Carleton's deadline for the Navajos to turn themselves in. Along the way he fed his animals from Navajo wheatfields and the already-harvested wheat they passed. His Ute allies, led by Kaniache, were scouting ahead and killed one Navajo man and captured twenty sheep on the very day the ultimatum expired. He encountered a party of nineteen Utes "operating against the Navajos on their own account," who told him there were other such war parties in the country. He hired five of the Utes as "spies." After spending two days at Fort Defiance, Kit set out with his staff, seventy soldiers, and the Utes toward Pueblo Colorado to view the proposed site of Fort Canby: "About one-third the distance from Defiance I left the command and pushed on with the Utes. . . . We came on a small party of Navajoes, and killed three men." A captive woman, a Paiute, told him that a large party of Navajos with sheep, horses, and cattle, were some thirty-five miles west, so he took the soldiers and the Utes and set off after them. They had left by the time he had arrived:

> I followed their trail for two hours, and until many of the horses had given out, and only returned on my own conviction, supported by

the superior knowledge of Kan-a-at-sa [Kaniache]: that it would be impossible to overtake them, without having to travel some ninety miles without water, and this my horses could not do. On my return route the Ute Indians killed eight Navajos, making a total of twelve since my arrival in this country.

He proceeded on to Pueblo Colorado. Concluding his report, Carson called Carleton's attention to "the valuable services rendered by the Ute Indians," and asked permission to employ another thirty.[85]

These first excursions would prove a forecast of the campaign. There was no large engagement; in fact, the soldiers were not in action at all. The Ute scouts found the enemy and inflicted the damage on them. Navajo crops found along the way were used to feed the column's animals. Women and children were captured. This pattern persisted, with variations, until the campaign ended the following spring. The actual casualties inflicted by the troops would be small, but the Navajos were deprived of their crops and animals, and of any security. The Utes and other Indian allies inflicted a substantial part of the damage and the casualties.

For Carson, the expedition commander, to be out ahead with the scouts was hardly standard military procedure, but it seems to have been his practice. H. R. Tilton, the surgeon who attended him in his last illness some five years later, gave an account he probably heard from Kit himself: "It is related of him, that while he was in command of his regiment and on a campaign against the Navajo Indians, he would leave camp very early each morning, taking his Ute Indian scouts, and let his lieutenant-colonel take charge of the regiment; before the command would have time to come up with the fugitive enemy, Carson and his Utes had finished the fighting." Tilton's story implies that Carson followed this procedure as a regular thing. In Indian warfare the scouts making the first contact often did all the fighting before the troops could come up. Kaniache later complained about this. If Carson made a practice of riding ahead with the scouts on occasion, it undoubtedly reflected his awareness of this reality. There were officers who could get the troops up, fed, and on the road in the morning as well as he, but few would have understood the business of scouting as well. Since it was not a matter of fighting sizable engagements but of catching elusive Indians, the soldiers served primarily as the support in case the scouts ran into more than they could handle. If Carson could trust his second in command to bring them up as quickly as possible, then he could justify being with the advance, which suited both his inclination and his skills, though not perhaps his age and physical condition. Later in the campaign he would be reported as "reeling in his saddle from fatigue and loss of sleep," but "still pushing forward."[86]

Carleton had not put Carson in command because of his talents as a disciplinarian, a drillmaster, or an administrator, but because he was Kit Carson, the great scout and Indian fighter who understood the principles of stealth, surprise, mobility, good scouts and trailers, and persistence in the face of adversity. That these principles were second nature to Carson, Carleton knew from their collaboration in 1854. Perhaps he himself had learned some of them from Kit. Certainly they must have discussed the conduct of this campaign before it began.

John Ayers, who served with both the California and the New Mexico volunteers and was closely associated with Carleton, may have reflected the general's opinion as well as common report in his description of Carson: "On the march he would never build fires if he wanted to surprise the enemy; he would creep up cautiously." Ayers also reports, "The troops sometimes accused him of cowardice because he was so cautious," an opinion Ayers clearly did not share. For nineteenth-century Americans, as Gerald Linderman argues, physical courage was the central male virtue, a courage defined as absolute fearlessness, or at least the refusal to acknowledge fear or the existence of danger. This was the standard that Civil War soldiers set for themselves and for others. Carson, however, had learned by hard personal experience, from Indians themselves, where that sort of courage could lead a man. Only one officer, Major Joseph Cummings, was killed during the Navajo campaign; his death was, in Carson's opinion, "the result of his rash bravery."[87]

Examination of the Pueblo Colorado site convinced Carson that it was unsuitable for a military post—lacking timber, grass, and water—and he moved his headquarters back to old Fort Defiance. The board of officers charged to survey the site agreed and so informed Carleton. Fort Defiance was instead renovated and renamed Fort Canby. Once again Carson, not just a submissive rubber stamp for the department commander, had modified his superior's orders and had his action approved.[88]

Nonetheless, "hands-off" management was definitely not Carleton's style, and he seldom hesitated to let Carson know when he was displeased with some action or the lack of it. In Robert Utley's judgment, "Carleton's own leadership supplied the catalyst that made the application [of Carson's knowledge] effective, for it was the general's paternalistic manipulation—now prodding, now scolding, now lecturing, now praising—that gave direction, energy, and success to efforts that could easily have foundered in confusion and lassitude." Certainly Carleton did not hesitate to apply the spur to all his subordinates, Carson included. He would write to a post commander that his troops were to look for Indians "well up toward or at the crest of the ridge" of a particular mountain range, admonish him that his men were not to go into any towns, and specify "bacon, flour, sugar, and coffee" carried in haversacks as their rations. (His instructions to Carson were seldom quite so detailed in regard to actual operations.)[89]

Displeased that Carson had not reported quickly enough about his first encounters with the Navajos, Carleton ordered him to send a weekly report "in detail," and added, "The value of time cannot be too seriously considered. . . . Much is expected of you, both here and in Washington." Carson replied by explaining what should have been obvious anyway, that when he was on a scout his movements would be "governed by circumstances," and he would have to send a strong detachment to carry a weekly report, which could not join him again and would weaken his striking force. Carson's deference to his formidable superior clearly had limits.[90]

One of Carleton's great concerns was that he was "greatly embarrassed for want of good officers, particularly in the New Mexican regiment." Although Major John Ayers believed Carson "had wonderful influence over the men," this did not extend to instilling formal military discipline and good behavior in his officers, some of whom were personal friends. Lawrence Kelly points out that, although only one officer would be killed by the Navajos, nearly half would face a court-martial or be forced to resign—"murder, alcoholism, embezzlement, sexual deviation, desertion, and incompetence" being among the problems that plagued the command. The population of Anglos in New Mexico was probably not a sufficient pool of officer material, and prejudice somewhat hampered the Hispanic officers, although from the evidence they were no less effective. (Major Rafael Chacon, a proud and sensitive man who was quick to resent slights from Anglo officers, had no complaint about Carson in this regard in his memoirs.) The officers of the First New Mexico were those picked during Canby's consolidation of the New Mexico regiments in 1862, but they apparently were not selected rigorously enough. Unlike many Civil War volunteer units, the First had not endured the weeding-out process of prolonged and bloody campaigning, including large-scale battles that rid the main armies of many unfit officers. The problem was to hamper Carson's operations, though the most serious difficulty would be caused by an officer from a California regiment. About Carson's own conduct, and his leadership in the field, there was evidently no doubt in Carleton's mind, though he would continue to admonish and to prod him to greater efforts.[91]

Having reestablished Fort Defiance as Fort Canby, his headquarters, Kit was soon out scouting again. Under a "broiling sun" he marched 490 miles in twenty-seven days. It was another march typical of the campaign, as shown both by his report and by a diary kept by one of his officers, probably Captain Eben Everett. They started from Pueblo Colorado on August 5, headed toward Zuni Pueblo, then west to the Hopi villages and eastward again, swinging around the Canyon de Chelly and back to Pueblo Colorado. Two of the six companies with him had to march on foot, because of the poor condition of their animals. The only grain they could get was in the fields of the Navajos. The diarist records that on the second day they came to "an Indian farm of large extent, planted with principally corn & fine wheat and some Beans Pumpkins and melons. Our animals were turned loose & enjoyed themselves. Wheat was pulled for them at night." During the day they also came to a cornfield, "which was destroyed." The next day the pack train set off ahead and the troops stayed long enough to destroy the remainder of the grain. The march was over "rolling country heavily timbered with Pine, Pinon & Cedar & scrub oak," with "many singular formations of rocks, towers, &c." On this day Captain Albert Pfeiffer's company joined the column with five prisoners and one hundred sheep.[92]

The rest of the march was much the same. Carson left one company behind with most of the pack train and headed west for the Hopi villages, near which he was informed there were many Navajos. One Navajo man was killed, two women and three children captured, with a number of horses and over a thousand sheep and goats. At that point Kaniache and the Utes left complaining that they had understood that they were to have all the stock captured during the campaign. According to Carson, "The real reason . . . was the fact they had now sufficient stock and captives." The diarist reported their complaint a little differently: "They brought some 20 or 25 horses with them & state that they had a fight with the Navajoes. That the command did not go until they, the Utahs, had whipped the Navajoes. . . . Col Carson took 8 horses 1000 sheep which they had captured in the fight from them. Kuniatche, the Chief would not stand this, as he wanted all the property captured, and so in high dudgeon he left." It is not clear whether Carson was with the scouts this time or not, but the Utes thought they were doing the work and should have their reward. It was not just the division of labor that bothered the Utes, but the division of the spoils. Though somewhat disgruntled at the army's mode of operation, they would continue to operate "on their own account"; the attacks of the Utes were as serious for the Navajos as those of the soldiers, and contributed much to their demoralization.[93]

On August 12 the diarist reported that "the Col. is after the Indians at full speed and is determined to overtake them if horseflesh will stand it." The horseflesh did not, and they had to turn back for water, a continuing weakness. Returning to base, Carson marched near the Canyon de Chelly but did not attempt to enter it, declaring that he was "satisfied that there are very few Indians in the Cañon," although there were reports to the contrary. In fact, he would not enter the reputed Navajo stronghold until months later, after prodding by Carleton, and he may simply have been reluctant to penetrate this spectacular chasm, where the defenders might well trap an intruder.[94]

During this march Major Joseph Cummings, the only officer casualty of the campaign, was killed while riding out with only one companion. The diarist noted that one Navajo man who was caught and killed after fighting to the last had been scalped: "This style of proceeding may inaugurate retaliation and a system of warfare in which we may be the sufferers. The Navajoes seldom or never scalp their prisoners and the barbarous practice should not have been commenced by us." This might imply that the man was killed while a prisoner, but the diarist himself contradicts this. The New Mexicans had been engaged in a long war with the Navajos and had their own ideas about the rules. Volunteer troops in the 1860s frequently scalped Indians, as frontier rangers and militia had done for generations. Indian fighting was warfare against "savages" who were assumed to do far worse things themselves. Mere retaliation for Cummings's death may also have been a factor. If Kit disapproved, he left no record of it in this instance, though the actions of some other volunteer troops toward living Indians would later earn his bitter condemnation.[95]

The march yielded no spectacular results in Navajo casualties. The few killed were in ones and twos in little skirmishes, at the cost of long marches and worn-out animals. The diarist records, day after day, the destruction of Navajo crops, either consumed by the expedition's animals, packed up and carried off, or simply destroyed: "It seemed a pity to destroy so much fine Corn & Fodder when not 50 miles from here at Fort Defiance it is so much needed." Carson himself believed that the march yielded two benefits: he had gained valuable knowledge of the country, and also "a knowledge of where the Navajos have fled with their stock, and where I am certain to find them."[96]

When Carson returned to Fort Canby on August 31, he found problems waiting for him that would seriously affect the campaign. Carleton had foisted Major Thomas Blakeney, a California volunteer officer, on Carson, urging that the major be given a chance to distinguish himself. Blakeney quickly antagonized the officers in Carson's regiment by conduct they deemed "overbearing and unbecoming an officer." More serious, however, was his treatment of four Navajos who came in to surrender. One man who had come in "to have a talk with his white brethren," in the words of Carson's report, was confined, "his statement not being believed by the Post Commander [Blakeney]," and was shot "while attempting to escape" a few days later. There was some doubt about the details of what happened to three others who came in some days later, for the provost-sergeant refused to write a report the way Blakeney wanted him to, saying instead that the major had made it clear that he was to kill the prisoners. At any rate, one was killed trying to escape, by Blakeney's account, and two others reportedly escaped. Carson's own report showed his displeasure: "From all I can learn these Indians came in with a flag of truce, and I cannot but regret that they were not better received (when received at all,) and kept until my arrival." The one man still alive in custody, named Little Foot, said that his party had come in to arrange the surrender of a number of Navajos on Carleton's terms. Carson believed him and set him free, "giving him twelve days to return with his people, at which time he promises to be here." The treatment of these men, Lawrence Kelly believes, may have prolonged the campaign, for Navajos who heard of it would hardly be encouraged to attempt surrender. Both honor and pragmatism gave Carson reason for indignation. He freed not only Little Foot but two New Mexico officers whom Blakeney had arrested, and placed the major himself under arrest. Carleton let

Blakeney off, but reprimanded him privately for creating trouble within Carson's command.[97]

In replying to the report just quoted, the general made his agreement with Carson plain: "You are right in believing that I do not wish to have those destroyed who are willing to come in. Nor will you permit an Indian prisoner once fairly in your custody to be killed unless he be endeavoring to make his escape." Any Navajos who wished to surrender must be informed that there was no alternative but to go to Bosque Redondo, that "this war shall be pursued against you if it takes years, now that we have begun, until you cease to exist or move. There can be no other talk on the subject." The obvious purpose of such tough talk was psychological, aimed at destroying the Navajos' hopes of gaining a temporary peace as in the past. A highly expensive, indefinitely prolonged war of attrition was actually the last thing frontier military commanders wanted. "You have deceived us too often and robbed and murdered our people too long—to trust you again at large in your own country," were the words Carson was instructed to use.[98]

On another matter Carleton also made his wishes quite clear. In one of his first reports Carson noted that the Utes had captured four women and seventeen children:

It is expected by the Utes, and has, I believe, been customary to allow them to keep the women and children, and the property captured by them, for their own use and benefit; and as there is no way to sufficiently recompense these Indians for their invaluable services, and as a means of insuring their continued zeal and activity; I ask it as a favor that they be permitted to retain all that they may capture. I make this request the more readily as I am satisfied that the future of the captives disposed of in this manner would be much better than if sent even to the Bosque Redondo. As a general thing the Utes dispose of their captives to Mexican families, where they are fed and taken care of and thus cease to require any further attention on the part of the government. Besides this, their being distributed as Servants thro' the territory causes them to loose that collectiveness of interest as a tribe, which they will retain if kept together at any one place.

Kit had summed up briefly the practice and results of the New Mexican "custom of the country" regarding Indian captives. This seems to be the only occasion on which he explicitly alluded to and approved the idea of detribalizing Indians, causing them to lose any sense of tribal identification, which would be popular as an ultimate goal with many reformers in later years, and which is of course anathema today. The hope was to make them autonomous individual citizens, according to the Anglo-American ideal. The reformers viewed the Indians' wishes as based on primitive ignorance and did not consider them paramount; apparently neither did Kit. It seems clear that he did not regard the New Mexican custom, as regards the actual treatment of the captives, as inherently evil. His prejudice in favor of the Utes probably entered into his attitude.[99]

Carleton replied promptly and decisively:

> I have the honor to acknowledge receipt of your letter of the 24th ultimo, in relation to the disposition to be made of captured Navajoe women and children—and to say in reply, that all prisoners which are captured by the troops or employes of your command will be sent to Santa Fe, by the first practicable opportunity. . . . *There must be no exception to this rule.*

He amplified the point about a month later: "No Navajoe Indians of either sex, or of any age, will be retained at Fort Canby as servants, or in any capacity whatever. All must go to the Bosque Redondo." Carleton may have had suspicions, based on long frontier military experience, about the "capacity" in which some women might be retained by officers at Fort Canby. Carson's suggestion that the captives might be better off in the hands of New Mexicans than at Bosque Redondo probably did not sit well with the commanding general.[100]

In the letter approving Carson's ideas on persuading Navajos to surrender, Carleton had also instructed him regarding the Zunis, whom the general had heard, or had somehow concluded, were aiding the Navajos. He wrote,

> I recommend unless you can produce the same results by more gentle measures that you seize six of the principal men of the Zuñi Indians and hold them as hostages until all Navajoes in and near their villages are given up, and all stolen stock surrendered. You will assure the Zuñi Indians that if I hear that they help or harbor Navajoes, or steal stock from any white man, or injure the person of any white man, I will as certainly destroy their villages as sure as the sun shines.

Carson arrived at Zuni on September 11, before these instructions were written, and found "more gentle measures" were all that was necessary, as he assured the general in his report, probably written after he had received the order:

The Governor of Zuñi furnished three men as Guides to the River, and I was accompanied by about twenty others, who desired thus to show their friendliness to the Whites and their enmity to the Navajoes. That they are not on friendly terms with the Navajoes and are desirous to aid us in every possible manner I am fully satisfied, not alone from their professions but from having seen the dead bodies of some Navajoes whom they had recently killed in an engagement.

The Zunis acted as scouts for the next few days until, in time-honored fashion, they had taken some Navajo sheep and goats and went home. Carson had avoided the needless trouble that might have resulted if a less experienced man had been in his place, and he let Carleton know it in a respectful manner.[101]

Otherwise the scout was, Carson reported, "a failure as regards any positive injury inflicted on the Navajoes." His animals had had only a little corn, scanty grass, and an uncertain supply of water, and as a result, "at no time since their arrival in this country have they been in an efficient condition for Field service." He wanted to send most of the mounts back to the Rio Grande for the winter: "I am now about to operate with detached parties on foot, which plan of campaign I shall continue during the winter. One party of 75 men will leave this Post to-morrow evening." Kit noted that Little Foot, the Navajo he had released to bring in his band, had not reappeared—hardly surprising in view of his reception by Major Blakeney. If the Navajos did not start to come in, then operations during the winter would be necessary.[102]

As far as General Carleton was concerned, they were indeed necessary. He had already written to Washington outlining his plans for a reservation at Bosque Redondo. He explained that the Navajos could not be trusted because of their "perfidy." More concretely, he pointed out that they had no government to make treaties binding all the Navajos. He believed they should all move to Bosque Redondo, and he was sure that a winter campaign would make them do it: "As soon as the snows of winter admonish them of the suffering to which their families will be exposed—I have great hopes of getting the most of the tribe." He added, "The purpose now is never to relax the application of force with a people that can no more be trusted than you can trust the wolves that run through their mountains." Putting aside the animalistic simile, which never appears in Carson's letters, and which is certainly "racist" by our standards, it seems clear that Carleton expected to achieve his result through hunger, the hardships of winter, and the insecurity caused by continual pursuit and harassment, not by the actual casualties inflicted in battle.[103]

Carson's decision to continue operations with smaller parties of dismounted men, instead of large, personally led sweeps, reflected recent experiences. The Navajos were not going to put up any large-scale resistance, or fight any big battles. The only effective way of fighting them was with small, mobile columns that could harass them, keep them on the run, and deny them subsistence. Some historians seem to assume that the lack of substantial resistance meant that the Navajos had no hostile intentions but were simply the victims of the predatory New Mexicans and the prejudices of Anglo-Americans. But evasion rather than organized resistance was the Navajos' historic response to invasion of their homeland. Neither their social organization, nor their resources, nor their ideas of warfare prompted them toward large-scale military operations.[104]

As winter came, operations against the Navajos continued. Carson's troops from Fort Canby and others from Fort Wingate crisscrossed the Navajo country, while others stationed near the Rio Grande pursued Navajo raiders. A chronology of expeditions and engagements in 1863, prepared by Carleton's headquarters, shows the extent of such efforts. Through much of the fall the Fort Wingate troops seem to have been able to show more concrete results than Carson's. One entry notes how Lieutenant Nicholas Hodt, of the First New Mexico, left Fort Canby on October 27 on a scout: "Result of this scout, four government mules worn out and shot."[105]

The same list shows that the uniformed troops were not the only ones harassing the Navajos. New Mexican militia, and self-constituted irregulars who were much the same as the slave raiders of years past, were in the field, and so were Utes and Pueblos operating without military supervision. In early September, Superintendent of Indian Affairs Michael Steck reported that some Utes had killed nine Navajos and captured forty children, while Pueblos had killed two. In November Ramón Baca reported that he had led a party of 116 men who left Cebolleta, traveled northwest for six days, killed six Indians, presumably Navajos, and captured three, and took three ponies. The prisoners, in this case, ended up in the hands of the army, as did three others who were discovered in the hands of some Mexicans arrested near Cebolleta in December; the Mexicans were apparently allowed to escape. A force of California and New Mexico volunteers from Fort Wingate, seeking to attack Navajos near the Sierra Datil, found that a force of Pueblos had anticipated them, killing Chief Barboncito (not the man who had talked with Carleton earlier) and sixteen other men and capturing forty-four women and children and one thousand sheep.[106]

Carson was concerned about the possibility that the Hopis, living on their mesas some eighty miles west of Fort Canby, might provide the Navajos with intelligence as to his movements. They were surrounded by the Navajos and, as he saw it, existed only by the sufferance of the stronger tribe: "Under these circumstances it is not surprising that the Navajoes are continually advised of the movements of any body of troops." He assumed that the Hopis, because of the barrenness of their land and lack of water, were living lives of extreme hardship and would benefit if they were removed to a better location. This he thought could be accomplished by peace commissioners rather than by force, "And until they are removed I am satisfied that there will always be a barrier opposed to the removal of the Navajos." It is doubtful if the Hopis, who still live on the same mesas today, would have appreciated Carson's concern for their well-being, or his notion of removing them from the homeland where they had lived since long before either Navajo or Spaniard had entered the Southwest.[107]

In the meantime he was suffering frustration and embarrassment, for his scouting parties were not making contact with the Navajos, while they were making their presence known by running off some of his sheep and mules. Deciding to try his own luck again (and undoubtedly conscious of the expectations of his superior in Santa Fe), he set out from Fort Canby on November 15 with five dismounted companies and some Zuni scouts, bound for the Hopi villages, "for the purpose of exploring the country west of the Oribi villages and, if possible to chastise the Navajoes inhabiting that region." This he thought would be "the last 'large scout' that Can be made this Winter, owing to the condition of the stock—many of which are dying daily."[108]

On the way west he sent out a small party under Sergeant Andrés Herrera, who managed to kill two Navajos, wound two, and capture some sheep and a horse—another action typical of this campaign. When he arrived at the Hopi towns, "I found that the inhabitants of all the villages except the Oribis [Oraibis] had a misunderstanding with the Navajoes, owing to some injustice perpetrated by the latter. I took advantage of this feeling, and succeeded in obtaining representatives from all the villages—Oribi excepted—to accompany me on the war path." His main purpose in recruiting these Hopis was to get them to commit to his side, "to bind them to us, and place them in antagonism to the Navajoes." He found that "they were of some service, and manifested a great desire to aid us in every respect." After viewing their country he observed "that these people numbering some four thousand souls are in a most deplorable condition. . . . They are a peaceable people, have never robbed or murdered the people of New Mexico, and are in every way worthy of the fostering care of the Government. Of the bounty so unsparingly bestowed by it on the other Puebla Indians—aye even on the marauding bands—they have never tasted." He recommended that some of the annuities meant for the Navajos be distributed to the Hopis instead. He said nothing further about removing them to a more fertile location, perhaps because he had suggested the idea to them and they had made their feelings plain.

At Oraibi his actions were somewhat different. He had been "credibly informed"—presumably by other Hopis—that the inhabitants of this Hopi town, the oldest continuously inhabited community in the United States, were in alliance with the Navajos. "I caused to be bound their Governor and another of their principal men, and took them with me as prisoners. The first day's march from their village I unbound them, and during the time they were with me they conducted themselves well." Apparently he had no further problems worth mentioning with the Hopis. With the Oraibis he took what he considered the minimum action necessary to impress them with his power, in case they were under pressure from the Navajos. There was apparently no talk of burning the town down, as Carleton threatened with Zuni.

The rest of the march was the same story of capturing a few captives and stock and destroying camps, while being hampered by the poor condition of the column's animals. More than once they saw signs that the Indians had just fled, and even saw them fleeing without being able to pursue. Carson and the troops may have found this discouraging, but the Navajos must have found such harassment and insecurity, especially with winter coming on, far worse. One encounter could have been more productive if the soldiers had acted more wisely. The few mounted troops met three Navajos, one of whom fired off his gun and approached them, making signs that he wanted to talk. They took both his guns

S O L D I E R

and allowed him to depart. When the Hopi allies saw the guns, they recognized one as belonging to Manuelito, one of the outstanding warriors and most influential men among the Navajos, reputedly the organizer of an 1860 attempt to capture Fort Defiance. As Carson observed, "It is more than probable that the Indian, whoever he was, desired to have an interview with me, but was deterred by the hostile attitude of the soldiers." Kit must have regretted not having been with the scouts, as on other occasions. Manuelito, however, would be one of the last Navajos to surrender. (That the soldiers did not simply kill the man suggests they were aware that the colonel did not want to kill every Navajo found. Possibly they did kill him and did not report it, but Kit was unlikely to be naive about such matters, and he had not concealed Blakeney's earlier brutality.) Carson made another attempt to induce Navajos to surrender by sending off a boy captured during the march, "that he might communicate to the Navajoes the intentions of the General Commanding in regard to them, of which I took particular pains to inform him." He wanted the Navajos to know that they would be required to go to Bosque Redondo, but that they would not be killed if they surrendered, as Blakeney's actions might have led them to believe.

Carson experienced some concern "that owing to the extended operations of our Armies elsewhere, that those of my command may be overlooked," but he thought "no troops of the United States has ever before been called upon to endure such hardships as did the men of my command on this Scout." As soon as his animals were rested, he intended to send a party to examine the Canyon de Chelly. He was of the opinion, however, that but few of the Navajoes were there, having "satisfied myself while in that vicinity in September." The question of an expedition to the Canyon de Chelly would be the focus of the most significant disagreement between Carson and Carleton during the Navajo campaign.[109]

Carson had made it plain before that he did not believe there were significant numbers of Navajos in the Canyon de Chelly, and that it was not worth his personal attention. In fact, he believed that there was no use in any further "large scouts" during the winter, considering that his animals were "dying daily." He communicated these ideas to Carleton at the beginning of November, well before the start of his expedition to the Hopi country, and requested a leave of absence, apparently not for the first time. As he saw it, his presence would not be necessary "until the weather opens sufficiently to permit of more extended operations." He wanted to tend to "some private business of importance," and "to avail myself of the opportunity . . . of consulting with the General Commanding personally—with regard to the plan of campaign to be adopted." Kit wanted to spend the winter at home with his family; he had last seen them six months before and Josefa was pregnant with their sixth child. He had had a hard, frustrating campaign, he was nearing his fifty-fourth birthday and was probably feeling his years, and domestic life in Taos was far more attractive than playing the great Indian fighter.[110]

Carleton here played the stern taskmaster. He wrote Carson: "As I have before written to you, I have not the authority to grant you a leave." Kit should, however, come to Santa Fe for consultation about future operations, "as soon as you have secured one hundred captive Navajoe men, women, and children"; then he could turn over command of the expedition and come on in. There was a catch, however: "It is desirable that you go through the Canyon de Chelly before you come."[111]

Carleton was convinced, in spite of Carson's contrary opinion, that it was important for the troops to penetrate Canyon de Chelly, and he would not let his lieutenant off until they did it. Winter, as Carleton and other frontier military commanders believed, was the time to increase, not slack off, the pressure on hostile Indians. The privation of having to hide out in the most inaccessible places at that season, after losing much of their food supply to the incursions of soldiers, New Mexicans, and Indian enemies, would be the final blow to their morale. Apparently Carleton also wrote, while Carson was absent on his November scout, to Captain Asa Carey, who commanded at Fort Canby in Carson's absence. Carey was a regular army officer and a West Pointer whom the general had assigned as Carson's quartermaster, to supply the administrative expertise otherwise lacking in the First New Mexico, and perhaps to act as Carleton's personal representative and keep Kit up to the mark on military matters in general. Unlike Carleton's Californians, he seems to have won the respect and liking of the New Mexico volunteers. Now Carleton wanted him to urge Carson to undertake the Canyon de Chelly expedition, convincing him of its importance. Carey wrote back on December 6, the day after Kit's return from his most recent scout, saying, "I am fully aware that now is the season for active operations and I think the Colonel agrees with me, I have just had a conversation with him about the Canyon de Chelly. In fact, I have often asked him why he did not visit the place. His mind is made up and he says that he shall go through it." One might say that Kit's mind had been made up for him.[112]

There were some further delays, however. A reconnaissance of the western entrance of the canyon that Carson had ordered was cancelled when Captain Francisco Abreu, who was to lead it, was promoted and transferred. Carson clearly trusted this New Mexican officer, but another New Mexican, Major José Sena, let some Navajos run off a number of pack mules and oxen, and others were lost in an attack on a supply train. (Kit "respectfully suggested" that the escort provided by department headquarters for the train was "entirely insufficient.") A party sent in pursuit took some prisoners, but not the stolen animals. They gave Carson some intelligence that must have increased his frustration over Major Blakeney's brutality toward the prisoners back in August:

> I have learned from one of the Captive Women that many of the Indians would be glad to come in and comply with our terms, but are deterred by the fate of one who was sent in by "Herrera Grandee"....
> This emissary is the Indian referred to in my report of August 31st . . . whose statement the then Comd'g Officer (Major J. F. Blakeney) doubted; and who was killed while attempting to escape. This woman assures me that this "Herrera" and his party are anxious for peace and have never been on the War Path. I cannot blame these people for distrusting the good faith of the Troops at this Post, from the manner in which their Messengers have been received at it on more than one occasion; I deplore it the more as I have only one way of communicating with them—through the barrels of my Rifles.

Without the bungling of amateurs like Blakeney, he might have been home by now with his family—and a good many Navajos might have been spared suffering and death.[113]

General Carleton applied the spur one more time in a letter of December 31, regretting the loss of the animals and suggesting that the herds might be used to lure the raiders into an ambush: "It is hoped, hereafter, your command will be able to protect its own stock." The loss, however, was not to be an excuse to delay the Canyon de Chelly expedition. If there were mules enough to carry provisions, the men could carry their own blankets and greatcoats and three or four days' rations: "The Army of the Potomac carries eight days rations in haversacks. Unless some fatigue and some privations are encountered by your troops the Indians will get the best of it," Carleton declared. "Now while the snow is deep is the true time to make an impression on the tribe." He concluded by reporting, "There is now a large party of citizens and Utes in the Navajoe country after Indians."[114]

Kit thus set out on what many historians have regarded as the crowning exploit of his career with reluctance, after much urging from his superior. Events were to prove that Carleton was right. If Carson was reluctant to stick his head into the potential trap of the Canyon de Chelly, because of his ingrained caution, he did not express this in his reports to Carleton, who would not have been the most sympathetic audience for such reasoning. His expressed reason was his belief that there were few Navajos hiding there, and in this he was proved wrong.

The Canyon de Chelly—derived from the Spanish version of the Navajo *Tségi,* "rock canyon"—is one of the most spectacular geological features of a region well endowed with them. Its sheer red sandstone walls, nearly one thousand feet high at the deepest point, were formed by stream erosion in the Defiance Plateau. There are really two main branches, Canyon de Chelly on the south, which extends some twenty-seven miles easterly from the canyon mouth on the west, and Canyon del Muerto, which branches off northeasterly; both have branching canyons. The dwellings of the ancient Anasazi can be seen at various points, but Navajos have lived there since the mid–eighteenth century. Since Spanish times the canyon was reputed a Navajo "fortress," a stronghold whites entered at their peril. In fact, at least one Spanish military expedition penetrated there, in 1805, and killed a number of Navajos. An Anglo-American military force first looked into the canyon for some miles in 1849. Colonel Edwin Sumner led a force up the main canyon, somewhat farther than the first party, in 1851; though not easily intimidated, he found the hail of rocks and arrows from Navajos on the rim more than he cared to face and retreated. In 1857 Colonel Dixon Miles took his column down a substantial portion of the gorge, again under Navajo fire, and declared, "No command should again enter it." At least one did, however, in 1859, and marched the length of Canyon de Chelly. Interestingly, neither Carleton nor Carson seems to have been aware of this last penetration.[115]

On January 6, 1864, Carson marched out of Fort Canby with fourteen officers and 375 enlisted men, going by way of Pueblo Colorado. At the same time Captain Albert Pfeiffer set out with his company of the First New Mexico to march directly to the eastern end of the canyon. A regimental poet had recently been moved to write some verses, which the bandmaster set to music:

> Come dress your ranks, my gallant souls, a standing in a row,
> Kit Carson he is waiting to march against the foe;
> At night we march to Moqui, o'er lofty hills of snow,
> To meet and crush the savage foe, bold Johnny Navajo.
> Johnny Navajo! O Johnny Navajo!
> We'll first chastise, then civilize, bold Johnny Navajo.

The "lofty hills of snow" were still present, causing what was ordinarily a one-day trip to Pueblo Colorado to take three days, and the loss of twenty-seven oxen forced Carson to leave behind one wagon when he pressed on to the west entrance of the canyon, at present Chinle, Arizona. (His route probably roughly paralleled U.S. Highway 191.)[116]

Carson's column arrived at the canyon entrance on January 12, and he reconnoitered a few miles up on the south rim, looking for a way down that he did not find, "the height of the sides averaging about one thousand feet and nearly perpendicular." Some Indians were seen on the opposite side, and Sergeant Andrés Herrera was able to round up a few prisoners and some sheep and goats, besides killing eleven Navajos. The next day Kit divided his command into two forces of two companies each, one commanded by the efficient Captain Carey to march along the south rim, the other under Captain Joseph Berney on the north side; Carson himself accompanied the first detachment. He was "very anxious about the safety of Captain Pfeiffer's command," and wanted to locate it as soon as possible. They found the site of Herrera's fight of the previous day and discovered there some wounded Navajos, who were given medical treatment. They were unable to locate Pfeiffer after marching to where, they believed, they could see the eastern end of the canyon, so they returned to the west entrance to find that Pfeiffer was already there.[117]

Albert Pfeiffer, as noted, had been subagent for the Capote Utes at Abiquiu when Kit was Ute agent. He was a Dutch immigrant who had come to New Mexico in the 1840s and had apparently served in the army. In 1860 he had accompanied some of his Utes in action against the Navajos, as part of Canby's campaign. Like Carson, he had married a New Mexican and settled down; like him, he had given up his agent's position to join the army when the Confederates invaded. When Canby reorganized the New Mexico volunteers Pfeiffer was dropped, but then was reinstated as a captain at Carson's request. A contemporary described Pfeiffer as "a mild-mannered, blue-eyed, kindly man, and, in the estimation of his fellows, probably the most desperately courageous and successful Indian fighter in the West." Like many of his fellow officers in the First New Mexico, he had a drinking problem, of which his commander was well aware. Carson, himself a very moderate drinker, wrote to Pfeiffer as an old friend, not as a commanding officer, in May 1863: "When will you have sense? Can't you try and quit whisky for a little while, at least until you get your face cured? If your face ain't well when I next see you, you had better look out." Pfeiffer's problem was not helped by an incident that happened soon after this letter was written; he went to a hot spring with his wife to treat the skin condition to which Carson alluded, and there Apaches attacked his party. Pfeiffer was wounded and his wife killed. Some accounts would have it that he became a ferocious Indian-hater thereafter, that accounting for his success in the Navajo campaign. Yet he seems to have retained the friendship of the Utes and had already campaigned with them against the Navajos.[118]

Pfeiffer had left Fort Canby on January 2, four days before Carson, headed northwesterly toward the eastern entrance of Canyon de Chelly, through snow six inches and more deep. On the eleventh he and his men reached what they thought was the eastern end of Canyon de Chelly, in fact the head of Canyon del Muerto, the northern branch. Along the way they captured eight Navajo women and children "in an almost famishing condition." Entering the canyon, Pfeiffer divided his men into three elements, within supporting distance of each other. At first they traveled on the frozen stream at the bottom of the canyon, taking a few more prisoners, "half-starved and naked." On the twelfth they had several skirmishes with the enemy, "Indians on both sides of the Cañon whooping and yelling and cursing, firing shots and throwing rocks down upon my command." They killed two "Buck Indians," and "one Squaw who obstinately persisted in hurling rocks and pieces of wood at the soldiers," and took a few more prisoners. At the wider parts of the canyon "the Corn Fields of the Savages are laid out with farmer-like taste, with *sacos* for irrigation." In the narrower places Pfeiffer observed the ledges and caverns high up on the walls, where the Navajos, he believed, sought refuge when pursued by their enemies, white or Indian: "[H]ere they were enabled to jump about on the ledges of the rocks, like Mountain Cats, hallooing at me, swearing and cursing, and threatening vengeance on my command in every variety of Spanish they were capable of mustering. A couple of shots from my soldiers with their trusty Rifles caused the Red Skins to disperse instantly, and gave me a safe passage through this celebrated Gibraltar of Navajodom." At one camp the smoke rose up toward "a large number of Indians resting over my head," but they were so far above that they "did not look larger than crows." The distance was too great for any harm to be done, and the shouts of the antagonists were barely audible.[119]

Pfeiffer reached Carson's base camp at the mouth of Canyon de Chelly on January 13, while the colonel was absent looking for him. The next day two Navajo men and a woman came in under a flag of truce, and the captain received them "kindly, friendly, and frankly, and treated them accordingly." Carson returned later the same day. Pfeiffer had taken nineteen prisoners and suffered no losses; he had, says Carson, discovered two Navajos frozen to death in the canyon. Carson himself had met some Navajos with a flag of truce, "requesting permission to come in with their people and submit." He agreed but, fearing they might be stalling for time, gave them until 10:00 A.M. the next morning, or "my soldiers would hunt them up and the work of destruction recommence." Sixty appeared before the deadline. Kit explained what was required, and they agreed to go to Bosque Redondo.

> They declare that owing to the operations of my command they are in a complete state of starvation, and that many of their women and children have already died from this cause. They also state that they would have come in long since, but that they believed it was a War of Extermination, and that they were agreeably surprised and delighted to learn the contrary from an old captive whom I had sent back to them for this purpose.

Carson fed the captives, who asked to go back and bring in the remainder of their people. He agreed and told them to join him at Fort Canby. Captain Berney returned from his scout along the north rim of Canyon del Muerto on the fifteenth, with a handful of captives.[120]

Carson now decided to return to Fort Canby to receive the incoming Navajos and to send out other scouting parties. Contrary to his earlier desire to wind down operations during the winter, he declared that "now is the time to prosecute the Campaign with vigor." He sent Captain Carey, "at his own request, he being desirous of passing through this stupendous Cañon," on a march up the main Canyon de Chelly. The captain was ordered to cut down the Navajo orchards in the canyon, but apparently this was not done until some months later. Large numbers of Navajos came to Carey offering their surrender and were told they must go to the Bosque Redondo or be treated as hostile. They agreed and asked only to be allowed to go and bring in their families. Carey, like Carson, agreed, and by the time he reached Fort Canby he had over a hundred with him and more following his trail.[121]

Legends grew up about the Canyon de Chelly expedition as writers sought a dramatic climax to a campaign consisting mainly of hard marches, petty skirmishes, crop destruction, taking of herds, and harrying of cold and hungry people. In the second edition of his biography of Carson, written less than a decade after the event but without Kit's help, Doctor Peters produced an account that shaped popular perception: "After a succession of skirmishes, Carson succeeded in getting the enemy into a bed or ravine, and had his own forces so disposed as to command every approach, and in doing this compelled the surrender of ten thousand Indians, being the largest single capture of Indians ever known." Once again, as Kit might have said, Peters had "laid it on a leetle too thick." Uncritically accepting what were presumably popular reports, he created the legend of a great military exploit by Kit Carson, the incomparable frontiersman and Indian fighter. Carson's own assessment was characteristically more down-to-earth.[122]

In a report written a few days after his return to Fort Canby, Carson summed up the immediate results of the expedition:

> Killed, 23
> Prisoners, 34
> Voluntarily surrendered, 200 souls
> Captured, 200 head of sheep

He declared, "We have thoroughly explored their heretofore unknown stronghold." More important, he believed, were the "ulterior effects" of the expedition:

> We have shown the Indians that in no place, however formidable or inaccessible, are they safe from the pursuit of the troops of this command; and have convinced a large portion of them that the intentions of the Government toward them are eminently humane; and dictated by an earnest desire to promote their welfare; that the principle is not to destroy but to save them, if they are disposed to be saved.

He was sure that, "When all this is understood by the Navajoes generally," they would begin to surrender in large numbers. Just after his return to Fort Canby, he had been visited by four Navajos who came from the Tunicha Mountains east of Canyon de Chelly, who admitted that they had "great fears of being killed on approaching our camp, but that their necessities overcame their fears." Many "rich Indians," they said, would come in but were afraid. One man agreed to go back with evidence of having been in the soldiers' camp and persuade them to come in. At the time of writing Carson had 170 Navajos, not counting small children, drawing rations at the post, and "They are arriving, almost hourly, and will I believe continue to arrive until the last Indian in this section of the country is en route to the Bosque Redondo."[123]

The Navajos had their own version of the Canyon de Chelly expedition. Howard Gorman, speaking in the 1970s, told how his ancestors had fled toward the canyon because "troops were on the move, destroying property, having no pity on anyone. . . . Canyon de Chelly was their only hope of survival." They were caught, however, in the canyon by troops because they were unable to climb the icy carved steps to their intended refuge in a cave. The troops were guided by a man called Small Mexican, a former captive among the Navajos who knew the area. Gorman does not say how many were killed, but he believed it was most of this group. A baby in a cradleboard was picked up and apparently cared for by the soldiers, and a wounded man was given medical treatment. The wounded man was taken to the soldiers' camp at Chinle (the canyon mouth), and a few days later sent into the canyon with instructions: "If you don't return, you will be killed just like the rest. Now go into *Tséyi'* and order all those that live in the canyon to move out. From here we'll go to *Tséhootsooí* (Fort Defiance). We'll be leaving soon." Sixteen Navajos came out of the canyon for fear of the Utes. Allowing for the transmission of the account over a few generations, this sounds like the story of Carson's expedition, with Carson sending in the captive to persuade other Navajos to surrender and giving them a deadline.[124]

Other traditional accounts relate the killing of Navajo women and children. Mrs. Akinabh Burbank was about ninety when she described what seems to be Carson's attack on Canyon de Chelly. The Navajos saw covered wagons coming up the Chinle valley. Former captives pointed out the hiding places of the people in the caves. She describes what could have been Sergeant Herrera's fight on the south rim of the canyon:

After more dreadful fighting, dead people were lying here and there, and many wounded were crawling around. Some fell from the cliff, including men, women, children and babies. After the fight, the leader of the enemy party observed the tragic scene, and it frightened him. He broke down and wept, saying, "What a terrible thing we have done to these people!"

The soldiers then went back to the mouth of the canyon, and the commander sent two captives to induce others to surrender, promising they would not be harmed if they did. Those who came in found the soldiers camped in tents. They were taken to the tent of the leader, who greeted them and again broke down and cried, according to Mrs. Burbank. Weeping in this manner does not at first seem characteristic of Kit Carson, if this was he. Perhaps the Navajos who passed on the story thought this was the way the commander should have reacted, or perhaps they exaggerated his actual expression of regret, whether genuine or intended to win the confidence of the Indians. It may be, as Lawrence Kelly suggests, that details from Spanish attacks of many years earlier have been added to the traditions about Carson's invasion. Or just possibly these Navajos glimpsed a side of Kit Carson seldom seen by his white acquaintances. (Remember Edward Beale's story about how Carson "mourned like a woman, and would not be comforted" over the families of the dead at San Pasqual.) In any case, the tough-minded Mrs. Burbank was not impressed: "If he was such a cry-baby, why was he waging war out here?" The commander gave the visitors food and promised that all who came in to Fort Defiance (Fort Canby) would be fed. Navajo messengers went out carrying the message "that the enemy wants peace and they have given us food. If you go to Fort Defiance you will be cared for and will have plenty to eat." Large numbers of people gathered at the fort. The whites, says Mrs. Burbank, had decided that the Navajos should be sent to Fort Sumner, where they would be safe from Indian enemies like the Utes and Hopis.[125]

Another traditional account came down to Teddy Draper Sr., who grew up in Canyon del Muerto, from his great-grandmothers through his grandmothers. He remembered one grandmother telling him, about 1932, "This is your canyon, my grandson. Did you know that you're not a slave to the United States soldiers?" His great-grandmother, Asdzaan Naakaii (Mexican Lady), was sixteen when the soldiers of Bi'éé' Łichíí'ii (Red Clothes, or Kit Carson) came to Canyon de Chelly; this is notable as one of the few traditional accounts that makes specific mention of Carson. Many Navajos had come to the canyon for safety, and a number took refuge on Fortress Rock, a massive, freestanding rock at the junction of Canyon del Muerto and Black Rock Canyon. They put up ladders to reach the top, and took up supplies of wood and dried meat. They saw a party of soldiers, perhaps Pfeiffer's men, coming down Canyon del Muerto; some three hundred people were on the rock, keeping quiet. Their leader, Dahghaa'í (Mustache) commented,

> There are about 75 more soldiers at the mouth of the canyon, and they have war commanding officers. The chief one's name is *Bi'éé' Łichíí'ii* (Kit Carson). He is a very pure White Man, and he has two commandants under him, and they will come back to fight us. *Bi'éé' Łichíí'ii* will never come to our stronghold. He is afraid he might get killed by the Diné. That why he stays back behind his soldiers and just gives orders.

Some soldiers, perhaps Captain Berney's men, fired at the people on the rock from the north rim of Canyon del Muerto; others came back up the two canyons, and the Navajos cursed at them. It snowed and the soldiers went away. "Some of our people were sick from the cold. Some of our families lost beloved ones, but it was natural to us." Some soldiers came back in February and camped in the canyon for several days, killing about twenty men. "The word we received was that many Navajos elsewhere were starving and dying. Many of them had already gone to Fort Defiance from Chinle." Eventually both Dahghaa'í and Asdzaan Naakaii went to Fort Canby to surrender.[126]

Lawrence Kelly concludes that the great importance of Carson's Canyon de Chelly expedition did not lie in the fighting that took place, but in what Kit called the "ulterior effects" of the incursion. Carson believed he had shown for the first time that a military expedition could penetrate the canyon and traverse its length, and the Navajos could not stop it. Moreover, he had been able to establish contact with the Navajos and tell them that he was not waging a "war of extermination," and that if they surrendered they would be fed and sent to Bosque Redondo. Even the Navajo accounts indicate that he made a point of treating kindly those who surrendered or were captured, feeding them, providing medical treatment, and expressing regret at their sufferings. In comparison with the privation, fear, and combat losses they were suffering, surrender, even at the cost of going far from home to a strange place, began to seem the better alternative. Navajos who wanted to go back and spread the word were allowed to do so. Earlier, he had lamented that he had only been able to communicate with them "through the barrels of my Rifles," and that the actions of Blakeney and others had aborted attempts by Navajos to negotiate surrender and led them to conclude that the army aimed at their destruction. Now they knew the true state of affairs and were coming in in increasing numbers.[127]

There were other factors operating at the same time to make surrender more attractive. Howard Gorman says that Navajos came to surrender to Carson "even though they didn't want to," because they knew the Utes "were on the loose, riding horseback, and that they were dangerously aggressive." In fact, Utes scouted the canyon after Carson's entry, and their chief, Grayhair, was supposedly killed by Navajo witchcraft. Even before the expedition one Navajo chief, Delgadito, who had surrendered in November, had been out spreading the word of Carleton's intentions to his people, and enjoying considerable success. By early February there were some twelve hundred at Fort Wingate.[128]

Dahghaa'í was reported as scornful that Carson himself did not enter the canyon but sent others instead. Lawrence Kelly's view is that Carson here showed his "essential humility" by letting junior officers gain the glory and the chance for promotion. Certainly, although he described the penetration and traverse of the canyon as a great accomplishment, he gave the praise for martial exploits to Pfeiffer, Carey, Berney, and Herrera. He could have paraded through the canyon himself if glory was his object. The Navajos may have taken pleasure in the idea that the man they described with such chauvinistic relish as "a very pure White Man" did not dare enter their canyon. But for Carson the expedition was not an eagerly sought chance for glory but an operation reluctantly undertaken at his superior's insistence to cover one more possible sanctuary of the Navajos. It was another duty to be carried out conscientiously and methodically, but without the younger Kit's enthusiasm for combat. The results went far beyond anything he had hoped for, especially in accelerating Navajo surrenders. In that sense it was certainly a victory, and he rightly reported it as such. Doctor Peters's grand vision of a brilliant piece of military strategy, resulting in the trapping of thousands of Navajos, would have astonished, embarrassed, and perhaps amused Kit.[129]

Soon after his return from Canyon de Chelly, some 500 Navajos had gathered at Fort Canby, fulfilling General Carleton's condition that Kit could come to Santa Fe when he had 100 captives. He set out promptly on January 26 with 240 of them, whom he took to the post of Los Pinos on the Rio Grande to be forwarded to Bosque Redondo. This was one of the first installments of the "Long Walk" so darkly memorable in the history of the Navajo people. This group was the only contingent of Navajos to make that journey under Carson's direct supervision, although some historians have held him directly responsible for the sufferings endured by all the Navajos forced on the "Long Walk." Carson would, in fact, be gone from the field for nearly two months, while operations continued and the stream of surrendering Navajos grew to a flood.[130]

There were so many Navajos at Fort Canby by early February that Captain Carey was unable to send most of them on to Bosque Redondo for lack of transportation. When important men and heads of families came in to inquire about the terms of surrender, the captain explained the requirements and allowed them to return to bring in their followers. In this, he explained, he followed Carson's directions: "The wisdom of the policy indicated by the Colonel Commanding, before leaving here, in permitting some of the leading men of the tribe to go out and bring in their families and friends, has been productive of the most salutary results." Carey had cancelled any scouting parties for fear they would only impede the process of surrender. By mid-February there were about one thousand Navajos at the fort, "and they are daily and hourly arriving." Carey noted, "Many of the Indians arriving here are almost unable to travel, resulting from hunger and destitution."[131]

Captain Joseph Berney headed east from Fort Canby on February 4 with 175 Navajos, under orders to pick up those at Fort Wingate on the way; he found there were too many there for the available transportation and went on with his original party. A little later twelve hundred Navajos in two parties were moved from Fort Wingate to Los Pinos, and Berney then took them all on to Bosque Redondo. Along the way he lost fifteen, "principally boys": ten died "from the effects of the cold &c.," two "strayed" or escaped, and three were "stolen"—carried off as captives by New Mexicans. Berney's party enjoyed a better survival rate than most groups who made the Long Walk, which stretched 375 to 500 miles from Fort Canby to Bosque Redondo, depending on the route.[132]

That notorious episode was already well under way when Carson returned to Fort Canby on March 19, 1864; over three thousand had already gone east from Forts Canby and Wingate. In later years the Long

Walk would be, for the Navajos, one of the most bitterly remembered phases of the period. Like the Cherokee Trail of Tears, it became for later generations a symbol of white injustice toward Indians. Kit Carson had little direct connection with the Long Walk itself. His campaign forced the surrender of thousands of Navajos and so made the Walk possible, but he himself conducted only one small party of Indians as far as Los Pinos. His principal contributions to the Walk were made in communications dictated shortly after his return to command. Captain Carey noted on March 20, 1864, that Carson had returned the previous day, "unwell and very much fatigued," and had resumed command the next day. His condition caused Carey to write, "I regret that there should have exhisted a necessity for the immediate return of Colonel Carson to this post." Kit's extended absence had not done much for his health; the disease that would kill him may already have been showing its effects.[133]

On the same day Carson himself wrote to department headquarters reporting the dispatch of 836 more Navajos from Fort Canby, and expressing the opinion that all who were likely to come in had now done so; the rest, who were relatively wealthy, had fled toward the Colorado River and would have to be "visited by the troops" before they would surrender. Carson then warned Carleton of a problem that would plague the general's future plans: "There is no doubt in my mind but that the strength of the Navajoe nation has been underrated, and that there is five or six thousand still at large." General Carleton had just written to Carey saying that he could feed six thousand Navajos at Bosque Redondo: "Will not that be the most of the tribe. I hardly think they will overrun 6000." Carey soon thereafter expressed a quite different opinion, with which Carson agreed. On March 27 the captain wrote headquarters that, "I am of the opinion that the Nation is nearly if not quite 12000."[134]

Carleton slightly revised his estimate of the number that could be fed at Bosque Redondo to 7,000, but that included 450 Mescaleros. "Will not 7000 cover all the Navajoes?" he asked with an unwonted note of anxiety. On April 1 he said flatly, "I think you overrate the number of the Navajoes." A little later he told Carson he could send in even 10,000, but some of them would have to bring their own flocks and herds to feed themselves. All the same, "I cannot believe but that 8000 will cover all the tribe."[135]

The general cannot have derived much comfort from Carson's communication of April 10, in which he wrote, "All the information which

I can collect on the subject confirms my belief that we have as yet not one-half the Tribe at the Bosque Redondo." Kit now thought, however, that it would not be necessary to go after them; they would come in of their own accord: "The vigor and energy which has characterized this campaign has fully convinced them of the folly of further resistance; and the hostility of the Pueblo and surrounding tribes of Indians, warns them that their only security is in that protection which the Government offers them."

Carson clearly did not see any need for further scourging of the Navajos. On a related point, he made a clear and emphatic recommendation concerning the Long Walk. Captain Francis McCabe had left Fort Canby on March 20 (the day after Kit's return to the post) with eight hundred Navajo prisoners to conduct to Bosque Redondo. He had, in his own words, "barely a sufficient supply of rations and forage" to reach Fort Wingate, and so had to push on through a snowstorm, which "occasioned great suffering amongst the Indians, many of whom were nearly naked and of course unable to withstand such a storm." The rations he could obtain at Fort Wingate amounted to half a pound of beef and half a pound of flour per day. Although he obtained more food at Los Pinos, other problems plagued the march, including New Mexican kidnappers and Pueblos who tried to induce Navajos to stay with them. In all, he declared that 110 people died and 25 were "enticed away."[136]

Carson apparently heard "unofficially" that one hundred people had run off from McCabe's party: "cause, want of a sufficiency to eat." Kit made his thoughts on the Long Walk clear to Carleton:

> I would respectfully suggest to you the propriety, and good policy of, giving to the Indians while at Forts Canby and Wingate, and while *en route* to the Bosque Redondo, a sufficiency to eat. It is while here, and *en route* that we must convince them by our treatment of them of the kind intentions of the Government towards them, otherwise I fear that they will lose confidence in our promises, and desert also. As suspicion enters so largely into the composition of the Indian character, the greatest possible care must be taken not to awaken it by acts contrary to our promises. I think one pound of Beef, or of flour, Wheat, or Corn, as entirely too small an allowance for an able bodied Indian for one day.

Carson had pointed out a major shortcoming in Carleton's management of the first phase of his "civilizing" program.[137]

The Long Walk would be remembered in Navajo tradition as a death march. Traditional accounts insist that people who could not keep up were sometimes shot, and that women were raped by soldiers. Others remembered insufficient food or unfamiliar food that they did not know how to prepare and that made them sick. Some even believed that the white men were trying to poison them; some refused to eat the food and starved. In these stories, the details on the Walk vary. Jake Segundo, who was six at the time, remembered that there were supply wagons drawn by mules and oxen, and "When people got sick or old people got tired they were allowed to ride awhile." Frank Mitchell, whose parents made the Walk, declared,

> The People were not tortured or separated as much as some people say they were during that time. When they were going to Fort Sumner, they were all gathered at Fort Defiance and from there, they were in the hands of those soldiers, the cavalry. They protected the People all the way to Fort Sumner, and they were well protected over there too. . . . My parents never really suffered because they were well taken care of as soon as they were turned over to the soldiers at Fort Defiance.

Mitchell thought the ones who really suffered were those who escaped and were caught by other Indians like the Utes. The stories of killing and rape occur too frequently to allow denial. A few such incidents in each contingent of Navajos, or even in one or two, would have made enough of an impression that in a generation or two of storytelling they would be recalled as a daily occurrence. That some of the New Mexican soldiers, with generations of conflict behind them, might have treated Navajo prisoners with contempt and brutality would not be surprising. Much must have depended on the quality and attitude of the officers in charge of each particular contingent; this would account for some of the variation in the accounts of treatment received. The relaxed discipline and the shortage of first-class officers in the New Mexico volunteers would not have helped—and Kit Carson must bear some responsibility for that state of affairs.[138]

Frank McNitt, the tireless researcher of the Navajo wars, broke down the official figures on the Long Walk and decided that 11,612 Navajos were sent to Bosque Redondo. Of these, 336 were officially reported to have died on the march, 220 escaped, 20 were stolen, and 158 were unaccounted for; 8,846 actually arrived according to the records.

McNitt was left with some 2,000 who were sent but whose arrival was not reported, and whose loss did not appear in any of the above categories, even as "unaccounted for." If we assumed that all these were unreported deaths, then we would indeed have a death march to rival that of Bataan. Historical experience does not allow us to say categorically that this cannot be true; too many graves, in too many places, in quite recent memory, say otherwise. McNitt says, "It is certain that some of them did reach the reservation (how many is purely conjectural), but their arrival went unreported. What happened to the others will never be known." Carson understood that some one hundred of the contingent escorted by McCabe escaped under a specific leader, and this would probably be true of a number of the missing in other groups. Some who escaped may have been recaptured and thus counted twice. Some were undoubtedly carried off by New Mexicans. Carson complained of the "citizen marauders" who came as far as Fort Canby to rob the Navajos near the post, and Lieutenant George Campbell, stationed at Cubero, warned, "At this place officers who have indians in charge will have to exercise extreme vigilence or the indians children will be stolen from him and sold." Some were persuaded to remain at Indian pueblos along the route, such as Acoma and Laguna. Jake Segundo recalled, "There were people in charge but they did not keep close watch at night." Allowing for all possible reductions, some, perhaps hundreds, must have died of hunger and sickness, and some by violence. Carleton simply had not planned adequately for moving so many people under such conditions.[139]

Although a campaign in winter was most feasible, the many surrendering Navajos either had to be fed at Forts Canby and Wingate until spring, requiring the transportation of large quantities of food and supplies under winter conditions, or they had to be moved to the Rio Grande or on to the Bosque Redondo, where they could more readily be supplied. This involved moving several thousand weakened people, whose numbers Carleton had underestimated, under harsh weather conditions. There were not enough wagons or mounts for everyone, rations were scanty and mostly unfamiliar, leading to diarrhea and other illnesses. Blankets, clothing, and shelter from the weather were also inadequate. A high death toll is hardly surprising. Large-scale deliberate killing by the soldiers is not necessary as an explanation, though there is no reason to doubt that Navajo traditions are correct in saying that some people were shot when they could not keep up. Carson—perhaps with the advice of Captain Carey—recognized the dangers and emphatically warned of the need for sufficient food and kind treatment, putting it in the practical terms to be expected in an official report. These recommendations were his most direct connection with the actual Long Walk.

On April 13 Carson wrote that "since active hostilities have ceased against the Navajos," New Mexicans were coming to the vicinity of Fort Canby to steal from the surrendered Indians. He wanted additional troops to enable him to pursue such raiders. A month later, probably at General Carleton's request, Governor Connelly issued a proclamation ordering the cessation of any hostilities by citizens and threatening "the severest penalties" for any violation. Carson, having been back at Fort Canby for a little over a month, once again relinquished command and left on April 21. For him the campaign that would always be associated with his name, for good or ill, was over.[140]

THIS CROWNING ACT

Most of Carson's white contemporaries regarded the campaign as a great achievement, as being what James Carleton said of the Canyon de Chelly expedition: "this crowning act in a long life spent in various capacities in the service of his country in fighting the savages in the fastnesses of the Rocky Mountains." Some New Mexicans would criticize the achievement as incomplete, insisting that large numbers of Navajos remained at large in the remoter corners of northeastern Arizona. That seems to have been true; perhaps as many as four thousand may have continued at liberty, either for months to come or until the remainder of their people returned from Bosque Redondo in 1868. Nonetheless, parties continued to come in to Fort Canby and Fort Wingate to surrender through 1864 and during the next two years. Troops continued to operate on a smaller scale against Navajo raiding parties who were still making off with the sheep of some western New Mexico settlers, who responded with their own forays. Criticism fell sharply upon General Carleton, whose increasingly numerous enemies accused him of exaggerating his achievement. Yet the power of the Navajos as the principal enemy of New Mexico was broken. Manuelito finally surrendered at Fort Wingate in September 1866, and many holdouts followed his example, although raiding never completely ceased.[141]

On May 20, 1864, Carson put his name to a final report on the Navajo campaign. It includes a lengthy sketch of the historical background and fulsome praise of Carleton, who is credited with "a perfect knowledge of the means to effect" the purpose of "freeing the Territory from these lawless Savages." One must suspect, from the language and the content, that the general or one of his staff had a hand in writing the report and advise some caution in searching for Carson's ideas in it. It asserts that the Navajo war had gone on for two centuries, subjecting the people of New Mexico to a "forced tax," besides the cost in lives and in children carried off as captives. After the United States took possession of the territory there were several expeditions against the Navajos, and several treaties, but no lasting peace, not because the troops did not carry out their orders, "but because the policy adopted was erroneous." The Texan invasion recalled the troops from the Navajo country, "when the war-whoop of their relentless foes smote the hearing of our peaceable citizens . . . the more appalling now from its being unexpected owing to their faith in the treaty just concluded." It was a fair summary of the history of the Navajo wars as New Mexicans, and General Carleton, would have seen it, although it makes no allowance for the Navajo view, or for the complex interactions and mutual hostilities between the various peoples of New Mexico. Does it reflect the actual views of Kit Carson, the ostensible author?[142]

As a matter of fact, Carson's own statement to the congressional committee in 1865, already cited, does seem to sketch the same history, much more briefly. There Carson declared, "We would hardly get back from fighting and making peace with them [the Navajos] before they would be at war again." Carson recognized the mutual nature of the hostilities. He noted "continual thieving carried on between the Navajoes and the Mexicans." He further declared that, "If located in different places [rather than at Bosque Redondo] it would not be long before they and the Mexicans would be at war." Here again Carson recognized the mutuality of the relationship while leaving little doubt that a reservation, under the guardianship of the army, was the only way to end hostilities: "If they were scattered on different locations, I hardly think any number of troops could keep them on their reservation."[143]

It should be apparent from the foregoing narrative that the word *genocide* cannot be applied meaningfully to Carson's Navajo campaign. To follow current fashion and call it genocidal is, in James Axtell's words, "to dilute our moral vocabulary to insipidity and to squander its intellectual and moral force." In spite of Carleton's tough talk, and his orders regarding the killing of males of fighting age, the purpose of the operation was always to force the Navajos to surrender and go to Bosque Redondo. Carleton was delighted when the Navajos began to surrender, and he endeavored to speed the process by sending Delgadito out as an emissary in November 1863, to spread the word that his goal was their surrender and not extermination. He was also eager to wind down the campaign, in spite of the complaints of vocal critics in New Mexico, and in spite of the fact that a significant number of Navajos remained at liberty in Arizona for many months. He had little concern for the wishes of the Navajos themselves, and little understanding of their profound reluctance to leave their land and put themselves in his hands. He would have preferred their immediate surrender. When they did come in and put an unanticipated strain on his available food supplies, he put his own soldiers on short rations in order to feed everyone. He even limited the number of Navajos he would accept as captives, based on his ability to feed them, while also slacking off on the military operations that were intended to force their surrender. None of this suggests indifference to their fate, or a desire to destroy them by whatever means offered.[144]

Actions that are not genocidal may nonetheless be reprehensible, and Carson's conduct of the Navajo campaign has occasioned severe attacks on his reputation, including allegations of genocide and racism, by some writers. Some have charged that he proceeded in a fashion worthy of Genghis Khan and Hitler's SS, killing and starving thousands of innocent people. One historian who has prosecuted these charges with particular zeal and detail is Clifford Trafzer, in his *Kit Carson Campaign*. Trafzer acknowledges that raiding was part of the Navajo economy, and that "once the raiding cycle was established, it was nearly impossible to break," and he also points out that the pattern followed by Carson in 1863–64 was already set by Canby in 1860–61. Nonetheless, he finds Carson's conduct of the war brutal and indiscriminate, killing "many innocent Navajos, people who had played no role in the hostilities before 1863." He acknowledges that Kit was not "a ruthless murderer" (though much of his narrative would lead to that conclusion), but the best he can say for him and for Carleton is that they showed "a sort of callous paternalism."[145]

Even if Kit Carson had remained at home in Taos and watched his children grow, instead of putting on a blue uniform, or if James Carleton had never returned to New Mexico at the head of the California Column, there surely would have been a military campaign of some sort against the Navajos during the Civil War period or soon thereafter. It probably would have followed much the same procedure, dictated by the realities of Indian warfare, worked out by Colonel Canby in 1860. Lacking Carleton or Carson, the operation might have failed, with a result much more bloody.

Modern-day critics of Kit Carson's Navajo campaign who know the historical background are aware that it was only the climax of a war that had gone on for generations, a war that Carson and Carleton brought to an end. They assume that Carson and Carleton saw only one side of the equation because of Indian-hating prejudice, preference for military solutions over peaceful negotiation, sheer callousness, or a desire for military glory—to which is added, in Carson's case, unquestioning subservience to a military and social superior.

These critics apparently measure the historical reality against an ideal solution based on negotiated peace, respect for the Navajos' culture and lifeway, trust in their ability to police themselves, and the use of force to restrain New Mexicans, whose raids on the Indians are seen as the real cause of the persisting hostilities. This last idea is based on the view that Indians were invariably the innocent victims of white European aggression throughout American history, a view that has much evidence to support it, as Kit increasingly realized, but which requires qualification. Carson, and most white inhabitants of New Mexico at the time, and most federal officials and soldiers who had to deal with the problem, would have said in all sincerity that they had tried the ideal solution repeatedly and it didn't work.

There were some Anglo-Americans in New Mexico who saw the Navajos as greatly wronged. The majority, like most Hispanic and Pueblo New Mexicans, saw it differently. It would have been asking a great deal of them to take on their own heads the guilt of the few who raided the Navajos and accept their losses in livestock, in blood, and in women and children taken captive, as retributive justice. The Navajos did not accept *their* losses in that spirit at the time. It is hard to imagine any military commander or civil governor in the territory tolerating the raids either, especially with the need to hold the region for a Union fighting for its existence, and with a renewed Confederate invasion considered a real possibility.

Nineteenth-century Americans tended to see "savage" warfare as wholly different—vastly more terrible and unrestrained—from "civilized" warfare, with its restrictions and soldierly codes of conduct. It would have been hard to sell that idea to Navajos who had experienced military operations as conducted by white soldiers—still less if they had seen war as the white men conducted it at Antietam or Gettysburg. Today there is a widespread tendency to see "primitive" war as a very mild, restrained thing, different in kind as well as degree from the bloody-mindedness of modern civilization—"more akin to full-contact sports like football, hockey, and rugby than anything else," in the words of one commentator. This idea would have been hard to sell to nineteenth-century New Mexicans, Hispanic and Pueblo, whose experience of Navajo warfare told them differently.[146]

Archaeologist Lawrence Keeley has recently made some useful observations: "Primitive war was not a puerile or deficient form of warfare, but war reduced to its essentials: killing enemies with a minimum of risk, denying them the means of life via vandalism and theft (even the means of reproduction by the kidnapping of their women and children), terrorizing them into either yielding territory or desisting from their encroachments and aggressions." This is exactly what New Mexicans and Navajos were trying to do to each other up to the 1860s, with little success so far as making the other side desist. Keeley also notes, however, that aggressive societies "may be pacified by defeat at the hands of equally aggressive but larger societies," and he cites the Navajos as one example.[147]

To say "the Navajos had it coming" is simpleminded, but we must understand why many people in the nineteenth-century Southwest saw them as an intolerable menace to peace and security. In his study of primitive warfare, Lawrence Keeley points out that certain groups or nations at certain periods in their histories become "bad neighbors," engaging in offensive actions and sparking continuing warfare and instability in their entire regions. Among various peoples from all over the world included in this category, such as the Iroquois, the Teton Sioux, the Zulus, and the Vikings, he places the Navajos and the Apaches of the Southwest. He also includes the nineteenth-century United States and twentieth-century Germany and Japan. The Navajos' Indian neighbors leaped at the chance to join in the last campaign against them, as in earlier ones, and they contributed to forcing the eventual surrender—which is consistent with many other "white" campaigns against Indians. Like many peoples, the Navajos had made enemies in the day of their power and prosperity, and when the tide turned there were many ready to help pull them down, for both revenge and profit. As the Navajos saw it, they all paid for the deeds of some over whom the rest had no control.[148]

The distinctive feature of Carleton's plan was his decision to relocate the Navajos at Bosque Redondo, hundreds of miles from their homeland. Even this was in the mold of the Indian removals of the Jacksonian period (when the young James Carleton first joined the army), when in fact eastern tribes were moved much farther from home; removals continued even into the 1880s, with present-day Oklahoma as the favorite dumping ground. Colonel Canby had intended to remove the Navajos to "points so remote from the settlements as to isolate them entirely from the inhabitants of the Territory," but he apparently never intended to take them so far from their homeland as the Pecos River. He seems to have had in mind an area on the Little Colorado River west of Zuni, which would have been near or within the western reaches of their present reservation, "remote from the settlements" on the Rio Grande at the time. Perhaps if Carleton had stuck to that part of Canby's strategy he could have secured the surrender of many of the Navajos with much less trouble and suffering.[149]

There were probably three main reasons for Carleton's determination to move them so far from home. First would be the need to separate "friendly" from "hostile" Navajos, ensuring that none of the latter would find temporary refuge among the former, and that the friendlies would not come under attack by troops eager to strike someone and inclined to believe that none could be trusted; separation over such a distance, with the surrendered Indians guarded by troops, would ensure that the distinction was real. Another reason was the general's liking for the Bosque Redondo site, which was indeed remote from New Mexican settlements of the time, though stockmen already had their eyes on the grazing in the area, and would oppose Carleton's appropriating it for Indians. He thought it would be easier to maintain both the Navajos and the military garrison on the Pecos than on the Little Colorado or some other area in Arizona where, he explained in 1865, barrenness and lack of water made it impossible to concentrate the Navajos in one place, and the cost of transporting supplies from the Rio Grande would be "immense." In addition, in Arizona "formidable ranges of mountains are near by, in which they could hide, and no force of troops could keep them together." In the same year Kit Carson agreed, declaring, "If they were scattered on different locations, I hardly think any number of troops could keep them on their reservation." To Carson and Carleton that meant another campaign, with all the attendant difficulty, death, and suffering.[150]

The third reason was probably Carleton's conviction that large mineral deposits were to be found in or near Navajo country. His efforts to promote the development of these potential mining areas have already been noted. Gold, silver, and other valuable minerals would draw miners like magnets, as in California and Colorado. Carleton was unlikely to ignore the service he could render to a Union needing every possible source of wealth. Miners were already swarming in central Arizona, and bitter fighting with local Apaches was the consequence. As far as Carleton could see, locating the Navajos on the Little Colorado or anywhere else near potential gold mines would only set up another such conflict. In 1865 he opposed a Navajo reservation on the San Juan River because "the San Juan runs through a country bearing gold, which will soon attract miners to the region; and even if the Indians were placed there they would soon come into conflicts with that kind of men." Carson had seen what happened when "that kind of men" moved into California and Colorado and met the Indians there. That should be remembered in connection with Carson's support for the Bosque Redondo reservation experiment, since he must have known of Carleton's belief in the mineral wealth of the San Juan.[151]

There were reasons, then, for making removal to the Bosque Redondo a condition of peace, although hindsight may question whether they were worth the increased reluctance of the Navajos to surrender. But the campaign itself has been the focus of the attack on Carson's, as opposed to Carleton's, reputation. The crux is the belief that Carson, as Harvey Carter summed up the charges, "starved, beat, and killed untold numbers of Navajo Indians and enslaved those who survived." Martin Green writes, without citing evidence, "It is said that Carson's sleep was haunted ever after by dreams of dying Navajo women and children." He adds that Kit used artillery on them, which is not supported by the evidence.[152]

Carson's campaign was typical of Indian warfare; there was a clear line of tradition stretching back at least to the Second Seminole War, with obvious precedents much earlier. The notion that "total war" methods developed during the Civil War were then applied to the Indian wars thus seems questionable. The same methods were used against "primitive" peoples by "civilized" armies the world over in the nineteenth century. Since the enemy refused to fight except when they possessed a great numerical or tactical advantage, since they possessed great mobility and knew the country much better than the soldiers, since they made evasion the basis of their strategy, and since they had no central government that could be forced into a binding surrender, conventional methods of warfare were of little use against them. Secretary Floyd's advice of 1860—that operations should be confined to killing enough warriors to force surrender without causing suffering to noncombatants—was based on the contemporary belief that it was honorable to kill great numbers of men in combat, but not to inflict suffering on the rest of their society. Lawrence Keeley argues that civilized armies were able to defeat primitive forces precisely because they put aside their artificial, limited ideas of warfare and adopted those of the "primitives." They became more mobile, relied on surprise and raiding tactics, destroyed the enemy's resource base, took advantage of superior logistical support to persist in campaigning over a long period, harassed the enemy without letup, engaged in slow attrition against the enemy's manpower in many small actions, and made extensive use of "primitive" allies.[153] If Carson had not fought the Navajos in the only way likely to bring about their final surrender, the cost to them would have been greater in the long run.

There can be no question that the period of the 1860s, the "Fearing Time," was for the Navajos a period of great suffering and loss. That suffering should not be minimized but neither, as Fritz Stern reminds us, should we dissipate the memory of the past by a facile analogy with such a uniquely terrible event as the Nazi Holocaust. Since there was no possibility of a decisive battle, the purpose of the campaign was to destroy the Navajos' resource base—more simply, to deprive them of food—and to harass them, taking away any sense of security, until the situation became intolerable and they gave up. The basic purpose was less to kill Navajos than to make them surrender as expeditiously as possible. Carleton did issue orders to kill male Navajos and Apaches who were capable of bearing arms, and this has naturally excited the indignation of later commentators. But at the very same time he was telling a subordinate, "Every Navajo or Apache man who may be found by your troops will be destroyed *or taken prisoner* [emphasis added]." When Kit Carson complained of the brutal acts of Major Blakeney, Carleton made clear that Indians coming in or taken prisoner were not to be killed. Carleton wanted to show his officers that he meant business, that there would be no peace agreements with a few chiefs or portions of tribes which left the Indians free to resume hostilities later—the sort of thing he considered had happened in the past, and that Carson saw in Meriwether's peace agreements. Complete and comprehensive surrender or destruction were to be the alternatives. By putting things in his customary style, he ensured later odium for himself and Carson. The general repeatedly coupled his instructions about killing men with orders that women and children were not to be harmed. Carson made a point of reporting the number of men killed in skirmishes and the number of women and children taken prisoner. (Again, one can always believe he concealed the truth if one wishes.) He made repeated efforts to secure the surrender of all Navajos, men included, from early in the campaign, ordering one subordinate that any agreeing to the surrender terms "will be permitted to take with them their families and all they possess," which obviously referred to male heads of families.[154]

Early on, Carson tried to induce Navajos to surrender by sending persons who surrendered or were captured as messengers to bear the word, and he bitterly lamented that actions of his own men, Major Blakeney in particular, had led the Indians to fear that the war was "one of extermination." The shaky discipline in the First New Mexico was to some extent his responsibility, but the worst offender, Blakeney, was an outsider imposed on him by Carleton. The men who sent away the Navajo, possibly Manuelito, who wanted to talk to Carson, blundered, though they did not kill him, presumably because they knew Carson's attitude. Carson considered that one of the most important results of the Canyon de Chelly expedition was the chance to explain to the Navajos there "that the principle was not to destroy them but to save them, if they are disposed to be saved." Whether or not he actually wept at the sight of Navajo casualties, he convinced them that they could safely come in and surrender. The campaign was undoubtedly an act of war, in which people were killed. The killing was done in small actions, amounting to a few casualties at a time. At the end of 1863 the official army count of Navajo losses stood at 78 killed, 40 wounded, and 196 captured; this was not negligible, but as Robert Utley points out, it was hardly a genocidal toll. As noted, Carson's report for the Canyon de Chelly expedition in January 1864 gave Navajo losses of 23 killed, 34 prisoners, and 200 surrendered. There seems little reason why reports to Carleton would have minimized the number of enemy casualties, considering the general's harsh orders and insistence on action.[155]

The official army record, of course, does not take into account the losses inflicted by Utes, Pueblos, and New Mexican irregulars, all acting independently except for Carson's Ute, Zuni, and Hopi scouts.

There are clear indications in Navajo tradition that the raids of the independent Ute war parties, in retrospect at least, were as effective as the actions of the army in inducing Navajos to surrender to the soldiers for protection. There can be no question that Navajos suffered greatly from deprivation, cold, and stress, as they had in previous campaigns. The losses would have been greatest among children, old people, and the physically frail. This is the reality behind phrases like "attacking the resource base," and it applies to blockades, economic sanctions, and bombing campaigns aimed at transportation and production, conducted by civilized states against each other. Carson's reports show that he was fully aware of the privations that the Navajos were enduring. Despite the destruction of their crops and the taking of their animals, he made a point of feeding those who came in.

Carson's opinions and actions make it clear that he wanted to end the campaign as soon as possible by persuading as many Navajos as possible to give themselves up. Captain Asa Carey commended the wisdom of his policy of sending out surrendered chiefs to bring their people in. For a time Carson thought that those who had fled into remote areas would have to be "visited" by the troops, but he soon changed his mind, believing they would surrender without further harassment, as many did. The end of the business meant, of course, that he could go home, but he saw no reason to continue the pressure, and he was anxious to have civilian raiding parties stopped once the Navajos had begun to surrender in large numbers.

The evidence does not permit certainty about Carson's emotions regarding the campaign. The notion that he eagerly "starved, beat, and killed untold numbers of Navajo Indians and enslaved those who survived," in Harvey Carter's summation of the charges, is disproved by the evidence of his conduct and his wish to be out of the campaign. Kit's persistent efforts to obtain the surrender of as many as possible must cast great doubt on his bloodthirstiness. His presence with the advance scouts in at least the early stages of the campaign and his pushing on when he was reeling in the saddle from fatigue indicate his temperamental inclination to be where the action was, once committed to the operation, and his equally characteristic determination to do his duty. The best evidence is that he regarded the whole campaign as an unavoidable necessity, which he would just as soon have let someone else carry out, and which he wanted to end with as little bloodshed and suffering as would achieve the result.

The story of his weeping at the killing of Navajos cannot be taken without reservations. It was after the Navajo war that he voiced his strongest recorded denunciations of white aggression against Indians, and his strongest expressions of compassion for them. One might see in this evidence of revulsion at what he had had to do in 1863–64. However, he never seems to have changed his mind about the necessity for the campaign, and obviously he had reasons, afterward, for wanting to believe it necessary. His later denunciations of white aggression seem to have spung from the desire to avoid unnecessary repetitions of such tragedies, rather than from consciously admitted guilt.

Finally we come back to Colonel Canby's assertion in late 1861 that the Navajos were now so "demoralized and broken up" there was no choice except "absolute extermination" or removal to "points so remote from the settlements as to isolate them entirely from the inhabitants of the Territory." The impoverishment of the Navajos by military cam-paigns and civilian attacks (including those of other Indians) had so increased the number of ladrones that "the depredations of the Navajos are constant." The cycle, as Canby saw it, would go on until the Navajos were brought under government control and placed on a reservation far enough from the New Mexican settlements to insure peace. Among those testifying before the congressional committee of 1865, even those who were most critical of the Bosque Redondo reservation and most inclined to blame Hispanics and Anglos for the troubles believed that it was necessary to have the Navajos on a reservation. James Collins, who thought he could have maintained peace in the late 1850s but for the conduct of the commander of Fort Defiance, believed that establishing Indians on reservations was "the only way they can be controlled or kept from hostilities" because "the condition became such they could not have been controlled in their own country." The people of New Mexico were "continually liable to get into difficulty with the Indians," and "it is a matter of security to the Indians themselves, and the women and children, to be placed under the protection of the United States upon a reservation." Chief Justice Benedict, a critic of General Carleton, thought that if the army had been able to protect the people of New Mexico from the Indians it would have been better for the latter to remain on their own lands; but that, he said, had not been the case.[156]

It is surely clear by now that the war Carson waged was neither geno-cidal in intent nor in practice. Direct battle casualties were relatively few, though not insignificant. The casualties due to destruction of the

Navajos' crops and loss of animals, and to the stress of harassment and flight in winter, were undoubtedly greater and more influential in compelling their surrender. When the Navajos understood that surrender was possible, the majority turned themselves in to Carson. But the campaign itself was only part of the trauma that made the entire period of the 1860s so memorable for them.

The other two phases of the Fearing Time—the Long Walk and the confinement at Bosque Redondo—probably inflicted far more casualties and more suffering on the Navajos than the military campaign. Kit Carson, as noted, had little to do with the Long Walk, except to warn General Carleton that he had probably underestimated the number of Indians to be transported and provided for, and to insist that they must be adequately fed and kindly treated. This Carleton and his subordinates failed to do, whether through miscalculation or lack of concern is hard to say.

The Bosque Redondo experiment was also James Carleton's responsibility and would do far more immediate harm to his reputation than any of his strictly military endeavors. The reservation has been described as a "concentration camp," and those who use that phrase definitely intend the comparison with the death camps of Nazi Germany. Gerald Thompson, the most thorough historian of the Bosque Redondo, sees it in less dramatic terms as a partial success, just enough of one to encourage proponents of the reservation system to maintain their faith in the idea over the next half-century. The Navajos, however, would remember it as a place of exile and suffering, and for too many it was a grave. A monument stands today on the banks of the Pecos, with an inscription in the Navajo tongue, commemorating the suffering of their people there.[157]

Bosque Redondo was almost a laboratory experiment in the efficacy of the reservation system. The underlying ideas were those laid down by the founders of the system in the 1840s and '50s, and advocated by Kit Carson in his official reports as an Indian agent: removing the Indians well away from white settlements, requiring them to support themselves by farming, and instructing them in the basics of white civilization and Christianity. James Carleton had in fact shown an interest in such matters as early as 1844, in a magazine article on his service with the dragoons in which he described the immigrant Pottawatamis on the eastern Great Plains. Lamenting the fading away of their old-time warrior virtues, he found them "a degenerate and dissipated race" that was "overshadowed and blighted" by white civilization—particularly by alcohol. Their "habits of idleness" prevented their benefiting from the good farmland on which they had settled. Instead of giving them annuities to spend on drink, Carleton opined that the government should spend the money on "the making of elegant farms, and in the purchase and rearing of stock," which could support them with a minimum of labor. In the late 1850s Carleton was stationed at Fort Tejon, California, near Edward Fitzgerald Beale's Tejon Indian Reservation, where the Indians were taught to support themselves by farming while the army post both protected and controlled them. This was one of the first full-fledged experiments in the reservation system, and it probably inspired the observant and activist dragoon officer.[158]

The epitaph for the Bosque Redondo reservation, as for so many well-intended enterprises, should probably be, "It seemed like a good idea at the time." Typically, its author persisted well past the point at which, hindsight would suggest, he should have given it up, because each setback seemed to be just a temporary problem that, once overcome, would yield to steady progress. The general and some dedicated subordinates worked very hard to make it a success, but they were defeated by adverse circumstances, some perhaps predictable, and by certain underlying flaws in their assumptions. Lynn Bailey writes, "While Carleton went to great lengths to learn the geography of Navajoland, he failed miserably to comprehend the geography of Navajo beliefs." The failure was no doubt characteristic of the man, but few members of his society would have known any better. The Navajos were plagued by malaria and by diseases related to crowding, unfamiliar food, food shortages, and stress. One of the most serious problems was simply that, accustomed to living dispersed over great areas of land, they were now crammed into a few square miles. Although they were familiar with agriculture and made serious efforts at planting, there were repeated crop failures due to insects, flooding, and climate. Carleton had received warnings about the shortcomings of the site from various people, notably New Mexico Superintendent of Indian Affairs Michael Steck, but he ignored them, believing that Bosque Redondo was the best available location. The continued failure to produce sufficient food forced Carleton to purchase provisions locally and bring them in from outside New Mexico. The entire cost of the reservation ran up to $1 million per year, and the large local food purchases, plus crop failures, inflated the price of food in New Mexico beyond the means of the poor. Many of the contracts, because of the pressing need, were awarded without competitive bidding, and they seemed to go to Carleton's fellow Democrats. Good Republicans (who also charged him with interfering in elections), and disappointed contractors in general, were numbered among the general's enemies who attacked him in the press and lobbied against him in Washington.[159]

Kit Carson's part in all of this was secondary. The reservation experiment was very much General Carleton's idea, and he gave it his intense and detailed attention. Whether counted as success or failure, it was definitely his responsibility. Carson, however, was in charge of the reservation for a few months, and he went on record various times in support of the project. As noted, his final report on the Navajo campaign, with its fulsome praise of Carleton, may not have been a wholly independent production. In it, however, Carson made some observations about the reservation experiment and its management that merit attention. After praising the wisdom that had inaugurated the policy, he expressed hope that the commanding general might be permitted to carry out his work. Kit then noted there was still a great deal to be done "in the way of teaching them to forget the old life, and in reconciling them to the new." To this end "some person well versed in Indian character—who knows these people, and by whom he is known, and in whom they have confidence, should be placed over them as Superintendent or Governor." Carson went on to describe this person's duties at some length. Although Carleton's influence cannot be ruled out, these recommendations are nonetheless Kit's fullest statement of his ideas on how a reservation should be run.[160]

The superintendent depicted by Carson was certainly a paternal figure:

> He would supply their wants, settle their disputes (which are often of a grave character), stand between them and the citizens in their limited intercourse, and instruct and direct their labors. One in fact to whom they could look for council and assistance in every and all emergencies.

As to how he should carry out these tasks:

> They should be governed with gentleness but firmness,—restrained without their being made to feel it. They should not be prematurely forced into the habits or customs of civilized life; and on the other hand care should be taken not to allow them to retrograde. I would

respectfully suggest that a few companies of troops should be stationed on the Reservation, not so much as a guard but as farmers. These by example in the use and application of farming tools would practically convey more instruction in the science of agriculture, and much more rapidly, than could be imparted in any other manner.

Until the Navajos learned white farming methods, they could be allowed to use their own: "That they can now raise good grain I can testify to, my command having destroyed over two millions of pounds during the past campaign." That last sentence helps explain Carson's and Carleton's optimism about the prospects for success of the experiment.[161]

Kit surely spoke with his own voice, from long experience, when he added,

It is of the utmost importance and should never be lost sight of, that every promise however trifling should be religiously kept in every particular, else the naturally suspicious mind of the Indian is alarmed, and distrust and want of confidence with their attending evils speedily follow.

Optimistically he concluded,

In this way I am confident that in a very few years they would equal, if not excel our industrious Pueblos, and become a source of wealth to the Territory instead of being as heretofore its dread and impoverishers: and they would cease to be a constant drain on the United States Treasury.

This last, echoing James Calhoun's observations of fourteen years earlier, was surely intended to appeal to the cost-counters in Washington. If these thoughts are paternalistic, they are also commonsensical.[162]

General Carleton believed he had just the man to fill the demanding role Carson had sketched, and it should come as no surprise that the man was Kit Carson. Opposition to the reservation was already mounting, notably on the part of Michael Steck, the superintendent of Indian Affairs in New Mexico, and the Bureau of Indian Affairs had refused to accept responsibility for the well-being of the Navajos there. The general needed his best man on the job. In fact, Kit took up the job of superintendent of the Bosque Redondo reservation shortly after he set out the requirements for the post, probably knowing he was to be the man. He would hold it for only a few months, however—from May until September 1864.[163]

The reservation was what Carson had been recommending for years as the best hope of saving the Indians and solving the problems created by white expansion. In vain he had urged the government to set up such reserves for the Utes and Jicarillas, remote from the settlements and guarded by soldiers, where the Indians could become self-supporting without coming into conflict with the whites. Agent Carson had never had a chance to try out the theory, but now Colonel Carson had several thousand Indians as his responsibility. It was only natural that he wanted the reserve to succeed, for the sake of the people themselves and because it was an idea invested with hope. Yet he was not to be in charge for long.

In July, after a council with Navajo leaders, Carson reported them content and pleased with their treatment at the reservation. They had planted a large corn crop and many vegetables, all of which seemed to be doing well. He recommended each family receive a small herd of sheep and goats, to provide wool and milk. They had already raised hay to sell to the army, and he thought the money should be used to purchase the animals, rather than letting the Indians spend it on trinkets. At times, clearly, Kit could be as paternalistic as General Carleton.[164]

The troubling note was the condition of the Mescalero Apaches, some 450 people living on the same reservation with 8,000 or so Navajos. Carleton was aware that the two groups spoke related languages, and thus he believed they could get along together on the same reservation. He was wrong: the two peoples had no sense of kinship and indeed saw each other as enemies. The Mescaleros felt overwhelmed, oppressed, and abused by the Navajos. They did not care much for farm work, and Carson found they had only a small acreage under cultivation. He criticized their agent, Lorenzo Labadie, for his performance of his duties and his overoptimistic reports. Kit sought to persuade the Mescaleros to try harder, but their discontent would only grow. When disease and short rations were added, it was too much; in the fall of 1865 the entire tribe fled, eluding pursuit, back to their mountains.[165]

With hindsight, Carson's optimism about the reservation seems sadly misplaced. Unquestionably, he was influenced by the belief that the reservation system was the only workable answer to the problems created by white expansion and Indian-white conflict. A war that had gone on long before he had come to New Mexico had been brought to an end, in considerable part through his own efforts and at considerable cost to the Navajos, and he was determined to see that it did not resume. It is not necessary to assume that he was Carleton's tool to explain his attitude, if one examines his recorded opinions since the 1850s, although loyalty to his military superior, a man he respected, was characteristic of him. He had differed with and criticized superiors and military men before, and he had differed with Carleton on various matters and said so. Carson's brief tenure as superintendent at Bosque Redondo came in the early stages of the experiment, when the first crop had been put in and seemed to be doing well. The Navajos may not have been so pleased with their situation as he thought, but they were making a real effort to become self-supporting in this strange place. They were no doubt relieved that the suffering of the war and the Long Walk was over, and they could see the necessity for making the best of it. Frank Mitchell, recalling his parents' descriptions, takes a characteristically moderate view:

> My parents said it was much worse before they were taken to Fort Sumner. . . . They really suffered during those times. But when they went to Fort Sumner things were altogether changed. I mean that while the People suffered there, it was not as bad as before they went there. That is what my parents said. . . . The Navajos may talk about how much they suffered at Fort Sumner and during that Long Walk, but that is nothing compared to the things my grandfather and father told me about; it was so much worse before they were taken to Fort Sumner.

Although they must already have been bearing a heavy burden of stress and grief, the demoralization produced by repeated crop failures and disease would come later after Carson left the reservation. In August 1864, after Carson's optimistic report, army worms destroyed the whole of the three-thousand-acre corn crop. Carleton recorded his frustration with an uncharacteristic admission: "The failure of the crop—a visitation of God—I could not contend against."[166]

Carson and Carleton both knew that Navajos were quite capable of raising respectable crops. They also knew that New Mexican farmers had for generations supported themselves in an arid land by irrigation from the Rio Grande and other streams. It did not seem impossible to them that the Indians could become self-sustaining in the valley of the Pecos, though in fact agriculture would not succeed in the area until the building of a dam on the river and the introduction of insecticides. The general, and Kit, would continue to believe, and hope, that once the misfortunes of the moment were past, the future would be bright. Criticism, they believed, came from Anglo and Hispanic New Mexicans with political and other selfish motives, like ranchers who wanted the grazing lands along the Pecos and those who had profited from the old raiding cycle. In 1865 Carleton observed "that much of the hostility manifested by many of the people of New Mexico against the reservation system grows out of the fact that when this system goes into succesful operation there will be no more tribes from which they can capture servants, and the military force being reduced . . . the millions of dollars annually expended here . . . will, in a great measure cease." Kit Carson declared, "Some Mexicans now object to the settlement of Navajoes at the Bosque, because they cannot prey on them as formerly."

The two were undoubtedly right regarding the motives of some who opposed the reservation, though these could not be the sole reasons. There is no reason, however, to believe that New Mexicans in general had suddenly become deeply concerned for the welfare of their old enemies. In fact, many thought that New Mexico was suffering as a consequence of providing a reservation for Indians who belonged in Arizona, a separate territory since 1863. Aside from the economic dislocations, many believed that Indians from the Bosque were raiding their livestock; in many cases this was true.[167]

Carson's enthusiasm for the reservation as an idea did not extend to his personal involvement in it. Three times during his few months in charge he offered his resignation, saying on one occasion, "The state of my health warns me that I can no longer render my country efficient service." His letter at the beginning of September 1864 may have given his real complaint; as superintendent, he had "no real power or control over the affairs of the Indians, except a moral one." He was in conflict with the Fort Sumner post commander, Captain Henry Bristol, a regular officer. With no direct control over the post, he had to ask for supplies and the assistance of troops: "This is not the position I contemplated occupying when I was ordered to supervise the Indians. I expected to order where I now have to request, nor do I think it is a position befitting an officer of my rank in the service."

Even Kit, like so many volunteer officers of the period, had apparently become rank conscious after a few years in the army. In addition, however, he felt hampered in doing his job by a regulation soldier who stood on his prerogatives and was perhaps not too impressed with an unlettered volunteer colonel, even if his name was Kit Carson.

Perhaps, too, his complaint reflected the simple fact that he found administration, as opposed to actual dealing with Indians, uncongenial. Carleton quickly assured him that "there is no disposition to place you in a position beneath your rank," and that he could of course give Captain Bristol orders by virtue of his rank. Nonetheless, he relieved Carson of the unwanted post in mid-September. Kit would not be spending much time with Josefa and the children, however. Carleton had another Indian problem looming, and once again he would call upon the indispensable man.[168]

KIT'S LAST FIGHT

As in most parts of the West, Indian-white relations on the Great Plains deteriorated during the Civil War as increasing white presence put pressure on the Indians and increased the occasions for friction. There was increasing settlement on the central plains, and a flood of people heading west toward the mountain gold fields. In 1862 came the Santee Sioux uprising against the settlers in Minnesota, one of the bloodiest in western history, which soon spilled out onto the plains of Dakota. Conflict increased between the Sioux and Cheyennes and the travelers along the westward trails through Nebraska, Kansas, and Colorado. The Comanches and Kiowas began to raid the Santa Fe Trail, New Mexico's principal line of communication with the East, in 1864. The bloodshed in Minnesota aroused the fears of whites in all the plains states and territories, and every raid seemed to herald a general uprising, while the federal government was distracted by the Civil War. The actions of the military commander in Colorado, Colonel John Chivington, would drive the Cheyennes into complete hostility.[169]

Although the troubles with the Cheyennes would eventually become Kit Carson's concern, General Carleton's immediate problem would be with the raids of the Kiowas and Comanches along the Santa Fe Trail. In October he would note that "we have been greatly embarrassed in getting . . . supplies from the States" because of these raids. In August, Kiowas and Comanches killed all five Anglo-Americans with a wagon train at Lower Cimarron Springs in southwest Kansas, letting the New Mexicans with the train return home; the New Mexicans said the Indians told them "they would kill every white man that came on the road." At Walnut Creek another train suffered ten men killed and two boys scalped and left alive. Other trains, military and civilian, had lost men and animals. Almost all the animals at Fort Larned in Kansas and other posts had been run off. In late August Colonel J. C. McFerran, chief of staff of the Department of New Mexico, who had just returned to Santa Fe over the trail, reported on the "unprotected and exceedingly insecure condition" of communications with the East. Many trains were immobilized out on the prairie by fear or loss of animals: "You cannot imagine a worse state of affairs than exists now on this route." But McFerran expected things to grow worse: "Unless prompt and efficient steps are at once taken our annual supplies for this department will be cut off and much suffering to the troops in this department ensue, not to mention the complete stoppage of our mails to and from the east." Carleton was, as always, eager to take "prompt and efficient steps" but faced serious difficulties.[170]

In the fall the three-year enlistments of most of his volunteer troops expired, which would leave his department "in a helpless condition," particularly regarding mounted troops. He would lose his California infantry, and most of the First New Mexico Cavalry, besides half of the California cavalry. His first concern was to escort the military and civilian trains safely in off the plains, after which he could consider taking the offensive. Under the circumstances, it is not surprising that his thoughts turned to the largest pool of experienced fighting men in New Mexico—its Indian tribes. In mid-August he wrote to Carson at Bosque Redondo, asking, "Will 200 Apaches and Navajoes go with troops to fight Comanches, in case of serious trouble with the latter Indians?"[171]

The more Carleton thought about the idea of utilizing Indian manpower, the better he liked it. After Carson's resignation as Indian agent, his successor at the Taos agency had moved the agency for the Utes and Jicarillas over the mountains to the vicinity of Lucien Maxwell's ranch on the Cimarron, although Kit had doubts about the move. Maxwell was now feeding them, at government expense, of course. In September Maxwell wrote Carleton, as the general reported to Carson, "that some 200 or more Ute Indians, now near Mr. Maxwell's place on the Little Cimarron, are anxious to go out on the plains and attack the Kiowas and other Indians . . . provided that they, the Utes, can be furnished with some rations, ammunition, perhaps a blanket apiece, and provided they may have whatever stock or other property they may be able to capture from the hostile Indians." Carleton wanted Carson to proceed immediately to Maxwell's and take charge of the

Indians for a foray against the plains tribes. Kit could have the services of a few companies of cavalry and infantry if he desired. The general feared the possibility that the Utes might join a confederation of plains tribes, and he wanted them committed on the side of the whites. (Tecumseh's ghost was still haunting some white men, and there were persistent rumors of a Confederate conspiracy with the western tribes.) Carleton told Kit, "Your knowledge of the haunts of the Indians of the plains, and the great confidence the Ute Indians have in you as a friend and as a leader, point to yourself as the most fitting person to organize, direct, and bring this enterprise to a successful issue." But once again it would be Carson who would make his commander modify his plans.[172]

From Taos, Kit wrote that he had talked to Kaniache, who was "disposed to go along with the whites on a campaign against the Indians of the plains." But Carson would require supplies and wagons for transport, and he wanted at least three companies of cavalry: "As my object will be to hunt and destroy their villages . . . it would be entirely useless for me to go with only the Indians." Something more than a horse raid was required. Here we see Carleton, the regular, trying to launch an operation primarily with Indian allies, and Carson, the old scout, insisting on the need for conventionally trained troops.[173]

Carleton hoped to have a force of Navajos and Mescalero Apaches from Bosque Redondo to cooperate with Carson's Utes and Jicarillas. The enlistment of recently hostile Indians to fight for their conquerors had been common since colonial times. However, Carleton would be disappointed, for the post commander at Fort Sumner informed him that the Navajos declined to go, saying "that by fighting they were ruined." It is impossible to know if they would have replied differently if Kit Carson himself had asked them. When Carson talked to the Utes in mid-October, he reported that about one hundred would go, and that he could get more if Carleton would arrange to have their families fed while they were gone—a reasonable request because their hunting skills were their families' principal means of support. The Utes, however, did not want any Navajos on the expedition. Carson had also upped the number of troops he deemed necessary, for the general wrote in some exasperation, "At Taos we agreed on 200 men and 100 Indians as the strength of the party. You now say 300 men. These I will try to raise." Carleton was anxious to get his campaign launched because winter was the time when the plains tribes would be concentrated along the river valleys for grass and timber, "and embarrassed by their families and by their stores of food, are easily overtaken."[174]

Finding troops was difficult, since the California and New Mexico cavalry had to be reorganized as smaller units after losing so many men, and Carleton was carrying on another campaign against Apaches in Arizona. But by early November Carson had an Indian contingent of seventy-five. The Utes included his old friend Kaniache and Buckskin Charley, later a prominent chief. A party of Jicarillas had also decided to go to war with "Gidi."[175]

Superintendent of Indian Affairs Michael Steck tried to dissuade Carleton, arguing that a campaign against the Comanches would only provoke unnecessary trouble with a tribe that had been at peace with New Mexico since the 1780s. Steck's opinion was not likely to weigh heavily with the general, but Carleton pointed out that witnesses implicated Comanches as well as Kiowas in the raids of the summer. Steck's information about the peaceful intentions of the Comanches he discounted as coming from comancheros anxious to preserve their business. However, no military commander was likely to ignore a threat to his line of communications, dependent as he was on supplies from the East to feed and clothe his Indian captives as well as his troops. The raiders' reported threats to kill Carleton himself if he came against them may have been an intolerable challenge, but that challenge, like the promise to "kill every white man that came on the road," could have been the big talk of a few warriors, not the settled determination of all Comanches—a tribe lacking any political centralization. ("White men" was taken as referring to Anglo-Americans, not Hispanics.) Or it could have come from the Kiowas, who were never as friendly to New Mexico as the Comanches. Kit Carson, in 1865, said he believed the Kiowas were "hostile against the government without cause," while he thought most of the Comanches "friendly disposed." Kit showed no signs before the campaign of doubts about its purpose. When some Kiowa and Comanche chiefs appeared at Fort Bascom in September, admitting they had committed aggressions and asking for peace, Carleton sent word that there would be no talk until they had returned the livestock and surrendered the men guilty of the killings at Lower Cimarron Springs. Evidently the tribes were aware that an expedition might be prepared against them. Carleton's demands, however, were unlikely to be met.[176]

Writing to Carleton from Maxwell's on October 10, Carson asked for at least three hundred cavalry, "as it will take that number of soldiers to attack a village of Indians with success." He also wanted two pieces of artillery, and was given two 12-pounder mountain howitzers; they were similar to the piece Frémont had hauled along on his second expedition, and the two General Kearny had taken to California in 1846, so Carson was quite familiar with them. These miniaturized artillery pieces, smooth-bore bronze muzzleloaders capable of transport over roadless terrain, accompanied innumerable frontier military expeditions from the 1830s to the 1870s, supporting troops against superior numbers of Indians. Carson clearly believed that attacking Plains Indians in large numbers would be altogether more serious than harassing the Navajos. He would be proved right.[177]

Carson and his Indian allies arrived at Fort Bascom on the Canadian River in eastern New Mexico, near present Tucumcari, on November 10, 1864, and found his troops waiting. He would have two and one-half companies of the First California Cavalry, two companies of the First New Mexico Cavalry, a company of California infantry, and a battery of two mountain howitzers, manned by California infantrymen. The cavalry was commanded by the trusty Major William McCleave, the infantry by Lieutenant Colonel Francisco Abreu, and the artillery by Lieutenant George Pettis, who would later write the best account of the expedition. Counting a surgeon and a quartermaster, Carson would have 14 officers, 321 enlisted men, and 75 Indian scouts when he headed east on November 12.[178]

Major General James Blunt was operating against Indians in western Kansas, and Carleton had written to him in October, expressing the hope that "you may be able to time your movements so as to reach the Indians on the Palo Duro, or near there, at the same moment with Colonel Carson." Carleton was trying to coordinate the sort of converging-column strategy that had already been tried in various Indian campaigns, and would be utilized repeatedly in later years, sometimes with great success, notably and unsuccessfully against the Sioux in 1876. Unfortunately, Blunt and his men were called east in October to meet a Confederate incursion into Missouri. Carson and his men would be on their own.[179]

The latest intelligence, obtained in October from comancheros, was that a large number of Comanches were camped on Palodura Creek (not to be confused with the more famous Palo Duro Creek further south), in the northern Texas panhandle north of the Canadian River. Carson's intention was to march down the Canadian from Fort Bascom to William Bent's old trading post, variously called Fort Adobe, Adobe Fort, and Adobe Walls, which he intended to use as a supply depot. From there he would operate with his cavalry using pack mules, while the infantry guarded the wagons and supplies. In his final orders Carleton, telling him of Blunt's expected cooperation, wrote, "You know where to find the Indians, you know what atrocities they have committed, you know how to punish them." The general reiterated his usual orders that only men were to be killed: "Of course I know that in attacking a village women and children are liable to be killed, and this cannot, in the rush and confusion of a fight, particularly at night, be avoided, but let none be killed willfully and wantonly." The problem Carleton described was always present in Indian warfare, where combatants and noncombatants were not segregated, and surprise attacks on camps were the most effective tactics.[180]

The column was marching east into Texas. The High Plains stretch, wide open and seemingly endless, for hundreds of miles eastward from the mountains of New Mexico; the country was roadless then and inhabited only by the people Carson's men were going to fight. The Comanches, a Shoshonean language–speaking people, had come south in the eighteenth century, acquiring the horse and becoming the dominant tribe on the southern plains. In the late 1700s they had formed an alliance with the smaller Kiowa tribe, also plains buffalo-hunters though quite different in language and culture. Although at peace with New Mexico since the 1780s, they terrorized northern Mexico with raids and were the bitter enemies of the Anglo-Americans in Texas, while regarding Americans and Texans as two different peoples. The powerful Comanches and the Kiowas were considered "bad neighbors" by other Indian tribes, including the Utes and Jicarillas, as indicated by the presence of the latter with Carson's force. The Texas Panhandle was the heart of their hunting grounds, and only once before had a U.S. military force challenged them there.[181]

Carson's force marched on the north side of the Canadian by "easy stages," losing two days to snowstorms. Carson kept his scouts well out on either flank, and each morning sent two out several hours ahead. The scouts danced a war dance every night, keeping the troops awake until all hours. On November 24 they camped early at Mule Spring, some thirty miles short of Adobe Walls. Near sunset the Indians jumped to their feet and stared eastward, talking excitedly. Carson explained to his officers that the two advance scouts were returning, and that they had found the enemy. The two rode through the camp, not deigning to speak to anyone until they had reported to the colonel (standard procedure on a war party). They had found the trail of a large village, with many animals, and in George Pettis's words, "We would have no difficulty in finding all the Indians that we desired."[182]

Carson set out just before dark with the cavalry, artillery, and Indian scouts on a night march to surprise the hostile camp, leaving the infantry to guard the wagon train. By midnight they were in the valley of the Canadian and had found the "deep-worn, fresh trail" of the Indians, at which time they halted, with no talking or smoking allowed, to wait until just before daylight. Dawn attacks were standard procedure, catching the enemy still asleep, with daylight to fight by coming soon. As the first light appeared in the east on the morning of November 25, they moved out again, Carson once again riding with the Utes and Jicarillas first, on the right near the river, followed by half the cavalry, then the battery, and then the remaining cavalry. Before long they heard someone calling in Spanish, from the south side, "Come here, come here." Three young Kiowas were out early collecting their horses and apparently thought the strangers were comancheros. Carson ordered McCleave with one company across the river, shots were fired, and the three Kiowas were seen racing for their village to give warning. The Indian scouts ducked into some brush, doffed their clothing, and emerged in their proper warpaint and feathers, dashing toward the enemy.[183]

Carson now sent the greater part of the cavalry to join McCleave and attack the enemy, while he himself and the remaining troopers brought up the artillery. The small-wheeled howitzers pushed on, slowed by the tall grass and driftwood of the river bottom, and the fact that the gunners were on foot. They passed herds of cattle the Kiowas had acquired on raids and Indian scouts gathering small herds of enemy horses, then mounting them and galloping off back to the fight. Then they crossed a low hill into the Kiowa village, the tipis standing abandoned following McCleave's attack. Firing continued to the front, so Carson pushed on, intending to return to destroy the village later. He threw his overcoat on a bush, expecting to pick it up on his return. Pettis stopped his men from doing likewise, and said it was the only time his judgment proved better than Carson's; Kit never saw his overcoat again. Finally they came within sight of the Adobe Walls and saw McCleave's men dismounted and fighting as skirmishers, their horses corralled inside the remains of the old post.[184]

McCleave's men had struck the village led by Dohasan (Little Mountain), head chief of the Kiowas, estimated by Carson at 150 lodges, by Pettis at 176. The Kiowas later said that most of their young men were away on a raid, but the remaining warriors made a fighting retreat, while the women and children, taking several white captives with them, took shelter along the river bluffs to the north. The elderly chief mounted and raced downriver to get help from nearby Kiowa and Comanche villages. George Bent said that Dohasan and Carson were old acquaintances, having met a number of times when Kit worked for Bent's father.[185]

The Kiowas, probably getting reinforcements, had made a stand near Adobe Walls, making "several severe charges" on McCleave's men, so the major dismounted to fight on foot. Carson's report says, "On my arrival on the ground I ordered the artillery to take a position, and the engagement ceased for a short time." According to Pettis's more dramatic account, when the howitzers came on the field Carson gave him the order, "Pettis, throw a few shell into that crowd over thar." Pettis put his guns into position on a small hill about a hundred yards from Adobe Walls. The cavalrymen were lying in the grass, fighting as skirmishers. In front, the Utes and Jicarillas were riding back and forth, facing about two hundred Comanches and Kiowas doing the same. Behind the latter was a larger number of Indians that Pettis put at twelve hundred to fourteen hundred, and whom he thought were preparing for a charge. Whether or not that was their intention, at the first shot from the howitzers they rose in their stirrups, turned, and galloped off downriver, and were out of range by the fourth shot.[186]

Carson says that, because his horses were in no condition to enable him to capture the enemy's stock, he decided to return upriver to the abandoned village that McCleave had struck and destroy the lodges and goods. However, Pettis (writing in the 1870s) says, "Colonel Carson now assured us that the fighting was over . . . and gave orders that after a short halt . . . we were to proceed and capture the Comanche village before us." This was a village Carson estimated at 350 or more lodges, in sight perhaps three miles downriver. The horses were unsaddled and watered in a nearby creek, and the men dug some food out of their haversacks. Before long, however, a large force of the enemy reappeared, "and seemed to be anxious to renew the conflict." The horses were resaddled and returned to the shelter of Adobe Walls and,

Carson says, "In a short time I found myself surrounded by at least 1,000 Indian warriors, mounted on first-class horses."[187]

The ensuing fight lasted all afternoon. Carson reported, "They repeatedly charged my command from different points, but were invariably repulsed with great loss." However, they avoided getting into masses that would have been good targets for the howitzers. A number lay down in the tall grass and fought as skirmishers, firing on the soldiers. The majority charged back and forth about two hundred yards in front, firing under the necks of their horses. Had some of the troopers begun to waver or retreat under the Indian skirmishers' fire, the mounted warriors might have taken advantage and charged in force. Such, at any rate, is one theory about what happened to Custer's detachment at the Little Bighorn.[188]

On the other side, Dohasan, Lean Bear, and Stumbling Bear distinguished themselves. Dohasan had a horse shot from under him. Stumbling Bear, who was credited with killing a Ute and a soldier, wore his daughter's shawl for good luck; it was pierced by several bullets, but he was unscathed. Someone in the Indian ranks had a bugle, and blew the opposite calls in response to the cavalry bugler; when the trooper sounded "advance," he sounded "retreat." Carson thought this was a white man, but it was more likely Satanta, a leading chief and warrior, who was noted for playing a bugle. Pettis says that hostile reinforcements kept arriving from villages downriver, reaching a number of at least three thousand; Carson says nothing of such a remarkable number. He believed they were mostly Kiowas, with some Comanches and Apaches. Carson says he became convinced they were trying to hold him in position at the Adobe Walls until dark, when they could save the tipis and supplies at the abandoned village, so he decided to return upriver to the village and destroy it. According to Pettis's account:

> The most of our officers were anxious to press on and capture the village immediately in our front, and Carson was at one time about to give orders to that effect, when our Indians prevailed upon him to return and completely destroy the village that we had captured, and after finding our supply train . . . we could come back again and finish this village to our satisfaction. After some hesitation and against the wishes of most of his officers, at about half-past three Carson gave orders to bring out the cavalry horses, and formed a column of fours.[189]

They started back up the Canadian.

One man in four led four horses; the remainder marched on foot, covering the flanks and rear. The howitzers brought up the rear. The enemy were not going to let them off easily. "Now commenced the most severe fighting of the day," reports Carson, who acknowledges that the hostiles' repeated charges caused him "serious doubts for the safety of my rear," but they were repulsed "with great slaughter." They then set the tall, dry grass on fire, forcing the troops to the bluffs, and charged behind the fire and smoke. One unfortunate California trooper was not only shot but lanced, showing that one Indian got very close indeed; the soldier survived nonetheless. Another warrior was shot off his horse and scalped by a young New Mexican soldier, the only scalp taken on either side during the fight.[190]

When they returned to the first village, some Kiowas were trying to save what they could. The howitzers drove them out, and the troops set to work to destroy the lodges, food, and household goods. Every man got a buffalo robe, and hundreds more were burned. Two Ute women had accompanied the scouts and in the village had found according to Pettis, "two old, decrepit, blind Kiowas and two cripples," whom they killed "by cleaving their heads with axes." Pettis says the troops knew nothing of this until the women themselves showed them the bodies. The last Kiowas, driven from the village, galloped off toward the river, one howitzer shell exploding in their midst as the sun set. It was the last shot of the Battle of Adobe Walls.[191]

Carson later reported two soldiers killed and ten wounded, while the Indian scouts counted one killed and five wounded. Pettis says there were twenty-one wounded soldiers, and that two or three more later died of wounds. Some sources say the dead scout was a Ute, but the Jicarillas say he was one of theirs. Pettis, on the basis of information given by comancheros who were in the hostile camp, estimates the Kiowa and Comanche losses at 100 killed and between 100 and 150 wounded. Carson more conservatively estimates their losses at 60 killed and wounded. The Kiowas, thirty years later, remembered their loss as only 5; this would probably not include the Comanche loss. Carson's estimate, based on his experience, would probably be more realistic than Pettis's, but he could only guess. As Robert Utley remarks, "As Indians traditionally set their losses absurdly low and military commanders tended to exaggerate, actual casualties doubtless fell somewhere between the extremes."[192]

After dark the column made its way upriver, carrying the severely wounded on the gun carriages and ammunition carts. Pettis says they were fearful of a night attack, though Indians seldom attacked in the dark, and they were greatly concerned about the fate of their wagon train carrying their food and spare ammunition. They were 250 miles from their base, and surrounded by aroused enemies. After about three hours, they spotted campfires and were greeted by the challenge, "Who comes there?" Now, Pettis says, "starvation would be averted for a season at least." They had been marching and fighting for thirty hours without sleep and with little food. The next morning, the twenty-sixth, they were up early in case the hostiles made their own dawn attack, but though mounted warriors were in sight there was no attack. At one point some men from each side rode out and exchanged shots, after which the hostiles rode off.[193]

On the morning of the twenty-seventh reveille sounded, and after breakfast Carson issued orders to saddle up for the return march to Fort Bascom. Pettis says the order was issued "much to the surprise and dissatisfaction of all the officers, who desired to go to the Comanche village that we had been in sight of on the day of the fight. It was learned afterwards that our Indians had advised Carson to return, and without consulting his officers the order was given and we commenced the return march." Carson says simply, "I now decided that owing to the broken-down condition of my cavalry horses and transportation and the Indians having fled in all directions with their stock, that it was impossible for me to chastise them further at present." We have, in fact, little other indication of what Carson's officers thought of his decision. Surgeon George Courtwright long afterward produced an account of the expedition largely plagiarized from Pettis, and he simply repeats the passage quoted above. Pettis himself never explicitly criticizes Carson's decision, but says Kit's judgment was virtually always better than his. William McCleave, in his recollections of his service as a California volunteer, gives a very brief, factual account of the battle, chiefly devoted to praising the Californians, especially Pettis and his gunners; perhaps he was too much the old sergeant to criticize the actions of a superior. This decision of Carson's may be the basis for John Ayers's statement, "The troops sometimes accused him [Carson] of cowardice because he was so cautious."[194]

Carson's report admits, "I must say that they [the enemy] acted with more daring and bravery than I have ever before witnessed." Challenged in the heart of their home territory, the Kiowas and Comanches had reacted with special aggressiveness and tenacity. Carson had asked for an increased force of cavalry and for artillery support, in case "I should strike the trail of a large village of Indians," and he must have been very glad he had, for he got even more than he bargained for. On the day of the battle, according to Pettis, he had taken the advice of his Indian scouts and, "against the wishes of most of his officers," ordered a retreat instead of pushing on to the next village, as he first considered doing. Again, two days later, he had consulted the scouts and decided to return to his base, instead of going after another village. Few frontier commanders, regular or volunteer, would have given the opinions of Indian allies more weight than those of their officers, but Carson was not a conventional commander, and he apparently considered Kaniache and his comrades to be the best judges. He was probably right to believe, on the basis of experience, that there was no hope of striking the Comanche village after two days, that the Indians would have scattered with their animals and tipis. But he also had to consider what would happen if they did not scatter, if they regrouped and kept after him. The following summer, on Patrick Connor's Powder River campaign in Montana, two strong cavalry columns were reduced to impotence and near starvation by the harassment of the Sioux and Cheyennes, and by logistical difficulties and their own ignorance. Another column, though led by an experienced commander with the aid of exceptionally capable Indian scouts, achieved only very limited success. Carson had no way of foreseeing this, and he apparently did not know that General Blunt's column would not be joining him, but he may have had some such danger in mind when he decided to retreat. The prospect, with weakening, irreplaceable horses and a dwindling supply of food and ammunition, could not have been encouraging.[195]

Any present-day assessment of Adobe Walls is inevitably affected by hindsight, by the knowledge that Plains Indians were often, in subsequent years, to prove more skilled and aggressive opponents than anticipated by white soldiers. In particular, we cannot forget what happened to another famous Indian fighter when his cavalry force attacked a large Indian encampment on the Little Bighorn on June 25, 1876. There were a number of significant differences between the two engagements, besides the obvious one. The level terrain of the Canadian valley differed greatly from the hilly ground on the east side of the Little Bighorn. The Kiowas and Comanches, though clearly aroused, were not as psychologically prepared as the Sioux and Cheyennes in 1876, who expected battle and had been promised victory by Sitting Bull's vision. After McCleave's advance in the morning, Carson kept his force united, not divided into separate bodies out of easy supporting distance, as with Custer's men. The Adobe Walls provided a corral for the horses, so that for much of the day all the men could be on the firing line, instead of one in every four serving as a horseholder, as usual when cavalry fought on foot; McCleave deserves credit for choosing this position. The howitzers, which Carson had insisted on bringing, were invaluable in defense, forcing the enemy to disperse and making a massed charge prohibitively expensive. Although Pettis and Carson both refer to the enemy's use of firearms, it is doubtful if they were as well armed as those at Little Bighorn. Certainly they would have had no repeating arms. Many of Carson's men had been fighting Apaches and Navajos for the past two years and were not, like many of the Seventh Cavalry in 1876, inexperienced and poorly trained. William McCleave, who spent most of his military career in the regular army, declared that "no better troops ever existed than the California volunteers," and there is no evidence that the New Mexicans were inferior to them on this day.[196]

George Bent, William Bent's half-Cheyenne son, was not at Adobe Walls, but he knew many Indians who were, on both sides, and he had experience fighting as an Indian warrior against soldiers. In his opinion, "But for the coolness and skill of Carson and his Indian scouts the retreat would have become a rout and few would have escaped." Elsewhere Bent related,

> Kit Carson told me in 1868, three weeks before he died, that the Indians whipped him in this fight. What saved him was Adobe Fort. When the Indians attacked him he ran back to the old fort to make his stand. Buckskin Charley, the Ute chief, was with Carson in this fight. He says the Kiowas, Comanches and Apaches had Carson whipped. He told me they had to fight fire to keep from being burned up. I bought a race horse from Carson in 1868, the horse he rode during the fight. The Indians followed Carson two or three days after leaving Adobe Fort. This horse I bought had white spots on each side of his back. Carson told me he had the saddle on the horse four days during this fight, and when he took the saddle off skin came with it.

For a horseman like Kit Carson to keep a saddle on a horse for four days argues a state of high alertness. In 1865 Colonel James Ford, a

Colorado volunteer officer stationed at Fort Larned, Kansas, reported, "The Indians attacked him as bravely as any men in the world, charging his lines, and he withdrew his command. . . . Carson said if it had not been for his howitzers few would have been left to tell the tale. This I learned from an officer who was in the fight." Ford's account suggests that at least one of Carson's officers may have rethought his opinion on the wisdom of withdrawing.[197]

If Carson had known the way he was to die, he might have considered a quick death in an Indian fight preferable. But he was responsible for the lives of some four hundred men under his command, and he had no intention of being a "damned fool," whatever younger, less experienced men might think of him. John Frémont credited him with "quick and complete perception, taking in at a glance the advantages as well as the chances for defeat." Kit anticipated that challenging the "Lords of the South Plains" on their home ground might involve more serious combat than the campaign against the Navajos. He was more right than he knew. During the battle and afterward, his perception of "the advantages as well as the chances for defeat," together with the judgment of his scouts, guided his decisions and overruled the eagerness of his officers.[198]

Carson's column returned to Fort Bascom "by easy marches" in order to save its animals; he arrived at the post on December 10. Although various witnesses noted his conviction that he was lucky to return, his report declared, "I flatter myself that I have taught these Indians a severe lesson, and hereafter they will be more cautious about how they engage a force of civilized troops." Nonetheless, if Carleton intended further campaigning, the animals would need six weeks' rest and forage, for they, unlike Indian ponies, could not function on grass alone. He would also need seven hundred more cavalry, and "two 6-pounder and two 12-pounder rifled guns." That would give him a force of one thousand men, "and no smaller command should go after these Indians with the expectation of chastizing them in a proper manner." No clearer evidence is needed of the impression made on him by the aggressiveness of the Kiowas and Comanches.[199]

Some other suggestions were more practical. Kit wanted to go back to Adobe Walls with four months' supplies, using the old post as a base as he had first planned: "Now is the time, in my opinion, to keep after them," because in winter they would have to stay near the Canadian, where there were many buffalo, and by summer they could be "brought to any terms." Comancheros had told him that the hostiles held five white women and two children, the thought of which inevitably moved him, and if some Indian women and children were taken, an exchange would be possible.[200]

The presence of comancheros among the hostiles just before or during the battle aroused Kit's ire. The trade between New Mexicans and Comanches had gone on for decades, but the Anglo-American authorities were casting an increasingly jaundiced eye on it, and Carson agreed. The traders could well have warned the Indians that the expedition was headed their way, but what infuriated him was their commerce with the hostiles. "On the day of the fight I destroyed a large amount of powder, lead, caps, &c., and I have no doubt that this and the very balls with which my men were killed and wounded were sold by these Mexicans not ten days before." What was worse was that Michael Steck, the territorial superintendent of Indian affairs, had issued trading licenses to these men after he knew of the expedition, in spite of the danger they would carry both information and ammunition. Kit said, "I blame the Mexicans not half so much as I do Mr. Steck . . . who gave them the pass to go and trade, he knowing perfectly well at the time that we were at war with the Indians, and that the Mexicans would take what they could sell best, which was powder, lead, and caps." Undoubtedly Kit's indignation was perfectly genuine, and justified, but he also knew that Carleton and Steck were badly at odds over the Bosque Redondo and other matters, and that the general would be happy to have something on the superintendent. Steck was in fact removed from his position a few months later.[201]

Kit proposed a winter campaign against the Indians, persistently harassing them on their hunting grounds in the season when their mobility was most limited. That, combined with Carleton's converging column strategy, was how the southern plains tribes would eventually be defeated, but not before another ten years had passed. In the meantime, Carleton lacked the resources for such an effort. Carson had inflicted damage on the Kiowas, but he had had to retreat. One column of troops, some four hundred men operating on their own, proved insufficient to subdue the "Lords of the South Plains."

The long-range effects of Adobe Walls were certainly not decisive. The Kiowas and Comanches did sign a peace treaty with the government in 1865, as we will see, and the knowledge that troops could attack them in the heart of their hunting range must have had its influence. But the treaty would prove a makeshift, because neither side could understand the other nor accommodate the other's minimum demands. After all, the bluecoats had had to withdraw in the face of the wrath of the allied tribes. Few battles of the Indian wars were decisive in themselves; it was the persistence of the white military that won these campaigns. Kit Carson understood that a large force operating for several months in the winter was necessary, and he also had understood the possibility of disaster for soldiers who underestimated the enemy. He judged he had accomplished all that was possible for a force the size of his.

Kit had, in fact, fought his last Indian battle, some thirty-five years after that first engagement, under the leadership of Ewing Young, with the Apaches on the Gila. General Carleton expressed no displeasure at the result of the Battle of Adobe Walls; he replied to Carson's first "very interesting and satisfactory report," expressing thanks to the officers and soldiers and to "our good auxiliaries, the Utes and Apaches . . . for the handsome manner in which you all met so formidable an enemy and defeated him." As for Carson, "This brilliant affair adds another green leaf to the laurel wreath which you have so nobly won in the service of your country." At the end of January the general replied to a letter from Carson: "It gratifies me to learn that you will not leave the service while I remain here. A great deal of my good fortune in Indian matters here—in fact nearly all with reference to Navajoes, Mescalero Apaches, and Kiowas—is due to you." Carson, in fact, remained in uniform as long as Carleton commanded in New Mexico; this was very likely at his superior's request, and it testifies to the mutual regard between the two men.[202]

Carson may have been in the service, but he seems to have spent the next few months on leave in Taos. Carleton nurtured some hopes that his expedition against the plains tribes would bring about peace; in the letter just quoted, he also noted, "The Comanche head chief has been into Bascom and wants peace." Strictly speaking, there was no "head chief," since the Comanches recognized no such office, but the general's hopes were aroused, and he permitted a number of traders to venture into the Comanche country. By May, however, word was coming in from the plains that the Comanches and Kiowas were not in a mood for peace. They robbed comancheros and sent them back to New Mexico with a warning that any more traders would be killed. The reason, recorded one man whom Carleton had sent out to negotiate the release of captives, was that they were "very much aggrieved by the attack having been made against them by Colonel Carson, and seek revenge." They even claimed to have made an alliance with the Texans, although the collapse of the Confederacy made this irrelevant even if true.[203]

If any of this proved true, the Santa Fe Trail and New Mexico's communications with the East would again be in danger. Carleton began to consider how best to protect the western reaches of the trail and his plans again involved Kit Carson. The general instituted biweekly escorts for trains eastbound as far as Fort Larned, Kansas, alternating between the two branches of the trail: the Mountain Branch along the Arkansas in southeast Colorado, and the Cimarron Cut-off that went through southwest Kansas, saving many miles but traversing a long waterless stretch. The force escorting the eastbound train would return from Larned to Fort Union, escorting a westbound train. He also decided to establish a temporary post on the Cimarron River branch near Cold Spring in the present Oklahoma Panhandle. Troops stationed there could give assistance to trains on this route, as he explained to Carson in a letter in early May, but there was another reason for giving Kit this assignment: "I believe if you go upon duty at that point you will be able to have a talk with some of the chiefs of the Cheyennes, Kiowas, and Comanches, and impress them with the folly of continuing their bad course." Once again, Carson's expertise was expected to provide the answer to the most difficult of problems. Carson accepted the mission, expressed approval of the general's ideas, and was pleased that Albert Pfeiffer, now a major, would accompany him.[204]

Carson set out from Fort Union on May 20 with two companies of the First New Mexico and one of the First California Cavalry, and two mountain howitzers. With Carson was Lieutenant Richard Russell of the First New Mexico, recently married to Marian Sloan, who as a little girl had known Carson during the 1850s in Santa Fe. She wanted very much to accompany her husband, and in her quarters at Fort Union she fixed Kit a buffalo pot roast with lots of red chili, the way she knew he liked it. It did no good, for he told her she could not come with the expedition. She remembered him as "a slight man with a frown between eyes that showed an infinite capacity for tenderness." At any rate, when her tears showed he promised to let her come to the post as soon as it was safe.[205]

Carleton's final orders, as usual, expressed "full faith and confidence in your judgement and your energy," and, as usual, gave advice on all sorts of practical details. Regarding the proposed talks, the general wrote, "If the Indians behave themselves, that is all the peace we want, and we shall not molest them. If they do not we will fight them on sight and to the end. . . . You know I don't believe much in smoking with Indians. . . . They must be made to fear us or we can have no lasting peace." Carson was to tell them that, with the end of the Civil War, the government could, if necessary, put ten thousand men in the field against them.[206]

Carson selected a site for what was called Camp Nichols on rocky bluffs some four or five miles east of the New Mexico line, a mile north of the Santa Fe Trail and west of Cold Spring. There was little water immediately at hand but, in the words of a later historian, "nothing obscured the view of the surrounding country from this high ground." Kit's first consideration was to keep anyone from sneaking up on him; he would have feared a surprise much more than a siege. The troops built a square enclosure of local stone, with small bastions at two corners for the howitzers; this served as a corral, with the living quarters outside. In an emergency the stockade would shelter the garrison, which included some three hundred troops and ten Indian scouts, most likely Utes or Jicarillas.[207]

Marian Russell came to Camp Nichols in June, when Colonel Carson considered it relatively safe (he himself rode with the escort detachment), and she provides the only detailed account of life there. Carson lived in a tent near the Russells and visited them often: "I remember his crude English, 'whar' for where, and 'thar' for there. I do not recall that he superintended to any great extent the work of the soldiers." The scouts rode out every morning, while pickets and sentinels were posted at "strategic places": "Colonel Carson's vigilance never relaxed for a moment." Although Russell says in one account that Kit often rode out with the scouts and was gone all day, something was clearly wrong with him, for in another account she says, "Some days his face seemed haggard and drawn with pain. The disease that was to claim his life in later years had even then fastened itself upon him." On hot afternoons he often lay on his cot in his tent, with the sides rolled up, scanning the prairie with his field glasses. He liked to play cards with the officers, and as they played, "I often heard his short, sharp little bark of laughter."[208]

Carson was at Camp Nichols only fifteen days after Marian Russell's arrival. At the end of June he came by her tent leading his big black horse, saying, "Little Maid Marian, I have come to say Good-bye." He was bound for Santa Fe and would not return. His last words to her were characteristic advice not to ride out "thar" on the trail: "Now remember the Injuns will get ye if you don't watch out." He rode off westward, merging into the mirage on the horizon: "I was destined never to see his face again."[209]

7. Peacemaker

Carson: I've seen as much of 'em as any man
liv'in, and I can't help but pity 'em, right or wrong.
They once owned all this country yes, Plains and
Mountains, buffalo and everything, but now they own
next door to nuthin and will soon be gone.
James F. Rusling in Edward S. Ellis, *Life of Kit Carson*

Black Kettle: We have all lost our way.
Report of the Commissioner of Indian Affairs, 1865

Carson and William Bent: The time is now fast
approaching when decisive action in regard to the
reservation policy for Indians must be taken . . . gradually
encircling them in its ever steady advance, civilization
now presses them on all sides.
Richard N. Ellis, "Bent, Carson, and the Indians, 1865"

General John Pope: Peace with these Indians is of all
things desirable, and no man is so certain to insure it as Kit Carson.
Edwin L. Sabin, *Kit Carson Days*

SMOKING WITH INDIANS

When Kit Carson rode back from Camp Nichols to Santa Fe through the heat of the summer of 1865, he was fifty-five years old. About this time a photograph was taken of him in uniform, showing the effects of time and of the hard campaigns of the past few years. The broad, round face of earlier years had hollowed out, and his habitually sober, even grim, expression seems downright fierce. Marian Russell had noted the frown between eyes in which she saw an "infinite capacity for tenderness." James Mead, who met him in the fall of this year, saw "a man of fierce, determined countenance," but with "a kind, reticent, and unassuming disposition." (The frown may have been partly due to failing eyesight; George Pettis says Kit wore spectacles to play poker, but could still "haul in the pot.") Months earlier he had declared, "The state of my health

warns me that I can no longer render my country efficient service."
His face had not yet taken on the sad dignity of his last year or two,
and perhaps he had not yet admitted to himself that an enemy he could
neither outwit nor outfight was on his trail. But some sense that time was
running out could come to a man at his age, and as he looked around
him he could see how the world he had known was ending.[1]

For the Indians too, time was running out, and the world they had
lived in was near its end. Many people besides Kit Carson saw a crisis
approaching that might decide the Indians' fate and were anxious to
influence it, one way or another. That foresight, in fact, explained why
Carson was called away from Camp Nichols. Although his career was
not over, his Indian fighting days were. General Carleton had sent him
out to that lonely spot on the Santa Fe Trail, not only to furnish military
protection to travelers but in the hope that he would "be able to have a
talk with some of the chiefs of the Cheyennes, Kiowas, and Comanches."
That hope was not fulfilled, but the assignment pointed to a shift in
emphasis in his official role. For the last few years he had been primarily
an Indian fighter, the role most people considered natural to him. But
he had already served as an Indian agent, and Doctor Peters had called
him the "Nestor of the Rockies" and a "safe counselor." In American
tradition the wise old scout was not only supposed to outfight and outwit
the Indians, he was supposed to be the fount of knowledge and good
advice about them, to act as an intermediary, explaining the Indians
to the whites and vice versa. Carleton, even though he did not "believe
much in smoking with Indians," clearly expected Carson to do so, as
many others would, too. He would spend much of his last few years
"smoking with Indians," and trying to get white people to do what he
believed was both sensible and just about the "Indian problem."[2]

In the spring of 1865 the United States could rejoice at the restoration of the Union and the end of slavery. But as the fratricidal killing
ceased, Congress and the public became aware that a series of wars was
going on in the western states and territories, including old conflicts
like those in New Mexico. A crisis loomed on the Great Plains. As congressmen looked forward to a drastic reduction in military expenditure,
they realized that several thousand federal troops were still engaged in
military operations over vast expanses of territory west of the Missouri
River. The scope and expense were enormous, most of the troops had
enlisted for another war and wanted to go home, and the justification
for fighting seemed dubious.

The complex causes of the conflict on the plains are hard to reduce to a neat synthesis. But one event leaps out because of its atrocious nature and because it turned a series of incidents along travel routes into a general outbreak of violence on the central plains. On November 29, 1864, just four days after Carson's fight at Adobe Walls, Colorado militia and volunteers under Colonel John Chivington had attacked a camp of Southern Cheyennes and Arapahos headed by Black Kettle on Sand Creek in eastern Colorado. The Indians had believed themselves safe because of a truce with the commander at nearby Fort Lyon, but Chivington chose to ignore this agreement and attacked at dawn, shooting men, women, and children indiscriminately. Estimates differ, but there may have been as many as one hundred fifty to two hundred killed, the great majority women and children. Troopers spent much of the day seeking out and killing people in hiding, and in scalping and mutilating the dead. Some one hundred scalps were displayed in Denver to an enthusiastic citizenry who believed the Indians to be the guilty parties in a series of raids in eastern Colorado and western Kansas.[3]

Some Southern Cheyennes had undoubtedly engaged in raids, and some of them may have been in Black Kettle's camp. Chivington's attack drove the great majority of the tribe into open hostility. They moved north, and in January and February, allied with the Teton Sioux, staged repeated raids on the Platte River Road and the routes to Colorado. Denver was virtually cut off from the East for a month. Julesburg, Colorado, was burned, and road ranches, stage stations, telegraph lines, and wagon trains all suffered; some fifty white people died. Added to the troubles already existing on the central and southern plains and the Santa Fe Trail, the whole situation constituted, in the words of one army officer, "no trifling Indian war."[4]

The news elicited two contradictory responses from Washington. First, the army made plans for an offensive against the various hostile tribes but faced logistical problems inherent in warfare on the Great Plains and confusion created by demobilization at the Civil War's conclusion. Congress, besides contemplating the expense, was shocked by the news of Sand Creek, which put the United States so obviously in the wrong. In March 1865, the lawmakers voted for a joint special committee, with Senator James Doolittle of Wisconsin as chairman, to go west and investigate "the condition of the Indian tribes and their treatment by the civil and military authorities of the United States." With such a vast area to cover, the committee split up. Three members, including Senator Doolittle, Senator Lafayette Foster of Connecticut, and Representative Lewis Ross of Illinois, would look into Indian affairs in Kansas, Indian Territory, Colorado, New Mexico, and Utah, and conduct an inquiry into the Sand Creek massacre. The congressmen, with suitable escort and staff, set out on the Santa Fe Trail in May. They held a brief session on Sand Creek, at Fort Lyon, Colorado, enough to convince them that Colonel Chivington had broken "the plighted faith of the government," and was "a monster that should be loathed and shunned by every Christian man and woman," in the words of a staff member. One of those interviewed was William Bent. They pushed on into New Mexico, where General Carleton showed them his reservation at Bosque Redondo, and then went on to Santa Fe on their way to Denver. They collected testimony from a variety of witnesses, soldiers, Indian agents, civil officials, and citizens who were thought to have ex-pert knowledge—or just a strong opinion—on the Indian affairs of New Mexico and the plains; they even talked to a few Indians. Some witnesses were also invited to fill out a questionnaire giving their opinions on the condition of the Indians and their recommendations for action. (General Carleton, not restrained by false modesty, provided a copious selection of his reports and correspondence for the nearly three years he had commanded in New Mexico; they were dutifully printed in the committee's report, making it a treasure trove for historians.)[5]

It was the committee's presence in New Mexico that called Kit Carson back from Camp Nichols, for of course the gentlemen from Washington wanted to hear the opinions of the great scout and Indian fighter who was believed to know as much about Indians as any man alive. They went through Taos on their way to Denver and met him there. Doolittle described to his wife how the people of Taos, "of all classes Rich & poor," turned out to greet them two miles outside of town, "with Kit Carson to control them." Among them were the people of Taos Pueblo, "in their full regalia, and riding & shouting, and going through the mimic war charges which Kit Carson who rode beside the buggy I was in, said was very good representation of their war maneuvers." The congressmen stayed at Carson's house that night, and years later Doolittle related: "Knowing him as a bear-hunter and Indian fighter you can hardly imagine the impression which this most modest and unassuming man with a voice almost feminine in accent and expression made upon us." He told them the story of being chased up a tree by grizzlies, and other tales, keeping them up "far into the small hours of the morning."[6]

It was what Kit had to say about the Indians, however, that they were there to hear, and on July 10 he spoke on that subject at some length. Presumably they asked questions to which he responded, having been sworn, but the record reads like an uninterrupted statement, in language obviously formalized by a secretary. Regarding his credentials he said simply, "I came to this country in 1826, and since that time have become pretty well acquainted with the Indian tribes, both in peace and at war." This was Kit's chance to state his views to men who might actually have influence over government policy. The committee members had read to him the statement his old friend William Bent made to them a few weeks earlier, and he opened by saying that Bent's "suggestions and opinions in relation to Indian affairs coincide perfectly with my own." Bent stated flatly that since his arrival on the Arkansas thirty-six years before, "nearly every instance of difficulties between the Indians and the whites arose from aggressions on the Indians by the whites." He recounted the circumstances leading up to Sand Creek in some detail, placing the blame on Colonel Chivington and other volunteer officers, and on Governor John Evans of Colorado. He denounced volunteer officers and troops, saying, "If officers from the regular army, with troops from the same, were stationed at the posts near the Indians, I think there would be no difficulty." Bent also denounced Indian agents, who he believed misappropriated the goods intended for Indians. Bent declared, "If the matter were left to me I would guarantee with my life that in three months I could have all the Indians along the Arkansas at peace, without the expense of war. These would include the Cheyennes, Arapahoes, Kiowas, Comanches, and Apaches." Bent thought a reservation could be established for the Cheyennes and Arapahos between the Arkansas and the Republican Rivers in northwest Kansas and southwest Nebraska. All these ideas Kit Carson, the former Indian agent and serving volunteer officer, declared he supported wholeheartedly.[7]

Beyond agreeing with his old friend, however, Kit had his own ideas, given frankly, and probably in blunter, more colorful language than the official version. Regarding the current troubles on the central plains, he said, "I think, as a general thing, the difficulties arise from aggressions on the part of the whites. From what I have heard, the whites are always cursing the Indians, and are not willing to do them justice." For instance, he believed that many accusations of theft of livestock by Indians on the trails were based on animals straying off. If Indians brought the stock in, expecting a reward, they were abused or even shot, "and thus a war is brought on." Regarding the war with the Cheyennes, he had heard that the authorities in Colorado had "determined to get up an Indian war" to keep their volunteers from being sent east, and he knew "of no acts of hostility on the part of the Cheyennes and Arapahoes committed previous to the attacks made upon them, as stated by Colonel Bent." Carson stated that he had been one of a party who made peace with the Arapahos in 1830 or 1831, an episode he says nothing about in his autobiography; this would have been a fur traders' agreement, not a government treaty. At any rate, he knew of no troubles between whites and Arapahos since then until 1864.

Like most old frontiersmen, Carson distinguished carefully between Indian tribes: "I think the Kiowas are hostile against the government without cause. The other tribes, I think, are rather compelled to be so. Most of the Comanches, I think, are friendly disposed." Like Bent, he believed that, "if proper men were appointed and proper steps taken," peace could be made with the Indians "on and below the Arkansas" without war. As to the proper men, "I believe that, if Colonel Bent and myself were authorized, we could make a solid, lasting peace with those Indians. I have much more confidence in the influence of Colonel Bent with the Indians than in my own." He thought that the plains tribes could be brought together for a council by September 10—that is, in two months' time.

When Kit went on to discuss the southwestern tribes, he clearly saw the Navajo war in a different light from the current troubles with the Cheyennes and Arapahos. To his knowledge, war "had about always existed" between the Navajos and New Mexicans, and no peace lasted long. Carson recognized that the hostilities were not one-sided, that "continual thieving" had been carried on by both sides. He believed many New Mexicans now objected to the reservation "because they cannot prey on them as formerly." He saw no answer to the problem except the reservation system as set up by General Carleton: "If they were sent back to their own country to-morrow, it would not be a month before hostilities would commence again."

He explained the distinction between the ricos and the ladrones among the Navajos, declaring the latter to be the majority. The Navajos could not be kept at peace in their own country, where they could scatter into the mountains and canyons, and where there was no place they could be concentrated for farming. Their customary dispersed, pastoral way of life was unacceptable because it made control and protection impossible. He particularly stressed the formidable nature of the Canyon de Chelly. The only real objection to the Bosque Redondo as a reservation, in his opinion, was the lack of wood other than mesquite.

Regarding other tribes, he thought the Apaches should be put on a reservation, but the Jicarillas would object to being placed at Bosque Redondo. (He was undoubtedly right; in the 1880s they showed their disapproval of being sent to the Mescalero reservation in southeastern New Mexico by leaving and returning to northern New Mexico, where they were finally given a reservation fairly remote from white settlements, as Carson had urged thirty years earlier.) His belief, which would prove seriously overoptimistic, was that the Arizona Apaches "would make very little objection to being placed on a reservation."

The Utes, about whom he could speak with special authority, and special regard, were another matter. It would be difficult to place them on a reservation, "as they know nothing of planting, and when spoken to on the subject have invariably objected." He went on, showing both his admiration and his realism: "They are a brave, warlike people; they are of rather small size, but hardy, and very fine shots. I would advise, however, that they be put on a reservation, as they cannot live much longer as now; they are generally hungry, and killing cattle and sheep, which will bring on a war. They are now at peace, and it would be the wiser policy to remain at peace with them." He thought a good place for their reservation would be north of the San Juan River in Utah; this was a remote area and would fulfill his belief that reservations should be far removed from white settlements.[8]

Carson closed his testimony with an earnest statement of opinion: "I think that justice demands that every effort should be made to secure peace with the Cheyennes and Arapahoes before any war was prosecuted against them, in view of the treatment they have received." He had another chance to make his ideas known to the congressmen, in answering the questionnaire that Doolittle had sent to him a little earlier. He wrote from Fort Lyon, Colorado, about a month after his meeting with the committee in Taos, apologizing for the delay and for having lost the questionnaire, but laying out at some length his ideas on the subjects they were curious about. Whoever helped him prepare this document boasted an elaborate, rhetorical prose style that seems especially roundabout compared to his earlier testimony. Although the letter was not dated from Santa Fe, one cannot help suspecting the influence, if not the actual hand, of General Carleton. On the other hand, Fort Lyon was near the home of William Bent, and there are similarities to a document that Kit and Bent produced together a little later. Nonetheless, Carson put his name to it, and it clearly reflects both experience and thought about the Indians and their relations with whites.

The letter declares that the rule for the "governance" of Indians must be

> firm, yet just, consistent and unchangeable; for the Indian, judging only by the effect of that which appeals to his senses . . . regards with contempt a weak and indecisive policy as the result of hesitation, fear, and cowardice, whilst a changeable and capricious one excites his apprehension and mistrust. . . . The rule for the government of Indians should be strong enough to inspire their respect and fear, yet protecting them from both internal dissension and external aggression.

Control of the Indians should therefore be turned over to the War Department. This opinion one would expect from a professional soldier like Carleton, but Carson would repeat it. He pointed out the conflicts that so often arose between army officers and agents of the Bureau of Indian Affairs—like General Carleton and Superintendent Michael Steck—which hampered the carrying out of policy. Indian agents were appointed "solely through political influence," and were "often swayed by feelings of personal gain in the transaction of their business, making the government appear to act in bad faith." Thus they aroused the hostility of the Indians: "To this cause, and that of repeated acts of aggression on the part of the numerous reckless frontiersmen that swarm upon the borders of the Indian territory, may be attributed many, if not most of our recent Indian wars, massacres, and murders, extending from Minnesota to California." These were exactly the sort of charges that regular army officers made repeatedly against Indian agents and frontiersmen, but again Carson would repeat them.

"The peculiarity of the Indians' position," he insisted, "now calls for prompt, decisive, and energetic action." The idea of moving Indians westward, beyond a frontier line, had been "exploded" by the discovery of gold in California and Nevada: "Instead of forcing them backwards in its steady advance, civilization now encircles them with its chain of progress, and each year, as it passes away, sees the chain drawing rapidly closer around the hunting grounds of the red men of the prairie." (Bent and Carson would use a similar metaphor of encirclement a few months later.) Then Kit came to the crux of the matter, though the language could hardly be his:

> A short-sighted policy might infer from, and leave to, this cause their extermination. That it would be accomplished is certain, but humanity shudders at the picture of the extermination of thousands of human beings until every means is tried and found useless for their redemption, while high motives of right impel us, out of respect to ourselves and duty to the Indians, to protect our citizens . . . and relieve and assist whilst controlling the red men of the west, as their hunting grounds vanish before the sturdy energy of the pioneer and backwoodsman.

The answer was to place the Indians on reservations "with wise rules enforced by military power," thus protecting the settlers from the Indians and the Indians from "the reckless injustice of those outlaws of society thronging upon the border, whose criminality has too often been the means of rousing the Indians to thoughts of vengeance, and carrying fire and desolation to many a homestead in the west."

Carson distinguished between "the bold, courageous, marauding Comanche—the wild, treacherous, nomadic Apache—the hardy, industrious, agricultural Navajo, or the lazy, degraded, almost brutalized Digger." Care should be taken that incompatible tribes were not located on the same reservation, a caution probably reflecting the increasing friction between Navajos and Mescalero Apaches at Bosque Redondo. He also noted a fact well known to frontiersmen, if expressed here in a particularly ethnocentric manner: "One wild tribe looks down on another with a contemptuous pride—strange to us but perfectly natural to their untutored minds, as they possess a less degree of skill in the barbaric virtues of murder, violence, and theft."

One of the leading queries in the Doolittle questionnaire was, "Are they increasing or decreasing in numbers, and from what causes?" Carson believed they were decreasing, and the causes included "cruel wars among themselves, prevalence of venereal diseases, and the inordinate use of intoxicating liquors." The first could be stopped by force, and should be, immediately. The other two were "due in a great measure to their intercourse with the white men," and "humanity and justice demand that prompt measures be taken to arrest their fatal progress."

He did not mention wars with the whites as a cause of the decrease, although that was clearly implied elsewhere in the letter.

He pointed out the Bosque Redondo reservation as an example of the way to deal with the problem; it showed "the propriety of military rule, and appears to be actuated by feelings of humanity, charity, and sound political economy." (Surely this last thought derived in some way from James Carleton.) The policy was aimed at "the welfare of hundreds of thousands of human beings," seeking "to convert them from fierce and reckless murderers to peaceful tillers of the soil." The document goes on to further flights of eloquence about the United States standing proudly among nations as "the exemplar of mercy, humanity, and philanthropy." Did Kit think the scribe was "laying it on a leetle thick," or was he lost in admiration and hoping that the grand words would add weight to his thoughts? He believed that commanding officers of posts on reservations should be "de facto Indian agents," as he had expected to be at Bosque Redondo. This officer could administer punishment and also dispense benefits as the representative of the government, while the system would "afford greater checks to the accomplishment of frauds, and greater facilities for their detection when perpetrated." The last point was one that army officers especially urged when advocating military control of the Indians; coming from Carson, the former Indian agent, it had a special force.[9]

Whatever Carleton's, or Bent's, direct influence on Carson's written statement, or his oral testimony, they certainly agreed on many points. Carleton's own testimony, given to the committee in Santa Fe a few days before Kit's, concentrated on the southwestern tribes and asserted the value of the Bosque Redondo reservation. The Navajo country lacked any location where they could be concentrated for farming, had too many mountains where they could hide, and was too near gold deposits that would attract miners. The general recognized that hostilities had been mutual between Navajos and New Mexicans, but attempts to make peace had not lasted. He was confident that the Indians at the Bosque Redondo would soon be self-supporting. There were, he thought, some three thousand Indians, chiefly Navajos, held captive by citizens in New Mexico. He believed they were treated with "great kindness" and seldom wanted to run away, but he acknowledged that the women "bear children from illicit intercourse," and that they were not allowed to leave. On the reservation, he pointed out, they would "run no risk of being stolen or attacked."[10]

In his answers to Doolittle's questionnaire, Carleton emphasized that the Indians were "decreasing very rapidly," the causes including "wars with our pioneers and armed forces," "intemperance," venereal and other diseases, and "the causes which the Almighty originates, when in their appointed time he wills that one race of men—as in races of lower animals—shall disappear off the face of the earth and give place to another race . . . the red man of America is passing away!" This was the doctrine of the Vanishing American in its purest form (not found in Carson's letter, and so casting some doubt on Carleton's influence on that document), but Carleton wanted to do as much as humanly possible to slow the process, and the reservation system, including a program of education to show "the evils to which their course of life tends," offered the best hope. Reservations must be set aside and then maintained against "the encroachments of the whites," because there would soon be no livable places remote from white settlement: "Therefore, place them upon reservations now, and hold those reservations inviolate." In anticipating that white settlement would soon surround even remote reservations, Carleton was more prescient even than Kit Carson or William Bent. Nonetheless, he feared that "the natural decay incident to their race must find its remedy in a power above that of mortals." The reservations would become islands in a white sea, and "as time elapses and the race dies out," the islands would be engulfed until "they become known only in history." Until then, the Indians should have lands, allotted in severalty: "We have taken quite enough from the Indian."[11]

Carleton was especially emphatic on the transfer of the Bureau of Indian Affairs from the Interior Department to the War Department, which would eliminate conflicts of authority and lack of coordination that dogged Indian policy under the current system. He believed army officers with long service knew more about Indians and Indian affairs than civilian agents, and of course understood military necessities and capabilities. If army quartermasters issued goods to Indians, fraud would be largely eliminated. The general clearly had no doubts on these points, and it is here that one would most suspect his influence on Carson's letter to Doolittle, since Kit did not touch on the subject in his oral testimony to the committee. But Carson would reiterate his belief in the benefits of War Department control of Indian affairs later.[12]

The Doolittle committee's report was not officially submitted to Congress until early 1867. Its conclusions were all summed up within a few pages, though based on a great mass of testimony gathered from all over the West. The first conclusion was that Indians were decreasing, from causes including disease, "intemperance," war, the "steady and resistless emigration of white men," the destruction of game, and "the irrepressible conflict between a superior and an inferior race." The committee also asserted "that in a large majority of cases Indian wars are to be traced to the aggressions of lawless white men." The principal expert opinions cited on this point in the report proper (as opposed to the attached testimony and letters) were those of William Bent and Colonel Kit Carson. Kit's words were the only ones directly quoted in support of this conclusion.[13]

On one point the committee differed with Carson, and with Carleton and virtually every other soldier who testified: they recommended against transferring the Bureau of Indian Affairs to the War Department. Acknowledging that the arguments for transfer, such as greater honesty and unity of control, were "not without force," they still saw many disadvantages in military control. Admitting the inefficiency and dishonesty of many civilian agents, they charged that army posts near reservations "have frequently become centres of demoralization and destruction to the Indian tribes." At Bosque Redondo, Navajo women were often prostitutes for the soldiers at Fort Sumner; this and Chief Herrero's testimony to the committee about mistreatment by some of the enlisted men at the post were probably the sort of thing they had in mind. Even more serious, "the blunders and want of discretion of inexperienced officers in command have brought on long and expensive wars." Carleton and Carson would have argued that Colonel Chivington and his ilk were not regulars, a distinction perhaps not wholly apparent to the congressmen, and that with the end of the Civil War, experienced frontier officers would again be in command in the West. The committee also thought that the two antagonistic agencies, army and Bureau, would "serve as a check upon each other," since "neither are slow to point out the mistakes and abuses of the other." The report stated emphatically that "as their hunting grounds are taken away, the reservation system, which is the only alternative to their extermination, must be adopted." There was nothing new or startling about that conclusion in 1867. About the only specific, new recommendation to come out of the fact and opinion gathering was for the establishment of "boards of inspection" to oversee the operations of the Indian Bureau in order to correct the abuses of the system.[14]

PEACEMAKER

Nonetheless, the committee's journey to the West did have an immediate effect on the situation on the plains, and it would give Kit Carson a chance to put his ideas into effect. As the committee members made their way west in May and June 1865, General John Pope, whose command embraced most of the Great Plains and would shortly expand to include New Mexico, was trying to initiate offensive campaigns against the hostile tribes north of the Platte and south of the Arkansas, in the face of logistical problems and the ongoing discharge of most of his volunteer troops. At the same time Jesse Leavenworth, an agent of the Bureau of Indian Affairs, was trying to arrange a peace council with the southern plains people. When the westbound congressmen had passed through Fort Larned at the end of May, Doolittle had observed the military preparations with deep disapproval. The troops would face up to seven thousand of "the greatest horsemen in the world," the expense might run up to $50 million, and the justification was scant. To the secretary of the Interior Department the senator wrote that the greatest bloodshed so far had been "the treacherous, brutal, and cowardly butchery of the Cheyennes on Sand Creek, an affair in which the blame is on our side." In fact, Doolittle had made up his mind about many of the matters under investigation before he ever heard any testimony about Sand Creek, or before he had ever talked to Kit Carson or William Bent. He believed that the proposed expedition would likely be beaten and forced to retreat, "as Kit Carson . . . was beaten last winter in his expedition gotten up by Carleton against the Comanches." Doolittle warned: "It is time the authorities at Washington realized the magnitude of these wars which some general gets up on his own hook which may cost hundreds and thousands of lives, and millions upon millions of dollars."[15]

Senator Doolittle believed that all the tribes wanted peace, except the outraged Cheyennes, and that "with some proposition of atonement" for Sand Creek, peace could be had, and he asked the president for authority to make the offer. The commissioner of Indian Affairs concurred. The offensive south of the Arkansas, already under difficulties, was eventually canceled. The operation north of the Platte, which is where most of the Southern Cheyennes were at the time, went forward at the end of the summer with very limited success. In the meantime, the committee had met with William Bent in Colorado and Kit Carson in Taos. Both asserted their belief that they could make a peace with the tribes "on the Arkansas"—the Southern Cheyennes, Arapahos, Kiowas, and Comanches—and they clearly made an impression, even if it only confirmed the congressmen's preconceptions. Doolittle telegraphed from Denver in July that "Colonel Bent says he will guarantee it [peace] with his head," in the absence of a military operation south of the Arkansas. The senator advised the authorities in Washington, including the secretaries of state and war, that Bent and Kit Carson should be allowed to make peace if possible.[16]

At about the same time, General Carleton wrote to the general escorting the committee, giving qualified approval to the peacemaking effort. Understanding that Commissioner of Indian Affairs William Dole, in addition to Jesse Leavenworth, Bent, and Carson, were all seeking to talk to the same Indians, Carleton feared some confusion might result, and the Indians might view the whole proceeding as "a practical joke of their Great Father." It would be better, he thought, to recall Dole and Leavenworth, let Carson and Bent "smoke through the preliminary protocols," and have the congressional committee step forward to make the treaty if matters were "propitious." As for himself, "I have no faith in treaties with Indians, and think none should be made as a rule. If they do right they should, in my opinion, be treated with great kindness and consideration. If they do wrong I believe in punishing them by war until they promise and do what is right again." Since the government believed it best to make a treaty with Indians who were "attacking our trains, running off our stock, and killing our people," then "Mr. Dole and Col. Leavenworth, not being men who understand Indian character as Col. Kit Carson and Mr. Bent do, should, in my opinion, retire from the treaty-making business." On August 5 Carleton issued orders to Carson for "Special Service upon the Plains for the purpose of seeing if the Comanches, Kioways, and other Indians living on, and south of the Arkansas River, cannot be induced to stop their acts of hostility"; at the same time, indicating once again his lack of faith in treaties, he wanted Kit to look out for a site for "a large post to be built in the place where the Kioways and Comanches spend their winters."[17]

General John Pope also recommended that Carson and Bent be included in the treaty-making commission. Jesse Leavenworth was able to get leading chiefs of the Kiowas and Comanches to agree to a council in October after a truce had been arranged in August. Black Kettle of the Southern Cheyennes, who had not gone north of the Platte with most of his people, agreed, as did important Southern Arapaho leaders.[18]

In mid-August 1865, Carson was at Fort Lyon, Colorado, "making preparations for special service on the plains" and conferring with William Bent, whose home was nearby. The two had known each other for many years, perhaps since 1829, and Kit had worked as a hunter at Bent's Fort in 1841–42. Carson had greatly admired William's older brother Charles, who became his brother-in-law, and Kit and William were devoted friends. Kit named two of his sons Charles and William. A witness described Carson, with some Indians, riding up to Bent's ranch on the Purgatoire River in 1864 or 1865, perhaps on his way to this proposed council. According to him, "Bill Bent pulled Kit off his horse and they hugged and kissed like a couple of children."[19]

Few white men, in 1865, could boast the length, breadth, and depth of experience among Indians that Carson and Bent could claim. People like Senator Doolittle were deeply impressed and hoped their knowledge would provide a key to solving the tragic situation on the Great Plains. Carson and Bent were, in fact, relics of an earlier age, in which whites and Indians could mingle and live together, in spite of occasional violence, on a "middle ground" of accommodation. Carson had married first an Arapaho and then a Cheyenne, had fought with Cheyennes against Crows, and had lived among the Cheyennes at Bent's Fort. Bent had twice married Cheyenne women, and all his children were half-Cheyenne. They knew the other side of Indian-white relations also. Carson's life had been threatened by Cheyennes in 1851. Bent had lost two brothers killed by Indians, Robert by the Comanches, Charles by men of Taos Pueblo. For Bent, indeed, the present war was uniquely painful. Four of his children had been at Sand Creek, one of them forced at gunpoint to guide Chivington's men there. Two of them, Charles and George, were now warriors with the hostiles north of the Platte. William's second wife, Yellow Woman, had also gone with her people north of the Platte, and although Bent probably did not know of it yet, in this same month of August she was killed and scalped by the army's Pawnee scouts.[20]

Carson's journey to the council took him through Fort Riley, Kansas, near which he camped for a few days on the Republican River. There, as he reported back to Carleton, he was visited on September 8 by General John Sanborn, the designated head of the proposed peace commission, who described his preliminary meeting with Kiowa and Comanche chiefs. According to Sanborn, the Comanches admitted they had no cause for hostility; they had been "drawn into" raids on the Santa

Fe Trail by the Kiowas. They were shifting the blame, but their statement more or less confirmed what Carson had told the congressional committee. Sanborn reported that "quite a number of both Comanches and Kiowas" said that they wanted peace, and would be willing to go on a reservation south of the Arkansas. In his own report Carson says, "I am of opinion that in all cases of locating reservations, it would be best where practicable to show some deference to the expressed wishes of the tribes (in point of locations) who are willing to remove peaceable to the place selected." Carson would repeat this opinion. It seems from this that he supported the compulsory settlement of the Navajos at Bosque Redondo because of the special situation in New Mexico and not because he lacked respect or concern for the needs and desires of Indians in general.[21]

In this report, dated September 11, Carson also commented on the government's wish to form two large reservations for the southern plains tribes, one north of the Platte, the other south of Kansas. This would leave the central plains travel routes open, but "to this the Indians will naturally raise objections, as it would remove them entirely from their great buffalo range." The plan would also cancel out Bent's proposal, which Carson had endorsed, of a Cheyenne and Arapaho reservation on Beaver Creek, but Kit had just heard of the reopening of the travel route along the Smoky Hill River, in west-central Kansas, "which the government appears determined to garrison, and maintain," and which "will effectually destroy the Indians hunting ground." Kit was sure that the road would block the buffalo migrations. "This road will also probably be strongly opposed by the Indians in council particularly the Cheyennes and Arrapahos." The news sharpened his sense of approaching crisis. If the government deemed it necessary to maintain the road "at all hazards," then "it will afford another powerful plea in the name of humanity, for their prompt removal to reservations . . . on the same plan so successfully pursued with the Navajos in the Dept. of New Mexico."[22]

He believed the tribes were faithfully observing the preliminary truce, committing no hostilities on the Santa Fe Trail. Several Cheyenne and Arapaho chiefs had also agreed to the truce and called on the hostiles north of the Platte to come to the council. He thought they were tired of fighting and afraid of "the long arm of the whites," and "if treated with a spirit of liberality, I am inclined to believe a treaty that will be permanently Kept, can be made with them." He had just been officially informed by telegram, on September 9, of his appointment to the treaty commission.[23]

Kit closed this report from Fort Riley with some thoughts less immediately related to the main subject, but which had apparently been on his mind for some time. "It has long been the practise to hold whole nations responsible for the bad actions of a single Indian, or a small party. The wrong if not criminality of this, must be apparent." No civilized country, he pointed out, could stop crime completely, "and how absurd to presume, that the nominal Chieftan of a band of wild nomads, should possess more power to seize and punish, or turn over to us for punishment, all turbulent spirits of his tribe, who scorning control commit some act of depredation along the road." During the gold rush of 1848 and 1849 across the plains, Kit observed, many Indians "were doubtless shot down in cold blood" by "ruthless outlaws," but there was no way to punish them "in the lawless state of society." Indian chiefs had even less power over independent hunting parties. As Kit saw it, "The Indians are entitled to at least the same consideration . . . [as] their more civilized neighbours in determining the responsibility to be attached to the nation for the criminal acts of an irresponsible savage. A careful consideration of this question, I shall consider it my duty to request at the council."

Carson had evidently been giving some hard thought to the state of affairs on the plains and in the entire West, and in particular to the principle of retribution. He had written a number of times of the need to "chastise" Indians for acts of hostility, or at least impress on them the power of the government to chastise them, and he would do so again. He had made war on the Navajos, knowing that not all of them were guilty of hostile acts, apparently believing there was no other way to end the cycle of hostility. Yet here he explicitly rejected the doctrine of retaliation against a whole tribe for the acts of certain members, emphasizing its "wrong if not criminality," and declaring that he felt a duty to raise the point at the coming council. Experience had shown how often individual acts led to greater conflicts, and he wanted to find some way of handling these incidents that would prevent war and satisfy both sides. (The treaty, when made, would include provisions for punishing individual Indians and whites for wrongful acts.) The letter was intended for the eyes of General Carleton, though addressed to his adjutant, and it might appear from the space given to the topic that they had not discussed the matter before (though this is hard to believe), and that possibly Kit was not sure how the general would react to his intention to bring it up in council.[24]

Although Kit was still optimistic about the chances of making a lasting peace on the plains, he was clearly aware of the complexities of the situation. The opening of the new Smoky Hill route only emphasized the increasing pressure on the Indians, and the need to find some means of averting disaster. Carson, the illiterate frontiersman, showed that he was quite capable of analyzing the dilemma. His thoughts show that he was also capable of growth, of reevaluating the principle of retaliation that he had once lived by.

The treaty council met in October in south-central Kansas, where the Little Arkansas River joins the Arkansas at the present site of Wichita. Besides Carson and Bent, a number of dignitaries were appointed as commissioners, including two generals, John Sanborn and William Harney; Thomas Murphy, the superintendent of Indian affairs for the central plains area; Agent Jesse Leavenworth; and James Steele, representing the Bureau of Indian Affairs. General Harney, now retired, had a long record as a frontier officer and had distinguished himself against the Seminoles, Mexicans, and Sioux before the Civil War. He and Carson, easily the most famous white men there, do not seem to have met before. Among the traders who gathered for the occasion was James Mead, who was struck by the contrast between the two heroes:

> [Harney], a noted Indian fighter and athlete, was six feet four in his moccasins, his luxuriant hair as white as snow. He was a famous story-teller. Kit Carson was his opposite in everything but fighting qualities. I found him to be quite a different man from what he is depicted in dime novels. . . . With a kind, reticent, and unassuming disposition, he combined the courage and tenacity of a bulldog. He had nothing to say about himself, though occasionally he might be drawn out by some question. He was bluff, but very gentlemanly in his conversation and manner, with nothing of the border bravado about him.

Mead considered Kit "one of the most intelligent and pleasant companions I had ever met with on the plains." Mead also noted Bent, who was "almost as dark as an Indian, with piercing black eyes, and a very prominent Roman nose." Carson and Bent, thought Mead, "had more influence with the Indians than any other two men of their time."[25]

Among other notables present were John Simpson "Blackfoot John" Smith, an old mountain man who had lived among the Cheyennes (and whose mixed-blood son had been killed at Sand Creek), and Jesse Chisholm, the famous Cherokee trader, interpreter, and "ambassador of the Plains," who would give his name to the Chisholm Trail and who had played an important part in persuading the Kiowas and Comanches to attend the council. The former would interpret for the Cheyennes, the latter for the Kiowas. Chisholm's biographer, admitting there is no evidence of it happening, imagines all these famous characters sitting around a campfire at the council ground, telling stories from their long and varied experience.[26]

There were some three thousand Indians, by Mead's estimate, camped along the Arkansas; their representatives also included noteworthy figures. For the Kiowas there were Dohasan, Satanta, Satank, and Lone Wolf, who would be great names in coming years. It is not recorded whether Dohasan and Kit Carson renewed old acquaintance and discussed events at Adobe Walls, although such conversations did take place between other Indian wars veterans over the years. Representing the Comanches were Horse Back, Buffalo Hump, and the grandfatherly, bespectacled Ten Bears. Little Raven was the leading man of the Southern Arapahos, and for the Southern Cheyennes there was the truly tragic figure of Black Kettle, whose camp had been struck at Sand Creek the year before—and who would be attacked again, and killed, by Custer, just three years later. Black Kettle still believed that peace with the whites was the only sensible future for his people, but in fact the majority of the Southern Cheyennes were still north of the Platte River, and the chief actually represented only a modest number of lodges who had remained with him after Sand Creek. Also present were a large number of Wichitas, Wacos, Caddos, and other southern plains people.[27]

There was one man who was not there, who would not have been welcome or even safe at this meeting, but whose symbolic presence no one could forget: Colonel John Chivington. General Sanborn, the president of the treaty commission, opened the proceedings on October 12 with an admission that "great wrongs have been committed" without the Great Father's knowledge, and assuring the Cheyennes and Arapahos that "we all feel disgraced and ashamed when we see our officers or soldiers oppressing the weak." He repudiated the actions of Chivington and his men and promised the restoration of all property lost at Sand

Creek, pledging to give individual plots of land to chiefs and to wives and children of men killed there. He told them that the government wanted them to move either north of the Platte or south of the Arkansas, preferably the latter, away from the main westward travel routes. It was best for the whites and Indians to be separated: "Our people are moving and scattering all over the country, and you should be in a country where white people can be kept away from you by positive law."[28]

Seeking to establish some kind of authority to be responsible for the acts of all people in a tribe, Sanborn said that the government wanted to recognize Black Kettle as the chief of the Southern Cheyennes. The Cheyennes were to have a reservation on which it was hoped that they would be able to support themselves by hunting "for many years." Sanborn made it clear that, however much the whites regretted the Sand Creek affair, they would not tolerate continued hostility by the Indians: "Any condition is better for them [Indians] than war. . . . War simply annoys and troubles the whites, while it destroys them."[29]

The chiefs in turn made clear their reluctance to accept the proposed reservation. Little Raven explained that it was "a very hard thing to leave the country that God gave them on the Arkansas; our friends are buried there, and we hate to leave that ground." All Sanborn could say in reply was, "We all have to submit to the tide of emigration and civilization." Little Raven, saying that his people could not stay north of the Platte where there were no buffalo, admitted that "he knows the game is most gone," and that they would have to settle down. He insisted that the Arapahos and Cheyennes did not deserve what Chivington had done to them, but that they would be happy to keep peace if the whites would do so. "Cheyennes and Arapahos suffered much. Colonels Bent and Carson were raised with them, and they were glad to see [both of] them." Repeating that "they did nothing to the whites until the affair at Sand Creek, but that was too bad to stand, and they had to go to war," Little Raven raised the usual complaint about the dishonesty of Indian agents, saying that he would like either Bent or Edward Wynkoop as agent. (Wynkoop, Carson's old acquaintance, was the commander at Fort Lyon who made the truce with the Indians that Chivington violated.)[30]

After Sanborn reiterated that the problems were caused by whites moving west to the goldfields, and that nothing could be done to stop them, Black Kettle shook hands with the commissioners and spoke. He insisted on his desire for peace, noting his fear of being attacked by soldiers. He had always been for peace with the whites, but since Sand

Creek, "it is hard for me to believe white men any more." He thought it would be best to wait until the majority of his people had returned from the north before discussing a reservation. He expressed some hope for the future, and said, "Now that times are so uncertain in this country I would like to have my old friend Colonel Bent with me." Black Kettle presented his wife, who showed the commissioners the nine wounds she had received at Sand Creek. After Black Kettle's speech and a few words by Jesse Leavenworth, the council adjourned for the day.[31]

The next day, October 13, William Bent spoke briefly. He admitted that both he and the Indians had been deceived in the past by white men, particularly in regard to Sand Creek. He had been asked to arrange a temporary agreement for the Colorado authorities that had put Black Kettle's village where Chivington could strike it. He believed, however, that the present commissioners were "a different kind of people," and that the Cheyennes and Arapahos could sign this treaty without hesitation. This was Bent's only contribution to the recorded speechmaking at the council, while Carson did not speak at all. But the recorded speeches were clearly only the formalities, not the real deliberations or efforts at persuasion. James Carleton had suggested that Carson and Bent "smoke through the preliminary protocols" and bring in more exalted government representatives if things looked favorable, and something not too different apparently took place. James Mead, an experienced trader well acquainted with the southern plains tribes and acting at the council for the Wichitas, applauded Bent and Carson and asserted, "Largely through their efforts and influence the treaty [council] terminated to the satisfaction of the government and the Indians"; historians have agreed. Donald Berthrong writes, "Undoubtedly, William Bent's presence and request that the Cheyennes and Arapahos sign whatever proposition the commissioners offered led to their accepting the treaty." Carson would probably have agreed with Berthrong. Bent had, after all, lived among the Cheyennes and Arapahos for over thirty years, had married among them, had helped them make peace with the Kiowas and Comanches back in 1840, and had been their agent for a time. They remembered Kit Carson, too; both Black Kettle and Little Raven expressed pleasure at seeing him, and indicated that his presence had something to do with their willingness to accept the agreement.[32]

A good deal of "smoking" probably went on both before and during the council that was not officially recorded, a good deal of slow deliberation and talk, with the pipe being passed around. This sort of diplomacy was almost second nature to men like Carson, Bent, Jesse Chisholm, John Smith, and General Harney. Someone like John Sanborn, a volunteer general only recently assigned to the Great Plains, was a novice, not likely to understand the intricacies of plains diplomacy. The belief that a particular man's word could be trusted, based on long personal acquaintance, counted enormously with the Indians, especially after recent events. It was all the more important because the Indian leaders had reasons for their reluctance to sign the treaty.

By the Fort Laramie Treaty of 1851, the government had recognized Southern Cheyenne rights to much of eastern Colorado, plus significant areas in western Nebraska and Kansas and southeast Wyoming. Ten years later they gave up much of that, and with the Southern Arapahos accepted a still sizable area north of the Arkansas in eastern Colorado, while still in fact roaming over much of their old range. But the advance of white settlement, and particularly the increased traffic to the Colorado goldfields, led to the frictions and violent incidents that outraged whites and culminated at Sand Creek. In addition, the commercial hide trade depleted the buffalo and other game on which the plains tribes depended. It seemed essential, if there was to be a lasting peace, to get the Indians away from the white men's travel routes, and there Carson and Bent and the other commissioners found themselves in difficulty.[33]

When Bent spoke to the Doolittle committee in June 1865, he stated that the best place for a reservation for the Cheyennes and Arapahos would be on Beaver Creek, in northwest Kansas and southwest Nebraska, between the Smoky Hill and Republican Rivers. As noted, however, by the time the treaty council met in October, the route to Colorado along the Smoky Hill had been reopened too close to Bent's proposed reservation. The ground was shifting under the feet of the Indians, and of those who wanted some kind of workable peace with them; the pace of events was speeding up.[34]

Three main roads—along the Arkansas, the Smoky Hill, and the Platte—now bracketed the Cheyenne and Arapaho hunting grounds. As Commissioner Thomas Murphy explained to the Indians, "These white men that travel these big roads do not know good Indians from bad ones, and say that if Indians come in sight they will shoot them." The only practical alternative for a reservation seemed to be south of the Arkansas. The treaty presented to the two tribes at the Little Arkansas council proposed a reservation between the Arkansas and Cimarron Rivers, in southcentral Kansas and northcentral Indian Territory (Okla-

PEACEMAKER

homa). All their other lands would be ceded to the government. Black Kettle was clearly reluctant to give up the old reservation, but there was a more immediate objection to the treaty. Some eighty lodges of Southern Cheyennes, figured at some five persons to a lodge, were on the Arkansas under his leadership. About four hundred more lodges, the active hostiles, were north of the Platte, and he was reluctant to sign for them. The Arapaho leaders had a similar problem. Black Kettle was assured that the absent Cheyennes would not be obligated to observe the treaty until they came south and their leaders signed it. Little Raven noted that the lands south of the Arkansas belonged to the Kiowas and Comanches, and moving there would lead to trouble between the tribes. As yet the full implications of the reservation system—confinement in a limited area, farming and not hunting for support, and an end to free movement on the plains—were either not apparent or not palatable to the Indians.[35]

George Bent, William's son, observes, "It was always easy to induce Indians to sign a treaty, even if they did not like its provisions." The Cheyenne and Arapaho chiefs signed the Little Arkansas treaty on October 14, 1865. Commissioner James Steele had explained to them the essential doctrine of the Vanishing American: staying near the whites meant that "you will gradually diminish, until you are swept away from the earth." "Wise and good men" in Washington had concluded "that it is best for the two races to be separated." When the two were in contact, the Indians "have gradually wasted away from the earth." That argument may have counted for less than the fact that, as Little Raven said, "You propose to give us land where we can live in quiet." Black Kettle wanted "the privilege of roaming around until it is necessary for me to accept the proposed reservation," which he may have hoped would be a long time yet. He tried to explain the shock and bewilderment his people felt: "We have all lost our way."[36]

After the agreement with the Cheyennes and Arapahos, signed on October 14, came the council with the Comanches, Kiowas, and Kiowa Apaches. Carson and Bent were present but did not figure in the formal speechmaking. The tone adopted by the commissioners was more militant than with the Cheyennes and Arapahos, for there was no Sand Creek to atone for; the raids on the Santa Fe Trail were considered just cause for military response. General Sanborn, using the classic simile, reminded the chiefs that the soldiers of the Great Father were "as numerous as the leaves of the forest or the grass on the prairies," but since the president's ear was "still open to the call of mercy," the council was called to attempt peacemaking. Nothing was said of the massive demobilization of the Union armies. Instead, the general reminded the chiefs that the whites could lose a thousand men without missing them, while the loss of ten was a tragedy for the Indians. The Kiowas and Comanches were asked to cede all lands north of the Canadian River, to remove them from direct contact with the Santa Fe Trail.[37]

The chiefs were not receptive. Dohasan said flatly, "The Kiowas own from Fort Laramie and the north fork of the Platte to Texas, and always have owned it." He did not want the country divided up or given to whites, he denied that the Kiowas had caused the recent troubles, and he asserted, "I want a big land for my people to roam over; don't want to stay long in one place, but want to move about from place to place." Sanborn finally said that the commissioners would not demand the surrender of lands north of the Canadian, though he insisted it was in the interest of the Kiowas and Comanches to do so. Jesse Leavenworth and Thomas Murphy spoke privately with the chiefs, and eventually persuaded the Kiowa and Comanche leaders to sign a treaty accepting a reservation encompassing the western part of Indian Territory and most of the Texas Panhandle.[38]

The final signing of the Kiowa and Comanche treaty came on October 24, but Bent and Carson had left on the nineteenth, bound for St. Louis. Samuel Kingman, one of the secretaries for the council, traveled with them; he had found the proceedings interesting but, in his opinion, likely to prove futile. The Cheyenne and Arapaho treaty was "very liberal in its terms to the Indians, probably more so than will be sanctioned by the senate." He thought the Indians "will probably keep the terms if we do." He had become quite friendly with Carson, Bent, and the other commissioners, but regarding their accomplishment he wrote, "Their fate as com[missione]rs will be that they died of too large views."[39]

Jesse Chisholm's biographer, Stan Hoig, says, "The Treaty of the Little Arkansas was far more notable for who attended the affair than for what it actually accomplished." When the five remaining commissioners— Sanborn, Harney, Steele, Murphy, and Leavenworth—transmitted the results on October 24, they implicitly acknowledged that they had been generous by contemporary standards regarding annuities to the Indians, saying that they wished to make certain that hostilities "shall never be induced by dissatisfaction or want on their part," and noting that the expense for annuities would be modest compared to the cost of military operations. The treaty, contrary to Kingman's expectation, was in fact ratified by the Senate, but the general verdict of historians has been that it brought about only a temporary lull in the hostilities on the central and southern plains.[40] The treaty and its aftermath illustrate the typical frustrations of Indian treaty-making, for both whites and Indians. Bent's plan for a Cheyenne and Arapaho reservation was thwarted. As in so many cases, the chiefs present could speak for only a portion of their people. Black Kettle's current following composed perhaps one-sixth of the Southern Cheyennes. The hostiles north of the Platte, who would have to be persuaded to accept the agreement, included the Dog Soldiers, a warrior society that had become virtually a separate band of the tribe, and would be the hard core of militant resistance to whites in coming years. When they did return south of the Platte, these bands would refuse, as Carson had feared, to accept the loss of the prized hunting grounds along the Republican and the Smoky Hill, and would force Black Kettle to repudiate that part of the treaty. The state of Kansas refused to sanction the use of any part of its territory for a reservation. Similarly, only a portion of the Comanches were represented at the Little Arkansas, and Texas would not relinquish any land for a Kiowa-Comanche reservation. The Indian Territory was thus the only place available for these tribes.[41]

The Treaty of the Little Arkansas, like nearly all such agreements, was compromised by mutual incomprehension and the inability of the signatories to provide what the other side really wanted. The basic causes of conflict remained, and neither the commissioners nor the chiefs could remove them. The chiefs could not exercise the kind of control over their young warriors that would prevent acts of robbery or violence, a requirement that whites would never yield, since it involved the safety and property of white citizens. The warrior culture of the plains tribes compelled young men to distinguish themselves in war, and to acquire horses, in order to achieve honor and status. The chiefs, wise in their maturity, were already established; for the young men, only total defeat could lead them to relinquish warlike activity. The peace commissioners could not alter the basic fact of continuing white expansion and settlement. The government they represented wanted peace on the one hand, but on the other it promoted expansion and settlement through the Homestead Act, by laying out roads through Indian lands and by encouraging the building of railroads. The Great

Father's ultimate purpose remained that of confining Indians on reservations, with the intention of "civilizing" them while appropriating the lion's share of usable land for white people. The commissioners at the Little Arkansas council had to accept those conditions as given. General Sanborn explained to the Cheyenne and Arapaho chiefs, "We have all got to submit to the tide of emigration and civilization," but that submission meant something quite different to him than to Black Kettle or Little Raven.[42]

Although they may have underestimated the actual pace of settlement, Carson and Bent seem to have been driven by a sense of time running out. After leaving the Little Arkansas, they proceeded to St. Louis, where General John Pope had requested their presence. Pope, usually remembered for his defeat by Lee at Second Bull Run, actually spent much of his military career in the West. As a topographical engineer before the Civil War he had served in New Mexico and on the plains, and he had apparently met Carson, and perhaps Bent; at any rate, he had requested their presence at the council. Pope believed very strongly in military control of Indian affairs, and he wanted the advice of the two experts to bolster his arguments.[43]

The document that the two presented Pope, dated October 27, 1865, was again produced by someone with a fine turn of phrase. Though Bent was more literate than Carson, he admitted he had almost forgotten how to spell during his years on the Arkansas, and he was probably not capable of the polished phrases of the finished letter. The ideas are very similar to those both Carson and Bent had expressed earlier to the Doolittle committee, and to those in Carson's letter to Doolittle from Fort Lyon, and indeed cover the same topics. Carson trusted Bent's judgment and may have deferred to him, but there are points where his opinions and experience show through clearly.[44]

Their first point, as Pope had hoped, was that the War Department should control Indian affairs. The two claimed "long continued personal observation of the working of the present system," and they believed it offered "no security" against "the rapacity and cupidity of the Agents," who, "with salaries barely sufficient for their support," often retired after a few years, comfortable if not indeed wealthy. In addition, "jealousies" between agents and army officers led to lack of "harmonious cooperation." At the Little Arkansas council, the chiefs complained that the Great Father meant well and sent out "big bales of goods for his Indian children," but they had to pass through many hands, and "when they get out to us they are hardly worth receiving." The result was that the government appeared to act in bad faith and, when the Indians became irritated, the agent would cover up by reporting them to the military as hostile, and the soldiers, "wearied of the monotony of frontier garrison life, gladly and without much enquiry as to its justice, [would] seize the opportunity for an active campaign." Nonetheless, Carson and Bent had more confidence in the soldiers than in the agents; if the former were in charge of the Indians, they would be able to judge "the necessity of action" more accurately. Transfer of Indian affairs to the War Department would "remove the control of the Indians from the hands of a set of irresponsible citizens," would "restore the confidence of the Indians by a faithful and scrupulous fulfillment of the promises of government," and would "justly and equitably distribute the presents, annuities, etc."[45]

Both Carson and Bent had been Indian agents, Carson for seven years, so their words constituted a powerful indictment of the honesty of agents and the effectiveness of the Bureau of Indian Affairs. Carson had perhaps transferred his loyalty to the army, but the Carson-Bent document included cautions about the readiness of officers to launch "an active campaign" without due consideration. The debate over civil versus military control of Indian affairs would draw considerable attention in coming years, until the army lost interest with the waning of actual Indian warfare. Soldiers believed that military control would ensure honesty and consistency, and would actually prevent many problems from reaching the point of violence. Humanitarian reformers and, of course, the Bureau of Indian Affairs, believed that the army only wanted control of the Indians so that its use of violence could be unrestrained. In his report for 1868, Commissioner of Indian Affairs N. G. Taylor summed up the antimilitary viewpoint, declaring that "the proposed transfer is tantamount, in my judgement, to perpetual war." He continued, "This war office management, now proposed, may look to the peace that follows extermination as the great desideratum of the service and the panacea for Indian troubles. . . . Is it to be supposed that [the Indians] can desire to be governed by those who have visited upon their race most of the woes they have experienced?" Indian agent J. H. Stout expressed it more succinctly in 1878: "If we accept as true the theory 'that a good Indian is a dead one,' then the red men should immediately be turned over to the Army, and in a very few years the complement of 'good Indians' in the happy hunting grounds will be complete." The military-versus-civil debate consumed time and energy that might have been spent in ways more beneficial to the Indians.[46]

The other point on which the two friends urged immediate action was the establishment of reservations. The reopening of the Smoky Hill route, making Bent's proposed reservation impossible, only emphasized the need for action while there was still some room for the Indians.

The time is now fast approaching when decisive action in regard to the reservation policy for Indians must be pursued, as each year passes away the game so necessary for the Red Man's subsistence is gradually dying off, in fact we know by personal experience, that there is not one buffalo at present, to one thousand that forty years ago swarmed upon the plains . . . in a few years the last herds of buffalo will have disappeared.[47]

As Carson had noted in his Fort Lyon letter, government policy had formerly relied on removing Indians westward, but could no longer do so: "Now emigration leaps forward from the West itself." Soon miners would be searching the length of the Rockies: "Gradually encircling them in its ever steady advance, civilization now presses them on all sides." Were the two old-timers expressing some of their own feeling of encirclement by strangers, and their own sense of loss in a changing world? But they explicitly addressed the plight of the Indians: "How pitiable a picture is presented for the preservation of any portion of that vast number of aboriginal nomads, that swarmed through the interior of our continent."[48]

The final result seemed all too clear. Again in terms similar to those in Kit's Fort Lyon letter, the Carson-Bent document admitted that "the cruel or the thoughtless might leave to this steady advance of a superior race, the ultimate destruction of the various Indian tribes." It would certainly occur if things went on as they were, "but humanity shudders at the idea of the destruction of hundreds of thousands of our fellow creatures until every effort shall have been tried for their redemption and found useless." The nation had a clear moral responsibility, for "by dispossessing them of their country we assume their stewardship." The way in which the duty was performed "will add a glorious record to American history, or a damning blot and reproach for all future times."

Once removal had been decided on, "a vigorous and determined war should be immediately made on those refusing to accept the Government offer, until all opposition is effectually destroyed." But when the

Indians agreed to move peacefully, as Carson had argued in September, "great care should be taken to consult as far as possible the Indians views with regard to point of location, etc."[49] In subsequent years the failure to consult Indians on this question would lead to episodes like the Modoc War of 1872–73 and the flight of the Northern Cheyennes in 1878.

Carson and Bent had both stated that the troubles on the plains in 1865 were the result of the aggressions of white men, that the Cheyennes and Arapahos had not gone to war as a whole until after Sand Creek. But no two men knew better that the plains tribes, and many other western peoples, were warrior societies, exalting the martial virtues. Although the two hoped desperately that their recent treaty would avoid further hostility, it was too much to hope that no one would resist confinement on reservations. And if reservations were not established soon, what would be the fate of the Indians as the "tide of emigration" continued to swell? The dilemma was inescapable.

Since military measures of some sort would be necessary, they gave advice on the location of forts on the southern plains, "both for the prevention of crime, and its prompt and speedy punishment when committed." Moreover, "we would earnestly recommend that all posts in the Indian country should be garrisoned by Regular troops, and officers of known discretion and judgement placed in command, with special instructions to be cautious, and not to rashly place the country in danger of a devastating Indian war, in consequence of any slight provocation on the part of the Indians." The incidents of the previous year involving Colorado volunteers, culminating in Colonel Chivington's atrocity at Sand Creek, provide the obvious reason for these recommendations. Nine years before, in his autobiography, Carson had urged the use of territorial volunteers in Indian conflicts in New Mexico. At the time of this letter he had been serving as a volunteer officer for over four years, participating in three Indian campaigns. He had now expressed a clear opinion that regular officers and troops were better suited to maintaining peace. During the Civil War years, volunteer troops had often proved highly effective in fighting Indians, but they had also proved harsher and more likely to seek a violent solution than the regulars.

Instead of launching an expedition on "any slight provocation," commanding officers should be governed by the procedures laid down by the Treaty of the Little Arkansas. The chiefs had agreed, in the case of any depredations, to deliver up the offenders to the commanding officer of the nearest fort. Any white men committing offenses against the Indians would also be arrested by the military for trial and punishment, on the Indians' written application through their agent. As Carson and Bent explained, "Could this system be successfully and practically carried into effect, many of these petty actions of wrong perpetrated by individuals on either side, that now unfortunately result in indiscriminate warfare, may be avoided." Carson had spent much of his time as an Indian agent trying to adjust "petty actions of wrong perpetrated by individuals," complaining that the perpetrators of crimes against Indians were seldom punished. The device of punishing individual wrongdoers, in place of the indiscriminate action against a whole group so often resorted to by both Indians and whites, was tried repeatedly, and often embodied in treaties, but it too often foundered on the reluctance of people on both sides to punish one of their own. Just as Indian chiefs lacked the authority to compel the surrender of their tribesmen, white authorities found it hard to lay hands on white offenders protected by public opinion. Both Indians and whites were to be tried by white men's law, and the whole purpose of government policy was to establish the superiority of the white man's law.

Carson and Bent pointed out some other leading causes of Indian-white conflict, such as the conduct of traders and hunters. Many of the former were of "reckless character," "unprincipled adventurers whose sole object is to secure the enormous profits incidental to illicit trade." They "treat with contempt all restrictive laws imposed by Congress respecting the sale of intoxicating liquors, and do not hesitate to sell weapons and ammunition to Indians." Carson's grudge is apparent against the comancheros who had traded ammunition to the Kiowas and Comanches he fought at Adobe Walls. William Bent had traded his share of whiskey, guns, and ammunition—staples of the fur trade—to Indians over the years since he had come to the Arkansas. It is easy to be cynical about Bent's motives, to accuse him of attacking his smaller competitors. Fly-by-night traders whose chief stock was bad whiskey and weapons were commonly regarded as a leading source of Indian-white friction, cheating the Indians and spreading bad feeling and alcoholism. Bent's possible self-interest certainly does not invalidate his charge. He undoubtedly considered himself a more responsible trader than the men he denounced, one who dealt in many other items besides guns and alcohol, and he would have said that times had changed since the advent of white settlement and Indian-white conflict.[50]

The hunters were hardly blameless. "Hunting game being the Indians natural mode of existence they look with jealousy and justly so to the indiscriminate slaughter of game by hunting parties of whites upon the prairies—all such parties should be prohibited by the Government from killing in excess of their actual want of provisions." Carson and Bent noted an incident when hunters had poisoned a buffalo carcass to kill wolves; a party of Cheyennes had dined upon the fresh animal and suffered the consequences. "The indiscriminate slaughter of game . . . leads to bad feelings, and frequently to quarrels, often resulting in bloodshed and murder, and in these transactions the blame is often with the whites, though invariably attached to the Indians." Occasionally one catches a note of weariness in the recommendations of Carson and Bent, as of men who have seen the same mistakes repeated too many times.

Echoing a number of Carson's reports as Indian agent, they believed that the Cheyennes, Arapahos, and Kiowa Apaches represented at the Little Arkansas council were "actuated by principles of good faith." They had agreed to "assist the soldiers against all Indians south of the Arkansas"—presumably the Kiowas and Comanches—"that may commit hostilities against the whites." In that event, "their services as scouts and guides, and [in] taking possession of stock from hostile Indians when in action, Col Carson from a number of years experience pronounces invaluable." They should be provided, while in service, with rations and allowed to keep captured stock. When the hostiles' stock could be destroyed or captured, Carson knew, they would be "effectually subdued."[51]

Bent planned to remain with the Cheyennes and Arapahos during the winter. He and Carson believed it best if the government allowed the portion of those tribes still hostile, and north of the Platte, to come south "with as little delay as possible." Clearly they hoped, too optimistically, that these people would agree to the treaty that Black Kettle and Little Raven had signed, and "would doubtless behave well under the advice and council of their Head Chiefs." If they came south, and were "still inclined for war," it would be easier for the military to control them than it would be if they were in the remote areas of Wyoming and Montana with the Sioux.[52]

In conclusion, the two pointed out the Bosque Redondo reservation as an example of how the reservation system could successfully convert hostile Indians into peaceable farmers. The Navajos, who until two years before had "waged a malignant war upon the frontier settlers of New

Mexico," carrying off stock and killing men, women, and children, "are now engaged in the pursuits of agriculture, and prior to the time of our leaving New Mexico, had, this season over five thousand (5,000) acres of corn planted." This had been done "solely by the labor of the Indians," and on August 1 "their corn crop presented as fine an appearance as any we have ever witnessed." The wording implies that Bent had visited the Bosque and shared Carson's enthusiasm. Perhaps Kit asked his old friend to visit the reservation with him, before they headed east for the treaty council, to see what could be done for Indians if the right plan was adopted. In fact, the 1865 crop would again prove a failure, thanks to the army worm, and the damage seems to have been under way by the beginning of August, when Carson and Bent reported they found the corn flourishing. Large purchases of beef and corn were once again necessary to prevent starvation. Possibly Carson and Bent were dishonest here, but very likely they saw what they wanted very much to see—an "alternative to extinction" for the Indians. At any rate, they believed the reservation to be "founded and carried on by a spirit of humanity and good faith," and "a successful example of the benefits to be derived from the system." In addition, it proved "the capacity of the Indians for the benefits to be received from civilization," that capacity doubted by so many whites, who questioned the use of expending money and effort in a hopeless cause.[53]

General Pope was well pleased with this report from Kit Carson and William Bent, which substantially agreed with his own ideas. He forwarded it to his own superior, General William Tecumseh Sherman, who sent it on to General U. S. Grant, the commanding general of the army, with the endorsement, "Probably no two men exist better acquainted with the Indians than Carson & Bent and their judgmt is entitled to great weight." The two friends, in their last years, had gained the ears of powerful men in Congress and the army, one of whom would be president in a few years. They had a chance to present their view that a crisis was at hand in the West which could decide the fate of the Indians, and that immediate action was necessary.[54]

In 1869 U. S. Grant became president and set about to reform government Indian policy. His program became known as the "Peace Policy," or the "Quaker Peace Policy" to contemptuous critics. In fact, the policy accepted from the first the necessity for military force in case of Indian resistance. In 1873 Grant's secretary of the Interior Department, Columbus Delano, said that the government would seek to combine "humanity and kindness" with "all needed severity, to punish them for their outrages." The basic idea remained that of placing the Indians on reservations, teaching them agriculture and white civilization, and eventually subdividing the reservations into individual farms. The transfer of Indian affairs to the War Department met with opposition, both from humanitarians and from politicians who did not want to lose a valuable form of patronage. When Grant tried to appoint army officers as Indian agents, hoping for greater honesty, Congress prohibited this by law, after which Grant turned to the churches, with whom the politicians (as he said) "dare not contend." We know that Carson's and Bent's recommendations went to Grant, with impressive endorsement from Pope and Sherman. Probably no single source shaped Grant's thinking on the subject because so many of these ideas were common currency. Still, that two men of their experience, particularly one with Carson's reputation, supported these ideas would have added to their weight. Moreover, their report reached Grant at a time, in late 1865, when his thoughts as commanding general were turning for the first time, with the end of the Civil War, to the "Indian problem" as a major concern. The only alternatives to the reservation system that contemporaries could readily imagine—"extermination," or simply "letting nature take its course," which seemed to amount to the same thing—were morally unacceptable, in spite of vehement voices from the frontier calling for such action. Thus many of Carson's and Bent's ideas would be carried out, if not as wisely, efficiently, humanely, or quickly as they might have hoped. (Grant, as commanding general, was also well aware of the details of the Bosque Redondo experiment, and of the controversy surrounding it. Some months after General Carleton left New Mexico in 1867, Grant wrote to him commending his efforts and condemning his critics, particularly agents for the Bureau of Indian Affairs.)[55]

"THE BEST MAN IN THE COUNTRY": CARSON AT FORT GARLAND

Bent had agreed to spend the winter of 1865–66 with Black Kettle's Cheyennes. Carson, still in the army, returned to duty in New Mexico. In late December he took command at Fort Union, the most important post in the territory, where he remained until April. There, at the beginning of the new year, he received notice from Secretary of War Edwin Stanton that he had been appointed brevet brigadier general of volunteers. The official date of the promotion was March 13, 1865. A great many officers received such promotions at the end of the Civil War as a reward for their services, and the official date of the majority was the same as Carson's. General Carleton had recommended him for promotion in October, "for gallantry in the Battle of Valverde, and for distinguished conduct and gallantry in the wars against the Mescalero Apaches and against the Navajo Indians of New Mexico, and for his gallantry in his brilliant engagement with the Comanche and Kiowa Indians . . . and for long, faithful, and meritorious services in New Mexico."

A brevet promotion carried no greater pay and, except under special circumstances, no greater actual authority than an officer's permanent rank—colonel in Carson's case. It simply entitled the recipient to be addressed by the brevet rank and served as a form of recognition at a time when there were few medals or other awards. Kit wrote to the secretary, sending in the required oath of loyalty and noting that the honor was "unsolicited by me." He accepted it "as a memento that during the late rebellion, the exertions of the New Mexican volunteers, though restricted in its sphere of usefulness to their own Territory, have not been overlooked by the United States Government." He did not mention that it was seventeen years since his commission as second lieutenant in the regular army had been rejected by Congress. The illiterate runaway apprentice had come a long way.[56]

Command at Fort Union, a supply depot, did not really call for Carson's particular talents, and in April 1866 he was transferred to Fort Garland, Colorado, which certainly did. The post lay on the western side of the Sangre de Cristo range and on the eastern edge of the San Luis Valley. Its principal purpose was to watch the Utes and Jicarilla Apaches in the area and maintain peace between them and the Hispanic and Anglo settlers, and the plains tribes. Far less imposing than Fort Union, it was a fairly typical small frontier post—not really a fort at all, but a collection of log and adobe buildings around a parade ground. It was over eight thousand feet above sea level, in a location of great natural beauty, but as Carson noted in one of his first reports, "in Very Bad Condition" for lack of repair. The garrison of sixty-three men and ten officers amounted to a motley collection of regulars and New Mexico, California, and Missouri volunteers. Kit feared that their weakness and lack of discipline had become apparent to the Indians. The frontier army was in a state of transition in 1866, with a few volunteers, most of them yearning for discharge, holding the line while the regular army, reorganizing and undergoing drastic "downsizing," prepared to reassume responsibility for the West.[57]

The reason for giving Carson this unprepossessing command was, as might be expected, because of the "Indian problem" in the area. In August, General John Pope reported that he planned to keep four companies of New Mexico volunteers in service at the fort under Carson, who would have to be reduced to the permanent rank of lieutenant colonel because so little of his regiment remained in service. As for Kit himself, he was yet again the indispensable man. As Pope noted: "Carson is the best man in the country to control these Indians and to prevent war if it can be done. He is personally known and liked by every Indian of the bands likely to make trouble."[58]

Carson must have had a strong sense of déjà vu, for the same old problems he had struggled with as Indian agent were still present, and in some ways more acute. The summer of the previous year a Colorado volunteer officer noted that the Utes and Jicarillas on the upper affluents of the Arkansas were killing settlers' stock because "their resources are very limited, being principally game." They could not hunt on the plains because of their enemies, and the settlers would continue to suffer until, the officer feared, some white man retaliated and a war started. Among them were some Muache Utes, including Kaniache, who had been with Carson at Adobe Walls and who insisted on their desire to remain friends with the whites.[59]

The factor that made the problem even more pressing than in the late 1850s was an increased influx of settlers and miners and new travel routes. The game was progressively scarcer, while whites had brought more livestock to the San Luis Valley and the upper Arkansas. As Governor Alexander Cummings of Colorado Territory explained to the commissioner of Indian Affairs in October of this year, 1866, "They [the Utes] are quite intelligent, and point with great earnestness to the condition of all the places where the whites have obtained a foothold. And they say with great force that if roads and settlements are allowed to be made in their present hunting grounds, which is all that is left to them, the game will vanish and they will soon be left to starvation." The governor added that the Utes often killed settlers' cattle, simply because of hunger, and "the natural anger of the settlers leads to the shooting of the Indians who attempt to steal cattle, and the bloody reprisals of the Indians is the cause of nearly every war."[60]

Three years earlier the previous governor, John Evans, had made a treaty with the Tabeguache Utes, who now had an agency at Conejos in the San Luis Valley. As Carson noted in June, not only were the Utes and Jicarillas "suffering from the greatest destitution," but the former "are also in a high state of Exasperation in Consequence of Certain Amendments to their treaty with Gov'r Evans (made in the U. S. Senate) which the Indians claim were never Explained to them." The Tabeguaches believed that the Great Father was cheating them; that, in Governor Cummings's words, "the treaty by which it is now claimed they are bound is not the treaty to which they agreed." The lands that they were supposed to give up, and those reserved for them, were "not in accordance with their understanding"; the amount of livestock they were to receive had been reduced; and their annuities had been cut from fifteen years to five. Cummings acknowledged that it would be difficult for "an intelligent reader" to understand the revised document as presented to the Indians. As Carson noted, the Indians "all declare themselves determined, not to abide by its provisions." Some three hundred lodges of them were hunting on the plains that June, without much success; they had already stolen horses and cattle, and if they did not find food, Kit warned, "the Settlers must tremble at Anticipated Misfortune in their unprotected State And no Assistance Can be at present Assured them."[61]

Carson estimated the strength of the nearby Utes at 800 warriors, and the Jicarillas at 250 (he probably did not choose to be conservative in his estimate), while he had some 60 men under his command. Post surgeon George Gwyther later described Fort Garland as "the point of strength and the protecting hope of many a small settlement and isolated rancho," but at the time Carson would have found this a highly exaggerated estimate of the garrison's military potential. He believed that with two cavalry companies, one company of infantry, and a battery of light artillery, he could maintain peace and "in Case of outrage . . . take prompt . . . measures for punishment." During a period of transition, the army seems to have hoped that Kit Carson's skill and reputation could substitute for troop strength.[62]

When Carson gave up the Taos agency in 1861, the Bureau decided to move the Jicarillas and Utes of that agency east across the mountains to Lucien Maxwell's ranch at Cimarron. The new agent, W. F. M. Arny, claimed that Carson had wanted the agency located there permanently, which Kit denied. The move was intended to get the Indians away from whiskey sellers and into a less settled area, thus addressing some of the complaints that Carson had made so frequently. But Maxwell's ranch was on the Santa Fe Trail; it was not far from Fort Union and from Las Vegas, which provided the soldiers with liquor; and there were ranchers in the area who objected to the presence of the Indians. Carson's idea for a permanent reservation was a location well away from white settlement, perhaps in the Four Corners area. The move to Cimarron had proved a great benefit to Maxwell, who was paid well for providing the Indians with beef, flour, and corn. He had a great deal more influence with them than Arny or subsequent agents. It was at Cimarron that Carson had recruited his Ute and Jicarilla scouts for the Adobe Walls expedition.[63]

These Jicarillas and Muache Utes by no means confined themselves to the Cimarron area but hunted into Colorado. Their "depredations" on livestock on the upper Arkansas roused the ire of the settlers, as in northeast New Mexico. Ignoring government orders and continuing to draw rations at Maxwell's, the Muaches had refused a treaty that would have moved them to Colorado. Another of Kit's old friends, Kaniache, had led the opposition to moving to a reservation farther west. The chief was perfectly happy to go to war with Kit Carson against Kiowas and Comanches, but regarding other matters their friendship may have been strained.[64]

On the other hand, Carson seems to have enjoyed an excellent relationship with Ouray, the leading man among the Tabeguache Utes. Ouray, whose father was a Jicarilla Apache, was in his thirties at this time; reportedly he had lived for some years with a New Mexican family near Taos and spoke fluent Spanish. According to the story, he observed or at least heard about the Taos revolt of 1847, in which Charles Bent was killed, and was impressed with the swift and bloody vengeance of the Americans; he concluded that resistance to the whites invited disaster. He had also made the customary trip to Washington in 1863, the sort intended to impress Indian chiefs with the power of the white men. At any rate, as a leader he consistently followed the path of negotiation and conciliation. For the western tribes, this was the beginning of a period in which men rose to leadership as much for their ability to negotiate with the whites as any other quality. Ultimately the government would designate Ouray the head chief of all the Utes, and he would be the most popular Indian in Colorado—among whites. Later historians would disagree whether he was a farseeing, statesmanlike leader, doing his best for his people, or a traitor, selling them out for his own advantage.[65]

Clearly Kit had his work cut out for him, and his knowledge and connections among the Utes, and the credit and reputation he enjoyed with them, would be as important as the firepower he could command. The following year some Ute chiefs would tell Randolph Marcy, the inspector general of the U. S. Army, that Kit Carson and Albert Pfeiffer headed a short list of former agents who "were all honest men, who gave them all the presents that were sent out by the Government," and whom they would be glad to have as agents again, in contrast to some more recent incumbents. Pfeiffer, in 1866–67, was Carson's second in command at Fort Garland.[66]

Dr. George Gwyther was much impressed by both of them, seeing Pfeiffer as a reckless hero, but also a tragic figure because of the loss of his wife to the Apaches. As for the commanding officer, "A more unmilitary man than Carson, in the strict sense of that definition, can scarcely be conceived. The trappings of war were thoroughly uncongenial to him, and I believe he was far more discomposed by the thought of wearing a uniform-coat, sash, and epaulettes, than by the proximity of powder and steel." Carson's eyes gave Gwyther "the impression of a man whose wits were in careful training, and who objected, both by instinct and education, to deceiving, or being deceived." Although he was short and long-bodied, with legs bowed like a jockey's, "His head and face once seen could never be forgotten."[67]

"At Garland," Gwyther relates, "Carson kept open house" for all passersby, including the Utes, over whom he had such influence, the surgeon says, "that no trouble ever took place when an appeal could be made to him." Any difficulty, however dangerous, "could be allayed by offering to send for 'Kitty,' . . . and it was a study to see him sitting, surrounded by them, talking as kindly and familiarly as to his own children; rolling cigarritos and passing the tobacco around, all the while laughing, joking, talking Spanish, or Ute tongue, with such abundant gesticulations and hand-movements, that it seemed to me he talked more with his hands and shoulders than with his tongue." (Since Carson was undoubtedly using the sign language, the common mode of intertribal communication, Gwyther was literally correct.) Four years after, the doctor could write of Carson's unfailing influence, but his commander's reports at the time show how anxious Kit really was, and how uncertain that he could keep the peace.[68]

In his June report describing the post and the overall situation, Carson explained the causes of the Utes' discontent, their "destitution" and their "high State of Exasperation" over the 1863 treaty, and declared,

> The time is fast approaching when the Government must take active definite measures for the Subjection And removal of these Indians on to Reservations—A war will necessarily first Ensue ere these wild men of the Mountains will Consent to leave their native haunts. . . . I Am fearful we are even now on the Verge of a war with these Indians—

Since "twice the amount of public funds had better be spent in the prevention than one half in the punishment of Crime," it would be advisable to "make the garrison of this Post strong Enough to overawe or punish these half Starved depredators." Carson was pessimistic, all the same: "Although war must Eventually ensue, And for the benefit of the American people the Sooner Measures Are taken for forcing the Indians of this Section, to remove to reservations the better it will be, and the less Expense finally to the Federal Government." When the crisis did come, Kit's actions varied from this belligerent prescription. He once again preferred to err on the side of caution, trying to persuade the army to send him as many troops as possible.[69]

A few days later Major Lafayette Head, the Utes' agent, brought word that Chief Shavano's band had raided a ranch east of the mountains, making off with cattle, sheep, and various goods, and whipping a herder. Then came a report of the killing of three men. Head asked for assistance and Carson gave him ten men, accompanied by six friendly Indians, "to Assist him in Apprehending or killing Chaveneau." Such civil-military cooperation, as he and William Bent had noted, was by no means invariable. The small number of men Kit sent may indicate just how weak Carson considered his force, or the presence of the friendly Indians may have reassured him that the incident was not going to turn into a general outbreak. Three days later Carson thanked General Carleton for sending reinforcements promptly. When he had enough horses he intended to visit the Utes. Though they had "expressed their disapprobation of the treaty in the Strongest terms," Kit was sure that he and Pfeiffer could talk to them and convince them "That their Grievances can be righted." From the Indians near the post, "With whom I can talk And reason, I have nothing to fear," but those at a distance were the danger, because "their destitution will be a powerful incentive to steal." If war came, "it will be forced partly by the Indians

Necessities." Even Shavano had expressed a desire for peace, though he wanted money and horses. The "weak State of the Garrison" had probably encouraged the Indians. He was waiting to hear from Head, and if the agent met Shavano and killed him, "it would have a good Effect." Shavano, however, came to no harm; he was present at a council at the fort in September, and would survive Carson by some years.[70]

By the end of June things were relatively quiet, but Carson had to inform Carleton that Agent Head had "neither funds nor Credit" with which to feed the Indians near the post. Kit had talked with some five hundred Utes, who all indicated "their intention of not complying with the terms of the treaty," as amended by the Senate, but part of them expressed "a Strong desire to be at peace with the whites." There was a strong war faction, which Carson blamed on the influence of the Jicarillas, who were trying to get the Utes to go to war along with them. As for the whites, "I have never Seen So great a feeling of Apprehension pervade a Community than does at present this Section of Colorado." Although hostilities "except in Extreme Cases Are Always to be deprecated," he thought the government ought to demand that the Jicarillas return any stolen property, and if they did not comply, "A Vigorous Campaign" should be carried out. A "temporizing policy" would only make the Jicarillas bolder and have a bad effect on the other tribes.[71]

In July Kit reported telling Maxwell to warn the Jicarillas near Cimarron about returning the stolen goods, or their annuities would be withheld and they would be "Severely punished." The Utes, on the other hand, appeared to be "friendly inclined," but "their destitution is so great . . . that I have Ordered issues of Meat & Flour," and he trusted the commanding general would provide some relief.[72]

The situation was calm enough in late July for Kit to travel to Santa Fe to meet General Pope, who was on an inspection tour. If Carson's verbal report was anything like his written ones, then Pope did not get a rosy picture. It was during this visit to Santa Fe that Kit met the artist Worthington Whittredge, who saw him as a real-life Natty Bumppo. Whittredge tells a comic, yet oddly touching, story of Carson's being so concerned about making a proper appearance at a dance that he insisted on carrying a pair of dancing shoes inside his uniform coat in addition to wearing his boots, so he could be sure of being properly clad. "He was all the time afraid," says Whittredge, "that he might do something which was out of place or not in strict compliance with the usages in the 'States' or of the Army." He could not simply play the part of the rough, uncouth frontiersman, as his old friend Joe Meek evidently enjoyed doing. The amused condescension of some well-dressed folk in big houses, of which he had complained to Jessie Frémont during his trips to Washington in the 1840s, must have been a painful and lasting memory. He knew the etiquette and protocol of an Indian council but not that of a ballroom, and it did not occur to him that the opinions of people to whom proper footwear was of major importance were inconsequential for a man of his standing. As Doctor Gwyther said, he could face "powder and steel" more readily than the prospect of appearing in a dress uniform.[73]

On this same trip to Santa Fe he also met Colonel James Meline, one of Pope's staff, who was impressed by his "great distinctness of memory, simplicity, candor, and a desire to make some one else, rather than himself, the hero of his story." One characteristic that struck Meline was Carson's reluctance to dogmatize about Indians: "He would frequently reply—unlike so many I have met who knew *all* about them—'I don't know'—'I can't say'—'I never saw that.' " He declared the Utes to be "the best rifle shots in the country, whether Indian or white," and he acknowledged that, although he had done a good deal of shooting, some Utes could beat him. Meline observed that most men of Carson's skill would have said, "I'll turn my back on no man for rifle-shooting."[74]

Inevitably, Meline asked about the Indians and their future. Carson still expressed some optimism that the "mountain Indians" (probably Apaches or Utes) would prosper if they settled down and cultivated the soil. Meline then quotes Carson as saying, "After the successful campaign against the Arrapahoes and Camanches in 1865, as usual, a treaty was made with them before half the tribes had been subdued." No treaty should have been made "as long as any portion of their nation remained insubordinate"; a further campaign, "at slight additional expense," could "have shown these Indians that they were dealing with a powerful government." There had, of course, been no successful campaign against the plains tribes in 1865, and Carson himself had helped negotiate the Little Arkansas treaty of that year and had expressed hope that it might lead to peace. Possibly he had become disillusioned by subsequent events, and by the unwillingness of so many Southern Cheyennes to accept the agreement. Just as likely, Meline, with no western experience or knowledge of Indians, misunderstood what Kit was saying. He may have been speaking about the Kiowas and

Comanches, who were more likely to be paired than the Comanches and Arapahos. Carson had emphatically stated, just the year before, that every effort should be made, for the sake of justice, to secure peace with the Arapahos and Cheyennes. He had tried to do so, while fighting the Kiowas and Comanches.[75]

Carson returned to Fort Garland in early August, in time to deal with some new problems. His own account is laconic, but Doctor Gwyther adds some colorful details that agree in essentials with Carson's version. On the morning of August 6 some Utes of Shavano's band, who were encamped in the vicinity, reported that one of their young men, missing for some days, had been found dead nearby. According to Gwyther, Carson had been discussing the disappearance with some Utes at the fort when they heard a woman wailing, at which Kit said, "Doctor, they've found him; he's been murdered; that's his mother crying, and thar will be trouble." Carson and the doctor examined the body; Carson says they concluded he had been struck with a blunt instrument, but Gwyther says he suspected poison. The boy had apparently staggered to the point where he was found. A party of New Mexicans was employed making adobes for the fort, and suspicion fell on one of them who had left shortly before, but Carson, after investigating, could find no good evidence against any of the group. According to Gwyther, the laborers all fled and the Anglo settlers in the area sent their families to the fort for protection.[76]

Gwyther describes a tense council with the Indians, at which the "majority were violent enough, advocating full reprisals against the citizens." Casador, whom Gwyther describes as "a young and very influential Chief," and who had been staying at the fort while receiving medical treatment, was seen by the doctor "holding a quiet conversation apart with Carson." The chief, says Carson, explained that a prominent medicine man had "ill feeling against the deceased boy" over a young woman. The medicine man was particularly vehement in his demands for vengeance, and Casador suspected him of the crime. According to Gwyther, Carson pointed out to the Utes that they had no real proof against anyone and had nothing to gain from "an unjust war," and persuaded them to accept "one hundred sheep and other presents." Carson's influence was "sufficient to smooth the tempest." When Carson reported the matter on August 9, however, he was pessimistic, saying that most of the Utes had departed "declaring their intention of having revenge."[77]

Kit believed "war with the Utes is inevitable," though he had "done everything in my power, short of compromising the dignity of the U.S.," promising justice when proof of the crime was found. The Utes were already inclined to war, he thought, by "the persuasions of the Jicarillas Apaches." He requested reinforcements of as many cavalry as could be spared, and two howitzers to protect the post.[78]

Ten days later, however, things had apparently been settled. The Utes had agreed to accept a payment for the life of the young man. Carson implies that Lafayette Head, the Indian agent, had a major part in the settlement. He himself found the agreement "distasteful as inferring that blame is to be Attributed to the whites for the Indian's death," which would be remembered by the Utes as another grievance. At the moment, however, "the Utes appear perfectly satisfied." Gwyther says the chiefs suspected the medicine man but considered him too powerful to move against. Carson had displayed his usual caution, insisting on as many reinforcements as possible, and once again, with the help of Casador and Agent Head, he had avoided bloodshed. If anyone had called him an alarmist, he probably would have pointed out that he was the man on the spot.[79]

In 1924 Kit Carson Jr. added some dramatic details to the story, saying that during the council Casador and his wife sat on either side of Carson holding knives, ready to "defend him with their lives." Josefa had taken the children into another room, and Albert Pfeiffer reassured her that "I have every soldier fully armed and ready to act the moment trouble starts and now the Indians know it." He also says that when his father rode out with forty troopers to make the payment, the Utes demanded more and when Carson refused, one threatened to strike him with a rawhide rope. Kit said to his men, "If he does I will kill him, then we will fight if we all have to die together." Kit Jr. was eight years old at the time and related his story fifty-eight years later; even if he was as truthful and as averse to exaggeration as his father, his account probably should be taken with a grain or two of salt. That Carson was capable of running such a bluff need not be doubted.[80]

The younger Carson also says that one of the soldiers had "fixed up a dose" for an Indian begging liquor, to make him sick, and that this had in fact caused the death of the young Ute. Gwyther had suspected poison, but he blamed the medicine man; Carson says nothing of such an explanation. If one of his men had foolishly poisoned the man, even though accidentally, there was ample reason not to let the Indians know of it, but his concealment of the truth even in an official report would cast doubt on his desire to do justice, though he could plead the danger of war as justification. He had repeatedly complained of the difficulty of punishing whites for crimes against Indians. He had condemned Chivington and the officer who flogged the Cheyenne, and he and William Bent had especially excoriated hunters who left poison where Indians might consume it.[81]

Carson had abundant reason for concern just then, for at about the same time there was similar unrest, for a similar reason, among the Utes at Cimarron. One of Kaniache's sons was shot dead by a Mexican herder in a dispute over a sheep. The killer fled to Fort Union for protection, and the Utes demanded that he be turned over to them. Colonel James Meline happened to be at Fort Union then, and he says that Kaniache was "not unreasonable," though his other sons could scarcely restrain their "devilish passion." A number of regular troops were passing through at the time, and their presence may have induced the chief to wait for legal redress. Carson, hearing about the trouble from Lucien Maxwell, thought matters at Fort Garland too tense for him to go to Cimarron, but he sent Albert Pfeiffer in his place.[82]

The Utes were temporarily assuaged, though a little later General Carleton himself had to take a detachment to Cimarron to quiet the Utes who, angry at the suspension of their rations, were even threatening Maxwell. The food issues at the agency had exceeded the appropriation for the purpose. (Lucien's inside knowledge enabled him to make the lowest bid, but purchases for Bosque Redondo had greatly inflated prices.) The general summed up the situation: "We have taken possession of their country, their game is all gone, and now to kill them for committing depredations solely to save life cannot be justified. . . . We have either to feed the Indians or let them kill the stock of the people at the risk of collision, which will lead to war. This is not only a true story, but the whole story." This was a familiar story to Kit Carson and demonstrated why he resisted locating the agency at Cimarron, in spite of the benefit to his old friend Maxwell.[83]

After Pfeiffer returned to Fort Garland with the details of events at Cimarron, Carson was even more worried. There was "great dissatisfaction" among the Indians, the settlers feared for their lives and property, and "distrust Existing among both parties renders war Still more imminent." The Indians were "Exasperated by broken promises, nearly desperate from want And fearful that justice will not be done them in the Case of the Mexican that Killed the Ute near Red River [Cimarron]." Kit was still hopeful that trouble could be avoided. At the next court session, the killer of Kaniache's son "should (I hope will) be promptly and legally punished"; the Indians should see that "the Scales of Justice Are evenly balanced and our obligations to them faithfully observed." Kaniache and another Ute chief had visited him on August 23; they were "Earnest for revenge" and would accept "no pecuniary Consideration." They would be satisfied if the Mexican herder were "found Guilty and hung." If not, the army must prepare for war. In fact, the case was transferred to a court in Santa Fe, then dismissed for lack of evidence. Kaniache eventually accepted a settlement of $400. What part Carson played in persuading him to settle is not evident; the chief's visit to Fort Garland indicates that he still trusted Kit, but his realization of the probable consequences of war must have been a major factor.[84]

Because of the general unrest, Carleton ordered the establishment of a small post, Fort Stevens, east of the Sangre de Cristo range across from Fort Garland. Kit wrote to the post commander, Captain A. J. Alexander, on September 12, praising his swift action in checking out reports of trouble at a ranch in the area, but characteristically pointing out that "perseverance And Caution in pursuit of Indians Are requisite." He promised prompt cooperation in case of trouble, including his personal services. Three days later he advised Alexander to check out another report of trouble, offering to reinforce him if necessary and adding that the captain should inform any Utes near his post, "for they will make the best Spies you Could have."[85]

Life at Fort Garland was seldom quiet for long. Colonel James Rusling, an army inspector, came by on September 20, in company with two other distinguished guests — Governor Alexander Cummings of Colorado and Kit's old California acquaintance, General William Tecumseh Sherman. When they had first met in 1847 Carson was already a national celebrity and Sherman an obscure lieutenant; now Sherman was one of the Union's greatest heroes and second in command of the U.S. Army, with a jurisdiction that included the Great Plains and the Rocky Mountains. Governor Cummings was there to negotiate a new treaty with the Utes. Rusling would write a book about his western travels, including some vivid and informative passages about Kit Carson.[86]

Sherman, who was making an inspection tour, came to Fort Garland with strong opinions about the "Indian problem." Everywhere on his travels citizens had besieged him with petitions for military protection from the Indians, and he had come to suspect that they were prompted by equal parts alarmism and the desire for profitable garrisons in their neighborhoods. He had traveled through Colorado without an escort, and he saw no sign, except for the constant petitions, that people expected an Indian war.[87]

Sherman was pleased to renew acquaintance with Carson. Rusling quotes him thus: "These Red Skins think Kit twice as big a man as me. Why his integrity is simply perfect. They know it, and would believe him and trust him any day before me." This was a considerable testimonial from a man notoriously tough-minded, acerbic, and unsentimental in his judgments. The general himself, in recalling the visit eighteen years later, spoke mainly of Carson's children, whom he remembered as "boys and girls as wild and untamed as a brood of Mexican mustangs," who "ran through the room in which we were seated half clad and boisterous." Clearly Kit's ideas on disciplining children were not those of General William Tecumseh Sherman. Carson expressed some concern about the children's future, which was "a source of great anxiety. . . . I value education as much as any man, but I have never had the advantage of schools, and now that I am getting old and infirm, I fear I have not done right by my children." Sherman offered to provide for the education of one of Carson's children, and did later take on William Carson as a ward for a few years, finding him "a good-natured boy, willing enough," but having "no taste or appetite for learning," which would probably not have surprised anyone who knew his father at the same age.[88]

Impressed as Sherman was with Carson's character and influence with the Utes, he was evidently not persuaded by his opinions about the situation in the Ute country. Writing from Fort Lyon a few days later, he said, "The Utes are harmless and peaceable, and the Cheyennes and Arrapahoes are off after the buffalo, God only knows where, and I dont see how we can make a decent excuse for an Indian war." Carson had convinced him that the Utes had "been reduced to a condition of absolute poverty that is painful to behold." Governor Cummings confirmed this, describing their appearance as "that of squalid wretchedness, many of them being nearly naked." Still, Sherman did not see them as much of a threat, believing the Fort Garland garrison, now four companies, strong enough to control them, and "if scattered hunting parties steal a cow or sheep now and then to keep from starving, I will not construe it war." This was a reasonable and humane sentiment from a man often depicted as an advocate of exterminating the Indians. What Sherman, who then had little experience of Indian war, failed to realize was that the owners of the animals would construe the stealing of "a cow or sheep now and then" as war, and react accordingly, as in the killing of Kaniache's son. What Carson feared was that the next such incident, on one side or the other, would be the last straw, given the current state of mutual apprehension and resentment. Either Kit had failed to convince the opinionated general, or he had expressed less concern than shown in his reports to Carleton.[89]

Governor Cummings's attempts to work out a new agreement with the Utes had little success. They complained bitterly about the Evans treaty of 1863 and the changes the Senate had made in it, and pointed out that even the revised version had not been fulfilled. Their agreement to the treaty was, they said, "such an agreement as the buffalo makes with his hunters when pierced with arrows: all he can do is lie down and cease every attempt at escape or resistance." When Sherman and Cummings argued that their only hope lay in going on a reservation, says Rusling, Ouray thought it would be hard to persuade his people of this until the Cheyennes and Comanches had gone first—in other words, until the whites had subdued their enemies and they could settle in one place without fear of raids. Sherman's comment was, "They will have to freeze and starve a little more, I reckon, before they will listen to common sense!"[90]

Rusling also was deeply impressed with Carson and described him at some length, both in his 1874 book about his journey and in a letter to one of Carson's biographers, Edward Ellis, in 1884. These two documents are important to any student of Carson because of the picture they provide of his character and his opinions about the Indians and their relations with the whites, and because of their lengthy, ostensibly verbatim quotes from his speech. Many of Rusling's impressions were conventional enough. He had expected a small, wiry, reticent man, and found "a medium sized, rather stoutish, florid, and quite talkative person instead." There was nothing of the "border ruffian" about him: "He impressed you at once as a man of rare kindliness and charity, such as a truly brave man ought always to be."[91]

In 1884 Rusling wrote, "He was very conscientious, and in all our talks would frequently say: 'Now, stop gentlemen! Is this right?' 'Ought we to do this?' 'Can we do that?' 'Is this like human nature?' or words to this effect, as if it was the habit of his mind to test everything by the moral law." All this sounds hopelessly Victorian, yet it also sounds rather elaborate for Rusling to have invented completely. Like some other things in his 1884 letter, it is not in his published book. Unlike many people, Rusling found Carson talkative, as Meline did at the same period. In these later years he had the confidence to express his opinions freely and to differ with important men. He had raised the question of moral responsibility in testifying before the Doolittle committee, in his letters to Doolittle and to Carleton from Fort Riley, and in his report with Bent for General Pope.[92]

Kit Carson, as Rusling saw him, was the Indians' "stout friend—no Boston philanthropist more so." "He did not hesitate to say, that all our Indian troubles were caused originally by bad white men, if the truth were known, and was terribly severe on the brutalities and barbarities of the border." The Indians, Carson said, were "very different from what they used to be, and were yearly becoming more so from contact with border-ruffians and cow-boys." According to Rusling, Kit "had never known an Indian to injure a Pale Face, where he did not deserve it; on the other hand, he had seen an Indian kill his brother even for insulting a white man in the old times." This does not, obviously, sound like a description of Carson's years as a mountain man, full of clashes with Blackfeet, Apaches, and other tribes, in which the trappers definitely considered themselves the wronged parties. Aside from the possibility of selective memory on Carson's part, it is likely that he was talking specifically about the Utes, and perhaps the Cheyennes and Arapahos, about whom Sherman would have asked especially. For Rusling, they were all just "Indians." Even with these tribes, as we have seen, Kit had had his uncomfortable moments; Rusling had obviously been impressed by Carson's general comments on the declining character of the tribes due to white contact and alcohol. He had certainly expressed himself forcefully about the "brutalities and barbarities of the border" on other occasions. Ironically, as if anticipating modern writers who would scorn him as a "brutal racist," Carson "pleaded for the Indians, as 'pore ignorant critters, who had no learnin', and did'nt know no better,' whom we were daily robbing of their hunting grounds and homes." Rusling quotes another sentiment: "What der yer 'spose our Heavenly Father, who made both them and us, thinks of these things?" No one else (with the exception, we will see, of Jessie Frémont) remembers him uttering such pious remarks. Yet he came from people who flocked to camp meetings, and Padre Martínez recorded him as having been

P E A C E M A K E R

baptized "according to the rite of the Anabaptists," who were surely known as Baptists back in Missouri. In his autobiography he had sought religious meaning in the death of Ann White. A little after this interview with Rusling, he reportedly called on Jesus in an hour of desperate need. Perhaps old, inherited patterns of speech and thought were now asserting themselves.[93]

It is important to note that Rusling himself, a volunteer officer from New Jersey with no previous western experience, was not especially humanitarian in his expressed attitudes toward Indians. He was impressed on meeting a Delaware chief who had served gallantly as a scout for the army, but he did not doubt that a single war-whoop "would speedily transform the gentle Fall-Leaf into a hideous savage again." The Sioux were "but little removed above the brute creation," and his brief observation of the Utes only confirmed stereotypes of their "shiftlessness" and "general squalor." The experience "dispelled many of the poetic ideas about the 'Noble Red Man' . . . that we cherish in the east." In fact, he "could not help regarding the great majority of them, as but little above the wild animals, that roam over the Plains"; they were even "infinitely below the colored race." The "noble exceptions," like Ouray, "only proved the rule." For Rusling, the best thing to be said for the Utes was that Carson thought well of them: "Kit Carson—a good judge—credited them with being the bravest and best Red Skins he had ever met, in all his wide wanderings."[94]

Rusling's longest quote from Kit is unsurpassed as a record of his manner of speech. Rusling gave two versions, in his 1874 book and his 1884 letter, and they differ slightly, the latter being fuller and slightly more convincingly colloquial. The subject was the most notorious "barbarity of the border" and its perpetrator. Kit's words here are taken from Rusling's 1884 letter:

. . . jist to think of that dog Chivington, and his dirty hounds, up thar at Sand Creek! Whoever heerd of sich doings 'mong Christians! The pore Indians had the Stars and Stripes flying over them, our old flag thar, and they'd bin told down to Denver, that so long as they kept that flying they'd be safe enough. Well, then, one day along comes that durned Chivington and his cusses. They'd bin out several days huntin Hostiles, and couldn't find none nowhar, and if they had, they'd have skedaddled from 'em, you bet! So they jist lit upon these Friendlies, and massacreed 'em—yes, sir, literally massacreed 'em—in cold blood, in spite of our flag thar—yes, women and little children, even! Why, Senator Foster told me with his own lips (and him and his Committee came our yer from Washington, you know, and investigated this muss), that that thar durned miscreant and his men shot down squaws, and blew the brains out of little innocent children— pistoled little papooses in the arms of their dead mothers, and even worse than this!—them durned devils! and you call sich soldiers Christians, do ye? and pore Indians savages! I tell you what, friends; I don't like a hostile Red Skin any more than you do. And when they are hostile, I've fit 'em—fout 'em—and expect to fight 'em—hard as any man. That's my business. But I never yit drew a bead on a squaw or papoose, and I despise the man who would. 'Taint nateral for men to kill women and pore little children, and no one but a coward or a dog would do it. Of course when we white men do sich awful things, why those pore ignorant critters don't know no better than to foller suit. Pore things! Pore things! I've seen as much of 'em as any man liv'in, and I can't help but pity 'em, right or wrong! They once owned all this country yes, Plains and Mountains, buffalo and everything, but now they own next door to nuthin, and will soon be gone.

Anyone who knows how people talk in the rural West and Midwest will have some idea of how Kit, with his "slow, quiet speech," might have sounded speaking these words.[95]

Although Kit had "no gift of swearing," it is possible that Rusling bowdlerized a bit in places. The reference to Chivington as a "dog" may have been the polite version of a familiar phrase meaning essentially the same thing. That Carson regarded the Colorado colonel and his men with contempt is implied in his testimony to the Doolittle committee in 1865. There may have been a special reason, aside from the obvious ones, for Kit's anger. The Doolittle committee, according to one of their staff, had been told that Chivington, returning to Fort Lyon after Sand Creek, had boasted of his deeds and "Striking his hand, red with the blood of innocents, upon his breast," had exclaimed "in effect" that "I have eclipsed Harney and Kit Carson, and posterity will speak of me as the great Indian fighter." Since Carson referred specifically to his conversations with Senator Foster and the committee, it is quite likely he had heard this story. Here was another example, recalling the Ann White incident, of the undesired consequences of his fame.[96]

Even so severe a critic as Clifford Trafzer was somewhat mollified by Carson's denunciation of Chivington. The "Fighting Parson" had violated a truce, as understood by the Cheyennes, in itself a crime to Indians and to mountain men who had adapted to their values. He and his men were, in Kit's eyes, cowards who would have run from active hostiles ready for battle. And they had killed primarily women and children, not fighting warriors. According to Rusling, Carson specifically and bitterly decried men who would deliberately aim at women and children, even infants, and "even worse than this"—probably a reference either to rape or to the mutilations reportedly inflicted on the dead Cheyennes.[97]

This all poses some interesting questions. Carson is quoted as saying that he "never yit drew a bead on a squaw or a papoose." Unless Rusling was elaborating here, which cannot be ruled out, Kit was saying that he had not, in the attacks on the Indians near Lassen's ranch in 1846, or in the retaliatory strike on the Klamaths a little later, or in any other of his many fights, actually aimed, knowingly and with intent to kill, on a woman or child. Certainly in his autobiography he never specifically refers to the deaths of noncombatants, for what that is worth. In any case where he was with a party attacking an Indian camp, the fighting men would have covered the retreat of their families. But saying that he had not drawn a bead on them is not to say that none were harmed. Thomas Martin, for instance, reported seeing a dead woman in a canoe after the Klamath fight. Carson knew that women and children had suffered and sometimes died from cold and deprivation during the Jicarilla war in 1854 and during his campaign against the Navajos. At Adobe Walls he had made a tactically necessary surprise attack on Dohasan's Kiowa camp—not under any truce, like Black Kettle's Cheyennes—and although the women and children had made good their retreat, casualties among them were always a possibility in this type of attack. But to Carson these would not have been the same thing as deaths deliberately inflicted with malice aforethought. General Carleton had prohibited any deliberate killing of women and children in all the campaigns Carson carried out for him, while recognizing that such deaths could not always be avoided "in the rush and confusion of a fight." This was an inescapable problem of Indian warfare, and of any war not fought by armies drawn up for formal battle well away from civilian habitation. Kit was perhaps allowing his conscience some leeway here, and he may have exercised a selective memory. Nonetheless, he was, in Rusling's judgment, expressing a convincing indignation, setting out the way things ought to be.

Rusling heard Carson say that, without urgent measures, the Indians would "soon be gone." It would appear, at least according to Rusling, that Ouray had come to the same conclusion. During the council with Governor Cummings, as the colonel reports his words, the chief observed, "Long time ago, Utes always had plenty," but then "White man came, and now Utes go hungry a heap." His conclusion was, "White man grow a heap; Red man no grow—soon die all." He and Carson were undoubtedly reasoning from the same empirical evidence.[98]

In early October, shortly after his visitors had left, Carson wrote to headquarters in Santa Fe, answering General Carleton's request for a report on "the present State And temper of the bands of Utes and Icarilla Apaches." Apparently, Sherman had let Carleton know that he thought the New Mexico commander's fears of Indian hostility, and his requests for troops, were exaggerated, and Carleton may have wanted the on-the-spot opinion of the man who happened to be one of the most respected experts on the subject. Kit was still apprehensive about the prospect of war. At the time he had returned from the plains last fall there had been reports of depredations, principally the killing of stock, from the Purgatoire River east of the mountains to Tierra Amarilla, some two hundred miles west. Three settlers had also been murdered and a young woman wounded. The Utes were discontented about their annuities and their agents. Albert Pfeiffer investigated and held a council, with no satisfactory result. "This was And is Still," said Carson, "the Condition of the Indians near the Tierra Amarilla."[99]

Both Carson and Pfeiffer were of the opinion "that an outbreak might occur At any moment," and if the outbreak could not be immediately subdued, "the loss of life and property in the Settlements would be Enormous." When Carson had arrived at Fort Garland, he had found the settlers "overwhelmed with Apprehensions of outrage"; his scribe went on to describe "A gloomy cloud of dread" hanging "like the Sword of Damocles" over the country. Horses and cattle were being stolen or killed and the Indians showed a "defiant bearing." The situation had not changed: "The Indians complain of frauds in their treaty by which they were despoiled of their lands and Cheated our of their annuities, And Yet Another And More potent Cause of danger is destitution." They would not be restrained by any white man's laws from satisfying their hunger. There were, Carson estimated, some forty-five hundred Utes and Jicarillas in the area; it would be impracticable for the army, so far from any supply depot, to feed such a number. If need forced them to begin raiding, "as it Apparently Must do," over 5,000 settlers would be at their mercy.[100]

In Carson's judgment, "The feelings of Utes Against Mexicans . . . Are those of undying hate and hostility, fostered by years of warfare, impossible to eradicate." The only remedy was "An Exhibition of force" strong enough to punish depredations, and therefore to "Awe into Quietude" the resentful Utes. It would be "impossible And unjust to try And Confine their outrages to our Mexican citizens," whose right to protection was the same as "our own."[101]

The Jicarilla Apaches were "undoubtedly the worst at present," and had for the past year been "trying to instigate the Utes into a general warfare." He recommended once again that they be ordered to return stolen animals, and if they refused, a military operation should be commenced against them. They were continually stealing and inciting others by their example. In the 1850s Carson had frequently negotiated the return of stock stolen by both Indians and settlers, blaming the latter more than the Indians who were driven to steal. Apparently the situation had changed, in his eyes, and he was fed up with the Jicarillas, who had never been favorites of his. He sensed that the situation between Indians and settlers had grown much worse: "From the Purgatoire to the Tierra Amarilla A feeling of discontent rages Among near 5000 Indians. . . . Any slight Circumstance may precipitate into a war, And Such Circumstances Are more likely to occur from the traditional hatred Existing between the Utes and Mexicans And the continuous Never tiring Exertions of the Icarillas." Carson and General Carleton knew that the Jicarillas, like the Utes, were desperate because they were dependent on government rations, which were not being issued because the commissioner of Indian Affairs, far away in Washington, would not let the New Mexico superintendent spend the money. There was no coordination, as Carson had pointed out, between the military and the Bureau of Indian Affairs, so the army's only way of dealing with the danger was to overawe the Indians or, at the worst, defeat them in war.[102]

One reason that Commissioner D. N. Cooley gave for not issuing rations to the Utes and Jicarillas at Cimarron was that they would have no incentive to settle down and start supporting themselves by farming as long as the government was feeding them and they could move about and hunt. As the Jicarillas' historian points out, the commissioner had no idea of the actual conditions under which these people were living. The notion of not feeding Indians as a means of forcing them into farming would occur to officials from time to time, with unfortunate if not tragic results. Although Carson had occasionally grumbled about Indians becoming dependent on government bounty, he had repeatedly insisted on providing subsistence to make stealing unnecessary. General Carleton accepted the responsibility of feeding the people at Bosque Redondo if their farming attempts failed. He and Carson were not so wedded to a theory about "civilizing" the Indians, or a principle opposed to supporting the idle, as to ignore the immediate well-being of actual human beings.[103]

Carson had, he reported, attended Governor Cummings's council with the Tabeguache Utes. Although "everything passed off well," only a small part of the Tabeguaches, themselves a small part of the Ute people, had been present. Carson denied any desire to create unnecessary apprehension—had someone suggested that old Kit was getting jumpy, or losing his nerve?—but his apprehensions were shared by Albert Pfeiffer and by "old Western Settlers." Considering the mountainous country and "My Knowledge of the habits and Character of the Indians," he believed that if it came to war the best troops to fight it would be Mexicans, "As they Are More Energetic And untiring in pursuit, Enduring a large Amount of physical fatigue And when well officered their Courage is unquestionable." This was a change from his opinions of some years earlier, but no one could have spoken with more experience on that subject than Colonel Kit Carson of the First New Mexico.[104]

The day after writing this report, Kit received word of an incident that seemed likely to confirm his worst fears. Kaniache and his band had been camped in the vicinity of Trinidad, Colorado, at the northern end of Raton Pass, arousing the apprehensions of the settlers. The details remain hazy, but apparently the alleged theft of some horses and corn by the Utes increased the tension; someone sent word to Captain A. J. Alexander at Fort Stevens, who moved quickly to the area with his company of the Third U.S. Cavalry. When the captain confronted Kaniache, the chief reportedly declared "that the land belonged to him, and when his children were hungry he would come and take food for them." Alexander thought the chief and his people displayed a "bad spirit." Calling Kaniache an "old scoundrel" and shaking a finger in the chief's face, he told him to come back and talk again in the morning.

When Kaniache did not appear the next day, Alexander declared that he would fight him, although he had only sixty men against a supposed Ute strength of several hundred. Word came that the Utes were attacking a ranch on the Purgatoire, and the cavalry galloped off. Supposedly, the Indians had taken some corn, and the Hispanic rancher's son had shot one of the Utes. By one account, the Indians ran to their horses to take up a defensive posture and at that moment Alexander and his troopers came into view, saw the Utes ready to engage them (or so the captain assumed), and charged. The Utes fled, leaving, by Alexander's count, thirteen comrades dead on the field, while the cavalry sustained one killed and two wounded.[105]

Carson got word of the affair from Alexander the next day, October 4, 1866. His first thought was, "This is bound to result in a general War with all the Utes." He sent warning to the settlers in the San Luis Valley, seeking to call up volunteers for the anticipated war: "Tell the Mexicans now is their Chance if they will now Meet . . . and pursue the Indians in the rear of these Mountains they Can do So." Two days later, some Utes, following good guerrilla strategy, attempted to make off with the Fort Stevens horse herd while Alexander was absent.[106]

Almost immediately, however, there was a break in the threatening situation. On October 6, Ouray rode in to Fort Garland to see Kit and tell him that he was not going to fight, "and would do his best to restrain his Young Men." Carson told the chief to bring his band in near the post and camp. He also wrote to Governor Cummings to bring the annuities intended for the Utes to Fort Garland and to make plans with him, Carson, for feeding the Indians near the post: "I shall have to feed them, until some other Arrangements Can be Made." He was a bit more hopeful as he wrote to headquarters in Santa Fe: "Events may probably occur during which I may if desirable to you be able to Make peace with them All—please Advise me how to Act Should Such opportunity occur." The next day, however, he was writing directly to Carleton that "war is inevitable, in fact it is already upon us," and requesting troops, pack saddles, and arms to issue to the settlers. He was already making plans to form a supply depot eighty to a hundred miles from the fort, "from which I can operate against the Indians." As he had told Rusling, fighting Indians, when they were hostile, was his business.[107]

His increased pessimism was caused by reports that Kaniache's band, pursued by Alexander, had killed several men on the Huerfano and captured "An American Lady" and four children. Kaniache was headed for Mosca Pass, leading into the San Luis Valley, and Alexander "I believe Cannot possibly overtake them." Mosca Pass was where Ouray had left his band when he came to Fort Garland to talk to Kit. If Alexander came upon them, especially in company with Kaniache's people, Carson feared the aggressive cavalryman would attack them all, and his hopes for making peace would be ruined. He still hoped "this unfortunate circumstance may be evaded," and sent a sergeant with Ouray "to assure any parties about to attack them that they were under the protection of the government." By the ninth, Ouray was back with perhaps a hundred lodges. Carson had sent out a detachment to escort them and "prevent any difficulties," and he had them camp near the post.[108]

Ouray had done more than this in the cause of peace, however. He had sent word to Kaniache to come in and quit fighting, and as Carson succinctly explained, "Yesterday all the hostile Indians came in under the guidance of Ulay [Ouray] and I made a treaty with them; they agree to return all stock stolen in the last disturbance." The grounds for Carson's action, as he explained it, were thoroughly pragmatic:

My action in this matter has been influenced solely by a desire for the public good; we were totally unprepared for a campaign. Citizens were not acquainted with the state of affairs and would be surprised and massacred and I could afford them no assistance; anxiety and dread prevailed everywhere; without sufficient troops or means of effecting successful war, I was forced into making terms with them, this may be only temporary, but it was the best I could do under the circumstances.

He began issuing rations immediately, subject to Carleton's approval.[109]

Kit pointed out that the Utes had allowed the captive white woman, Mrs. McGuire, and her children to return home unharmed, "and none of those outrages that makes humanity shudder have been perpetrated here—the loss of life and property will be small." Outrages against humanity were a well-established feature of the stereotype of Indians held by most white Americans. Carson knew from experience that they were also sometimes a reality, if not quite so common as inflamed imaginations made them. He also knew that, for many white people—the folks back in Boonslick, for example—even a small loss of life among frontier settlers was ample justification for massive retaliation—for a Sand Creek. In the past, he himself had talked of punishing hostile Indians severely enough to insure that they would never dare take the warpath again. During the Mescalero and Navajo campaigns, General Carleton had made it quite clear that his subordinates were not to make local "treaties" on their own initiative before the hostiles had been thoroughly subdued. Now Kit had seized the first opportunity for peace, merely on the condition that all captured stock be returned, explaining, "Uninfluenced by personal feeling, I have acted in this matter solely for the benefit of the public and confidently rely on the approbation of the General Comdg." In his opinion the war was over for the present, and it was not necessary to send more troops. Carleton, however, ought to come and talk to Kaniache personally; his "long Knowledge of Indian character" would allow him to judge what further action to take.[110]

Carson's stated reasons for making peace were undoubtedly genuine, so far as they went. He had a handful of troops, and if any large number of Utes chose to retreat into the mountains and wage a prolonged war, the cost in blood and money could be considerable. At the same time, he obviously wanted to convince Carleton and other superiors that his actions had been both wise and proper. After all, the Utes had not done a great deal of damage, and some of the loss of life, he pointed out, had been due to the fact that some settlers had disregarded Ouray's timely warnings. Perhaps Kit's special feeling for the Utes can be read between the lines. (He said nothing of his past relations with Kaniache, who had once saved his life.) An unsympathetic observer could have said that he was making excuses for them, minimizing their depredations. He praised Ouray's "straight forward conduct" during the crisis: "No white man could act better, he was not only prompt in notifying me of his intention to keep peace, but he also warned all the settlers of the Upper Huerfano." In emphasizing Ouray's role as peacemaker, and in minimizing the damage the Utes had done, Carson made the best case for his own decision to make peace at the first opportunity while deflecting any charge that he was soft on Indians who committed "outrages." The Utes with Kaniache were anxious about women and children left at Cimarron, who should be returned to them at once; and a woman and children held prisoner by whites on the Purgatoire should also be restored, "I having promised it to them." He was also anxious that "no unfortunate circumstance" should happen "to the prejudice" of Ouray, "he having acted in better faith than most white men in the recent troubles." In other words, he feared some whites, military or civilian, might take some action against the chief in the heat of emotion.[111]

Kit Jr. tells of an incident which he says happened when his father gave a feast for the Utes, after the talk that produced the peace agreement. His sister Teresina, shocked at a Ute's declaration that the shoes he was wearing came from a white woman he had killed, refused him food, and he struck her with his quirt. Kit was so angry that he "rushed at the fellow and would have punished him severely and perhaps have killed him then and there, but mother seemed to realize what the result would be and begged father to let it go." The backcountry man's reaction to an insult to one of his womenfolk is credible, but he, like Josefa, realized very well "what the result would be" when he cooled down a little. The suggestion that she could indeed cool her husband down, coming from their son, is perhaps more reliable than the details of the incident.[112]

One reason why Kit thought Carleton should talk to Kaniache personally was that he had heard a story, apparently not from the Ute chief himself, that an army officer at Cimarron had given some Utes whiskey, had gotten drunk himself, and had tried to kill Kaniache, being prevented by Lucien Maxwell. The truth of this tale remains obscure (there are widely differing versions), but Kit believed that if true it would "account in a great measure" for the subsequent trouble with Captain Alexander, and in his opinion, "it cannot be too severely dealt with." It is possible that there was another reason for getting Kaniache's side of the story, though the record is not clear. At any rate, on October 16 Carson, on instructions from Carleton, ordered Captain Alexander to forward a detailed report of his actions, which would "embrace the reasons why you commenced operations of hostilities against the Ute Indians before receiving instructions from the District Commander [Carleton] and your justification for attacking them."[113]

It is not clear whether Carson himself had doubts about Alexander's actions. Kaniache reportedly claimed that his only casualty in the fight with Alexander was the man shot by the rancher just before the cavalry arrived and attacked him, whereas Alexander claimed that thirteen warriors were killed. Alexander's judgment in the matter is hard to assess. He had an excellent record as a cavalry commander in the Civil War, but he had only recently come to the West. Believing the settlers near Trinidad in danger, he had taken a tough line, attacking when he thought the Indians were defying him and menacing the ranch on the Purgatoire. If the rancher had indeed killed a Ute, the people on the place might well have been in danger from Ute retaliation. What Kit Carson would have done in the same situation is hard to say, but

General Carleton, not generally considered soft on Indians, apparently had some questions. Carleton's own superior, General Winfield Scott Hancock, eventually commended Alexander for "promptness to determine, bravery in the encounter, and vigor in the pursuit," preventing the difficulties that "a more timid policy" might have caused. At the same time, Hancock also praised the "sound discretion of Brevet Brig.-Gen. Carson, who, in the absence of detailed instructions, arranged a peace with the beaten Indians, when honor had been satisfied and they had been sufficiently punished." Let no one say that the army had made any errors in the affair, or was letting the Indians off easy![114]

The lion's share of credit for restoring peace should obviously go to Ouray, who took immediate action to assure Carson of his peaceful intentions and then persuaded not only his own band but Kaniache's to go to Fort Garland, ending the "war" a few days after it had begun. Kaniache too, after the initial encounter with Alexander and some acts of retaliation, evidently realized that his only good option was to surrender to his old friend and hope for the best. If the two had played the part of warrior chiefs they would only have subjected their people to misery—especially with winter near—and for many, death. Carson also deserves credit, however, for in spite of his stated belief that war was inevitable, and his plans for conducting it, as soon as the opportunity for peace appeared, he seized it, "in the absence of detailed instructions" as General Hancock said, and seemingly with some misgivings about whether his superiors would approve. He had done everything he could to prepare for war, and he was happy to have peace instead. The pattern, as we have seen, was one he had followed before. His official reasons were quite pragmatic and might be deemed sufficient if he had not revealed other feelings at various times. At any rate, Ouray and Kit had accomplished something more difficult in its way than the fictional feats of Hawkeye and Chingachgook: they had prevented a possible repetition of the disastrous war of 1854–55.

Shortly after, Carson, Lucien Maxwell, and Indian agent John Henderson met with Kaniache and Ancotash, another Ute chief, in Taos to discuss the recent events. Henderson at least became convinced that the troubles were caused by Captain Alexander's hasty action. They decided that Kaniache and his people should return to Maxwell's place at Cimarron for now, and Carson himself took them there, leaving Fort Garland on October 22. Alexander's wife reports that Kit told her that he had deposed Kaniache as chief, putting Ancotash in his place.

White authorities did on occasion "depose" chiefs who displeased them, elevating others in their places, without necessarily affecting the chiefs' actual standing with their people, as Carson would surely have realized. Certainly Kaniache remained a prominent figure among the Utes for years to come.[115]

If Carson had any doubts about Alexander's actions, they do not seem to have affected his relations with the captain when his company joined the Fort Garland garrison immediately after the outbreak. Kit charmed, and was apparently charmed by, Alexander's young wife Eveline, who found him "a most interesting, original old fellow." She rode out with him to visit the nearby Ute camp and reported on his reception there: "It was pleasant to see the effect old Kit's appearance had on these savages. Instead of the sullen, stolid appearance I had always noticed on them before, their faces brightened with smiles as they held out their hands to him with the salutation, 'Como le va?' or the Indian, 'Hough!' " He shook hands with one old woman who, he said, had accompanied his Ute scouts during the Navajo campaign.[116]

Ouray evidently met Eveline Alexander's expectations as a Noble Savage, being "the finest Indian I have seen yet, good looking, dignified, and from all I can learn, honest and reliable." This information probably came from Carson, who declared, "I shall always treat Oulay just like a white man, for he is a good Injun." To twentieth-century ears this may sound condescending. Perhaps Kit meant it that way, or perhaps he had no better words readily available for expressing his respect and liking for the Ute leader. What white person in his time would not have thought that the highest compliment to a "nonwhite" was to be treated "just like a white man?" What he meant may have been more like the words his amanuensis found, praising Ouray's "straight forward conduct" and declaring that the chief had "acted in better faith than most white men."[117]

JUST ANOTHER CALL TO DUTY

Affairs in the San Luis Valley were relatively quiet for some time after the trouble with Kaniache was settled. Kit took Josefa (pregnant once more) and the children back to Taos for the winter, and apparently stayed there himself for some time. He may have decided at about this time to resign from the army. The volunteer troops were being discharged, and he had no rank in the regular army. He had promised General Carleton that he would remain in the service until the general left New Mexico. In October 1866, Carleton received word that he would be relieved of the command of the District of New Mexico in the near future. The Bosque Redondo experiment had proved fearfully expensive, and the strong-willed, dictatorial commander had made many enemies in the territory who charged him with a variety of financial irregularities, political offenses, and even with disloyalty. He asked for a court of inquiry, but General Grant thought "no good to the service could result." He remained in command until the following April, but in December 1866 he was ordered to turn the Bosque Redondo over to the Bureau of Indian Affairs. For Carson, the impending departure of Carleton, with whom he had made a seemingly mismatched yet effective team, provided another reason to give up the military life as he had proposed to do nearly four years before.[118]

He was back at Fort Garland in early 1867, and once again he saw the situation as gloomy. On February 15 he wrote to Carleton, apparently in answer to inquiries through channels from General Hancock about the attitude of the Utes toward the 1863 treaty. Once again he had the chance to explain some complicated and uncomfortable facts of life to people in power. He was trying to obtain the best possible conditions for the Indians, but also to point out to the authorities what they might have to face if those conditions were not met. The government had tried for some time to make Kaniache's Muaches join Ouray's Tabeguaches on one reservation. Carson pointed out that the Muaches had not been represented at the making of the 1863 treaty and, as far as he knew, had never consented to join the Tabeguaches. The two "would not make peaceable neighbors," for the men of each band were "each jealous of the sagacity and prowess of the other, which would lead to continual brawls," rendering the security of the frontier settlements "very precarious." That all these people were designated as "Utes" by whites, or even that they shared language and culture, did not make them one "tribe." Their perception of themselves was very different from the white man's. The old mountain man found it necessary to explain these important facts to the greenhorns.[119]

"When I arranged the peace which now exists with the Mohuaches," he said, he had made no promises and had told them they could not go east of the mountains. They would have observed that rule, he believed, if he had not been ordered to take them back to Cimarron. They appeared to be "well satisfied that they must eventually succumb to the advancing step of civilization, and, that in a War with the whites, they have nothing to gain, and everything to lose." The Muaches, he noted, claimed territory from the San Luis Valley to the "Rabbit Ears" on the plains in northeast New Mexico as their reservation.[120]

He recommended that, if the Jicarillas were removed somewhere, it be with the Tabeguache Utes, not anywhere near the still hostile southern Apaches: "They are a brave and warlike tribe, and should be kept apart from those Indians not at peace with us."

Ouray and the Tabeguaches had "expressed themselves much dissatisfied with the present treaty," declaring that the agreement they had signed "is very different from the treaty as it now exists." Ouray was absent somewhere, but Carson intended to get a statement from him to forward to Carleton. In the meantime, if the government intended to remove the Indians west of the mountains, in accordance with the treaty, "I would urge upon the necessity of preparation for War—," for "the Tabequaches will not relinquish their claim to the 'San Luis Valley,' without a Desperate and Sanguinary struggle." Though friendly to the whites, "they will not give up their birthright until the last man of the 'Great Utah Nation' lies beneath his native soil." Kit must have impressed the seriousness of the situation on his scribe, by calling forth this Cooperian rhetoric. He closed by assuring Carleton that "your knowledge of Indians" would suggest that these "forebodings" were no "Chimera," but were "'facts' stern in their nature and terrible in their effect." If the authorities decided that the Utes must move, "We must be prepared for a War to the knife, and knife to the hilt."[121]

Whether due to Kit's warnings or not, the government made no attempt to coerce the Utes into accepting the 1863 treaty, and the war he had feared did not come to pass. If it had, he probably would have been unable to fight it, for his health was now failing visibly, as evidenced by photographs from the period. As his face and body thinned, he lost the old fierce expression, acquiring a rather wistful look. The man who had thought nothing of riding horseback across half a continent now traveled in an army ambulance. He submitted his resignation from the volunteer service in July 1867.

Kit had kept his promise to General Carleton, who had been relieved of the New Mexico command in April, though he remained in the territory for a few months more. The general's many enemies rejoiced, anticipating the end of the Bosque Redondo reservation. But in his nearly five years as military commander in the Southwest, Carleton had made dramatic and irreversible changes, summed up by Howard Lamar: "Carleton had by no means solved the Indian question in New Mexico and Arizona, but henceforward it would center around the problem of controlling specific outbreaks in specific regions. Warfare and anarchy—the natural state of New Mexico since Juan de Oñate [c. 1600]—was now to be the exception rather than the rule." Carleton had freely awarded much of the credit for this accomplishment to Kit Carson. Although hostilities with some Apache groups would continue until the 1880s, the resistance of the Navajos was broken. The Bosque Redondo experiment might eventually be judged a failure, but the endless cycle of Navajo wars was ended. The Navajos themselves concluded from the disaster that they must avoid war with whites at all costs. Latter-day critics of Carleton's Navajo war would hold that, if the raids on and enslavement of Navajos had been stamped out earlier, the campaign and the Bosque Redondo would have been unnecessary—an argument resting on the assumption that the responsibility for conflict lay chiefly on the heads of New Mexicans.[122]

While Carson waited for his release from military service, he was still in command at Fort Garland, and still on call for the kind of job for which Kit Carson the great scout was uniquely qualified. In 1866 Congress had authorized the enlistment of Indian scouts on a regular basis, and in August 1867 Carleton's successor, Colonel George Getty, ordered Kit to Maxwell's place to enlist and organize three companies of Ute and Apache scouts. He was not expected to command them, for it was recognized that he was no longer physically capable of that, but he was the man who could persuade them to sign up. Among the reasons for such recruitment, aside from the clear military necessity for their services, was the belief that scouting would keep the active younger men occupied and out of trouble, while their pay and rations would help support their families and reduce the need to prey on settlers' livestock.[123]

Around this time Captain Henry Inman, a quartermaster officer at Fort Union, became acquainted with Carson and Lucien Maxwell, both of whom he later celebrated in his book *The Old Santa Fe Trail*. Romantic and imaginative, Inman provides a good deal of misinformation about Carson's life, but also some eyewitness anecdotes that may deserve more credence. He was greatly impressed by the "barbaric splendor" of Maxwell's "baronial" lifestyle, and he describes sleeping on the floor of the main hall of the Cimarron ranchhouse, with "the mighty men of the Ute nation laying heads and points all around me."

I have sat there in the long winter evenings, when the great room was lighted only by the cheerful blaze of the crackling logs roaring up the huge throats of its two fireplaces . . . watching Maxwell, Kit Carson, and half a dozen chiefs silently interchange ideas in the wonderful sign language. . . . But not a sound had been uttered during the protracted hours, save an occasional grunt of satisfaction on the part of the Indians, or when we white men exchanged a sentence.

Like others, Inman noted that Carson was a devoted player of seven-up, and that he usually won, "for he was the greatest expert in that old and popular pastime that I have ever met." Inman says that Carson was at Cimarron on July 4, 1867, when Maxwell celebrated the day by firing off a rusty old cannon, and managed to mutilate his thumb so badly it had to be amputated a few days later. Inman and Carson held kerosene lanterns while an army surgeon performed the operation at Fort Union, Maxwell refusing an anesthetic.[124]

Inman was surprised to find his boyhood hero, Kit Carson, to be "a delicate, reticent, undersized, wiry man, as perfectly the opposite of the type my childish brain had created as it is possible to conceive." It is Inman who tells one of the most famous Kit Carson stories. At the Fort Union sutler's store he purchased a sensational periodical on whose front page was depicted "a gigantic figure dressed in the traditional buckskin," his arm around the waist of "the conventional female of such sensational journals," whom he had just rescued from the several Indians now lying dead around them—the figure, supposedly, of Kit Carson. When Inman showed this interesting publication to Carson, Maxwell, and several army officers, Kit "wiped his spectacles, studied the picture intently for a few seconds, turned round, and said, 'Gentlemen, that thar may be true, but I hain't got no recollection of it.' " The twinkle in his eye can only be imagined, but the discrepancy between his actual and fictional lives must have been old hat to him by now.[125]

Carson gave up command of Fort Garland in early November 1867, and soon after was mustered out of the volunteer service, after more than six years. He was nearly fifty-eight, in poor health, had no regular source of income, and had several young children and a wife to support. With the help of William Bent, he was seeking an appointment as superintendent of Indian affairs for Colorado. Had the citizens of the territory been aware of the great Indian fighter's denunciation of Colonel Chivington and the Sand Creek massacre, and of his insistence that the troubles with the Cheyennes and Arapahos arose largely "from aggressions on the part of the whites," many of them might have opposed the appointment, in spite of his reputation. As it happened, he received the position in January 1868.[126]

By then he must have known that his time was running out. In the fall of 1867 he met Doctor H. R. Tilton, the post surgeon at Fort Lyon, Colorado, on the Arkansas River near William Bent's home. They took to each other immediately. Tilton, being an amateur trapper, was happy to receive advice from a professional who declared, "Some of the happiest days of my life were spent in trapping." Like many others, the doctor was delighted to be on friendly terms with a living legend. It is not certain if Tilton was the first medical man to diagnose Carson's condition, the most notable symptom of which was a pain in the chest, nor is the doctor clear on whether he did diagnose the problem at the time of their first meeting, though it was probably far enough advanced at the time for him to do so. Carson was suffering—quite literally—from an aneurysm of the aorta. A weakness in the wall of the blood vessel had caused a portion within the chest to swell like a balloon. Physicians at the time could diagnose the condition but could do nothing for it. (Sherlock Holmes fans will remember that, in *A Study in Scarlet*, Doctor Watson was able to diagnose an aortic aneurysm by placing his hand on the victim's chest; Arthur Conan Doyle, a physician himself, knew whereof he wrote.) According to Tilton, Carson blamed the problem on a fall he had suffered while riding in the mountains in 1860. He was leading his horse down a steep slope by a lariat, intending to let go if the animal fell. When the horse did fall, he released the rope, but it caught him and dragged him several feet over rocks, causing severe bruises.[127]

In fact, such an accident is unlikely to have caused damage of this sort to the aorta, especially within the chest cavity. Likely causes for such a condition include a hereditary weakness, high blood pressure, or syphilis, any of which could have affected a man his age. Kit was stocky and stout in his middle age, and many people remarked on his ruddy complexion; he was also a heavy smoker. Venereal disease was common in nineteenth-century America, and one of the effects of the fur trade was to spread it far and wide among the western tribes, from whence it would be passed back to other trappers and traders. It would be an especially bitter irony if Carson's intimacy with the Indians as a young mountain man led to his contracting his fatal illness in this manner, yet it would once again reflect the way in which his life and his fate were linked with theirs. There is, however, little indication of his suffering from any other symptoms of the disease, except failing eyesight (he wore spectacles to play cards), which was hardly remarkable at his age. It is also conceivable that the bullet wound he suffered in the skirmish with the Blackfeet in 1835 had caused some damage to the blood vessel, although his description of the wound is not precise enough to make this more than conjecture; if so, it took a very long time to catch up with him.[128]

Having received his new appointment, Kit moved his family from Taos to Boggsville, Colorado, on the Arkansas a few miles above Fort Lyon, just outside present Las Animas, in the spring. It was a considerable family, with six children and a seventh on the way, and probably some Indian dependents besides, the sort of large, patriarchal family that he had grown up in. William Bent lived nearby.

Some time in 1867 the artist Henry Cross painted Carson, as he says, from life. In conformity with the legend, he could not portray Kit Carson as a uniformed military commander, and certainly not as a civil servant, even though in photographs he invariably appears in uniform or respectable broadcloth. Instead, he painted the Old Scout, dressed in buckskins and moccasins, with powder horn and shot pouch, and leaning on a long, muzzle-loading plains rifle, pointing off into the distance as a scout or guide should. The background is a rugged landscape of red rocks that might well be found in the Navajo country. Behind and below him, apparently standing on a ledge below the lip of a ravine, is an Indian with long hair and a simple headband, also holding a rifle, his gaze following Carson's pointing finger. They are obviously allies, and here the artist showed a certain insight, quite possibly intending the Indian to represent a Ute scout. If the picture was painted at Fort Garland, there would have been plenty of Utes available for models. Perhaps he is Chingachgook to Kit's Hawkeye, but his position makes him clearly subordinate to the white man, following a tradition in American portraiture from the eighteenth century of using Indians as an allusion to frontier achievement. Kit himself is clearly aged, wasted and hollow-cheeked, much of his stockiness gone. Cross has painted the sky behind his head as dark and threatening, perhaps because he knew he was painting a man who did not have much time left.

Soon after the move to Boggsville, Kit received another summons. The government had decided to negotiate a new, definitive treaty with the Utes in Washington, where the chiefs could be given the traditional tour to impress them with the power and grandeur of the United States. As superintendent, Carson was to accompany them and assist in the negotiations. Though in no shape for such a trip, he went along.[129]

Kit Jr. said many years later that his father "felt it was just another call to duty." Having accepted the position of superintendent, he had a responsibility to assist in treaty negotiations. When the younger Kit told the story in 1924, most white people would have found that a perfectly satisfactory explanation. In the late twentieth century, many would charge that he was simply participating in another operation for cheating the Indians out of their birthright, another treaty that the Indians did not understand and that the government would discard when the occasion suited. (In fact, within a few years Washington would abandon the whole procedure of making treaties with Indian tribes, in favor of treating them as "wards of the government.") Carson does not seem to have left any specific record of his reasons for going, but Doctor Tilton wrote a few years later, "It was a great tax on his failing strength to make this journey; but he was ever ready to promote the welfare of the Utes, who regarded him in the light of a father." Tilton's most likely source for such an interpretation is Carson himself. It is hard to see what reason Kit would have had for dissembling with the man who attended him in his final days, and there is no way of knowing if he deceived himself. As agent and later as superintendent, and as an elder and important man, he was in any case addressed as "Father Kit." The Indians would have expected him, as representative of the Great Father, to observe certain paternal obligations, in seeing to their welfare. Tilton saw him as "a true knight-errant ever ready to defend the weak against the strong, without reward other than his own conscience." This is Cooper's hero again, but in this case, Tilton is giving his interpretation of Carson's motives for going to Washington. Kit might well have found it necessary to explain to his physician why he would undertake such a journey in his condition, and Tilton would describe his motives in the most Romantic language. In addition, however, he could consult with eastern doctors about his illness.[130]

Carson had, since 1854, been urging the need for a reservation for the Utes, a refuge from the effects of white expansion. During all that time the government had put the question off, failing to ratify treaties or radically modifying them in the interests of economy, adopting tempo-rary expedients like the Cimarron agency, and all the while whites had settled on Ute hunting grounds. Now through much of the Colorado

Rockies, the San Luis Valley, and east of the mountains, there were white men's towns, ranches, and travel routes. There was ample reason to think that something had to be done, and few white men had Kit's understanding of the situation with the Utes. His ideas on the subject remained much the same—establish the Utes on a reservation remote from white settlement, provide food, livestock, and farm implements, and educate them in the ways of "civilization." Nothing he had seen in the last fourteen years had altered his belief that close contact with advancing white settlement was destructive to the Indians. Moreover, he knew that whites once established in an area were unlikely ever to give it up. As the relentless pace of expansion continued, the need to set aside an "inviolate" area for them became more urgent. The question was whether any reservation would remain inviolate, and whether the Utes could be persuaded to accept the situation. Kit had helped negotiate the Treaty of the Little Arkansas, and just two years later it had been deemed necessary to work out another agreement with the same tribes, at Medicine Lodge in 1867, which also began unraveling within a short time.

Carson set out by stage to Fort Hays, Kansas, where he boarded the railroad for Washington. Ouray, Ancotash, and some other chiefs had already left for Washington in January. Kaniache may have made the trip east with his old friend. The government had designated Ouray the chief spokesman for the Utes, but his support among his own people was far from unanimous. Carson was present at the White House when the Ute chiefs were presented to President Andrew Johnson on February 5, 1868, along with the governor of Colorado, Agent D. C. Oakes, and other whites charged with negotiating the treaty.[131]

Treaty negotiations were apparently combined with the grand tour of Washington, but the document was eventually signed on March 2. Frank Reeve, in his study of federal Indian policy in New Mexico, says, "The proceedings were probably expedited by a round of 'fire-water.' " This is the stereotypical view of Indian treaty negotiations, which assumes that Indian chiefs were all childish fools easily duped into signing anything by use of beads and alcohol, and white negotiators were all unscrupulous swindlers. But the Utes were not under serious illusions about the main outlines of the situation. Many of the purposes of the whites were a mystery to them, and the concept of exclusive land ownership was particularly alien. But in 1866 they had told Governor Cummings that the 1863 treaty, even in its original form, was "such an agreement as the buffalo makes with his hunters when pierced with arrows—all he can do is to lie down and cease every attempt at escape or resistance." Ouray may well have spoken those words to Cummings in 1866, yet Ouray and other chiefs had signed that treaty, and the 1868 agreement was essentially the same; its provisions now extended to all the Utes. It is very likely that Kit Carson told them, at length and with all the persuasiveness that his experience and his standing with the Utes could provide, that this was the best deal they were likely to get, and that time was not on their side. From the less than perfect historical accounts, this was the view of Ouray, whose biographer goes so far as to say, "The 1868 treaty contained all the elements of Ouray's strategy for the Utes."[132]

The treaty set aside most of the western slope of Colorado, roughly one-third of the present state or over fifteen million acres, for the Ute tribe. The basic elements of the "civilizing" program were written in: a schoolhouse, with teacher, for the children at each agency; carpenters, farmers, millers, and blacksmiths to assist and teach the adults; sawmills and gristmills; and a homestead provision to encourage the Utes to take up separate farms. They would also receive annuities of clothing and blankets for thirty years, plus cattle and sheep, and these provisions were probably more immediately compelling to a people in great need than the long-range prospect of drastic cultural change. Moreover, whites were to be excluded from the Ute lands, with the significant exception of roads and railroads—an unavoidable exception, given the extent of the reservation and its location in this era of railroad building, but a potentially fatal one.[133]

The Ute chiefs had signed over their hunting grounds east of the Rockies, in the San Luis Valley, the North and Middle parks, and the Yampa River valley. In fact, they had really lost those lands years before. The white man's towns, ranches, and mines were everywhere; his cattle and sheep drove out the game and grazed on the grass that had fed the Utes' horses and the buffalo. The Utes were hard-pressed wanderers on what had been their own land, increasingly less tolerated by the newcomers who believed themselves to possess an unquestionable right to the soil. Little Raven, the Arapaho, had said of the lands on the Arkansas that "our friends are buried there, and we hate to leave that ground." Undoubtedly, the Utes felt the same grief at giving up what they had always considered theirs. The new treaty, like all such documents, promised that the reserved lands would be theirs "forever." They did not yet know just how finite a period that could be in Indian-white relations.

Carson apparently did not leave a record of his thoughts about the treaty of 1868. Since he had for so many years urged the need to set aside for the Utes lands far removed from white settlement, we can only assume that he saw the treaty as the closest thing to his hopes that was possible under the circumstances. If whites would actually respect the reservation, the Utes might have room and time to adjust to the radical transformation of their world. He knew that frontier whites, Anglo and Hispanic, wanted whatever western lands seemed valuable and believed that an Indian had no rights that a white man was bound to respect. These were Carson's own people, and he knew their ways. For that very reason he had a powerful sense of a crisis at hand, demanding action before it was too late.

The alternative, of course, is to view Carson as the "good company man," the good soldier who served his government and his society by helping negotiate an agreement dispossessing the Utes of their homeland—just one more job. However, for a desperately ill man to undertake several thousand miles of travel by stage and railroad, leaving his pregnant wife and young children without knowing if he would ever return, would require a monumental sense of duty indeed, especially when the basic outline of the result was already clear. If the summons to Washington was "just another call to duty," as his son believed, the question of whom he owed the duty to may never have occurred to him. It simply did not fit the realities of the situation as he understood them.

The treaty being signed, the chiefs made a tour of the East, visiting New York and Boston. On the way Kit consulted at least one distinguished medical man, a Doctor Sayre in New York, and met an old friend. Jessie Benton Frémont provides some interesting information about Carson in these last days, although her details may be suspect (she places the events in "the summer of '67"). John Frémont wrote her from Washington that he had met Kit there, "greatly altered by suffering," and asked Jessie to meet Carson in New York and persuade him to stay at their home on the Hudson. She met him at the home of a friend, where he came into the library leaning on the shoulder of her son. He would not let her come to him where he was staying, saying, "No, you couldn't do that—I'm alive yet," but he was so exhausted he had to rest before talking.[134]

The boy had come to the door of the hotel room, where he met several Indian chiefs and saw Carson lying down. Kit knew immediately that the youngster was a Frémont, and introduced him to the chiefs. He had, he explained to Jessie, told Doctor Sayre that he only wanted to get home with the chiefs and "die among his own people." The doctor could only confirm that he was near death, and that it might be postponed until he got home if he avoided fatigue or excitement. Kit showed amusement when he noted, "And the doctor said I must not do any drinking." The "border ruffian" image was hard to shake. He explained to Jessie: "I must take the chiefs to see Boston. They depend on me. I told them I would. Then we go home, straight. My wife must see me. If I was to write about this, or died out here, it would kill her. I must get home, and I think I can do it." He would not let Jessie show her grief, saying he must avoid excitement: "No don't—you must help me get home."[135]

After seeing Doctor Sayre, he told her, he had returned to the hotel room, then lay down.

Suddenly the bed seemed to rise with me—I felt my head swell and my breath leaving me. Then, I woke up at the window. It was open and my face and head all wet. I was on the floor and the chief was holding my head on his arm and putting water on me. He was crying. He said "I thought you were dead. You called your Lord Jesus, then you shut your eyes and couldn't speak." I did not know that I spoke. . . . I do not know that I called on the Lord Jesus, but I might— It's only Him that can help me where I stand now.

This is another of the very few instances where Carson is reported as expressing his religious ideas. One may suspect Jessie Frémont of a desire to edify her readers, but such words would not have seemed strange to people in backcountry Missouri or New Mexico. She did not record the identity of the Ute chief who aided Carson.[136]

Kit took the Union Pacific to Cheyenne, Wyoming, then went by stage to Denver, where he had to rest for three days before returning home to Boggsville. It is said he made his last campfire twenty-five miles south of Denver. Josefa met him with a carriage at La Junta on April 11. His daughter Josefita, or Josefine, was born two days later. Kit Jr. says, "It was not until then, I believe, that father realized how far gone he was and was forced to go to bed." Perhaps it was the boy who had not realized his father's condition before. Doctor Tilton saw him shortly after his return, and found him much worse: "His disease, aneurism of the aorta, had progressed rapidly; and the tumor pressing on the pneumo-gastric nerves and trachea, caused frequent spasms of the bronchial tubes which were exceedingly distressing." It might have seemed that things could not get worse, but they did. On April 27 Josefa Carson died suddenly, presumably from complications resulting from childbirth, leaving seven children, the youngest two weeks old. She and Kit had been married twenty-five years. Tilton, who describes her simply as "tall and spare" and as having "evidently been a very handsome woman," says, "Her sudden death had a very depressing effect upon him."[137]

He wrote asking Josefa's sister, Ignacia Bent, to come and help with his children. Guild and Carter find his letter "remarkably cheerful and optimistic," even speaking of her staying "until I am healthier," but according to Tilton he realized his time was short. His backcountry conception of manhood required, above all else, courage in the face of death. The doctor visited him frequently, but the spring rise of the Arkansas made fording the river difficult, so on May 11 he was moved to Tilton's quarters at Fort Lyon.

Kit passed the time, "in the interval of his paroxysms," telling of his experiences, and Tilton sometimes read to him from Peters's biography. The doctor, writing some six years later, clearly treasured the memory of their brief association, but it was bound to be brief, for "his disease rapidly progressed and he calmly contemplated his approaching death." Several times he pointed to his chest and said, "If it was not for this . . . I might live to be a hundred years old."

Tilton explained to him that he might die of suffocation, or more likely by the rupturing of the aneurysm. "He expressed a decided preference for the latter mode. His attacks of dyspnoea were horrible, threatening immediate dissolution." Chloroform, which gave some relief, threatened his life, but Carson preferred the risk. He could face death, but he did not pretend indifference to suffering: "He begged me not to let him suffer such tortures, and if I killed him by chloroform while attempting relief, it would be much better than death by suffocation." His dependence must have troubled him, for he asked Tilton, "What am I to do, I can't get along without a doctor?" When Tilton replied, "I'll take care of you," Kit said with a smile, "You must think I am not going to live long."

On the night of May 22 he was a bit more comfortable, but he had to sit up nearly all the time. He was coughing up some blood. Alois Scheurich, an old friend who had married Carson's niece, Teresina Bent (whom Kit and Josefa had raised after Charles Bent's death in 1847), had come to Boggsville with Ignacia Bent, and was staying with him at the fort. He and Tilton were with Carson on the afternoon of May 23 when Kit suddenly called out, "Doctor, Compadre, Adios." Tilton saw a gush of blood from his mouth and said, "This is the last of the general." The doctor remembered: "I supported his forehead on my hand, while death speedily closed the scene. The aneurism had ruptured into the trachea. Death took place at 4.25 P.M., May 23rd 1868." Carson was buried with military honors beside Josefa at Boggsville. The next year the bodies were moved to Taos. Although Kit had been a Mason since 1856, they were reburied with the rites of the Catholic Church. Nearby lay the bodies of Charles Bent and Padre Martínez.[138]

Five days after Carson's death, at Fort Sumner, General Sherman and Samuel Tappan, acting as peace commissioners, opened a conference with the chiefs of the Navajos. The commissioners had already decided, from reports they had received, that the Bosque Redondo experiment was unlikely to prove successful in the foreseeable future. The question was whether the Navajos could be trusted to remain peaceful if they were allowed to return to their homeland in northwest New Mexico and northeast Arizona, or if they should be removed to Indian Territory. There was considerable opposition in New Mexico to the tribe going back to its old lands, both because of fear of renewed raiding and the belief that great mineral wealth lay in that region. The Navajos, on the other hand, were determined to return home and planned to resist any attempt to send them anywhere else. One writer has suggested that Kit Carson had advised Sherman to allow the Navajos to return home, and has even quoted words he supposedly used at this very conference, saying, "General, I'm not so sure the Great Spirit means for us to take over Indian lands. . . . Let me lead them back while they still have the will to live." Kit had, of course, been dead five days when the conference opened, which casts doubt on this quote. It is not clear when, if ever, he might have spoken such words to Sherman. General Carleton had written in February to the adjutant general of the army, protesting strongly against the idea of returning the Navajos to their old home or to Indian Territory, giving all his old arguments about the renewal of hostilities. He noted that Carson was then in Washington and urged that he be consulted on the matter. There seems to be no clear record of Carson's having changed his mind about the Bosque Redondo, though the continued failure to produce crops there, the deaths from disease, and the attacks on the reservation by Comanches, might have caused him to rethink the experiment. It would not have been surprising if Grant or Sherman had consulted him on the question while he was in Washington. However, Sherman said nothing of such a consultation in his 1884 letter to Carson's biographer, Edward Ellis, seemingly indicating instead that their last meeting was at Fort Garland in 1866. The general seems to have been in the West during most of the period when Carson was back east. When Sherman suggested moving the Navajos to Indian Territory, Barboncito spoke for his people: "I hope to God you will not ask me to go to any other country except my own." The Navajos had suffered greatly at Bosque Redondo—from disease, deprivation, Comanche raids, and demoralization from their dependence on government rations. They were not willing to try another strange place. Sherman concluded that it would be best to remove them to a part of their traditional lands as far as possible from white settlements, and a treaty to that effect was signed on June 1, 1868.[139]

For the Navajos, their release from Bosque Redondo was a deliverance from bondage and exile, as their traditional accounts make clear. They returned home determined never again to endure such experiences as they had undergone during the Fearing Time. The cycle of raid and counterraid with the New Mexicans did not resume, even though federal legislation ending peonage and Indian slavery proved difficult to enforce in New Mexico. Arguments over the return of captives went on for many years. General Sherman's opinion of the Southwest was that it was a barren region that cost the government more than it was ever likely to repay. He undoubtedly believed that there was no great loss to whites in turning a considerable area over to Indians, and apparently he was convinced that the Navajos would keep the peace on their home ground, while removing them elsewhere might lead to war. Events proved him right. The federal government would actually increase, rather than decrease, the size of the Navajo reservation in later years, testifying to the general belief in the valuelessness of the land the Navajos considered the most beautiful and desirable on Earth.[140]

Sherman had acted on one of the cardinal points of the reservation system, the "alternative to extinction" that had been developed after the mid–nineteenth century. He had removed the Navajos away from contact with the whites to give them space and time, in the hope of averting conflict and decline. In this case, it worked. Kit Carson would probably have been disappointed by the failure of the reservation experiment at Bosque Redondo, but he would almost certainly have found the establishment of peace and the eventual resurgence of the Navajos pleasing. He would also have seen it as proof that the essential idea, which he had so often reiterated, of saving something for the Indians before it was too late, was right. But by a particular historical irony, while he would receive both credit and blame for many things he neither did nor thought, he would receive no credit for his real ideas or intentions.

8. Conclusion

A man's a man for a' that.
Robert Burns, "Is There For Honest Poverty"

Kit Carson was a good type of a class of men most
useful in their day, but now as antiquated as Jason of the
Golden Fleece, Ulysses of Troy, the Chevalier La Salle of the
Lakes, Daniel Boone of Kentucky, [Jim] Bridger and Jim
Beckwith of the Rockies, all belonging to a dead past.
William Tecumseh Sherman in Edward Ellis, *The Life of Kit Carson*

Carson's early biographer, Edward Ellis, quotes an undated tribute to
him from a Salt Lake City paper, perhaps an obituary notice, proclaiming, "To the red man he was the voice of fate. . . . To them he was a voice
crying the coming of a race against which they could not prevail; before
which they were to be swept away." Ellis finds this an eloquent tribute
to "the matchless scout, hunter, and guide." Ellis, the dime-novel writer,
was a creator of the type of fiction that depicted Carson as "a great hero,
slaying Indians by the hundred," but few of Kit's contemporaries would
have doubted the truth of those words. Kit Carson was the symbolic
hero of white expansion in the trans-Mississippi West, expansion at the
expense of Indians. Ever since Benjamin Church, the frontier hero had
been first of all an Indian fighter.[1]

In the twentieth century, as popular attitudes toward the Winning of
the West shifted, so did the Kit Carson image. In the 1920s Stanley Vestal
could celebrate both Kit Carson and Sitting Bull as representatives of a
heroic age with no sense of incongruity. In the 1950s Jack Schaefer could
condemn James Carleton's Indian policy and still admire Kit Carson. But
about 1970, with the Vietnam-era revulsion at the purified, triumphal
version of America's past, Carson had to take on a new role.

Then, Carson's very fame as the Western Frontier Hero, fame gained
largely in contests with Indians, made him suitable for a new role as villain. George Armstrong Custer had always been an equivocal figure—to

some a gallant cavalier, to others a glory-hunter—but came to be re-garded by many as the representative bloodthirsty, manic military man, prefiguring the U.S. commanders in Vietnam. But to effect the drastic revision in Western history that seemed appropriate and necessary, to underline the profound injustice now deemed to be the essence of that history, the villain should be someone who had always been held up for unequivocal admiration. Who better for the role than Kit Carson?

It is often asserted that Carson was hated, in his lifetime and since, by Indians in general and Navajos in particular. Beyond doubt, Navajos in the late twentieth century regard Carson as the persecutor of their ancestors. "It is not to be expected," write Guild and Carter, "that Kit Carson will ever become popular on the Navajo Reservation any more than General W. T. Sherman will ever become popular in the state of Georgia. The reasons are the same in both cases." But while Sherman has been the South's favorite devil for many years, there is some question whether Carson's dark eminence dates from the 1860s or developed more recently with the rise of Indian political consciousness in the 1960s and '70s.[2]

Aside from his position as a frontier hero, the supposed Navajo hatred of Carson rests upon the assumption that, since he administered their final military defeat, they must have despised him. Traditional Navajo accounts collected up to the early 1970s, while telling in often harrowing detail of the sufferings of the narrators' ancestors, seldom mention Carson at all. Although one account reports the contempt of a Navajo chief for that "very pure White Man" Kit Carson, who would not dare venture into the Canyon de Chelly, there is little indication that Kit was considered the sole author of their troubles by the generation that endured those trials, or by their descendents who heard the stories directly from them.[3]

In *Navajo Stories of the Long Walk Period*, the principal compendium of these traditional stories, Kit Carson is referred to, when mentioned at all, as Bi'éé' Łichíí'ii' (Red Clothes). In one account where the term is translated as "Kit Carson," it is also said to mean, "Red Clothes, referring to the soldiers," with no reference to a specific person. One of these traditional stories was told by a Navajo with the English name of Chester Arthur, before 1930. His unnamed translator may have added some assumptions. Arthur says, "About 1863, a Captain in the United States Army, called Red Shirt by the Indians, came to Red Lake, north of Fort Defiance, to make a treaty with the Navajos." Red Shirt told the Indians "they would have to stop stealing from the Mexicans, and from the neighboring tribes and each other. He told them they had made other treaties and broken them, but if they broke this one, it would be the last." The chiefs signed the treaty, but the young men stole the presents Red Shirt had brought, so he left to get more gifts. After he left the orator Nahtahlith made a speech scolding the young men and describing his vision of disaster. The white man would come back, not with presents but with "many soldiers, and Mexicans and Zuñis and Utes and Moquis—all armed with guns to kill them." The Navajos would be driven out of their country into the barren desert, running from place to place to place, hiding: "Many would starve, many more would be killed," and there would not be a single Navajo in the land, "not even a moccasin track." The people were afraid at first, but when summer came they planted corn, "even around Fort Defiance, which the Indians had burned down." Then Red Shirt came back with soldiers, and also Mexicans, Utes, and Zunis, all armed. He called in the chiefs and told them, "Yes, my friends . . . it is war." He smoked with them and explained, "My government has given orders to kill you all unless you come in and surrender. So come in to the fort to-day or else take your families and flee to the wildest mountains."[4]

Red Shirt thanked the chiefs for trying to keep the people from stealing: "But there is only one way to do that now, and tomorrow we begin to kill them." Beginning the next day, says Arthur, the soldiers rode out and killed the Navajos' herds, killed the herders, took the wheat for their animals, and cut down the corn. The Mexicans, Utes, and Zunis robbed them and stole their women and children. As winter came on, the people began to starve: "all except a few were rounded up and caught and taken away to Hwalte [Bosque Redondo]."[5]

Arthur describes what sounds much like the Carson campaign, and the story as given places the beginning of these events in 1863, as does the reference to Fort Defiance having been burned down, which happened after its abandonment in 1861. Red Shirt and his soldiers returned in the summer, when the wheat was ready to cut, and Carson marched to Fort Defiance and began his campaign in July 1863. The problem is with the name Red Shirt, or Red Clothes, assigned to the leading character in Chester Arthur's story. The most successful government agent for the Navajos before the Civil War was Henry Dodge, who served from 1853 to 1856 and was apparently highly regarded. According to Frank McNitt, the Navajos called him Bi'éé' Łichii, or Red

Shirt, because of his fondness for that color. This is recognizably the same name given to Kit Carson in other traditional accounts. Dodge was killed by Apaches in 1856 and obviously played no part in the wars of the 1860s. Yet Arthur's detailed story of Red Shirt's negotiations with and warning to the Navajo chiefs seems to fit Dodge better than Carson. The latter came to the Navajo country with his troops in 1863, after General Carleton's deadline had run out, and played no significant part in earlier councils. Perhaps Arthur had compressed events that occurred over several years, and the campaigns he describes include those of the 1850s and Canby's in 1860–61, all part of a time of great stress for the Navajos. Still, Arthur's dating of the council with Red Shirt at Red Lake in 1863 is confirmed by Henry Chee Dodge, a distinguished Navajo of the twentieth century, who specifically says that the Red Shirt referred to was "the man I am named after, Colonel Henry Dodge"—who by some accounts was Henry Chee Dodge's father by a Navajo wife.[6]

Seemingly, there was some confusion between Henry Dodge, the popular agent of the 1850s, and Kit Carson, the conqueror of the 1860s, at least in the mind of Chester Arthur, who told his story four decades nearer the events than the narrators of *Navajo Stories of the Long Walk Period*. Moreover, Henry Chee Dodge, the namesake and alleged son of Henry Dodge, also seems to identify the original Red Shirt as the leader of the soldiers of the Civil War period, or at least closely associated with them. It is hard to see how this could happen if Kit Carson had lived in infamy as the scourge of the Navajo people from the 1860s on. Arthur says, "Red Shirt was their friend, but the young men would not listen to him. They were so bad that nothing could be done with them and so they were destroyed." Whatever confusion may have occurred between Dodge and Carson, this is not the description of a man considered the Navajos' greatest enemy. Betty Shorthair says that one Navajo leader at Bosque Redondo, who helped give out rations, was named Bi'éé' Lichíí'ii' (Red Clothes or Kit Carson). Probably this man had adopted the name from Henry Dodge, but it seems unlikely he would keep it if it became associated with the man Navajos most hated. Certainly these questions indicate the difficulty of using traditional accounts for specific details and events, as opposed to general impressions. Perhaps this confusion between Dodge and Carson accounts for the charge made by recent writers that Carson is remembered by the Navajos as "a pretended friend who betrayed them," in Tony Hillerman's words. Carson is not known to have had a long and intimate association with the Navajos, such as would justify a feeling of betrayal. Possibly as Ute agent he was involved in some negotiations between that tribe and the Navajos. But Dodge was the one who could be considered a friend of the tribe over some years. Chester Arthur specifically describes Red Shirt as an army officer, and Dodge did serve as an officer in the New Mexico militia in a campaign in Navajo country in 1849.[7]

One story of the Long Walk period may prove an exception to this thesis. In the 1980s Tiana Bighorse and her white collaborator, Noel Bennett, set down her recollections the stories of her father, Gus Bighorse. Bighorse, born about 1846, was one of the holdouts who never went to Bosque Redondo. Here we have a record only one generation removed from the *Nahondzod*, though it is possible she may have mixed her own later knowledge with her memories of the stories her father told. The book's verdict on Kit Carson is succinct: "Once Kit Carson was our good friend. We called him Rope-Thrower. He could do tricks with the rope; that is why we called him that. We never [before 1863] think of him as a soldier, fighting against us or taking us prisoners. We Navajos will never have the heart to forgive Kit Carson—he has done the damage already." Here we may have an authentic record of specific animosity against Carson by a member of the *Nahondzod* generation, speaking for his people. Once again Carson is described as a onetime friend of the Navajos, sufficiently well known to have a name representing a well-known trait. Although some sources give Rope-Thrower as Carson's Navajo name, it is hard to find any others crediting him with such a skill. Because the book appeared in the 1980s, there is the possibility that a latter-day attitude has been placed in Gus Bighorse's mouth. The author is literate in English and her coauthor clearly regards the Long Walk as a shameful episode that has been covered up by white historians.[8]

If indeed the animosity of Navajos and other Indians toward Carson is of fairly recent vintage, arising from his prominence in Anglo-American written history, then we must review his past and present position in that history, in the light of ascertainable fact and historical context. What can we say about his relationships with Indians that is neither shallow polemic nor special pleading?

In 1914 Edwin Sabin wrote, "Kit Carson was not a great man, nor a brilliant man. He was a great character; and if it was not his to scintillate, nevertheless he shone with a constant light." Sabin was thinking in terms of the Carlylean great man, a model Carson clearly did not fit. It would be hard to prove that the history of the American West would have been

CONCLUSION

radically different if Kit had stayed in Missouri and made saddles for a living. The Utes and Jicarillas might have had a worse agent in the 1850s, yet given Anglo and Hispanic expansion and the overall policy and specific neglect of the federal government, the overall situation would surely have been much the same. James Carleton credited Carson with much of his success against Indians in the 1860s, but those operations would most likely have been carried out by someone, perhaps less effectively and thus at greater cost to whites and Indians alike. Carson and William Bent may have influenced the development of U. S. Grant's ideas on Indian affairs, leading to the famous Peace Policy, but that policy followed the basic outlines of the reservation system as devised years before.[9]

Nonetheless, there are reasons for taking an interest in Carson besides his symbolic status as a hero. He lived his life on or beyond the frontier, the zone of contact between cultures, and so he offers us some insight into the complexity of ethnic or "racial" relations in the West. Moreover, he was an adaptable man who played several representative roles in the changing West, a fact obscured by his image as the buckskin-clad scout. At different times he was a teamster, interpreter, trapper, guide, scout, rancher, Indian agent (i.e., a civil servant), field commander in major Indian campaigns, government peace commissioner and diplomatic representative, and an expert whose advice was sought by federal legislators and administrators. Above all, he was "the man who knows Indians," able to stand between the cultures in peace and in war.

Unquestionably, his fortuitous reputation had much to do with this versatility. After 1845 the name Kit Carson suggested on one hand the sort of heroism associated with Daniel Boone and Cooper's Leatherstocking, and on the other a special expertise—he had become "pretty well acquainted with the Indian tribes, both in peace and at war." He would be called on repeatedly to serve in one capacity or another as Indian-white conflict intensified. His reputation did not diminish as his responsibilities increased. The military and civil authorities who called on his services, with the notable exception of David Meriwether, were not disillusioned. Even granting the undoubted power of publicity—of the commercial hype that he did not encourage and that embarrassed him—his performance must have been satisfactory in the eyes of his superiors. Admittedly, most of them, in dealing with the Indians, were not the superiors of experienced mountain men and traders.

The previous pages have documented Kit's pride, sense of honor, and courage in combat. By all accounts, he was kind and tenderhearted—but when one so described is famous primarily as a fighting man, some questions must arise. The image of the soft-spoken, gentlemanly killer, "the mildest-mannered man who ever cut a throat or scuttled a ship," is quite familiar in American culture. Nathan Bedford Forrest, who came from a very similar backcountry family and culture, was noted for his soft-spoken demeanor in ordinary social life, yet he was notorious for his savagery in combat, especially toward Union black troops, and even toward his own men. Is the resemblance to his fellow backcountry man Kit Carson more than superficial, as many would urge today?[10]

Carson makes no bones about his hostile encounters with Indians and other people in his autobiography. His upbringing taught him that violence could be necessary for self-defense, and even obligatory in defense of honor and in retribution for wrong. Often in the autobiography he describes violent episodes in matter-of-fact, even clinical fashion. One Indian horse thief, he says, "showed fight. I was under the necessity of killing him." In the attack with Godey on the Indian raiders he gives more detail, but says nothing of his emotions and leaves out Godey's scalping of a man not yet dead, who had to be "put out of his misery," in Frémont's words. This apparent detachment offends Martin Green, who finds in it a "lack of feeling or emphasis, the absence of reflection and responsibility." But the narrator here was an illiterate man speaking to a scribe of limited fluency. It is doubtful if John Mostin thought to ask, "How did you feel when you did that, Kit?" Mostin and Carson both accepted that there were certain things you did not talk about, that were better left unsaid. One cannot conclude that he killed without emotion simply because he did not beat his breast in public; the social conventions of the time did not really allow a man to do that.[11]

Admittedly, the emotions that Carson reveals are sometimes unedifying. Describing the fight with the Crow horse thieves in 1833, he emphasizes that he was with the majority who insisted on "satisfaction" beyond recovering their horses—that is, on having a fight. In fact, fighting the more numerous Crows with the advantage of surprise could well have been safer than being pursued in turn, but Kit does not mention that, apparently thinking his audience would understand the trappers' motives. Recalling the retaliatory attack on the Klamaths in 1846, he describes the burning Indian huts as "a beautiful sight," explaining, "I thought they should be chastized in a summary manner." He adds that Frémont "arrived too late for the sport," words Martin Green finds deeply offensive. But most of Carson's associates, probably most of his American contemporaries, would have regarded a pursuit of thieves to recover property, even if violence was necessary, as perfectly legitimate. So would most members of the Indian tribes with whom he associated, including the Crows; two Cheyennes accompanied the trappers in the first incident. Certainly most frontier whites, and most Indians, would have seen retaliation on those who killed their friends as legitimate, even obligatory.[12]

Carson had spent much of his life in regions where there was no law or system of justice that all the diverse peoples recognized as legitimate or would submit to. Between Indian tribes there was no way of redressing serious grievances—except by the occasional peace agreement—other than war. War was usually small-scale, raids for taking livestock or captives, or revenge expeditions to kill some of the enemy. Although many writers describe this activity as a sort of dangerous game, different in kind from the bloody wars between nation-states, it was deadly indeed for the people involved, especially when it persisted over years and even generations. In Lawrence Keeley's judgment, "primitive" warfare was far more costly, proportionately, than that of "civilized" societies, and massacres did occur from time to time that were highly destructive to these small societies. Keeley points out how the "savagery" of "primitives" has been used to justify colonialism and conquest, but nonetheless, he rejects the idea of the unique bloodlust and destructiveness of Western civilization.[13]

The mountain men whom Kit Carson joined in his youth sought not dominion but profit. They did not intrude their violent presence into a world of peace and natural harmony. They would have snorted at the "Noble Savage" in the abstract, but he made his appearance in their thinking and their writing nonetheless. Flatheads, Nez Perces, and Shoshones were popular in that role; Kit Carson extolled the courage and general virtue of the Utes. Not surprisingly, the tribes pointed out for their noble qualities were also distinguished as friends and sometime allies of the mountain men and were, like the trappers, the enemies of the powerful and aggressive Blackfeet.

Undoubtedly, the mountain men came to the Rockies with a full roster of prejudices. But in the mountains they had to live in the Indians' world, to a great extent by the Indians' rules. Those who celebrated unbridled freedom, and the occasional sociopaths, probably did not flourish, for life as a trapper in the Rockies demanded the ability to get along with people different from oneself.[14] Skill in violence was valuable, but indiscriminate violence was another matter. When Joseph Walker found that members of his party had killed Paiutes on suspicion of stealing, he quickly and effectively brought them under control—too late, as it turned out.

Almost no one suggests that Kit Carson was an antisocial loner or a casual killer; those who knew him indicate quite the contrary. The closest thing to an exception among those with extended acquaintance is Charles Preuss, who deplored Carson's attack, with Godey, on the horse thieves on the Old Spanish Trail. Like so many then and later, Preuss found the stealth and surprise of guerrilla warfare to be cowardly and dishonorable. The scalping, in spite of statements to the contrary, was a widespread Indian custom, and was practiced by the tribes with which Carson and Godey were best acquainted. There is no clear evidence that Carson ever took a scalp, and also no strong reason to believe that he did not.[15]

Edward Beale described how Kit "mourned like a woman, and would not be comforted" after San Pasqual, not so much for the dead but for the women at home. Admittedly, the expression "tenderhearted as a woman" was conventional at the time. Joshua Chamberlain, the Union hero of Gettysburg and many other bloody battles, took it as a great compliment when a fellow officer told him, "General, you have the soul of the lion and the heart of the woman." Such tenderness, of course, was permissible when a man's courage was considered beyond question, as with Chamberlain or Carson.

Nineteenth-century Americans were generally far less troubled than we are by the idea of a warrior, a man with blood on his hands, who was also kind, tenderhearted, and chivalrous. Indeed, the two strains seemed to many to be complementary, likely to be found in the same man. Although they were familiar with the "fighting mad" warrior, the "incarnate devil in an Indian fight," they believed that the highest and truest courage was associated with control of the passions, with strength of will. Thus, a truly brave man would have the strength to be kind and compassionate; cruelty was likely to be the attribute of a coward. When Chamberlain's comrade said he had "the heart of the woman," he meant he had retained his compassion and sensitivity in the face of massive violence. After fighting the bloodiest war in American history, Carson's contemporaries had compelling reasons for wanting to believe

426   CONCLUSION

such men to be both brave and decent. Except for Charles Preuss, they did not raise a question about Carson's humanity, which seems so obvious to us.[16]

On occasion Carson himself made the connection between cruelty and cowardice. Notably, he found those qualities inseparable in the Sand Creek massacre, calling the leader, Colonel John Chivington, a "dog" and his men "hounds." They had been unable to find hostile Cheyennes, "and if they had, they'd have skedaddled from 'em, you bet!" He was outraged by the atrocities committed at Sand Creek. Whatever questions we may have about some of Carson's actions, or about the nineteenth-century association of "true" courage with tenderness and sensitivity, it seems he accepted in principle the contemporary belief that a truly brave man recognized limits to violence and was capable of mercy. In the instances cited, moreover, he specifically condemned acts of cruelty against Indians: "and you call sich soldiers Christians, do ye? and pore Indians savages."[17]

But does all the testimony about Carson's kindness and tenderness of heart absolutely rule out the possibility that, in Allan Nevins's words, he was kind and gentle "except to Indians and Mexicans"? Historians of white American attitudes toward Indians often cite Herman Melville's chapters in *The Confidence-Man* on "The Metaphysics of Indian-Hating," in which he reviews the career of Colonel John Moredock, a respected citizen of Illinois, benevolent and generous, credited with a "loving heart," "a moccasined gentleman, admired and loved," who was also a vicious Indian-hater and killer. Though he was clearly a pathological case, his society tolerated his activities, directed against people outside the white community. There certainly were obsessed Indian-haters on the frontier, usually not on the social level of a Colonel Moredock; they were popular in nineteenth-century fiction as foils to the more restrained heroes. They were probably less common than men like John Chivington, who seems to have sought self-advancement through exploiting the hatred and fear of his fellow Coloradans for the Cheyennes, although he may also have been somewhat unbalanced.[18]

It should be evident from the present account of Carson's life that he was not the sort of Indian-hater described by Melville and less talented writers, and sometimes seen in real life. In his later years he had to be persuaded by James Carleton to undertake the campaigns that crowned his reputation as an Indian-fighter. He spent years as an Indian agent trying to avoid conflict, as he did later at Fort Garland, going to great lengths to maintain peace, even after declaring war inevitable and talking about the need to chastise the Indians. While campaigning against the Mescalero Apaches and the Navajos, he repeatedly sought ways of persuading them to surrender, lamenting when his peace overtures were at first frustrated by the acts of a subordinate. He argued that justice required an attempt to negotiate a peace with the Cheyennes and Arapahos after Sand Creek. However pragmatic, these are not the acts of an obsessive Indian-hater or a man who believed that the only good one was a dead one. Nor are they the acts of an unscrupulous opportunist and demagogue such as Chivington seems to have been.

In his younger days Carson was involved in a number of violent encounters with Indians; these were either acts of self-defense, as construed by Kit and his comrades, or acts of retaliation, including forcible recovery of stolen property. Carson and most of his contemporaries accepted without question a man's right to defend himself using deadly force. Of course most of these acts occurred in Indian country, but they would have asserted their right, as free men, to go where they wanted; those who attacked them took the responsibility for any violence. A man was not born, Justice Holmes observed, to run away. Indians raided each other, defended themselves, and carried out retaliatory campaigns. Why should the mountain men (they would have asked) show more regard for the well-being of hostile Indians than did other Indians? The white men were one more tribe in the mountains. They did not see themselves as intruders. They went where the beaver were, and if the local people were friendly, especially the women, that was vastly preferable to hostility. That they committed a wrong by reacting violently to hostility probably never occurred to most of them.

Carson also participated in acts of retaliation. Among western tribes this was often the only means of redressing intertribal wrongs, and the mountain men readily adopted a principle that came naturally to many. They must pay back offences or no trapper in the mountains would be safe. Thus the cycle of hostility kept turning. The mountain men often undertook retaliation in alliance with other Indians, frequently in the pursuit of horse thieves. Anglo-Americans have a strong sense of property, and many still believe strongly in a person's right to shoot trespassers and thieves. The western tribes generally reacted to the theft of their animals in the same way, and raiders detected in the act or overtaken usually suffered a hard fate.

Were mountain men's acts of retaliation bloodier or more destructive than those of Indians? Accounts like Zenas Leonard's tale of Joseph Walker's preemptive attacks on Paiutes suggest a bloodthirsty enthusiasm going beyond what was necessary to drive off an enemy. But we cannot say that Indians never pursued a fleeing enemy, trying to kill as many as possible, in the excitement of combat.

Trapping brigades like those of Jim Bridger aggressively invaded the Blackfoot country, not unlike certain mountain tribes who hunted buffalo in the same regions, and while there conducted themselves as if at war, sometimes attacking Blackfoot villages without immediate provocation, believing that the Indians would soon attack them. Kit Carson comments, "We determined to trap wherever we pleased, even if we had to fight for the right."[19]

The same mountain men were happy to fight alongside other Indians against common enemies, especially the Blackfeet, and to spend long periods in company with these same Indians. Carson notes how Bridger's men camped near a Crow village: "They were friendly and [we] remained together during the winter." They would have been greatly puzzled by any suggestion of incongruity in their actions, that they displayed vicious prejudice in one case or commendable lack of it in the other. The distinction between good and bad Indians was as old as European presence in the New World. It was later whites, settlers and miners, who radically simplified the distinctions into "Red" and "White."[20]

As a young man, Carson displayed an eagerness for combat that at times compromised his judgment. Later on, he told Albert Richardson he had learned caution from the fatal mistakes of his comrades, but he also clearly learned from some close shaves of his own. Some of this may have been natural impetuosity and aggressiveness, some the need of a backcountry man (who had been an undersized boy) to prove his manhood, some a young man's faith in his own immortality. Many combat veterans have confessed the excitement of battle. Those of us who find such disregard of fear personally unimaginable must nonetheless acknowledge the possibility in others, without dismissing it simply as bloodlust.[21]

He was in his thirties when he participated in Frémont's first three expeditions, the period that saw some of his most famous exploits and also, from a later viewpoint, some of his most dubious actions. The foray against horse thieves on the Old Spanish Trail struck Frémont as a disinterested act of chivalry, righting the wrongs of some New

Mexicans he had never met. The attack on the Indians near Lassen's ranch was another matter, seen by white participants as necessary to prevent a clear and present danger to settlers. Carson says only, "The number killed I cannot say. It was a perfect butchery." Twenty years later, according to James Rusling, Carson would deny ever having knowingly drawn a bead on a woman or a child and would bitterly denounce John Chivington for such killing at Sand Creek, in a manner that deeply impressed—and convinced—Rusling. It may be too much to see his vehemence as reflecting uneasiness about his participation in the California episode, but his use of the word *butchery* is unique, suggesting a sense of something excessive.[22]

If he had any doubts about the California fight, he seems to have had none about the attack on the Klamaths a little later. These people, "a mean, low-lived, treacherous race," had, as he saw it, attacked Frémont's men without justification. Carson mourned three comrades killed in that attack, two of them Indians, describing their burial in some detail after ten years. This was hardly the reaction of a callous and insensitive man, but it helps explain his eagerness in the retaliatory attack, in which, according to Jessie Frémont, he insisted that "the women and children we did not interfere with."[23]

Dave Grossman, in his study of the psychology of killing in combat, argues that the killing of a "noble enemy," a brave man who fights well to the last, causes relatively little guilt in soldiers, though they respect his courage. Hence, perhaps, Carson's words about the brave Indian who "deserved a better fate"; he won Kit's respect, but was too dangerous to be allowed to live. Yet the killing of enemies who commit atrocities, says Grossman, is also easy to justify, and Carson and his friends clearly saw the "treacherous" attack by the Klamaths as an atrocity.[24]

The question of atrocities also entered into one of the least excusable episodes in Carson's life, the killing of the three Californios during Frémont's Mexican War operations. Two Americans had been murdered by Californios, reportedly in a most brutal fashion. The only account Carson gave emphasized the deaths of the two Americans. He says nothing of the matter in his autobiography, probably because he knew the matter would not stand inspection, and quite possibly because he felt shame and remorse in retrospect. He was quite frank about most killings in combat.

He also says nothing about the incident during his trip with George Brewerton when he and others tried to bring down a fleeing man, believed to be a hostile scout, detected near their camp. Yet Carson was not the type of man who shot Indians on sight as he traveled through their country, and he later expressed his contempt for those who did. His fight with Shunar at the 1835 Rendezvous was different, for he reportedly still felt animosity toward the man years later, with no sign of shame; nor does he indicate any more personal motive than "I did not like such talk from any man." Just twelve years later he was reported as calling this "the only serious personal quarrel" he had ever had, certainly the only one he mentions in his autobiography, in contrast to the record of prominent backcountry men such as Andrew Jackson and Nathan Bedford Forrest, who were notorious for "serious"—potentially deadly—personal quarrels. The prominence he gave the affair suggests that it was, indeed, a unique occurrence in the life of a man who generally avoided the kind of "matter of honor" confrontations that were common in his culture. A writer of 1847 judged him "of a peaceable and gentle temper."[25]

Yet Carson did, on occasion, display anger and act belligerently. Governor David Meriwether found him so "boisterous" on one occasion that he had him arrested; he does not admit that he was afraid of Carson, whose courage he had just impugned. The New Mexican ranchero whom Kit knocked into the Rio Grande with the flat of his sword must have thought him a man of some temper, but Carson would have said he was protecting women whom the ranchero was endangering, the man's obstinacy forcing him to take action; he immediately rescued the man, jumping into the river himself. Concerning the officers of the eighteenth-century British navy, N. A. M. Rodger writes, "It was characteristic of the age that . . . genuine and practical humanity coexisted with a tolerance for personal violence which would today be considered the mark of coarse brutality." The same could be said of the nineteenth-century backcountry and the frontier.[26]

On many occasions Carson used threatening language, as when he told the Paiute chief, "Your life's in danger," or when he bluffed a Jicarilla war party that caught his men inadequately armed. During Ewing Young's California trip, he warned some Indians to leave camp within ten minutes or be shot because he had spotted some concealed weapons. In such episodes, Carson believed, he and his companions were in imminent danger. Kit was a good poker player; he knew the value of a good bluff. In later years he pointed out the need for a convincing force, or the appearance of one, in tense periods in Indian-white relations.

Dave Grossman in his study of reactions to killing in combat argues that most men find it extremely difficult to kill other humans face to face, and that if forced to do so they pay a heavy psychological price, at the time or later. Grossman makes a convincing case, allowing for many exceptions and factors that ease the guilt. A small percentage of men feel little or no guilt over the act of killing in combat. Some of these men lack any empathy for others and are, in fact, dangerous sociopaths. There are others, however, who seem capable of killing in battle without suffering crippling emotional trauma, yet who are still capable of empathy. Grossman compares the first category to wolves and the second to sheepdogs. The "sheepdogs," he argues, are not pathological cases but are often valuable citizens whose special characteristics become evident only in war; they are often found in military or police forces. In words that might have been intended to describe Kit Carson, he writes, "These men are quite often armed and always vigilant." They may yearn for a righteous battle, but they are not a danger to their community. (Grossman acknowledges that many will see his theory as simply a romanticizing of killers.) Although Grossman's pattern may not fit Kit Carson in all respects, it may help explain the seeming paradox of a warrior who was described by so many as kind, gentle, even tenderhearted.[27]

This theory, however, does not entirely rule out the possibility that Carson harbored prejudices against Indians that lessened his guilt at killing them. According to Grossman, racial and ethnic difference is one of the distancing factors that make killing easier. But evaluating Carson's attitudes toward Indians in terms of racial prejudice is not as easy as it might seem.

That Americans attach great importance to "racial" distinctions hardly needs demonstration. We tend to feel a vague discomfort about people whom we cannot easily classify until we get a clarification of their standing. That a large proportion of present-day "Indians" have some white ancestry seems somehow less important than what group, Caucasian or Indian, they are identified with. A white man of my acquaintance in northern Nebraska was surprised to learn that an elderly man of distinctly Indian appearance whom he had known for years had never told him that his father was a white man, which would have raised his standing considerably. The importance of racial identification in America is demonstrated by the fact that those who denounce most stoutly the evil of racism cannot help speaking and writing of people in these categories, in order to describe the very injustices they decry.

Writing of current criticism of certain nineteenth-century white antislavery men as racially prejudiced, James McPherson says, "Perhaps by modern absolutist standards of racial egalitarianism (which few could meet today), these men harbored some mildly racist or paternalistic feelings. But to call these 'powerful racial prejudices' is to indulge in what William Manchester has called 'generational chauvininsim—judging past eras by the standards of the present.' " Similarly, Carson's attitudes toward Indians, insofar as we can discern them, have to be measured against those of his time and place. The question is, how did Carson think about and treat Indians compared to his white American contemporaries on the frontier, not compared with the ideal behavior espoused by latter-day advocates of equal rights, and actually achieved by some of them.[28]

Some of Carson's own words suggest condescension at least. Of the Utes he observed, "They are in no way industrous," and for Carson's contemporaries, with their devotion to the work ethic, this was a grievous fault. The stereotype of the lazy Indian was very much alive.[29] Jessie Frémont says that on seeing a picture, illustrating Byron's poem, of Mazeppa tied to the back of a horse, Kit commented, "It looks like Indian work—they're devils enough for just such work as that." If true, then the idea of tying a helpless man to the back of a horse and running him off onto the steppe to perish or survive as chance dictated made Kit think of Indians. Or did he name a specific tribe, like the Blackfeet? Such generalizations about Indians are rare in Kit's more directly transcribed words. His description of the Klamaths is the harshest indictment to be found in his autobiography.[30]

When Kit reportedly said, "I shall always treat Oulay [Ouray] just like a white man, for he is a good Injun," he expressed his liking, indeed admiration, for the man in terms then deemed unobjectionable. The same observer, Eveline Alexander, reports his enthusiastic reception in the Ute camp, where he shook hands with everyone. The Utes could undoubtedly pick up on any very evident contempt or condescension as well as anyone. Alexander herself reports without embarrassment that she would not dismount and accept Ouray's offer of hospitality. It is tempting to imagine that a man with little formal education lacks finer feelings or sensitivity because he cannot find words different from those in common currency to express fine shades of meaning.

When Kit described Indians as "pore ignorant critters," he expressed his understanding of the cultural differences between Indians and whites in the only words available to him, explaining why they did things whites found repugnant. White contemporaries would have objected to the description only because they found it too lenient. He was well aware that, in many people's eyes, he was himself a "pore ignorant critter."[31]

Since his society found it natural to classify people according to race and ethnicity, it should not be surprising if Carson did so. His contemporaries also routinely ranked people "in the order of their merits," in Francis Parkman's words, with white Anglo-Americans clearly the most meritorious. Kit probably did put people in some such informal ranking by merit, not questioning the fundamental assumptions of his culture. But how far did he go in this direction, how rigid were his categories, how important were these categories to his sense of himself, and how far were these notions subject to modification by experience and other principles? Southern whites of his time, for instance, had so much invested in the idea of white superiority over blacks that they fought a long and bloody war in defense of it. Carson never addressed such questions directly, and would not have recognized the problems he dealt with if put in those terms. Today we assume that those who reject racism should observe a scrupulously egalitarian attitude toward all "minorities," but few nineteenth-century Americans saw it that way, and most had no doubt of their right to rate Indians, blacks, and Mexicans as higher or lower. Colonel Rusling, based on the most superficial acquaintance, had no difficulty rating the Utes "infinitely below the colored race."[32]

Carson simply never addressed the problem of "racism" in the abstract, and probably never realized there was such a thing. He almost certainly had no carefully formulated ideology on the subject, but neither do most people condemned for racism today; they simply know what "those people" are like, and it would take a great deal to change their ideas on the subject. This sort of prejudice is anterior to, and the basis for, racism as a formal, intellectualized ideology of the sort so conspicuous in the nineteenth and twentieth centuries. It is the attitude of ordinary people who do not examine most of their received ideas.

But what did Kit Carson do with received ideas in his everyday life? Carson was married to two Indian women, Waanibe and Making Out Road. Carson and other mountain men were "in another country," far from the home folks who might have discountenanced such marriages;

indeed such unions were not unknown in frontier Missouri. Kit's first marriage ended with his wife's death, the second by divorce. He cared for his children by Waanibe as well, probably, as circumstances permitted. One died young. Adaline Carson was brought up by his family and educated in Missouri. Kit clearly did not conceal her existence or her parentage from his Missouri relatives or from Josefa Jaramillo's family in New Mexico, either of whom were probably far less disturbed than folk back east would have been, but he never mentioned her or his Indian wives in his autobiography. His private affairs were nobody else's business. He undoubtedly knew how respectable folk "back in the States" regarded unions with Indian "squaws," unblessed by the church, and the "half-breed" children of such couples. He feared that the ladies of the Benton family might not want to associate with a man who had been married to an Indian, although he insisted that she had been a good wife. He probably did not consider his wife his equal any more than most men of his culture and generation. As with his friend William Bent and many other traders and mountain men, his children were his children and his half-Arapaho daughter was acknowledged and brought up to be "white." Carson's Indian marriages do not offer definitive insight into his general attitude toward Indians, other than his desire for the approval of respectable people and his reticence about his private affairs.[33]

Prejudice in favor of some Indian tribes was a recurring phenomenon of the frontier. Mountain men found Nez Perces, Flatheads, and Shoshones admirable; the women made good wives. Kit Carson married among both the Arapahos and the Cheyennes, and his acquaintance with both probably influenced his later outrage over the Sand Creek massacre and his insistence that a special effort should be made to negotiate peace with those tribes. Carson's special fondness for the Utes has been noted, but on occasion he was also in danger from Utes. There is no record of a relationship with a Ute woman, though this would have been possible at various times. The point is not that a sexual relationship alone predisposed a white man in favor of certain tribes, but that a wider range of human relationships was possible with those tribes.

It is harder to say how the Utes regarded Carson, given the paucity of evidence and the lack of an adequate tribal history. According to report, one Ute chief, Blanco, tried to shoot Kit in front of his house, and another, Kaniache, saved his life. Some Utes agreed to hold a council with their enemies, the Cheyennes, on the condition that Carson was present. Apparently the leaders of Taos Pueblo were prepared to do the same on a similar condition. Utes assigned to Kit's agency and some assigned to other agents all came to his Taos office seeking government food and clothing. Uninterested in bureaucratic jurisdiction, they may have found Father Kit more generous than his colleagues. In 1867 some chiefs remembered Carson, along with a few other agents, as an honest man who gave them what they were supposed to receive, and they said they would be happy to have him as agent again.[34]

Of the Jicarilla Apaches, also his responsibility as agent, Carson was less fond and wrote more critically, pointing out their increasing drunkenness and accusing them of trying to involve the Utes in a war with the whites. Yet he recognized their grim situation, pointed out the need to feed them to prevent "depredations," and sought thus to prevent the outbreak of hostilities in 1854. When that effort failed, he scouted for the forces against the Jicarilla warriors; yet they went with "Gidi" against the Kiowas and Comanches ten years later.

Carson's regard for the Utes may have influenced his attitude toward their enemies the Navajos. He agreed with the Utes' unwillingness to make peace with the Navajos in 1859. But, like his neighbors, he would have seen the Navajos as the great enemy of New Mexico, and the Utes' hostility toward them as a military advantage for whites. He was quite willing to help make treaties between tribes like the Utes and Cheyennes, of whom he thought well.

Carson's attitudes about Indians as a mountain man, guide, and scout were shaped by personal experience. As an Indian agent he had to consider things from a broader perspective, thinking about how his actions affected Indians, Anglos, and Hispanics. It is hard to say how much he had considered these matters before becoming an agent, because he confines himself largely to narrative in his autobiography. These pages have detailed his concern about the catastrophic decline in Indian populations, observed during his California trip in 1853, and his awareness of the effects of white expansion on their old nomadic hunting life. He saw how various stresses and violent conflicts generated by increasing contact threatened the Indians' very existence, as well as the safety of frontier settlers. New Mexicans lived in a state of perpetual insecurity. His years as a trapper had shown the possibilities of complex, often friendly interaction between whites and Indians, but the changed conditions worked against peaceful coexistence.

CONCLUSION

By 1856 Carson had become an advocate of separating Indians and whites, removing the Indians to reservations remote from white settlements where they could be taught to live like white farmers. It was a policy, as he saw it, that served the interests of both Indians and whites. Jacksonian Indian removal, officially justified as preserving the Vanishing American, also opened up large areas to white settlers. As Carson knew, New Mexicans did not want Indian reservations near them, in the San Luis Valley or near Abiquiu (or later at Bosque Redondo), because they wanted those areas for themselves: "Such treaties were not of a character to suit the people." Carson himself, with Lucien Maxwell, had started a settlement on Jicarilla hunting grounds. Was his advocacy of the reservation system simply a means of serving his own people by dispossessing the Indians?[35]

Westward expansion was a basic fact of the first century of American history, seen by most Americans as good and necessary. Though it seemed for a time that the Great Plains might be a barrier to settlement, and hence a refuge for Indians, the Permanent Indian Frontier west of Missouri was quickly negated by the leap to the Pacific, and the surrounding of the western tribes began in earnest. In 1865 Kit Carson and William Bent would write, "Civilization now presses them on all sides." They had seen virtually the whole process. The frontier gave way to the pressure of a restless people. The politicians and reformers who shaped government Indian policy in the mid–nineteenth century took for granted the continued expansion of the settlement frontier and the constriction of the Indians' living space. They could work on no other assumption.[36]

Whites had come to believe that the advance of civilization meant the destruction of the Vanishing American. There was much objective evidence supporting this conclusion. Whites of the time often preferred to believe in the Indians' "inability to stand civilization," an inherent weakness (those of a later date are more likely to see them as set up for "genocide"). The fact seemed indisputable, and the debate was over whether anything could or should be done for the Indians. Many, including respected scientists, were pessimistic. For a vocal segment of opinion, especially in the West, their extinction was a highly desirable result, best hastened; those who disagreed were sentimental fools whose ideas of Indians were derived from Cooper and not from real life. Those who wanted to save the Indians could see only one solution: removal to areas remote from white settlement where they would be safe and uncontaminated and self-supporting. Proponents of the idea thought "civilizing" the Indians on the Anglo-American model was desirable; the only question was whether it was possible. The ideals of both the Enlightenment and evangelical Christianity, as opposed to recently developed racial theories, argued for the "civilizing" process.

The selfish callousness of those who eagerly anticipated the end of the Indians and the ethnocentrism of the civilizers alike appall many modern Americans, obscuring the fact that the two were enemies at the time. For the latter, the reservation system was the only practical, humane solution. As an Indian agent, Kit Carson repeatedly urged the establishment of reservations and the commencement of a civilizing program on a government that was slow to begin the process in remote New Mexico. It was his job to promote the government's policy, to look after the Indians, and to avoid or minimize conflicts as much as possible, and he would do it to the best of his ability. His repeated urging of his superiors to get on with the program and his constantly repeated descriptions of the progressive impoverishment and degradation of the Utes and Jicarillas suggest his genuine belief in the need for action. He feared that the Utes, whose virtue he praised and whose peaceful intentions he repeatedly vouched for, would be degraded by alcohol and the bad influence of New Mexicans and Anglos: "Every visit an Indian makes to a town, it is of more or less injury to him." When the government dragged its feet about establishing a permanent agency, his frustration increased.[37]

Carson was surely not free of the ethnocentric assumptions on which he was raised, though he had had intense exposure to human beings raised on different assumptions. He probably understood those differences better than all but a few white men, but he never seems to have lost his sense of who he was, a part of Anglo-American culture. He knew that all Indians were not alike, that the simple dichotomy of "Red" and "White" was inadequate, but he was unable to articulate an alternative theory. He did not try to pretend that he was an Indian, nor propose an Indian lifeway as preferable to that of white America. Perhaps the very sense of who he was that kept him from taking his own legend too seriously also kept him firmly anchored in his identity as a white man.

He surely understood better than most proponents of the reservation system the cultural gulf between Indians and whites, and the difficulty the Indians would have in adopting a different culture. Perhaps the younger generation, brought up on the reservation, would have an easier time adjusting.

It is, in fact, impossible to offer indigenous societies a free, uncoerced choice between their culture and Western industrial civilization. By the time they know enough about that civilization to make an informed choice, they have already been too much changed by it to go back. Only if whites had stayed entirely out of the West and had avoided any interchange of goods or infectious diseases could drastic change in the Indians' lifeways have been avoided, even if white Americans had been far less sure of their cultural and "racial" superiority than they were.

Without a radical change in Anglo-American society, preserving Indian lifeways and landholdings unchanged was not a workable option. Carson, as Indian agent, was somehow supposed to serve the needs of his own society and those of his Indian charges, keeping a precarious balance. Some of his statements from his last years suggest a sense of emotional conflict: "I've seen as much of 'em as any man liv'in, and I can't help but pity 'em, right or wrong." His correspondence as agent shows his awareness of the conflict between the interests of settlers and Indians. Increasingly he tended to blame the conflicts on the settlers.[38]

Indian-white relations in New Mexico during Kit's tenure as Indian agent (1854–61) were in a confused, transitional state. Attempts to put the reservation system into practice failed because Congress neither ratified the treaties made by government representatives nor appropriated funds. Carson maintained his agency at his home in Taos and doled out food, blankets, and other supplies as he deemed necessary, trying to avert trouble by adjusting quarrels between New Mexicans and Indians. In the war of 1854–55, after his initial attempts to avert conflict failed, he took the field as a scout. During the entire period he was engaged in a holding action, while repeatedly reminding his superiors of the need to act.

Carson's decision to act as a scout in 1854–55 might seem to be in conflict with his duty to the Indians, but it is doubtful if he saw it that way. Once the war had started, the boy whose family had been forted at Boonslick and whose father had been wounded by a hostile Indian could not ignore the danger. When it seemed to him that hasty actions by army officers had precipitated the war, he urged peace negotiations. Later, frustrated by the unsettled situation in New Mexico and the policies of his nemesis, David Meriwether, he declared that the war with the Jicarillas should have been pressed to a decisive conclusion. He harshly criticized Meriwether for buying peace by promises of food and supplies, yet he constantly urged the need to feed the Indians to keep them from stealing.

After the war, much of his time was spent trying to adjust the difficulties between Indians and settlers. Eventually, Kit in exasperation declared that, if citizens would not steal from Indians, he would never have to report Indian "depredations," forecasting his later, more sweeping denunciations of white aggressions as the prime cause of "Indian troubles." The fur trade modus vivendi, the "middle ground" with all its complex interactions, was being replaced by a simplified, polarized division between "Red" and "White," in which the latter had "no need for the Indian." Kit's years as an Indian agent make it impossible to regard him simply as an Indian-hater; he tried continually to avoid Indian-white conflict and to protect the Indians from the worst effects of white expansion. The Utes expressed their trust in him and found him honest. By later standards he was paternalistic in his attitude toward the Indians in his charge, for he believed that he knew what was good for them better than they did, and was prepared to make them accept it if necessary. The late twentieth century, holding cultural pluralism an undoubted good, finds such an attitude unacceptable. Knowing some of the actual results of the program for "civilizing" the Indians as we do, we view the advocates of such ideas as arrogantly ethnocentric.

Anglo-Americans in the mid–nineteenth century, when the reservation system was formulated, were certainly ethnocentric, convinced of the superiority of their civilization and their religion. Indians were seen as having not alternate cultures and religions but none at all to speak of, as living in a state of nature little different from the higher animals, except for a few repulsive customs and superstitions.

There are almost no references to such ideas in Carson's writings. As a mountain man he lived much like an Indian, adjusting to many Indian practices and customs. He understood well the protocol of an Indian council. There is no evidence that he ever delved into Indian religious beliefs or views of the meaning of life; he may have known much that no white interviewer ever bothered to ask him about. (The noted soldier-ethnographers of the post–Civil War period, like John Bourke, missed him by a few years.) He certainly knew of the cultural gulf between his people and the Indians, however little he could express this understanding. But he could easily see that the material basis of the Indians' way of life was being destroyed by white settlement, that the warrior cultures could not persist unaltered without being destroyed, and that alcohol, disease, and demoralization were themselves eroding Indian cultures. The idea that Indians lived in a completely traditional, "natural," and unchanging way until being forced onto reservations does not hold up under inspection.

Carson concerned himself with the immediate evils he saw around him. By training and position he was an intermediary between peoples, though he knew where his final allegiance lay. He had to use his knowledge and experience to serve his government and his people, yet he knew much more about what was happening and was going to happen than the Indians could. He knew how the government operated and how white expansion worked, and he believed he knew better than the Indians how to give them a chance of surviving. It is easy, with more than a century's hindsight, to see the harm done by the assimilation program and the reservation system (together with individual land allotments) to Indian peoples. This does not mean that these harmful results should have been equally evident to Carson and his contemporaries in the mid-nineteenth century. They were concerned with immediate problems, at a point of crisis as they saw it, of the impending destruction of the western Indian peoples, and of preventing violent, costly conflicts between the races.

Like other government officials, he believed that force might be necessary to implement policy. People with warrior traditions might not submit passively. Chiefs might see the need to change in order to survive, but not everyone would accept the chiefs' authority. The acts of a few, white or Indian, could trigger a conflict affecting thousands of people.

Carson's use of words like *chastisement* emphasizes the most negative aspect of white paternalism—the treatment of Indians as errant children who must be shown the error of their ways by stern punishment. "Chastisement" may be John Mostin's word, but Kit surely meant that hostile Indians must be defeated badly enough to convince them to remain at peace. In 1856 he expressed his exasperation that the punishment had not been severe enough to have a lasting effect. A decade later, he had some different thoughts on the subject.

Still, Carson spent most of his time and effort as an Indian agent, and later after Adobe Walls, trying to avert conflict, moderating disputes, recovering stolen animals, distributing food to Indians, and repeatedly seizing the opportunity to make peace, often with people about whom he had just been using quite belligerent language. During the Mescalero and Navajo campaigns he was eager to accept the surrender of any who would go to Bosque Redondo. He interpreted Carleton's "draconian" orders as allowing this, and the general approved.

Carson's attitude toward Indian captives shows his paternalism in the worst light. There are two recorded instances in his younger years of his purchasing or selling young Indian boys. These boys were certainly captives when Carson bought them and were surely no worse off in his care. There is no indication that he engaged in slave-trading on a regular basis. The trade in captives was well established among the western tribes, even before the arrival of the Spanish in New Mexico.

When Carson brought Navajo captives into his home in Taos, he also followed well-established custom. Navajos were the enemies of New Mexico, and New Mexicans regularly ransomed Navajo captives from the Utes and took them on their own. Supposedly, these women and children were treated as members of the family, even being baptized with their masters as godparents. Their treatment must have varied, but they were not free and were separated from their own families and culture. In the 1860s Kit and Josefa Carson held two young boys and a young woman, all Navajos and all baptized. They were ransomed from the Utes and, as Carson said, were probably better off under his care. None of that alters the essential nature of the practice. He probably saw taking the captives in as the best answer to an immediate, individual problem. There is no evidence that he believed every Indian should be a slave to whites, simply for being an Indian, as contemporary southern whites believed of blacks.

It appears that he had no essential quarrel with the practice, since he desired to reward his Ute allies during the Navajo campaign by letting them keep and sell their captives, thus encouraging the Utes while sparing the government expense in supporting the captives; they would be even better off, he suggested, than at the Bosque Redondo. Becoming integrated into New Mexican society, the captives would be "detribalized." By our present standards of respect for cultural integrity, this is wholly unacceptable. Carson and his New Mexican neighbors thought of Navajos as the enemy, the scourge of New Mexico, and breaking up their power was of paramount importance. There is no indication, however, that he thought every Navajo should be detribalized.[39]

Although the heroic Kit Carson myth emphasizes his derring-do as mountain man and scout, the current countermyth centers on his

CONCLUSION

military service in the 1860s. The Old Scout of fiction lacked this versatility or capacity for growth, but Kit's fame gave him the opportunity to play a role unlike any other mountain man. Two successive military superiors believed he had the wisdom, as well as the fighting prowess, to command important military operations. Carson himself, having joined up to help expel Confederate invaders, was not personally tempted by the opportunity to clean out the Mescaleros and Navajos, preferring to go home and look after his family. As Kit Jr. might have put it, it was "just another call to duty," an attitude that in his time aroused only admiration, but that now raises questions.[40]

Historians who understand the nature of genocide are reluctant to apply the term to Indian-white conflicts in the United States. The federal government undoubtedly placed the interests of the white population first, but it never adopted or sanctioned a policy of genocide — of wiping out all Indians or all members of a particular tribe — nor did any regular military commander of high rank ever issue orders to that effect. Talk of "extermination" by commanders like Sherman or Sheridan, reflecting frustration over guerrilla resistance, were neither statements of policy nor orders and were not construed as such by their subordinates. Many acts of brutality did take place, sanctioned by the atmosphere of guerrilla warfare against people of a very different culture and "race."

When Kit was a boy at Boonslick, some Indians were apparently accepted, with reservations, as friendly visitors, a phenomenon not unknown in the backcountry. But Indians were also the enemy who ravaged the countryside and made everyday life hideously insecure. The attempt to kill the Indians captured by Henry Dodge's rangers in 1814 shows the impulse toward retribution typical of the frontier settlers.[41]

Virtually all that Kit recorded of his childhood was the impression of the war years from 1812 to 1815. He does not mention his father's being wounded by Indians when he was four going on five, but he could hardly have forgotten it. These memories must have recurred whenever he saw a frontier population menaced by Indian attack.

But the federal government was not obliged to carry out frontier settlers' calls for "extermination," and Kit Carson as an agent of federal Indian policy was not asked to carry out genocide, nor the kind of action for which he denounced John Chivington, the deliberate massacre of people who believed they were protected by a peace agreement. He was asked to carry out military campaigns against people who fought as guerrillas, forcing them to surrender and accept internment at a reservation distant from their homeland. Historical denunciation of him centers on this campaign, the way it was carried out, and the effects on the people.

Indian-white conflict had meant perpetual insecurity in New Mexico, for Indians and New Mexicans, for generations: raid and counterraid, theft of livestock, carrying off of women and children, violent death, and the enslavement of the living. Each side believed it had good cause and damned the other as aggressor. Old residents of New Mexico thought the Navajos did better stealing stock, while the New Mexicans took more captives. Neither community seemed willing or able to control the acts of its own members, and on this failure repeated peace efforts had foundered. The holding of captives by New Mexicans was so thoroughly sanctioned by the Hispanic community that it seemed impossible to end it.

In 1861 Colonel Edward Canby declared that it was futile and irrelevant to inquire into who had started the Navajo conflict. The fact remained that it could only be ended by exterminating the Navajos or bringing them under the control of the government on a reservation. Since the former was not acceptable, the only solution, Canby believed, was a decisive military campaign to force the surrender of all Navajos. Some retrospective Navajo accounts suggest that many Navajos also believed that their destruction was at hand if things did not change.

Kit Carson clearly believed in the necessity for bringing the Navajos under federal control. In 1865 he several times blamed most of the Indian troubles of the period on the aggressions of white frontiersmen and the misconduct of Indian agents, urging negotiations to end these troubles without further fighting. Yet, regarding the Navajos, he thought confining them to a reservation was the only way to end the war and prevent its resumption. He recognized the reciprocal nature of the conflict, in which "forays were made into each other's country, and stock, women and children stolen," and he thought that some New Mexicans objected to placing the Navajos at Bosque Redondo "because they cannot prey on them as formerly." Carson did not make war on the Navajos because of a hatred for all Indians, nor because he blamed Indians for all conflicts between them and whites. Nor did he think the Navajo wars the exclusive fault of one group of people. He may have been prejudiced by his connections with New Mexicans and Utes, though he saw how they contributed to the problem. But whether or not one accepts his conclusion, something more than blind, unthinking prejudice clearly shaped his opinion.[42]

The general principles of military campaigns against Indians had become clear through years of experience, and the strategy to be pursued against the Navajos had been developed by 1860. Like most guerrilla fighters, the Navajos and Apaches relied on mobility, dispersal, and knowledge of the country to evade pursuit, refusing to fight or to take heavy casualties. Since there was no hope of a decisive battle, the only military option was continual harassment, attacking small groups as opportunity offered, driving the enemy into the most uninhabitable parts of the country, preferably in winter. The Navajos, with their herds, fields, and orchards, were especially vulnerable to this strategy. The soldiers might surprise and kill or capture a few here and there, but it was the denial of security and sanctuary, the fear, hunger, and cold, that would bring about the surrender of the majority. This strategy inflicted suffering on women and children as well as on fighting men. Although General Carleton specifically ordered that women and children were not to be killed, it was the children, the sick, and the elderly who suffered most.

Carson accepted the surrender of most of the Mescalero Apaches, even though he could have interpreted his written communication from Carleton as orders to keep fighting. Carleton approved, either because Kit carried out his actual intention or because he trusted his subordinate enough to allow modification of his orders. Carleton believed that the war could be ended only by forcing the Navajos to go to the Bosque Redondo, insuring both federal control over them and their protection from New Mexican and Indian raiding. He had no faith in formal treaties with them, because their chiefs had no power to compel obedience. Therefore, his troops would treat all Navajos in their country as hostile until they surrendered.

Carleton's orders in the Mescalero and Navajo campaigns have been characterized as "extermination orders." If carried out as some historians have interpreted them, as mandating the killing of all adult males of these tribes, they would merit that description. But Carson did not carry them out in that fashion, and Carleton does not seem to have found fault with him. The general wished to emphasize that he had no faith in any treaties with these tribes, and that he would accept no arrangement allowing them to remain on their own territory, where he believed they would continue to be a menace to the peace and security of

New Mexico. Certainly none of the earlier treaties had worked, whoever was to blame. Hence the campaign would continue without letup until all had surrendered.[43]

Carleton ratified Carson's acceptance of the Mescalero surrender. Regarding the Navajos, he told Carson that he, Carson, was right to believe that he, Carleton, did not desire to destroy any who surrendered, and that no Indian "once fairly in our custody" should be killed. However, only surrender could bring safety. This was the essence of counterguerrilla operations, based on decades of experience, notably in the Seminole War and past Navajo campaigns. Indian warfare was seen as different from conventional, "civilized" warfare; the enemy did not fight "honorably" and had to be treated differently. Apache and Navajo fighting men did not live as separate armies apart from their noncombatants; to deny them subsistence, shelter, and security meant to deny these things to all.[44]

Kit Carson's military reports deal with pragmatic affairs, not with his emotional reactions to the Navajo campaign. He made it clear very early that he wanted to establish communication with Navajo leaders and persuade them to surrender, the sooner the better. He bitterly regretted that the actions of some subordinates made things more difficult: "I deplore it the more as I have only one way of communicating with them—through the barrels of my Rifles."[45]

Of Benjamin Church, ranger commander in King Philip's War, Richard Slotkin and James Folsom write, "Pragmatism, not moral scruple, made Church relatively more humane than his commanders—that and his ability to see some Indians as human beings." There were clearly pragmatic reasons for Carson to try to secure the surrender of the Navajos—in particular, the enormous difficulty of killing a large portion of them in combat. The Navajo report, handed down over a generation or two, that the commander of the Canyon de Chelly expedition wept over the loss of life among the Indians, cannot be taken as reliable, even if the man could be identified as Kit Carson. Some of his later statements show that he could indeed see Indians as human beings. His desire to call off his efforts during the winter, and his reluctance to march to Canyon de Chelly, show that however strong his sense of duty, he found no pleasure or deep satisfaction in the work.

The Canyon de Chelly expedition, in January 1864, which Carson had to be prodded into carrying out, seems to have been the climax of the campaign. Although tales of Kit's corralling thousands of Indians there were gross exaggerations, the expedition gave him a chance to talk to a number of Navajos and convince them that they could safely surrender on the condition of going to Bosque Redondo. Afterward, the surrenders increased to a flood, though the fear of Indian and New Mexican raiders and the efforts of previously surrendered Navajo chiefs also helped. It was while Carson was on leave that most of the notorious Long Walk to Bosque Redondo took place. The majority of the Navajos spent four years at Bosque Redondo, a period they remembered as a long agony of disease and short rations, of confinement in an alien land where the crops they labored over failed year after year. The basic idea of "civilizing" the Indians on the reservation was General Carleton's; Carson supported and defended the reservation experiment, though he was only in charge for a few months at the beginning, when things seemed most hopeful. Many modern scholars, if they do not accuse him simply of being a brutal, or at least callous, racist, charge that his sense of duty and his deference to his commander led him into carrying out brutal, even genocidal, policies.

Dee Brown charged that Carson never got over "his awe of the well-dressed, smooth-talking men at the top," and that Carleton, a well-educated, articulate, and strong-willed member of the officer class, was able to persuade him to do things against his better judgment and moral sense. Alvin Josephy and Clifford Trafzer have echoed this opinion. Jessie Benton Frémont, however, reported Kit's sharp resentment of the arrogant and condescending gentry. His criticism does not mean that he did not wish for the approval of well-educated folk, nor that those elites who treated him with respect and accepted him as he was could not have used his sense of duty to manipulate him. Carleton persuaded him to stay in uniform and go on campaign by, apparently, assuring him that his experience and skill made him indispensable. The demanding, authoritarian New Englander, who raised so many people's hackles, might not seem the man to manipulate someone of such different character and background, but as we have seen, Carleton was more complicated that his image suggests.[46]

Martin Green argues that Carson became a "proto-administrator and soldier," that is, he was coopted by the class of officers and civil servants. Carson did become "the perennial public servant." His reputation made him the man to call on in case of problems with Indians, and public employment was a convenient way of supporting his wife and children, although he never accumulated any great fortune. In his autobiography he praises army officers in the conventional language of that class, most conspicuously in the case of Frémont, using expressions like "a noble and brave officer." They were brave men who did their duty in the face of hardship and danger. His unqualified praise of Frémont, whose judgment on a number of occasions appears questionable, suggests an uncritical attitude toward those whom he liked and respected. But Colonel Frémont had saved his life and put him on the path to fame. A backcountry man was loyal to his friends.[47]

Carson could, nonetheless, be sharply critical of army officers and other "smooth-talking men at the top" if he found their judgment faulty. Governor David Meriwether, with whom he differed both personally and over Indian policy, and who treated Carson with disdain, is the most conspicuous example. He also differed with, and criticized, General Kearny, Captain James Grier, and Colonel Edwin Sumner. He was not automatically subservient and unquestioning with his alleged betters, and they had to show respect to a man who, however humble and self-effacing, had his backcountry man's pride and a faith in his own judgment.[48]

When Carleton took command in New Mexico in 1862 the two men already respected each other's knowledge and judgment. Carleton never hesitated to let Carson know of his displeasure or to apply the spur as well as dangle the carrot of praise. He knew he needed Carson to carry out his plans as no one else available could. To take advantage of Kit's skills, he had to tolerate, within limits, the volunteer colonel's shortcomings as an administrator and disciplinarian and to grant him a freedom of judgment that he might not have tolerated in anyone else. Carson did, on occasion, modify the general's orders and even let him know, diplomatically, that certain recommendations were impracticable or unnecessary.

Carrying out Carleton's orders in conducting the Mescalero and Navajo campaigns does not prove that Carson was "a good company man" who would comply with any and all orders. The assumption that these military operations were a form of genocide, motivated by racism, prompts the accusation. If Carleton's policy and strategy were unequivocally immoral in the context of the times and Carson's own understanding, then his obedience would require explanation. But that verdict rests on latter-day assumptions about the situation in New Mexico and the conduct of the campaign, and on what Carson should have thought.

CONCLUSION

Carson apparently accepted the necessity of carrying out these campaigns; his judgment essentially concurred with Carleton's. He recognized that New Mexicans contributed to the situation, and he blamed other Indian-white conflicts of the time on white men's blunders and aggressions, but he could see no other solutions to the situation in New Mexico.[49]

Although Carson believed that he was carrying out a task necessary to insure peace and security there, the Long Walk was a poor beginning to the job of ensuring the Navajos' survival. The Bosque Redondo reservation was a paradigm of the federal government's Indian policy in the mid-1800s, Carleton's innovation being military control of the process. The location was Carleton's idea. Carson agreed in essentials with the general's reasoning, including the need for a reservation far from the Navajo country. An advocate of the reservation system for a decade, he had become disillusioned with the Bureau of Indian Affairs and now favored military control, identifying himself with the soldiers.

Repeated crop failures forced General Carleton to feed the Indians at Bosque Redondo, often inadequately, at enormous expense. Twentieth-century critics have not hesitated to call the reservation a concentration camp, with the comparison to the Nazi death camps definitely being intended. The intentions of Carleton and his subordinates, including Kit Carson, were certainly quite different from those of the men who planned and ran Auschwitz and Treblinka. Nevertheless, the Navajos rightly remember the Bosque as a place of suffering and death.

When Carson served as superintendent of the reservation in the summer of 1864, things seemed hopeful. Kit apparently believed in the goals, and the Navajos were trying to farm. Considering the alternative as he saw it—renewed war—what could he do but try? Regarding his own participation, he seems to have become disgruntled within a few months, but he continued to support the idea. After the reservation had been in operation for over a year, he and William Bent described it as "a successful example of the benefits to be derived from the system."[50]

While New Mexicans, the Bureau of Indian Affairs, and military superiors lost faith, Carleton continued his experiment, insisting each setback was only a temporary "visitation of God." If Carson believed that the reservation system offered the only workable solution to a worsening situation, he also believed that a reservation in Navajo country would not end the cycle of conflict. Too many past peace agreements had failed. Kit had stressed the need to prove the government's humane intentions by keeping all promises made to the Indians. If the Indians went hungry and died, his and Carleton's hopes would come to nothing.

They conducted this experiment without the consent of the people most concerned, believing that they knew best, ignoring or failing to foresee factors that hindsight suggests should have been obvious. Even so, some twentieth-century Navajos apparently believed that the military campaign and the reservation were indeed intended to preserve the Navajos from extinction. The question might at least be asked, though it would be hard to answer, whether several more years of conflict might not have cost the Navajos as much. The tragedy came from the failure to find a peaceful solution, which few then believed possible.

By 1868 Carleton's superiors had given up on the Bosque Redondo, for financial and political reasons as much as humane ones. General Sherman let them return to their own country if they would keep the peace. Perhaps such a solution would have been possible before the Kit Carson campaign and the years at Bosque Redondo, but now the Navajos had an even greater incentive to remain at peace, and a heightened sense that the actions of a few could affect everyone. Gerald Thompson argues that these factors and a better understanding of the white man's ways changed the Navajos permanently, making peace possible.

That the Navajos are today the most numerous tribe in the United States is due first of all to their toughness and the adaptability of their culture. Nonetheless, it was in the 1860s that the destructive cycle of hostility between them and the New Mexicans came to an end without the destruction of their people, and this was the intention of James Carleton and Kit Carson.

Carson's last Indian campaign, to punish the Kiowas and Comanches for attacks on the Santa Fe Trail, was significantly different from the others. Carleton's strategy to harass them in winter forecast future campaigns on the plains. The engagement at Adobe Walls validated Carson's request for substantial numbers of white troops. His subsequent retreat was contrary to the wishes of many officers but accorded with the judgment of his Ute and Jicarilla allies, ensuring that his last battle is remembered quite differently from that of George Armstrong Custer.

Carson saw no more combat after Adobe Walls; his role shifted increasingly toward trying to find solutions to the burgeoning Indian-white conflicts of the 1860s. Soon civil and military officials were consulting him, hoping his knowledge and experience would provide the key to these western conflicts. Several times in 1865 he, with his friend

William Bent, set down his opinions, and he and Bent helped negotiate the Treaty of the Little Arkansas.

Although others may have influenced some of Carson's written statements, his opinions seem consistent. He thought the chief cause of current troubles was "aggressions on the part of the numerous reckless frontiersmen" and the dishonesty and bad management of Indian agents. He credited reports that the Sand Creek massacre happened because the Colorado authorities "determined to get up an Indian war," and did not blame the Cheyennes and Arapahos for the current warfare. He believed that he and Bent could make peace and that "justice demands that every effort should be made to secure peace with the Cheyennes and Arapahoes before any war was prosecuted against them."[51]

Carson and William Bent collaborated in presenting their ideas to the government and trying to devise a peace settlement on the southern plains. Their notions were similar to those of serious reformers and military men of the time, which, considering their breadth of experience, is significant in itself. It appears that the ideas that gave rise to the reservation system were so pervasive in American culture that even the white men best acquainted with the Indians and the situation were unable to imagine anything better. And perhaps realistic, workable alternatives to the "only good Indian is a dead Indian" school, or to the Vanishing American theory, were in fact extremely limited.[52]

In urging the transfer of Indian affairs to the War Department, Carson and Bent differed sharply with civilian policymakers and the increasingly vocal Indian rights reformers. The reformers believed that military control meant "extermination." Bent and Carson had in mind the regulars, not volunteers like the perpetrators of the Sand Creek massacre.

Neither Carson nor Bent believed all Indian-white conflicts could be resolved without the use of force. The government, Carson emphasized, "should be strong enough to inspire their respect and fear, yet protecting them from internal dissension and external aggression." They hoped that well-located reservations, their integrity respected, might minimize conflict if set up before too late.

As white civilization pressed the Indians on all sides, Carson and Bent had a sense of approaching crisis, of time running out. Carson insisted on the government's moral obligation to save the Indians from the fate that some of his countrymen welcomed, others were resigned to. Carson was more likely to speak of moral obligation in concrete situations; the plight of the Indians was hardly an abstraction to him.[53]

The Treaty of the Little Arkansas immediately faced a hurdle. Carson and Bent were perhaps compelled to hope that the Cheyennes and Arapahos would accept a peace, and that a proper reservation could be found. The first area they recommended, in northwest Kansas and southwest Nebraska, was rendered impossible by a new travel route. The pace of settlement was overtaking the Indians even faster than they had feared. Because most members of the two tribes were unwilling to surrender any of their hunting grounds, the treaty Bent had guaranteed with his head brought only a lull in hostilities. Carson had participated in the negotiations, after urging the effort and volunteering his services, while knowing that General Carleton lacked enthusiasm for the process.

Carson's last military assignment was the command of Fort Garland, Colorado, where he was expected to maintain peace with the Utes and Jicarillas, as much by his personal influence as by military strength. He struggled to do so for over a year, all the while seeing hostilities as imminent. In the worst outbreak of violence, he once again seized an opportunity for peace opened up by Ouray.

Carson knew both the insecurity and fear of isolated frontier settlers and the suffering of the Indians when the white men struck back. In a sense he knew too much and could not always maintain the cool consistency and objectivity of one well removed from the situation in space or time. In 1856 he complained of David Meriwether's purchasing a peace with Utes and Jicarillas before they were properly chastised—the same people he feared had been provoked into hostility by the hasty actions of army officers. He denounced Meriwether, yet at the same time insisted that the Utes were sincere in their desire for peace.

The disgruntlement with the Bureau of Indian Affairs he expressed in the 1860s probably arose from his frustrations in the 1850s: the disputes with Meriwether, the failure to set up reservations, and the persistent state of warfare and insecurity in New Mexico, especially the Navajo troubles. The disgust was shared by many frontiersmen. Carson occasionally implied that he had had to issue food to Indians who were not being fed by their own agents. By 1865 he was convinced that military control of Indian affairs would be firmer, more consistent, more efficient, and above all more honest. Yet in 1867, needing a job, he sought the appointment as superintendent of Indian Affairs for Colorado, no doubt believing he could do things right. The Utes had said they would be happy to have him as agent again.

Carson was not an eager campaigner in the conflicts of the 1860s, but he saw the military operations as a necessity. By 1866, James Rusling reports, "he declared all our Indian troubles were caused originally by bad white men, and was terribly severe on the barbarities of the border." Rusling might have been describing one of the "Friends of the Indian" of the period, a breed despised by frontier Indian-haters. In their ranks few would have expected to find Kit Carson, the great scout and Indian-fighter. Many westerners would have laughed, or cursed, to hear an easterner say that "pore ignorant" Indians could not be expected to do better than imitate white men who did such things. They would hardly have expected such words from Kit Carson, the "incarnate devil in an Indian fight" of the dime novels.

Kit had come a long way from the Boonslick militiamen who wanted to murder the Miami prisoners, and he was out of step with the Denver citizens who were delighted by the Cheyenne scalps taken at Sand Creek. He had apparently come to a realization of the limits and dangers inherent in the retaliatory principle, denouncing the practice of punishing whole tribes for the actions of a few. Like many frontiersmen, he had experienced a range of human relationships possible in a world where the simple polarity of "Red" and "White" broke down into a kaleidoscope of individuals and groups. It has been demonstrated how white settlement reinforced the polarity.[54]

Men like Rusling and Henry Tilton, who knew Carson in his last years, believed that "the Indians had no truer friend." Tilton wrote, "He was ever ready to promote the welfare of the Utes," seeing this as the reason for Kit's last journey to Washington when he was desperately ill. Carson's journey to Washington in 1868 may have been "one more call to duty," his responsibility as superintendent of Indian affairs in Colorado, and he may have hoped that eastern doctors could prolong his life. Doctor Tilton believed that Carson, "ever ready to defend the weak against the strong," wanted to help the Utes.[55]

Carson helped negotiate the treaty by which the Utes gave up much of their hunting grounds, receiving in return the supposed title to much of the western slope of Colorado. Today there are only two small Ute reservations in southwest Colorado. Did Carson assist cynically in persuading the Ute chiefs to accept what he knew was only another step in their ongoing dispossession? Or did he think that the treaty really offered the last, best hope for the Utes, the "alternative to extinction" he had been urging since the 1850s? Given his sense of urgency, he may have seen no alternative but to try. The treaty allotment, much larger than the Bosque Redondo reserve, he may have hoped would provide sufficient hunting ground, and a cushion against white expansion, until the Indians learned to farm.

As noted, the reservation system grew out of widely held assumptions about Indians and about the results of white expansion. Carson accepted the major premises, apparently until his death. His opinions, and William Bent's, were passed up to U. S. Grant, and just may have had some influence on Grant's "Peace Policy," which incorporated some of these ideas.

Carson's belief that a new generation of Indians might find reservation life more congenial may have been naive or overly optimistic. Clifford Trafzer accuses Carson of "callous paternalism," but other evidence suggests that he was so concerned with the immediate problems, war and the survival of the Indians, that he spared far less thought for the long-range problems. What was happening now seemed the worst thing possible. In the last days of his life, he went to extraordinary lengths, for a dying man, to acquire a reservation for the Utes.

Detailed self-revelation, except in the context of "getting religion," was not favored by Carson's culture, and he did not explain his motives at length. James Rusling found him "very conscientious," frequently asking if it was right to do something, "as if it was the habit of his mind to test everything by the moral law." Rusling's impression that Carson judged things according to a strong ethical standard would help explain why so many implicitly compared him to Cooper's Leatherstocking—bearing in mind that that was just what many wanted to see. This may seem hard to reconcile with the many episodes of violence narrated in this work. Carson's standards of right and wrong were formed first of all in the backcountry, where justice was often based on an intuitive perception of right and wrong, often administered by one's own hand. Carson increasingly avoided the use of violence in specific cases, seeing both sides all too clearly, but he apparently never imagined that force could be ruled out as a last resort.[56]

Kit did not have much to say about abstract principles of justice in his day-to-day reports as an Indian agent, but in 1865, asked about larger considerations, he spoke of the justice of seeking peace with the Cheyennes and Arapahos, of the United States' moral obligation to help the Indians. With William Bent he declared, "By dispossessing them of their country, we assume their stewardship." Failure to perform this duty would be "a damning blot and reproach" to the American people. If Rusling's impression of his character was correct, then these words may be more than rhetorical window dressing added by a scribe.[57]

It does seem that Carson's ideas changed somewhat from the 1850s to his last years. He became more doubtful about volunteer troops, became dissatisfied with the Bureau of Indian Affairs, and placed the lion's share of blame for Indian-white conflict on whites. Not everyone can make such adjustments in viewing the world after reaching middle age.

Rather than measuring Kit Carson by the absolutist standard of the late twentieth century, we should consider where he got to from where he started. Frontier whites tended to see themselves as the victims of Indians, whose hostile acts were not a defense of their birthright, or an attempt to survive, but criminal acts prompted by innate savagery against innocent people, whose deaths, particularly those of women and children, enraged white men. The attacks, however much exaggerated, were real enough, and fear and hatred combined with desire for Indian land to create a powerful stereotype. Carson, from childhood experience, could understand these feelings. He had felt terrible frustration at his failure to rescue Ann White, whose fate embodied so much of what white people believed and feared about Indians. Although Carson never forgot Ann White or the reality her death represented, experience had taught him much more. Like the hero of Conrad Richter's novel *The Light in the Forest*, a former captive among the Delawares, Carson had the misfortune of being able to see people on both sides—in a situation where whites and Indians had become mutually hostile categories—as human beings.

Carson was not so bitterly divided as Richter's hero; he knew who he was and which side he would be on if the choice had to be made. But like William Bent and others of his "class of men," he also knew too much; he had learned to see Indians as individual, varied, and human, not a single disposable collection of dehumanized beings. He did not apologize for the violence he had seen, but the extinction that many of his fellow Americans saw as inevitable, perhaps desirable, was more than he could swallow, though he feared it might come true. In his years as a soldier he was not the enthusiastic scourge of the Indians but an aging warrior undertaking a necessary duty his superiors insisted only he could do—a duty to his fellow citizens to end the terror and destruction he had known from his childhood.

Kit Carson knew that people had wildly distorted ideas about him, that "some of these newspaper fellows know more about my affairs than I do." Being illiterate, he may never have fully appreciated the extent to which people saw him in terms of a fictional model, always clad in buckskin, ever scouring the prairies and slaying Indians by the hundred. He never seems to have confused himself with the fictional character who appeared under his name on the printed page, and who sometimes irked and sometimes amused him. He knew that he was plain old Kit Carson from Boonslick, Missouri (which he probably pronounced "Missoura," like so many natives). Americans have a special place in their hearts for heroes who do not forget where they came from, who keep the common touch, who can still laugh at themselves. This is surely one reason why Abraham Lincoln has become the supreme national hero. We often tear down heroes who seem to have forgotten that they are common clay. Historians, until recently, have always treated Carson with a respect they did not give Davy Crockett, and certainly not Buffalo Bill Cody.[58]

Of a backcountry hero of a later generation, Sergeant Alvin York, John Bowers writes, "He bore his fame with a sly chuckle, a little uncomfortable"—words that might have been written about Kit Carson; they both came from people who would not tolerate too obviously inflated self-esteem, however much they practiced aggressive male self-assertion. Doctor Tilton believed that "Carson had great contempt for noisy braggarts and shams of every sort." Not surprisingly, he strove, probably without thinking about it very much, to avoid any appearance of being a noisy braggart or a sham himself. He would not insist on being addressed as "General": "Oh call me Kit at once and be done with it." On his last trip to Washington, he declined to be photographed with other peace commissioners, saying, "Oh, I guess I won't be in it, this time." Since he had just been photographed with General Carleton and other military men, the commissioners thought he had become too proud to be photographed with mere civilians. In fact, he was probably too ill and tired. The next morning he said to three of them, "Boys, let's us four go out and have those pictures." When they signed the picture, he asked if he should sign "Christopher," or "just Kit," and of course they insisted on "Kit." That he might appear to be so puffed up by vanity as to be rude to friends was intolerable. This modesty and humility was one of the qualities that endeared him to so many, but Kit had his pride, as these pages have illustrated.[59]

CONCLUSION

Whether or not Carson was a hero, he certainly fit many of the criteria established in western culture since the time of the ancient Greeks. He traveled to far places; he did battle with men of many breeds and performed deeds of valor, as such deeds were viewed by his friends and his enemies; he fought for his people against their traditional enemies and vanquished them. He was respected as a man who kept his word, told the truth, was loyal to his friends, and did his duty as he and his contemporaries conceived it. He was an old-fashioned American who believed that courage, loyalty, doing one's duty, and keeping one's word were of paramount importance. He asserted his belief in honorable conduct toward friend and foe. A famous and rather cynical general thought his integrity "simply perfect." This is the sort of material from which heroes have traditionally been made for centuries. Today many believe that we should adopt new criteria, that the heroes of the future should more closely resemble Martin Luther King Jr., Mahatma Gandhi, and Mother Teresa. This might well be a desirable development, but if it comes to pass it will signal radical changes in our society and culture. Patricia Limerick argues that the old Western heroes need to be replaced. They are "a pretty battered and discredited lot," who "often affirm the wrong faith entirely—the faith in guns and violence—or serve solely as individual examples of courage and determination, attached to no particular principle." She prefers "sustainable" heroes, one of whose qualifications is their inconsistency, their record of doing the right thing some of the time, a kind of heroism we can all aspire to. The Kit Carson depicted in these pages is surely inconsistent enough to meet her criteria, although she would undoubtedly place him beyond the pale simply for his involvement in violence, especially against Indians. Still, his human fallibility and his efforts to do what seemed right in a changing world make him more interesting, more down-to-earth, and perhaps even more "sustainable" as a hero, than the cardboard caricatures who have borne his name. In an age of hype, when style counts for more than substance, there may be something to be said for a hero who deprecated his own legend.[60]

When Carson's contemporaries looked at him, they tended to see the Old Scout, exemplified in fiction by Cooper's Leatherstocking, who was in turn inspired by Daniel Boone. The real Kit Carson displayed some of the characteristics of both: he came from the same backcountry culture as Boone, and Cooper may well have incorporated traits of frontiersmen he had known or heard about. Like both Boone and Bumppo, he was not an Indian-hater, but had much more complex feelings about them. For all of them, relations encompassed fear and friendship, love and hate, mutual respect and paternalism, hostility and alliance. Not surprisingly, Kit was far more complex than Leatherstocking, more adaptable than the fictional scout, or even than the real-life Boone. As his world changed around him, he changed with it. He was indeed the Old Scout, the trapper and hunter, and on occasion he was the Indian-fighter, both in personal combat and as a military commander.

Daniel Boone, in popular mythology, was the eternal frontiersman, always in search of "elbow-room," never able to secure a permanent place and so doomed to keep heading west toward a new frontier. To his countrymen he exemplified a necessary stage of white American expansion, breaking the trail and subduing the Indians, but thereby destroying the wilderness that he loved. Cooper portrayed Natty Bumppo playing the same role; preferring the wilderness—the life, in fact, of an Indian—Natty leads the advance of white civilization and, however unwittingly, helps clear away the Indians so white people can safely settle on the land. The process was seen in the nineteenth century as inevitable, and the result desirable, in spite of the tragic overtones. In the 1880s General Sherman placed Carson with Boone in a "class of men" who were "most useful in their day," but were already as antiquated as Jason and Ulysses. Richard Slotkin sees all these stories as part of a myth of "regeneration through violence," in which white men become like Indians in order to conquer them in a blood ritual, so validating their claim to the land.[61]

This book has tried to show that Kit Carson lived in a real world with real Indians, and his relations with them were not simple. He was a man of the frontier, the meeting place of peoples and cultures. He lived much of his life, physically and psychologically, in the "middle ground," and he knew that there were more than two different kinds of people.

He played his part in Anglo-American expansion, probably unconsciously as a trapper, perhaps with more intent as Frémont's guide, and certainly knowing what was going on as a settler, Indian agent, soldier, and peacemaker. In each phase he was intimately involved with Indians, profiting from what he had learned from and about them. As time went on, he understood more and more clearly what the expansion of his people meant for the Indians, and he was forced to think about the consequences. He could not abandon his commitment to his own people, his duty as he saw it. Neither could he ignore the fate of the Indians, who for him were undeniably human. The middle ground eroded away around him, and its values were increasingly hard to sustain. He tried, inconsistently and imperfectly because he was human, and a man of his time and culture, to do what he thought might best serve the interests of all parties.

It would be presumptuous to try to speak for Kit, but perhaps he would be willing to have some words he once used in a particular situation applied to his life as a whole: "I do not know whether I done rite or wrong, but I done what I thought was best."[62]

Notes

A&W   *Arizona and the West*
CIA   Commissioner of Indian Affairs
DOK   Harvey Lewis Carter, *"Dear Old Kit": The Historical Christopher Carson.*
    [1968] Norman: University of Oklahoma Press, 1991.
MHQ   *MHQ: The Quarterly Journal of Military History*
NARS   National Archives and Record Service, Washington DC
NMHR   *New Mexico Historical Review*
NR   Lawrence Kelly, *Navajo Roundup: Selected Correspondence of Kit Carson's Expedition Against the Navajo, 1863–1865.* Boulder CO: Pruett Publishing Company, 1970.
OR   *War of the Rebellion: A Compilation of the Official Records of the Union and Confederate Armies.* Washington DC: Government Printing Office, 1880–1901. Series 1 unless otherwise noted.
RCIT   *Condition of the Indian Tribes: Report of the Joint Special Committee, Appointed Under Joint Resolution of March 3, 1865, With an Appendix.* Washington DC: Government Printing Office, 1867.
WHQ   *Western Historical Quarterly*

PREFACE

1. Robert M. Utley, "An Indian before Breakfast: Kit Carson Then and Now," in R. C. Gordon-McCutchan, ed., *Kit Carson: Indian Fighter or Indian Killer?* (Niwot: University Press of Colorado, 1996), 91.

2. Gale E. Christianson, *Writing Lives Is the Devil! Essays of a Biographer at Work* (Hamden CT: Archon Books, 1993), 10.

3. Richard Slotkin, *Gunfighter Nation: The Myth of the Frontier in Twentieth-Century America* (New York: Atheneum, 1992), 14, 16.

4. Douglas S. Freeman, *R. E. Lee: A Biography* (New York: Charles Scribner's Sons, 1934), 1:viii.

5. Lawrence C. Kelly, "The Historiography of the Navajo Roundup," in Gordon-McCutchan, *Kit Carson*, 49–71; Gordon-McCutchan, "'Rope Thrower' and the Navajo," in *Kit Carson*, 21–47; Marc Simmons, "Kit and the Indians," in *Kit Carson*, 73–90.

1. Richard Boyd Hauck, *Davy Crockett: A Handbook* (1982; reprint, Lincoln: University of Nebraska Press, 1986), 55–105.

2. Herman Melville, "Mr. Parkman's Tour," in *The Piazza Tales and Other Prose Pieces, 1839–1860* (Evanston IL: Northwestern University Press, 1987), 233.

3. Kent L. Steckmesser, *The Western Hero in History and Legend* (Norman: University of Oklahoma Press, 1965), 25, 35–44; Daryl Jones, *The Dime Novel Western* (Bowling Green OH: Popular Press, 1978), 57–61, 180–81, 183; Darlis A. Miller, "Kit Carson and Dime Novels: The Making of a Legend," in Gordon-McCutchan, *Kit Carson*, 1–19. Carson appeared as a character in a magazine serial soon published as a novel in 1848 in Great Britain; see George Frederick Ruxton, *Life in the Far West*, ed. LeRoy R. Hafen (Norman: University of Oklahoma Press, 1951).

4. DOK, 15–17. DeWitt C. Peters, *The Life and Adventures of Kit Carson, the Nestor of the Rocky Mountains, from Facts Narrated by Himself* (New York: W. R. C. Clark and Meeker, 1859).

5. Edwin L. Sabin, *Kit Carson Days (1809–1868)* (Chicago: A. C. McClurg and Company, 1914); Stanley Vestal [Walter Stanley Campbell], *Kit Carson: The Happy Warrior of the Old West* (Boston: Houghton Mifflin Company, 1928); Blanche C. Grant, ed., *Kit Carson's Own Story of His Life* (Taos NM: n.p., 1926); Milo Milton Quaife, ed., *Kit Carson's Autobiography* (1935; reprint, Lincoln: University of Nebraska Press, 1966); Bernice Blackwelder, *Great Westerner: The Story of Kit Carson* (Caldwell ID: Caxton Printers, 1962); M. Morgan Estergreen, *Kit Carson: A Portrait in Courage* (Norman: University of Oklahoma Press, 1962); DOK; Thelma S. Guild and Harvey L. Carter, *Kit Carson: A Pattern for Heroes* (Lincoln: University of Nebraska Press, 1984.

6. Bernard DeVoto, *Across the Wide Missouri* (Boston: Houghton Mifflin Company, 1947); David Lavender, *Bent's Fort* (1954; reprint, Lincoln: University of Nebraska Press, 1972); Jack Schaefer, *Company of Cowards*, in *The Short Novels of Jack Schaefer* (Boston: Houghton Mifflin Company, 1967), 321–460.

7. Dee Brown, *Bury My Heart at Wounded Knee: An Indian History of the American West* (New York: Holt, Rinehart and Winston, 1970), 23, 100.

8. Harvey L. Carter, "The Curious Case of the Slandered Scout, the Aggressive Anthropologist, the Delinquent Dean, and the Acquiescent Army," *Denver Westerners Brand Book* 28 (1973): 95, 98.

9. Tony Hillerman, introduction to Haniel Long, *Piñon Country* (1941; reprint, Lincoln: University of Nebraska Press, 1986), xiv; Tony Hillerman, in *Hillerman Country* (New York: Harper Collins, 1991), 131, confuses General James Carleton and Governor Henry Connelly.

10. Russell Thornton, *American Indian Holocaust and Survival: A Population History Since 1492* (Norman: University of Oklahoma Press, 1987), 183–84.

11. Alvin M. Josephy, *The Civil War in the American West* (New York: Alfred A. Knopf, 1991), 284–87, 291.

12. Clifford E. Trafzer, *The Kit Carson Campaign: The Last Great Navajo War* (Norman: University of Oklahoma Press, 1982), xv-xvi.

13. Trafzer, *Kit Carson Campaign*, 58, 59, 62.

14. Ibid., 237.

15. Bob Scott, *Blood at Sand Creek: The Massacre Revisited* (Caldwell ID: Caxton Printers, 1994), xii.

16. Stephen Tatum, review of *Kit Carson* by Guild and Carter, *Great Plains Quarterly* 6 (fall 1986): 310–11.

17. Daniel Boorstin, introduction to William T. Hagan, *American Indians* (Chicago: University of Chicago Press, 1979), xi; Francis Jennings, *The Invasion of America: Indians, Colonialism, and the Cant of Conquest* (Chapel Hill: University of North Carolina Press, 1975).

18. Vestal, *Kit Carson*, viii.

19. DOK, xv, 18.

20. Carter, "Curious Case."

21. Tatum, review of Guild and Carter, 311.

22. Josh Kurtz, "The Second Battle for the West," *Santa Fe Reporter* 19 (1993): 11–12.

23. Kurtz, "Second Battle," 11; see also R. C. Gordon-McCutchan, "Revising the Revisionists: Manifesto of the Realist Western Historians," *Journal of the West* 33 (July 1994): 3–7.

24. DOK, 124–26.

25. Patricia N. Limerick, "Making the Most of Words: Verbal Activity and Western America," in William Cronon et al., eds., *Under an Open Sky: Rethinking America's Western Past* (New York: W. W. Norton, 1992), 167–68.

26. DeWitt C. Peters, *Kit Carson's Life and Adventures, From Facts Narrated by Himself . . .* , rev. ed. (Hartford CT: Dustin, Gilman and Company, 1874), 356–57.

27. See DOK, 217–21; Guild and Carter, *Kit Carson*.

28. DOK, 188–91.

29. William Tecumseh Sherman, *Memoirs* (1875; reprint, New York: Da Capo Press, 1984), 46–47.

30. George D. Brewerton, *Overland with Kit Carson*, ed. Stallo Vinton (New York: A. L. Burt, 1930), 38.

31. Steckmesser, *Western Hero*, 36–37.

32. Ibid., 35–46; Jones, *Dime Novel Western*, 57–60; Richard Slotkin, *The Fatal Environment: The Myth of the Frontier in the Age of Industrialization, 1800–1890* (New York: Atheneum, 1985), 203–7.

33. James I. Robertson, *Soldiers Blue and Gray* (Columbia: University of South Carolina Press, 1988), 26.

34. James Fenimore Cooper, "Preface to the Leatherstocking Tales [1850]," in *The Deerslayer; or, The First Warpath*, ed. James Franklin Beard (Albany: State University of New York Press, 1987), 6–7.

35. Brewerton, *Overland with Kit Carson*, 38.

36. *Rough and Ready Annual* (1848), quoted in Steckmesser, *Western Hero*, 25.

37. Edward Fitzgerald Beale, in Gerald Thompson, "'Kit Carson's Ride': E. F. Beale Assails Joaquin Miller's Indecent Poem," A&W 26 (summer 1984): 145–47. Thompson reprints the whole of Beale's 1872 article.

38. Worthington Whittredge, "The Autobiography of Worthington Whittredge, 1820–1910," ed. John I. H. Bauer, *Brooklyn Museum Journal* 1 (1942): 47.

39. Steckmesser, *Western Hero*, 24–34; Slotkin, *Fatal Environment*, 203–5.

40. Brewerton, *Overland with Kit Carson*, 143.

41. Beale in Thompson, "'Kit Carson's Ride,'" 146–47.

42. Jessie Benton Frémont, *The Will and the Way Stories* (Boston: D. Lathrop Company, 1891), 30; Jessie Benton Frémont to Carson, May 1863, in Pamela Herr and Mary Lee Spence, eds., *The Letters of Jessie Benton Frémont* (Urbana: University of Illinois Press, 1993), 353.

43. Whittredge, "Autobiography," 1:48.

44. Frank Chalk and Kurt Jonassohn, quoted in James Axtell, *Beyond 1492: Encounters in Colonial North America* (New York: Oxford University Press, 1992), 261.

45. Axtell, *Beyond 1492*, 261. See also Steven T. Katz, "The Uniqueness of the Holocaust: The Historical Dimension," in Alan S. Rosenbaum, *Is the Holocaust Unique? Perspectives on Comparative Genocide* (Boulder CO: Westview Press, 1996), 19–27, who finds United States Indian policy unjust but "contragenocidal in its intent."

46. Fritz Stern, *The Failure of Illiberalism: Essays on the Political Culture of Modern Germany* (New York: Alfred A. Knopf, 1972), xii.

47. Richard Drinnon, *Facing West: The Metaphysics of Indian-Hating and Empire-Building* (Minneapolis: University of Minnesota Press, 1980), 458–59.

48. Martin Green, *The Great American Adventure* (Boston: Beacon Press, 1984), vii, 124–25, 126; D. H. Lawrence, *Studies in Classic American Literature* (London: Penguin Books, 1971), 68.

49. Francis Parkman, *The Oregon Trail*, ed. E. N. Feltskog (Madison: University of Wisconsin Press, 1969; reprint, Lincoln: University of Nebraska Press, 1994), 293; Mark Twain, *Roughing It* (Berkeley: University of California Press, 1972), 145.

50. James F. Meline, *Two Thousand Miles on Horseback* (1868; reprint, Albuquerque: Horn and Wallace, 1966), 246.

51. Sabin, *Kit Carson Days*, 2:505.

52. John Mack Faragher, *Daniel Boone: The Life and Legend of an American Pioneer* (New York: Henry Holt, 1992), 351.

2. BACKCOUNTRY

1. DOK, 38–39; William E. Foley, *The Genesis of Missouri: From Wilderness Outpost to Statehood* (Columbia: University of Missouri Press, 1989); Larry C. Skogen, *Indian Depredation Claims, 1796–1920* (Norman: University of Oklahoma Press, 1996), 37, notes that Indian claims to the area had not been relinquished.

2. David Hackett Fischer, *Albion's Seed: Four British Folkways in America* (New York: Oxford University Press, 1989), 605–8, 618–21.

3. George MacDonald Fraser, *The Steel Bonnets: The Story of the Anglo-Scottish Border Reivers* (London: Barrie and Jenkins, 1971), 2, 21–30; Fischer, *Albion's Seed*, 621–28.

4. Blackwelder, *Great Westerner*, 13; Guild and Carter, *Kit Carson*, 1–2; Fischer, *Albion's Seed*, 629–32.

5. Fischer, *Albion's Seed*, 633–34, 639.

6. Peters, *Kit Carson's Life and Adventures*, 19.

7. Fischer, *Albion's Seed*, 680.

8. Estergreen, *Kit Carson*, 8–13.

9. Guild and Carter, *Kit Carson*, 4–5; Faragher, *Daniel Boone*, 278–79, 290; Foley, *Genesis of Missouri*, 187–88; Henry Marie Brackenridge, *Views of Louisiana . . .* (1814; reprint, Chicago: Quadrangle Books, 1962), 211; DOK, 38.

10. Foley, *Genesis of Missouri*, 220; William T. Hagan, *The Sac and Fox Indians* (Norman: University of Oklahoma Press, 1958), 16–25.

11. John K. Mahon, *The War of 1812* (Gainesville: University of Florida Press, 1972), 134, 289; Foley, *Genesis of Missouri*, 224–33; Arrell M. Gibson, *The Kickapoos: Lords of the Middle Border* (Norman: University of Oklahoma Press, 1963), 73–75.

12. Paul Horgan, *Josiah Gregg and His Vision of the Early West* (New York: Farrar, Strauss, Giroux, 1979), 15.

13. Foley, *Genesis of Missouri*, 231; Louis Houck, *A History of Missouri* (Chicago: R. R. Donnelly and Sons, 1908), 3:114–20; Gibson, *Kickapoos*, 74; Horgan, *Josiah Gregg*, 16.

14. Houck, *History of Missouri*, 3:117, 118–19; Estergreen, *Kit Carson*, 20.

15. Gibson, *Kickapoos*, 75–77; Estergreen, *Kit Carson*, 21.

16. Foley, *Genesis of Missouri*, 220.

17. Houck, *History of Missouri*, 3:120–23; Louis Pelzer, *Henry Dodge* (Iowa City: State Historical Society of Iowa, 1911), 23–26.

18. Oakah L. Jones, *Pueblo Warriors and Spanish Conquest* (Norman: University of Oklahoma Press, 1966); Thomas W. Dunlay, *Wolves for the Blue Soldiers* (Lincoln: University of Nebraska Press, 1982), 11–15.

19. Benjamin Church, "Entertaining Passages Relating to King Philip's War . . . ," in Richard Slotkin and James K. Folsom, eds., *So Dreadfull a Judgement: Puritan Responses to King Philip's War* (Middletown CT: Wesleyan University Press, 1978), 433, 441, passim; David H. Corkran, *The Cherokee Frontier: Conflict and Survival, 1740–62* (Norman: University of Oklahoma Press, 1962), 208–13, 216, 246–54; James H. O'Donnell, *Southern Indians in the American Revolution* (Knoxville: University of Tennessee Press, 1973), 71; Robert Frazier, *The Mohicans of Stockbridge* (Lincoln: University of Nebraska Press, 1992), 116–43; Robert Rogers, *Journals of Major Robert Rogers* (1765; reprint, New York: Corinth Books, 1961), 55, 70, passim; James K. Greer, *Texas Ranger: Jack Hays in the Frontier Southwest* (College Station: Texas A&M University Press, 1993), 43, 50–51.

20. Slotkin and Folsom, *So Dreadful a Judgement*, 373; James Smith, *An Account of the Remarkable Occurrences in the Life and Travels of Col. James Smith* . . . (1799; reprint, Cincinnati: Robert Clarke Company, 1907), 108; Greer, *Texas Ranger*, 29–32.

21. George A. Jellison, *Ethan Allen, Frontier Rebel* (Syracuse NY: Syracuse University Press, 1969), 137; Smith, *Account*, 157–58; James Axtell, *The European and the Indian: Essays in the Ethnohistory of Colonial North America* (New York: Oxford University Press, 1981), 273, 284–85; 297–303.

22. Estergreen, *Kit Carson*, 18–19; Foley, *Genesis of Missouri*, 228–29.

23. Fischer, *Albion's Seed*, 687–90.

24. Foley, *Genesis of Missouri*, 186; Richard Maxwell Brown, *No Duty to Retreat: Violence and Values in American History and Society* (New York: Oxford University Press, 1991).

25. Fischer, *Albion's Seed*, 766–68; John Bowers, "The Mythical Morning of Sergeant York," MHQ 8(Winter 1996): 39.

26. Fischer, *Albion's Seed*, 769.

27. Fischer, *Albion's Seed*, 662–68, 720–21, 768: DOK, 214; Meline, *Two Thousand Miles on Horseback*, 246.

28. Brian Steel Wills, *A Battle from the Start: The Life of Nathan Bedford Forrest* (New York: Harper Collins, 1992); Horgan, *Josiah Gregg*; Bowers, "Mythical Morning," 39.

29. Jacqueline D. Meketa, *Legacy of Honor: The Life of Rafael Chacon, a Nineteenth-Century New Mexican* (Albuquerque: University of New Mexico Press, 1986), 123; William T. Sherman, in Edward S. Ellis, *The Life of Kit Carson: Hunter, Trapper, Guide, Indian Agent and Colonel U.S.A.* (Chicago: M. A. Donahue, 1889), 249.

30. Guild and Carter, *Kit Carson*, 10.

31. Ibid., 10–11.

32. DOK, 188–91; Jessie Frémont, *The Will and the Way Stories*, 40–42; Fischer, *Albion's Seed*, 721–24.

33. DOK, 39n.

34. Guild and Carter, *Kit Carson*, 11.

3. MOUNTAIN MAN

1. DOK, 38; Guild and Carter, *Kit Carson*, 16–17.

2. William E. Brown, *The Santa Fe Trail* (St. Louis: Patrice Press, 1988); Max L. Moorhead, *New Mexico's Royal Road: Trade and Travel on the Chihuahua Trail* (Norman: University of Oklahoma Press, 1958).

3. David J. Weber, *The Taos Trappers: The Fur Trade in the Far Southwest* (Norman: University of Oklahoma Press, 1971), viii, 3–4, 34–58;

4. David J. Wishart, *The Fur Trade of the American West, 1807–1840* (Lincoln: University of Nebraska Press, 1979), 127–28.

5. DOK, 42–44; Guild and Carter, *Kit Carson*, 26–34.

6. Henry Nash Smith, *Virgin Land: The American West as Symbol and Myth* (Cambridge MA: Harvard University Press, 1950), 81–82; Albert Pike, *Prose Sketches and Poems Written in the Western Country* (1834; reprint, Albuquerque: Calvin Horn, Publisher, 1967); Ruxton, *Life in the Far West*; William Drummond Stewart, *Edward Warren* (1854; reprint, Missoula MT: Mountain Press, 1986); Washington Irving, *Astoria; or, Adventures of an Enterprise beyond the Rocky Mountains*, ed. Edgeley W. Todd (Norman: University of Oklahoma Press, 1964); Washington Irving, *The Adventures of Captain Bonneville, U.S.A.*, ed. Edgeley W. Todd (Norman: University of Oklahoma Press, 1961); for a fuller history, see Harvey L. Carter and Marcia C. Spencer, "Stereotypes of the Mountain Man," WHQ 6 (January 1975): 17–32.

7. William H. Goetzman, "The Mountain Man as Jacksonian Man," *American Quarterly* 15 (fall 1963): 402–15; Irving, *Adventures of Captain Bonneville*, 12; see also Jerome O. Steffen, *Comparative Frontiers: A Proposal for Studying the American West* (Norman: University of Oklahoma Press, 1980), 29–50.

8. Goetzman, "Mountain Man," 408–10; James O. Pattie, *The Personal Narrative of James O. Pattie* (1831; reprint, Lincoln: University of Nebraska Press, 1984), 111; Lewis H. Garrard, *Wah-to-yah and the Taos Trail* (Norman: University of Oklahoma Press, 1955), 63; George Frederick Ruxton, *Adventures in Mexico and the Rocky Mountains* (1847; reprint, Glorieta NM: Rio Grande Press, 1973), 242.

9. Carter and Spencer, "Stereotypes."

10. Ibid., 22–23, 24, 28–29.

11. Winfred Blevins, *Give Your Heart to the Hawks: A Tribute to the Mountain Men* (Los Angeles: Nash Publishing, 1973), 299.

12. Carter and Spencer, "Stereotypes," 22; Francis Paul Prucha, *The Sword of the Republic: The United States Army on the Frontier, 1783–1846* (New York: Macmillan, 1969), 155–57, 236–38, 365–94.

13. Blevins, *Give Your Heart*, 299; Wishart, *Fur Trade*, 146.

14. Howard R. Lamar, *The Far Southwest, 1846–1912: A Territorial History* (New Haven CT: Yale University Press, 1966), 250; William R. Swagerty, "Marriage and Settlement Patterns of Rocky Mountain Trappers and Traders," WHQ 11 (April 1980): 179; Richard White, *The Middle Ground: Indians, Empires, and Republics in the Great Lakes Region, 1650–1815* (Cambridge: Cambridge University Press, 1991), ix–x.

15. Frances Fuller Victor, *The River of the West: Life and Adventures in the Rocky Mountains and Oregon* (Hartford CT: R. W. Bliss and Company, 1869), 142; Bernard DeVoto, *Across the Wide Missouri* (Boston: Houghton Mifflin Company, 1947), 97.

16. Gary E. Moulton, ed., *Journals of the Lewis and Clark Expedition* (Lincoln: University of Nebraska Press, 1993), 8:157, 302; Burton Harris, *John Colter: His Years in the Rockies* (1952; reprint, Lincoln: University of Nebraska Press, 1993);

Thomas James, *Three Years among the Indians and Mexicans* (Philadelphia: J. B. Lippincott, 1962), 26.

17. Blevins, *Give Your Heart*, 298; John C. Ewers, "Indian Views of the White Man Prior to 1850: An Interpretation," in Daniel Tyler, ed., *Red Men and Hat Wearers: Viewpoints in Indian History* (Boulder CO: Pruett Publishing Company, 1976), 10–13.

18. Peter Skene Ogden, *Traits of American Indian Life and Character* (1853; reprint, New York: AMS Press, 1972), 12; John C. Ewers, *The Blackfeet: Raiders on the Northwestern Plains* (Norman: University of Oklahoma Press, 1958), ix, 52; Ewers, "Indian Views," 16–17; Frank R. Secoy, *Changing Military Patterns of the Great Plains Indians (Seventeenth Century through Early Nineteenth Century)* (Seattle: University of Washington Press, 1953; reprint, Lincoln: University of Nebraska Press, 1992), 51–59.

19. Ewers, "Indian Views," 8, 14–15; Anthony McGinnis, *Counting Coup and Cutting Horses: Intertribal Warfare on the Northern Plains, 1738–1889* (Evergreen CO: Cordillera Press, 1990), 16, 45 (Atkinson quote), and passim.

20. Ewers, "Indian Views," 8; W. P. Clark, *The Indian Sign Language* (1885; reprint, Lincoln: University of Nebraska Press, 1982), 223.

21. Ewers, "Indian Views," 8–9; Secoy, *Changing Military Patterns*, 58–59; James, *Three Years*, 26; McGinnis, *Counting Coup*, 9–10, 30; Frederick E. Hoxie, *Parading through History: The Making of the Crow Nation in America* (Cambridge: Cambridge University Press, 1995), 76–77.

22. Warren A. Ferris, *Life in the Rocky Mountains*, ed. LeRoy R. Hafen (Denver: Old West Publishing Company, 1983), 379–80; DeVoto, *Across the Wide Missouri*, 418; Charles E. Hanson, *The Plains Rifle* (New York: Bramhill House, 1960); Hanson, *The Hawken Rifle: Its Place in History* (Chadron NE: Fur Press, 1979).

23. Lewis O. Saum, *The Fur Trader and the Indian* (Seattle: University of Washington Press, 1965), 26, 87.

24. Wishart, *Fur Trade*, 122, 190; John C. Ewers, *Indian Life on the Upper Missouri* (Norman: University of Oklahoma Press, 1968), 17; Fred R. Gowans, *Rocky Mountain Rendezvous: A History of the Fur Trade Rendezvous, 1825–1840* (Layton UT: Peregrine Smith Books, 1985); Alfred Jacob Miller, *The West of Alfred Jacob Miller* (Norman: University of Oklahoma Press, 1951), 82, 110, 159, 175, 186, 189, 199 (text and illustrations); John Fahey, *The Flathead Indians* (Norman: University of Oklahoma Press, 1974), 39–40; Virginia Cole Trenholm and Maurine Carley, *The Shoshonis: Sentinels of the Rockies* (Norman: University of Oklahoma Press, 1964), 61–62; John Kirk Townsend, *Narrative of a Journey across the Rocky Mountains to the Columbia River* (1839; reprint, Lincoln: University of Nebraska Press, 1978), 82–83.

25. Saum, *Fur Trader and the Indian*, 46–59.

26. Ibid., 55–56.

27. Moulton, *Journals of the Lewis and Clark Expedition*, 8:128–36; James, *Three Years*, 26, 35–48; Ewers, *Blackfeet*, 45–57; Hoxie, *Parading through History*, 76–77; McGinnis, *Counting Coup*, 53–54; Miller, *West of Alfred Jacob Miller*, 148; Wishart, *Fur Trade*, 145–46, 163–65; DOK, 61.

28. Saum, *Fur Trader and the Indian*, 57–59, 93; Ferris, *Life in the Rocky Mountains*, 162–63; Irving, *Adventures of Captain Bonneville*, 33–34; Keith Algier, *The Crow and the Eagle: A Tribal History from Lewis and Clark to Custer* (Caldwell ID: Caxton Printers, 1993), 47–81; Fahey, *Flathead Indians*, 27–63; Victor, *River of the West*, 189–93; Osborne Russell, *Journal of a Trapper*, ed. Aubrey L. Haines (1955; reprint, Lincoln: University of Nebraska Press, 1965), 33; Daniel T. Potts to Dr. Lukens, July 8, 1827, in Dale L. Morgan, ed. *The West of William H. Ashley* (Denver: Old West Publishing Company, 1964), 167.

29. Ferris, *Life in the Rocky Mountains*, 200; Fahey, *Flathead Indians*, 41; Russell, *Journal of a Trapper*, 41; Victor, *River of the West*, 248–49.

30. Victor, *River of the West*, 259–60; Dorothy O. Johansen, ed., *Robert Newell's Memoranda: Travels in the Territory of Missourie . . .* (Portland OR: Champoeg Press, 1959), 39; E. Willard Smith, "Journal of E. Willard Smith . . . 1839–40," *Quarterly of the Oregon Historical Society* 14 (September 1913): 266–67; Bil Gilbert, *Westering Man: The Life of Joseph Walker* (New York: Atheneum, 1983), 159.

31. Townsend, *Narrative*, 104–5.

32. Irving, *Adventures of Captain Bonneville*, 150–53; Saum, *Fur Trader and the Indian*, 55–56.

33. Roy Harvey Pearce, *Savagism and Civilization: A Study of the Indian and the American Mind* (Baltimore: Johns Hopkins University Press, 1953), epigraph (Webster quote); Francis Parkman, *The Conspiracy of Pontiac and the Indian War after the Conquest of Canada* (1851; reprint, Lincoln: University of Nebraska Press, 1994), 1:41.

34. Fischer, *Albion's Seed*, 766–67; McGinnis, *Counting Coup*, 69; Richard J. Fehrman, "The Mountain Men—A Statistical View," in LeRoy R. Hafen, ed., *The Mountain Men and the Fur Trade of the Far West* (Glendale CA: Arthur H. Clark Company, 1972), 10:9.

35. Josiah Gregg, *Commerce of the Prairies*, ed. Max L. Moorhead (Norman: University of Oklahoma Press, 1954), 329; Fischer, *Albion's Seed*, 617.

36. DOK, 43–44; Weber, *Taos Trappers*, 142–43.

37. Gilbert, *Westering Man*, 159, 166–70, 43, 161.

38. Faragher, *Daniel Boone*, 19–22; Irving, *Astoria*, 211; Don Berry, *A Majority of Scoundrels: An Informal History of the Rocky Mountain Fur Company* (New York: Harper and Brothers, 1961), 316–17; Irving, *Adventures of Captain Bonneville*, 69–70.

39. Axtell, *The European and the Indian*, 272–73, 284–85; Blevins, *Give Your Heart*, 300.

40. Drinnon, *Facing West*, xvi–xvii, 51.

41. See William Stanton, *The Leopard's Spots: Scientific Attitudes toward Race in America, 1815–59* (Chicago: University of Chicago Press, 1960); Reginald Horsman, *Race and Manifest Destiny: The Origins of American Racial Anglo-Saxonism* (Cambridge MA: Harvard University Press, 1981); Robert E. Bieder, *Science Encounters the Indian, 1820–1880* (Norman: University of Oklahoma Press, 1986), 55–103.

42. Russell, *Journal of a Trapper*, 51, 109; Frederick A. Wislizenus, *A Journey*

to the *Rocky Mountains in the Year 1839* (St. Louis: Missouri Historical Society, 1912), 130.

43. Drinnon, *Facing West*, xvii–xviii, and passim.

44. Octave Mannoni, *Prospero and Caliban: The Psychology of Colonization* (Ann Arbor: University of Michigan Press, 1990), 39–48, 126; Ewers, "Indian Views," 10–20.

45. Blevins, *Give Your Heart*, 300; Parkman, *The Oregon Trail*, 332; David J. Weber, "Scarce More Than Apes: Historical Roots of Anglo-American Stereotypes of Mexicans," in David J. Weber, ed., *New Spain's Far Northern Frontier: Essays on Spain in the American West* (Albuquerque: University of New Mexico Press, 1979), 295–307.

46. Fehrman, "Mountain Men," 9; Swagerty, "Marriage and Settlement Patterns," 161–62; Ewers, *Adventures of Zenas Leonard*, 51–52, 139, 147–49; Bonner, *Life and Adventures of James P. Beckwourth*, 248–50; Willis Blenkinsop, "Edward Rose," in Hafen, *Mountain Men*, 9:334–45; Weber, *Taos Trappers*, 148–51; Harvey L. Carter, "Mariano Medina," in Hafen, *Mountain Men* 8:247–50; Janice K. Duncan, *Minority without a Champion: Kanakas on the Pacific Coast, 1788–1850* (Portland: Oregon Historical Society, 1972).

47. Ferris, *Life in the Rocky Mountains*, 386; Russell, *Journal of a Trapper*, 59; Morgan and Harris, *Rocky Mountain Journals of William Marshall Anderson*, 132–35, 333–34; Russell, *Journal of a Trapper*, 49.

48. Theodore Karamanski, "The Iroquois and the Fur Trade of the Far West," *The Beaver* 62 (spring 1982): 5–13; John C. Ewers, "Iroquois Indians in the Far West," *Montana, The Magazine of Western History* 13 (spring 1963): 2–10; Russell, *Journal of a Trapper*, 87, 89; Merle Wells, "Pierre Tevanitagon (Old Pierre, the Iroquois)," in Hafen, *Mountain Men*, 4:351–57; Gowans, *Rocky Mountain Rendezvous*, 65; James Meline, *Two Thousand Miles on Horseback* (1868; reprint, Albuquerque: Horn and Wallace, 1966), 249.

49. Frank G. Speck, "The Wapanachki Delawares and the English: Their Past as Viewed by an Ethnologist," *Pennsylvania Magazine of History and Biography* 67 (October 1943): 321–24; Washington Irving, *A Tour on the Prairies* (Norman: University of Oklahoma Press, 1956), 86–88; Harvey L. Carter, "Jim Swanock and the Delaware Hunters," in Hafen, *Mountain Men*, 7:293–300.

50. Francis Haines, "Tom Hill—Delaware Scout," *California Historical Society Quarterly* 25 (June 1946): 139–47 (note that the existence of the "Carson Men," as described by Haines and others, has been disproved by Harvey Carter in DOK, 20–22); Victor, *River of the West*, 227.

51. John Brown, *Mediumistic Experiences of John Brown, the Medium of the Rockies . . .* (San Francisco: Office of the Philosophical Journal, 1897), 23–26; Russell, *Journal of a Trapper*, 87–88.

52. Roger G. Barker, "The Influence of Frontier Environments on Behavior," in Jerome O. Steffen, ed., *The American West: New Perspectives, New Dimensions* (Norman: University of Oklahoma Press, 1979), 61–91.

53. Ferris, *Life in the Rocky Mountains*, 420.

54. Samuel Parker, *Journal of an Exploring Tour Beyond the Rocky Mountains* . . . (1838; reprint, Minneapolis: Ross and Haines, 1967), 80; DOK, 50–52.

55. Swagerty, "Marriage and Settlement Patterns," 164–65, 170.

56. Swagerty, "Marriage and Settlement Patterns," 164. On the Canadian experience, see Sylvia Van Kirk, *Many Tender Ties: Women in Fur-Trade Society, 1670–1870* (Norman: University of Oklahoma Press, 1980); Jennifer S. H. Brown, *Strangers in Blood: Fur Trade Families in Indian Country* (Vancouver: University of British Columbia Press, 1980); William J. Scheick, *The Half-Blood: A Cultural Symbol in Nineteenth-Century American Fiction* (Lexington: University Press of Kentucky, 1979); Steckmesser, *Western Hero*, 16–17; Slotkin, *Fatal Environment*, 206.

57. James B. Marsh, *Four Years in the Rockies; or, the Adventures of Isaac Rose* . . . (1884; reprint, Columbus OH: Longs College Book Company, n.d.), 92–93, 157–58; Slotkin, *Fatal Environment*, 206; Aubrey L. Haines, "Isaac P. Rose," in Hafen, *Mountain Men*, 7:255–60, says "most of what is said about Isaac Rose as a trapper in the Rocky Mountains is suspect"; Beale's statement reported in John C. Frémont, *Memoirs of My Life* (Chicago: Belford, Clarke and Company, 1887), 1:74; Guild and Carter, *Kit Carson*, 65, 89.

58. Guild and Carter, *Kit Carson*, 95, 96, 179, 190.

59. Swagerty, "Marriage and Settlement Patterns," 173–78; Janet Lecompte, *Pueblo, Hardscrabble, Greenhorn: The Upper Arkansas, 1832–1856* (Norman: University of Oklahoma Press, 1978); Rebecca M. Craver, *The Impact of Intimacy: Mexican-Anglo Intermarriage in New Mexico, 1821–1846* (El Paso: Texas Western Press, 1982).

60. Swagerty, "Marriage and Settlement Patterns," 176–77.

61. DOK, 48; George H. Phillips, *Indians and Intruders in Central California, 1769–1849* (Norman: University of Oklahoma Press, 1993), 63, 83–84, 118.

62. Guild and Carter, *Kit Carson*, 41–42.

63. DOK, 48; Guild and Carter, *Kit Carson*, 42.

64. DOK, 49. If these Indians were Mojaves, they had been in conflict with mountain men before; see Dale L. Morgan, *Jedediah Smith and the Opening of the West* (1953; reprint, Lincoln: University of Nebraska Press, 1964), 253, 337–38.

65. DOK, 50–52.

66. DOK, 52; Ferris, *Life in the Rocky Mountains*, 200; Fahey, *Flathead Indians*, 41.

67. DOK, 53–55; George E. Hyde, *Life of George Bent, Written from His Letters*, ed. Savoie Lottinville (Norman: University of Oklahoma Press, 1968), 65–67.

68. Green, *Great American Adventure*, 121. On the fate of horse thieves, see McGinnis, *Counting Coup*, 28–29; Ewers, *Blackfeet*, 135–36; Edwin Thompson Denig, *Five Indian Tribes of the Upper Missouri: Sioux, Arickaras, Assiniboins, Crees, Crows*, ed. John C. Ewers (Norman: University of Oklahoma Press, 1961), 144–47.

69. Hyde, *Life of George Bent*, 64–67; Green, *Great American Adventure*, 126; Allan Nevins, *Frémont: Pathmarker of the West* (1939; reprint, Lincoln: University of Nebraska Press, 1992),100; DOK, 54n.

70. Victor, *River of the West*, 154–57; DOK, 55–56n.; Janet Lecompte,"Levin Mitchell," in Hafen, *Mountain Men*, 5:238–47; Haines, "Tom Hill."

71. DOK, 56–58; Guild and Carter, *Kit Carson*, 56–57.

72. DOK, 58–60.

73. Guild and Carter, *Kit Carson*, 60–61, 304n; DOK, 67.

74. DOK, 61; J. Cecil Alter, *Jim Bridger* (Norman: University of Oklahoma Press, 1962); Wishart, *Fur Trade*, 145–46, 163–65; DeVoto, *Across the Wide Missouri*, 271.

75. DOK, 61–63; Victor, *River of the West*, 141; Carl P. Russell, *Firearms, Traps, and Tools of the Mountain Men* (New York: Alfred A. Knopf, 1967), 64–70.

76. DOK, 63–65; Guild and Carter, *Kit Carson*, 305n.

77. DOK, 65; Peters, *Kit Carson's Life and Adventures*, 110–16.

78. Sabin, *Kit Carson Days*, 165–66, 632n; Vestal, *Kit Carson*, 115–25; Vestal in Milo Milton Quaife, ed., *Kit Carson's Autobiography* (1935; reprint, Lincoln: University of Nebraska Press, 1966), 44n.

79. DOK, 63–66 and n. 225; Guild and Carter, *Kit Carson*, 69.

80. Marsh, *Four Years*, 150–53.

81. Parker, *Journal of an Exploring Tour*, 79–80.

82. Vestal in Quaife, *Kit Carson's Autobiography*, 44n.; Parker, *Journal of an Exploring Tour*, 77, 79. Marc Simmons has reached the same conclusion about Parker's source of information independently; Simmons to author, August 4, 1995.

83. The author's brother made this last point.

84. DOK, 65–77; Guild and Carter, *Kit Carson*, 70–89; Wishart, *Fur Trade*, 163.

85. Wishart, *Fur Trade*, 165; DOK, 67.

86. Irving, *Astoria*, 253; Richard Glover, ed., *David Thompson's Narrative, 1784–1812* (Toronto: Champlain Society, 1962), 305–6, 392–93; Hoxie, *Parading through History*, 79; Francis Haines, *The Nez Perces: Tribesmen of the Columbia Plateau* (Norman: University of Oklahoma Press, 1955), 36, 44–45; McGinnis, *Counting Coup*, 33–34, 38–39, 54–55; Ewers, *Blackfeet*, 53.

87. Johansen, *Robert Newell's Memoranda*, 35; Victor, *River of the West*, 217–18; Blevins, *Give Your Heart*, 299.

88. Victor, *River of the West*, 169–72, 195, 197, 225, 227; Russell, *Journal of a Trapper*, 47–49; Haines, "Tom Hill," 140; Shawnees were sometimes counted as Delawares because the two tribes frequently associated in the West.

89. DOK, 69–71; Russell, *Journal of a Trapper*, 86–89; Victor, *River of the West*, 228–31.

90. DOK, 73–74; Russell, *Journal of a Trapper*, 53–54; Victor, *River of the West*, 196, 227.

91. Wishart, *Fur Trade*, 165–66; William C. McGaw, *Savage Scene: The Life and Times of James Kirker, Frontier King* (New York: Hastings House, 1972), 106–53; Gustive O. Larson, "Walkara, Ute Chief," in Hafen, *Mountain Men*, 2:339–50; Alfred G. Humphreys, "Thomas L. (Peg-leg) Smith," in Hafen, *Mountain Men*, 4:311–30; Johansen, *Robert Newell's Memoranda*, 39; DOK, 71; Gowans, *Rocky Mountain Rendezvous*, 194–98.

92. DOK, 71n.; Guild and Carter, *Kit Carson*, 87; Howard R. Lamar, *The Trader on the American Frontier: Myth's Victim* (College Station: Texas A&M University Press, 1977), 19; L. R. Bailey, *Indian Slave Trade in the Southwest: A Study in Slave-taking and the Traffic in Indian Captives* (Los Angeles: Westernlore Press, 1973); Erwin G. Gudde, ed., *Sutter's Own Story: The Life of General John Augustus Sutter . . .* (New York: G. P. Putnams Sons, 1936), 17; LeRoy R. Hafen and Ann W. Hafen, *Old Spanish Trail: Santa Fe to Los Angeles* (1954; reprint, Lincoln: University of Nebraska Press, 1993), 259–83.

93. Smith, "Journal of E. Willard Smith," 265, giving the man's name as Spillers; Meline, *Two Thousand Miles*, 250–51.

94. DOK, 71–74; Harvey L. Carter, "The Divergent Paths of Frémont's Three Marshals," NMHR 48 (January 1973): 11–16.

95. Johansen, *Robert Newell's Memoranda*, 39; Hafen and Hafen, *Old Spanish Trail*, 227–57; DOK, 79.

96. Lavender, *Bent's Fort*; Thomas J. Farnham, *Travels in the Great Western Prairies . . .* (London: Richard Bentley, 1843), 1:173–80, 186–91; DOK, 214; testimony of Col. Kit Carson, RCIT, 96, 97.

97. DOK, 79–82.

98. DOK, 79; Henry Tilton in John S. C. Abbott, *Christopher Carson, Familiarly Known as Kit Carson* (New York: Dodd, Mead and Company, 1873), 342–43; Albert D. Richardson, *Beyond the Mississippi: From the Great Salt Lake to the Great Ocean* (Hartford CT: American Publishing Company, 1867), 257.

99. Lamar, *Trader on the American Frontier*, 37; Fehrman, "Mountain Men," 9–15; Swagerty, "Marriage and Settlement Patterns," 162.

100. Mark Twain, *Roughing It* (Berkeley: University of California Press, 1972), 146.

101. Swagerty, "Marriage and Settlement Patterns," 161, 179; Irving, *Adventures of Captain Bonneville*, 69; Lamar, *Trader on the American Frontier*, 33, 36; Fehrman, "Mountain Men," 9, 15.

102. Victor, *River of the West*, 259; Simmons, "Kit and the Indians," 79–80; McGinnis, *Counting Coup*, 49.

103. William H. Ellison, ed., *The Life and Adventures of George Nidever* (Berkeley: University of California Press, 1937), 15–16; Farnham, *Travels*, 1:293.

104. Brewerton, *Overland with Kit Carson*, 65; Whittredge, "Autobiography" 1:48.

105. Moulton, *Journals of the Lewis and Clark Expedition*, 5:68–80, 104–6; Irving, *Adventures of Captain Bonneville*, 97–142; Richardson, *Beyond the Mississippi*, 258.

106. DOK, 77.

107. Green, *Great American Adventure*, 130–31; Albert Seaton, *The Horsemen of the Steppes: The Story of the Cossacks* (New York: Hippocrene Books, 1985); Irving, *Astoria*, 211; Lamar, *Trader on the American Frontier*, 33.

108. DOK, 79.

109. Swagerty, "Marriage and Settlement Patterns," 178; Lamar, *Trader on the Frontier*, 52.

1. William H. Goetzmann, *Army Exploration in the American West, 1803–1863* (1959; reprint, Lincoln: University of Nebraska Press, 1979), for the period and the organization.

2. DOK, 81.

3. Frémont, *Memoirs*, 1:74.

4. DOK, 121–22.

5. Nevins, *Frémont: Pathmarker of the West*, 94–95.

6. Andrew Rolle, *John Charles Frémont: Character as Destiny* (Norman: University of Oklahoma Press, 1991), 278–84 and passim.

7. Rolle, *John Charles Frémont*, 39, 63.

8. Rolle, *John Charles Frémont*, 35; Frémont, *Memoirs*, 1:76, 242; Lawrence R. Murphy, *Lucien Bonaparte Maxwell: Napoleon of the Southwest* (Norman: University of Oklahoma Press, 1983), 39.

9. Charles Preuss, *Exploring with Frémont*, trans. and ed. Erwin G. and Elisabeth K. Gudde (Norman: University of Oklahoma Press, 1958), xix–xxix, 3, 47–48; DOK, 90.

10. DOK, 81–84; John C. Frémont, *The Exploring Expedition to the Rocky Mountains* (Washington DC: Smithsonian Institution Press, 1988), 15 (a reprint of Frémont's official report of 1845).

11. DOK, 81; Preuss, *Exploring with Frémont*, 21; Frémont, *Exploring Expedition*, 37–38.

12. Frémont, *Exploring Expedition*, 41–42.

13. Ibid., 45; DOK, 84.

14. DOK, 84.

15. Preuss, *Exploring with Frémont*, 40, 45–46.

16. Ibid., 47, 118.

17. Claudius Antony, "Kit Carson, Catholic," NMHR 10 (October 1935): 326; Lewis H. Garrard, *Wah-to-yah and the Taos Trail . . .* (Norman: University of Oklahoma Press, 1955), 181.

18. Craver, *Impact of Intimacy*, 21–22 and passim; Lavender, *Bent's Fort*, 176–77.

19. Antony, "Kit Carson, Catholic," 325; DOK, 94; Note on baptism in Christopher Carson Papers, New Mexico State Records Center and Archives, Santa Fe; Fray Angelico Chavez, *But Time and Chance: The Story of Padre Martinez of Taos* (Santa Fe: Sunstone Press, 1981); Lavender, *Bent's Fort*, 218–19; Craver, *Impact of Intimacy*, 58–60.

20. Craver, *Impact of Intimacy*, 32.

21. Weber, " 'Scarce More Than Apes,' " 293–307; Parkman, *Oregon Trail*, 332; Henry Tilton in Abbott, *Christopher Carson*, 348; Murphy, *Lucien Bonaparte Maxwell*, 118–20, 206.

22. DOK, 84–85.

23. DOK, 85–87.

24. Rufus B. Sage, *Rocky Mountain Life . . .* (1846; reprint, Lincoln: University

of Nebraska Press, 1982), 300–28; Lavender, *Bent's Fort*, 232–40.

25. DOK, 87–88.

26. Guild and Carter, *Kit Carson*, 110–11; Harvey L. Carter, "The Divergent Paths of Frémont's 'Three Marshals,'" NMHR 48 (January 1973): 8–9; Frémont, *Exploring Expedition*, 105; Goetzmann, *Army Exploration*, 85.

27. Goetzmann, *Army Exploration*, 89–101.

28. Ibid., 102–4.

29. Frémont, *Memoirs*, 1:196, 206, 264.

30. Frémont, *Memoirs*, 1:298; Goetzmann, *Army Exploration*, 96–98; Frémont, *Exploring Expedition*, 228–45.

31. Frémont, *Exploring Expedition*, 232, 237, 240–43, 245; DOK, 90.

32. See Hafen and Hafen, *Old Spanish Trail*.

33. Frémont, *Exploring Expedition*, 261–62; DOK, 92.

34. DOK, 92–93.

35. Frémont, *Exploring Expedition*, 262–63; Frémont, *Memoirs*, 1:facing p. 374.

36. Frémont, *Exploring Expedition*, 263; Frémont, *Memoirs*, 1:374.

37. Preuss, *Exploring with Frémont*, 127.

38. Frémont, *Exploring Expedition*, 264–65.

39. DOK, 93; Frémont, *Memoirs*, 1:503.

40. Frémont, *Exploring Expedition*, 266–67; Preuss, *Exploring with Frémont*, 129.

41. Frémont, *Exploring Expedition*, 268–69; DOK, 93–95.

42. Frémont, *Exploring Expedition*, 269; Preuss, *Exploring with Frémont*, 130; Hafen and Hafen, *Old Spanish Trail*, 259–83; Bailey, *Indian Slave Trade in the Southwest*, 139–72.

43. Frémont, *Exploring Expedition*, 272; Preuss, *Exploring with Frémont*, 133.

44. Preuss, *Exploring with Frémont*, 134; Lamar, *Trader on the American Frontier*, 17–19; Hafen and Hafen, *Old Spanish Trail*, 277.

45. Frémont, *Exploring Expedition*, 283–87.

46. DOK, 95; James Josiah Webb, *Adventures in the Santa Fe Trade, 1844–47*, ed. Ralph P. Bieber (1931; reprint, Lincoln: University of Nebraska Press, 1995), 64–65.

47. DOK, 95.

48. See the original title page in Frémont, *Exploring Expedition*, 1; David H. Coyner, *The Lost Trappers*, ed. David J. Weber (Albuquerque: University of New Mexico Press, 1970), 2.

49. William T. Sherman, *Memoirs of General William T. Sherman* (1875; reprint, New York: Da Capo Press, 1984), 46–47; Brewerton, *Overland with Kit Carson*, 38.

50. Slotkin, *Fatal Environment*, 198; Steckmesser, *Western Hero*, 17–19, 35–36; Joseph T. Downey, *The Cruise of the Portsmouth, 1845–1847* . . . , ed. Howard R. Lamar (New Haven CT: Yale University Press, 1958), 183; DOK, 15.

51. Slotkin, *Fatal Environment*, 200–201.

52. Rolle, *John Charles Frémont*, 68–69.

53. Murphy, *Lucien Bonaparte Maxwell*, 62; Thomas S. Martin, *With Frémont*

to California and the Southwest, 1845–1849, ed. Ferol Egan (Ashland OR: Lewis Osborne, 1975).

54. DOK, 95–96; Frémont, *Memoirs,* 1:427.

55. Frémont, *Memoirs,* 1:427; see Harvey Carter's reflections in DOK, 199; Carter, "Divergent Paths."

56. Murphy, *Lucien Bonaparte Maxwell,* 62; Rolle, *John Charles Frémont,* 68.

57. Frémont, *Memoirs,* 1:435, 436–38.

58. Frémont, *Memoirs,* 1:444–46; Phillips, *Indians and Intruders,* 102–16.

59. Murphy, *Lucien Bonaparte Maxwell,* 64–65; Frémont, *Memoirs,* 1:445.

60. DOK, 100; Frémont, *Memoirs,* 1:448–51.

61. DOK, 101.

62. DOK, 101–3 and note; Guild and Carter, *Kit Carson,* 152.

63. Frémont, *Memoirs,* 1:502–3, 516–17.

64. Martin, *With Frémont,* 7; Frémont, *Memoirs,* 1:516–17.

65. Green, *Great American Adventure,* 124; Carson quoted by James Rusling in Ellis, *Life of Kit Carson,* 239.

66. Martin, *With Frémont,* 35n., and Alan Rosenus, *General M. G. Vallejo and the Advent of the Americans* (Albuquerque: University of New Mexico Press, 1995), 250n., give differing identifications of the Indians.

67. Werner H. Marti, *Messenger of Destiny: The California Adventures, 1846–47, of Archibald H. Gillespie, U.S. Marine Corps* (San Francisco: John Howell—Books, 1960), 34–37 and passim; Neal Harlow, *California Conquered: War and Peace on the Pacific, 1846–1850* (Berkeley: University of California Press, 1982),77–78; DOK, 103.

68. Frémont, *Memoirs,* 1:490–91; DOK, 103–4.

69. Frémont, *Memoirs,* 1:491–92; DOK, 89; Green, *Great American Adventure,* 125.

70. Guild and Carter, *Kit Carson,* 152; Lawrence H. Keeley, *War before Civilization: The Myth of the Peaceful Savage* (New York: Oxford University Press, 1996), 128; Frémont, *Memoirs,* 1:492.

71. Frémont, *Memoirs,* 1:492–93; Martin, *With Frémont,* 10; DOK, 105.

72. DOK, 105; Frémont, *Memoirs,* 1:494; Martin, *With Frémont,* 11; Jessie Frémont, *Will and the Way Stories,* 34.

73. DOK, 104.

74. Frémont, *Memoirs,* 1:494–95; DOK, 105–6.

75. DOK, 106–7.

76. DOK, 107.

77. Harlow, *California Conquered,* 97–136; Frémont, *Memoirs,* 1:519–40.

78. Frémont, *Memoirs,* 1:525.

79. Hubert Howe Bancroft, *History of California* (San Francisco: History Company, 1886), 5:171–74; Harlow, *California Conquered,* 110; Marti, *Messenger of Destiny,* 60–61.

80. DOK, 110; LeRoy R. Hafen, ed., "The W. M. Boggs Manuscript about Bent's Fort, Kit Carson, the Far West and Life among the Indians," *Colorado*

Magazine 7 (March 1930): 62–63; Bancroft, *History of California*, 5:160–61, 172, where O'Ferrall indicates Carson was reluctant.

81. Harlow, *California Conquered*, 129–30; Frémont, *Memoirs*, 1:533; Jessie Frémont, *Will and the Way Stories*, 26–27.

82. Guild and Carter, *Kit Carson*, 154–55; K. Jack Bauer, *Surfboats and Horse Marines: U.S. Naval Operations in the Mexican War, 1846–48* (Annapolis MD: United States Naval Institute, 1969), 160–61, 165–74; Harlow, *California Conquered*, 137–52; Harold D. Langley, "Robert F. Stockton: Naval Officer and Reformer," in James C. Bradford, ed., *Command under Sail: Makers of the American Naval Tradition, 1775–1850* (Annapolis MD: United States Naval Institute, 1985), 273–304.

83. Frémont, *Memoirs*, 1:567; DOK, 111.

84. DOK, 111–12.

85. K. Jack Bauer, *The Mexican War, 1846–1848* (New York: Macmillan Company, 1974),127–37; George Walcott Ames, ed., *A Doctor Comes to California: The Diary of John S. Griffin, Assistant Surgeon with Kearny's Dragoons, 1846–1847* (San Francisco: California Historical Society, 1943), 20.

86. Dwight L. Clarke, *Stephen Watts Kearny: Soldier of the West* (Norman: University of Oklahoma Press, 1961), 166–74; DOK, 112; Frémont, *Memoirs*, 1:585–86; Dwight L. Clarke, ed., *The Original Journals of Henry Smith Turner: With Stephen Watts Kearny to New Mexico and California, 1846–1847* (Norman: University of Oklahoma Press, 1966), 100–101; Ames, *Doctor Comes to California*, 29–30; Ross Calvin, ed., *Lieutenant Emory Reports* (Albuquerque: University of New Mexico Press, 1951), 118–19 (a reprint of the narrative portion of the report of Lieutenant William H. Emory, Corps of Topographical Engineers).

87. Harlow, *California Conquered*, 159–92; Clarke, *Stephen Watts Kearny*, 195–232; DOK, 112–15; Sabin, *Kit Carson Days*, 2:537–38; Joseph T. Downey, *Filings from an Old Saw: Reminiscences of San Francisco and California's Conquest*, ed. Fred Blackburn Rogers (San Francisco: John Howell, Publisher, 1956), 89–90, gives the Indian's name.

88. Harlow, *California Conquered*, 193–218; Clarke, Stephen Watts Kearney, 233–55; DOK, 116; Downey, *Cruise of the Portsmouth*, 215.

89. Harlow, *California Conquered*, 219–62; DOK, 116–17; Beale in Thompson, "'Kit Carson's Ride': Joaquin Miller's Indecent Poem," 145–47; Green, *Great American Adventure*, 126.

90. Stephen Bonsal, *Edward Fitzgerald Beale: A Pioneer in the Path of Empire, 1822–1903* (New York: G. P. Putnam's Sons, 1912), 30.

91. Guild and Carter, *Kit Carson*, 164–67; Garrard, *Wah-to-yah*, 181–82.

92. Jessie Frémont, *Will and the Way Stories*, 39–42; Herr, *Jessie Benton Frémont*, 152–53, 156; DOK, 222–30.

93. DOK, 117–18; the commission is in Christopher Carson Papers, New Mexico State Records Center and Archives, Santa Fe; Albert G. Brackett, *History of the United States Cavalry* (1865; reprint, Freeport NY: Books for Libraries Press, 1970), 60–61.

94. DOK, 118.

95. Brewerton, *Overland with Kit Carson*, 38, 40, 65, 75–82.

96. Ibid., 83–86, 94–98.

97. Brewerton, *Overland with Kit Carson*, 100–140; DOK, 119.

98. Brewerton, *Overland with Kit Carson*, 139–41.

99. DOK, 121; Frémont, *Memoirs*, 1:427.

100. DOK, 121; Herr, *Jessie Benton Frémont*, 176–77; J. B. Frémont to Carson, May 1863, in Herr and Spence, *Letters of Jessie Benton Frémont*, 352.

101. DOK, 121; Frémont, *Memoirs*, 1:586.

102. Lavender, *Bent's Fort*, 331; Hyde, *Life of George Bent*, 355–56 and n.

103. DOK, 122; Guild and Carter, *Kit Carson*, 182.

104. DOK, 122–23; Lawrence R. Murphy, "The United States Army in Taos, 1847–1852," NMHR 47 (January 1972): 35–36.

105. DOK, 123; Murphy, *Lucien Bonaparte Maxwell*, 53–55, 71, 84.

106. Murphy, *Lucien Bonaparte Maxwell*, 85; Guild and Carter, *Kit Carson*, 182–84.

107. Lawrence R. Murphy, "Rayado: Pioneer Settlement in Northeastern New Mexico, 1848–1857," NMHR 46 (January 1971): 38, 40; DOK, 123–24.

108. Morris E. Opler, "Jicarilla Apache Territory, Economy, and Society in 1850," *Southwestern Journal of Anthropology* 27 (winter 1971): 309–21; Veronica E. Velarde Tiller, *The Jicarilla Apache Tribe: A History, 1846–1970* (Lincoln: University of Nebraska Press, 1983), 13–31; Murphy, *Lucien Bonaparte Maxwell*, 78–79.

109. Paul A. F. Walter, "The First Civil Governor of New Mexico under the Stars and Stripes," NMHR 8 (April 1933): 111–12; George Archibald McCall, *New Mexico in 1850: A Military View*, edited by Robert W. Frazer (Norman: University of Oklahoma Press, 1968), 104–5.

110. Anna P. Hannum, ed., *A Quaker Forty-Niner: The Adventures of Charles Edward Pancoast on the American Frontier* (Philadelphia: University of Pennsylvania Press, 1930), 208–10.

111. Murphy, *Lucien Bonaparte Maxwell*, 87, 99–100, 116–18; Charles L. Kenner, *A History of New Mexican–Plains Indian Relations* (Norman: University of Oklahoma Press, 1969), 121.

112. DOK, 124 and n; James Calhoun to CIA William Medill, October 29, 1849, in Annie Heloise Abel, ed., *The Official Correspondence of James S. Calhoun . . .* (Washington DC: Government Printing Office, 1915), 63–66; Paul Horgan, *Josiah Gregg and His Vision of the West* (New York: Farrar, Strauss, Giroux, 1979), 16.

113. DOK, 124–25; Tiller, *Jicarilla Apache Tribe*, 25, 35; *Jicarilla Apache Tribe: Historical Materials, 1540–1887* (New York: Garland Publishing, 1974), 101.

114. DOK, 125; Meline, *Two Thousand Miles on Horseback*, 267–68; Faragher, *Daniel Boone*, 139.

115. DOK, 125–26; Simmons, "Kit and the Indians," 83; Faragher, *Daniel Boone*, 131–38.

116. Tiller, *Jicarilla Apache Tribe*, 35.

117. Murphy, "Rayado," 42; DOK, 126–27; see Holbrook's and Grier's reports in Sabin, *Kit Carson Days*, 351–52.

118. DOK, 127–28; Murphy, "Rayado," 44–45; Abel, *Correspondence of James S. Calhoun*, 230–31.

119. Murphy, "Rayado," 44–45; DOK, 146; Robert M. Utley, *Frontiersmen in Blue: The United States Army and the Indian, 1848–1865* (New York: Macmillan Company, 1967; reprint, Lincoln: University of Nebraska Press, 1981), 14–15, 21, 101–2, 210; Abel, *Correspondence of James S. Calhoun*, 300–303.

120. DOK, 129, 132; Guild and Carter, *Kit Carson*, 190.

121. DOK, 129–30; Simmons, "Kit and the Indians," 80–81.

122. DOK, 130–31 and n.

123. DOK, 130–31.

124. DOK, 131–32; Green, *Great American Adventure*, 124–25.

125. DOK, 131–32.

126. DOK, 132–33; Meline, *Two Thousand Miles*, 250; Robert F. Heizer and Alan J. Almquist, *The Other Californians: Prejudice and Discrimination under Spain, Mexico, and the United States, to 1920* (Berkeley: University of California Press, 1971), 23–64; Robert F. Heizer, ed., *The Destruction of California Indians* (1974; reprint, Lincoln: University of Nebraska Press, 1993), passim.

127. Benjamin D. Wilson, *The Indians of Southern California in 1852: The B. D. Wilson Report . . .*, ed. John W. Caughey (1952; reprint, Lincoln: University of Nebraska Press, 1995); Gerald Thompson, *Edward F. Beale and the American West* (Albuquerque: University of New Mexico Press, 1983), 54–59, 63–79; James J. Rawls, *Indians of California: The Changing Image* (Norman: University of Oklahoma Press, 1984), 148–58; Albert L. Hurtado, *Indian Survival on the California Frontier* (New Haven CT: Yale University Press, 1988), 141–44, takes a more negative view of Beale's work, seeing him as serving principally white interests.

128. Guild and Carter, *Kit Carson*, 194–96; Thompson, *Edward F. Beale*, 66; Wilson, *Indians of Southern California*, 110.

129. DOK, 133–34.

130. DOK, 133–34; Guild and Carter, *Kit Carson*, 185, 308n.

131. Lamar, *The Far Southwest*, 270.

5. INDIAN AGENT

Note: Unless otherwise noted, all correspondence cited in this chapter is from Letters Received from and Relating to Kit Carson, 1854–1860. National Archives Microfiche FMT21, Roll 1, NARS, Washington DC.

1. DOK, 133–34; Marshall D. Moody, "Kit Carson, Agent to the Indians in New Mexico, 1853–1861," NMHR 28 (January 1953): 2.

2. Moody, "Kit Carson, Agent," 8.

3. James Calhoun to CIA William Medill, October 15, 1849; Calhoun to CIA Orlando Brown, March 30, 1850, in Annie Heloise Abel, ed., *The Official Correspondence of James S. Calhoun*, 53–55, 178–79.

4. George Catlin, *Letters and Notes on the Manners, Customs, and Conditions of the North American Indians* . . . (1844; reprint, New York: Dover Publications, 1973), 2:245; see Lee Clark Mitchell, *Witnesses to a Vanishing America: The Nineteenth-Century Response* (Princeton NJ: Princeton University Press, 1981), for romantic regrets.

5. Robert A. Trennert, *Alternative to Extinction: Federal Indian Policy and the Beginnings of the Reservation System, 1846–51* (Philadelphia: Temple University Press, 1975); Henry F. Dobyns, *Their Number Become Thinned: Native Population Dynamics in Eastern North America* (Knoxville: University of Tennessee Press, 1983), 8; Russell Thornton, *American Indian Holocaust and Survival: A Population History Since 1492* (Norman: University of Oklahoma Press, 1987), 91; Brian W. Dippie, *The Vanishing American: White Attitudes and U.S. Indian Policy* (Middletown CT: Wesleyan University Press, 1982), 34–43 and passim.

6. Francis P. Prucha, *The Great Father: The United States Government and the Indians* (Lincoln: University of Nebraska Press, 1984), 1:179–269, 315–18; Heizer and Almquist, *Other Californians*, 23–64; John K. Mahon, *History of the Second Seminole War, 1835–1842* (Gainesville: University of Florida Press, 1967); Trennert, *Alternative to Extinction*, 94–130; James Calhoun to CIA Orlando Brown, March 30, 1850, in Abel, *Correspondence of James S. Calhoun*, 176.

7. Lonnie J. White, ed., *Chronicle of a Congressional Journey: The Doolittle Committee in the Southwest, 1865* (Boulder CO: Pruett Publishing Company, 1975), 62; see Utley, *Frontiersmen in Blue*, 182; Robert W. Mardock, *The Reformers and the American Indian* (Columbia: University of Missouri Press, 1971), 88.

8. Utley, *Frontiersmen in Blue*, 101 and n., 178, 181–82; John G. Bourke, *With General Crook in the Indian Wars* (Palo Alto CA: Lewis Osborne, 1968), 34–35.

9. Carson to James L. Collins, June 24, 1857, Letters Received from and Relating to Kit Carson; Prucha, *Great Father*, 1:319–23; James Calhoun to CIA William Medill, October 1, 1849, in Abel, *Correspondence of James S. Calhoun*, 32; Trennert, *Alternative to Extinction*, 196.

10. Hamilton Gardner, "Philip St. George Cooke and the Apache, 1854," NMHR 28 (April 1953): 117; see Utley, *Frontiersmen in Blue*, 10–17.

11. David Meriwether's annual report, 1854, in U.S., Congress, 33rd Cong., 2nd sess., *House Executive Document No. 1*, pt. 1 (Serial 777), *Annual Report of CIA, 1854*, 376, 378.

12. DOK, 150n.

13. Testimony of Col. Kit Carson, RCIT, 96; Utley, "An Indian Before Breakfast," 91–98.

14. Meriwether's annual report, *Annual Report of CIA, 1854*, 374–77; David Meriwether, *My Life in the Mountains and on the Plains*, ed. Robert A. Griffen (Norman: University of Oklahoma Press, 1965), 165 and n.

15. Jefferson et al., *Southern Utes*, 22–23; Tiller, *Jicarilla Apache Tribe*, 96–97.

16. Robert M. Utley, *The Indian Frontier of the American West, 1846–1890* (Albuquerque: University of New Mexico Press, 1984), 36, 43–45; Prucha, *Great Father*, 1:209.

17. Morris F. Taylor, "Campaigns against the Jicarilla Apache, 1854," NMHR 44(October 1969): 271–73.

18. Carson to David Meriwether, January 1, 1854; Carson to Meriwether, n.d.

19. Carson to William J. Messervy, March 21, 1854.

20. Carson to Messervy, March 21, 1854.

21. Carson to Messervy, March 27, 1854.

22. Taylor, "Campaigns . . . 1854," 274–76; Tiller, *Jicarilla Apache Tribe*, 45–47; Robert W. Frazer, "The Battle of Cienguilla," *La Cronica* (March 1980): 3–5, provides a good, brief summary of events leading up to the battle; Jerry Thompson, introduction to James A. Bennett, *Forts and Forays: A Dragoon in New Mexico, 1850–1856*, ed. Clinton E. Brooks and Frank D. Reeve (1948; reprint, Albuquerque: University of New Mexico Press, 1996), xxi–xxvii and see Bennett's brief account, 53–54; Homer K. Davidson, *Black Jack Davidson, A Cavalry Commander on the Western Frontier . . .* (Glendale CA: Arthur H. Clark, 1974), 70–72; DOK, 134–35.

23. Murphy, *Lucien Bonaparte Maxwell*, 98, accuses Carson of inciting the military to aggressive action; Taylor, "Campaigns . . . 1854," 275; DOK, 135–36 and n; Cooke's report, May 24, 1854, in Gardner, "Philip St. George Cooke and the Apache," 120–21; James H. Quinn, "Notes of Spy Company under Colonel Cooke. Furnished by the Capt. at the request of Wm. H. Davis. April 13, 1854 to May 2, 1854," MS, New Mexico Highlands University, Las Vegas NM (courtesy of Robert M. Utley); Carson to Messervy, April 2, 1854.

24. DOK, 136.

25. Taylor, "Campaigns . . . 1854," 277; Cooke's report in Gardner, "Philip St. George Cooke and the Apache," 121–24; DOK, 136–38; Quinn, "Notes of Spy Company," 1–2.

26. Cooke's report in Gardner, "Philip St. George Cooke and the Apache," 121–23; Pliny E. Goddard, *Jicarilla Apache Texts*, Anthropological Papers of the American Museum of Natural History (New York: American Museum of Natural History, 1911), 8:243 and n.

27. Carson to Messervy, April 12, 1854; Carson to Messervy, April 9, 1854; DOK, 138; Meriwether's annual report, *Annual Report of CIA, 1854*, 378.

28. Tiller, *Jicarilla Apache Tribe*, 48; John W. Dunn to Messervy, April 14, 1854, reports the guilty Jicarillas in the Raton Mountains (Dunn was Carson's secretary at the time).

29. DOK, 137, 139.

30. DOK, 139–40; Taylor, "Campaigns . . . 1854," 278–79.

31. Taylor, "Campaigns . . . 1854," 279–84; Cooke's report, June 5, 1854, in Gardner, "Philip St. George Cooke and the Apache," 126–30; DOK, 140–42; Carson to Messervy, June 12, 1854.

32. Carleton's report quoted in Aurora Hunt, *Major General James Henry Carleton, 1814–1873: Western Frontier Dragoon* (Glendale CA: Arthur H. Clark Company, 1958), 141; Cooke's report in Gardner, "Philip St. George Cooke and the Apache," 130, paraphrases Carleton; DOK, 142; Sabin, *Kit Carson Days*, 384; Carson to Messervy, June 12, 1854.

33. Carson to Messervy, June 12, 1854; Carson to Messervy, June 25, 1854.

34. Meriwether, *My Life*; Calvin Horn, *New Mexico's Troubled Years: The Story of the Early Territorial Governors* (Albuquerque: Horn and Wallace, 1963), 53–69.

35. Meriwether's annual report, *Annual Report of CIA, 1854*, 378.

36. Tiller, *Jicarilla Apache Tribe*, 51–52; Carson to Meriwether, September 25, 1854.

37. Carson to Meriwether, October 11, 1854; DOK, 142–43.

38. DOK, 143; Meriwether, *My Life*, 200–202.

39. Carson to Meriwether, November 23, 1854.

40. Morris F. Taylor, "Campaigns against the Jicarilla Apache, 1855," NMHR 45 (April 1970): 119–20; Lecompte, *Pueblo, Hardscrabble, Greenhorn*, 237–53; Carson to Meriwether, January 7, 1855.

41. Taylor, "Campaigns . . . 1855," 121–22; DOK, 144–45.

42. Taylor, "Campaigns . . . 1855," 124–25; Morris F. Taylor, "Action at Fort Massachusetts," *Colorado Magazine* 42 (fall 1965): 295–98.

43. Taylor, "Action at Fort Massachusetts," 298–300; Jacqueline D. Meketa, ed., *Legacy of Honor: The Life of Rafael Chacon, A Nineteenth-Century New Mexican* (Albuquerque: University of New Mexico Press, 1986), 100–102; DOK, 145–46.

44. Taylor, "Campaigns . . . 1855," 123, 126–29; Meketa, *Legacy of Honor*, 103; DOK, 146.

45. DOK, 144, 146; Carson's annual report for 1855, in U.S., Congress, 34th Cong., 1st Sess., *House Executive Document No. 1*, pt. 1 (Serial 840), *Annual Report of CIA, 1855*, 512.

46. Carson's annual report, 1855, *Annual Report of CIA, 1855*, 511–12, with Meriwether's note; DOK, 147; Kenner, *History of New Mexican–Plains Indian Relations*, 120–22.

47. Horn, *New Mexico's Troubled Years*, 64–65.

48. Meriwether, *My Life*, 226–28.

49. Ibid., 228–30.

50. Ibid., 231–32.

51. Ibid., 232.

52. See Carson's and Meriwether's annual reports, *Annual Report of CIA, 1855*, 507–12; Carson to Meriwether, September 17, 1856.

53. Meriwether, *My Life*, xvi; Guild and Carter, *Kit Carson*, 209; DOK, 128–30 and n.; Percy G. Hamlin, *"Old Bald Head" (General Richard S. Ewell): The Portrait of a Soldier* (Strasburg VA: Shenandoah Publishing House, 1940), 49; Percy G. Hamlin, ed., *The Making of a Soldier: Letters of General R. S. Ewell* (Richmond VA: Whittet and Shepperson, 1935), 82–83, 95; Murphy, "Rayado: Pioneer Settlement," 47.

54. Michael D. Heaston, "The Governor and the Indian Agent: 1855–1857," NMHR 45 (April 1970): 140.

55. Carson to Messervy, April 4, 1854; Carson to CIA George W. Manypenny, June 30, 1854; Moody, "Kit Carson, Agent," 8; Guild and Carter, *Kit Carson*, 209.

56. Horn, *New Mexico's Troubled Years*, 65; DOK, 136n; Carson to Meriwether, August 29, 1855.

57. Horn, *New Mexico's Troubled Years*, 64–65; Moody, "Kit Carson, Agent," 9.

58. Carson to CIA, January 22, 1858; CIA Manypenny to W. W. H. Davis, January 3, 1856.

59. Carson to Davis, January 9, 1856; Carson to Davis, February 9, 1856; Carson to Davis, February 28, 1856.

60. Carson to Meriwether, August 9, 1856.

61. Carson to J. L. Collins, March 23, 1859.

62. Account for John Mostin, March 23, 1859; Carson to Collins, November 9, 1859; Horn, *New Mexico's Troubled Years*, 68.

63. DOK, 197; Peters, *Kit Carson's Life and Adventures*, 534–35.

64. DOK, 144, 147.

65. DOK, 146; Trennert, *Alternative to Extinction*, 195–96; Martin F. Schmitt, ed., *General George Crook: His Autobiography* (Norman: University of Oklahoma Press, 1960), 229; Annual Report of the Board of Indian Commissioners, in *Report of the Commissioner of Indian Affairs to the Secretary of the Interior for the Year 1871* (Washington DC: Government Printing Office, 1872), 15 (hereafter cited as *Annual Report*, with year, distinguishing separately printed CIA reports from those in congressional documents).

66. Carson's annual report, in *Report of the Commissioner of Indian Affairs, Accompanying the Annual Report of the Secretary of the Interior, for the Year 1859* (Washington DC: George W. Bowman, 1860), 343; Carson to Collins, June 24, 1857.

67. Prucha, *Great Father*, 1:372–73; DOK, 147.

68. Tiller, *Jicarilla Apache Tribe*, 52, 56–58; Guild and Carter, *Kit Carson*, 207.

69. Carson to Collins, June 24, 1857; DOK, 149.

70. Noah Smithwick, *The Evolution of a State, or Recollections of Old Texas Days* (Austin TX: Gammel Book Company, 1900), 194; Utley, *Indian Frontier*, 55–56.

71. Carson's annual report, in U.S., Congress, 35th Cong., 1st Sess., Senate Executive Document No. 11 (Serial 919), Annual Report of CIA, 567–68.

72. DOK, 147; Carson to Meriwether, September 17, 1856; Guild and Carter, *Kit Carson*, 209.

73. Carson to Collins, June 29, 1857; Carson to Collins, May 26, 1857; Prucha, *Great Father*, 1:373.

74. DOK, 147–49.

75. DOK, 149.

76. Guild and Carter, *Kit Carson*, 210–11; Peters, *Life and Adventures*, 19; Sabin, *Kit Carson Days*, 2:506.

77. DOK, 147, 149.

78. Carson to CIA Manypenny, July 2, 1856; Carson to Manypenny, July 30, 1856; Carson to Collins, May 26, 1857; Carson to Collins, June 6, 1857.

79. William Bent to Carson, October 17, 1856; Carson to Meriwether, November 3, 1856.

80. Carson to Meriwether, January 20, 1854; Carson to Meriwether, n.d.; Carson to Messervy, March 21, 1854.

81. Carson to W. W. H. Davis, October 11, 1855.

82. Carson to Davis, November 29, 1855.

83. Carson to Davis, December 5, 1855.

84. Carson to Davis, December 13, 1855; Carson to Davis, March 5, 1856.

85. Carson to Meriwether, August 29, 1856.

86. Carson to Meriwether, December 5, 1856; Morris F. Taylor, "Ka-ni-ache," pt. 1, *Colorado Magazine* 43 (fall 1966): 281–84 (hereafter cited as Taylor, "Ka-ni-ache," pt. 1).

87. James L. Collins's annual report, in U.S., Congress, 35th Cong., 2d Sess., *Senate Executive Document No. 1*, pt. 1, Annual Report of CIA (Serial 974), 536–38.

88. Carson to Meriwether, January 22, 1857; Carson to Collins, July 14, 1858.

89. Carson to Yost, February 18, 1858; Carson to Yost, February 28, 1858; Frank McNitt, *Navajo Wars: Military Campaigns, Slave Raids, and Reprisals* (Albuquerque: University of New Mexico Press, 1972), 286–333; Carson to Yost, March 31, 1858.

90. Carson to Collins, November 2, 1858; Carson to Collins, September 30, 1858; Carson to Collins, November 30, 1858; see Jones, *Pueblo Warriors and Spanish Conquest*, for the Spanish utilization of Indian allies.

91. Carson to Collins, December 8, 1858.

92. Bailey, *Indian Slave Trade in the Southwest*, 73–137; Russell M. Magnaghi, "The Genizaro Experience in Spanish New Mexico," in Ralph H. Vigil, Frances W. Kaye, John R. Wunder, eds., *Spain and the Plains: Myths and Realities of Spanish Exploration and Settlement of the Great Plains* (Niwot: University Press of Colorado, 1994), 114–30; Fray Angelico Chavez, "Genizaros," in Alfonso Ortiz, ed., *Handbook of North American Indians*, Southwest 9 (Washington DC: Smithsonian Institution, 1979), 198–200; Richard L. Nostrand, *The Hispano Homeland* (Norman: University of Oklahoma Press, 1992), 44, 63–64, 68; Frances L. Swadesh, "Hispanic Americans of the Ute Frontier from the Chama Valley to the San Juan Basin, 1694–1960" (Ph.D. diss., University of Colorado, 1966), 37–56; Marc Simmons, *Coronado's Land: Essays on Daily Life in Colonial New Mexico* (Albuquerque: University of New Mexico Press, 1991), 47–50; McNitt, *Navajo Wars*, 12–13, 73, 205, 374–75.

93. Murphy, *Lucien Bonaparte Maxwell*, 112; Swadesh, "Hispanic Americans," 88–90; testimony of Kirby Benedict, RCIT, 326.

94. Parish records translated in J. Lee Correll, "Long Ago in Navajoland: Navajos Adopted by Kit Carson at Taos, New Mexico," *The Navajo Times*, n.d., article in Archives, Kit Carson Historical Museums, Taos NM, Section 1, Folder 17.; A. B. Sanford, "Reminiscences of Kit Carson, Jr.," *Colorado Magazine* 6 (September 1929): 180–81; Fray Angelico Chavez, *But Time and Chance: The Story of Padre Martinez of Taos* (Santa Fe: Sunstone Press, 1981), 148, on Martinez's displacement by Ussel.

95. Carson to Collins, January 12, 1859; Carson to Collins, April 27, 1859; see Schmitt, *General George Crook*, 171–72, for an instance of Indian children being unwilling to return to their own people.

96. Carson to Collins, July 21, 1858.

97. Carson to Collins, July 28, 1858.

98. Collins's annual report, *Annual Report of CIA, 1858*, p. 538.

99. Carson's annual report, Ibid., 546–47.

100. See Henry Inman, *The Old Santa Fe Trail: The Story of a Great Highway* (New York: Macmillan Company, 1899), 375; George Gwyther, "A Frontier Post and Country," *Overland Monthly* 5 (December 1870): 524–25.

101. Carson to Collins, December 31, 58.

102. Dan L. Thrapp, ed., *Dateline Fort Bowie: Charles Fletcher Lummis Reports on an Apache War* (Norman: University of Oklahoma Press, 1979), 119–20.

103. Carson to Collins, November 17, 1858; Carson to Collins, February 10, 1859; Carson to Collins, April 20, 1859.

104. Carson to Collins, February 23, 1859; Kenner, *New Mexican-Plains Indian Relations*, 78–97, 129–32, and passim; William Y. Chalfont, *Without Quarter: The Wichita Expedition and the Fight on Crooked Creek* (Norman: University of Oklahoma Press, 1991).

105. Carson to Collins, March 1, 1859; Thompson, *Edward F. Beale*, 111–16.

106. Jesus Ma. Velasques to Carson, May 1, 1856 (translated by Patricia Wendt).

107. Carson to Collins, April 27, 1859.

108. Ibid., June 8, 1859.

109. Ibid., June 8, 1859.

110. Ibid., June 15, 1859.

111. Ibid., June 20, 1859; ibid., July 20, 1859.

112. Ibid., July 27, 1859.

113. DOK, 143.

114. Carson to Collins, August 17, 1859.

115. Collins's annual report in *Annual Report, CIA, 1859*, 336, 338.

116. Ibid., 1859, 342–44.

117. Ibid., 342–43.

118. Carson to Collins, August 21, 1859; Carson to Collins, August 24, 1859; Carson to Collins, August 27, 1859.

119. Ibid., September 1, 1859.

120. Ibid., September 21, 1859.

121. Ibid., October 27, 1859; Ibid., November 9, 1859.

122. Carson to Collins, November 30, 1859; Ibid., January 18, 1860; Kenner, *New Mexican–Plains Indian Relations*, 94–96; Arrell M. Gibson, *The Kickapoos: Lords of the Middle Border* (Norman: University of Oklahoma Press, 1963), 175–76.

123. Carson to Collins, January 4, 1860; Carson to Collins, January 7, 1860; affidavit of Salvador Lucero, January 7, 1860.

124. Carson to Collins, January 31, 1860.

125. Carson to Collins, February 7, 1860; Carson to Collins, February 29, 1860; McNitt, *Navajo Wars*, 402–3.

126. Carson to Collins, June 30, 1860.

127. Carson's annual report, in *Annual Report, CIA, 1860*, 163.

128. Ibid., 164.

129. Reginald Horsman, "Scientific Racism and the American Indian in the Mid-Nineteenth Century," *American Quarterly* 27 (May 1975): 152–68; Prucha, *Great Father*, 1:334–38; Francis P. Prucha, *Indian Policy in the United States: Historical Essays* (Lincoln: University of Nebraska Press, 1981), 180–97.

130. Horsman, "Scientific Racism," 160, 162.

131. Testimony of John Greiner, RCIT, 328.

132. Warren A. Beck, *New Mexico: A History of Four Centuries* (Norman: University of Oklahoma Press, 1962), 179; Prucha, *Great Father*, 1:315–18; Utley, *Indian Frontier*, 51–52, 56–58.

133. Pauline Weaver to Charles Poston, October 30, 1864, quoted in A. L. Kroeber and C. B. Kroeber, *A Mohave War Reminiscence, 1854–1880* (1973; reprint, New York: Dover Publications, 1994), 75; Hunt's annual report, in U.S. Congress, 40th Cong., 3rd Sess., *House Executive Document No. 1* (Serial 1366), Annual Report of CIA, 1868, 643.

134. Carson to Collins, January 2, 1860 [1861?].

6. SOLDIER

1. Sabin, *Kit Carson Days*, 1:394, 2:648n.; information about Smith Simpson's list, courtesy of Skip Miller, Kit Carson Historic Museums, Taos, NM.

2. Luther Perry Wilmot, "'A Pleasant Winter for Lew Wilmot,'" *Colorado Magazine* 47 (March 1970): 10–15.

3. Michael Fellman, *Inside War: The Guerrilla Conflict in Missouri during the American Civil War* (New York: Oxford University Press, 1989), on the Missouri struggle; Darlis A. Miller, "Hispanos and the Civil War in New Mexico: A Reconsideration," NMHR 54 (April 1979): 105–23.

4. Chris Emmett, *Fort Union and the Winning of the Southwest* (Norman: University of Oklahoma Press, 1965), 228–44; Donald S. Frazier, *Blood and Treasure: Confederate Empire in the Southwest* (College Station: Texas A&M University Press, 1995), 48–72.

5. Emmett, *Fort Union*, 228, 242–43.

6. Miller, "Hispanos and the Civil War," 105–9.

7. *Official Army Register of the Volunteer Force of the United States Army for the Years 1861, '62, '63, '64, '65. Part 8: Territories of Washington, New Mexico . . .* (Washington DC: Adjutant General's Office, 1867), 7.

8. Emmett, *Fort Union*, 242–45.

9. Meline, *Two Thousand Miles on Horseback*, 250.

10. Edward S. Wynkoop, Manuscript 2, Colorado State Historical Society Library, Denver, 19–20 (hereafter cited as Wynkoop MS).

11. Wynkoop MS, 20–21; *Official Army Register*, 2.

12. Don E. Alberts, ed., *Rebels on the Rio Grande: The Civil War Journal of A. B. Peticolas* (Albuquerque: University of New Mexico Press, 1984), 120; George H. Pettis, in Sabin, *Kit Carson Days*, 1:425–26.

13. John Ayers, "A Soldier's Experiences in New Mexico," NMHR 24 (October 1949): 262; Wynkoop MS, 19–20.

14. Wynkoop MS, 19–20.

15. Morris Janowitz, *The Professional Soldier: A Social and Political Portrait* (Glencoe IL: Free Press, 1960), 21–36; this point was also made by the author's brother, a former air force officer.

16. Frazier, *Blood and Treasure*, 71–100, 137; Miller, "Hispanos in the Civil War," 106.

17. See John Taylor, *Bloody Valverde: A Civil War Battle on the Rio Grande, February 21, 1862* (Albuquerque: University of New Mexico Press, 1995), for a complete history of the battle.

18. Ibid., 78–96.

19. Wynkoop MS, 21–22; William Clarke Whitford, *Colorado Volunteers in the Civil War: The New Mexico Campaign in 1862* (1906; reprint, Glorieta NM: Rio Grande Press, 1971), 64; the only eyewitness account is from William Mills, in Meketa, *Legacy of Honor*, 175; David P. Perrine, "The Battle of Valverde, New Mexico Territory, February 21, 1862," in Leroy H. Fischer, ed., *Civil War Battles in the West* (Manhattan KS: Sunflower University Press, 1981), 76; Taylor, *Bloody Valverde*, 119.

20. Frazier, *Blood and Treasure*, 186–275.

21. Utley, *Frontiersmen in Blue*, 216–18; Frazier, *Blood and Treasure*, 64–67.

22. Utley, *Frontiersmen in Blue*, 231–53.

23. John C. Cremony, *Life among the Apaches, 1850–1868* (1868; reprint, Glorieta NM: Rio Grande Press, 1969), 198; Utley, *Frontiersmen in Blue*, 233; C. L. Sonnichsen, *The Mescalero Apaches* (Norman: University of Oklahoma Press, 1958), 97; Arrell M. Gibson, "James Carleton," in Paul A. Hutton, ed., *Soldiers West: Biographies from the Military Frontier* (Lincoln: University of Nebraska Press, 1987), 72.

24. Hunt, *Carleton*, is an uncritical biography containing useful information, but it does not address the important questions; Constance Wynn Altshuler, *Cavalry Yellow and Infantry Blue: Army Officers in Arizona between 1851 and 1886* (Tucson: Arizona Historical Society, 1991), 55–57; Carleton to Henry D. Wallen, December 24, 1863, RCIT, 152–53; Gibson, "James Carleton," 59–77.

25. DOK, 142; Hunt, *Carleton*, 337; Utley, *Frontiersmen in Blue*, 233.

26. Constance Wynn Altshuler, *Chains of Command: Arizona and the Army, 1856–1875* (Tucson: Arizona Historical Society, 1981), 242, 255–56; Emmett, *Fort Union*, 125–27.

27. Herman Hattaway and Archer Jones, *How the North Won: A Military History of the Civil War* (Urbana: University of Illinois Press, 1983), 502.

28. General Orders No. 81, Headquarters, Department of New Mexico, September 9, 1862, NR, 3–4; this work is indispensable to any student of the Navajo campaign. Edward R. S. Canby to Lorenzo Thomas, Demember 1, 1861, in *War of the Rebellion: A Compilation of the Official Records of the Union and Confederate Armies* (Washington DC: Government Printing Office, 1880–1901), Series 1, 4:77–78 (hereafter cited as OR; all citations to Series 1 unless otherwise noted).

29. Special Orders No. 176, Headquarters, Department of New Mexico, September 27, 1862, NR, 8–10.

30. Carleton to Joseph West, October 11, 1862, RCIT, 99–100; Carleton to Carson, October 12, 1862, RCIT, 100.

31. Sonnichsen, *Mescalero Apaches*, 57–94 and passim.

32. Collins's annual report, in *Annual Report, CIA, 1861*, 122; Sonnichsen, *Mescalero Apaches*, 94–95; Lorenzo Labadi's annual report, *Annual Report, CIA, 1862*, 247–48.

33. William A. Keleher, *Turmoil in New Mexico, 1846–1868* (1952; reprint, Albuquerque: University of New Mexico Press, 1982), 279; Sonnichsen, *Mescalero Apaches*, 99.

34. Jerry D. Thompson, *Desert Tiger: Captain Paddy Graydon and the Civil War in the Far Southwest* (El Paso: Texas Western Press, 1992), 52–54; William McCleave, "Recollections of a California Volunteer," MS, Bancroft Library, University of California, Berkeley, 9–10; Sonnichsen, *Mescalero Apaches*, 99–101.

35. NR, 12; Sonnichsen, *Mescalero Apaches*, 101.

36. Carleton to Carson, November 25, 1862, RCIT, 101–2; Thompson, *Desert Tiger*, 56–61; Carleton to Carson, November 26, 1862, RCIT, 102–3; Dale F. Giese, ed., *My Life with the Army in the West: Memoirs of James E. Farmer* (Santa Fe NM: Stagecoach Press, 1967), 50–51; Farmer does not indicate that he was an eyewitness to either the shooting or Carson's reaction.

37. Frank McNitt, "Fort Sumner: A Study in Origins," NMHR 45 (April 1970): 101–17; Carleton to Lorenzo Thomas, March 19, 1863, NR, 16–17.

38. Chavez, "Genizaros," 198–200; Magnaghi, "Genizaro Experience," 117–23; testimony of John Greiner, RCIT, 328; testimony of Louis Kennon, RCIT, 334; Carleton to James Doolittle, July 3, 1865, RCIT, 323.

39. Sonnichsen, *Mescalero Apaches*, 102–3; Utley. *Frontiersmen in Blue*, 237; Carleton to Lorenzo Thomas, February 1, 1863, RCIT, 104–5.

40. Carson to Carleton, February 3, 1863, NR, 15–16.

41. Schaefer, *Company of Cowards*, in *The Short Novels*, 423.

42. Raymond Friday Locke, *The Book of the Navajo* (Los Angeles: Mankind Publishing Company, 1986), 354.

43. Testimony of Col. Kit Carson, RCIT, 96–98.

44. Grant quoted in Brooks D. Simpson, *Let Us Have Peace: Ulysses S. Grant and the Politics of War and Reconstruction, 1861–1868* (Chapel Hill: University of North Carolina Press, 1991), 21; Crook quoted in H. B. Whipple's introduction to Helen Hunt Jackson, *A Century of Dishonor* (1881; reprint, New York: Indian Head Books, 1993), viii.

45. Richard J. Perry, *Western Apache Heritage: People of the Mountain Corridor* (Austin: University of Texas Press, 1991); Jack D. Forbes, *Apache, Navajo and Spaniard* (Norman: University of Oklahoma Press, 1960), 281–85.

46. Ruth M. Underhill, *The Navajos* (Norman: University of Oklahoma Press, 1956), 33–71; McNitt, *Navajo Wars*, 10–65; Locke, *Book of the Navajo*, 181.

47. Robert L. O'Connell, *Ride of the Second Horseman: The Birth and Death of*

War (New York: Oxford University Press, 1995), 69–83; John Keegan, *A History of Warfare* (New York: Alfred A. Knopf, 1993), 160–65, 177–82.

48. Edward H. Spicer, *Cycles of Conquest: The Impact of Spain, Mexico, and the United States on the Indians of the Southwest, 1533–1960* (Tucson: University of Arizona Press, 1962), 217.

49. Testimony of Kirby Benedict, RCIT, 325–26; testimony of Henry Connelly, RCIT, 332.

50. Testimony of Henry Connelly, RCIT, 332; testimony of Louis Kennon, RCIT, 334; Marc Simmons, *Coronado's Land*, 47–48.

51. McNitt, *Navajo Wars*, 201, 295, 402–3 and passim; James Calhoun to CIA Luke Lea, March 22, 1851, in Abel, *Official Correspondence of James S. Calhoun*, 299–300; Calhoun proclamation, March 18, 1851, ibid., 300–301; Proposal of Manuel Chaves, March 18, 1851, ibid., 302–303; testimony of James Collins, RCIT, 332; Richard L. Nostrand, *The Hispano Homeland* (Norman: University of Oklahoma Press, 1992), 64; Simmons, *Coronado's Land*, 48–49; Utley, *Frontiersmen in Blue*, 84.

52. See McCall, *New Mexico in 1850: A Military View*, 82–85, 180.

53. Testimony of Col. Kit Carson, RCIT, 97; Utley, *Indian Frontier*, 81.

54. Robert M. Utley, ed., "Captain John Pope's Plan of 1853 for the Frontier Defense of New Mexico," A&W 5 (summer 1963): 152–53.

55. Utley, "Captain John Pope's Plan," 153.

56. Testimony of John Greiner, RCIT, 328; McNitt, *Navajo Wars*, 195–264.

57. McNitt, *Navajo Wars*, 285–384.

58. Max L. Heyman, "On the Navaho Trail: The Campaign of 1860–61," NMHR 26 (January 1951): 44–63; Utley, *Frontiersmen in Blue*, 171–72; McNitt, *Navajo Wars*, 390–409; Giese, *My Life with the Army*, 30–37.

59. Heyman, "On the Navaho Trail," 54–63; McNitt, *Navajo Wars*, 415–16, on the defects of Canby's treaty.

60. Collins's annual report in *Annual Report of CIA, 1861*, 124–25; Collins's report in *Annual Report of CIA, 1862*, 241; Michael Steck's annual report in *Annual Report, CIA, 1863*, 105–6; McNitt, *Navajo Wars*, 421–28, on the Fort Fauntleroy incident; Trafzer, *The Kit Carson Campaign*, 67–70, dates the affair a year too late.

61. Testimony of John Greiner, RCIT, 328; testimony of Louis Kennon, RCIT, 333–34.

62. McNitt, *Navajo Wars*, 410.

63. Canby to Assistant Adjutant General, Western Department, December 1, 1861; OR, 4:77–78.

64. Canby to Governor Henry Connelly, November 22, 1861, OR, 4:75–76.

65. Sherry L. Smith, *The View from Officers' Row: Army Perceptions of Western Indians* (Tucson: University of Arizona Press, 1990); Robert Wooster, *The Military and United States Indian Policy, 1865–1903* (New Haven CT: Yale University Press, 1988).

66. *Between Sacred Mountains: Navajo Stories and Lessons from the Land* (Tucson: University of Arizona Press, 1994), 143; Carleton to Joseph Walker, June 22,

1863, RCIT, 115; Carleton to Nathaniel Pishon, June 22, 1863, RCIT, 115–16; Carleton to Henry Halleck, May 10, 1863, RCIT, 110; Carleton to Halleck, June 14, 1863, RCIT, 113–14; Carleton to Secretary of the Treasury Salmon Chase, September 20, 1863, RCIT, 140; Altshuler, *Cavalry Yellow and Infantry Blue*, 57; A. J. Alexander to John Rawlins, May 5, 1867; John Y. Simon, ed., *The Papers of Ulysses S. Grant* (Carbondale: Southern Illinois University Press, 1967–), 18:76, regarding Carleton's mining interests.

67. Clyde Kluckholm and Dorothea Leighton, *The Navaho* (1946; reprint, Garden City NY: Doubleday, 1962), 41.

68. *Between Sacred Mountains*, 142–43.

69. Ruth Roessel, introduction and acknowledgements to *Navajo Stories of the Long Walk Period* (Tsaile AZ: Navajo Community College Press, 1973), ix–x, xv–xvi; hereafter cited as *Navajo Stories*.

70. Roessel in *Navajo Stories*, x; Howard Gorman, ibid., 23; Rita Wheeler, ibid., 79; Eli Gorman, ibid., 200; Hascon Benally, ibid., 229; Henry Zah, ibid., 156; see also Charlie Mitchell in Edward Sapir and Harry Hoijer, eds., *Navaho Texts* (Iowa City: Linguistic Society of America, University of Iowa, 1942), 339–45.

71. Curly Tso, *Navajo Stories*, 103.

72. Canby to Assistant Adjutant General, Western Department, December 1, 1861, OR, 4:77; Hascon Benally, *Navajo Stories*, 229; Dugal Tsosie Begay, ibid., 213; Frank Goldtooth, ibid., 152.

73. Recollections of Ahson Tsosie (Slim Woman), in Franc Johnson Newcomb, *Hosteen Klah: Navaho Medicine Man and Sand Painter* (Norman: University of Oklahoma Press, 1964), 48–50; Canby to Assistant Adjutant General, Western Department, December 1, 1861, OR, 4:77.

74. Erna Fergusson, *Dancing Gods: Indian Ceremonials of New Mexico and Arizona* (1931; reprint, Albuquerque: University of New Mexico Press, 1990), xxiv; Laura Bayer and Floyd Montoya, and the Pueblo of Santa Ana, *Santa Ana: The People, the Pueblo, and the History of Tamaya* (Albuquerque: University of New Mexico Press, 1994), 115, 123–24, 134; James Calhoun to CIA William Medill, October 4, 1849, Abel, *Official Correspondence of James S. Calhoun*, 48.

75. Calhoun to CIA Luke Lea, August 31, 1851, Abel, *Official Correspondence of James S. Calhoun*, 415; T. J. Ferguson and E. Richard Hunt, *A Zuni Atlas* (Norman: University of Oklahoma Press, 1985), 60–61; Harry C. James, *Pages from Hopi History* (Tucson: University of Arizona Press, 1974), 78–81; Mitchell in Sapir and Hoijer, *Navaho Texts*, 345; Underhill, *The Navajos*, 116.

76. Floyd quoted in Utley, *Frontiersmen in Blue*, 172; Heyman, "On the Navajo Trail," 51; Canby to Assistant Adjutant General, Western Department, December 1, 1861, OR, 4:77.

77. Heyman, "On the Navajo Trail," 52–53; Max L. Heyman, *Prudent Soldier: A Biography of Major General E. R. S. Canby, 1817–1873* (Glendale CA: Arthur H. Clark Company, 1959), 40–45; Mahon, *History of the Second Seminole War*; Sam C. Sarkesian, *America's Forgotten Wars: The Counterrevolutionary Past and Lessons for the Future* (Westport CT: Greenwood Press, 1984), 163–65; Barbara Graymont, *The*

Iroquois in the American Revolution (Syracuse: Syracuse University Press, 1972), 192–222.

78. Antony T. Sullivan, *Thomas-Robert Bugeaud, France, and Algeria, 1784–1849: Politics, Power, and the Good Society* (Hamden CT: Archon Books, 1983), 87–88; Douglas Porch, "Bugeaud, Gallieni, Lyautey: The Development of French Colonial Warfare," in Peter Paret, ed., *Makers of Modern Strategy from Machiavelli to the Nuclear Age* (Princeton NJ: Princeton University Press, 1986), 380–81; Keeley, *War before Civilization*, 75.

79. Mark Grimsley, *The Hard Hand of War: Union Military Policy Toward Southern Civilians, 1861–1865* (Cambridge: Cambridge University Press, 1995); Mark E. Neely, "Was the Civil War a Total War?" *Civil War History* 35 (March 1991): 5–28; Russell F. Weigley, *The American Way of War: A History of United States Military Strategy and Policy* (1973; reprint, Bloomington: Indiana University Press, 1977), 153–63; Lance Janda, "Shutting the Gates of Mercy: The American Origins of Total War, 1860–1880," *Journal of Military History* 59 (January 1995): 7–26.

80. Janda, "Shutting the Gates"; William B. Skelton, "Army Officers' Attitudes toward Indians, 1830–1860," *Pacific Northwest Quarterly* 67 (July 1976): 16, 121.

81. Carleton to Lorenzo Thomas, December 20, 1862, RCIT, 103; NR, 17.

82. NR, 20; Carleton to Carson, April 11, 1863, NR, 18–19.

83. NR, 19; General Orders No. 15, Headquarters, Department of New Mexico, June 15, 1863, NR, 21–24.

84. Carleton to Lorenzo Thomas, June 17, 1863, RCIT, 114.

85. Carson to Acting General, Department of New Mexico, July 24, 1863, NR, 26–29.

86. Henry Tilton in John S. C. Abbott, *Christopher Carson*, 347; Sergeant George Campbell quoted in NR, 53.

87. Ayers, "Soldier's Experience," 262; Gerald Linderman, *Embattled Courage: The Experience of Combat in the American Civil War* (New York: Free Press, 1987), 7–23; Carson to Ben C. Cutler, August 19, 1863, NR, 53.

88. Lawrence C. Kelly, "Where Was Fort Canby?" NMHR 42 (January 1967): 49–62; Carson to Assistant Adjutant General, Department of New Mexico, June 28, 1863, NR, 32–33; Carleton to Carson, August 9, 1863, NR, 33.

89. Utley, *Frontiersmen in Blue*, 234; Carleton to Samuel Archer, August 3, 1863, RCIT, 123.

90. Carleton to Carson, August 7, 1863, NR, 35; Carson to Carleton, August 19, 1863, NR, 36.

91. NR, 15, 49; Ayers, "Soldier's Experience," 262; Joseph T. Glatthaar, *The March to the Sea and Beyond: Sherman's Troops in the Savannah and Carolinas Campaigns* (New York: New York University Press, 1985), 20–21; see Chacon's various references to Carson in Meketa, *Legacy of Honor*.

92. Carson to Cutler, August 19, 1863, NR, 38–41; Raymond E. Lindgren, ed., "A Diary of Kit Carson's Navajo Campaign," NMHR 21 (July 1946): 228–31.

93. Carson to Cutler, August 19, 1863, NR, 39–40; Lindgren, "Diary of . . . Navajo Campaign," 231.

94. Lindgren, "Diary of . . . Navajo Campaign," 233; Carson to Cutler, August 31, 1863, NR, 42.

95. Carson to Cutler, August 19, 1863, NR, 40; Lindgren, "Diary of . . . Navajo Campaign," 242–43.

96. Lindgren, "Diary of . . . Navajo Campaign," 243; Carson to Cutler, August 31, 1863, NR, 43.

97. NR, 44–50; Carson to Cutler, August 31, 1863, NR, 43.

98. Carleton to Carson, September 19, 1863, NR, 52.

99. Carson to Carleton, July 24, 1863, NR, 30.

100. Carleton to Carson, August 18, 1863, NR, 31; see Hunt, *Major General James Henry Carleton*, 55–65, for Carleton's court-martial in connection with another officer's shooting of the husband of the officer's part-Cherokee mistress in 1842.

101. NR, 52–53.

102. Carleton to Carson, September 19, 1863, NR, 52; Carson to Carleton, October 5, 1863, NR, 53–54.

103. Carleton to Lorenzo Thomas, September 6, 1863, NR, 57.

104. See Trafzer, *Kit Carson Campaign*, 87, 89, passim.

105. General Orders No. 3, Headquarters, Department of New Mexico, February 24, 1864, RCIT, 254; NR, 59.

106. General Orders No. 3 . . . February 24, 1864, RCIT, 253–55; Edward Willis to B. C. Cutler, October 6, 1863, OR, 26:315–16.

107. Carson to Cutler, October 20, 1863, NR, 61–62.

108. Carson to Cutler, October 20, 1863, NR, 61–62; Francis McCabe to L. G. Murphy, October 12, 1863, NR, 62–64; Francis Abreu to Cutler, October 16, 1863, NR, 64–65; A. B. Carey to L. G. Murphy, October 13, 1863, NR, 65; Carey to Murphy, October 15, 1863, NR, 66; Jose Sena[?] to Murphy, October 29, 1863, NR, 66–68; Carson to Carleton, November 1, 1863, NR, 68–69; Carson to Cutler, November 10, 1863, NR, 73; Carson to Cutler, December 6, 1863, NR, 75–77; General Orders No. 3 . . . , RCIT, 254.

109. Carson to Cutler, December 6, 1863, NR, 75–77.

110. Carson to Carleton, November 1, 1863, NR, 68–69.

111. Carleton to Carson, December 5, 1863, NR, 69–70 (Carleton's emphasis).

112. Carey to Carleton, December 6, 1863, NR, 78.

113. Murphy to Abreu, December 13, 1863, NR, 81; Carson to Abreu, NR, 82; Carson to Cutler, December 20, 1863, NR, 83–84; Sena to Murphy, December 13, 1863, NR, 84–85; Donaciano Montoya to ?, December 20, 1863, NR, 85–87.

114. Carleton to Carson, December 31, 1863, NR, 87–88.

115. Campbell Grant, *Canyon de Chelly: Its People and Rock Art* (Tucson: University of Arizona Press, 1978); McNitt, *Navajo Wars*, 341; L. R. Bailey, ed., *The Navajo Reconnaissance: A Military Exploration of the Navajo Country in 1859* . . . (Los Angeles: Westernlore Press, 1964), 37–55.

116. Carson to Cutler, January 24, 1864, NR, 98; Keleher, *Turmoil in New Mexico*, 314.

117. Carson to Cutler, January 24, 1863, NR, 98–99.

118. Laura C. Manson White, "Albert Pfeiffer," *Colorado Magazine* 10 (November 1933): 217–22; A. A. Hayes, *New Colorado and the Santa Fe Trail* (New York: Harper and Brothers, 1880), 166; NR, 25–26 and n.; Carson to Pfeiffer, May 8, 1863, in Sabin, *Kit Carson Days*, 617–18; McNitt, *Navajo Wars*, 402–3.

119. Pfeiffer to Murphy, January 20, 1864, NR, 102–4.

120. Pfeiffer to Murphy, January 20, 1864, NR, 104–5; Carson to Cutler, January 24, 1864, NR, 99–100; Carey to Murphy, January 21, 1864, NR, 105–7.

121. Carson to Cutler, January 24, 1864, NR, 104; Carey to Murphy, January 21, 1864, NR, 105–6; Stephen C. Jett, ed., "The Destruction of Navajo Orchards in 1864: Captain John Thompson's Report," A&W 16 (winter 1974): 365–78.

122. Peters, *Kit Carson's Life and Adventures*, 553; Jacob P. Dunn, *Massacres of the Mountains: A History of the Indian Wars of the Far West, 1815–1875* (1886; reprint, New York: Archer House, n.d.), 396.

123. Carson to Cutler, January 24, 1864, NR, 100–101.

124. Howard Gorman, *Navajo Stories*, 25–28.

125. Akinabh Burbank, *Navajo Stories*, 127–31; NR, 16.

126. Teddy Draper, *Navajo Stories*, 43–51.

127. NR, 97, 110; Carson to Cutler, January 24, 1864, NR, 100–101.

128. Howard Gorman, *Navajo Stories*, 28; NR, 110–11.

129. NR, 97.

130. NR, 110.

131. Carey to Cutler, February 4, 1864, NR, 111–12; Carey to Cutler, February 14, 1864, NR, 112–13 ; Carey to Cutler, February 21, 1864, NR, 113.

132. Joseph Berney to Assistant Adjutant General, Department of New Mexico, April 7, 1864, NR, 115–16.

133. Carey to Assistant Adjutant General, Department of New Mexico, March 20, 1864, NR, 133.

134. Carson to Assistant Adjutant General, Department of New Mexico, March 20, 1864, NR, 140–41; Carleton to Carey, March 16, 1864, NR, 137–38; Carey to Assistant Adjutant General, Department of New Mexico, March 27, 1864, NR, 138.

135. Carleton to Carson, March 19, 1864, NR, 139; Carleton to Carson, March 21, 1864, NR, 141–42; Carleton to Carson, April 1, 1864, NR, 142; Carleton to Carson, April 8, 1864, NR, 143.

136. Carson to Carleton, April 10, 1864, NR, 143–44; Francis McCabe to Assistant Adjutant General, Department of New Mexico, May 12, 1864, NR, 134–36.

137. Carson to Carleton, April 10, 1864, NR, 144.

138. Howard Gorman, *Navajo Stories*, 30–31; Rita Wheeler, ibid., 82–84; Curly Tso, ibid., 103–4; Crawford R. Buell, "The Navajo 'Long Walk': Recollections by Navajos," in Albert H. Schroeder, ed., *The Changing Ways of Southwestern Indians: A Historic Perspective* (Glorieta NM: Rio Grande Press, 1973), 171–79, including recollections of Jake Segundo; Charlotte Frisbie and David P.

McAllester, eds., *Navajo Blessingway Singer: The Autobiography of Frank Mitchell,* *1881–1967* (Tucson: University of Arizona Press, 1978), 18.

139. Frank McNitt, "The Long March, 1863–1867," in Schroeder, *Changing* *Ways of Southwestern Indians,* 156, 160; Carson to Acting Assistant Adjutant General, Department of New Mexico, April 13, 1864, NR, 150; George Campbell to Carleton, March 3, 1864, NR, 149; McCabe to Assistant Adjutant General, Department of New Mexico, May 12, 1864, NR, 135.

140. Carson to Acting Assistant Adjutant General, Department of New Mexico, April 13, 1864, NR, 150; Proclamation of Governor Henry Connelly, May 4, 1864, NR, 150–51.

141. Carleton to Lorenzo Thomas, February 7, 1864, NR, 106; Neil C. Mangum, "Old Fort Wingate in the Navajo War," NMHR 66 (October 1991): 404–10.

142. Carson to Acting Assistant Adjutant General, Department of New Mexico, May 20, 1864, NR, 155–58.

143. Testimony of Col. Kit Carson, RCIT, 97.

144. Axtell, *Beyond 1492,* 261.

145. Trafzer, *Kit Carson Campaign,* 50, 224–25, 237–38; Kelly, "Historiography of the Navajo Roundup," 49–71.

146. Ward Churchill, *Indians Are Us? Culture and Genocide in Native North* *America* (Monroe ME: Common Courage Press, 1994), 246.

147. Keeley, *War before Civilization,* 130, 175.

148. Ibid., 128.

149. McNitt, *Navajo Wars,* 428.

150. Testimony of James Carleton, RCIT, 323; testimony of Col. Kit Carson, RCIT, 97.

151. Testimony of James Carleton, RCIT, 323, 325.

152. Carter in DOK, xv; Green, *Great American Adventure,* 128.

153. Keeley, *War before Civilization,* 74–75; Geoffrey Parker, "What Is the Western Way of War?" MHQ 8 (winter 1996): 90–91.

154. Fritz Stern, *The Failure of Illiberalism: Essays in the Political Culture of Modern* *Germany* (New York: Alfred A. Knopf, 1972), xli; Carleton to William Lewis, August 3, 1863, RCIT, 122; Carleton to Joseph Updegraff, August 19, 1863, RCIT, 129; Carleton to Joseph Smith, August 19, 1863, RCIT, 129–30; Carleton to Joseph West, March 3, 1863, RCIT, 105; Carleton to Carson, September 19, 1863, NR, 52.

155. Utley, *Frontiersmen in Blue,* 241; Carson to Cutler, January 24, 1864, NR, 100; Utley, "An Indian before Breakfast," 96.

156. Canby to Assistant Adjutant General, Western Department, December 1, 1861, OR, 4:77; testimony of James Collins, RCIT, 331–32; testimony of Kirby Benedict, RCIT, 327.

157. Lynn R. Bailey, *Bosque Redondo: An American Concentration Camp* (Pasadena: Socio-Technical Books, 1970); Gerald Thompson, *The Army and* *the Navajo: The Bosque Redondo Reservation Experiment, 1863–1868* (Tucson: University of Arizona Press, 1976).

158. James Henry Carleton, *The Prairie Logbooks: Dragoon Campaigns to the Pawnee Villages in 1844, and to the Rocky Mountains in 1845*, ed. Louis Pelzer (1943; reprint, Lincoln: University of Nebraska Press, 1983), 131–33; Thompson, *Army and the Navajo*, 12–14; Thompson, *Edward F. Beale*, 45–79.

159. Bailey, *Bosque Redondo*, 153; Thompson, *Army and the Navajo*, passim.

160. Carson to Assistant Adjutant General, Department of New Mexico, May 20, 1864, NR, 157.

161. NR, 157.

162. Ibid.

163. NR, 155; Thompson, *Army and the Navajo*, 42.

164. Thompson, *Army and the Navajo*, 42.

165. Carleton to Lorenzo Thomas, September 6, 1863, NR, 57; Thompson, *Army and the Navajo*, 42–45, 99; Carson to Carleton, July 14, 1864, OR, 41, pt. 2, 192–94.

166. Carleton to Lorenzo Thomas, October 29, 1864, RCIT, 207; Frisbie and McAllester, *Navajo Blessingway Singer*, 15, 18–19.

167. Testimony of Col. Kit Carson, RCIT, 97; testimony of James Carleton, RCIT, 324; William Haas Moore, *Chiefs, Agents and Soldiers: Conflict on the Navajo Frontier, 1868–1882* (Albuquerque: University of New Mexico Press, 1994), 5–6.

168. NR, 169.

169. Utley, *Frontiersmen in Blue*, 281–87.

170. Carleton to Marcellus Crocker, October 22, 1864, RCIT, 201; Carleton to Steck, October 29, 1864, RCIT, 204–6; Nicholas Davis to Carleton, October 30, 1864, OR, 41, pt. 1, 212–13; J. C. McFerran to Carleton, October 28, 1864, OR, 41, pt. 2, 927–28; since McFerran must have reported verbally to Carleton on his arrival in Santa Fe, the general presumably asked for a written version for the record.

171. Carleton to Lorenzo Thomas, August 27, 1864, OR, 41, pt. 2, 897; Carleton to Thomas, August 29, 1864, 927; Carleton to Carson, August 15, 1864, 723.

172. Murphy, *Lucien Bonaparte Maxwell*, 122–23; Carleton to Carson, September 18, 1864, OR, 41, pt. 3, 243–44.

173. Carson to Carleton, September 21, 1864, OR, 41, pt. 3, 295; Carleton to Cyrus DeForrest, September 26, 1864, 400.

174. Crocker to Cutler, September 30, 1864, OR, 41, pt. 3, 525; Carson to Carleton, October 18, 1864, pt. 4, 99–100; Carleton to Carson, October 14, 1864, pt. 3, 877; Carleton to Lorenzo Thomas, October 9, 1864, 743.

175. Carleton to Thomas, October 9, 1864, 743; Taylor, "Ka-ni-ache," 291; Goddard, *Jicarilla Apache Texts*, 8:250.

176. Carleton to Steck, October 29, 1864, RCIT, 204–6; Kenner, *History of New Mexican–Plains Indian Relations*, 146–47; Robert M. Utley, "Kit Carson and the Adobe Walls Campaign," *American West* 2 (winter 1965): 7, 9–10; testimony of Col. Kit Carson, RCIT, 97.

177. William A. Kupke, *The Indian and the Thunderwagon: A History of the Mountain Howitzer* (Silver City NM: n.p., 1992); Warren Ripley, *Artillery and*

Ammunition of the Civil War (New York: Van Nostrand Reinhold Company, 1970), 48–49, 198–99, 268, 376; Utley, *Frontiersmen in Blue*, 28; Carson to Carleton, October 10, 1864, OR, 41, pt. 3, 771.

178. Carson to Cutler, December 4, 1864, OR, 41, pt. 1, 939–40.

179. Carleton to James Blunt, October 22, 1864, OR, 41, pt. 4, 197–98.

180. Francisco Abreu to Cutler, October 10, 1864, OR, 41, pt. 3, 771; Carson to Cutler, December 4, 1864, pt. 1, 940; Carleton to Carson, October 23, 1864, pt. 4, 214; Thrapp, *Dateline Fort Bowie*, 111, quoting Crook.

181. Ernest Wallace and E. Adamson Hoebel, *The Comanches: Lords of the South Plains* (Norman: University of Oklahoma Press, 1952); T. R. Fehrenbach, *Comanches: The Destruction of a People* (New York: Alfred A. Knopf, 1974); Kenner, *History of New Mexican–Plains Indian Relations*; Mildred P. Mayhall, *The Kiowas* (Norman: University of Oklahoma Press, 1962).

182. George H. Pettis, *Kit Carson's Fight with the Comanche and Kiowa Indians* (Santa Fe: New Mexican Printing Company, 1908), 11–13; Carson to Cutler, December 4, 1864, OR, 41, pt. 1, 940.

183. Carson to Cutler, December 4, 1864, OR, 41, pt. 1, 940; Pettis, *Kit Carson's Fight*, 13–15; James Mooney, *Calendar History of the Kiowa Indians* (1898; reprint, Washington DC: Smithsonian Institution Press, 1979), 315.

184. Carson to Cutler, December 4, 1864, OR, 41, pt. 1, 940–41; Pettis, *Kit Carson's Fight*, 15–19.

185. Mooney, *Calendar History*, 315; Hyde, *Life of George Bent*, 246; Wilbur S. Nye, *Carbine and Lance: The Story of Old Fort Sill* (Norman: University of Oklahoma Press, 1969), 36 (an account based on Nye's interviews with Kiowas and Comanches in the 1930s).

186. Carson to Cutler, December 4, 1864, OR, 41, pt. 1, 941; Pettis, *Kit Carson's Fight*, 19–21.

187. Carson to Cutler, December 4, 1864, OR, 41, pt. 1, 941; Pettis, *Kit Carson's Fight*, 21–22.

188. Carson to Cutler, December 4, 1864, OR, 41, pt. 1, 941; Pettis, *Kit Carson's Fight*, 22–24; Richard A. Fox, *Archaeology, History, and Custer's Last Battle: The Little Big Horn Reexamined* (Norman: University of Oklahoma Press, 1993).

189. Mooney, *Calendar History*, 315; Nye, *Carbine and Lance*, 37; Carson to Cutler, December 4, 1864, OR, 41, pt. 1, 941; Pettis, *Kit Carson's Fight*, 24–25.

190. Carson to Cutler, December 4, 1864, OR, 41, pt. 1, 941; Pettis, *Kit Carson's Fight*, 25–26; Darlis A. Miller, *The California Column in New Mexico* (Albuquerque: University of New Mexico Press, 1982), 21.

191. Carson to Cutler, December 4, 1864, OR, 41, pt. 1, 941–42; Pettis, *Kit Carson's Fight*, 26–28.

192. Carson to Cutler, December 4, 1864, OR, 41, pt. 1, 942; Pettis, *Kit Carson's Fight*, 29; Goddard, *Jicarilla Apache Texts*, 250; Mooney, *Calendar History*, 315; Utley, "Kit Carson and the Adobe Walls Campaign," 74.

193. Pettis, *Kit Carson's Fight*, 28–31.

194. Pettis, *Kit Carson's Fight*, 31; Carson to Cutler, December 4, 1864, OR,

41, pt. 1, 942; Carson to Carleton, October 10, 1864, pt. 3, 771; George S. Courwright, *An Expedition against the Indians in 1864* (Lithopolis OH: Canal Winchester Times Press, 1911), 29; McCleave, "Recollections of a California Volunteer," 12–13; Ayers, "Soldier's Experience," 262.

195. Pettis, *Kit Carson's Fight*, 24–25, 31; Utley, *Frontiersmen in Blue*, 323–32, on the 1865 Powder River campaign.

196. Fox, *Archaeology, History, and Custer's Last Battle*; McCleave, "Recollections of a California Volunteer," 14; One Who Was There, "The Old Adobe Walls," *Santa Fe Gazette*, April 22, 1865, quoted in Utley, "Kit Carson and the Adobe Walls Campaign," 7.

197. Hyde, *Life of George Bent*, 246; Bent quoted in Sabin, *Kit Carson Days*, 2:747; testimony of James Ford, RCIT, 65.

198. Frémont, *Memoirs*, 1:427.

199. Carson to Cutler, December 12, 1864, OR, 41, pt. 1, 942; Carson to Carleton, December 16, 1864, 943.

200. Carson to Carleton, December 16, 1864, OR, 41, pt. 1, 943.

201. Ibid., 943.

202. Carleton to Carson, December 15, 1864, ibid., 944; Carleton to Carson, January 30, 1865, OR 48, pt. 1, 689.

203. Carleton to Carson, January 30, 1864, OR 48, pt. 1, 689; Kenner, *History of New Mexican–Plains Indian Relations*, 150–52; A. Morrison to Carleton, May 10, 1865, OR, 48, pt. 1, 310; see also J. H. Leavenworth to James Ford, May 30, 1865, pt. 2, 687–88.

204. Leo E. Oliva, *Soldiers on the Santa Fe Trail* (Norman: University of Oklahoma Press, 1967), 161–63; Carleton to Carson, May 4, 1865, OR, 48, pt. 2, 317; Carson to Carleton, May 6, 1865, 318.

205. Special Orders No. 15, Headquarters Department of New Mexico, May 7, 1865, OR, 48, pt. 2, 344; Mrs. Hal Russell, *Land of Enchantment: Memoirs of Marian Russell along the Santa Fe Trail* (1954; reprint, Albuquerque: University of New Mexico Press,1981), 103.

206. Carleton to Carson, May 8, 1865, OR, 48, pt. 2, 360.

207. Carson to Cutler, June 19, 1865, ibid., 341–42; Albert W. Thompson, "Kit Carson's Camp Nichols in No Man's Land," *Colorado Magazine* 11 (September 1934): 179–86; Herbert M. Hart, *Old Forts of the Southwest* (1964; reprint, New York: Bonanza Books, n.d.), 98–100; Gregory M. Franzwa, *Maps of the Santa Fe Trail* (St. Louis: Patrice Press, 1989), 130–31.

208. Thompson, "Kit Carson's Camp Nichols," 184. The account Russell gave Thompson seems to contradict that in Russell, *Land of Enchantment*, 104–5, regarding Carson's riding out with the scouts, raising the question of how much Mrs. Hal Russell, Marian Russell's daughter-in-law, added to the record. Although the former version does not mention Carson's accompanying the scouts, indicating that he lay on his camp bed much of the time, it remains possible that, being Carson, he went out when he felt able.

209. Thompson, "Kit Carson's Camp Nichols," 184; Russell, *Land of Enchantment*, 105.

1. Russell, *Land of Enchantment*, 103; James R. Mead, *Hunting and Trading on the Great Plains, 1859–1875*, ed. Schuyler Jones (Norman: University of Oklahoma Press, 1986), 176; Pettis quoted in Sabin, *Kit Carson Days*, 2:818; NR, 169.

2. Carleton to Carson, May 5, 1865, OR, 48, pt. 2, 317; Carleton to Carson, May 8, 1865, 360.

3. Stan Hoig, *The Sand Creek Massacre* (Norman: University of Oklahoma Press, 1961); Utley, *Frontiersmen in Blue*, 293–97.

4. Utley, *Frontiersmen in Blue*, 300–303.

5. Utley, *Frontiersmen in Blue*, 309; Lonnie J. White, ed., *Chronicle of a Congressional Journey: The Doolittle Committee in the Southwest, 1865* (Boulder CO: Pruett Publishing Company, 1975), 3–60; Donald Chaput, "Generals, Indian Agents, Politicians: The Doolittle Survey of 1865," WHQ 3 (July 1972): 269–82.

6. James Doolittle to Mary Doolittle, July 11, 1865, Doolittle Papers, Archives and Manuscripts Division, State Historical Society of Wisconsin; Doolittle to Mrs. L. F. S. Foster, March 7, 1881, NMHR 26 (April 1951): 155–56.

7. Testimony of Col Kit Carson, RCIT, 96; testimony of William Bent, RCIT, 93–95.

8. Testimony of Col. Kit Carson, RCIT, 96–98.

9. Testimony of Col. Kit Carson, RCIT, 438–39; Carson to Ben C. Cutler, August 19, RCIT, 438–39.

10. Carleton to Doolittle, July 25, 1865, RCIT, 432, quoting questionnaire; Carson to Cutler, August 19, 1865, RCIT, 439.

11. Carson to Cutler, August 19, 1865, RCIT, 439–40.

12. Testimony of James Carleton, RCIT, 324–25.

13. Final Committee Report, January 26, 1867, RCIT, 3–5.

14. Final Committee Report, 6–8; testimony of Herrero, RCIT, 356.

15. Doolittle to Secretary of the Interior James Harlan, May 31, 1865, OR, 48, pt. 2, 868–69.

16. Doolittle to Harlan, OR, 48, pt. 2, 869; CIA William Dole to Harlan, June 12, 1865, OR, 869–70; Richard N. Ellis, *General Pope and U.S. Indian Policy* (Albuquerque: University of New Mexico Press, 1970), 68–86; testimony of William Bent, RCIT, 95; Doolittle to Secretary of State William Seward and Secretary of War Edwin Stanton, July 19, 1865, OR, 48, pt. 2, 1094.

17. Carleton to A. M. McCook, July 17, 1865, OR, 48, pt. 2, 1088–89; Chris Emmett, *Fort Union and the Winning of the Southwest* (Norman: University of Oklahoma Press, 1965), 308, quoting Special Order No. 22.

18. Ellis, *General Pope*, 108; Donald J. Berthrong, *The Southern Cheyennes* (Norman: University of Oklahoma Press, 1963), 240.

19. Carson to Cutler, August 19, 1865, RCIT, 438; Lavender, *Bent's Fort*, 105, on possible first meeting of Carson and Bent; Asa F. Middaugh quoted in DOK, 214.

20. Lamar, *The Far Southwest,* 250; Lavender, *Bent's Fort,* 203, 386–90; Hyde, *Life of George Bent,* 227.

21. Carson to B. C. Cutler, September 11, 1865, NARS RG 108, Register of Letters Received.

22. Carson to Cutler, September 11, 1865, NARS.

23. Ibid.

24. Ibid.

25. Treaty council held in camp on the Little Arkansas River, October 1865, *Annual Report of CIA, 1865,* 516; Berthrong, *Southern Cheyennes,* 240–41; Richmond L. Clow, "William S. Harney," in Hutton, *Soldiers West,* 42–58; Mead, *Hunting and Trading,* 176–77.

26. Stan Hoig, *Jesse Chisholm: Ambassador of the Plains* (Niwot: University Press of Colorado, 1991), 145.

27. Treaty council, *Annual Report, CIA, 1865,* 517, 528; Stan Hoig, *The Peace Chiefs of the Cheyennes* (Norman: University of Oklahoma Press, 1980), 104–22.

28. Treaty council, *Annual Report, CIA, 1865,* 517–18; Hyde, *Life of George Bent,* 247–48.

29. Treaty council, *Annual Report, CIA, 1865,* 518.

30. Ibid., 518–20.

31. Ibid., 520–21.

32. Ibid., 519, 522, 524; Mead, *Hunting and Trading,* 177; Berthrong, *Southern Cheyennes,* 242; Hoig, *Peace Chiefs,* 104.

33. Berthrong, *Southern Cheyennes,* 11.

34. Testimony of William Bent, RCIT, 95; Berthrong, *Southern Cheyennes,* 241.

35. Berthrong, *Southern Cheyennes,* 11, 242; *Annual Report, CIA, 1865,* 520–21, 523–24, 526.

36. Hyde, *Life of George Bent,* 248; *Annual Report, CIA, 1865,* 522–25. See Treaty with the Cheyenne and Arapaho, 1865, in Charles J. Kappler, ed., *Indian Treaties, 1778–1883* (1904; reprint, New York: Interland Publishing, 1972), 887–91.

37. *Annual Report, CIA, 1865,* 528–30.

38. *Annual Report, CIA, 1865,* 530–33; William H. Leckie, *The Military Conquest of the Southern Plains* (Norman: University of Oklahoma Press, 1963), 26. See Treaty with the Comanche and Kiowa, 1865, in Kappler, *Indian Treaties,* 892–95.

39. *Annual Report, CIA, 1865,* 534–35; Samuel A. Kingman, "Diary of Samuel Kingman at Indian Treaty in 1865," *Kansas Historical Quarterly* 1 (November 1932): 446–48, 450.

40. Hoig, *Jesse Chisholm,* 156; Leckie, *Military Conquest,* 26; Utley, *Frontiersmen in Blue,* 338–39; Berthrong, *Southern Cheyennes,* 243–44; *Annual Report, CIA, 1865,* 527.

41. Berthrong, *Southern Cheyennes,* 256–61; Leckie, *Military Conquest,* 26.

42. *Annual Report, CIA, 1865,* 518.

43. Ellis, *General Pope;* Richard N. Ellis, ed., "Bent, Carson, and the Indians, 1865," *Colorado Magazine* 46 (winter 1969): 59–60; Wallace J. Schutz and Walter

N. Trenerry, *Abandoned by Lincoln: A Military Biography of General John Pope* (Urbana: University of Ilinois Press, 1990), 42.

44. Berthrong, *Southern Cheyennes*, 146.

45. Ellis, "Bent, Carson, and the Indians," 62–63.

46. Mardock, *Reformers and the American Indian*, 42–45; Prucha, *Great Father*, 1:549–60; U.S. Congress, 40th Cong., 3rd Sess., *House Executive Document No. 2* (Serial 1366) Report of the CIA, annual report of CIA N. G. Taylor, 469–72; annual report of J. H. Stout, agent for the Pima Indians, in *Annual Report, CIA, 1878*, 5.

47. Ellis, "Bent, Carson, and the Indians," 63.

48. Ibid., 63–64.

49. Ibid., 64.

50. Ibid., 65–66.

51. Ibid., 67.

52. Ibid., 70.

53. Ibid., 68; Thompson, *The Army and the Navajo*, 92–94.

54. Ellis, "Bent, Carson, and the Indians," 61; Robert G. Athearn, *William Tecumseh Sherman and the Settlement of the West* (Norman: University of Oklahoma Press, 1956), 25–26. Pope's endorsement, November 6, 1865, described Carson and Bent as "men of standing and reliability, thoroughly acquainted with Indians and Indian management by the experience of their whole lives," declared that their statements "may be entirely relied on," specifically in connection with "any measures adopted by congress"; see endorsement in Simon, *Papers of Ulysses S. Grant*, 15:622.

55. Prucha, *Great Father*, 1:481; Francis Paul Prucha, *American Indian Policy in Crisis: Christian Reformers and the Indian, 1865–1890* (Norman: University of Oklahoma Press, 1976), 51–52; Thompson, *Army and the Navajo*, 121–22, 130–32, 147–48.

56. Emmett, *Fort Union*, 412; Carson to Stanton, January 2, 1866, Letters received from and relating to *Kit Carson*, 1854–60, NARS Microfiche, FMT21, Roll 1, National Archives and Record Service, Washington DC; Francis B. Heitman, *Historical Register and Dictionary of the United States Army* (Washington DC: Government Printing Office, 1903), 286; Utley, *Frontiersmen in Blue*, 32–33; Carleton to Adjutant General, U.S. Army, October 27, 1865, OR, 48, pt. 2, 1247; Mark M. Boatner, *The Civil War Dictionary* (New York: David McKay Company, 1987), 84, on brevet rank; Roger D. Hunt and Jack R. Brown, *Brevet Brigadier Generals in Blue* (Gaithersburg MD: Olde Soldier Books, 1990), v–viii, xiii, 103.

57. Thelma S. Guild and Harvey L. Carter, *Kit Carson*, 259; Gene M. Gressley, ed., "Report on Fort Garland Made by Christopher (Kit) Carson to Major Roger James [sic], June 10, 1866," *Colorado Magazine* 32 (July 1955): 216–22 (this is a published version of Carson to Roger Jones, June 10, 1866, in Records of Fort Garland, Correspondence of Brev. Brig. Gen. Christopher Carson, NARS Record Group 98, copy in Fort Garland Collection, Colorado Historical Society, Denver; all correspondence relating to Fort Garland is from the latter source unless otherwise noted.)

58. Pope to William T. Sherman, August 11, 1866, quoted in Sabin, *Kit Carson Days* (1935 edition), 2:761; DOK, 121.

59. Frank Murrell to Commanding Officer, Fort Fillmore, CO, June 20, 1865, OR, 48, pt. 2, 952–53.

60. Annual report of Alexander Cummings, *Annual Report, CIA, 1866,* 154.

61. Carson to Jones, June 10, 1866; annual report of Alexander Cummings, *Annual Report, CIA, 1866,* 155.

62. Carson to Jones, June 10, 1866; Gwyther, "Frontier Post and Country," 520.

63. Lawrence R. Murphy, *Frontier Crusader—William F. M. Arny* (Tucson: University of Arizona Press, 1972), 103, 109; A. B. Norton, Superintentendent of Indian Affairs, New Mexico, to CIA D. N. Cooley, July 29, 1866, *Annual Report, CIA, 1866,* 152, citing Carson's opinion regarding the location for a Ute reservation; Frank D. Reeve, "The Federal Indian Policy in New Mexico, 1858–1880," pt. 2, NMHR 13 (January 1938): 53 and n.; Murphy, *Lucien Bonaparte Maxwell,* 122–32.

64. Morris F. Taylor, "Ka-ni-ache," *Colorado Magazine* 43 (fall 1966): 290.

65. P. David Smith, *Ouray, Chief of the Utes* (Ouray CO: Wayfinder Press, 1986).

66. Randolph Marcy to William Nichols, August 29, 1867, quoted in Simon, *Papers of Ulysses S. Grant,* 18:308.

67. Gwyther, "Frontier Post," 521–24.

68. Ibid., 524.

69. Carson to Jones, June 10, 1866.

70. Carson to C. H. DeForrest, June 14, 1866; Carson to Carleton, June 17, 1866.

71. Carson to DeForrest, June 30, 1866; second letter, Carson to DeForrest, same date.

72. Carson to DeForrest, July 14, 1866.

73. Sabin, *Kit Carson Days* (1935 edition), 2:761; Whittredge, "Autobiography," 48.

74. Meline, *Two Thousand Miles on Horseback,* 246–49.

75. Ibid., 249.

76. Carson to DeForrest, August 9, 1866; Gwyther, "Frontier Post," 524–25.

77. Carson to DeForrest, August 9, 1866; Gwyther, "Frontier Post," 525.

78. Carson to DeForrest, August 9, 1866.

79. Carson to DeForrest, August 19, 1866.

80. Sanford, "Reminiscences of Kit Carson, Jr." 182.

81. Ibid., 181–82. Kit might not have wanted to admit that one of his own soldiers had committed such an act. If one of the adobe makers had drugged the Indian's liquor, the younger Kit could easily have confused the perpetrator with a soldier many years later. In that case there would be little reason to conceal the facts from Carleton, though Carson would still have been reluctant to let the Indians know of it. The younger Carson's story, related nearly sixty years later, would seem dubious if the post surgeon had not suspected poison. If Carson and Gwyther had cooked up a cover story together, they would presumably

have agreed on the details, and if the doctor knew of the poisoning story, he made the cover story a central part of his reminiscence. If the story was current enough for the commanding officer's son to pick up, would the surgeon or the commanding officer be ignorant? Or did young Kit pick up the story from a local source years later? The truth is probably unrecoverable.

82. Meline, *Two Thousand Miles*, 289–91; Carson to DeForrest, August 9, 1866.

83. Murphy, *Lucien Bonaparte Maxwell*, 133–34.

84. Carson to DeForrest, August 24, 1866; Reeve, "Federal Indian Policy in New Mexico," pt. 3:170; Taylor, "Ka-ni-ache," 295–96.

85. Guild and Carter, *Kit Carson*, 263; Carson to A. J. Alexander, September 12, 1866; Carson to Alexander, September 15, 1866.

86. James R. Rusling, *Across America; or, The Great West and the Pacific Coast* (New York: Sheldon and Company, 1874), 113.

87. Athearn, *William Tecumseh Sherman*, 76–82.

88. Rusling, *Across America*, 137; Sherman to Edward Ellis, June 25, 1884, in Edward S. Ellis, *The Life of Kit Carson*, 248–50.

89. Sherman to John Rawlins, September 30, 1866; Simon, *Papers of Ulysses S. Grant*, 16:334–35; Athearn, *William Tecumseh Sherman*, 82–83; annual report of Alexander Cummings, *Annual Report, CIA, 1866*, 155.

90. Annual report of Alexander Cummings, *Annual Report, CIA, 1866*, 155; Rusling, *Across America*, 114, 125–27.

91. Rusling, *Across America*, 135–36; Rusling to Edward Ellis, June 23, 1884, in Ellis, *Life of Kit Carson*, 253–54.

92. Rusling in Ellis, *Life of Kit Carson*, 254.

93. Ibid., 257–58; see Francis Jennings, *The Invasion of America: Indians, Colonialism, and the Cant of Conquest* (Chapel Hill: University of North Carolina Press, 1975), 146–70.

94. Rusling, *Across America*, 29–31, 56, 115–25, 133–35.

95. Rusling in Ellis, *Life of Kit Carson*, 258–59; as to whether Ellis, the dime-novel writer, might have elaborated on Rusling's text, it should be noted that Rusling lived for a number of years after the 1889 publication of Ellis's book, which would presumably have inhibited any tendency toward creative additions.

96. White, *Chronicle of a Congressional Journey*, 27; see also the testimony of A. C. Hunt in "Massacre of Cheyenne Indians," in *The Sand Creek Massacre: A Documentary History* (New York: Sol Lewis, 1973), 46, suggesting that Chivington was directly influenced by dime-novel portrayals of Carson and other frontier heroes. See Slotkin, *Fatal Environment*, 206, on the racism of dime novels.

97. Trafzer, *Kit Carson Campaign*, 237.

98. Rusling, *Across America*, 125–26.

99. Carson to DeForrest, October 3, 1866; Athearn, *William Tecumseh Sherman*, 83–84.

100. Carson to DeForrest, October 3, 1866.

101. Ibid.

102. Ibid.; Tiller, *Jicarilla Apache Tribe*, 66–68.

103. Tiller, *Jicarilla Apache Tribe*, 67.

104. Carson to DeForrest, October 3, 1866.

105. Taylor, "Ka-ni-ache," 297–99; Sandra L. Myres, ed., *Cavalry Wife: The Diary of Eveline M. Alexander, 1866–1867* (College Station: Texas A&M University Press, 1977), 92–95; James H. Wilson, *The Life and Services of Brevet Brigadier-General Andrew Jonathan Alexander, United States Army* (New York: n.p., 1887), 97–98.

106. Carson to DeForrest, October 4, 1866; Carson to Charles Deus, October 4, 1866.

107. Carson to DeForrest, October 7, 1866; Carson to Carleton, October 8, 1866.

108. Carson to Carleton, October 10, 1866, a second letter of this date.

109. Carson to DeForrest, October 11, 1866.

110. Ibid.

111. Ibid.; Carson to DeForrest, n.d. (follows previous item on film).

112. Sanford, "Reminiscences of Kit Carson, Jr.," 181.

113. Carson to DeForrest, October 11, 1866; Murphy, *Lucien Bonaparte Maxwell*, 135, for another version of this occurrence; Carson to Alexander, October 16, 1866.

114. Taylor, "Ka-ni-ache," 301; Myres, *Cavalry Wife*, 95; Wilson, *Life and Services*, gives Alexander's record; Hancock's General Orders No. 31, Headquarters Department of the Missouri, December 12, 1866, in Wilson, *Life and Services*, 98; this may reflect the version of events given Hancock by Carleton.

115. Taylor, "Ka-ni-ache," 301–2; Myres, *Cavalry Wife*, 99, 109; Murphy, *Lucien Bonaparte Maxwell*, 135–36.

116. Myres, *Cavalry Wife*, 97–99.

117. Ibid., 97–98.

118. Ibid., 101; Guild and Carter, *Kit Carson*, 276; Emmett, *Fort Union*, 319; see the correspondence in Simon, *Papers of Ulysses S. Grant*, 18:73–76; Grant's endorsement of December 23, 1867, to Carleton's request states, "no good to the service could result from granting the application." Grant quoted a report by A. J. Alexander, May 5, 1867, made at Grant's request, which praised Carleton for the conquest of the Navajos and stated that much of the criticism came from Indian agents and contractors, whose motives were purely selfish, but found Carleton at fault for influencing elections and using military resources to develop areas where he and his staff had "large pecuniary interests." Thompson, *Army and the Navajo*, 121–22, 131–33.

119. Guild and Carter, *Kit Carson*, 276; Carson to Carleton, February 15, 1867; Reeve, "Federal Indian Policy," pt. 2, 60–61; ibid., pt. 3, 168.

120. Carson to Carleton, February 15, 1867.

121. Ibid.

122. Guild and Carter, *Kit Carson*, 277; Thompson, *Army and the Navajo*, 133; Lamar, *Far Southwest*, 130.

123. Guild and Carter, *Kit Carson*, 277.

124. Inman, *Old Santa Fe Trail*, 374–75, 379–80.

125. Ibid., 380–81.

126. Guild and Carter, *Kit Carson*, 277–78.

127. H. R. Tilton to John S. C. Abbott, January 7, 1874, in Abbott, *Christopher Carson*, 543–44.

128. I wish to thank Drs. Robert Settles and Stephen Youngberg for answering my questions about Carson's illness.

129. Guild and Carter, *Kit Carson*, 278–79.

130. Sanford, "Reminiscences of Kit Carson, Jr.," 183; Tilton in Abbott, *Christopher Carson*, 344, 345–46.

131. Guild and Carter, *Kit Carson*, 279; Morris F. Taylor, "Ka-ni-ache 2," *Colorado Magazine* 44 (spring 1967): 140 (the second installment of Taylor's biography of the Ute chief); Smith, *Ouray*, 72.

132. Reeve, "Federal Indian Policy," pt. 3, 148; Taylor, "Ka-ni-ache 2," 141–42, bases his account on Reeve; Hyde, *Life of George Bent*, 248; annual report of Alexander Cummings, *Annual Report, CIA, 1866*, 155; Smith, *Ouray*, 75.

133. Smith, *Ouray*, 73–75; see Treaty with the Ute, 1868, in Kappler, *Indian Treaties*, 990–96.

134. Frémont, *Will and the Way*, 43–45.

135. Ibid., 45–47.

136. Ibid., 48.

137. Guild and Carter, *Kit Carson*, 280–81; Sanford, "Reminiscences of Kit Carson, Jr.," 183–84; Tilton in Abbott, *Christopher Carson*, 344–45.

138. Guild and Carter, *Kit Carson*, 281; Tilton in Abbott, *Christopher Carson*, 345–47.

139. Thompson, *Army and the Navajo*, 151–55; Athearn, *William Tecumseh Sherman*, 203–4; Carleton to Lorenzo Thomas, February 18, 1868, in Simon, *Papers of Ulysses S. Grant*, 18:518–19; Barboncito quoted in council proceedings, *Treaty between the United States of America and the Navajo Tribe of Indians* (Las Vegas NV: KC Publications, 1968), 5 (a reprint of the council and treaty). See Treaty with the Navaho, 1868, in Kappler, *Indian Treaties*, 1015–20.

140. Lawrence R. Murphy, "Reconstruction in New Mexico," NMHR 43 (April 1968): 99–115; Thompson, *Army and the Navajo*, 161–65; Moore, *Chiefs, Agents and Soldiers*, xix, 19.

8. CONCLUSION

1. *Salt Lake City Tribune*, n.d., quoted in Ellis, *The Life of Kit Carson*, 260.

2. Guild and Carter, *Kit Carson*, 291.

3. Draper, in *Navajo Stories*, 45–46.

4. Gorman, in *Navajo Stories*, 23, 35; Chester Arthur, in Dane Coolidge and Mary Roberts Coolidge, *The Navajo Indians* (Boston: Houghton Mifflin Company, 1930), 20–22.

5. Arthur, in Coolidge and Coolidge, *Navajo Indians,* 22–23.

6. McNitt, *Navajo Wars,* 267, 287; Henry Chee Dodge, in Coolidge and Coolidge, *Navajo Indians,* 20.

7. Betty Shorthair, in *Navajo Stories,* 114; Tony Hillerman, introduction to Haniel Long, *Pinon Country* (1941; reprint, Lincoln: University of Nebraska Press, 1986), xiv; Tiana Bighorse, *Bighorse the Warrior,* ed. Noel Bennett (Tucson: University of Arizona Press, 1990), 27–28; McNitt, *Navajo Wars,* 134–44.

8. Bighorse, *Bighorse the Warrior,* 27–28.

9. Sabin, *Kit Carson Days,* 2:503.

10. Jack Hurst, *Nathan Bedford Forrest* (New York: Alfred A. Knopf, 1993), 4, 6, 9.

11. DOK, 60, 92–93; Green, *Great American Adventure,* 124.

12. DOK, 53–55, 105.

13. Lawrence Keeley, *War Before Civilization: The Myth of the Peaceful Savage* (New York: Oxford University Press, 1996), 59–69.

14. Saum, *Fur Trader and the Indian,* 26.

15. Preuss, *Exploring with Frémont,* 118, 127–28.

16. Beale in Thompson, " 'Kit Carson's Ride,' " 147; Joshua L. Chamberlain, *The Passing of the Armies* (New York: Bantam Books, 1992), 44; Rusling, *Across America,* 136.

17. DOK, 130; Rusling in Ellis, *Life of Kit Carson,* 258.

18. Herman Melville, *The Confidence-Man: His Masquerade,* ed. Stephen Matterson (London: Penguin Books, 1990), 168–88; Hall's sketch in Melville, *The Confidence-Man,* 345–51; for a historical example, see William Sterne Randall, "Tom Quick's Revenge," MHQ 4 (summer 1992): 70–75; see also William M. Ramsey, "The Moot Points of Melville's Indian-Hating," *American Literature* 52 (May 1980): 224–35, which argues that Melville's Indian-hater, and his Indian-hating ethos, is intended as a fiction, unrelated to reality.

19. DOK, 67.

20. Ibid.

21. See J. Glenn Gray, *The Warriors: Reflections on Men in Battle* (New York: Harper and Row, 1970), 43–46.

22. DOK, 101.

23. DOK, 89, 103–5; Frémont, *Will and the Way,* 34.

24. Dave Grossman, *On Killing: The Psychological Cost of Killing in War and Society* (Boston: Little, Brown, 1995), 195–96, 216; DOK, 107.

25. DOK, 63, 225.

26. David Meriwether, *My Life in the Mountains and on the Plains,* ed. Robert A. Griffen (Norman: University of Oklahoma Press, 1965), 230, 232; N. A. M. Rodger, *The Wooden World: An Anatomy of the Georgian Navy* (New York: W. W. Norton, 1996), 217.

27. Grossman, *On Killing,* 180–84.

28. James M. McPherson, *Drawn with the Sword: Reflections on the American Civil War* (New York: Oxford University Press, 1996), 91.

29. Carson to James Collins, July 28, 1858, Letters Received from and Relating to Kit Carson.

30. Carson to Collins, September 21, 1859, ibid.; Frémont, *Will and the Way*, 41; DOK, 89.

31. Myres, *Cavalry Wife*, 98–99; Rusling, in Ellis, *Life of Kit Carson*, 259.

32. Rusling, *Across America*, 56, 135.

33. DOK, 82.

34. Randolph Marcy to William Nichols, August 29, 1867, Simon, *The Papers of Ulysses S. Grant*, 18:308.

35. DOK, 147.

36. Richard N. Ellis, ed., "Bent, Carson, and the Indians, 1865," *Colorado Magazine* 46 (winter 1969): 63.

37. DOK, 149.

38. Carson quoted by James Rusling, in Ellis, *Life of Kit Carson*, 259.

39. Carson to Carleton, July 24, 1863, NR, 30.

40. Sanford, "Reminiscences of Kit Carson, Jr.," 183.

41. White, *Chronicle of a Congressional Journey*, 62.

42. Testimony of Col. Kit Carson, RCIT, 97; Carson to Cutler, August 19, 1865, RCIT, 439.

43. Carleton to Carson, October 12, 1862, NR, 11–12; Carleton to J. Francisco Chavez, June 23, 1863, NR, 20–21; General Orders No. 15, Headquarters Department of New Mexico, June 15, 1863, NR, 21–22.

44. Carleton to Carson, September 19, 1863, NR, 52.

45. Carson to Cutler, December 20, 1863, NR, 84.

46. Brown, *Bury My Heart at Wounded Knee*, 23; Frémont, *Will and the Way*, 40.

47. Green, *Great American Adventure*, 127; DOK, 121, 131, 132, 134; John Charles Frémont, *Memoirs of My Life* (Chicago: Belford, Clarke, and Co., 1887), 1:586.

48. DOK, 143; Carson to Carleton, April 10, 1864, NR, 147; Guild and Carter, *Kit Carson*, 204.

49. Ellis, "Bent, Carson, and the Indians," 68.

50. Sonnichsen, *The Mescalero Apaches*, 97.

51. Testimony of Col. Kit Carson, RCIT, 97.

52. Carson to Cutler, August 19, 1865, RCIT, 439; Ellis, "Bent, Carson, and the Indians," 62, 66–67.

53. Ellis, "Bent, Carson, and the Indians," 63–66.

54. Testimony of Col. Kit Carson, RCIT, 96; Sanford, "Reminiscences of Kit Carson, Jr.," 181; Rusling in Ellis, *Life of Kit Carson*, 259.

55. Tilton in Abbott, *Christopher Carson*, 345–46.

56. Rusling in Ellis, *Life of Kit Carson*, 254.

57. Ellis, "Bent, Carson, and the Indians," 44.

58. Mead, *Hunting and Trading*, 178.

59. John Bowers, "The Mythical Morning of Sergeant York," MHQ 8 (winter

1996): 39; Tilton in Abbott, *Christopher Carson*, 346; DOK, 63; Meline, *Two Thousand Miles*, 250;

60. Rusling, *Across America*, 137; Patricia N. Limerick, in Geoffey C. Ward, et al., *The West: An Illustrated History* (Boston: Little, Brown and Company, 1996), 212.

61. William Tecumseh Sherman to Edward Ellis, June 25, 1884, in Ellis, *Life of Kit Carson*, 252.

62. Carson to Collins, September 20, 1859, Letters Received from and Relating to Kit Carson.

INDEX

Bourke, John, 154, 440
Bowers, John, 33, 35, 456
Brackenridge, Henry Marie, 27
brevet rank, 376
Brewerton, Lt. George, 13, 14–15,
    16, 82, 107–8, 128–31, 430–31
Bridger, Jim, 35, 42, 48, 68–69,
    75–76, 83, 85, 86, 91, 239, 429
Bristol, Capt. Henry, 323–24
Brooks, Capt. William, 257
Brown, Dee, 3, 447
Buckskin Charley (Muache Ute), 327,
    336
buffalo, 49, 61, 74, 136, 157, 169,
    337, 340, 364, 373, 388
Buffalo Hump (Comanche), 361,
    411
Bumppo, Natty (fictional character),
    14, 22, 49, 140, 186, 382, 401, 423,
    454, 457–58
Burbank, Mrs. Akinabh, 297–98
Burdett, Charles, 2
Bureau (Office) of Indian Affairs,
    155, 182, 204, 320, 353, 354–55,
    360, 369, 375, 403, 449; KC on,
    350, 354, 452
Burns, Robert, 127

Cadete (Mescalero Apache), 244
Calhoun, James S., 148, 150–53, 155,
    156, 269, 320
California Column, 236, 239, 308
California Indians, 62–63, 68,
    110–14, 119, 145–46, 153, 187,
    224, 436
California Trail, 10, 38, 150
California volunteer troops, 236, 241,
    245, 262–63, 282, 286, 290, 325,
    327–28, 333–34, 336, 376
Californios, 62, 120–21, 430
Campbell, Lt. George, 305
Camp Nichols OK, 341–44, 346
Canadian River, 133, 138, 231,
    328–30, 333, 335, 337, 366
Canby, Col. Edward, 230–31, 234–36,

241, 255, 257–58, 260–62, 264,
    267–68, 271–72, 274, 279, 308–9,
    311, 315, 444
Cantonment Burgwin NM, 163–64
Canyon de Chelly AZ, 280–81,
    289–90, 349; described, 292;
    expedition to, 292–300, 306, 314,
    419, 446–47
Canyon del Muerto AZ, 292, 294–95
Capote Utes, 197–98
captives, Indian, 76, 200–204, 251–
    54, 283–84, 286, 442, 444, 449;
    KC and, 76, 105–6, 137, 200–204,
    283–84, 442
Carey, Capt. Asa, 290–91, 293,
    295–96, 300–302, 306, 314
Carleton, Gen. James H., 167–68,
    191, 236, 241, 251, 264, 277, 287,
    316, 354, 355, 418; ; achievement
    of, 404–5; assimilation plans
    of, 246, 317–18, 320, 395; and
    Bosque Redondo, 5, 246–47, 302,
    311–12, 317–23, 346, 375, 403,
    415, 447; character and personality
    of, 236–39, 248, 262–63, 279,
    308, 318, 325, 386, 441, 447;
    and command of Department of
    NM, 241, 260, 325, 448; critics
    of, 259; described, 5, 236–37;
    intentions regarding Indians,
    244–47, 262–63, 273, 285–86,
    305, 307–8, 311, 313, 318, 340,
    396, 445–46, 450; and KC, 3, 5–6,
    11, 34–36, 144, 168, 237, 241,
    247–48, 278–79, 280–81, 283–85,
    289–92, 300–301, 302–3, 306–7,
    324, 326, 328, 338–41, 344, 349,
    351, 359–60, 363, 376, 381, 390,
    394–95, 397, 398–400, 402–3, 404,
    423, 427, 442, 445–47, 448–50,
    452, 453; orders given by, 241,
    243–45, 270, 275, 284, 291–92,
    307, 313, 325–26, 328, 329,
    340–41, 393, 394, 399, 441–42,
    445; on peace negotiations, 356

Carson, Adaline (daughter of KC), 60–61, 84, 87, 142, 146, 435

Carson, Alexander (great-grandfather of KC), 25–26

Carson, Charles (son of KC), 146, 357

Carson, Christopher (Kit), Jr. (son of KC), 201–2, 385–86, 443

Carson, Josefita (daughter of KC), 413

Carson, Juan (Navajo), 201

Carson, Juan Bautista (Navajo), 201–2

Carson, Kit (Christopher): and Adobe Walls campaign, 328–37; attempted resignation of, 247–48; autobiography of, 19–21, 24, 41, 60, 63–64, 74, 82–83, 89, 92, 100–104, 111–13, 116–18, 119, 123–24, 128, 133–34, 139, 142–44, 158, 164, 170, 171–72, 177–78, 190, 391, 424, 431, 433, 435, 447–48; background and upbringing of, 21, 26–29, 32–36, 85, 424, 429, 443, 448; baptism of, 94; and William Bent, 3–4, 96, 133, 192, 348, 350–51, 357, 368–75, 386, 390, 406, 408, 437, 449, 450–52, 484–85; biographical sketch of, 11–12; on Bosque Redondo, 319–20, 323, 370; brevet promotion of, 376; and James Carleton, 5–6, 144, 237, 238–39, 241, 243–44, 247–49, 275–76, 278–79, 280–81, 283–85, 289–92, 302–3, 306–7, 324, 326, 328, 338, 240–41, 344, 348–49, 351, 359–60, 381, 390, 394, 397, 400, 402–3, 404, 442, 445–46, 447, 448–50, 452, 456; caution shown by, 34, 63, 81–82, 91–92, 278, 334–35, 337, 341–42, 450; character and personality of, xv, 3, 15–17, 20, 21, 35–36, 65–66, 71, 78–79, 88–89, 109, 117–18, 121, 126–27, 130–31, 133, 139–40, 144, 158–59, 163,

175–76, 187–88, 190–91, 210, 226, 248–50, 277–78, 287–88, 289, 294, 298, 300, 315–16, 322–24, 337, 364, 370, 382–83, 389–94, 400–402, 406, 409, 412, 416–17, 424–59; on comancheros, 338; correspondence as agent, 158, 173, 193, 197–98, 204, 205–6, 216–17; criticism of, 4, 5, 6, 20, 85, 89, 112, 115, 126, 144, 248–49, 250, 271, 278, 308–9, 312, 442–43, 444, 447, 454; death of, 415; described, 1–2, 10, 12–13, 15, 87, 125, 126, 130–31, 137, 191, 232–34, 341–42, 346, 360, 380, 382–83, 388, 389, 402, 406, 408; duel with Shynar, 69–73, 175; ethical standards of, 454–55; on extinction of Indians, 343, 370; final illness of, 12, 302, 341–44, 404, 407–8, 409, 412–13, 414–15; and John C. Frémont, 87–88, 89, 92–93, 97, 97, 118, 124, 132, 134, 429, 430, 448; as government advisor, 344, 368–75, 403–4, 423, 450–52; and Hispanics, 95, 120–21, 396; illiteracy of, 12, 19, 158, 177–79, 180, 232–33, 249, 352, 368, 456; indispensability of, 247–48, 377, 447; as Indian agent, 147, 156–58, 162, 164, 185–86, 191, 193, 195, 207, 214–15, 216–17, 221–27, 347, 369, 372–73, 423, 427, 435, 439, 458; and Indian captives, 76, 105–6, 137, 200–204, 283–84, 442; and "Indian problem" 147, 154, 250; on Indians, 20, 74, 103–4, 111–13, 115, 127–28, 137–38, 160, 249–50, 433–34, 438–39 (see also individual tribal names); on Indian-white conflict, 184–86, 193, 204–7, 210, 225, 250, 315, 327, 347–48, 350–51, 368–75, 390–94, 398–99, 407, 439, 440, 449, 451–52, 455; and Little Arkansas treaty, 360–68, 451–52; marriage to Josefa Jaramillo, 93–95; marriage to Making-Out-Road, 60, 66, 78, 357, 434–35; marriage to Waanibe, 60, 357, 434–35; and David Meriwether, 166, 170, 173–89; as military commander, 231–34, 277–78, 280, 289, 292, 313, 323, 327, 328–29, 339, 341–42, 347, 376, 423, 443–47, 450, 453, 458; as mountain man, 49, 50, 52, 59, 64, 76, 78, 83–84, 105, 159, 182, 239–40, 403, 407–8, 425–26, 443, 458; modesty and humility of, 21, 35, 127, 133, 231, 300, 360, 406, 438, 456; myth and reputation of, xii–xiii, xiv, xv, xvi, 1–3, 5–9, 10, 13–14, 16, 22, 46, 67, 69–70, 85–86, 107–8, 110, 122, 132–33, 139–40, 190, 240, 248–49, 296, 306, 308, 344, 374, 380, 400, 408–9, 413, 418–22, 423, 442–43, 457, 459; on Navajos, 249–50, 311; and paternalism, 205, 225, 308, 319–20, 442, 450, 454; and peace negotiations, 355–56, 358, 363–64, 366, 368, 400–401, 408–12, 423, 441–42, 450–52, 453, 458; as rancher, 107, 135, 159, 423; and religion, 94, 390–91, 413; on reservation system, 135, 158, 319, 321, 437–38; responsibility of, 264, 301, 317, 370, 409; and retaliation, 52, 64–65, 80–81, 116, 118, 120–21, 127–28, 137, 143, 359–60, 424–25, 428–31, 441; as scout and guide, 9–10, 21, 86, 133–34, 138–40, 159, 164–65, 167–68, 171, 423, 436, 439, 458; speech of, 20, 77, 126, 389, 390, 391–92; as superintendent of Indian affairs (CO), 406–7, 408–9, 453; and Union, 229–30; on use of force, 155, 163, 164, 370–71, 431, 441, 451; on U.S. Indian

policy, 158–60, 182, 185, 222, 226, 350–51, 368–75, 403–4; and violence, 80, 89–90, 101–3, 111–13, 115–18, 121, 424, 426, 428–32, 484; wounded, 69, 408; Carson, Lindsey (father of KC), 26–27, 28, 35, 86, 144, 248, 443

Carson, Maria Dolores (Navajo), 201, 202

Carson, Maria Josefa Jaramillo (Josefa; wife of KC), 10, 60, 93–95, 106, 127, 131, 135, 142, 146, 147, 201–2, 238, 290, 324, 385, 400, 402, 413–14, 415, 435, 442

Carson, Moses (brother of KC), 121, 235

Carson, Rebecca Robinson (mother of KC), 27, 36, 86

Carson, Susan. *See* Nelson, Susan Carson

Carson, Teresina (daughter of KC), 201, 400

Carson, William (grandfather of KC), 26

Carson, William (son of KC), 201, 357, 388, 400, 409, 412

Carson City NV, 3

Carson County TX, 3

Carson National Forest NM, 3

Carter, Harvey L., xi, xii, 6, 7–8, 40, 41, 62, 66, 71, 116, 176, 312, 315, 414, 419

Casador (Ute), 384

Casa Maria (Jicarilla Apache), 172

Catlin, George, 152, 223

Caudill, Boone (fictional character), 40

Cebolleta NM, 254, 286–87

Chacón (Jicarilla Apache), 140, 169

Chacón, Maj. Rafael, 35, 171, 279

Chacón, Tomas, 209

Chamberlain, Joshua, 426

Chase, Salmon, 263

Chato (Mescalero Apache), 244

Chavez, Lt. Col. J. Francisco, 240

Getty, Col. George, 405
Gibson, Arrell, 236–37
"Gidi": KC as, 165, 172, 327, 436
Gila River, 39, 122, 124, 125, 126, 146
Gilbert, Bil, 52
Gillespie, Lt. Archibald, 114–15, 120, 122
Glorieta (NM), battle of, 228
Godey (Godin), Alexis, 97, 100–103, 108, 109–10, 115, 119, 131, 163, 176, 424, 426
Godin, Antoine (Iroquois), 57
Goetzmann, William, 39–40
gold: and Navajo war, 262–63, 312, 352
gold rush: Arizona, 312; California, 145–46, 159, 187, 312, 350, 359; Colorado, 210, 211, 218, 312, 324, 362, 364
Goldtooth, Frank (Navajo), 268
Goodale, Tim, 10, 141
Gordon-McCutchan, R. C., xv, 8, 271
Gorman, Eli (Navajo), 266
Gorman, Howard (Navajo), 265, 297, 300
Grant, U. S., 251, 374–75, 403, 415, 423, 454
Graydon, Capt. James, 244, 245, 249
Grayhair (Ute), 300
Great Basin, 47, 98, 110, 200
Great Plains, 35, 38, 86, 132, 437; Indians of, 45, 80, 136, 224, 272, 324, 335; war on, 344
Green River, 43, 46, 49
Green, Martin, 20, 65, 83, 113, 115, 126, 144, 312, 424, 425, 447
Greenhorn CO, 61, 229
Gregg, Josiah, 34–35, 51
Gregg, Patsy, 28, 138
Greiner, John, 222, 259
Grier, Capt. William, 138–40, 141, 143–44, 180, 448
Grossman, Dave, 430, 432
guerrilla warfare. See Indian warfare; primitive warfare

Guild, Thelma, xii, 6, 8, 39, 62, 112, 116, 176, 414, 419
Guthrie, A. B., 40
Gutierrez, Ramon, 9
Gwyther, George, 378, 380, 383, 384, 385

Hafen, Leroy R., 79
Halleck, Gen. Henry, 262–63
Hancock, Gen. Winfield Scott, 401, 403
Harney, Gen. William, 360, 364, 366, 372
Haro, Francisco de, 120–21
Haro, Ramon de, 120–21
Hawkeye (fictional character). See Bumppo, Natty
Hays, Capt. Jack, 32
Head, Lafayette, 383, 385
Head, Mark, 69
Henderson, John, 401
Hernandez, Pablo, 100, 103
Herrera, Sgt. Andrés, 287, 293, 297, 300
Herrero Grande (Navajo), 291, 354
Hill, Tom (Delaware), 53
Hillerman, Tony, 4, 5, 421
Hodt, Lt. Nicholas, 286
Hoerster, H., 216
Hoig, Stan, 366
Holbrook, Sgt. William, 140–41
Holmes, Oliver Wendell, 428
Homestead Act, 367
Hopis, 266, 267–68, 270, 280, 287–88, 298, 314; KC on, 287–88
Horgan, Paul, 28
Horse Back (Comanche), 361
horses and livestock, stolen, 62–63, 64–65, 81, 119, 195–96, 216, 226
"Horsethief Indians" (CA), 110, 111
Horsman, Reginald, 54
Houck, Lewis, 28
Houston, Sam, 185, 186
Hudson's Bay Company, 44, 56, 57, 73, 86–87, 98, 116

Russell, Osborne, 49, 54, 56–58, 68, 75
Russell, Lt. Richard, 340
Ruxton, George Frederick, 39, 41

Sabin, Edwin L., 2, 70, 226, 227, 422
Sac and Fox Indians, 25, 27–28, 29, 33, 185
Saguache Pass (CO), 171
Sagundai (Delaware), 115, 116, 118
San Antonio CO, 215
Sanborn, Gen. John, 357, 358, 360, 361–62, 364, 365–66, 368
Sanches, Jesus Maria, 193
Sand Creek massacre, 6, 154, 155, 275, 345, 346, 355, 360, 361–63, 364, 365, 371, 398, 453; KC on, 348, 391–94, 406, 427, 428, 430, 451
Sangre de Cristo Mountains, 17, 107, 135, 167, 376, 387
San Juan River, 312, 349
San Luis Valley CO, 130, 160, 164, 171, 179, 184, 376, 377, 378, 397, 398, 402, 404, 410, 411, 437
San Pasqual (CA), battle of, 124–25, 126, 163, 298, 426
Santa Ana Pueblo NM, 270
Santa Fe NM, 38, 228, 231, 235, 382–83
Santa Fe Trail, 9, 11, 34, 36, 38, 39, 94, 123, 131, 150, 235, 324, 325, 340, 341, 344, 345, 346, 357–58, 365, 366, 379, 450; Cimarron Cut-off, 340; Mountain Branch, 78, 142, 340
Santo Domingo Pueblo NM, 270
Satank (Kiowa), 361
Satanta (Kiowa), 332, 361
Saum, Lewis, 46, 68
scalp-hunters, 76
scalping, 28, 41, 61, 100–103, 119, 141, 281, 333, 345, 424, 426, 453
Schaefer, Jack, 3, 248, 418
Scheurich, Alois, 414–15

Scheurich, Teresina Bent, 414
Segundo, Jake (Navajo), 304, 305
Seminole wars, 19, 37, 152, 272, 312, 360, 446
Sena, Maj. José, 291
Senate, U.S. See Congress, U.S.
Seventh U.S. Cavalry Regiment, 336
Shavano (Ute), 381, 382, 384
Shawnees, 27, 29, 30, 57–58, 75, 79
Sheridan, Gen. Philip, 79, 443
Sherman, Gen. William Tecumseh, 12, 13, 21, 35, 107, 128, 374, 375, 387–89, 394, 415–16, 418, 419, 443, 450, 457, 458
Shorthair, Betty (Navajo), 421
Shoshones, 43–50, 52, 56, 59, 60, 77, 80, 82, 93, 98, 425, 435
Shunar (Chouinard), 69–73, 175, 233, 431
Sibley, Gen. Henry, 234, 235
Sierra Nevada Mountains, 62, 98, 99, 108, 110, 144
sign language, 45, 380, 406
Simmons, Marc, xv, 8, 80, 143, 253–54, 271
Simpson, Smith H., 70, 229
Sioux, 45, 49, 59, 77, 91–92, 310, 324, 335, 336, 345, 360, 391
Sitting Bull (Sioux), 336, 418
Skelton, William, 273
slavery, Indian. See captives, Indian; Navajos, captives
Sloan, Marian. See Russell, Marian
Slotkin, Richard, xiv, 13, 108, 446, 458
Small Mexican (New Mexican scout), 297
smallpox, 159, 170
Smith, E. Willard, 49, 77
Smith, James, 31–32
Smith, John Simpson, 361, 364
Smoky Hill River (KS), 358, 360, 364, 367, 370
Snively, Jacob, 95, 97
sociopaths, 425–26, 432